Fundamentals of Human Communication

Social Science in Everyday Life
Third edition

Margaret H. DeFleur

Louisiana State University

Patricia Kearney

California State University, Long Beach

Timothy G. Plax

California State University, Long Beach

Melvin L. DeFleur

Louisiana State University

Boston   Burr Ridge, IL   Dubuque, IA   Madison, WI   New York   San Francisco   St. Louis
Bangkok   Bogotá   Caracas   Kuala Lumpur   Lisbon   London   Madrid   Mexico City
Milan   Montreal   New Delhi   Santiago   Seoul   Singapore   Sydney   Taipei   Toronto

Higher Education

FUNDAMENTALS OF HUMAN COMMUNICATION: SOCIAL SCIENCE IN EVERYDAY LIFE

Published by McGraw-Hill, a business unit of The McGraw-Hill Companies, Inc.,
1221 Avenue of the Americas, New York, NY, 10020. Copyright © 2005, 1998, 1993,
by Margaret H. DeFleur, Patricia Kearney, Timothy G. Plax, and Melvin L. DeFleur.
All rights reserved. No part of this publication may be reproduced or distributed in
any form or by any means, or stored in a database or retrieval system, without the
prior written consent of The McGraw-Hill Companies, Inc., including, but not
limited to, in any network or other electronic storage or transmission, or broadcast
for distance learning.

Some ancillaries, including electronic and print components, may not be available to
customers outside the United States.

This book is printed on acid-free paper.

2 3 4 5 6 7 8 9 0 FGR/FGR 0 9 8 7 6 5

ISBN 0 07 286293 9

Publisher: *Phillip A. Butcher*
Senior sponsoring editor: *Nanette Giles*
Developmental editor: *Josh Hawkins*
Senior marketing manager: *Leslie Oberhuber*
Media coordinator: *Christie Ling*
Senior project manager: *Diane M. Folliard*
Associate production supervisor: *Jason Huls*
Associate designer: *Srdjan Savanovic*
Media project manager: *Kathleen Boylan*
Associate photo research coordinator: *Natalia C. Peschiera*
Cover design: *Jenny El-Shamy*
Typeface: *10/12 Sabon*
Compositor: *Thompson Type*
Printer: *Quebecor World Fairfield Inc.*

Library of Congress Cataloging-in-Publication Data
Fundamentals of human communication / Margaret H. DeFleur ... [et al.].–3rd ed.
    p. cm.
    Includes index.
    Rev. ed. of: Fundamentals of human communication / Melvin L. DeFleur. 2nd. ed.
c1998.
    ISBN: 0-07-286293-9 (softcover : alk. paper)
    1. Communication.   I. DeFleur, Margaret H.   II. DeFleur, Melvin L. (Melvin
Lawrence), 1923– Fundamentals of human communication.
P90.D4415 2005
302.2–dc22
                                                            2004045698

www.mhhe.com

Contents in Brief

Contents

chapter 3 Nonverbal Communication: Communicating Without Language   64

chapter 4 The Importance of Listening   95

chapter 12 Coping with Conflict 329

part four   Understanding Communication Media

chapter 13 Using Media to Communicate Interpersonally 349

Preface

The authors wish to thank the many instructors and students who have sent us invaluable comments and advice as to how to craft this third edition. We hope it will continue to meet the needs of those who adopt it for their courses. We also hope that it will prove useful to the students who use it.

Our Goals

One of the goals of this third edition was to recognize the contribution of the field of communication to the social sciences. Communication is the basis of both social life and of personal cognitive functioning. As such it is perhaps the single most important form of human behavior. We all communicate, all day, every day, in an enormous variety of contexts, to many kinds of people and for an enormous variety of purposes. It follows that the better we understand that process the more effective we will be in relating to other human beings.

For that reason an effort was made to incorporate relevant theories and findings from all of the social science disciplines into the study of human communication. Contributions from those fields provide significant insights into the ways people communicate and the influence that communication has on their lives. By pursuing this objective we hope to bring social science into the everyday lives of our readers so that they may develop a better understanding of the processes, problems, and consequences of human communication.

Within that framework, this book presents a number of innovative theories and perspectives as well as the more traditional introductory material in order to help students develop strategies for thinking about and engaging in communication. We do not want students to leave the course with only a list of memorized concepts and definitions. We want them to cultivate a working command of the tools of effective communication so that they can competently manage everyday situations long after they have completed the course. We have drawn from a growing body of classical and contemporary theory and research and have brought together ideas and findings from several disciplines—communication, psychology, sociology, biology, anthropology, and education—that provide a rich variety of insight into the communication process.

Another major goal is to discuss communication in ways that are sensitive to the needs and interests of diverse categories of students. Although most fundamental communication theory and its applications are not unique to either gender or to any particular racial, ethnic, or cultural category, we have tried to provide material that acknowledges the variety of communication styles and customs that exist in the American society. Related to this, we use many examples, concepts, and explanations that are relevant to the workplace so that the content will be of value to students when they enter the labor force. Of course, many students are already in the labor force.

In short, the purpose of this book is to present basic theoretical and practical analyses of the human communication process. To do that, the book makes extensive use of examples, concepts, theories, and research from many sources that help clarify multicultural issues that are an important part of that process.

Organization

After an overview of the communication process, the book moves from the discussion of simple messages between two people to more complex communication contexts, such as intercultural, organizational, and mass communication. Part One presents the basics of verbal and nonverbal interaction, their personal and social implications (Chapters 1–4). Part Two explains how communication takes place in distinct contexts (Chapters 5–8). These beginning chapters provide the student with a strong foundation of concepts, principles, and research-supported theories that explain the nature and consequences of human communication.

The third part of the book (Chapters 9–12) focuses on practical applications and is intended to improve the student's ability to communicate effectively in a variety of situations and settings. The final part of the book looks at four major topics. These are effective communication with new media technologies (Chapter 13), the process and effects of mass communication (Chapter 14), applications of communication skills in two professional industries—advertising, and public relations (Chapter 15), and, finally, the design and conduct of research on the communication process (Chapter 16).

Features

A number of innovative approaches make this book unique. For example, starting with the first chapter, both linear and transactional approaches are used to analyze the basics of the communication process. A second example is the developmental format used to discuss interpersonal communication (Chapter 5). That format discusses how people use particular forms of messages to initiate interpersonal relationships, to maintain them, and (possibly) to disengage from each other if things do not work out.

Another innovative theoretical perspective is used in the discussion of small groups (Chapter 6). This expands on traditional approaches by showing the influence of patterns of behavior based on norms, roles, ranks, and controls that indicate who can talk to whom, in what way for what purpose. Still another innovation is the development in Chapter 7 of a theory of group cohesion based on such factors as sentiment, personal reward considerations, interlocking work assignments, or mutual role dependency.

A feature that has been retained and updated from the second edition is *A Closer Look*, boxes which provide skills-based tips, bulleted summaries, narrative examples, or relevant theories in each chapter. In addition, many chapters feature *Ethical Concerns* boxes which underscore ever-important questions and issues of ethics within the field of communication.

Changes in the Third Edition

In every chapter an effort has been made to incorporate recent research developments and to cite noteworthy contributions of communication scholars. Many new examples have been added. Definitions of key terms have been simplified. Selected chapters contain new *Workplace Perspective* boxes which highlight important communication issues in career settings, including such topics as office e-mail etiquette and how to communicate effectively with your manager.

Of particular note is the addition of Chapter 15, Professional Communication. This has been added to acquaint students with the fields of advertising and public relations—where the kinds of communication skills and perspectives derived from communication courses can have direct applications in the labor force. Increasingly, the field of communication is providing preparation for individuals who want to develop careers in communication-intensive industries.

Acknowledgments

We are indebted to the following people who made important contributions to this book, including the reviewers who provided many insightful comments for the previous editions as well as in revising this book for the third edition: Terre and Scott Allen, California State University, Long Beach; Jack M. Bain, Michigan State University; Michael J. Beatty, Cleveland State University; Julie A. Burke, Bowling Green State University; Karen Buzzard, Southwest Missouri State University; Ann L. Darling, University of Utah; Sharon Downey, California State University, Long Beach; Lawrence W. Hugenberg, Youngstown State University; Robert Kastenbaum, Arizona State University; Richard A. Katula, Northeastern University; Joann Keyton, University of Kansas; Anne F. Mattina, Northeastern University; Matt McAllister, Virginia Tech; Raymie E. McKerrow, Ohio University; Heidi M. Rose, Villanova University; Carolyn Shepard, University of California at Santa Barbara; Jennifer Thackaberry, University of Colorado; Bryan C. Taylor, University of Colorado; Jennifer Waldeck, University of California at Santa Barbara; Larry J. Whatule, University of Pittsburgh at Greensburg; John L. Williams, California State University, Sacramento; and Donald D. Yoder, University of Dayton.

The authors would like to offer a special thanks to the following from McGraw-Hill for their important contributions to this book: Nanette Kauffman Giles, sponsoring editor; Joshua Hawkins, editorial coordinator; and Diane Folliard, project manager.

The Communication Process: An Overview

Well son," Mr. Andrews said. "It's really nice to have you home, even if it's only for the few days of the Thanksgiving holiday. Your mom and I are so proud of you. But it is a bit hard to believe that you are going to college already. It seems like only a short time ago that you were just a little guy sitting on my lap."

Tom chuckled, saying, "Well, Dad, it's sure nice to be here. The dorms are really OK, and I like the friends I've made. But as they say, 'There's no place like home.' College is cool, but it's nice to get away, and I'm really looking forward to mom's Thanksgiving dinner."

"Tell me how things are going," Mr. Andrews said. "How are the grades shaping up?" Recognizing the note of parental concern in his Dad's voice, Tom explained that he had a solid grade point average, and that with some hard work he might be able to raise it even higher.

"Well that's just fine, Tom," Mr. Andrews replied with a smile. "Maybe next year you will be able to qualify for a scholarship. With both you and your sister in college, those tuition bills are really starting to add up. Mom and I are glad to do it though, we want both of you to have the best possible chances to get really good jobs when you finish."

"I really appreciate that Dad. I know that it has been a financial sacrifice. But I think that it will be worth it once I finish my degree and start working."

"Have you given any more thought to what you will major in?" Mr. Andrews asked.

"Yes I have. I have to finish my required courses in sciences and humanities first, of course, but I've thought about it a lot, and I have looked into what kind of work I might really want to do after I graduate. Dad, I have decided to major in communication, and I have already taken an introductory course in that program. It's really interesting."

Tom saw his father's eyes widen and his mouth drop open, with a disbelieving look on his face. Tom sensed immediately that he had a problem.

"You're going to major in *what*? Did I hear you say you're going to major in 'communication'? Am I hearing wrong?"

"Yes, Dad, communication!"

"Oh, for heaven's sake Tom. Get real! Mom and I want you to be able to earn some money after you graduate. We have been hoping that you would select something practical like accounting or computer science. Those people get real jobs. But communication . . . good grief!"

"But it is really an interesting major, Dad. It means working with people rather than in a lab, or with numbers or computer codes. I don't want to just juggle some company's profit and loss statement, or sit in a cubicle staring into a computer all day—unable to have an intelligent conversation with another human being."

"Well I'll tell you what kind of 'intelligent conversation' you will probably have if you major in communication."

(Tom detected the obviously negative tone that his Dad used with the word "communication.")

"You'll be able to have great discussions with people that you drive around in your taxi-cab. Or, with luck, you can talk things over with customers to whom you will be selling shoes. There just aren't decent jobs for people who major in stuff like that. You might as well have selected Medieval studies, Latin, or Icelandic literature. In fact, people who pick those majors may actually have a better chance."

"I don't think that you understand the situation very well, Dad. I have looked into the employment picture pretty thoroughly. People who have a solid command of communication skills have excellent chances in the labor force. The study of communication is a social science—one devoted to understanding how we communicate and how we can do it well. It really does help people who want to excel in their jobs."

"I don't know how to break this to your mom." Mr. Andrews said, as he walked away, shaking his head and looking disgusted.

As the days of the brief vacation slipped by, the rift between Tom and his dad did not heal easily. His major was a sore point with both of his parents and everyone tried to talk about something else.

In spite of his parents' views, Tom became even more firmly committed to his major during his sophomore year, and he went on to establish an outstanding record in the communication courses he took. Although his father was worried that he and his wife would never get "a decent return on their investment" in Tom's tuition, they learned over time that communication was indeed a practical skill after all.

They discovered how much employers valued communication skills in virtually every field in the workplace. Employees who can communicate complex information effectively have an edge over those who cannot.

While Tom had decided to study communication, it is clear that his father had serious reservations about the field. That is hardly surprising, many people have no idea about what it is or what value it may have. So, an appropriate way to begin the first chapter is to ask, what is the field of communication anyway? Where did it come from? What do people in the field study? A second important question is to ask what value does the knowledge it develops have for someone like Tom who decides to major in it?

Answers to the first question can be both simple and complex. The simple version is that the central focus of the field is **human communication** *in all its aspects.* Stated briefly, then, communication is the study of the many ways that human beings relate to each other by exchanging messages, using a number of different processes of communication in a variety of settings and **contexts,** and the consequences of those exchanges.

A more complex answer to the first question above is that communication is an academic field that makes use of the strategies and perspectives of social science to discover and teach others about the processes and consequences of human communication. Actually, the field had its origins centuries before any kind of social scientific strategies for study were available. Its prescientific roots extend back to ancient Greece, and the writings of philosophers such as Aristotle and Quintillian. In the fourth century B.C. they recognized the importance of communication in human affairs and they systematically studied the use of *rhetoric*. The term refers to the art of expressive discourse, including the rules of message composition used in speaking (and writing) to achieve specific kinds of results and influences on audiences. Indeed, public speaking remains one of the field's central concerns today. In addition, contemporary communication scholars conduct research, using the intellectual tools of science. They seek to push forward the cutting edge of knowledge about how human beings communicate, well or badly, either orally or with media, and what consequences results from such exchanges. To do this they not only conduct their own research projects but they also incorporate knowledge about human communication that has been discovered by several related social sciences—anthropology, linguistics, social psychology, psychology, and sociology. Thus, this complex field is an *interdisciplinary* one focusing on human communication in all its many aspects. It includes how communication takes place between individuals, in various kinds of group settings, and through the use of many kinds of media.

Using this broad explanation of communication as a guide, the purpose of the present chapter is to explain in considerable detail how human beings communicate at an interpersonal level, and the consequences of doing it well. That explanation will be based on an examination of two so-called "models" of the process. These are detailed discussions and portrayals of the exact stages and steps that take place when *one person communicates with one other in a face-to-face setting.* First, however, why is the study of communication so important?

The Significance of Communication in Human Life

An old joke, familiar to any sixth grader, begins with the question, "Where in the jungle does the 800-pound gorilla sleep?" The answer, of course, is "Anywhere he wants!" Perhaps a more relevant version of that question is this: "Where does a person with a degree in communication work?" Perhaps, surprisingly, the answer is much the same: "Anywhere he or she

what can you do with a communication degree?

Left profile list:

Community Relations Director • Publications Editor • Communication Trainer • Museum Curator • Editor • Publicist • Quality Inspector • **Radio News Director** • Radio Talk-Show Host • Webmaster • Activities Director (retirement center) • Wedding Consultant • Camp Director • Career and Training Advisor • Recreational Coordinator and Supervisor • Residential Housing Director • Salesperson • Accreditation Specialist • **Advertising Executive** • Alumni Coordinator • Arts Administrator • Sales Representative • Script Writer • Newspaper Publisher • Special Events Coordinator • **Secondary School Speech Teacher** • **Speechwriter** • **Sports Announcer** • Sports Marketer • **Public Affairs Director** • Training Specialist • Travel/Conference Manager • Sports Publicist • News Anchor • Paralegal • Student Activities Director • Student Services Director • Symphony Orchestra Media Relations • **Human Resources Specialist** • Human Rights Officer • Instructional Designer • Tour Guide • Department Administrator • Leasing Consultant • Legal Communication Consultant • Legislative Assistant • Legislative Correspondent • Linguist • Health Services Manager • Telecommunications Specialist • Telemarketing Manager • **Television Producer** • **Television Reporter** • National Fraternity Chapter Consultant • National Sorority Chapter Consultant • Account manager • Hotel Manager • Human Resources Manager • Child Welfare Worker • Claims Adjuster • College Admissions Counselor • Private Investigator • Production Assistant • **Promotional Specialist** • **Motivational Speaker** • Multicultural Specialist • Patient Rights Advocate • International Students Coordinator • **Journalist** • Labor Negotiator • Labor Relations Consultant • Language Arts Teacher • Law Firm Recruiter • Maintenance Supervisor Manager • **Market Researcher** • **Media Account Executive** • Media Buyer • Media Critic • **Mediation Specialist** • Hospital Volunteers Membership Coordinator • **Information Analyst**

Right profile list:

College Dean • College Recruiter • **Government Relations Officer** • **Public Opinion Researcher** • Communication Consultant • Communication Statistician • Property Manager • Administrative Aide • **Lobbyist** • Assistant to the President (college) • Broadcasting Floor Manager • **Public Information Officer** • Public Relations Coordinator • Communication Researcher • **Community Affairs Liaison** • Proofreader • **Community College Speech Instructor** • Business Manager • **Instructional Development Consultant/Specialist** • Arena Director/Manager • Personnel Development Specialist • **Conference Leader** • **Community Outreach Director** • Theatre Manager • Company Spokesperson • Consulting Analyst • **Copywriter** • Counselor • University Administrator • Technical Recruiter • University Information Specialist • University Communication Professor • Volunteer Coordinator • Crisis Manager • Database Analyst • **Customer Service Representative** • Parliamentarian • **Nonprofit Organization Director** • Debate Coach Associate Producer • Developmental Officer • **Child Language Specialist** • **Political Activist** • Disc Jockey • Mental Health Professional • College Admissions Counselor • Director of Admissions (college) • Director of Corporate Communications • Diversity Consultant • Drug Company Representative • Educational Media Specialist • Systems Administrator • Broadcasting Production Supervisor • Lawyer • Employment Interviewer • Environmental Lobbyist • **Editor** • Events Planner • Executive Administrative Assistant • Fashion Merchandiser • **Political Analyst and Campaign Director** • Film Marketing • Film Director • **Forensics/Debate Director** • Fundraiser • Gallery Manager/Owner • Government Lobbyist • **Governmental Press Secretary** • Graduate Dean • International Program Coordinator • Intercultural Communication Consultant • Marketing Communication Manager • Marketing Product Manager • Corporate Communication Director

NCA

NATIONAL COMMUNICATION ASSOCIATION
1765 N Street, N.W. Washington, DC, 20036
www.natcom.org

---

wants!" Of course that is an overstatement, because there are many occupations that require very specific technical training. These would include such pursuits as civil engineer, brain surgeon, computer programmer, bulldozer operator, airline pilot, and submarine captain—to name only a few. Nevertheless, in contemporary society there is one kind of skill that stands out sharply as more critical to success in the workplace than any other. That skill is the *ability to communicate effectively*—that is, to communicate clearly and accurately in such a way that others have no difficulty whatever in understanding what you are saying or writing.

In virtually any survey, or other research study, of what employers say they want when they hire new people, they say "the ability to communicate effectively."[1] There is no question that other skills are also important in the workplace. Some employers want people who can start immediately and expertly perform the duties of accountants, investment managers, nurses, or other specialized roles. Yet, the vast majority of people in the American labor force do not perform these highly specific technical duties. After graduation from college, the majority begin work in entry-level jobs in companies, corporations, agencies, and industries. There they learn the specific duties that they need to perform. If they prove to be valuable and dedicated employees, they soon move up in responsibility and reward. For the most part, in such work, they deal with *people,* not numbers or things. They use communication skills to relate to customers, colleagues, and clients in ways that bring them to buy, invest, perform, donate, cooperate, join, be satisfied, vote, approve, or engage in some other form of action that their employers value. Becoming an expert **communicator,** therefore, *lays the foundation for success* in the largest segment of the contemporary labor force.

Jobs are not the only setting in which communication can be critical. There are compelling reasons beyond the world of work for developing refined skills as a communicator. We must all relate effectively to those whom we like, love, honor, admire, or otherwise value. People who are unable to do this often experience problems. If they fail to interact comfortably with their families, friends, lovers, neighbors, and others with whom they are in frequent contact, they may remain "outsiders" who live lonely and unrewarding lives. The divorce courts constantly process people who were unable to communicate effectively with their spouses. Children in homes where effective communication with parents is not possible are at risk. Effective communication is crucial in the relationship between physicians and their patients, and for designing campaigns to persuade individuals to adopt behaviors that promote good health.[2] Men or women who cannot communicate in acceptable ways with persons of the opposite gender don't get a second date—and maybe not even a first one! And so it goes. The bottom line is that ability to communicate effectively at both a *personal* level and in the *workplace* is one of the most important skills characterizing modern life.

Human communication is a truly remarkable process. Think about it! It is our most complicated form of behavior. Because it is so complicated, it sharply separates us from other members of the animal kingdom. Through the use of words, along with other signs and **symbols** for which we share meanings, we do all kinds of important things. We perceive, evaluate, and respond to the physical and social world around us as only human beings can.

Communication can be looked at from both an individual and a social or collective viewpoint. For example, it is not only the means by which we are able to engage in human *thought* (an individual activity), but also it provides us with the ability to develop and maintain a *society* (clearly a social activity). At a personal level communication enables each of us to acquire a *personality.* That is we become a separate and unique individual—with our own special patterns of beliefs, attitudes, and habits of behavior that are not identical to those of anyone else in the world. Not only that, but because we engage in extensive communication with other people we develop shared understandings about what is expected and acceptable in social relationships—a host of *shared guides for behavior* (informal norms, laws, etc.). In an overall sense, then, communication is critical to everything that we are. It is the foundation of virtually everything that is human and that we do not share with other biological organisms.[3]

But how important is the ability to communicate *effectively* to each of us personally? As we noted, communicating well or poorly can spell the difference between success and failure in almost every kind of human relationship. The American society today is no longer one in which those who work with their hands can achieve significant economic success—as was the case only a few decades ago. For most of the 1900s, blue-collar workers producing "things" of many kinds could earn relatively high incomes, even though they were not skilled communicators. Those days have all but come to a close. By the mid-20th century, the United States was already becoming an "information society" in which more people were working with symbols—words and numbers—than were producing things with their hands.[4] Today, educated workers who are skilled communicators command the highest salaries. Those who lack the ability to communicate ideas persuasively and accurately are at a distinct economic disadvantage.

Improving your ability to communicate is precisely what this book is about. It examines the fundamental nature of human communication and discusses how this process is influenced in a variety of settings. No one will claim that this is easy. You will have to work hard to achieve this goal, but it will be worth it. In other words, this text is not just a "how-to" manual like the ones people get with a new software program. Acquiring effective communication skills requires *detailed analysis of every feature of the process.* Becoming a truly competent communicator rests upon a full understanding of the nature of speech and language as used in both verbal and nonverbal communication, as well as how different situations influence the communication process, and of how to listen effectively. In other words, practical skills are built on an understanding of concepts, principles, and theories that explain the human communication process as it takes place in a variety of contexts for many purposes. That knowledge has emerged from decades of systematic study and research on how communication takes place, how it can go wrong, and what the consequences are likely to be. This text will help in understanding these issues. It brings together the main ideas from these analyses and shows how they can be usefully applied.

Why is human communication complex? For many reasons. For example, the number of *settings* or *contexts* in which people communicate is almost unlimited. Think about it. The range includes such settings as intimate conversations between lovers, discussions in small groups such as families and friends, sending or receiving messages that move through large organizations, and making public speeches with one person talking to a large audience—to name only a few. People also communicate using various *media* such as the telephone, fax machine, the Internet, and various computer systems for sending and receiving e-mail—as well as by using traditional mass media such as newspapers, magazines, the movies, and television, whereby messages may go out to millions of people. Unique factors characterize communication in each such context, with each medium posing its own problems. OK, so communication can be complex, but how it works in various settings and what difference it makes will be addressed in chapters that follow.

Defining Communication

But wait a minute! What exactly is communication? That may sound like an obvious question, because you do it all the time and you undoubtedly do it very well. However, the exact nature of the process has fascinated human beings and has been debated throughout history.[5] From ancient times to the present, philosophers, scholars, and teachers have examined how people are influenced, both in personal terms by thinking and knowing the world around them, and in terms of rational discourse and public speaking as forms of human communication.[6] They have left a legacy of important treatises on many topics, such as oratory, rhetoric, dialogue, persuasion, elocution, syntax, and grammar, that deepen our contemporary understanding of human communication.[7] We need not plow through this entire legacy, but a brief look at what a few of them have said can be helpful.

By the beginning of the 1900s, social scientists had put together comprehensive definitions of human communication that more or less included all its basic features. For example, pioneer student of communication Charles Horton Cooley, writing in 1909, developed the early foundations of a broad *paradigm*—that is, a general and comprehensive theory—explaining that the origins and nature of the human mind as well as society itself was in the use of language. That paradigm came to be called "symbolic interactionism," and it remains an important way today to look at individual human personality and the social order. This view stresses the idea that *human nature* (what makes us different from animals) is developed in a process of communication using language symbols (mainly words) that are passed on as part of culture through generations. His definition was an interesting one:

> By Communication is here meant the mechanism through which human relations exist and develop—all the symbols of the mind, together with the means of conveying them through space and preserving them in time. It includes the expression of the face, attitude and gesture, the tones of the voice, words, writing, printing, railways, telegraphs, telephones, and whatever else may be the latest achievements in the conquest of time and space.[8]

If you look closely at Cooley's definition you can see that it recognizes that communication can take place not only by *verbal* means but also by *nonverbal* means as well. He also noted that communicating via *media* that surmount space and time can be part of what he called the "mechanism" (by which people relate to each other). Although he had no knowledge of media to come—such as radio, television, movies, and the Internet—his definition is as modern as the latest technological triumphs of digital television, wireless cellular phones, and the Internet. However, note also that his definition says nothing about exactly how the "mechanism" works. That is, it really does not explain *how* communication actually takes place, either between individuals or via media. That really is a limitation of any definition. A necessary feature of an acceptable definition today is that it must set forth the nature of the *process* by which the intended meanings of a person sending a message are reconstructed by a **receiver** in such a way that both of their meanings are reasonably similar. Nevertheless, Cooley's definition did set forth the important ideas of *verbal, nonverbal,* and *mediated* communication.

We noted earlier that communication scholars make use of perspectives and findings from all of the social sciences that are concerned with communication. In that spirit, let's look at what psychologists have to say about the process. First, however, we need to understand that their discipline is a very general one, which tries to find ways in which all living organisms share patterns of behavior. Thus, in recent times, psychologists have taken an interesting approach to try to identify the nature of communication *as it occurs across species.* In other words, they have done so by studying communication among both animals and human beings to see what they have in common.

The classic strategy of psychology is to develop a *comparative perspective*—comparing the ways in which communication occurs among all animal forms, from simple to complex, and then sorting out what is common to all, or different among them. This strategy can be a very useful one and it has led to a very general definition of communication that actually can be applied to all living forms. Perhaps there are some important clues here that will help us to develop a really useful definition of human communication:

> Communication occurs when one organism (the source) encodes **information** into a signal that passes to another organism (the receiver), who decodes the signal and is capable of responding appropriately.[9]

This very broad definition from comparative psychology is one into which both human and animal communication can fit. However, that may be of only limited help in understanding what is actually unique about human communication. That is, what is there about human communication that very clearly *sets it apart* from that of animals? Or, is there actually little or nothing that makes the human communication process unique and distinct?

In spite of its limitations, this very general definition from psychology does add to the factors that were included in Cooley's definition in that it provides an elementary view of his "mechanism." For example, it shows that when an act of communication takes place, one "organism" initiates the process by serving as a **source** or **sender**. Then, some sort of **encoding** occurs. Following that, "information" *moves across space.* Following that, **decoding** is accomplished by a *receiver.* Finally, a *response* is made.

These ideas are important because they are indeed essential features of any act of communication—whether among animals or human beings. However, more is needed for understanding this form of behavior among human beings because people communicate in very complex ways that never occur among animals. For example, while animals clearly do signal each other about food, mating, and danger, they do not chat with friends, give speeches, write letters, or read the newspaper, making use of verbal and nonverbal communication in both oral and written form. So, human communication *is really not just like that of animals,* and much more has to be added to describe the process more realistically. Indeed, a brief comparison of animal and human communication will be one of the objectives of Chapter 2. Meanwhile, bringing together both Cooley's sociological concepts and those from comparative psychology, we can (finally) formulate a foundation definition for discussing how two human beings in face-to-face settings communicate with each other:

> Human communication is a *process* during which a *source* (individual) initiates a *message* using *verbal and nonverbal symbols* and *contextual cues* to express *meaning* by transmitting *information* in such a way that similar or parallel *understandings* are constructed by the intended *receiver(s).*

At first glance, this definition looks complicated. Yet, if you look more closely, it is essentially a sort of *list* of the important factors that are involved when two people communicate with one another.

Let's look carefully at each of the factors that is included in this definition. For example, note that the definition begins by stating that communication is a *process*. That is really an important idea—and it is not very difficult to understand. To explain, any "process" is a series of *stages* in which something undergoes *transformation* at each step. Lots of things that you already know about take place as "processes." An example would be transforming food that you chew, eat, and digest (in a series of stages) into energy for your body plus waste. Or, transforming the expansive characteristics of an explosion of gasoline vapor into the power running your car (plus waste gases that pollute the air).

In the communication process human beings serve as *sources* and begin by selecting meanings that will make up their messages. It is these meanings that are transformed during the process. In the first stage, the source's thoughts and ideas—his or her meanings—are transformed into messages by selecting appropriate symbols. This is the stage that is referred to as *encoding*. Then, these messages are transformed once again, this time into *information*—that is, physical events, like verbal sounds, visible nonverbal signals (like printed letters), or both, that can move across space. In the next stage, receiving individuals then see or hear the messages and transform them back to the person's own symbolic understandings of thoughts and ideas—meanings—aroused by the message. For communication to be accurate, of course, the meanings constructed by both sender and receiver must be similar. So, communication can be thought of as a series of stages—that is, a process.

A critical idea included in the definition is the idea that a message typically consists of a set of words with agreed-upon meanings, plus arrangements of grammar and syntax that are part of language. It may also include standardized nonverbal cues and contextual factors that imply meanings. Thus, a source normally expresses intended meanings with words, gestures, and actions. However, features from the social and physical settings within which the communication takes place can *add additional meanings*. All these concepts—words, nonverbal symbols, and contextual cues—are discussed here only in brief overview, but each of these ideas will be discussed in full detail in subsequent chapters.

Note also that the definition highlights the idea of *parallel meanings* in each of the communicators. As we will see, *meaning* is a form of internal or subjective behavior that occurs as responses *within a person* to words or other standardized signs and signals. To the degree that the subjective meanings aroused in each person are *similar*, they can be said to be "parallel." If that is the case, the communication between the individuals is reasonably complete or accurate. If the meanings are *different*, the communication process has suffered some kind of **distortion**, and the result is limited **accuracy.**

Although the word *communicator* in everyday language commonly designates the person who initiates a message, in the present analysis both the source and the receiver are "communicators." Therefore, the term *source*, or *sender*, will be used to identify a person who formulates and transmits a message. The term *receiver* will identify the communicator to whom that message is directed and who constructs his or her version of what it means.

Now here is an unusual notion: The foundation definition stated above conceptualizes communication somewhat artificially as a **linear** process—one that starts, goes through stages, one after the other like a straight line, and then stops. Is this realistic? Is it a truly adequate way to describe the complex process of human communication? The answer is definitely "No!" In many ways this linear description of the process is *unrealistic*. This view implies that communication occurs when one person begins the action and another, who waits for the message to arrive, completes it. That is, a person serving as a source begins the process by formulating a message and transmitting it to another person, who then receives and interprets it—ending the process! In reality, ongoing communication between two interacting parties is *far more complex* than this linear view implies. However, even though this is not the final way that we will define and discuss human communication, it does provide a good point of departure.

An important advantage of looking first at communication as a linear process is that it provides a foundation for understanding in some detail what two human beings do when they communicate. In reality, human communicators engage in a complex and ongoing *exchange*. As will be clear, they repeatedly go through linear stages as they communicate back and forth. Thus, when one person is acting as a sender, she or he can also be acting as a receiver while formulating an outgoing message to be transmitted to the other. Similarly, the receiver can be serving as a source, both listening and sending back a response.

Usually, people quickly take turns in such interactions. However, they may perform them *simultaneously*, providing subtle messages to each other before, during, and after their turns. However, even subtle messages must be formulated, transmitted, and received. Thus, ongoing stages of message transmission and reception, as in a conversation, are made up of patterns of linear exchanges that are embedded in a complex process of simultaneous interactions. That sounds complicated, and in many ways it is. We will discuss it after beginning with the linear view. As will be seen, it is very helpful, even if it is not the final answer.

Using the linear view, then, we can *analyze* the process—that is, break it down into each of the components and activities that make up each stage or step and each transformation. Again, as we have indicated, such a step-by-step analysis of communication is in a sense artificial, just as it would be to analyze breathing or walking as a series of stages. Everyone communicates so automatically that it scarcely seems necessary to look at it one stage at a time. However, to improve our communication skills, we must first understand every feature of the process thoroughly in order to identify potential problems and to minimize the effects of various pitfalls. Thus, the linear view of communication provides a convenient initial way of looking at the process, breaking it down into the stages involved. Once these are understood, the more complex simultaneous and interactive view can be discussed.

Communication as Linear Process: An Analytic Model

The stages or steps involved in the person-to-person human communication process can be illustrated by considering an elementary communicative act involving only two people. The source will initiate the exchange with a sentence consisting of three words, and the receiver will respond with a single nonverbal gesture. Using that example, we can examine a very basic linear model of the communication process.

A *model* in science is a "representation"—a careful and concise *description* that summarizes and illustrates what takes place in some situation or process. All sciences use them for that purpose. Some models are verbal—set forth in ordinary words and descriptive sentences. These are probably the easiest to understand. Others use graphics, abstract symbols, or even mathematical equations in some cases to portray what they represent. The model of communication presented in Figure 1.1 is both verbal and graphic.

How about a "linear" model? This is really a simple idea. As noted earlier, the term *linear* indicates that the process being depicted moves rather like a straight line, from a beginning point to an end point through specific stages—one after the other. Our basic strategy of analysis using the linear model will be to start a conversation between two people at a point when one person decides to transmit a message to another. That sounds simple enough. We will then enter the process and artificially *slow it down* to look at what happens stage by stage—like looking at a film projected slowly, one frame at a time. We will examine every stage of

the communicative act in detail. We will start from the point at which one human being constructs a meaningful message, transmits it to another, who attends to it and then reconstructs the meaning and ultimately understands the message. We will also indicate that the receiver then transmits an acknowledgment back to the initiator. Although these stages may sound simple and straightforward, they involve many aspects of human capacity and complex behavior.

We can start with the example shown in Figure 1.1, our linear model. The sender says to the receiver, "Nice work, John," and the receiver smiles in return. Despite its simplicity, this exchange, using only three words (and a nonverbal gesture) provides a basis for understanding each of the steps or stages involved in human communication. Essentially, the process involves *five distinct stages*, summarized as follows:

Stage 1: *Deciding on the message.* A person serving as a source decides on a message to be sent to a receiver (or receivers) to achieve a desired *goal.*

Stage 2: *Encoding the intended meanings.* The source searches his or her *memory* for specific *symbols,* such as words and gestures, and their associated *meanings* that can be put together into a *pattern* that will describe the desired facts, ideas and images.

Stage 3: *Transmitting the message as information.* The message is transformed by voice or other means into physical *information* (like sound waves) so that it can overcome distance, and the message moves in this form from sender to receiver.

Stage 4. *Perceiving the information as a message.* The receiver attends to the physical information as it arrives and *perceives,* that is, identifies, the symbols into which it has been coded.

Stage 5: *Decoding and interpreting the message.* The receiver searches and compares

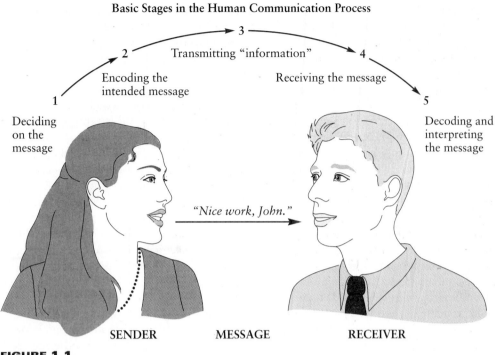

Basic Stages in the Human Communication Process

3

2   Transmitting "information"   4

Encoding the   Receiving the message
intended message

1   5

Deciding   Decoding and
on the   interpreting
message   the message

"Nice work, John."

SENDER   **MESSAGE**   **RECEIVER**

FIGURE 1.1

A Linear Model

With the basic linear perspective, we can understand what is happening at each stage in the communication process: A message is decided on and formulated by the sender; the message is encoded and transmitted; it is decoded and interpreted by the receiver, who applies meanings stored in memory.

the incoming symbols with meanings stored in her or his memory and selects those that seem best for *interpreting* the message.

Look at those steps again. There are a lot of concepts in them that need to be discussed more fully. These include *encoding, decoding, symbols, goal, memory, meaning, pattern, information, perceiving,* and *interpreting.* This is quite a list. However, to understand human communication fully, each step has to be explained because these steps are the human activities that make the process possible. Therefore, let's take a closer look at each of the five stages, and see how these concepts are involved:

Stage One: Deciding on the Message

Any person initiating an act of communication has some *intention* in mind—that is, a *goal.* The goal may be to sell something, improve a relationship, fire back an insult, or teach something to another person. Of the many goals that people attempt to achieve through communication, most are simple and obvious, but others can be complex, and vague, and are often difficult to ascertain. Indeed, on many occasions, the person initiating a message may not have consciously thought much about achieving some sort of "goal." For example, when you see your friend walking toward you in the morning, and you say, "Hi, how are you?" you do not consciously think, *Hmmm, I have a goal of sending a nice greeting to this person who is my friend because that will help maintain that relationship, which I value.* Nevertheless, on close analysis, that is what such a communication is all about. You plan and execute it so fast that you are not even aware of having a goal in mind.

Even though such planning and stating such a greeting takes place swiftly, it is a deliberate act. We do not just randomly run off at the mouth with any sort of message. We formulate messages so that they fit with what we are involved in and intending at the moment. For example, in Figure 1.1, where the three-word message is, "Nice work, John," the source's purpose is simple: *to express a sentiment that will reinforce a meaningful relationship.* Whatever the intention, a key principle here is that communication begins when the sender mentally constructs a message that she or he feels the receiver can interpret with reasonable accuracy so as to accomplish whatever goal or purposes the person seeks.

Stage Two: Encoding the Intended Meanings

After the goal or goals have been set, whether vaguely or clearly, the source must construct (mentally) a message consistent with his or her purpose. This is done by selecting from *memory* whatever *signs and symbols*—usually words and maybe gestures—are needed to represent the *intended meanings.* This is what takes place in the encoding stage and it can be complex. It is sometimes complex because it is more than merely selecting particular words. Often, our messages include gestures, postures, or even objects and other nonverbal symbols associated with particular meanings.

The term *symbol,* as used here, is an important one, but the idea is quite simple. A symbol is any word, number, gesture, object, or other cue (verbal or nonverbal) that has associated with it in our "language community" a *conventional* meaning. The term **convention** implies that people share a rule as to how they are ex-

pected to understand it. In other words, the symbol arouses in our minds an interpretation that is very similar to the interpretations that others are likely to experience when they use, see, read or hear the same one. Even a bodily posture can serve as a symbol. Imagine a person who is uptight, has folded arms, is glaring at you with a frown, and is tapping his or her foot. Few of us would assume that such a person is a happy camper. Physical objects can serve as symbols. Examples are a police badge, a flag, a cross, and even a limousine. Clothing is often used to send messages (as when we wear a military uniform, a tuxedo, or a long evening gown, versus when we are in shorts and sandals).

While actions and objects can be important, our principle "mechanism" (as Cooley stated it) for communicating with other people is the use of *words* as standardized symbols. That is, in verbal communication words are most often the tools that permit meanings to be encoded. Moreover, words are the most deeply established of all signs and signals in our language culture. Words are truly a remarkable invention. Because words have such well-standardized meanings in our language community, and can be translated with reasonable accuracy from one to another, we can interpret the thoughts and ideas of writers who have been dead for thousands of years. No animal can even remotely do this. Cooley explained the idea in a colorful way:

> A word is a vehicle, a boat floating down from the past with the thought of men we never saw; and in coming to understand it we enter not only into the minds of our contemporaries, but into the general mind of humanity continuous through time.[10]

The term *sign* refers to much the same idea, but it is even broader. Words are one form of signs, but even events can serve as signs. For example, a lightning stroke can be a "sign" that a peal of thunder will follow, or a snarling dog may be a "sign" for an intruder that an attack is likely. Animals use signs to adjust to their world, as when a dog whines at the door to be let out. Symbols, on the other hand, are a form of signs that are used *exclusively by human beings* who share their links to meanings in a specific language community. However, people do communicate with signs that are not really words. For example, two persons who live together quickly learn to read signs in the behavior of one another that tell them what mood the person is in, or what has pleased or angered them. They don't need verbal messages to understand such meanings. So, signs in this sense are part of the human communication experience as well—although they may be used at a less conscious level than when we use words.

Although the example shown in Figure 1.1 is elementary, involving only the symbols "nice," "work," and "John," plus a slight smile, most people in the English-speaking language community will have conventional (standardized) meanings for each of these words. Even so, selecting just the right symbols is not all the sender must consider. Not only must each of the symbols selected be *linked in our language community with our desired meanings,* but also we must believe that they will be *understood in the same way by both sender and receiver.*

In addition, there is the problem of the *sequence* or pattern of these signs and symbols. This is called *syntax.* For example, suppose we rearranged the order of the three words of the message in Figure 1.1 into another pattern, such as "Work nice John." Hold it! Hold it! That expresses a very different overall meaning—even though it contains exactly the same three words! Or consider this case: "The bear ate the man." That's clear enough. But what about "The man ate the bear?" Obviously, in each case, these are very different overall meanings that are introduced by the distinct patterns. So, meaning is associated not only with specific symbols, but the *order* in which they are presented. In other words, syntax matters, and it matters a lot! The lesson here is that our language community sets rules, not only about the meanings aroused in our heads for specific symbols (words, numbers, gestures, objects,

and so on), but also for the sequences or patterns in which they are used.

The next step in gaining a perspective on the human communication process is to examine the *nature of meaning* itself and the relationship it implies between symbols, patterns, and memory. Then we can look at ways in which senders try to anticipate whether the receiver actually will understand their encoded message.

The meaning of meaning. Quite obviously, understanding the concept of meaning is essential to a full understanding of the encoding process. Meaning can be difficult to define, study, and analyze. Nevertheless, we need to do it because it is at the very heart of the human communication process. We can start by noting that meanings are *subjective.* What that means is that they are experiences that occur "in our heads," where only we—and no one else—can experience them. For that reason, we have no way of directly observing another person's meanings. Nevertheless, we can make some *assumptions* about meaning that will make it less mysterious and easier to define.

First, meanings are not ethereal, spiritual, or in any other way unnatural. They are a form of internal, that is, "mental" *behavior.* In short, meaning consists of *responses* we make (within ourselves) to objects, events, and situations we encounter in the world around us. Those subjective responses are the different kinds of images, feelings, and beliefs that are aroused within us when we encounter some part of reality—a dog, a house, mom, a football game, and so on. Thus, meanings are *learned* internal behaviors. We encounter such realities (dog, mom, house, etc.) through our senses—by seeing, feeling, hearing, smelling, or even tasting. After many such encounters, we learn to make a specific pattern of internal subjective responses (a set of meanings) that we and our fellow members of our language community assign to each kind of object, event, and situation.

What about meanings for words, as opposed to objects and events? We learn to make responses to words or other symbols *in the same way we experience meaning for things that exist in reality*. In other words, the term *meaning* has a double implication: Not only does it imply subjective responses to aspects of reality—when we actually see, hear, or feel something that exists—but it also implies the same kinds of responses *to the words that we use to label that reality*. To illustrate this point, consider this: We will have an internal meaning experience when we see a small animal, such as a squirrel. At the same time, we have a very similar internal experience when we hear or read the *word* "squirrel." If we were talking and I mentioned that I saw a squirrel, you would have a kind of internal image (a meaning) of that nice little animal associated with that word. Thus, both the reality and the symbol we use as its label arouse much the same inner meaning. Recognizing this double implication of *meaning* (as a response both to reality and to labels for that reality), we can set forth a rather simple definition. *Meaning* can be defined as:

> Subjective responses that individuals in a given language community learn to make, either to things they directly experience in reality or to particular symbols they use to label that reality.

We learn such links between reality, symbols, and meaning because we live among other people, all of whom have been taught the rules to be used to associate specific patterns of inner experiences with particular words we share with them. It is this remarkable "language community" feature of human social life that permits human beings to communicate *with each other* as they do. In addition, this ability also makes it possible to communicate *with ourselves* (to think) by using language to arouse internal meanings. Meaning, then, is the key to understanding human beings as both thinking and communicating creatures.

But are we sure that others in our language community understand reality as we do? Interesting question, and one that has been debated for centuries. The answer is that we can't be certain, but we normally assume that the meanings one person experiences for a particular aspect of reality or a word used to label it are basically the same as another's. For example, we assume that a banana looks the same to everyone and has the same smell, feel, and taste. The symbol we use to label that reality, "banana," is also supposed to arouse pretty much the same experiences in everyone. Unfortunately, a sender's subjective meanings may not always be precisely and exactly the same as the receiver's, which can result in distortion and misinterpretation of the message.

Types of meanings: Denotations versus connotations. One potential source of confusion in communication is the problem of *unique personal meanings* versus shared or *standardized meanings*. This can be a significant source of inaccuracy in communications. For the most part, a symbol in a message transmitted to a receiver will evoke only its *denotative* or standardized meaning within the relevant culture. If that is the case, accuracy will be high. The meanings aroused in each will be restricted to those set forth in dictionaries. However, there is always the problem of *connotative meanings*. These may be part of the personal meanings that an individual uniquely associates with a word because of past experience, or as a result of membership in a specific culture. If that is the case, use of the symbol in a message will arouse those private and unshared meanings and reduce the accuracy of the communication.

Connotative meanings can be illustrated easily. For example, in 2001, President George W. Bush initially described to the public the struggle against terrorism that he was designing as a "crusade." What he meant, of course, was a spirited and determined effort to apprehend and bring to justice those who commit attacks against civilians—such as the assault by airliner on the World Trade Center that occurred on Tuesday, September 11, 2001.[11]

In contemporary English, a "crusade" can be conducted against anything that needs to be strongly opposed—disease, poverty, crime, ignorance, or whatever. The meaning of *crusade* in that context was clear to most Americans who heard the president's speech. However, that term has additional and much more emotional meanings for those of Muslim faith. They remain deeply aware of the great armed expeditions initiated by Pope Urban II, beginning in the 1100s to force the Muslims out of Jerusalem. Over two centuries there were a number of bitterly fought crusades, led by knights and their followers, who were intent on ejecting Muslims from the Holy Land, and indeed the complete destruction of Islam. To many in the Arabic world, then, the president's use of the word *crusade* had ominous connotative meanings indeed.

In less global terms, suppose that you ask me if I have a pet and I say, "Yes, I have a dog." It may appear that communication has been complete and accurate. After all, the word *dog* has a specific denotative meaning set forth in English language dictionaries. However, I may have private (connotative) meanings for the word that bring to mind the attributes of my large, brown, friendly, and gentle dog that wags its tail when petted. Your dog, however, is different. It is a mean, little, white mutt that barks nastily and nips at the heels of strangers. Our mutual connotative meanings have limited the degree to which our communication can be accurate.

Although connotations often bring about inaccuracy, they are not always undesirable. They can be a source of delight in certain kinds of messages. Poets, novelists, and even spellbinding orators often try to arouse a flow of colorful subjective meanings within their audiences by a rich attachment of connotative meanings to the symbols they select.

While the use of connotative meanings may be accepted for some purposes, accurate communication normally requires denotative meanings. It is a simple idea, really, and one that virtually everyone understands. To do otherwise, and let people use whatever meanings they wished for a particular word or nonverbal symbol, would result in an *Alice in Wonderland* world of chaos and would make communica-

tion impossible. It is for this reason that dictionaries provide relatively fixed meanings—at least for verbal symbols.

Storing symbols and meanings in memory. The way symbols and meanings are stored in memory is also an important consideration for understanding the encoding stage. But how does this work? No one is completely certain, but scientists in recent years have developed a couple of theories to explain how our memories work.[12] One way of explaining the process (by analogy) is to think of our memory structure as like that of a computer that records information on a magnetic disk, but infinitely more intricate. The key concepts that scientists have identified are *traces* and *schemas*.

Traces are imprinted records of experience registered in the brain's nerve cells. The computer analogy would be the magnetic areas on a disc that record the digital patterns for letters and numbers. But a word of caution: It may not be helpful to carry the computer analogy too far. We are talking about a biological rather than a mechanical process. In any case, traces can be thought of as neural "imprints" of the images, recollections, and other elements of experience that we associate with every word or symbol we know. This gets a bit murky because neurologists differ in their explanations of exactly how traces are imprinted. It may be a biochemical process, the result of tiny electrical currents, or alterations of nerve-cell structure. But one thing seems clear: A large body of research indicates that everything we experience, either in waking life or in our dreams, *leaves memory traces in our brain cells.* Even though we may not be able to recover those traces into consciousness at will, they appear to be there. We do know that many memories can be recovered through hypnosis, drugs, or psychotherapy.

Looking at memory *psychologically* (rather than physiologically), how do we recover into consciousness memories of our experience from these traces? That is, how do we *organize our memories* so that we can recall past episodes in our life, meanings for words, and so forth? Psychologists who study memory conclude that as we send our experiences to our memory system, our brain organizes them into *schemas*. *A schema is a pattern or configuration of traces of symbols, images, experiences and their meanings that have been organized and recorded in a person's memory.*[13] What this implies is that our memory is not just a random jumble of imprinted traces. We store and recall organized schemas made up of all the memory traces of understanding, feeling, imagery, or other interpretations that we associate with experiences that we have, or even with the word labeling that aspect of reality.

To illustrate, some schemas are simple, like the organization of the recall we experience for such words as *chair, fork,* or *shoe*. Others are more elaborate, like *circus*. Here we have a number of ideas in a kind of hierarchy, with big tents, animals, people, acts, and so on. The ideas included get more and more specific as one goes down the levels, with the most general and inclusive at the top and the most detailed at the bottom. (See Figure 1.2.)

You have used schemas many times—indeed every day. For example, when your friend says the phrase "Fourth of July," what organized meanings will you both recall? Probably you will experience a pattern of meanings that includes fireworks, flags, parades, and perhaps picnics or barbecues. But shame on you! You forgot the Declaration of Independence, which was announced on that date, and all the other patriotic reasons we celebrate that date. In any case, the Fourth of July schema brings together a number of meanings into an organized configuration.

Some schemas are related to more abstract terms, like "democracy" or "freedom." But even though those these terms are abstractions, we do have some experiences that "come to mind" when we hear or read them. We also have schemas for particular episodes in our life, such as our high school graduation ceremony, the wedding of a good friend, or a scary movie we have seen. Thus, we organize our meanings psychologically into schematic patterns of varying complexity that help in the recall of "clusters" of related traces.

What do all these ideas and concepts—memory traces and schemas—have to do with encoding intended meanings in a message? The schema idea is essential in describing the structure of a particular message that is selected and encoded for transmission to others. We can think of any message we formulate as *a number of organized schemas*, one associated with each word we select. Referring again to the example in Figure 1.1, the sender constructs an organized message from the separate schemas for "nice," "work," and "John." The sender then organizes these individual schemas into a sequence that meets the requirements of syntax (and of course grammar) in our language community. We noted earlier that these rules are also recorded as traces that can be recalled as organized schemas. For example, the sender in this case uses the recalled schemas of meanings for each word and rules of syntax to bring together the message of "Nice work, John" into one overall configuration of meaning. The sender fully believes that the message represents her intended meanings and that good old John will be able to interpret it in his own head by experiencing parallel meanings.

These issues of encoding include a lot of ideas, to be sure; but they are necessary for understanding how communication works. In summary, at the encoding stage the sender has to sort among his or her traces and organized schemas and decide which symbols match the meanings he or she intends. The individual then selects those symbols, plus the appropriate rules for their combination, in order to form a message that is both appropriate to the occasion and consistent with the goal. Then, as the encoding stage of the process proceeds, he or she tentatively constructs the message pattern to be used.

Role-taking to assess probable receiver interpretations. Even when the message has been tentatively constructed, the encoding process is not complete. A remaining problem for the sender

FIGURE 1.2
A Schema for "Circus"
The schema for "circus" includes meaningful categories of experience, such as animals, people, and things. Each person's schema for "circus" will vary according to the person's subjective experiences and memories.

is to decide whether the receiver is likely to understand the message as formulated. Will good old John understand what his boss is saying? The sender decides this by an activity called **role-taking**—which means "taking the role of the other."[14] Role-taking refers to an activity of the sender or source, who figuratively places herself or himself (psychologically) in the position of the receiver. The purpose of role-taking for the sender is to try to understand the best way to encode intended meanings so that the receiver will be able to interpret them as they were intended. This is not difficult if the sender knows the receiver well, but it can be a problem if the receiver is a complete stranger. In either case, if role-taking suggests the receiver is *not* likely to understand the message as formulated, the sender must quickly revise the message before transmission. (See Figure 1.3.)

Role-taking may sound complicated, but it is not difficult to understand. We all do this every time we communicate, and we do it in different ways, depending on the nature of the receiver. For example, we engage in role-taking when we communicate with a child—encoding the message in simple symbols associated with

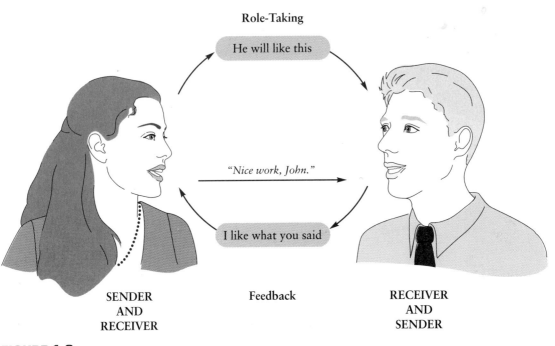

Role-Taking

He will like this

"Nice work, John."

I like what you said

SENDER
AND
RECEIVER

Feedback

RECEIVER
AND
SENDER

FIGURE 1.3

Role-Taking and Feedback
Adding feedback to the linear model modifies the communication process by making the
receiver now a sender and the original sender now a receiver. Role-taking further modifies the model by making it more interactive.

appropriate meanings the child is likely to understand. We also use role-taking with adults
every time we hope to convey a message that
may not be easily understood or that could
arouse unwanted feelings. The assessment of
probable interpretations by role-taking, then, is
a significant part of the message-encoding
process.

An important, and more complex, role-taking
activity is the construction of an *implicit personality*. That is, when we look at someone, especially for the first time, we observe what are
called "salient characteristics." These are prominent, or at least readily noticeable, features of
the person—a nice smile, excessive jewelry, a big
nose, an attractive hair style, obesity, or anything that stands out. We use these features to
make assumptions about that person's character and probable behavior. (This idea will be explained in greater detail in Chapter 9).

Encoding as automated behavior. By explaining the encoding process in such great detail, it
may seem cumbersome and slow. That is totally
incorrect. In fact, the encoding process is *unbelievably fast*—so fast that it rivals the speed of
even the most sophisticated computer. In an instant we can formulate a message, engage in
role-taking, and revise what we want to say if
needed. We do this all the time, even when
using long strings and patterns of symbols. We
can achieve this speed because encoding behavior is *automated*. That is, it takes place so fast
and automatically that we are not usually
aware of the steps we follow while doing it.[15]

Examples of automated behavior, other than
what we do when communicating, include typing on a keyboard, playing a piano, and driving a car. When we do these things, we do not
carefully plan, select, and then execute each
finger or arm movement or other action with

conscious awareness. In the communication process, encoding messages that incorporate the meanings we intend is done even faster.

Stage Three: Transmitting the Message as Information

The third stage in the linear model of the communication process requires that the message span the distance between the parties as *information*.[16] The term *information* refers to *patterned physical events*. For example, in the example in Figure 1.1 the message "Nice work, John" is transformed into agitations of air molecules that we know as sound. That transformation is accomplished by the parts of the body the sender uses to produce the sound waves relevant to the phrase "Nice work, John." In this form, the information moves across space in physical patterns representing words and related aspects of the message. This information serves as *stimuli* (a term from psychology) that the receiver's sensory organs can detect.

If the message had been transmitted in written form, the information would conquer distance as visible patterned marks on paper. In a movie the information is patterns of light waves. Here, in both cases, the information stimuli are visual. If a medium such as a telephone, computer, or broadcasting had been involved, electronic impulses traveling along a wire or radiated electromagnetic waves would move the information from one communicator to another.

Stage Four: Perceiving the Information as a Message

In the fourth stage of our linear model, the person to whom the message is directed becomes the principal actor. Briefly stated, the receiver first *perceives* the incoming information stimuli and then assigns meanings to it so as to interpret it as a message. Perception is a rather complex psychological process. What happens is this: Patterns of information transmitted by the message source are picked up as stimuli by the receiver's sensory organs—usually eyes or ears. These are then identified as specific words, in a recognizable pattern, along with any nonverbal or other observable cues. Only then will the assignment of meanings (decoding) actually begin.

The term *perception* is a very important one in understanding human communication. It comes from psychology and has both common-use and technical meanings. Many people use the term loosely as a synonym for *belief* when they say something like, "It is my perception that our candidate will win the election." A more precise and technical meaning is used by psychologists and other social scientists. When they use the term *perception*, it means seeing, hearing, or feeling something (with the senses) and then *identifying* what it is, based on knowledge and prior experience that the person has obtained from his or her culture. To illustrate, when we see a person with a round semispherical shape of cloth on the end of a shaft held over the individual's head while it is raining (a stimulus) we have no trouble in identifying (perceiving) it as an "umbrella."

Thus, perceiving refers to identifying and classifying a stimulus apprehended by the senses. It could be a physical stimulus—like recognizing a small, red spherical object as an apple—or it could be identifying the pattern of sounds for the spoken word *apple* as a label for that fruit. Other stimuli may be identified as abstractions, such as "triangle," or as complex ideas, such as "justice" or "the Middle Ages." Perception is of critical importance in human communication because receivers have to identify the words that make up a message before they interpret it in full by arousing within themselves the appropriate meanings they have stored for those words.

Stage Five: Decoding and Interpreting the Message

After the words and other symbols of the message have been perceived and identified, the process of *decoding* can take place. This occurs at a very rapid rate (again, automated). That is, we are able to receive and interpret very quickly shared meanings associated with long clusters of words and the patterns used by the sender. One need not listen step by step to a message, then carefully decide what specific words have been used, then figure out each word's meaning, then decide what their overall pattern implies, and then interpret what has been said. That would take a while, to say the least. Thus, decoding, as well as encoding, is automated behavior that takes place almost instantaneously.

How can all of this take place so fast? The automated memory processes that enable the sender to sort and select appropriate symbols for the message are also used by the receiver to interpret the information. Stored in the receiver's memory are many thousands of schemas, organized structures of verbal and nonverbal symbols and grammatical patterns that have standardized and recognizable meanings that are *part of our shared language culture.* The incoming symbols are quickly distinguished from others similar to them and specifically identified. For each symbol, a quick search is made for possible interpretations. In the case of our simple three-word example (Figure 1.1), the receiver (John) almost instantly perceives the message as "Nice work, John"—and then instantly sorts out the associated meanings stored in his memory. When these are understood, the linear process is complete.

Note that even within this linear view of the communication process, it is the receiver who actively constructs meanings for the incoming information. In so doing, he or she draws on enormous personal resources of learned meaning responses, based on traces organized into schemas, plus habits, opinions, beliefs, attitudes, values, and factual information stored in memory. Clearly, the receiver's interpretations are certainly related to the sender's intended meanings, but they are not just passive duplications of the sender's meanings. They are *active reconstructions of meanings* derived from the receiver's own traces, schemas, and other experiences stored in memory. Because each participant constructs and interprets meanings separately, things can always go wrong!

Let's pause at this point and reconsider for a moment. As we have already indicated, face-to-face communication is seldom as simple (and never as slow!) as in this example. And, as mentioned repeatedly, it is much more than the start-stop linear process that has been discussed up to this point. In reality, communication *flows back and forth* between people as they engage in ongoing conversations, and what they have said or done earlier shapes what they say next. It is for these reasons that we need to look at a more realistic *interactive model* of the process.

Interactive Communication: A Simultaneous Transactions Model

The basic linear model can be easily transformed into a much more realistic interactive representation of ongoing human communication by recognizing that both people in a conversation are communicators. They constantly respond to each other, simultaneously initiating messages and sending responses back and forth. This calls attention to the importance of messages *sent back by the receiver to the source as responses.* For example, depicted in the linear model, after the source said, "Nice work, John," the receiver responded with a smile. In other words, John sent a message back! Stated a bit more technically, a smile under such circumstances is a nonverbal gesture used as *feedback.*[17] The term **feedback** indicates that some sort of message is returned to the sender as the message is being perceived and interpreted by the receiver. The smile is a good example of nonverbal communication—a conventionalized gesture that functions like a word because it has a standardized meaning in our society. We all understand that it implies a positive, rather than a negative, interpretation of meaning—something like "I like what you said."

Introducing feedback into the model makes the process *interactive.* That is, the communication process is no longer simply linear—a one-way series of stages from sender to receiver—but one in which both parties are *simultaneously* sending and receiving messages to and from one another at the same time. This simultaneous interaction feature of the process makes it necessary to develop a somewhat different model to portray human communication more realistically.

You will be relieved to know that to understand feedback, no new concepts or stages are required. A feedback message may be little more than a simple facial expression, like smiling or yawning, or the feedback may be a complex verbal statement or question, as in ordinary conversation. A feedback message, like any other, begins with a goal—to supply the sender with a return message. Words or gestures are selected to arouse an intended meaning. The message is transmitted (the smile in our example), and it is then perceived and decoded for interpretation by the source, *who is now a receiver*. Thus, feedback follows the step-by-step linear process between the two communicators that was discussed earlier.

However, we can now put together a more realistic model of human communication by incorporating both the role-taking and feedback activities of sender and receiver. This new version can be called a *simultaneous transactions model*. It is simply a broader and more inclusive portrayal of the process that describes in more realistic terms how it usually takes place. Although the phrase "simultaneous transactions" may sound like complex jargon, neither term implies any special meaning beyond common dictionary definitions. When used to describe the communication process, "simultaneous" implies that both communicators are undergoing the same kind of experience *at the same time*. That is not a complex idea. Equally simple is the term **transaction.** It refers to any kind of *exchange*—that is, an activity that occurs between, and mutually influences, all individuals acting with each other in some way. You have transactions every time you buy something, like

exchanging money for beer (oops! we mean milk or soft drinks, of course).

The simultaneous transactions model does not challenge the validity of the linear view of the communication process. On the contrary, it subsumes or *incorporates* it. To explain, the linear model helped us to *analyze* the act of communication, to break it down into its constituent parts and stages. Our task now is to take that linear process and *synthesize* (combine) it with other critical features of the process to provide a more realistic description of what happens when people communicate. (See Figure 1.4 on the next page.)

We can sum up the essential ideas of a simultaneous transactions model of the human communication process in six basic propositions. Communicators *simultaneously:*

1. *Encode and decode messages.* All individuals involved act as sources and receivers at the same time.

2. *Engage in role-taking and feedback.* These processes take place as each person decodes messages and encodes replies.

3. *Are influenced by their prior acts of communication.* What people say and the way they respond during a given transaction depend greatly on what has been said before.

4. *Are influenced by the physical surroundings within which their transaction takes place.* People communicate differently in different places.

5. *Are influenced by the sociocultural situation within which their communication takes place.* What people say is almost always part of an ongoing social situation that has behavioral rules, such as a family dinner, a date, or workplace activity.

6. *Are influenced by the relationship that exists between them.* The type of social relationship between communicators (they may be strangers or intimates) significantly influences their transaction.

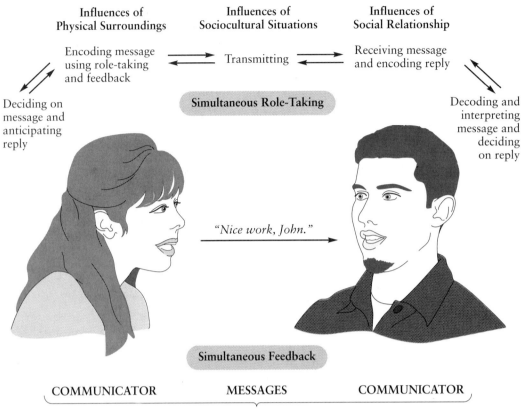

Influences of Physical Surroundings | Influences of Sociocultural Situations | Influences of Social Relationship

Encoding message using role-taking and feedback → Transmitting ← Receiving message and encoding reply

Deciding on message and anticipating reply

Decoding and interpreting message and deciding on reply

Simultaneous Role-Taking

"Nice work, John."

Simultaneous Feedback

COMMUNICATOR | MESSAGES | COMMUNICATOR

Influences of Prior Communication

FIGURE 1.4

A Simultaneous Transactions Model

The simultaneous transactions model depicts the process of face-to-face communication as reciprocal activities that both parties engage in at the same time. While the messages are encoded and decoded, transmitted and received, role-taking and feedback are also applied. Moreover, significant influences on the process arise from what they have said before, the physical setting, the sociocultural nature of their activity, and the relationship between them.

Taken together, these six propositions form a realistic description of the nature of face-to-face communications. They provide the basis for setting forth a model of how it occurs under a wide variety of circumstances, ranging from an intimate conversation between friends to a speech before a live audience of strangers.[18] Figure 1.4 illustrates this model. It is most applicable to face-to-face communication, and is less applicable to "mediated" communication, such as when communicators write letters, talk on the telephone, or use e-mail. It is clearly not relevant to communication with mass media, where professional writers or broadcasters transmit messages to large audiences of individuals whom they do not know and never see.

Encoding and Decoding

The first proposition in the model indicates that while encoding messages, people also receive and decode incoming verbal or nonverbal messages from others. Thus, even as one person is speaking, the other may be encoding a reply.

This is not inconsistent with the linear model described earlier. What this proposition implies is that those processes occur *simultaneously* as each party formulates and interprets messages continuously, speaking and responding, listening and replying.

Role-Taking and Feedback

The second proposition in the model is an extension of the first: The messages of each party, and the interpretations constructed by each, are simultaneously influenced by the role-taking assessments and the feedback they mutually provide. Thus, even as a person speaks, he or she is simultaneously assessing the listener's response on the basis of feedback and may be modifying parts of the message as that feedback is being transmitted.

Influences of Prior Communication

The third proposition in the model is obvious: What people have already said or heard determines what will follow. Thus, the encoding, decoding, and interpretation of messages usually builds on, or is an extension of, prior message content. Communicators simultaneously take this prior message content into account as the exchange continues.

Influences of Physical Surroundings

The influence of physical surroundings on communication is not always clear, but in many cases the setting in which it takes place has a strong influence on both what and how messages are exchanged. Consider how the physical context influences a discussion among close friends at a favorite bar, in the home of one's parents, at a funeral, or at a rowdy New Year's Eve party.

Influences of Sociocultural Situations

People do not usually get together in random groupings and begin communicating. Instead, communication is part of social situations that have meanings within their culture. These can be one-time get-togethers such as weddings, parties, or religious ceremonies, or ongoing situations such as at home, school, or work. What is said, to whom, and in what way is heavily influenced by the sociocultural situation. At a party where people have only recently met, for example, the conversation will likely focus on *small talk,* as people size up one another without revealing much about themselves. When it's a fishing vacation among close friends, however, conversation topics are quite different, and a great deal of self-disclosure takes place. Thus, the situation that brings people together is an important feature of a transactions model.

Influences of Social Relationships

Finally, the model's sixth proposition states that communicators are simultaneously influenced by any *social relationships* that already exist between them. That is, relationships such as those between spouses, friends, acquaintances, or supervisors and subordinates at work, can strongly influence both the content of messages and the way in which they are transmitted and received. Even if the communicators have never met before, the absence of a relationship heavily influences what they communicate to each other. Thus, the social expectations and rules of relationships shape many aspects of the exchange. These include the way messages are encoded or decoded, the effectiveness of role-taking assessments, the amount and kind of feedback, and even the amount of self-disclosure each party provides for the other.

In summary, the simultaneous transactions model is a general view that applies to a broad spectrum of situations, relationships, and contexts within which people communicate. It brings together all the elements and stages discussed in the linear model and adds the influence of factors that affect the human communication process as it takes place in various settings for various purposes. The simultaneous transactions model will be used extensively in the

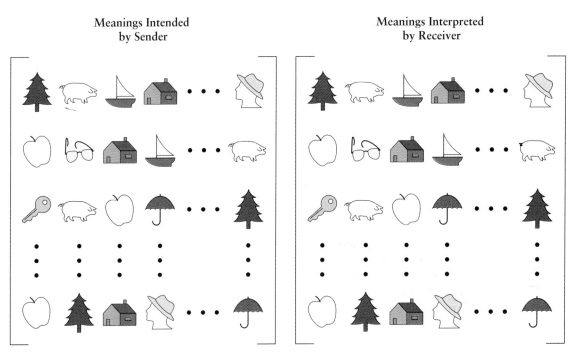

FIGURE 1.5

Totally Accurate Communication
In totally accurate communication, every element and nuance of meaning in the message encoded by the sender would be decoded and interpreted by the receiver precisely as the sender intended. This accuracy is probably only possible for very trivial messages.

chapters that follow as we explore ways in which people communicate for different purposes in different kinds of contexts.

Accuracy in Communication

Totally accurate communication means that all the source's intended meanings, element by element, are reconstructed by the receiver so that they match each other perfectly and completely. Unfortunately, however, communication between human beings is seldom if ever completely accurate in this sense. The meanings of the message as interpreted by the receiver almost always differ to some degree from those intended by the source. It was the realization of this fact during the 1940s that led two physical scientists to put together the very first linear

model of the communication process—on which our discussion is based. (See Figure 1.5.)

Claude Shannon and Warren Weaver, physicists working in Bell Telephone Laboratories, were considering the problems of distortion and inaccuracy that can take place in a mechanical communication medium—in this case the telephone. At first, they were not concerned with how the words or patterns of a message could become distorted by language problems or misunderstandings on the part of human communicators. They were trying to understand the *physical* problems that could introduce what they called "noise" into the exchange.[19] To do this they set about to design a model of the mediated communication process.

What they came up with was a linear view of mediated communication that included a *source*, a *transmitter*, a *signal*, a *receiver*, and,

FIGURE 1.6

The Shannon and Weaver Conceptualization of the Communication Process.

finally, a *destination*. As is obvious, these terms look very much like those used in our linear model. The reason they seem similar is that the Shannon-Weaver model was adopted by communication scholars considering how people communicate interpersonally—with or without media. Thus, ideas from physical science provided a useful way of looking at interpersonal communication as we are discussing it.

The Shannon-Weaver view of the communication process (see Figure 1.6) was a mathematical one. It incorporated a number of ideas that did not become a part of the models later developed by communication scholars. However, one that was long regarded as useful was the term "noise." What that means is that various kinds of distortions that reduce accuracy can be introduced in the exchange between source and destination. Obviously, *physical* factors can reduce accuracy—such as trying to communicate over some sort of racket. In interpersonal communication, many kinds of *psychological, social,* and *cultural* factors can reduce accuracy. These would include problems of perception, lack of familiarity with language, faulty memory, and perhaps animosities between the communicators. All of these can introduce "noise" (reduced accuracy) into an exchange. In fact, there are an almost unlimited number of ways in which unintended meanings, constructed by a receiver, can displace or become compounded with those that the sender wanted to arouse. In large part, distortion arises because communi-

cation is much more than just using words and other symbols to express ideas. (See Figure 1.6.)

Three broad categories of techniques are used, either deliberately or unwittingly, to arouse meanings in others. Each offers abundant opportunities for distortion. First, messages can be distorted *verbally*, through the spoken, written, or printed symbols and patterns (grammar and syntax) of language itself. Although words are deliberately selected, the sender may make poor choices that distort meaning for the receiver. For example, the use of the term *man* to refer to all human beings implies a lesser status for women. Although the sender may not intend this implication, poor word choice caused the distortion.

A second opportunity for distortion is provided by **nonverbal communication,** which can be very complex and confusing. For example, winking at a child while scolding her in front of others can be intended to negate the meanings included in the verbal scolding. However, the child may not understand. Whether nonverbal cues are used deliberately or unintentionally, they can cause others to construct distorted meanings. Third, distortion may arise from features of the setting or *context* within which the communication takes place. A message such as "I love you" said sincerely after a romantic candlelight dinner, may be interpreted differently from the same words uttered to someone met an hour earlier in a singles bar. Later chapters will discuss the influences of

BOX 1.1   *A Closer Look*

Distortion in Communication

Although achieving complete and accurate communication is virtually impossible, examining those factors that interfere with our ability to get our intended meaning across to others will help us minimize distortion.

- *First, select your words carefully.* Even though you and your communication partner may both speak English, you probably do not share the exact same connotative meaning for any given word or phase. Verbal word choice becomes increasingly more important when you communicate with people whose experiences have been very different from yours. They may not understand what you mean or, worse, they may think you intend to hurt, demean, or exclude them by the words you use. For example, to refer to Asian-Americans as "Orientals" or adult women as "girls" can unintentionally distort what you mean to convey.
- *Second, give special attention to the nonverbal messages you send.* Nonverbal gestures, hand movements, eye contact, smiling or frowning, and leaning body forward or backward all send a message—whether intended or not. Know that others will read those nonverbal signals even if you did not consciously send them. In fact, should you happen to send a nonverbal message that appears to contradict your words, you may confuse people.
- *Third, consider what you say always takes place within a certain context.* People often look to the context to help them understand the meanings of your message. A verbal message that may be appropriate and reinforced in one context might be totally distorted in another. For example, suppose you say "I do" when standing before a justice of the peace. Contrast the meaning of those same words when spoken as a trial witness in a county courtroom. Although both may connote a promise, what is being promised is altogether different.

contexts at length. For now, note the sociocultural and physical settings within which communication takes place can introduce subtle or obvious cues into the process. These cues often influence the meanings intended by the source and those constructed by the receiver, resulting in distortion without awareness on the part of either. Shannon and Weaver would refer to such distortions as "noise." (See Box 1.1.)

Remember that receivers are always *active parties* in the communication process. They bring their own individual memories and meanings to the act of interpreting the message. The receiver's private and subjective meanings or connotations for words, things, actions, and settings may not be shared by the source. Nevertheless, they may be used in the receiver's construction and interpretation of the source's message. It is little wonder, then, that human communication can often be a flawed process.

This discussion of incompleteness and distortion may make it seem that we can never communicate with other human beings at a level of accuracy needed to conduct our affairs. In reality, we seldom need to communicate perfectly. Other features of the human communication process permit people to get along pretty well *without* totally complete and perfectly accurate meaning constructions. To illustrate, let us assume that you're at work and your boss comes by one morning and says:

"I wonder if you would mind going down to the legal department and talk with Mr. Murakita. He has a mortgage contract that was signed a couple of days ago, and we may need it for the

| BOX 1.2 | *Ethical Concerns* |

DILEMMAS IN COMMUNICATION

Communication ethics develops guidelines to help us make good communication decisions. Consider the following ethical dilemmas. How would you answer each? What set of moral rules or principles do you rely on to help you respond to various communication situations? In other words, what are your personal ethics about communicating?

- Should I always tell the truth, even if the truth may hurt? Shouldn't some people be protected from the truth?
- Is there a difference between self*less* lies (Lying to protect someone else) and self*ish* lies (lying to protect myself)? Is one more acceptable than the other?
- Should others always be able to trust my word? Should I assume that I can trust someone else's word?

- Am I obligated to listen intently to my friend's concerns even when I think her problems are trivial?
- Should I attempt to persuade my partner to vote for the Democratic presidential nominee, or should I let him make up his own mind?
- If I am anxious to get off the phone and back to work, should I lie and say, "Someone's at the door. I have to go now"?
- When is it okay to reveal a confidence?
- When is it okay to interrupt someone else's talk? What if his or her topic is boring and I want to talk about something else?
- In an effort to avoid conflict, is it okay to be intentionally ambiguous or to simply refrain from stating my opinion?
- What responsibility do I have to keep the conversation going in social situations? Can't I just sit back and listen quietly if I want to?

three o'clock meeting this afternoon. You might want to go over it with him so that you will understand the terms."

Suppose now that another person comes up a few moments later and asks, "Exactly what did the boss say?" Your response might be:

"Well, she told me to go see Mr. Murakita to get a contract that was just signed. Then she said she wanted me to read it in time for the meeting this afternoon."

Your version may sound pretty close, but looking at the two it is clear that it is different in a number of ways. In fact, if the two messages are directly compared, the accuracy level is rather low. For example, the boss asked you "if you would mind"—but you didn't say that. Furthermore, she did not specifically say that she wanted you to *read* the document; she merely implied that by saying that, "You might want to go over it."

Thus, the two messages above contain a number of differences between the version encoded and transmitted by the boss and that decoded and interpreted by you. At the same time, the basic elements of meaning *are close enough* so that you can do what the boss expects. The source's and receiver's combinations of meaning schemas contain enough similarity *for practical purposes*. That is: (1) You understand that there is a document, (2) you know that you are to get it, and (3) you realize that you are supposed to read it and be ready for the meeting. Those elements are all you really need to comply rather closely with the boss's wishes.

The point is that in any message there are two levels of meaning in most messages we initiate and transmit: The **surface meaning** refers to the whole range of intended elements we formulate into our message, exactly as we word it, but the **deep meaning** is the basic ideas that can be understood well enough for practical purposes. Despite this flexibility, even deep meanings are often interpreted incorrectly. However, if a reasonable amount of accuracy can be attained at the deep meaning level, the transaction can usually serve well enough. Unfortunately, even modest levels of accuracy are not always easy to attain. (See Box 1.2.)

Communication that is complete and relatively free of distortion doesn't just "happen." The most important lesson that can be learned from all of these considerations is that the messages we put together for any purpose that is important to us must be *carefully managed at every stage*. That is true whether we are among family, friends, work associates or others with whom we need to have effective communication. The chapters that follow offer insights into the ways in which all of us, as either senders or receivers, can improve our ability to communicate.

Brief Chapter Review

- The central focus of the field is *human communication in all its aspects.* Stated briefly, communication is the study of the many ways that human beings relate to each other by exchanging messages, using a number of different processes of communication, and the consequences of those exchanges.

- In today's society, whether in the workplace, among friends, family, or in other kinds of settings, understanding the process of communication and acquiring effective communication skills is essential. Communication is defined in a basic way as a process in which an individual initiates messages using verbal and nonverbal symbols to express meanings in such a way that similar or parallel understandings are aroused in all the communicators involved.

- The act of human communication can be visualized using a "linear model," which has been derived from an earlier version developed by Shannon and Weaver. The model is somewhat unrealistic in that it does not take into account the processes or role-taking or feedback, but it does break down the act of communication into a series of stages for purposes of detailed analysis.

- The linear model depicts communication as taking place when a person identifies a goal, constructs a message, and then transmits that message using various parts of the body and brain. With the use of the senses, a receiver then detects and identifies (perceives) the symbols, decodes the message, and interprets the meaning. Often, the receiver formulates a return message to provide feedback to the original source.

- Meaning is at the heart of communication. *Meaning* is the internal or subjective responses we make, either to aspects of the reality around us or to the labels we impose on that reality.

- A more accurate depiction of the human communication process is provided by the "simultaneous transactions model," which indicates that communicators simultaneously encode and decode messages and engage in role-taking and feedback. The model also indicates that communicators are influenced by their prior interactions, the physical setting, the social situation, and the nature of their relationship.

- Complete and totally accurate communication between communicators is unlikely because a variety of factors create distortion. However, total accuracy is not necessary in routine exchanges. Most message transactions arouse deep meanings that serve the practical needs of the communicators. Even so, it is likely that inaccuracies will occur in communication, even at a deep meaning level.

Key Terms

human communication	decoding	role-taking
context	distortion	perception
communicator	accuracy (in communication)	feedback
symbols	linear	transaction
receiver	convention	nonverbal communication
information	trace	meaning (surface)
source or sender	schema	meaning (deep)
encoding		

Notes

1. See, for example: Stewart, J., & Knowles, V. (2000). Graduate recruitment and selection: Implications for HE, graduates and small business recruiters. *Career Development International,* 65–80; Ritter, M. A., Starbuck, R. R., & Hogg, R. V. (2001). Advice from prospective employers on training BS statisticians. *The American Statistician,* 14–18; Napoli, P. M., Taylor, M., & Powers, G. (1999). Writing activities of public relations practitioners: The relationship between experience and writing tasks. *Public Relations Review, 25,* 3, 369–380; Ugbah, S. D., & Majors, R. E. (1992). Influential communication factors in employment interviews. *The Journal of Business Communication,* 145.

2. McNeilis, K. S. (2001). Analyzing communication competence in medical consultations. *Health Communication, 13,* 1, 5–18; Miller, K., & Ryan, D. J. (2001). Communication in the age of managed care: Introduction to the special issue. *Journal of Applied Communication Research, 29,* 2, 91–96; Slater, M. D. (1999). Integrating applications of media effects, persuasion, and behavior change theories to communication campaigns: A stages-of-change framework. *Health Communication, 11,* 4, 335–354.

3. The relationship between language, thought, and social life has been well established for many decades in such fields as anthropology, linguistics, philosophy, social psychology, and sociology. See, for example: J. B. Carol, *Language, thought and reality.* Cambridge, MA: MIT Press; Mead, G. H. (1934). *Mind, self and society from the standpoint of a social behaviorist.* Chicago: University of Chicago Press; Bronowski, J. (1978). *The origins of knowledge and imagination.* New Haven, CT: Yale University Press, and Hymes, D. (1964) *Language in culture and society.* New York: Harper and Row, Publishers.

4. See: Bell, D. (1973). *The coming of post-industrial society: A venture in social forecasting.* New York: Basic Books.

5. Locke, J. (1975). In P. Nidich (Ed.), *An essay concerning human understanding* (p. 402). Oxford: Clarendon Press. (First published in 1690.)

6. Becker, H., & Barnes, H. E. (1961). *Social thought from lore to science* (3rd ed., pp. 3–131). New York: Dover Publications. Also: Cornford, F. M. (Trans.). (1941). *The Republic of Plato.* London: Oxford University Press. See especially Part III, Books XXIV–XXVIII, pp. 221–264.

7. See: Harper, N. (1979). *Communication theory: The history of a paradigm.* Rochelle Park, NJ: Hayden Book Company; Trenholm, S. (1991). *Human communication theory* (2nd ed.). Englewood Cliffs, NJ: Prentice-Hall.

8. Cooley, C. H. (1909). *Social organization.* New York: Charles Scribner's Sons (p. 61).

9. Ellis, A., & Beattie, G. (1986). *The psychology of language and communication* (p. 19). New York: Guilford Press.

10 . Cooley, *Social organization,* p. 69.

11. See Kornblut, A. E., & Radin, C. (Sept. 18, 2001). Bush image of crusade upsets some potential allies. *The Boston Globe,* p. A22; Ford, P. (September 19, 2001). Europe cringes at Bush "crusade" against terrorists. *The Christian Science Monitor,* p. 12.

12. Detailed reviews of this rapidly developing field are found in the following sources: Cermak, L. S., & Craik, F. I. M. (Eds.). (1979). *Levels of processing in human memory.* Hillsdale, NJ: Lawrence Erlbaum; and Bower, G. (Ed.). (1977). *Human memory: Basic processes.* New York: Academic Press; Green, J. (1984). A cognitive approach to human communication: An action assembly theory. *Communication Monographs, 51,* 289–306; Green, I. (1989). Action assembly theory: Metatheoretical commitments, theoretical propositions, and empirical allocations. In B. Dervin, L. Grossberg, B. J. O'Keefe, & E. Wartella (Eds.), *Rethinking communication* (Vol. 2, pp. 117–128). Newbury Park, CA: Sage.

13. The schema concept was first used by Frederick C. Bartlett in his classic work *Remembering* (1932). London: Cambridge University Press. See also: Crocket, W. H. (1988). Schemas, affect and communication. In L. Donahue, H. E. Sypher, & E. T. Higgins (Eds.), *Communication, social cognition and affect* (pp. 32–51). Hillsdale, NJ: Lawrence Erlbaum; Trenholm, S. (1991). *Human communication theory* (2nd ed., pp. 65–68). Englewood Cliffs, NJ: Prentice Hall.

14. The activity of role-taking, sometimes called "taking the role of the other," comes originally from the writings of George Herbert Mead, a philosopher and sociologist of the early 20th century. He developed a general theory called "symbolic interactionism," which maintains that human communication, using symbols with conventional rules of meaning, is the basis for the thinking abilities of human beings, and of the social rules that we share for behaving predictably in society. See: Mead, G. H. (1934). *Mind, self and society. From the standpoint of a social behaviorist.* Chicago: University of Chicago Press. For excellent discussions of role-taking and of symbolic interactionism more generally, see: Littlejohn, S. W., Symbolic interactionism as an approach to the study of human communication. *Quarterly Journal of Speech, 63,* 84–91; and Delia, J. G., & Grossberg, L. (1977). Interpretation and evidence. *Western Journal of Speech Communication, 41,* 32–42.

15. For a readable account of the implications of automaticity, see: Bargh, J. A. (1988). Automatic information processing: Implications for communication and affect. In L. Donahew, H. E. Sypher, & E. T. Higgins (Eds.), *Communication, social cognition and affect* (pp. 9–32). Hillsdale, NJ: Lawrence Erlbaum.

16. The term *information* as physical events that permit a message to conquer long or short distances, such as sound and light waves, electric pulses moving along a wire, or electromagnetic radiations that instantly transverse space, was developed in the work of Claude Shannon and Warren Weaver. See: Shannon, C., & Weaver, W. (1949). *The mathematical theory of communication.* Urbana: University of Illinois Press.

17. The term *feedback* comes from the field of cybernetics, which is the study of the automatic control systems formed by the nervous system and the brain that stabilize functions of the human body. It came into the study of communication through the work of Norbert Wiener (1954) in his seminal book, *The human use of human beings: Cybernetics and society.* Boston: Houghton Mifflin.

18. This view of human communication parallels in part what has been described as the "rules perspective." Communication scholars arguing this perspective indicate that people learn the rules for communication within differing situations and that the use of these rules is highly contextualized. For complete discussions of the rules perspective, see: Shimanoff, S. B. (1980). *Communication rules: Theory and re-*

search. Beverly Hills, CA: Sage; and Sigman, S. J. (1980). On communication rules from a social perspective. *Human Communication Research, 7,* 31–51.

19. The term *noise* is often used to lump together and label various kinds of physical and other influences that reduce the accuracy of communication. It comes originally from the classic formulation of Shannon and Weaver's information theory (page 25). For elaborations of Shannon and Weaver's formulation, see: Broadhurst, A. R., & Darnell, D. K. (1965). An introduction to cybernetics and information theory. *Quarterly Journal of Speech, 5l,* 442–435; Krippendorf, K. (1975). Information theory. In G. Hanneman & W. McEwen (Eds.). *Communication and behavior* (pp. 351–389). Reading, MA: Addison-Wesley; and Littlejohn, S. W. (1989). *Theories of human communication* (3rd ed., pp. 42–64). Belmont, CA: Wadsworth.

Chapter 2

Verbal Communication: Using Speech and Language

L ook, Jennifer, I know I'm right," Gary said firmly. "My dog
Sparky understands every word I say. He even talks back!
When I get my car keys out and say 'Do you want to go for a
ride?' he barks with enthusiasm. Or, when he's been bad, and I scold
him, he hangs his head and looks sorry. Don't tell me that animals
can't use language. Sparky is a smart dog and, I say again, he understands every word I say. I have no doubt that he can engage in verbal
communication."

"But Gary," Jennifer replied, patiently. "What you are seeing is
not really verbal communication. What is actually happening is that
Sparky is an intelligent animal. He has lived with you long enough to
pick up on your every action, your every tone of voice and even all
the distinctive patterns of sounds and signals that you use with him
frequently—like letting him see the keys and asking him if he 'wants
to go for a ride.' He does not remotely understand the words in the
same way we do. He recognizes that particular pattern of signs and
signals, and he has learned that a pleasant experience is likely to follow. It's no wonder that Sparky gets excited and barks.

"Psychologists have a term for this kind of animal habit-pattern.
They call it 'learning to respond to natural signs that occur in their
environment.' You are Sparky's environment. All animals are capable
of learning, and they catch on quickly about what will follow when

they detect a particular stimulus. It's like pigeons who see someone eating from a sack of popcorn on a park bench. They have learned that if they approach and strut around they are likely to get some. They don't have to understand language at all. Neither does Sparky. Let me say it again, and watch my lips. Animals just do not understand or use language."

"Oh yeah! What about whales? I read that they have their own language. Human beings can't understand it yet, but whales are highly intelligent and can make complex sounds that other whales can detect, even miles away. Their singing has even been recorded and set to music! I think dolphins also have their own language. I saw a thing on TV where dolphins followed the commands of a trainer who asked them to do all kinds of really complicated things."

"It is a wonderful idea, Gary, and I am sure that it was fun to watch on TV. People love whales and dolphins, and want to think they are able to speak. I personally would love to have a conversation with a whale or a dolphin. It is a very romantic idea, but it just isn't going to happen. It is certainly true that they engage in complex signaling to each other, but all animals in the wild do that. Geese, deer, wolves, and even insects provide signals to indicate the presence of danger, their readiness to mate, or the availability of food. Some do it with sounds, others with body movements or even odors. But they are not having conversations about the weather or setting up meetings for later in the week. They are using inherited or learned systems of signals to communicate basic messages. So, I am saying that animals can certainly communicate. But they do not develop and share languages."

"Jennifer, I hate to say it, but you're being a stupid jerk on this issue. You need to read up on the experiments psychologists have done in teaching chimpanzees and even a gorilla to use sign language. Some of those animals were able to learn more than a hundred different signs and use them to understand various messages that their trainers sent to them. Sure, they couldn't actually speak, as we do, but they were able to respond to signs. You have to agree that this clearly is verbal communication, even if it is not speaking like we are now."

"Gary, I'm not going to argue with you any more. Your head is filled with incorrect interpretations and false conclusions. I don't want to waste my time discussing this any more. So don't call me again asking me for a date, or for any other reason for that matter. You can just stay home and have a nice chat with your dog."

We can hope that Gary and Jennifer made up and found some other topic to discuss. But who was right? Was Jennifer correct in her conviction that animals can communicate, but only by using a variety of nonverbal and nonlanguage behaviors? Or, is Gary right in concluding that his dog, Sparky, and indeed other kinds of animals, such as whales, dolphins, and chimpanzees, have been able to master forms of verbal communication and the use of a language of their own under the right circumstances?

First, why is this important? Or is it important at all? One answer is that the study of how animals communicate has been an important topic in the social sciences—particularly in psychology. Psychologists search for "universal laws of behavior"—conduct and actions that can be found among many kinds of species. The question is this: Do human beings communicate in ways that are *unique* to them, or are they just one more animal that communicates in basically

Communication using language is unique to humans. Verbal communication is based on learning but also requires shared conventions of meaning among those who use a language.

the same way? We can find the answer to that question by a very brief look at the communication process in *comparative perspective*—which means comparing and contrasting the communication processes used by animals with that used among human beings. Are they essentially the same or starkly different?

It can be instructive to look very briefly at what takes place among animals as a starting point for gaining a better understanding of human verbal communication using speech and language. As Jennifer pointed out, animals certainly are able to communicate with each other—using **natural signs**—sounds, movements, odors, and postures that they are capable of performing—often in remarkably complex ways. But is it the equivalent, as Gary claimed, to the use of language to communicate the way people do constantly? The value in sorting out this issue as a foundation for discussing verbal behavior among human beings is *not* to become an expert in the ways of animals. Its value lies in un-

derstanding more thoroughly the unique nature of words, their meanings within a language, and what human communication does for us as thinking, remembering human beings who know their environment, develop solutions to problems, and lead complex social lives.

The Animal Kingdom: Communicating without Language

The idea is an old one that animals can communicate as do human beings, and at least in some cases, understand **language** as fully as we do. The idea of talking animals can be found in legends and tales in almost every society throughout history. Talking animals were common in classic Greek fables (e.g, Aesop's tale of "The Fox and the Grapes") as well as in more modern literature (e.g., Lewis Carol's *Through the Looking Glass*) and on into today's funny papers. But there is one account that for our purposes truly stands out. Over a hundred years ago, a particular animal came to public attention that seemed to offer convincing proof that an animal could understand language in remarkably complex ways. The animal seemed to possess an extraordinary level of intelligence. It was startling because no one had ever before suspected such capacity among members of the animal kingdom. This case not only astonished everyone who saw the animal in action, but it raised truly important ethical questions as to whether human beings had been treating their fellow creatures in acceptable ways by using them for food, making them beasts of burden and assuming that they were simply "dumb animals." This is what happened:

The Case of Clever Hans

In 1900 a retiring Berlin schoolteacher of high school mathematics, Wilhelm von Osten, bought a horse. He called him Hans. The horse was an attractive animal who soon bonded with his master. As a kind of hobby, Herr von Osten began to train Hans in a most unusual way. With the aid of a blackboard and other devices, he taught the horse to recognize numbers and count out their value by tapping his forefoot on a small wooden platform. This took time. At first, he had to assist Hans in learning the tapping routine, but the schoolteacher was very patient with his new pupil and aided him in getting it right. In the early lessons he had to take the horse's hoof in his hands and show him just how to tap, over and over, until Hans could do it by himself. He then taught him the right answers to some very basic problems. For example, when shown a number (such as 7 or 9) on a blackboard that Hans could see, and then when asked verbally what it was, Hans would obediently tap the correct number of times. Hans progressed rapidly and could soon do fairly large numbers, even those over one hundred.

The teacher was pleased with his pet and decided to go on to more advanced problems. To his delight, Hans caught on very quickly, and

soon the horse could answer amazingly complex arithmetic questions put to him by his trainer. He seemed to be able to add and subtract, and even to multiply and divide, always signaling the correct answers to his trainer by taps of his hoof on the little platform. There was no fakery here. Herr von Osten was not a showman or a professional animal trainer, and he was certainly not trying to deceive anyone by displaying the abilities of his horse. He was as much surprised as anyone at how clever Hans turned out to be.

As the neighbors saw what Hans could do, and stories began to appear in the press, the horse's reputation grew rapidly. After several years Hans was attracting nationwide, and later even worldwide, attention. The idea that an animal could communicate with human beings was very exciting. Furthermore, the level of intelligence required to perform the tasks accomplished by Hans was far beyond what anyone had attributed to a horse before. Finally, experts were coming from all over Europe, and even other parts of the world, to see *Kluge Hans* ("Clever Hans," as he became known).

Some were convinced that it was all a fake, and they tried to expose Herr von Osten as a fraud. But no one was able to detect any deception. As time went on, many came to believe that Clever Hans might provide the key to a whole new understanding of animals. Some authorities felt that the discovery of the horse's amazing capacity posed an important ethical breakthrough. It seemed clear that the animal—and perhaps all animals—had a level of intelligence very close to that of human beings. In particular, it appeared that Hans was *understanding and using language as effectively as a human being*. Although he lacked a voice, his hoof-tapping seemed like an acceptable alternative. If true, continuing to use animals as food and as beasts of burden was a troublesome idea, to say the least.

Then, in 1904, a new perspective on *Kluge Hans* was developed. A German psychologist, Professor Oskar Pfungst, persuaded the owner to let him make a thorough study of the remarkable horse to determine once and for all whether the animal was actually able to understand and use human language.[1] With the owner's permission, the psychologist conducted all kinds of tests to determine the animal's true abilities.

What Professor Pfungst discovered was that Hans was a very clever horse indeed—but not in the way people thought. Actually, Hans was receiving unintentional "cues" from his owner that enabled him to start and stop tapping in exactly the right way! The bond between the animal and his owner was so strong that Hans could detect the *most subtle movements and facial expressions* of the schoolteacher when he was standing in front of Hans and waiting for him to tap out answers. What Herr von Osten was doing, without realizing it, was nodding his head in an almost undetectable manner as he silently counted to see whether Hans would reach the correct number of taps. Such unintended movements (some as small as a fraction of a millimeter) were cues to Hans to keep tapping. When the owner stopped moving his head, changed expression, moved back, or smiled as the correct number was reached, Hans simply stopped tapping.

What confused many observers for a long time was the fact that Hans was able to tap out the right number to answer problems posed by a stranger—even if his master was not present. That certainly ruled out deliberate deception with secret signals; but eventually, Professor Pfungst found out that Hans could not correctly solve a problem if the answer was not known to the questioner or if Hans could not see or hear the person standing in front of him.

The conclusion finally reached was that Clever Hans had no grasp of human language whatsoever. What he was doing was much simpler. The horse had learned to read a great variety of *subtle cues* as to when he should start and stop tapping. In fact, he learned to read amazingly subtle forms of behavior from strangers as well as his master. When other people came to watch Hans perform he was able to read their expressions of anticipation, encour-agement, and satisfaction, just as well as those of his master. When such cues were absent, Hans was just another nice horse.

Communicating with Learned Signs

The story of Clever Hans helps us understand the nature of language by showing the *sharp contrast* between human and animal communication. It is very easy to be misled by clever animals that seem to understand language. What can be observed in their behavior is often called the **Clever Hans effect**—responses to subtle actions and cues provided unwittingly by owners or experimenters. Nevertheless, the question whether animals are capable of using language still remains an open one within the scientific community.

It is easy to assume mistakenly that a clever animal, like Hans, can learn to use language. Anyone who has lived with a much-loved pet understands that communication between a human being and an animal can be both subtle and extensive. Like Hans, dogs, cats, and parrots are much more intelligent than most people realize. It doesn't take them long to figure out how to master their environment, whether it is a backyard or an urban apartment. They develop ways to let people know that they want to be fed, that they want out (or in), that strangers are present, and so forth. They have little trouble in initiating *signals* to beg for treats, to indicate that they want to go along in the car, or that they want to play. Like Clever Hans, pets quickly learn to pick up subtle cues related to human habits and family routines. Anyone who has seen pets suddenly make themselves scarce at bath time will realize the subtlety of the cues they can read. No wonder owners sometimes conclude that their pets really can understand human language.

Where are we in this debate now? At present, psychologists who compare animal and human behavior have concluded that animal communication is based on inherited biological abilities, that is, *instincts* (among simpler animals

FIGURE 2.1

(a) The bee uses a dance to indicate to other bees the distance (*x*) to food source; (b) the bee circles in the hive to direct other bees to direction and distance to food.

like cockroaches) and on *learned* **signs** for those closer to human beings on the evolutionary scale. Human beings, in contrast not only learn various kinds of **symbols** but also learn to interpret them in ways that are parallel to their meanings to others in their **language community**. Animals do not do this. Individually, they can respond to signs, often in remarkable ways as was the case with Hans, but they have yet to develop a system of language in which meanings for signs are shared with others of their species in a language community. (See Figure 2.1.)

In spite of all these considerations, there is one important question that needs to be addressed: Isn't it possible that some intelligent animals would be capable of learning to use language *if human beings took the trouble to teach them?* This question has been vigorously studied in recent decades, and a considerable controversy has raged around the conclusions reached.

Trying to Teach Apes to Talk

Are *any animals at all* capable of learning to speak and use language, even at a very elementary level? We saw that Clever Hans seemed to use language, but in the end it was not true. But can any creature *other* than a human being be taught to speak? This is a very interesting, even critical, question—and it has, in fact, been systematically explored.

The capacity to learn is at a maximum among animals near the top of the **phylogenetic continuum** or scale (those nearest us in the evolutionary chain), such as chimpanzees, gorillas, and other large primates. All these remarkable animals have fascinated human beings for centuries. Most Americans easily recognize chimpanzees. These animals seem intelligent, and in some ways apes look rather like human beings. Because of this, some people think they ought to be able to behave like people—especially when it comes to the use of language. In fact, some decades ago a number of systematic attempts were made by psychologists to teach chimpanzees to speak and also to instruct gorillas or other primates to use sign language, special symbols, and computers. In many ways, the results of these attempts are surprising. They also remain controversial.

In the first of a series of classic experiments, psychologists Winthrop and Louise Kellogg decided in 1931 to see whether a chimpanzee could learn to speak.[2] At the time, they did not understand the limitations of chimpanzee anatomy that would make this impossible (like the problem with early human beings). They believed that one reason apes did not do so was because they were not raised in a language environment. Human infants, on the other hand, are in constant contact with language-using adults who offer rewards and encouragement for attempts to learn to talk. Why not, then, raise a chimp in a completely human environment and teach the animal to speak as though it were a human child?

As it happened, the Kelloggs were expecting a baby. They decided to conduct an experiment by acquiring an infant chimpanzee to raise in an identical manner with their own child. As soon as their infant son, Donald, was born, they were able to get a baby chimp. Donald and the baby chimp, Gua, were bathed, fed, diapered, and treated affectionately in exactly the same manner. Both were equally encouraged to use words and were coached extensively.

It didn't work. The chimp and the baby got along very well, but at the end of three years, Donald was growing up to be a normal boy while Gua was developing into a normal chimp. Donald learned speech in the manner typical of his age, putting together words into simple sentences. Gua was never able to speak a word. On the other hand, Gua was a bright animal and quickly learned to respond to a number of simple verbal commands. Furthermore, the chimp far outstripped Donald in manual dexterity and within a year could swing about in vigorous chimp-like fashion while the boy could only toddle awkwardly.

In 1947 a somewhat similar project was undertaken. There was no human baby present, but Keith and Catherine Hayes raised a chimp, Vicki, in their home.[3] They coached her constantly in the use of specific words, helping her to form sounds by manipulating her lips. After six years, however, the chimp had learned to vocalize only three crude approximations of English words— "mama," "papa," and "cup." She did so only on command in a hoarse whisper with great difficulty, and there was no firm indication that these "words" had the same meanings they have for people. Vicki's accomplishments were not much different from those of a dog that learns to "speak" at the owner's command.

The home-rearing experiments with Gua and Vicki were generally failures in terms of their original goals. Yet, in one way they were great successes. They forced a clear recognition that the animals had difficulty because their vocal physiology was not able to form speech sounds. We know now that the vocal tract, larynx, and other soft tissue structures that human beings use to generate and control complex sounds are quite different in other primates.

Even more significant, an elaborate brain is required for speech. The chimpanzee brain does not appear to have clear counterparts of the areas in the human brain that are essential to human speech (Broca's and Wernicke's areas).[4] What all of this means is that apes are not going to learn to talk, no matter how they are coached. So don't plan on having a conversation with one next time you visit a zoo! Their bodies are not designed for it, and it would be rather pointless to make further attempts along these lines.

If apes can't speak, is there another way that they can communicate using language? As an alternative to speech, sign language has been the subject of several classic experiments. Young apes are far better at manual dexterity than are young human beings. They spontaneously make many expressive gestures and finger movements. This fact led comparative psychologists to conclude that they should try to take advantage of their manual dexterity, by using a means of communication not requiring the apes to speak. If this could be done, then perhaps apes could be taught to "talk" with human beings without the use of the voice.

Thinking along these lines, psychologists Beatrice and Allan Gardner decided to try to teach a chimp the finger positions, movements, and other language signs and symbols used by people who are deaf. In 1966 they acquired Washoe (whom they named after the Nevada county where they lived). They immediately began to teach her ASL—American Sign Language—which is used by the deaf community.[5] Here, no vocalization was involved, and the chimp could take advantage of her natural agility.

Teaching Washoe the signs wasn't easy. The chimp was housed in a special trailer surrounded by a big yard with a high fence—a rich environment somewhat like a human home.

Both the Gardners and other teachers spent long periods with Washoe every day, conditioning her to make the right signs for various objects and actions. At the end of the four-year experiment, the researchers believed she was able to respond to some 160 signs.

What seemed even more exciting to them was that the chimp sometimes spontaneously put two, or even three, signs together. At least some of these combinations appeared to "make sense." The chimp produced such combinations as "gimme tickle," "go sweet" (which the experimenters interpreted as a request to be taken to raspberry bushes to eat fruit), and even "Roger Washoe tickle" (seen as a request to play with her trainer).

While the results seemed gratifying, there were serious limitations in what Washoe could do. On no occasion did she put together anything abstract, novel, or inventive, although she lived in an environment where there were numerous possibilities to make such combinations. Her signing behavior was restricted to the *here and now,* never referring to the past or future. Virtually all her spontaneous signing was related to food, treats, or other personal needs of the moment. Most important, there was no evidence that she developed an understanding of **syntax,** that is, rules for putting signs together in consistent patterns that themselves provide meaning. In short, the effort was inconclusive.

Perhaps the most dramatic of the sign language experiments was the effort by psychologist Francene Patterson to teach Koko, an African gorilla, to communicate with ASL. She acquired the animal as an infant and established it in special quarters. Gorillas are large and powerful, with a reputation for being bad-tempered and ferocious; but, working with several assistants, Patterson patiently taught the animal to make signs and associate them with specific meanings (such as "food," "drink," and "more"). Later, this was extended to include many more signs and their associated meanings. No dangerous behavior was encountered, and the animal was able to make a great many signs which she produced in many sequences.

Some of them seemed to Patterson to be appropriate to communicate simple requests and responses to queries from the trainers. Generally, Koko seemed to be the equal or even superior of Washoe in the use of signs.[6]

Many critical psychologists have rejected the conclusion that these animal experiments show any language usage or capacity at all. They base their rejection on two grounds. First, careful studies of films and videotapes taken to record the training of many of the chimps, and the gorilla Koko, seem to show the Clever Hans effect. That is, there was evidence that these intelligent animals could detect what their trainers wanted them to sign, and they obligingly complied to get approval or rewards. This interpretation has raised serious doubts about whether the animals involved had any real conceptual ability or had mastered even the crudest idea of syntax.

In more recent years, psychologists have tried to go beyond the close contact between trainer and chimp required by learning sign language. In various experiments chimps learned to use "artificial languages." For example, a chimp called Sarah was taught by David Premack to manipulate pieces of plastic of various colors and random shapes.[7] Through conditioning, the ape was taught to associate various objects and actions with these plastic "words." Then, to try to develop primitive rules of syntax, various combinations were given meanings. Sarah did learn to use sequences of her pieces of plastic. In fact, after extensive training it seemed to the experimenters that she had mastered simple abstractions and conceptual relationships, such as identifying things by color and indicating whether an object was "over," "under," or "beside" another.

Perhaps the most significant finding from the work with Sarah was that she could learn and use simple rules for associating meaning with combinations of her plastic pieces. On the other hand, she was limited by the characteristics of all apes: She had a very short memory span and her use of the synthetic "language" was restricted completely to the here and now.

Even more recently, elaborate experiments have been tried in attempts to rule out the Clever Hans effect. Chimps have been placed in computer-controlled environments that did not require the presence of a human handler.[8] Typically, these are laboratory-like rooms that contain a kind of keyboard. Each key corresponded to a "word" in an artificial language called "Yerkish" (after Robert Yerkes, a famous comparative psychologist). Pressing the key, on which is displayed a special symbol, causes a visual display with the same symbol to light up. The chimp subject can press several keys and get a string of symbols lit up on the special display. Outside the room, the experimenter has a similar keyboard. Because it is also wired to the visual display, two-way signaling with the ape is possible. A computer interfaces the two devices and keeps track of the results.

These more technologically sophisticated experiments appear to show, once again, that chimps are very intelligent, and that they quickly learn to manipulate whatever environment they are in to get food and other rewards. Overall, however, no startling findings have come forth. Chimps still seem to be chimps and their capacity to learn and use language appears very limited indeed, in spite of the enthusiastic claims of some experimenters.[9]

The most damaging criticism of the animal communication studies comes from statistical evidence. The number of times the animals used various signs and signals both singly and in various combinations has been carefully tallied in a number of these experiments. Out of the thousands of such usages, a certain number of combinations would be expected *if only chance were at work*. That is, even in the most random set of events, at least some combinations will be found that "look" meaningful. In fact, such analyses reveal that the combinations of sign usage occur almost exactly in proportion to what one would expect in distributions produced solely by chance. Thus, enthusiastic experimenters may have focused on those few random accidental occurrences and unrealistically concluded that they represent language

usages, while ignoring the huge numbers of meaningless combinations far more typical of animal behavior.

In the end, the question of animal communication remains open. At present, it seems that even the animals closest to human beings on the phylogenetic continuum will not be shown to be able either to speak or to use language in any realistic way as do human beings. Yet, studies of this issue should continue. Who knows? Perhaps a clever experimenter in the future will show us a way in which Gary can have that nice chat with his dog Sparky.

The Human Experience: The Development of Speech and Language

OK, so animals and human beings do not communicate in the same way. But have we always, since our very beginnings, been able to use speech and language? Or, were we like animals long ago, at some prehistoric point before we acquired those remarkable features of human life? Analysis of fossil remains reported in 2002 indicate that the earliest hominids (human-like creatures) split off in the evolutionary tree of apelike animals about 8 million years ago.[10] Those prehistoric human ancestors (*homo australopithicus*) were only about three feet tall and they looked rather like today's chimpanzees. To communicate they could use only signs and signals. That is, they could use their arms, hands, and various bodily actions to transmit simple commands or other signals to each other. It seems likely that they could supplement these signs and signals with sounds, but these appear to have been relatively uncontrolled vocal noises, rather like the grunts and hoots that apes and monkeys make today. They would not be able to speak as we do until their brains became much larger, their vocal chords moved to their present position (from a much lower area in the upper chest) and their lip and tongue structures became more refined to resemble those of contemporary human beings. All of that gradually took place over millions of years as *Homo sapiens, sapiens* (modern human beings) gradually evolved through a number of intermediate earlier forms.

The Beginnings: Gaining the Ability to Talk

What all this means is that we began speaking and using language—that is engaging in verbal communication—only a relatively short time ago, considering the millions of years that human creatures have lived on this planet.[11] According to the best available evidence put together by paleoanthropologists (who study ancient human beings), *speech*—the ability to pronounce words using vocal chords with refined movements of tongue, lips, and air passages—as we know it today did not come until the appearance of the *Cro-Magnon people,* our immediate human ancestors. These were people who looked pretty much like us. Our current variations in skin color, eye shape, and other minor physical characteristics among different racial categories were probably local adaptations to specific climates. In fact, if a *Cro-Magnon* individual had somehow survived, and were to pass us on the street dressed in modern clothes, he or she would not look much different from anyone else. The most important feature of the *Cro-Magnon* is that they were the first in the chain of human evolution *who could make and control the sounds* that we use today when we talk.

Our best estimates place these changes back somewhere between 90,000 and 35,000 years ago. (No one really knows in any more precise way.) It seems very likely that by about 30,000 years ago, the ability to speak was well-developed and local groups in many parts of the world could talk with each other, tell stories, teach their young, and generally communicate with speech, much as we do now. To do so they had to use a *language*—that is, a standardized vocabulary, with agreed-upon rules of pronunciation, syntax, and grammar.

Was there a "mother tongue" developed by the Cro-Magnon, from which localized tribal or regional versions of languages evolved? Obviously, some languages are older than others, but no one really knows whether human beings began speaking one initial language early on, which spread and got modified, or whether distinct languages were developed locally in various places. In any case, by modern times (the last 10 millennia) there were literally thousands of different languages in use.

Expanding Verbal Communication: Conquering Time and Distance

Acquiring the ability to speak and use language brought remarkable benefits to human beings. For example, somewhere around 10,000 years back our ancestors began to invent *agriculture*—techniques for farming and the domestication of animals. This enabled them to make a transition from hunting and gathering as a means of subsistence to living in fixed locations—in villages where they could tend their crops and raise their animals. Agriculture along with techniques for preserving food made life far easier. It also meant great progress toward a more stable existence.

Being able to talk allowed each new generation to invent at least some new and additional ideas, procedures, and technologies for solving problems and pass them on orally. One consequence was a development of ever more efficient techniques of agriculture and food preservation. As a result, there was a steady and significant growth in world's human population and a gradual increase in life expectancy (average age at death). Still, the ability to pass on knowledge was limited to the capacity of human memory, so even small advances took many generations. The expansion of human knowledge, then, was slow and limited in an era of purely oral communication. More rapid improvements in life would not come about until more recent times with the invention of writing. Improvements would accelerate greatly after the 15th century, with the invention and widespread use of printing. Finally, in very recent times, over the last two centuries, human communication would cease to be bound by time or distance with the invention and adoption of modern mass media.

Writing: Recording and recovering thoughts. Today, few of us truly understand that the development of writing was one of the most remarkable human accomplishments in verbal communication of all time. Some authorities link it to cave paintings, such as those found in southern France and in Spain. In some cases, these go back at least 15,000 years. Yet, their purpose remains unclear and no one really knows whether they were the first steps in developing writing.

Much clearer are techniques for using graphic pictures and abstract symbols for *recording ideas* that began between 5,000 and 6,000 thousand years ago. At first they were very simple, to be sure, but they were indeed systems for writing as we think of it today. What happened was that people of the time (in various parts of the Mesopotamian area) began to carve or scratch simple pictures on flat stone slabs. They used lines to separate different parts of their messages into small squares (like is still done in the comic strips in the daily paper). Within such squares they carved representations of objects that had associated familiar meanings, such as animals, parts of the human body, or other features of their environment. For example, a simple depiction of a foot represented a man walking. A simplified sun indicated one day, and a wavy line meant water, such as a lake. A person seeing these symbols and recovering their meaning would read them as: "A man walked for one day alongside a lake." It was a remarkable achievement. *It even permitted living people to communicate with the dead!* That hitherto impossible feat gave even early writing a special significance.

The key to understand such a written message using *pictographs* (simplified pictures representing ideas) was that agreements had to be in place (among both those who prepared them and those who tried to interpret them) that a particular little pictograph (e.g., a sun) was always supposed to arouse the standardized meaning of *one day.* With such agreements in place, such a system of writing really worked. Each symbol represented a particular word or idea and could indeed be prepared by, or later interpreted by, anyone who knew the rules. In fact, many of the writing systems used in the world today are still based on this process. Examples are Arabic, Chinese and Japanese—to mention only a few.

Eventually, some of the ancient people who inhabited regions around the Mediterranean began to improve their way of writing. One great improvement was that they began to have the graphic forms—the symbols—whether carved, painted with a brush, or written with a pen represent *sounds,* rather than words or whole ideas. This was a really important advance. To develop "sound" writing, a way had to be invented so that each of the different noises human beings can make with their voice boxes, lips, tongues and so on, has its own characteristic written mark. Over time a link was made between sounds and written symbols or *characters* to represent them.

Eventually, by around 900 b.c., the Greeks produced a remarkably different system based on *letters,* each of which represented its own sound. The letters could be placed into sequences to make the sound of an entire word. Eventually, they standardized these characters throughout their various regions. This made written communication based on the oral sounds of spoken language much simpler, easier to learn, and far easier to write. The Greeks used common names of things in their environment, such as *alef* (the bull), to label their letters. Thus the first letter was *alpha* from that source. Their second was *beta,* and from those two we get *alphabet.*

Using an alphabet to represent sounds greatly simplified learning both reading and writing. There are only a certain number of distinct sounds that a human being can make with his or her voice. Generally, we can make sounds that we know today as *vowels* (softer ooohs, aaahs, and eeehs). We can also make a bunch of harsher sounds—consonants like the *t*, the *k*, *b*, and *d*. There are a few others, of course, like the *z*, the *f* and the more guttural *g*. Although it took thousands of years to produce and standardize the way we do this today, using a set of letters for sounds did get conventionalized. The standardized Greek alphabet made it possible for Plato (428–348 b.c.) to write his *Republic*, and for his student Aristotle (384–322) to produce not only his great works *Ethics* and *Politics*, but also his system of Aristotelian logic, which became the established route to valid knowledge for religious scholars more than a thousand years afterward. Their ideas have remained a part of Western culture since that time. They also made it possible for children to learn to read.

Beginning in about the first century before Christ, the Romans developed a modified alphabet derived from the Etruscan and Greek versions. They also standardized the appearance of the letters. The Roman letters they developed are still widely used when we write in English as well as in many other languages. (In fact, on your computer there is a font called Times Roman which has the same letter forms that Cicero and Caesar used—with no computer, of course, and without the benefit of the *New York Times*, which adopted and popularized it.) Today, we have only 26 letters, plus some punctuation characters, that represent in graphic form the phonograms we use in speech.

In overview, it took many centuries for human verbal communication to get here from there, but both human speech and the ability to record it as writing represent advances of staggering proportions. We often think today that inventions like the telephone, the automobile and the computer represent immense steps forward. And, of course they do. But they all pale in comparison with the development of speech and writing as modes of verbal communication which made possible the very foundations of human existence and civilization.

Printing: Expanding the dissemination of ideas.
With speech and writing well developed, hu-
mankind still faced a significant problem. There was a serious need for extensive written documents that could preserve the growing bodies of knowledge that were being produced by the world's great religions, by early mathematicians and astronomers, by some of the founding fathers of science and other intellectuals. Books were badly needed to record that knowledge and to pass it on to others. The skill of writing books by hand did not provide well for that need. Books written by hand, that is, *manuscripti*, prepared letter by letter, word by word and sentence by sentence, were very difficult to produce and demand far outstripped supply.

Not only were handwritten books difficult to prepare, but there came a time when the very skill of writing itself was threatened and nearly lost. What happened was that Rome went into a period of serious decline over the several centuries that followed the birth of Christ. During the second century, the Romans were decimated by plagues. Then, their territories in outlying regions of their empire were overrun by fierce people from both their north and their south. Later, even what is now Italy was repeatedly overrun. In fact, the city of Rome itself was sacked twice during the 400s—first by the Germanic Visigoths who had overrun Spain, and then by the ruthless and destructive Vandals from North Africa (from whom we get our current term "vandalize").

Neither the Visigoths nor the Vandals had a written language. Not understanding the idea of writing but fearing its power, they were determined to stamp it out. Consequently they destroyed Roman libraries, burned all the books that they found there, and tried systematically to kill those who were able to prepare them.

As Europe moved on into what came to be known as the Dark Ages, Rome, and Italy generally, gradually reverted back to a simpler agricultural society. To be sure, Rome had a glorious past, but it had lost its power and status. Meanwhile, those who were able to write (largely Christian monks) built fortified monasteries in remote places to protect themselves and continued to produce handwritten books—mostly of a religious nature. Thus, for several centuries, the critical skill of writing using an alphabet was preserved within the *scriptoria* of religious orders.

During the 1200s, a new kind of more secular institution began to be established in major capitals of European countries. At the time they were called *studia generalia*. Today we call them "universities." They were schools whose curricula focused on the "learned professions." These were the liberal arts, canon and civil law, medicine and theology. While they educated students who were mainly from the upper levels of society, their importance for the study of verbal communication is that *they required both libraries and textbooks*. But at the time, books for both uses were still dreadfully difficult to obtain. All were handwritten in (secular) *scriptoria* to be sold for very high prices, or were copied word for word from rented chapters by students themselves. A new technology for producing books was sorely needed. However, it was simply not available.

The person who developed the technology for printing was Johannes Gutenberg, the son of a goldsmith in Mainz (in what is now Germany). It was a remarkable new technology. He experimented for more than 20 years and finally developed a press (based on the principles of a wine press). He cast individual letters in metal, one letter at a time, and prepared a suitable printers' ink (made of lampblack and varnish). Finally he had all the procedures needed to produce a large number of identical pages free from the usual errors of the *manu-scriptus*. His first effort was an elegant Bible. However, he did not profit from his invention. He had to borrow money for supplies but was unable to repay the loan. The lender threw him out of his print shop, took over his press and the 200 copies of the Bible he had printed. He had the Bibles bound and sold them at a considerable profit. The penniless Gutenberg wandered around for a few years after that, living miserably on charity, went blind, and died in utter poverty. As you read these lines today, think of the remarkable contribution that he made to

your personal education, and indeed human existence.

By the time that Columbus set out for the new world, there was a printing press in virtually every major city in Europe, from which it quickly spread to most other parts of the world. The use of print as a means of extending speech as a mode of verbal communication entered a new and truly important era. Now, books could be printed in large numbers of identical copies. With the alphabet as a basis for written language, and books available to read, the rate of literacy in populations rose sharply. The new books not only served the universities and churches well, but it expanded the ability of humankind to pass on culture to new generations. As science began, religion expanded and writers produced an increasing body of literature. Thus, verbal communication was serving human beings as never before. By the 1500s, a few primitive news sheets began to appear on the street of major cities. Limited though they were, they were the forerunners of the newspapers we know today. The era of mass media based on print as verbal communication was getting its earliest start.

Contemporary media: The proliferation of channels. The pace of development in conquering distance and time in verbal communication gradually accelerated in Western societies. However, at the time the first settlers arrived in the new world (early in the 1600s), printing technology was virtually identical with that first used by Gutenberg. Books and other printed documents (e.g., simple newspapers) were produced with a hand-operated flatbed press, with letters individually cast in metal, and indeed with all the technology that had been used by Gutenberg to print the pages of his Bible. As newspapers gradually developed during the 1700s, they played an important part in defining the ideals underlying the American Revolution. They were not like those of today. Subscribing was very expensive and distribution beyond the city where they were published was very limited, but the newspapers were developing. The political information they contained was important in developing a new form of government in the colonies, but they were of interest primarily to the commercial elite who were well educated and affluent. Nevertheless, in the British Colonies in North America, literacy was slowly expanding, books were being printed, and even a few magazines began to appear (most failed financially very quickly).

The great breakthrough in extending human verbal communication beyond print and across the barriers of time and distance took place in the first half of the 1800s. Within a few decades after the 19th century began, the steam engine was rapidly replacing wind, water, and muscle as a source of power. The great Industrial Revolution had begun.

Within a remarkably short time, steam power was used for a long list of applications. Ships were built to be driven by steam. Carriages on rails moved goods and people far more swiftly than ever before. Above all, factories made use of steam to power their machines. Along with these, steam was applied to the printing press. When the publishers began to pay the costs of production by selling advertising, the modern mass newspaper was born (in New York in 1834). Newspapers were sold for only a penny, which made it possible for ordinary people to participate in a rapid and extended flow of information for the first time ever. Channels for verbal communication were expanding.[12]

A decade later, the telegraph was developed. The name itself indicates what it did (*tele*, the Greek word for "at a distance," plus *graphos*, "to write"). Samuel F. B. Morse sent his first message, "What hath God Wrought?" over 35 miles of wire (between Washington, D.C., and Baltimore, Maryland) at the speed of light (186,000 miles per second). At that point, verbal communication between human beings entered a totally new era. Device after device greatly expanded the channels available for verbal (and even visual) communications—the telephone at the end of the 1800s, the wireless telegraph (dot and dash radio) at the turn of the century, the radio-telephone in the first decade of the 1900s, the movies during the same period, regularly scheduled broadcasts to radio receivers in peoples' homes in the 1920s, television in homes by the late 1940s, and the Internet and the World Wide Web by the end of the 1900s.

The relatively short time from the beginnings of speech to the widespread use of the Internet (say somewhere around 40,000 years) was one of the most remarkable periods in the existence of human beings; but compared to the period in which human beings have lived on this planet, it has been a wink of the eye. For example, if that 40,000 years were to be represented by a clock with a face of 60 minutes, the time since the telegraph was shown to the world by Morse and the present would represent a mere *15 seconds!* From the development of home television to the present has been *only 4.5 seconds,* and the use of the Internet would represent *a mere 0.9 of a second* more. Clearly, our ability to conquer time and distance with both verbal and visual communication has accelerated at an incredible pace.

Where is all this development leading? No one can tell. People talk of a "global village," united by common interests and brought together by open channels of communication. Obviously, we are not there yet. Divisions between peoples remain sharp and sometimes exceedingly bitter. Yet, as we continue to travel through the centuries ahead, perhaps that is not really such a far-fetched dream after all. Our ability to engage in human verbal communication, overcoming distance and time, to relate to each other in more harmonious ways may prove to be the most remarkable of all of the accomplishments of our species.

The Basic Nature of Language

Human beings use many different kinds of cues, signs, and labels to refer to the various types of organized and shared meanings we have discussed. We noted in Chapter 1 that one convenient way of referring to all of those many kinds is simply to call them "symbols." This term has come into wide use for that purpose.

Language Symbols and Their Referents

Human beings communicate with patterns of *symbols* whose meanings are understood by both the individual initiating a message and the person or persons who perceive, decode and construct its meanings. As explained in Chapter 1, this can be a complex process involving a number of stages. It can also include role-taking, feedback, and considerations of contexts. In interpersonal communication this complex process is best understood in terms of simultaneous transactions in which each of the communicating parties plays an active part.

Included in any spoken language are two basic categories of symbols—*verbal* and *nonverbal*—plus a number of patterns (i.e., grammatical structures, word order, or syntax) that serve the same functions as words (in that they too arouse meanings in people who are communicating). In each case, such symbols and patterns are used to encode and decode meanings. An important point here, one that aids in understanding the basic nature of language, is that there is a socially accepted and standardized *rule* or "convention" that defines the relationship between *every symbol in a language and its referent*. The term **referent** is used by language scholars to indicate whatever the symbol "refers to"—that is what it "labels," or "stands for." Each of these ideas requires clarification.

Most of the symbols we use in communication are ordinary words that are formally or "officially" defined in standard dictionaries in terms of their **denotative meanings**. The most significant point that can be made about this broad category of symbols is that each of them serves as a *label* in some way for some organized set or sets of meanings. That is, each provides an identifier, or a guide to how people are expected to respond to its sound or appearance in writing by experiencing internal images,

feelings, and understandings. In terms of the explanations developed in previous sections, we can put all the ideas together in the following definition:

> Symbols are socially agreed-upon labels that we use to identify and arouse conventionalized meanings stored in schemata within our memory system.

This formulation provides an extension of the definition of communication that we formulated in Chapter 1 (page 7). It does so by specifying more precisely the nature of symbols—including nonverbal symbols and signs.

Nonverbal symbols: Communicating without words. Much of what human beings communicate takes place without words. Included in the messages we transmit to each other are actions, gestures, and tones of voice. These too have referents. That is, they arouse conventionalized meanings in ourselves and others in much the same way as words.[13] For example, a frown is an action that communicates an emotional state as its referent. In addition to such actions, many other symbols we use in communication are also not actually words but nonverbal cues, such as special clothing (e.g., a police officer's or nurse's uniform that implies a specific set of meanings). These are also used to identify and arouse within us particular *connotative* (that is subtle) meanings and interpretations. The list is long and can include military insignia, tattoos, and jewelry. In each case, however, the nonverbal symbol has an associated meaning that is more-or-less standardized.

Sources of symbols: The principle of arbitrary selection. Where do such verbal and nonverbal symbols come from? That is, how does a given language community originally select a particular word, a nonverbal gesture, an object, or another symbol for its members to use as a label for a given set of meanings? The fact is that there is no clear answer to that question. No clear rules precisely explain the origins of most of our words or other symbols. The most

BOX 2.1　🔍 *A Closer Look*

The Principles of Symbols

Symbols are the labels we agree to use to arouse meanings that are associated with some reality we've experienced. Most of the symbols we use are words. But where do these symbols come from? And why do all of us, within the same language community, decide that we should use this word as a label, and not some other symbol? The following principles apply to symbols:

- *The principle of arbitrary selection.* The particular symbol or word we select is arbitrary. In other words, we could just as easily have chosen the symbol *chair* to refer to table or *dad* to refer to *mother.* Consider how this principle is applied by special groups, like teenagers: *Bad, tight,* and *phat* all refer to something that is good. What other labels have you or your friends arbitrarily chosen to refer to something else?
- *The principle of conventions.* Once a symbol has been arbitrarily assigned, the rules change. To use the symbol to communicate, we need to stabilize its use. That is, all individuals within a shared language community must now agree to use that particular symbol. This principle, then, asserts that once a symbol is assigned, we must always use that particular symbol, and no other, to refer to that particular thing. Without this principle, people would arbitrarily use any word at any time to refer to anything at all. Imagine how difficult it would be to communicate with others without this principle!

common. No one can say exactly how these very different labels came to be associated with that particular kind of animal. Someone in the history of the people speaking those languages decided that the word was an acceptable label for that aspect of reality. Most of our words are like that—their original selection was arbitrary.

For some words, clearly, we can uncover historical origins. Many contemporary words in English, which is a composite of a number of ancient and relatively modern languages, can be traced back to historic or even prehistoric sources. For example, the term *father* is an obvious derivation of the Latin and Greek *pater.* That, in turn, is almost identical to the earlier term *pitar* found in ancient Sanskrit. In fact, there are indications that it originated as part of the very earliest languages used by human beings. Thus, a number of words that appear in many modern languages can be traced back to an ancient common source—which some people call a "mother tongue" that was probably spoken in northern and eastern Europe and parts of Asia somewhere between 6,000 and 8,000 years ago.[15]

Aside from this heritage, the process of selecting words to signify and arouse particular meanings appears to be rather capricious. Whoever those ancient people were who began using *pitar* to signify male parenthood could just as easily have chosen something quite different. Thus, their choice was also arbitrary. In fact, in other parts of the world totally different sound patterns came into use to signify that particular human relationship.

The same can be said about nonverbal symbols. Why does a middle finger, pointed upward, with the other fingers pointed down, have as its referent a rude meaning? Why does a tongue sticking out imply an insult, or a thumb and finger held in a circle imply *"OK"* or general approval (at least for English speakers)? There probably are historical origins, but someone back then selected those gestures in an arbitrary manner.

The principle of arbitrary selection, then, indicates that when new sets of related meanings

accurate statement we can make is that the selection process is **arbitrary.** This means that it is often rather random and sometimes even capricious.[14] For example, in English we say *horse,* in Spanish *caballo,* and in German *pferd.* These sounds and spellings have nothing in are formed, the process of labeling them does not follow some rigid or systematic rule. The reason a particular sound comes into use is seldom easy to explain. Someone proposes a label; it starts to be used, becomes more common; and when usage stabilizes it has become a part of the standard vocabulary within a language community. For that reason, Americans use "gasoline" in their cars, the British use "petrol," and people in Argentina use *nafta,* even though they are all chemically the same.

Language as Conventions

The term *convention* refers to a standard *rule* that has been accepted by a particular community or society to engage in some action in a particular way. For example, it is a convention among the military that enlisted personnel will always salute an officer who approaches them. There are many kinds of conventions, and those of concern here are the ones that link certain symbols and their standardized meanings.

While the original assignment of a symbol as a label for a common set of meanings can be arbitrary, once the assignment has been made the situation changes sharply. To be used as a tool for communication, the link between a symbol and its referent—the object, situation, or event to which it refers—has to be *predictable, stable, and relatively unchanging.* Otherwise, its use in communication would be impossible. No one could be sure of what meaning was implied. This stability is achieved by the use of the *principle of conventions* for defining and using symbols.

Convention has a broad meaning, implying any kind of rule that a given people agree to follow. In verbal (and nonverbal) communication, it refers to a rule that people within a given language community have devised and accepted. That rule links a particular meaning to a particular word (or nonverbal symbol). Such conventions state that whenever a person initiates a particular sound pattern or written mark (as in a given word) or a specific nonverbal symbol, the expected meaning experience is standardized.

We can now bring together the ideas and principles we have discussed concerning symbols, their referents (the objects or situations that are labeled), and their meanings to raise again the issue of how we know the world outside our heads. The relationships between all three can be represented by the simple diagram. This diagram is a version of one that was first proposed in 1946 by Ogden and Richards, who aptly called it the **meaning triangle.**[16]

The diagram shows that meaning, the symbol, and referent constitute a kind of system. That is, within a specific language community, each pair of elements is linked by a convention. The referent is the object, situation, or thing (or even make-believe idea) to which we have assigned some meaning. The meaning, as was explained in detail earlier, is the internal psychological configuration or *schema* of memory traces subjectively aroused in us. That arousal takes place either by apprehending the referent itself with our senses or by receiving a communicated cue from another person. The symbol, of course, is the word, gesture, object, or behavior we use as a cue to arouse the meaning in another person (or even in ourselves).

The conventions, C1, C2, and C3 are the rules of our particular language community that stabilize the meaning triangle. The first, C1, links the *referent* and the *person's meaning* with a rule that a specific pattern of internal experiences is the expected way of perceiving and understanding that aspect of reality. A second convention, C2, links the *symbol* and the *person's meaning* with an agreement that **perception** of the symbol will arouse the same meanings (in us or in another person) as does the referent itself—even though the latter may not actually be present. Still another convention, C3, completes the system with a shared agreement that the particular symbol *will stand for,* and *will be the socially accepted label of,* the referent. The arrows in the meaning triangle show these relationships.

Conceptualizing language symbols in terms of configurations of schemata and meaning triangles probably will not, just by themselves, be

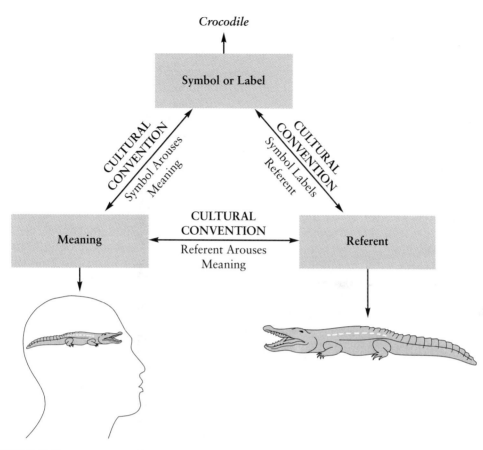

FIGURE 2.2

The Meaning Triangle
Every symbol in our vocabulary can be thought of as a *meaning triangle,* depicting the
relationship between the symbol, what it labels in reality, and the meaning experience
we have for both. Cultural conventions provide rules for linking the symbol, referent,
and meaning.

of immediate practical utility in communicating effectively with one's boss, roommate, or special friend. Nevertheless, such theoretical models do identify the nature and definitions of the most basic features of the communication process that may otherwise be difficult to understand—and they do so far better than vague descriptions. For that reason, models are an important part of the foundation on which effective communication skills are acquired.

Mastering a particular language requires a thorough familiarity with a host of different types of conventions. For example, every language has a large formal or official *vocabulary,* specific words with particular meanings that must be well understood, both to express meanings and to understand the meanings of others. These are the building blocks out of which messages are constructed. The authoritative *Oxford English Dictionary* lists about 500,000 words. To this could be added about another half-million terms used in specialized technical and scientific fields by English speakers.[17] In contrast, German has about 185,000 words, and Chinese has at most about 50,000 characters, each standing for a word. However, each of these languages provides for the same level of richness of expression as words can be combined to indicate virtually any intended meaning.

To represent the entire English vocabulary, including all technical words, in the form of meaning triangles we would need up to 1 million diagrams (there would have to be a separate diagram for every word). This is a staggering thought, to say the least. However, none of us carry around anything even close to a million meaning triangles in our head. In order to conduct our daily routine, most of us can get by nicely with about 5,000 words. On average, an educated person will have a vocabulary of about 15,000 words. Truly able communicators will have many more. For example, William Shakespeare, who had one of the largest vocabularies of any English writer, used an estimated 30,000 different words to write his plays and sonnets.[18] Included in the vocabulary of every language are numerous synonyms—words that actually are associated with very similar meanings.

Each language has conventions of *pronunciation*. Even minor errors in the way a word is pronounced can cause confusion. Significant regional accents can also muddy meanings for people not familiar with them. The rules of pronunciation are acquired in a language community, starting at a very early age.

To the conventions of vocabulary and pronunciation we can add those of *grammar*—a critical aspect of any language. The important point is that grammatical structures themselves imply meanings. That is, different variants of symbols (tenses, verb forms, and so on) arranged into grammatically conventionalized sequences, indicate meanings that are not implied in the specific words in a message. The same words in different grammatical patterns form distinct messages.[19]

The grammatical conventions of some languages are far more complex than those of others, and many languages use forms that have no counterparts in English. For example, English speakers do not assign a masculine or feminine status to nouns, as some languages require. In Spanish, any house (*casa*) is feminine and takes an "a" ending, whereas any "building" (*edificio*) is masculine and takes an "o" ending. For every noun one must remember whether it is masculine or feminine and pronounce it accordingly. Native English speakers learning Spanish often find this difficult.

By comparison with those of some languages, English grammar is simple. We use nouns to indicate objects and verbs for action. Our system of nouns is neuter in terms of the masculine-feminine distinctions noted above. We do make an important distinction between actions that occurred in the past, those that are occurring in the present, and those that will occur in the future, and we conjugate our verbs differently in each of these tenses. Furthermore, we use separate sets of adjectives and adverbs to modify the meanings of nouns and verbs.

Some languages do all of this very differently. For example, the Navajo language uses only two major categories of verbs—neuter and active—for which English has no counterparts. However, in each category, the Navajo have from five to seven different ways of conjugating their verbs that imply important distinctions. In addition, the implications of nouns, verbs, adjectives, and adverbs can be compounded into a single term. In the Navajo language it is possible to indicate, with only one word, the meaning "the round solid object that was formerly in motion is now at rest."[20]

Finally, as we have noted and illustrated earlier, using the accepted rules for syntax is essential to avoid serious misinterpretations. Thus, the principle of conventions extends beyond linking words and nonverbal symbols to meanings. It is also the foundation for the use of pronunciation, grammar and syntax in verbal communication.

How Language Serves Us Today: Individually and Collectively

As has been suggested, human life changed greatly and continuously in that short period

BOX 2.2　　*A Closer Look*

Using Symbols Appropriately and Sensitively

One way to avoid the hazard of using the wrong labels to refer to a particular group is to use the names or symbols that individuals or groups choose to use for themselves. See if you can identify culturally sensitive alternatives to the following labels:

old people	_____
drunk	_____
dope addict	_____
fat people	_____
mentally retarded	_____
poor	_____
handicapped	_____
homosexual	_____
salesman	_____
waitress/waiter	_____
unwed mother	_____

cleaning lady	_____
the deaf	_____
Indians	_____
Orientals	_____
illegal aliens	_____
cops	_____
mailman	_____
religious fanatics	_____
pro-abortionists	_____
old maid	_____
womanizer	_____
illegitimate children	_____
housewife	_____
femi-Nazi	_____
children from a broken home	_____
Mrs. or Miss	_____

between the first development of language by the *Cro-Magnon* and the present with our current world-wide use of instantaneous mass media. But how has the use of speech and language made a difference in our lives today? There are two important questions. First, how does language shape the way we function psychologically as individual human beings who continuously experience and respond to our environment? The answer is that it does so in very complex ways. Second, how has language enabled us to live together collectively and harmoniously in groups and societies with stable and predictable ways of life and with a continuous development of new solutions to problems of living? Again, the answer is in complex ways.

First, language made it possible for people to *know the world* through internal meanings. We are able to understand our physical environment through a process of *perception* that is dependent on the language community in which we exist. Second, language enabled human beings to *think analytically*—to solve problems by examining facts and premises, to reason from them to reach conclusions and decide on what actions to take or what interpretations should be reached. Third, language enabled human beings to *remember* the events of their daily experiences in an organized manner. Thus, our language provides each of us with the means to *accumulate knowledge,* records of experience, that can guide future decisions and actions. Those three great changes in psychological functioning are what psychologists currently call "cognitive processing."

Language also changed the way people *relate collectively* to their fellow human beings. After acquiring the ability to speak, our ancestors evolved from small hunting and gathering

BOX 2.3   *Ethical Concerns*

WHAT SIGNIFICANCE SHOULD WE PUT ON GRAMMAR?

Not too long ago when my sister was visiting from out of state, I invited her to accompany me to a public speaking class that I was teaching. Together we listened to a young Latina student give a heartfelt presentation on the status of illegal immigrants trying to make a living in southern California.

After class, I turned to my sister and asked, "What did you think of Dolores's speech?" Dianne replied that she really enjoyed it and thought Dolores had made several good points.

But I persisted, "Yes, but what did you think of Dolores's presentation?" Again, Dianne discussed the relative merits of the student's arguments.

"Okay, but let me ask you this: What if your daughter spoke the way Dolores had? How would you have evaluated her presentation then?"

Dianne was quick to respond. "I would expect my daughter to talk with a better vocabulary and grammar than this student did. After all, Dolores mispronounced and misused a number of words and phrases in her presentation."

Do we, should we, hold others to the same high standards of grammar and vocabulary that we do ourselves? Do we, should we, lower our standards when the speaker represents a culture that is different from our own? Does incorrect grammar or word pronunciation interfere with our ability to understand a speaker? Does it influence our perceptions of a speaker's credibility? Does it make it more difficult to listen?

What happens when individuals do not follow the conventions for "good" grammar? What does "poor" grammar communicate about the individual, if anything? Should we expect everyone to share our grammatical conventions—even people for whom English is not their first language? Should we expect individuals who represent different ethnic groups to share U.S. standards for grammar? Why or why not?

This chapter discusses the importance of grammar and conventions: that is, different word arrangements, word pronunciations, and verb tenses all communicate particular meanings. The grammatical conventions or rules for English are very complex. Children are taught rules for English grammar even before they begin school, and that instruction continues through grade school, high school, and college. What ethical responsibility do we have to comply with the conventions of grammar that we are taught? What ethical responsibility do we have to overlook another's grammatical mistakes?

---

groups of related families to ever-larger populations living in fixed villages and practicing agriculture. Eventually, large societies developed, composed of many kinds of groups with complex relationships. To stabilize those relationships between people, shared rules for acceptable behavior were needed, so that individuals and families could lead well-regulated lives. Language made this possible. Putting it very simply, language permitted the development of a uniquely human existence that forever separated us from other species on our planet.

Language and the Social Construction of Reality

For more than 2,000 years, philosophers have pondered how it is that human beings can develop internal understandings that enable them to cope with the physical and social worlds that exist outside their heads. This seemingly arcane question was of great concern to ancient scholars who were first trying to understand human mental processes. They posed the issue in terms of the question "How do we know reality?" Indeed, that question has continued to hold the attention of many kinds of scholars right up to the present day.[21]

The answer to this very basic question provides the key to understanding how human beings interpret their physical and social environment, think about the world around them, and communicate their thoughts to others and themselves. Thus, the issue of how we know reality must be resolved before insight can be gained into communication transactions as well as into such critical "mental" activities as perceiving, reasoning, and remembering. As we have noted, it is these activities that enable human beings to lead elaborate social lives and to develop and pass on complex cultures.[22]

Constructing reality by communicating. Almost 400 years before the birth of Christ, a remarkable man began to clarify the issue of how we know reality. Plato wrote in his *Republic* of an imaginary experiment that wonderfully illustrates the issue. In his "Allegory of the Cave," he set forth this passage:

> Imagine the condition of men living in a sort of cavernous chamber underground, with an entrance not open to the light and a long passage all down the cave. Here they have been from childhood, chained by the leg and also by the neck, so that they cannot move and see only what is in front of them, because the chains will not let them turn their heads.[23]

Obviously, such an experiment would not actually or ethically be possible, but suppose there were men in such a condition. Now we can add additional conditions that Plato described. Behind the men (who are presumably seated on a bench), he wrote, is a high wall. The men, facing outward, cannot see this, but on the back of the other side of the wall is a walkway, along which other men can move while holding up long sticks, each of which has a shape attached (like a silhouette figure of men or animals, or any kind of shape formed of wood or other material). Still farther back from the wall, and high up, is a brightly burning fire. The fire casts a bright light onto the wall of the cave that the chained men can see (Plato obviously did not have electricity for this purpose).

These arrangements result in the chained men seeing *shadows* on the cave wall in front of them—shadows with various silhouette shapes moving along (as the men behind the wall on the walkway march along holding up their sticks with the figures).

These shadows *are all the reality that the chained men ever see.* As they talk to each other, they discuss the shadows, give each different one a name, and try to see who among them can best forecast their sequences of appearances. Since the shadows are their only reality, they come to know them well indeed.

Now suppose that one of the men were unchained, released, shown the fire, the sticks, the walkway and the silhouette shapes that the other men used to produce the shadows. He would be told that the reality that he and his fellows had worked out with the shadows was only an illusion! Then, imagine further that he was taken out of the cave altogether, and shown the real world that existed out there— its stars, sun, moon, houses, roads, sheep, wagons, and all the other things that the Greeks of the time saw and used.

Finally, suppose that he were to be brought back into the cave and chained once again in his original position. Now he would have the task of explaining to his comrades where he had been and what he had learned. He would try to explain to them that what they regarded as reality was *only an illusion,* and that he had a true grasp of the real world. He would describe what he had seen and heard during his absence.

Would those still in the chains believe him? Plato said no. After all, they already knew the nature of reality. They had worked it out together, communicating again and again about the shadows and agreeing on the names and meaning of each. They would laugh at the man who had returned, and at his preposterous ideas. In fact, they would probably see him as a raving lunatic. Indeed, said Plato, the men who had remained in the cave might be inclined to kill him because he was a dangerous madman.

If you and I encountered a person who claimed to have been transported to a totally different reality—say to a remote planet, by aliens from outer space—we might react in a manner similar to Plato's chained men. We would surely not contemplate killing the poor soul. But we might be inclined to question his or her sanity and would probably make phone calls to tell someone to come with a straight jacket.

The lesson from Plato? *It is through an extended process of verbal and nonverbal communication within our language community that we come to know reality.* Plato had an incredible insight that is as true today as it was in his time. Today we can revise that principle by adding the influences of *mass-mediated visual communication*—and especially its *visual* forms (such as movie and television). To illustrate this revised principle and show its practical implications, a recent large-scale study of teenagers in 12 countries shows the influence of mass-communicated entertainment on teenagers who have little or no direct knowledge of Americans or their society. From their exposure to American popular culture (which they enjoy greatly) they gain impressions of the reality of ordinary people and their ways of life in the United States. As they lack contact with Americans, the impressions, beliefs, and attitudes that they unwittingly form about Americans from media-delivered entertainment are often *seriously distorted.* This comes about because many countries have no facilities for producing their own movies or TV programming. However, they do have cinemas for providing movies and cable or broadcast systems to deliver TV content to their populations. Satellite dishes are also common, from which they can receive programming from U.S. sources. Their local entertainment entrepreneurs (or sometimes their governments) import films and television programs so that the people can enjoy popular culture produced in Western societies (mainly the United States).

In this way, people even in developing countries receive entertainment and news programs on their TV sets, and see films at their local cinemas. Many own VCR players, for which they can rent tapes cheaply in the street. Others, who do not own receivers, can see much content in group settings at village centers or in the homes of more affluent neighbors. In all areas of the globe, then, people see soap operas, *Oprah, Sex and the City, Baywatch, The Sopranos,* crime and cop dramas, and much the same programs depicting Americans that are seen by families in cities and towns in the United States. This popular content seems to them to depict life among ordinary people in the United States. It seems obvious to such viewers (who have no other sources from which to gain knowledge) that Americans and life in the United States are characterized by crime, violence, open and nonmarital sexual liaisons, materialism, and little or no interest in religious or spiritual matters. American movies and TV entertainment are designed as *entertainment* and not as documentaries or educational materials, but it is from such popular mass communications that millions of people around the world build **social constructions of reality** concerning the nature of American people and their ways of life.

Needless to say, the consequent understandings and beliefs about Americans and lifestyles in the United States are seriously flawed.[24] Such verbal and visual communications provide a basis for strong condemnation of the United States and Americans (who are portrayed as immoral people who deserve to be punished). Indeed, in some countries, the United States and the American people are seen as the "Great Satan," with all the meanings this term implies. One need look no further than the tragic events of September 11, 2001, and other terrorist events, to understand that very real and dire consequences can result from such views.[25] At the same time, Americans often receive incorrect views of other nations and their people.

Thus, modern mass communications have been added to what existed in Plato's time. The social construction of reality is a process of communication during which labels and definitions are provided for all the things that make up the physical and social worlds that we experience. This is a process that has been going on since language came into existence.

Linguistic relativity: Different cultures, different names, different realities. As the foregoing suggests, not all language communities construct the same interpretations of reality. Even without considering the influence of television and movies, the way a language is organized can bring people to define and experience reality in quite different ways. This is a simple way of defining the principle of **linguistic relativity.** When populations began to grow (as agriculture produced more food) people began to live longer. Slowly, people began to drift away from where humankind originated (much evidence exists that it was in Africa). When this dispersion of populations to what is now Europe, Asia, and the Americas took place, new languages were developed and older ones were modified. Distinct cultures came to be developed as people adapted in different ways in different regions and continents. Some remained as hunting and gathering people (e.g., many Native American and Eskimo groups as well as others in Africa and Australia). Others improved their agriculture and built remarkable cities and monuments (e.g., the Aztecs and Maya in the Western Hemisphere). Still others industrialized to become modern societies.

One major result of all these changes was the development of thousands of local languages, each very different from all others. Different word categories developed with distinct meanings attached to each symbol. For example, among Native American language groups even the realities of colors are divided up differently from one group to the next. Some indigenous people lumped all the greens and blues together and gave them a single name,[26] and some had dozens of different names for what we currently refer to simply as "snow." For example, among the Greenland Eskimos there are many kinds of snow—some suitable for building igloos, others unsuitable. Still other named categories provide excellent surfaces for sleds; others make sled travel more difficult. Each type has a different name.

That principle that different kinds of people divide up what they see around them and name them in special ways is not confined to people who live in remote places. The same principle can be observed by comparing males and females in the United States on the degree to which they can name and recognize colors. Females have an elaborate vocabulary for naming colors—in the same way Eskimos name and make distinctions about different types of snow. Most females can recognize such colors as puce, aubergine, taupe, or chartreuse. Males often have little command of these names, and when asked the color of a sweater, or some other object that is not obviously black or white, they resort to clumsy phrases like "sort of light purple" (for lavender), or "kind of yellowish-green" (for chartreuse), and so on.

Thus, when people construct specific sets of labels and meanings through a process of communication, they interpret the physical and social world in distinct ways. Plato established the principle long ago and it is still relevant today. People watching a TV set in a neighbor's mud or grass hut, and seeing the United States portrayed in programs produced to entertain, are likely to develop a set of terms to describe the characteristics of Americans that is different from the set of terms developed by suburbanites in the American Midwest who view the same content.

Human Cognitive Processing

The individual counterpart to the social construction of reality—which is a *collective process* that takes place between people—is what takes place *within each of us* as we personally experience the reality to which we must respond. This activity is profoundly influenced by our language. Today, more than 2,000 years after Plato, we understand that human beings continuously engage in complex internal or subjective processes as they sort out meanings for, and respond to, what they encounter in their environment. An everyday term for this is "mental" activity, but this description fell into disrepute among psychologists long ago. As their field advanced, they substituted the phrase "cognitive processing" to refer to such human activities as *perception, judgment* (that is, systematic reasoning or thinking), and *memory.* Cognitive functions are distinct from other internal human behaviors such as emotions, including fear, hate, and love, although there may be mutual influences.

The point is that words and their standardized meanings in our language play a critical part in shaping the cognitive processing of information that is provided by our senses. Our eyes and ears, plus our senses of touch, smell, and taste, provide us with our initial contacts with the world outside our heads. The sensations that are received by these organs have to be "processed" within our brains so that meanings we will understand can be assigned to them. Those meanings have been learned by each of us as we participated in our language community. The first way in which cognitive processing takes place, then, is in our initial perception of features of our environment.

Perception: Using the pictures in our heads to interpret the world outside. The words of our language and the meanings associated with them enable us to identify people, objects and situations that we encounter as we constantly apprehend our physical and social world. We refer to this as *perception.* It is the process by which we as individuals *assign meaning to and interpret* what we experience with our senses on an ongoing basis. We engage in perception constantly. We have to, or the world we experience would be a meaningless and confusing jumble.

To illustrate the process and show the importance of language, suppose you are walking along and you suddenly see what appears to be some sort of large bird and hear it making a distinctive sound. For a tiny fraction of a sec-

ond you are not sure what it is. Clearly you have tentatively classified it in a general way by using the word *bird,* which is stored in your memory, with its associated meanings. That is, you "apprehended it with your senses"—your eyes and ears in this case—and assigned to it a preliminary but very general meaning. At this stage, you have not yet completed the process of perception. You want to narrow down what your senses are revealing to a familiar category of bird that you will understand much better.

Now comes a process of matching and comparing the information your eyes and ears are providing with words and their meanings stored in your memory. Looking more closely, you see that *it looks like a duck* (a named category in your memory). Then you notice that *it walks like a duck* (a feature of that category stored in your memory). Finally, you realize that *it quacks like a duck* (another remembered feature of that category). Aha! You instantly conclude that *it is a duck.* Perception has taken place!

Perception takes place at unbelievable speed—indeed, it is virtually instantaneous in most cases. What were initially just neural impulses sent to your brain from your eyes and ears have swiftly been transformed into a category of meaning that you recognize. The point is that we can perceive a stimulus, such as a duck, because we have the words and their related meanings already stored in our memory, ready to go, to enable us to make this interpretation.

In summary, perception is a critical part of the verbal communication process. We are totally immersed every waking moment in a complex physical and social environment, constantly confronting thousands of objects, people, messages and situations with which we have to deal. Our skills in perception—one of the most essential features of verbal communication—has made this possible because human beings long ago developed language.

Thinking: Using language to analyze situations and decide on actions. A second part of cognitive processing is analyzing what we have perceived and forming an appropriate response. Once we understand what we are perceiving, we can make orderly judgments about it. This is the second important feature of cognitive processing. Perceiving a duck, for example, calls for a different analysis of what to do than perceiving a snake. If we identify the object in our path as a duck, we might just smile and walk on. If we interpret it as a snake, however, we have some immediate thinking, analyses, and decision making to do. Is it a harmless garden critter? Or, is it a dangerous rattlesnake? We sort through that problem (using what we know about the two types of snakes), make a judgment, and choose an appropriate action (running from the rattler or ignoring the garden variety). Our stored words and their meanings for various categories of snakes and their relationships to possible danger, then, provide what we need to make that judgment. Again, our language enables us to engage in this internal verbal behavior as we process the situation cognitively.

Memory: Using language to store experiences for later recall and retelling.   Finally, whatever the bird or the snake turned out to be, we will retain the experience in memory—stored in physical terms as traces within the brain and organized psychologically into a *schema* of what happened, what we thought and how we acted. This will not only permit us to recall the event and recount our adventure to others, but also to formulate an appropriate response if a similar situation is perceived again. Thus, cognitive processing in the form of memory functions is also based on words, meanings, and language.

Language and the Accumulation of Culture

Once human beings gained the capacity to speak and developed language, their ability to invent solutions to problems of living accelerated at a remarkable pace. Within a period of only a few thousand years (again, a wink of time in evolutionary terms), people trans-

formed their lifestyle from a precarious existence based on constant wandering around in search of food to a stable existence based on agriculture. Instead of trying to exist on whatever animals that they could kill, or on plants they could find growing wild, they began to raise their own livestock for food and to plant crops to sustain them.

Inventing solutions to problems: The process of innovation.   As ways of obtaining a living by using the technology of agriculture were increasingly refined, people moved into *fixed villages*, where they built permanent shelters. It is clear that this remarkable transition took place only because they had become physically capable of speech and had begun to develop languages, which in turn enabled them to remember complex ideas, to think, and to invent. Thus, a remarkable period in human existence took place as our prehistoric ancestors developed *Neolithic culture*. (The term *neo* means "new." The other part of the word, *lithic*, refers to "stone." *Neolithic*, then, means "new stone age"—a time of considerable cultural development, but before metals came into use.)

The Neolithic era was a time when remarkable new arts and technologies were invented and slowly accumulated—including agriculture, weaving, clothing, pottery, and the wheel. There was more: The practice of burying the dead with weapons and food indicates that they also developed theories of the nature of life, death, and an afterlife. It was during this period, in other words, that the foundations for the great cultural institutions we know today were developed. With the *family* and the process of educating the young already well established, they added the forerunners of the *political, economic,* and *religious* institutions we now have in our societies. At the same time, progress was slow because these were people who remained in the oral tradition. Their development and ability to pass on solutions to succeeding generations was limited by the capacity of human memory.

Cultural accumulation.   For thousands of years after human beings acquired the ability to talk and develop language, each new generation was able to develop and add at least *some* new solutions to problems of living to those that had already been discovered. New ways of harnessing animal power for plowing and pulling were developed. Then, the ability to capture the wind to move boats, and to use the weight of water to turn wheels for power were discovered. New beliefs were developed, along with new ways to maintain a stable government, to use coins as a medium of exchange, to use a bow and arrow for hunting and defense, and to use the wheel to solve problems of transportation. Slowly but surely, people orally passed on from one generation to the next those solutions already at hand and the new ones that each generation invented. Thus, it was the ability to speak and to use language that made *cultural accumulation* possible.

This process accelerated greatly when it was freed from the limitations of human memory that characterized societies in the oral tradition. The development of *writing* made it possible to record achievements, rather that relying on people's memories to pass them on. Later, printing and all the rest of the communication media that followed increased the pace. Cultural accumulation today goes forward at a speed that could not have been even remotely imagined thousands of years ago. Even in the lifetime of our most elderly generation living today, such remarkable cultural innovations as the airplane, the automobile, the refrigerator, and the computer have become commonplace.

Symbolic Interaction: The Key to Developing Mind, Self, and Society

An important *paradigm* (broad theory) that helps in understanding how human beings make use of language and verbal communication to live together in orderly groups and society as a whole is called the "symbolic interaction perspective." Initially developed by Charles Horton Cooley in the late 1800s and early 1900s, it was later elaborated upon by George Herbert Mead and other sociologists. The paradigm explains how people are able to understand both other persons and themselves so that they can relate to each other effectively in human groups.[27] In this sense, symbolic interactionism provides additional insights into what verbal communication does for us both individually and collectively.

Cooley's idea was this: As a baby slowly begins to develop, it begins to interact with other people. At first, the voices, facial expressions, and activities of surrounding adults are only a part of the environment and have no special meaning in themselves. Gradually, however, the baby learns that certain family members are associated with its care, feeding, and comfort. Thus, these beings assume an increasing importance to the baby.

Gradually the child begins to perceive the limits of its own body and to define itself (develop a **self image,** or **self-concept**) as distinct from those other human beings. The word the child learns to label such a distinction becomes important. The social nature of *self-realization* is implied by the word *I*. Once this is learned, it automatically indicates the existence of persons who are "not *I*"—other distinct persons who have to be taken into account. In time, these persons come to be identified by other labels ("momma," "papa," and so on). This provides the beginning of an understanding of a social reality.

As the child matures, it becomes increasingly clear that relating to other people requires an *understanding of their expectations*. If one does not behave according to those expectations—certain rules—rewards may not follow. And indeed, in some cases, punishments may follow. Thus, three things take place in the development process as the child increasingly commands speech and language and engages in symbolic interaction with an ever-enlarging number of people. The first is the maturing cognitive ability to *perceive, think, and remember* through the use of the language that is being learned. A second is the recognition by the child that he or she is a *distinct being* with unique personal characteristics. The third is the under-standing that *social behavior is patterned* and one is expected to follow predictable rules.

These three outcomes of engaging in a complex process of symbolic interaction—that is living in a language community and relating to others with speech and language—were characterized by these early sociologists as the development of *mind, self, and society.*[28] Thus, the symbolic interaction paradigm (and its perspective on verbal communication) attempts to explain the foundation for *cognitive functioning,* for *understanding one's self,* and for gaining a command of the *rules and requirements for interacting in groups.*

We have explained in some detail the first of these processes—developing understandings of reality within a language community and how cognitive and processing is influenced by that language. But what about the other two? That is, how is language important in obtaining an understanding of self? Also, in what way does language serve in acquiring a command of the expectations of others—knowing the patterns and rules of human groups?

The looking-glass self. Cooley provided a very clear answer to the first question—the one about the process of developing a concept of self through a process of symbolic interaction. In an insightful poetic phrase he said this:

> Each to each a looking glass
> Reflects the other that doth pass.[29]

What he meant is that we see *reflections and definitions of ourselves* in the ways that other people react to us. For example, if we walk into a room and people come over, and smile, and say how glad they are to see us, that sends one message—one definition of what we are. If, on the other hand, we walk into the same room and people look the other way, or even get up and leave without saying anything, that sends a quite different definition. The reactions of others to our presence, comments, or actions, then, serve as a kind of "social mirror" in which we can see what we are.

Mirrors were called "looking glasses" in Cooley's time, and he called the general idea just expressed the *looking-glass self.* Clearly, then, gaining a concept of what we are, as others see us, and consequently what we come to believe about ourselves, emerges from symbolic interaction, that is communication through language, with others who provide us with their definitions.

Social organization: The rules of human groups. The final feature of human life explained by the symbolic interactionists was *society*—how we learn the patterned expectations of social life. Through the process of verbal communication, the paradigm explains, we learn the *orderly rules for behavior*—the expectations that characterize any human group, ranging from the smallest to the largest. Every group—from the two-person family to the huge corporation or the bureaucratic government agency—has an organization of expectations. These expectations, or rules, bring order, predictability, and stability to the actions of their members. Essentially, there are four features of any such group that provide for predictable relationships within the group.

One feature of the social organization of a group is its *general norms.* Every group has rules that apply to all its members more or less equally. These may deal with such matters as dress codes, modes of greeting, acceptable and unacceptable language or actions, and cleanliness. Everyone who is a member of the group is expected to observe these norms.

A second feature of a group's pattern of social organization is the expectations that apply to individuals who play specialized parts within the group. These are the *roles* that are associated with particular activities in the group. In a baseball team, for example, the roles of pitcher, catcher, outfielder, and so on involve all quite different activities. In other groups the specialized roles may be doctor and patient, boss and worker, parent and child, or professor and student. In each case, such specialized activities are understood and defined in terms of the expectations of members as a whole.

A third pattern of social organization is the group's *ranking* arrangement. Some members of any group—even informal ones made up of friends—have more respect, more power, or more authority than others. Some are at the top of the hierarchy and others at the bottom. Most members are somewhere in between. Generally speaking, those who rank high in the pattern receive more rewards. Members must live with these arrangements. They are part of the general social expectations—the social organization—of group life, not only in small groups like families but also in communities and even in society at large.

Finally, all groups have ways of maintaining their stability. This feature of social organization refers to the expectation that those who fail to follow the rules, and deviate in significant ways, risk the application of *social controls*. They can be positive or negative. These controls may be minor in groups of friends—perhaps only amounting to praise as a positive reward or mild verbal criticism for annoying behavior. In families, where parents dominate, allowing or withholding privileges may be a form of control if children do not do well or fail to conform. In the workplace, the control may be a promotion or raise, or more drastically, separation from the group (getting fired). At the most extreme, for violating certain official rules of society, the offending deviant may be executed. Thus, norms, roles, ranks, and controls are the patterns of social organization developed through a process of symbolic interaction. They have been worked out through verbal communication in one form or another for maintaining the stability of human groups.

Chapter Review

- Early in the 1900s, a great controversy began about whether or not animals could communicate with language. The value of this controversy was that it brought about enthusiastic efforts to clarify the nature of language and the question of whether only human beings use it. After decades of animal studies, it appears there is a huge gap between the communication abilities of human beings and those of the animals nearest to us on the phylogenetic continuum.

- Human beings require shared language in order to develop normally. If they are denied such an environment, their processes of perception, thought, and memory, along with their social relationships, are impaired. They remain at an animal-like level.

- Engaging in verbal communication requires that each of us has to command an enormous set of labels for internal and subjective images, interpretations, and experiences that are associated with specific aspects of the world outside our heads. By participating in our language community we learn inner meanings not only for concrete objects that make up the physical world, but also for situations, relationships, activities, and conditions that make up our complex social life. In addition, we learn meanings for ideas that have no physical counterparts and even for things we know do not exist. A broad term for acquiring these processes is the "social construction of reality."

- By using symbols, human beings attach labels to configurations of meaning. Then, by establishing conventions of usage, those same symbols refer to both the object and the meaning. The three ideas—meaning, symbol, and referent—form a triangular system, with each pair stabilized by a convention. The initial choice of a symbol to label a referent and its meaning may be arbitrary, but once consensus is reached regarding the convention, meanings are stabilized.

- Language is composed of thousands of such systems, plus elaborate conventionalized rules for putting symbols together, as in sentences composed of words. The subtlety and complexity of human communication can be appreciated by realizing that just to get by at a simple level requires knowledge of about 5,000 words and their meanings, and an educated person will, on the average, command about 15,000 such meaning systems. Truly able communicators may be able to use up to 30,000. Important structural aspects of language governed by conventions include connotative meanings, grammar, and syntax. These can introduce meanings that are not contained in the conventional usage or that go beyond the meanings of the separate words used in a message.

- The human ability to learn and use language provides the individual with not only a sophisticated means for communicating with others but also the means by which inventions and innovations are achieved and cultural accumulation takes place to constantly enrich human life.

- Engaging in verbal communication is the process by which each person develops the ability to engage in cognitive processing—including perception, thinking, and remembering. It also enables the person to develop self-understanding. Finally, verbal communication—what sociologists call symbolic interaction—has for more than a century been identified as the critical process enabling human beings to develop mind, self, and society.

Key Terms

natural signs	language community	arbitrary (selection)
language	phylogenetic continuum	meaning triangle
Clever Hans effect	syntax	perception
signals	referent	social constructions of reality
sign	denotative meanings	linguistic relativity
symbols	connotative (meanings)	self-image (or self-concept)

Notes

1. Pfungst, O. (1907). *Das pferd des Herr von Osten: der Kluge Hans* (Clever Hans: The Horse of Mr. von Osten). Leipzig: Johan Ambrosius Barth.

2. Kellogg, W. N., & Kellogg, L. A. (1967). *The ape and the child: A study of environmental influence upon early behavior.* New York: Hafner. (First published by Whittlesey House in 1933.)

3. Hayes, C. H. (1951). *The ape in our house.* New York: Harper.

4. Geshwind, N. (1970). The organization of language and the brain. *Science, 170,* 940–944.

5. Gardner, T., & Gardner, R. A. (1969). Teaching sign language to a chimpanzee. *Science, 165,* 664–672.

6. Patterson, F., & Linden, E. (1981). *The education of Koko.* New York: Holt, Rinehart, and Winston.

7. Premack, A. J., & Premack, D. (1972). Teaching language to an ape. *Scientific American, 227,* 92–99.

8. One of the first of these experiments is reported in: Rumbaugh, D. M., et al. (1975). Conversations with a chimpanzee in a computer-controlled environment. *Biological Psychiatry, 10,* 627–641.

9. For recent discussions on the controversial issue of animals' ability to use language, see: Marler, P. (1999). How much does a human environment humanize a chimp? *American Anthropologist, 101,* 2, 432–436; Sundberg, M. L. (1996). Toward granting linguistic competence to apes: A review of Savage-Rumbaugh, et al.'s language comprehension in ape and child. *Journal of the Experimental Analysis of Behavior, 65,* 477–492.

10. Gugliotta, G. (April 18, 2002). Suddenly humans age three million years. *The Washington Post,* p. A-03; Moffett, N. (April 18, 2002). Monkey's great-grandpa older than we thought? *Chicago Sun-Times,* p. 10.

11. The family *Hominidae* (humanlike creatures) began to develop as a variation of the order *Primata* (primates) several million years ago. As evolution proceeded, such creatures grew larger and their brain-to-body mass ratio increased. By about 1.8 million years ago they were walking upright, as we do now. After the genus *Homo* emerged, our ancestors began making tools and using fire. However, cultural development remained at a stone-tool level throughout the Pleistocene period. Modern *Homo sapiens, sapiens,* in the form of *Cro-Magnon,* can be traced back no farther than around 90,000 years. They were the first human beings physiologically capable of using speech and language, which may have been fully developed only as recently as about 35,000 or perhaps 45,000 years ago. It was this communication ability, enabling *Cro-Magnon* to engage in reasoning, organized recall, and the transmission of solutions to complex problems to new generations, that provided the foundation for a rather sudden and increasing elaboration of human culture. By 15,000 years before the present, *Homo sapiens, sapiens* was widely dispersed in Europe, Asia, and Africa, and about 10,000 years ago the great Neolithic era of agriculture and village life began. For a detailed discussion of the fossil record and its implications, see: Lieberman, P. (1984). *The biology and evolution of language.* Cambridge, MA: Harvard University Press.

12. For more information on the development of the mass media, see: DeFleur, M., & Dennis, E. (2002). *Understanding mass communication* (7th ed.). Boston: Houghton Mifflin.

13. Remland, M. S. (2000). *Nonverbal communication in everyday life.* Boston: Houghton Mifflin.

14. Goss, B., & O'Hair, D. (1988). *Communicating in interpersonal relationships.* New York: Macmillan.

15. McCrum, R., Cran, W., & MacNeil, R. (1986). *The story of English* (pp. 51–53). New York: Elisabeth Sifton Books, Viking.

16. Ogden, C. K., & Richards, I. K. (1946). *The meaning of meaning.* New York: Harcourt Brace. See also: Adler, R. B., Rosenfeld, L. B., & Towne, N. (1995). *Interplay: The process of interpersonal communication.* New York: Holt, Rinehart, and Winston.

17. McCrum, Cran, & MacNeil, *The story of English,* p. 19.

18. Ibid., pp. 102–103.

19. Schegloff, E. A. (1972). Notes on a conversational practice: Formulating place. In D. N. Sudnow, (Ed.), *Studies in social interaction* (pp. 75–119). New York: Free Press.

20. Hoijer, H. (1964). Cultural implications of some Navajo linguistic categories. In D. Hymes (Ed.), *Language and culture in society: A reader in linguistics and anthropology* (pp. 142–153). New York: Harper and Row.

21. Cherwit, R. A., & Hikins, J. W. (1986). *Communication and knowledge: An investigation in rhetorical epistemology.* Columbia: University of South Carolina.

22. A large body of scholarly writing from such fields as anthropology, sociology, and social psychology support this position. See, for example, DeFleur, M.L., & Ball Rokeach, S. (1989). Stages in the development of human communication, in *Theories of Mass Communication* (3rd ed., pp. 3–45 Longman.)

23. Plato (1945). "Allegory of the Cave." In F. M. Cormford (Trans.), *The Republic of Plato.* London: Oxford University Press. p. 227.

24. For a detailed research report on these issues, see: DeFleur, M. L. & DeFleur, M. H. (2003). *Learning to hate Americans: How the U.S. media shape negative attitudes among teenagers in twelve countries.* Spokane: Marquette Books.

25. Perlmutter, D. D. (September 30, 2001). Why do they hate Americans and America? *The Buffalo News,* p. H5; Why the world loves to hate America: Anti-U.S. sentiment comes in different forms (December 7, 2001). *Financial Times (London),* p. 23.

26. See: Hoijer H., (1960). The Sapir-Whorf hypothesis. In *Language in culture* (pp. 92–115). Chicago: The University of Chicago Press.

27. See: Cooley, C. H. (1902). *Human nature and the social order.* New York: Charles Scribner's Sons.

28. See: Mead, G. H. (1934) In C. W. Morris, (Ed.), *Mind, self and society: From the standpoint of a behaviorist.* Chicago: University of Chicago Press.

29. Cooley, *Human nature and the social order,* p. 184.

Chapter 3

Nonverbal Communication: Communicating Without Language

Jerome knew he was late for the interview, and he suspected that Mr. Kim, the personnel director, would be annoyed to be kept waiting. However, Mr. Kim didn't say anything about it, and, after shaking hands and introducing himself, he smiled and said warmly how nice it was to meet Jerome. He invited him to have a seat. Jerome really wanted the job, and he knew he could do the work. After all, he did have a degree in communication, and he had gotten good grades in all his courses. All he had to do was explain to this guy how well qualified he was, and he would be in.

They sat facing each other in comfortable leather chairs in Mr. Kim's attractive office. Jerome noticed right away that Mr. Kim was slim and neatly dressed. His conservative blue suit and tasteful maroon tie seemed somehow to suggest competence and dignity. Even his shoes looked expensive, and Jerome noticed that Mr. Kim's socks were much longer than his own, covering Mr. Kim's entire lower legs. He suddenly felt awkward because his own short socks revealed his hairy legs. He squirmed to get his cuffs down.

I probably should have bought a new suit, Jerome thought. He had gained a lot of weight last year, and his coat and trousers were stretched and wrinkled from being too tight. He hoped that Mr. Kim wouldn't notice the small spots on the lapel. Then he observed that Mr. Kim's hair was neatly trimmed. Darn, thought Jerome, I should have gotten a haircut too. He suddenly realized that he looked shaggy and he should have done something about his dandruff.

Mr. Kim reached into an expensive-looking leather case and took out a pad and a beautiful gold pen. Then he glanced at an elegant watch and said, "Well, Jerome, let's begin." As Jerome looked at the pen, he realized that Mr. Kim's fingernails were neatly trimmed and immaculate. Suddenly, he felt like sitting on his hands to hide the grime under his own ragged nails.

By this time, Jerome was getting nervous and felt that somehow he wasn't making just the right impression. He cleared his throat several times and squeezed his hands together. Finding it hard to look Mr. Kim directly in the eye, he shifted his gaze from the floor to the ceiling and then glanced quickly at the different objects in the room.

As the personnel director asked various questions, Jerome felt less and less confident. He realized that the interview was not going as well as he had hoped. Even when Jerome talked about his good grades and how much he liked to work with people, Mr. Kim did not seem enthusiastic. However, he remained polite. Jerome hoped for the best.

Finally it was over. As they were walking toward the door, Mr. Kim explained rather briskly how pleased they were that Jerome had applied. He told him that there were a number of candidates, but that if they decided he was the one they would be in touch right away.

Needless to say, Jerome did not get the job. Obviously, there were a number of things that sent the wrong messages to the personnel director. It wasn't so much what Jerome said in verbal terms that posed a problem, it was the accompanying *nonverbal meanings* interpreted by Mr. Kim that did him in. Such factors as Jerome's lateness, gestures, clothing, and body appearance were not helpful. Mr. Kim's dress, office, and *artifacts* (pen, leather case, and watch) sent other kinds of messages. Thus, the interview illustrates ways in which human communication includes exchanges of both verbal and nonverbal messages.

This chapter examines **nonverbal communication**—how an enormous variety of gestures, postures, tones of voice and many other factors—play a part in human communication. As we will see, they are far more than mere additions to or extensions of what we say. Our nonverbal activities are an inseparable part of the way human beings communicate.

The Relationship Between Verbal and Nonverbal Communication

Many people are convinced that meanings associated with our actions, facial expressions, and similar nonverbal activities are even more important than what is said.[1] Indeed, some scholars maintain that nonverbally transmitted meanings contribute as much as 90 percent to our interpretation of other people's behavior.[2] That is a considerable exaggeration. Neither the verbal dimension nor the nonverbal dimension of communication should be interpreted without considering the other.

There is no question that the signs and signals we send as nonverbal communication provide meanings that can alter, amplify, or limit people's understandings of the words we use. However, nonverbal factors are, like our words, a part of the overall human communication process. Thus, an effective command of communication skills is not possible without understanding fully how meanings encoded and transmitted nonverbally are part of the process.

Nonverbal communication can be defined as *the deliberate or unintentional use of objects, actions, sounds, time, and space so as to arouse meanings in others.* It is difficult to distinguish neatly between verbal and nonverbal processes. People do not communicate just in one mode or the other, or even rapidly shift back and forth. Their ongoing communication uses both systems at the same time. That is, while speaking words and sentences, all parties in the transaction simultaneously supplement or even modify their meanings with the use of a host of gestures, actions, and other nonverbal cues.

A simple illustration of the use of nonverbal cues to include different meanings in a verbal message is the emphasis provided by the sounds we make when speaking. For example, consider the sentence "I hate chocolate ice cream." Each of its words can be pronounced a number of different ways with stress and emphases supplied by various tones of voice. If accompanied by specific actions or gestures (such as crossed fingers or a wink), the message can take on still other meanings, even though the words remain the same.

There is an unlimited number of ways in which a sender can include subtle implications and nuances of meaning in a message while using words. Posture, movement, time sequence, space, eye contact, clothing, gestures, facial expressions, and even odors can all stimulate meanings in a receiver. This chapter reviews how all parties in communication transactions use nonverbal means to modify meanings in messages conveyed by words or to transmit meanings without using words at all.

There is considerable misunderstanding in popular thinking about the idea of nonverbal communication. Some people refer to it as "body language." It has been popularly touted as a means by which the "true" feelings and intentions of people can be read and understood by a shrewd observer armed with knowledge of what nonverbal signs "really mean."[3] What this implies is that you can't tell what speakers

Our gestures, actions, and postures can modify what we say with words. Such nonverbal communication often makes use of objects, actions, vocal sounds, the eyes, space, and time.

really mean by what they say with words. Instead, the claim goes, true intentions must be read in what the speakers communicate nonverbally. In fact, nothing could be further from the truth, and this implication is not intended in this book.

One writer has recently pointed out some of the mistaken ideas associated with this aspect of human communication:

A phrase that comes readily to mind is "body language," and there has been a book from the popular press with that phrase as its title. The topic has everything: the hope of reading the romantic intentions of one's girl- or boyfriend, the adventure of outsmarting a shrewd salesman, the sure thing of predicting the next move of a poker-faced gambler, the surprise of "reading through" the white lies of one's friends, the advantage of knowing what a prospective employer wants to hear.[4]

Even though nonverbal cues are an important part of the behaviors that human beings use to arouse meanings in others, they do not provide a separate code that has a life of its own. Indeed, they can often be misread to a point where serious consequences follow.

Communication scholars note that there are four fundamental ways in which we use nonverbal cues to extend, enrich, or modify our verbal messages to others. Most commonly, we use them to *complement or reinforce* the meanings we intend in our verbal messages. Equally important is the fact that we rely extensively on nonverbal behaviors to *regulate the flow* of our ongoing communication transactions with others. However, nonverbal cues on some occasions can serve as *substitutes for words*. Or, more rarely, they may actually *contradict what we say*.

Complementing Our Verbal Meanings

The most frequently found relationship between verbal and nonverbal communication is a complementary one. That is, almost everything we say verbally is accompanied by nonverbal actions, expressions, and other behaviors that *supplement or reinforce* the meanings contained in our talk. One common form is the case where nonverbal communication serves to **frame** our verbalizations. That is, as we talk to another person, we may jab the air with our finger for emphasis, extend our palms upward, roll our eyes, tick off points by touching the tips of the fingers one after the other, shrug our shoulders, and so on.

Usually, such actions are subtle or even barely noticeable. At times, however, such framing is done with great enthusiasm. A student may jump up and down, clapping his hands while saying such things as "I got an A in chemistry!"

Or, if the student crumples up his report card, throws it on the floor, and says "Damn!" through clenched teeth, such nonverbal cues clearly indicate less enthusiasm. Whatever their form, such actions are important in that they assist others in understanding the emotional meanings we attach to the message we are transmitting. An important part of learning to communicate and understand the meaning of others is a full understanding of the implications of such framing cues.[5]

This need to complement and frame our meanings with nonverbal signs and signals runs very deep. It is even done when people can't actually see each other, such as when they talk on the phone. As they speak into the phone, they nod, smile, shrug, and point to supplement what they are saying. Some even make elaborate pointing and body movements to accompany such verbal instructions as "Make a right turn" and "Go to the second light."

Regulating Verbal Interaction

Although supplementing the meanings of our verbal messages may be the most obvious use of nonverbal behavior, one of the most subtle is in **regulating** our conversations.[6] Here, the nonverbal cues are not used as part of an encoded message, but as signs and signals making up informal "rules of order" that make conversations orderly. Employing nonverbal actions and gestures to regulate the flow of talk among people is almost always done with little awareness on the part of the participants. Even for observers, it can be difficult to detect such efforts unless one knows exactly what to look for.

For example, in ordinary conversation we usually take turns talking. Normally, we wait until the current speaker stops before responding. Then, when we have the floor, others listen until we signal that it is appropriate for someone else to talk. These *turn-taking* rules are intricate, but they are really quite powerful in regulating the flow of conversation. Now try to imagine a conversation among several people where there were no such rules. It would be chaos! No one would know whose turn it was to talk, when to start, when to stop, or when to listen. Individual speakers would be constantly struggling to hold the floor, and everyone would be chattering at once.[7]

What are the *turn-yielding* cues that we send to one another to regulate who talks when? Careful studies of people conversing shows that eye contact is certainly one such cue.[8] Looking away from a person talking to you and focusing on someone else, for example, tells the speaker "OK, I listened to you, but now it is the next person's turn." The person who is talking may "sign off" with a shrug, a hand gesture, or simply a change in vocal tone as she or he winds down. On the other hand, if the person wants to continue and someone else tries to take over, the speaker might send the signal "but, but, but," in a kind of stutter that says "Hey, I am not through; I want to say more." Similarly, to head off a competitor, a speaker may increase voice volume and continue, or nod his or her head, as if to say "Sure, I know you want to say something, but wait a minute." Other cues include catches of breath, head turns, eye movements, and gestures. Most of us learn these things as a part of everyday life. A command of such nonverbal cues is an important part of learning to be a good conversationalist.

Substituting Actions for Words

Even though nonverbal communication generally parallels, extends, and supports our verbal messages, occasionally we substitute actions for words. For example, people commonly use nonverbal gestures or facial expressions rather than words when trying to communicate such emotions as dismay, disgust, frustration, hostility, or love. The facial expressions, gestures or other patterns of behavior that people use in doing this vary from one culture to the next. In the United States, many nonverbal gestures have relatively straightforward meanings that can be translated into direct verbal terms.[9] Conventional gestures that most people understand include the hitchhiker's raised thumb, ro-

tating the first finger around one's ear, sticking out one's tongue, and blowing a kiss. Communication specialists have chosen the term **emblems** as a name for this category of nonverbal gestures—ones that have direct verbal translations that are widely understood.[10] Box 3.1 lists some common emblems that are widely used in the United States.

Although the meanings of standardized emblems are reasonably clear, other nonverbal substitutes for words may be vague and difficult to read as we relate to others. For example, consider the meanings of the following: After a minor argument one person says, "OK, let's forget it," and the other shrugs. One interpretation of such a response might be that it represents a good-natured shrugging it off. However, another might be "It's useless to argue with you." Thus, interpreting nonverbal behavior that does not have clear conventional meanings can be risky. Indeed, the very impreciseness in the link between nonverbal messages and their intended meanings can be a source of serious errors.

Contradicting Our Verbal Meanings

Although it is not common, nonverbal actions or expressions sometimes openly contradict what we are transmitting in verbal terms. For example, when the husband shouts angrily, "Look! I said I was sorry!" the wife is likely to interpret the nonverbal message as, "I'm not sorry at all; I'm just mad!" Rather than being accidental, this form of nonverbal communication is usually deliberate. That is, people are usually quite aware when they are transmitting or receiving contradictory nonverbal cues. For example, as children, we all at one time or another received a stern reprimand or warning communicated in front of others by an authority figure, such as an aunt or a grandparent. But a single wink accompanying such a message and seen only by the child could simply turn the entire meaning around: "What I am saying in words is for public consumption in this situation, but you and I understand privately that my real message is quite different."

BOX 3.1   *A Closer Look*

Common "Emblems" Used in the United States

Recall that emblems have direct verbal equivalents established by conventions. Can you translate verbally what each of the following emblems supposedly means to many Americans? How many of these do you suppose are interpreted similarly in other societies or cultures?

Placing an imaginary halo above your head

Poking your index finger back in your cheek and twisting it back and forth

Mimicking a talking mouth with rapid finger and thumb movements

Licking a forefinger and marking the air with it

Blowing on your fingertips and then rubbing your nails on your shirt

Pretending to pull up each trouser leg to the knees

Making a telephone with thumb and little finger alongside your cheek

Licking your lips back and forth

Rubbing your thumb across your fingertips over and over again

Pretending to play an imaginary violin

Holding two fingers in the air in the shape of a "V"

Twirling your index finger in the air to make horizontal circles

Nodding your head up and down and from side to side

Cupping your ear and leaning forward

As was suggested earlier, some people believe that our nonverbal messages are both *unwitting* and *unintentional*. This leads them to the conclusion that the true meanings of our verbal messages are revealed by nonverbal cues. It would be an interesting world if we could somehow discover a person's true intentions or real message just by careful attention to their nonverbal cues. Poker buffs are particularly fond of this idea. They scrutinize every twitch and eye movement of their competitors in a game to try to divine whether the player is holding a powerful hand or is merely bluffing. At the same time, the ability to show a "poker face" (a total absence of nonverbal cues) is considered essential to the accomplished player. However, as many an impoverished, but wiser, poker player has discovered, making decisions on the basis of such cues can be an uncertain business at best. The really successful poker player telegraphs *disinformation* with the subtle use of nonverbal cues intended to deceive the others.

The detection of lying is another area that focuses on nonverbal cues that somehow "leak" the truth. Some people maintain that it is possible to identify nonverbal gestures, expressions, and postures that indicate when an individual is lying, or is arguing a position counter to her or his beliefs.[11] The best-known form of such detection is the use of a *polygraph* (commonly called a lie detector) to identify activity in the autonomic nervous system that presumably occurs when people are not telling the truth. The assumption is that people have little or no control over such indicators as changes in heart rate, increased electrical conductivity of the skin, and other physiological activities that take place when they lie. The major problem with this assumption is that it does not always hold for many people. Some subjects who are telling the absolute truth blow the needles off the graph, whereas others who are lying through their teeth seem to be able to control their reactions. For that reason, lie detector findings have not been admitted as evidence in courts and have recently been banned from use by employers.

The belief that true meanings are revealed by certain types of nonverbal cues may have merit when verbal and nonverbal messages are

BOX 3.2 🔍 *A Closer Look*

Four Major Ways We Use Nonverbal Communication

Nonverbal communication is a very important aspect of the communication process. In fact, much of the meaning that is derived from a verbal message is contingent upon the nonverbal behaviors that accompany it. Exactly how do nonverbal behaviors function in this interpretive process?

1. *Complementing.* When a verbal message is transmitted, it is usually also accompanied by a nonverbal message. In this way, nonverbal behaviors function to reinforce or support the meaning intended in the verbal message.

2. *Regulating.* When we communicate with others, we must follow certain rules, such as when to talk and when to listen. Nonverbal cues, such as eye contact and tone of voice, help to regulate the ongoing flow of conversation. We call these subtle nonverbal behaviors turn-taking or turn-yielding cues.

3. *Substituting.* Sometimes we can actually substitute or replace spoken words or phrases with simple nonverbal symbols. These nonverbal symbols that take the place of words are known as emblems.

4. *Contradicting.* Nonverbal behaviors can also be used to contradict or undermine a verbal message. A common form of nonverbal contradiction used by adults is sarcasm. We say the words in such a way that our tone of voice, pitch, and rhythm contradict the general meaning of the verbal message. These mixed messages may be difficult for children and (some adults) to decipher.

---

inconsistent or in conflict. For example, the individual who tells another "I love you," but who at the same time is rummaging through the refrigerator, seems to be saying, "You're okay, but at the moment a sandwich is more important to me." This apparent inconsistency is unlikely to inspire confidence in the verbal message. At the same time, it would not be wise to conclude that the speaker is lying and really does not love the other person; it is possible that the speaker is just hungry.

One of the most interesting ways in which verbal and nonverbal messages can convey different meanings is with the use of *sarcasm.* Adults understand this mode of communication very well and usually have little trouble sorting out the true meaning of a verbal message delivered sarcastically. They recognize that the nonverbal message implied by the sarcastic tones of voice and facial expressions represents a more subtle dimension of meaning. Children, on the other hand, are often relatively unskilled in identifying subtle meanings when sarcastic cues are used in communication. Generally,

they are more literal: In a contradictory message where the words say one thing and the nonverbal cues another, children are more likely to believe the verbal.[12]

In summary, then, the relationship between verbal and nonverbal communication is primarily one of *symbiosis,* or mutual dependence. Human communication in its richest sense relies heavily on both. Although we sometimes substitute nonverbal cues for words or even contradict our verbal messages with gestures, facial expressions, and actions, most of the time the two systems complement each other. Box 3.2 summarizes the four major ways we use nonverbal communication.

Interpreting Nonverbal Communication

Although much of our nonverbal communication is subtle, there are occasions when it is loud and clear. For example, students who get restless near the end of a lengthy lecture are experts at sending blatant nonverbal signals. They send unmistakable *leave-taking cues,* shuffling books, putting pens and pencils away, yawning, and transmitting other conspicuous signals that carry meaning. The basic message? "Professor, it is time to stop talking and let me escape."

Communication difficulties arising from inadequate understanding of the nature and importance of nonverbal communication are commonplace. Unless the nonverbal communication is well understood—and used effectively—it is inevitable that we will confuse others and become confused ourselves. For example, most of us have been in situations where we have been truly tired and have yawned while someone was presenting a message that he or she judged to be very important. Although we might understand completely that the act was involuntary, the other person will surely read it as "I am bored by you" and will probably feel some resentment.

One reason that speaking (as a mode of communication) is often more effective than writing is that we can include nonverbal cues to enrich and emphasize our meanings. That is, the absence of nonverbal cues in writing can pose problems. For example, in the world of work, a manager who relies solely on written memos will be unable to transmit nonverbal messages that might express the urgency of what is being communicated. Consequently, employees receiving the message may glance at it and then toss the memo into a pile of other papers for future examination. Days or weeks later, that manager may be irate at the lack of employee responsiveness. When a fuss is made about the memo, the employees may express surprise at the manager's spontaneous outburst. Thus, the absence of nonverbal cues on even the most basic level of interaction can be problematic at times, especially if there are incomplete understandings of the intended meaning of a verbal message.

"Things" That Communicate

This section takes a look at three major nonverbal strategies that are used to inform others about ourselves or about some topic. Each of these strategies depends on the use of "things." These include the *body itself,* as well as the *artifacts* we own or carry, including the clothing we wear.

Using the Body to Send Messages

Most of the things used to send nonverbal messages are under the sender's control and can be manipulated, modified, selected, or excluded to incorporate intended meanings transmitted to others. An exception is the use of the body itself. Some so-called **body language** can be controlled through various means, but others—those related to age, height, skin color, and perhaps weight—are not subject to voluntary change.

To illustrate, being tall or short is a matter of genetics rather than choice. Nevertheless, even such a simple fact as one's height can carry a nonverbal message. Many short men feel at a disadvantage among their taller peers. In our culture, commanding height among males implies greater authority, leadership qualities, and power. Being short suggests the opposite. Similarly, a woman can be tall and be thought of as glamorous—up to a point, after which she may be regarded as ungainly. Short women complain that they suffer a special disadvantage in competitive arenas, such as the business world, where those who are taller are taken more seriously.

Skin color is obviously related to social meanings in our society. Among African Americans, particularly prior to changes during recent decades, a longstanding rule was that lighter-skinned individuals had social advantages over those of darker skin. This situation is common in many societies in which skin colors vary from light to dark, but among those of any race, skin condition can also carry powerful nonverbal messages. For women and men alike, appearance of the skin—especially on the face—has powerful emotional connotations. Wrinkles, oil, hair, blemishes, and scars typically communicate less socially desirable meanings. The preferred conditions are those that communicate youth, sexual desirability, and robust health.

An enormous skin-care industry designed to control such messages thrives on every continent.

Although it may be tempting to dismiss efforts at body beautification as mere vanity, an abundance of research on the experiences of attractive versus unattractive people shows that being handsome or pretty can have definite advantages.[13] Doors open for physically attractive people that sometimes remain closed for those who are not. It may not be fair, socially just, or acceptable, but in the simplest terms, the majority of U.S. Americans fully believe that "beautiful is good." The opposite of that proposition is all too obvious.

Along these lines, one body condition that has long conveyed troublesome meanings in contemporary society is being overweight. Because of the message that excessive weight sends to one's self and others, a large proportion of the U.S. population is dieting, thinking about dieting, or feeling bad because they can't seem to lose weight. Our language contains a long list of epithets (negative terms) for those who are obese. These messages are so powerful that a significant number of people regularly prod themselves into jogging, weight-lifting, dancing, and going to gyms or exercise spas to punish off excess pounds. In more extreme cases, being fat is so feared that individuals undergo liposuction, stomach staples, or other surgery, or deny themselves food to a point of virtual starvation.

Modifying the body in one way or another to make it seem more attractive to self and others has been a feature of human existence since prehistoric times. Tattoos, filing the teeth, extending the lips or ears, and binding the feet to prevent normal growth are all ways that have been used to communicate beauty or some special status. People in the United States today are no exception. In addition to dieting and exercising, some rather drastic approaches to body modification are in use. Some women have silicone surgically inserted to make their breasts look larger and firmer. A growing number of young males take steroids and pump iron to make their muscles bigger. An increasing number of males and females of all ages troop to plastic surgeons to have big noses made smaller, facial skin made tighter, and thighs and bottoms made shapelier. The message of these transformations: "Look at me—I'm young, slim, attractive, and sexy."

Even those of us who do not care for such draconian measures do not hesitate to use more widely accepted means to make us took better. We have our hair curled, dyed, razor-cut, streaked, and styled—all to achieve that "natural" look. If we can afford it, we get manicures and pedicures, facial massages, wax applications, or tanning treatments; we apply layers of cosmetics, insert artificial lenses into our eyes, and generally suffer whatever it takes to modify our body so that it will send the messages we desire to others.

The point is that our bodies are available to us as communication devices. Although we can scarcely make ourselves taller or shorter, our bodies are subject to considerable manipulation and change, depending on how far we want to go and what we want to communicate.

Communication with Artifacts

We noted in Chapter 1 that the physical surroundings in which communication takes place can add meanings to the messages we exchange with others. (See simultaneous transactions model.) Those surroundings include not only places but the use of **artifacts**—that is, various kinds of physical objects that we possess. Such "things" can communicate meanings to others about our personal and social attributes. Artifacts are important for people who want others to believe that they are physically attractive or have other qualities that people admire. For example, many want others to believe that they enjoy a social rank of significant status and prestige, or that they are accepted by groups they feel are important. Those needs may be based on the proposition that if others respond to them favorably, then they can take comfort in feeling favorable about themselves.[14] Still others use artifacts to express their individuality—or even in some cases for a kind of shock value (e.g., hair dyed green or blue, or various metal rings attached to parts of the head or face).

Most commonly, artifacts are used by individuals in our impersonal society to signal their position in the social order. Generally speaking, this translates into messages about personal wealth, status, and power. One of the most obvious ways in which we communicate to others our position in the social order is through the display of things, both large and small, that symbolize *rank*. These include artifacts as obvious and expensive as homes, furniture, and automobiles, and as seemingly insignificant as eyeglasses, earrings, purses, and briefcases. These possessions can communicate to others a great deal about us as individuals concerning where we belong in the social class system; our financial resources; and our tastes, hobbies, interests, and so on.

In the United States, perhaps no single possession communicates more than one's dwelling, including its location and contents. Even the address of one's home or apartment can speak volumes. People form impressions based simply on whether the dwelling is large or small, well or poorly furnished, and in a nice neighborhood or on the wrong side of the tracks. At work, an office can become a stage upon which an individual communicates his or her power and status. One kind of message is transmitted by a large and elegant corner office with a nice view, paintings on display and handsome wood furniture. Add an outer office with a secretary and the person's rank goes up even more. In contrast, a small windowless room with metal furniture and linoleum flooring—or even worse, a cubicle with walls that do not reach the ceiling, places the person much lower in the pecking order.

An automobile can also communicate a person's position in the society. Different messages are transmitted by a limousine, a sports car, a minivan, a late-model Sports Utility Vehicle (SUV), a rusting pickup truck (with gun rack), an older station wagon, and a heavily reworked "muscle car" with a homemade air scoop on the hood. These are more than mere indicators of preferences in types of vehicles: They are artifacts that send loud and clear signals that define locations in our complex social system in terms of the financial resources, tastes, and values of their owners.

In recent years, one type of vehicle, the large and relatively new SUV, has come to have different meanings for different categories of people. Originally designed for off-road use by hunters, campers and so forth, the SUV has become the vehicle of choice for many relatively affluent families who live in the suburbs, for whom it means practical advantages. SUVs have been replacing the minivan and the earlier family-oriented station wagon. Although the SUV is more expensive to buy and operate, many people see it as providing reliable and safe transportation. SUV drivers are less likely to be injured in a crash than are drivers of small automobiles. SUVs serve many functions important to suburbanites. They can haul kids. They are easy to load and can haul large amounts of such things as groceries, plants, or stuff that has to be taken to the recycling center. Moreover, with their four-wheel drive, they can get home even in snowy and icy conditions.

Other people assign very different meanings to these vehicles, and have come to despise and denounce the SUV. They see SUVs as merely expensive status symbols for people who want to flaunt their affluence. They maintain that, because of their size, they are dangerous to drivers of smaller vehicles. They denounce them as "gas hogs" that contribute to the wealth of oil-producing Middle Eastern nations that support terrorism. Some groups go so far as to vandalize SUVs—with spray-painted slogans, slashed tires, broken windows, or other physical damage—justifying their actions as a way to protest their drivers' assumed lack of interest in saving the environment.

Even small artifacts—such as rings, wristwatches, eyeglasses, and briefcases—send messages about our personal qualities. Consider the message sent by a gold fountain pen favored by affluent lawyers (versus the modest ballpoint model that most of us carry). A crucifix or Star of David on a slender gold chain sends a message. Other artifacts that send nonverbal signals are wedding and engagement rings, alligator handbags (versus plastic copies), leather briefcases (versus vinyl models), designer sunglasses, Rolex watches, and heavy gold chains worn by men with their shirts unbuttoned to the waist.

In summary, "things" provide us with almost unlimited choices for transmitting messages to other people about meanings we value. That is not to say the interpretations they construct will be the ones we have in mind. Indeed, the very artifacts we regard as signaling high status and good taste may be seen by others as tacky signs of low class and poor judgment. For that reason, the use of artifacts in communicating significant information about ourselves must be approached with care and sensitivity.

Communicating with Clothing

The use of clothing as artifacts to signify one's place in society is an ancient form of nonverbal communication. Today, it remains a very important way of using artifacts to communicate a variety of meanings. The technology of weaving to make cloth—replacing animal skins for clothing—goes back over 20,000 years to the Neolithic era. By biblical times, clothing had become deeply established as one of the ways in which a person's social level could be identified instantly. The poor wore shapeless garments woven of coarse gray wool (or other fiber in warmer areas) that was left natural (not colored). Those of higher rank had much finer clothing made of woven fabrics colored with dyes. Fashions for the elite changed quickly, making garments obsolete even when they had been used only slightly. Only the wealthy could afford such changes.

Dressing to communicate status and power. During the 1400s and 1500s, as the rigid structure of medieval society began to erode somewhat, those in power were concerned about

preserving their social ranks. One means of preserving the status quo was specifying by law who could dress in what manner. Both the nobility and the Church backed laws that prescribed *elaborate dress codes*, setting forth what colors, types of cloth, and decorations were allowed at each level and severely limiting what those of lower ranks could wear.

Later, as Western societies moved into modern times, particularly during the late 1800s, ready-made, factory-produced clothing was developed. Early in the 1900s, volume production, low cost, and wide distribution made such clothing available to virtually everyone. This caused great change: As the use of such mass-produced garments spread, status and power could no longer be determined readily on the basis of what people were wearing in public. The shop girl and the heiress, or the banker and the clerk, began to dress rather similarly. Thus, both appearance and styles in clothing became less obvious as overt signs of rank, especially as the designs of the great fashion houses were copied, mass-produced, and marketed through nationwide retail chains.

What has happened in more recent times is that very subtle codes of dress have come into use for both men and women. These provide nonverbal cues that enable those in the know to recognize those of "gentility" (presumably of higher social status). Thus, clothing continues to distinguish those who believe themselves to have more refined tastes from those who do not understand or choose to ignore the rules of proper dress.

Many of these codes identify appropriate attire for individuals in positions of power and status in the business and professional world. Among women in such settings, a relatively clear set of rules prevails as to appropriate garments to be worn at work. A dark business suit, conservative blouse, and plain pumps with high heels are thought to command respect. Similarly, men in the business world have dress codes that communicate status, financial means, and good taste (read "high rank"). For example, men who adhere to such rules would never think of wearing a striped seersucker suit to a board meeting.

Moreover, in the overall ensemble, the business professional must be conscious of color. For women, black suits and dresses supposedly connote strength and potency. For men, somber gray or dark blue are preferred. Patterns, other than a faint pin stripe or a subdued chalk stripe, are regarded as gauche. Brown shoes worn with a gray or blue suit are a disaster. Hosiery is a must for women. For men, stockings should always cover the lower leg to just below the knee. A clear view of a naked stretch of hairy male leg between stocking and trousers is perceived as gross and disgusting. Ties with hula dancers or other gaudy decorations are to be avoided at all costs.

How much attention should be paid to such rules? Whether you personally think such elaborate codes are important, trivial, or even silly, a significant number of people in our society will make judgments about your social nature and inner characteristics on the basis of what you wear. It is important to keep in mind that those who do feel such dress codes are important are likely to be the ones in charge. Often they are the bosses who have the power to hire, fire, promote, and give raises. Finally, because the way we dress signals rank and power, it influences how we are treated even in the most casual and impersonal encounters, such as when we are customers in stores, banks, car dealerships, and so on.

Dressing to fit in. There is far more to clothing as nonverbal communication than just the dress code idea that we inherited from ancient sources.[15] For one thing, on many occasions we dress so as to be *socially acceptable,* that is to "fit in" with others when we engage in certain activities. An obvious case is the uniforms characteristic of some occupations; distinctive uniforms are worn by nurses, police officers, and airline pilots, for instance. However, prevailing dress codes are similar to uniforms in that they identify what one should wear as a member of a particular group. Students do not usually wear formal dress in the classroom, nor does the president of the university wear blue jeans to the graduation ceremony. Appropriate dress can also be important in recreation. Those who play tennis dress differently from those who jog. Such recreations as skiing, sailing, hiking, fly-fishing, riding, and hunting all require different costumes to "fit in."

Although people widely believe that clothes make a difference in social acceptability and popularity, is it really true? Researchers Madelyn Williams and Joanne Eicher found that it is. Their research showed that both popularity and liking are related to the clothes people wear.[16] Even ordinary social events are governed by clothing rules. It is not uncommon to be asked to an informal gathering, such as an outdoor pool party, and be told to "dress casually." On the other hand, sometimes it is difficult to forecast just what that means. A woman, taking the hostess at her word, may arrive at the party dressed in white cotton slacks and a new T-shirt. To her mortification, she may discover that all the other guests interpreted "casual" to mean silk sport jackets rolled up at the sleeves!

Dressing to communicate inner feelings. Clothing is often used to communicate how we feel—or at least how we want others to think we feel. For example, people traditionally wear dark colors at a funeral to communicate that they feel grief and respect for the deceased, whether they do or not. They generally dress in restrained colors to go to church so as to signal their religiosity and concern for the dignity of the service. To demonstrate that they too are just plain folks, politicians campaigning in rural areas commonly wear open-collared shirts with their sleeves rolled up, or farm jackets and feed company caps.

In summary, then, clothing is far more than something we wear for modesty or to keep from getting cold. It is also an extraordinarily complex system of nonverbal communication that can be used to signal what we are as persons, where we are (or would like to be) in the social class structure, that we fit in, and how we feel at a given time.

Nonverbal Sexual Communication in the Workplace

One area of nonverbal communication in contemporary life that has become increasingly difficult is that of *gender relationships* in the workplace. Men and women often have different conceptions of how to interpret nonverbal behavior related to the body as well as various artifacts and clothing in the context of working together. As more and more women have entered the workplace in recent decades, these differing conceptions may contribute to significant sexual misunderstandings.

Many working women today are troubled by nonverbal (or verbal) messages of a sexual nature that make them uncomfortable, afraid, or even unable to continue their employment. These women often maintain that men "just don't get it"—and that even after repeated protests men fail to understand that gestures, actions, hints, and other verbal messages with sexual meanings are *unwelcome* and can cause female workers great distress. On the other hand, when women who feel victimized define those messages as *sexual harassment,* the men involved are often astonished to learn that what they said or did was interpreted as offensive.

There is no misunderstanding about some of the more obvious behaviors, such as misuse of power for sexual advantage, coarse propositions, obscene language, or physical abuse; but sometimes other nonverbal behaviors are misunderstood. These include staring, whistling, facial expressions, and gestures often used in flirting. They also include certain kinds of "touching."[17] Verbal messages can also be misunderstood, such as telling a woman that she "looks sexy," telling off-color stories, or making mild sexual innuendos. Indeed, many men "just don't get it" with respect to such communication. They can't understand why women object to such messages, which they see as just "joking around"—as men have always done in the workplace—in ways that they think mean no harm.

How can such misunderstandings occur? Are men simply being immoral when it comes to women in the workplace, or are women being overly sensitive? An alternative explanation is that *neither of these is true.* What may be happening is that, in the workplace, meanings associated with the body, and with various artifacts and types of clothing, are no different than in other walks of life. For example, for working women, remaining slim; using modest amounts of makeup and scent; wearing a nice suit, stockings, high heels, matching accessories; and a flattering hair style may simply be attempts to follow the norms of appropriate dress in the contemporary world. For men, these same features of the body, artifacts, and clothing may seem to send messages of sexiness or enticement. This is because, in part, meanings used by men to interpret women's nonverbal behavior continue to be based on traditional interpretations of women *outside* the workplace.

Where do such traditional meanings come from? One major source is the content of a virtual sea of mass media. Media entertainment products often stress the theme that women seek and welcome the attentions of men. Media entertainment poses such behavior models daily. These are a source for the construction and reinforcement of social interpretations of reality for both men and women. For example, the movies began to emphasize the role of "sexual enticer" for women during the silent picture era when they created the model of the seductive "vamp." That industry continued all during the 1900s, and on into the 21st century, to promote the enticing vision of the "sex goddess."

Today, the entertainment products produced by a small number of multinational conglomerates for worldwide distribution emphasize the sexy-woman-interested-in-men. The fact is that such entertainment *sells*, and produces profits both in the United States and worldwide. For example, motion pictures, designed with younger age categories in mind, often show women willing to have sex on the first date. The reality is quite different, much to the chagrin of males who come to the United States from other countries with such expectations and go on their first dates.[18] Even American men who construct their beliefs about women from media sources may not understand this. The sources for such social constructions are ubiquitous. Television places heavy emphasis on the erotic woman in sitcoms, soap operas, and evening dramas—and even in popular game shows.

Another source of male misconceptions is advertising. Huge industries focus on selling a long list of womens' products with openly sexual appeals. Women are portrayed as preoccupied with being seductive and attractive to men. After seeing such advertising and media content day after day, men may believe that women deliberately engage in sexual enticement and value male sexual attention. Furthermore, it has always been the accepted role of men, stemming from training since childhood and frequently reinforced by communication among peers, to take the lead in male-female relationships. Thus, taking the sexual initiative seems natural for many men, in or out of the workplace.

In contrast, the women's movement poses entirely new role models for women. Rejecting the image of sexual enticer, women today promote the concept of *gender equality,* especially in the workplace. Many women feel that the role of sexual enticer has absolutely no place on the job, and they insist on a gender-neutral work environment. However, at this point in our nation's history, this is not fully understood by many of their male co-workers.

In summary, misunderstandings concerning both nonverbal and verbal messages of a sexual nature can be confusing. They can seem natural and appropriate to men and objectionable and inappropriate to women. Until traditional men are able to engage in more sensitive role-taking, sexual communication in the workplace will undoubtedly remain a problem, and confusion over what constitutes sexual harassment will continue.

Actions That Communicate

A number of actions, postures, and activities are part of the nonverbal dimensions of human communication. Among them are facial expressions and gestures, variations in voice, and messages transmitted by eyes. The use of space, touch, and time can also introduce special meanings into ongoing transactions.

Body Movements and Gestures

The study of body movements—including gestures, posture, and facial expression—as forms of human communication has a long history.[19] In fact, it is so important that this aspect of human communication has its own name. As a specialty, this study is called *kinesics.*[20] The reason it is so important is that people's overall body orientation or posture typically communicates their level of interest, liking, and openness. For example, simply by watching a couple engage in conversation from afar we can sometimes guess rather accurately whether or not they are intimate, interested in one another, or strangers who have just met. Some of the indicators are displaying direct, frontal body orientation or close side-by-side seating, open arm gestures (as opposed to folded arms across the chest), and leaning forward. The presence of such postures and movements—along with head-nodding, smiling, and direct eye contact—is a good indicator that the couple are enjoying each other's company a great deal.

Nonverbal gestures are even easier to decipher. Earlier we discussed emblems, noting that they are gestures that have specific conventions of meaning in our culture.[21] Because this is the case, emblems are often used as effective *substitutes for talk.* A good example is simply putting your index finger to your lips, which everyone sharing our culture understands to mean "Shhh" or "Be quiet."

Another category of gestures is *illustrators*—hand and arm movements that demonstrate and reinforce meanings intended by verbal messages.

For example, pointing to your sweater on the chair while explaining "It's lying over there" is an illustrator. Others include stretching your arms over your head to emphasize your level of fatigue, slapping your hand against your head in an effort to recall a thought, punching the air with your fist to accentuate a word or phrase, and using your hands to show length when describing the fish you caught (or the one that got away).

Another category of gestures is *adapters*. These are unintentional hand, arm, leg, or other body movements used to reduce stress or relieve boredom. For example, waiting endlessly for your turn at the doctor's office may elicit such actions as pencil tapping, nail biting, or chewing on eyeglass frames. We may use such adapters excessively when we are anxious or afraid and they are common among students giving their first talk in front of a class. Many people try to calm themselves by pacing or dancing across the room, twisting their hair or moustache, rocking back and forth on their heels, pulling on their ears or nose or shuffling notecards.

Although these body activities are common, most of us are unaware that we are using them. However, observers are quick to interpret nonverbal adapters as indicators of nervousness, insecurity, or anxiety. In this sense, they can be a problem if not controlled. The last thing we want is for others to perceive us as lacking confidence during such communication situations as job interviews, public presentations, or date invitations.

Nonverbal Uses of the Voice

Our vocal tones often indicate to others that we are happy, sad, confident, nervous, culturally refined, boorish, and so on. This is another area of nonverbal communication that is so important that it has a name. The study of such nonverbal uses of the voice is called **vocalics**. The idea is not complex. We surround the words we use with many kinds of voice-quality cues that contribute significantly to people's judgments about us, and directly or indirectly, to the meanings of our messages. Put simply, *how* you say something can at times be as important as *what* you say.

Nonverbal vocal cues can take many forms: Pitch, tone, rate, volume, and accent patterns in speech all make big differences in how verbal messages are interpreted. For both men and women, voice quality is often associated with suggestions of size, intelligence, and sexuality. For example, if a woman greets a man by saying "Hello," what are the implications when her voice quality is flat and matter-of-fact? Now suppose her voice is breathy and a bit drawn out. Does the subtle meaning change? Of course it does; it sounds sexy, adding an important dimension of meaning to what she said.

Accents are another category of vocalics. These can cause endless problems in misjudging the intelligence, emotions, and personalities of people who speak in ways that seem different and strange to us. For example, people from the Midwest seem to talk through their noses, and such a nasal voice quality may be perceived negatively by listeners from other geographic areas. The same can be true of the Texas drawl, the Boston accent, and the speech patterns heard in the Deep South. Sometimes speakers are assigned characteristics of laziness and ignorance on the basis of their accents. A Kentucky hill-country accent can result in a mental subtraction of about 10 IQ points when the listener is from another part of the country.

Speech patterns used by many poor urban Americans may be judged very negatively by the well-educated. Pronunciations characteristic of people raised in some parts of New York City (especially Brooklyn) do not inspire confidence among those from Western states. Regional, racial, and ethnic accents, then, bring with them a curious baggage of positive and negative attributions about the speaker's personality.[22] However, there is absolutely no relationship between any accent and level of intelligence. It is a serious mistake to assume that because a person pronounces words in an unfamiliar way, his or her intelligence is low (or rs of our immediate family or with our iends. Similarly, Asians, Indians, Pakista- d northern Europeans (except Germans) o noncontact people. In contrast, Arabs, mericans, and southern Europeans (par- y male Italians) are identified as more oriented.[36] In fact, for many U.S. Amer- ttempting to maintain space with Latin ic friends or business acquaintances may ke a fencing match; as they move for- he Americans keep moving back.

erences also exist among African Ameri- European Americans, and Hispanics or s. African Americans maintain the clos- raction space and Hispanics the farthest. ch suggests that those variations are function of socioeconomic status than al or ethnic identification. Shawn Scherer that such cultural differences were not t when the people interacting were all he middle class or all from lower strata social system.[37]

he of the more interesting research on ter- lity and personal space involves *en- ment*, or space invasion. Experiments on achment require a confederate (who is of the purpose of the study). The confed- deliberately violates subjects' territories rsonal space. The subjects remain un- that they are in an experiment or of what but to happen. As the experiment pro- s, an observer records each subject's re- e to the encroachment.

he of the best-known experiments of this was pioneered by Robert Sommer.[38] He onfederates approach tables in a library ied by one other person. Each confeder- ould sit at the table directly across from ccupant, or right next to him or her, or a eats away. Observers sitting at nearby ta- reported that subjects' reactions to this invasion were fairly consistent. In almost ses, victims of the invasion experienced ty and then attempted to reduce it by in- ing the distance between themselves and ncroacher. Some set up barriers by redis-

tributing their books, book bags, or other materials around them. Some shifted themselves away from the intruder. Only a few defied the invader by glaring. Others gave up and took flight by switching tables or leaving altogether.

Subsequent studies confirm these findings. Almost always, people respond to space invasion in one of two ways—"fight" or "flight." The most common response to encroachment on public or territory occupied temporarily is *flight*.[39] Evidently, people recognize that no one really owns such space. For example, if someone stands too close to you in an elevator where you are the only other occupant, you are more likely to move over (flight) than you are to complain or to shove the person aside (fight). Nevertheless, some individuals may become agitated and engage in fight responses to territorial violations. You may have seen an angry driver yell or even get out of his car when someone took the only parking space available. Box 3.3 describes a number of strategies people use to prevent encroachment.

Fight responses are more common when invasions occur within primary or exclusive territory. The legal system, police force, and insurance carriers provide services, penalties, and financial restitution to victims of territorial invasion. By such formal means, homeowners are supposed to be protected from thieves, men and women from rapists, authors from plagiarists, and rock bands from overly zealous groupies. Across all these instances, a fight response is expected and typically condoned by our society. Note, however, that (in this sense) fight need not necessarily involve hitting someone or other types of physical force. Fight reactions can range from polite forms of requests ("Would you please move your books to the other end of the table so that I can have the room I need to study?") to enraged commands ("Just what the hell do you think you're doing? Get away from me!"). Whether our response to space invasion is fight or flight, personal space, distance, zones, and territory are very important to all of us.

high) or that the individual has any other personality trait.

Not only do we assign personal and social qualities to those who talk differently from the way we do, but we also make judgments about people's *emotions* based on vocalics.[23] Hearing two people in the next room or upstairs speaking loudly can lead us to assume that they are arguing, and that they are angry with each other. We may not be able to understand the words, but the level of hostility often seems unmistakable because of the vocalics.

Research suggests that negative emotions are much more likely to be identified accurately from vocalic cues alone than are positive ones.[24] It appears to be easier to tell if someone is sad, disappointed, or angry from voice tone, level, and pitch than if someone is happy, relieved, or thrilled. Some individuals are more skilled than others in deciphering vocalics to determine how someone feels.[25] Obviously, then, our judgments about emotions based on a person's vocalics are not always accurate.

Although the rules for interpreting the meanings of vocalics are not entirely standardized, we commonly use nonverbal aspects of the voice to make judgments about people because they are so noticeable. That is, the nature of a person's voice and speaking style is one of the first and most salient things we notice about that person. When we are in a communication situation with a stranger, or a mere acquaintance, we have to try to understand what that person is like in order to deal with the situation. Vocalics may be one of only a few discernible guidelines we have available.

Eye Contact

Novelists, poets, and songwriters have always been fascinated by eyes. Their works lyrically describe the character traits that different types of eyes supposedly reveal and the subtle messages that eyes presumably can transmit. In such sources one finds a great deal of lore about eyes that are shifty, steely, beady, innocent, or jaded. The idea that we communicate with our

eyes, then, is deeply rooted in popular culture. The only problem with such rich descriptions is that they do not seem to have a basis in fact. Nevertheless, we do communicate using our eyes.

A less romantic view of the role of eyes in nonverbal communication is called **oculesics** by communication scholars. The term refers to the study of eye contact and pupil dilation in nonverbal communication. People clearly do use their eyes to indicate their degree of interest, openness, and even arousal as they communicate. Even simple eye contact with another has meaning on some occasions. For example, one of the rules of public address is that speakers are supposed to maintain eye contact with people in their audience.

To illustrate, what assumption do we make when receivers of our message look down or away? Most of us conclude they're not interested in what we have to say. Similarly, teachers, politicians, clergy, and others who make public presentations can become threatened and concerned when the audience fails to meet their gaze. A parent may scold a child, saying, "Look at me when I'm talking to you!" (the kinesics here is usually a finger vigorously shaken at the hapless child). Another example is loss of personal eye contact when you happen to be browsing through a magazine during an exchange with a friend. He or she is likely to ask, "Am I boring you?"

Research on eye contact as communication supports our popular beliefs only up to a point.[26] Even though eye contact with another generally communicates positive feelings toward that person, staring can be interpreted as a sign of hostility or aggression. Keep in mind that eye contact communicates the degree of interest or arousal between persons. Whenever we feel extreme sentiment, whether that sentiment is anger or love, a degree of interest or arousal is triggered. Thus, we are likely to express both emotional extremes through eye gaze, and we have to look to other communicative behaviors to determine the particular emotion that is revealed.

In addition, popular lore has it that the lack of eye contact is a certain clue that someone is lying. So firmly established is this so-called fact that people who suspect another person is lying may demand, "Look me in the eye when you say that." Supposedly, this will solicit the truth. The problem with this idea is that a considerable number of studies on detecting deception have failed to confirm its validity.[27] In truth, most people learn early on to lie quite successfully while steadily holding eye contact with an accuser. As children, most of us were able to fool our parents in this way. A recent study found an average accuracy rate (percentage of correct answers) of only 56.6 percent—barely above chance—when observers were using nonverbal behavior to judge when people were lying.[28]

Law enforcement agencies recognize that the detection of deception is a necessary and challenging task. For example, a recent FBI law enforcement bulletin states:

> From heated knife blades across the tongue to electric prods, people have sought ways throughout history to test the truthfulness of others. Fortunately, researchers in criminology and psychology have identified verbal and nonverbal behaviors that detect deception in a more humane manner. Nonetheless, detecting deception remains a difficult task. In fact, multiple studies have found that lie detection, like a coin toss, represents a 50/50 proposition, even for experienced investigators . . . Unfortunately, no particular nonverbal or verbal cue evinces deception.[29]

However, the bulletin describes certain "clusters" of behaviors that at least some experienced investigators believe increase the likelihood that an individual is not being truthful. For example:

> Feet that fidget or point to the door communicate discomfort. . . . Deceivers often use soda cans, computer screens, and other objects, both large and small, to form a barrier between themselves and investigators. Objects used in this manner create distance, separation, and par-

tial concealment—behaviors consistent with dishonesty.[30]

Although the degree to which such behaviors indicate untruthfulness is uncertain, the FBI's bulletin also states that many investigators rely too much on eye contact. In fact, they say that frequent liars may actually *increase* eye contact because they have learned that investigators use strong eye contact as an indicator of veracity.

On the other hand, for the most part, we do gaze at others less when we feel embarrassment, guilt, or sadness.[31] If we feel such emotions, our most common response is to avoid interacting with them. For example, at a dinner party, the last thing you want your host to do is focus undue attention on the fact that you spilled red sauce all over the white linen tablecloth. If you contribute further to your embarrassment by spilling the wine as you try to wipe up the mess with your napkin, you do not appreciate eyes on you at such a time. Similarly, when we experience either guilt or sorrow, we would rather hide than face the open confrontation implied by eye contact.

Many conventions are used in connection with oculesics in nonverbal communication. For example, the rules of eye contact between professor and student in the college classroom are well understood. When the instructor poses a question, students quickly learn to escape from having to provide an answer by avoiding the professor's gaze. They examine their fingernails, glare at their books, study the floor, or gape at the ceiling—anything to avoid being singled out and called upon. Equally understood are the rules of flirting with the eyes. Gazing or even repeatedly glancing at someone across a crowded room is likely to result in some kind of response—at best a smile, at worst bored indifference.

Using Space and Distance

Some of the most subtle aspects of nonverbal communication are associated with the use of space and distance. Both can influence mean-

ings we arouse in others. People seldom consider such things, but they have important implications for communication. Again, this feature of communication has a special name. The study of the meanings communicated by the use of space and distance is called **proxemics.**

Two uses of space are important in understanding human communication behavior: These are **territoriality** and **personal space.** The term *territoriality* refers to a common tendency that is characteristic of both animals and human beings.[32] That is, many species define some fixed or semifixed space to claim or stake out as their own. When we as individuals engage in this behavior, we feel that some territory belongs to us exclusively, but we willingly share other territory with family or friends. Still other territory involves only temporary ownership.

Regardless of the level of exclusivity, we respond to territorial "invasion" as if we have a right to that space. For instance, the most primary form of territory may include your office, your room, your side of the bed, or even your chair. Should others attempt to encroach on your rightful domain, you may feel frustrated, angry, or downright hostile. More public, and thus less exclusive, are forms of territory that provide only temporary ownership, such as a parking spot, a table reserved at a restaurant, or a seat or desk in a particular class. Even though technically we have no rightful claim to such public territories, we may behave as if we actually own that parking spot, table, or seat.

The second proxemic concept, personal space, refers to the *immediate zone* we carry around with us during our daily interactions with others.[33] It is like a bubble that stays with us, contracting and expanding as we move, depending on where we are, what we are doing, and whom we are with. In other words, the degree of personal space we allow with others is determined by the nature of our relationship with them; the topic under discussion; and our gender, age, and cultural background.[34]

Anthropologist Edward T. Hall has identified distinctive zones of personal space that determine or are determined by our interpersonal

transactions.[35] The first [...] tance of zero (touching) [...] and is called the *intimat[...]* from 18 inches to 4 feet [...] *personal zone.* Then, 4 [...] *socio-consultative zone[...]* feet is the *public zone.* E[...] us something about the [...] ship those conversing sh[...] tance between lovers, c[...] members during intimate[...] be limited. When a teac[...] class, the interaction prob[...] boundaries more typical [...]

Hall's zones have impo[...] the study of nonverbal co[...] difficult, if not impossib[...] mate topics from a dista[...] Instead, we "move in" to[...] wish to discuss a secret, s[...] experience, or make very[...] Thus, as we move in close[...] a change in the meaning [...] messages.

Both *gender* and *age* a[...] ritoria[...] *croach[...]* termining the size of an i[...] encro[...] space. Women tend to in[...] aware[...] tances with other womer[...] erate[...] other men. Not surprising[...] or pe[...] (male-female couples) int[...] aware[...] tances than do either fem[...] is ab[...] male pairs. Furthermore, [...] gress[...] use space differently. Becau[...] spons[...] the rules concerning the ap[...] to maintain in communicat[...] Or[...] ing that young children cc[...] kind[...] percentage of "space invad[...] had [...] each other's territories and[...] occu[...] the distance zones of adult[...] ate w[...] they learn to follow the rule[...] the o[...]

Great variability exists [...] few s[...] group to the next as to the ru[...] bles [...] emics. For example, compar[...] space[...] societies, people in the Uni[...] all ca[...] most paranoid about space. W[...] anxi[...] oriented people. That is, [...] creas[...] close (intimate zone) intera[...] the e[...]

membe[...] close fr[...] nis, an[...] are als[...] Latin A[...] ticular[...] contac[...] icans, [...] or Ara[...] seem l[...] ward, [...]

Diff[...] cans, [...] Latino[...] est int[...] Resea[...] more a[...] of raci[...] found[...] presen[...] from [...] in the [...]

Sor[...]

BOX 3.3   *A Closer Look*

Techniques to Prevent Territorial Encroachment

Dogs, cats, and other animals are pretty good at staking out their territory by "spraying" the boundaries with their urine. If you've ever moved your dog or cat to a new house or apartment, you've probably had a lot of cleaning to do initially. This is especially true of environments that were inhabited previously by another animal.

In many ways, human beings are little different from animals. Although we seldom stake out our territory with urine, we do construct elaborate fences or walls around our property, post "keep-out" signs on our doors or gates, and sign legal documents of ownership. These are all ways we ward off potential encroachers. Researchers categorize our stakeouts in four ways:

1. *Markers.* We strategically place objects to "mark" our spot, like leaving a sweater on the table to let others in the cafeteria know that the table now belongs to you. Book bags, a partially filled glass or cap, or caps or hats all make excellent markers. Such markers allow us to leave the territory temporarily without worrying that someone else will take over. Curiously, feminine markers (a girl's jacket or a woman's purse) are less likely to ward off invaders than are masculine markers. Why do you suppose that is so?

2. *Labels.* Labels are markers with your name or some other symbol on them. Mothers may label their kids' clothes before the kids leave for college. Checks and credit cards are labeled with your legal name. Signs marked "reserved" com-municate to others that the table (or chair or room) is being held for someone else. T-shirts, baseball caps, license plates, and brass door plates use a variety of labels, not only to communicate a slogan but also to identify the owner.

3. *Offensive displays.* Clenching your fists, leaning forward, glaring, and just looking mean are example of offensive displays. Such displays are very effective at preventing invasion. After all, who would want to mess with Wesley Snipes or Jean Claude Van Damme when he gives you that look that means business?

4. *Tenure.* By being there first and staying the longest, we can prevent others from taking over the space. One of the authors comes from a family of seven kids and happens to be one of the youngest members. Like all families, they had so-called assigned seats around the table. Now that they are older and living elsewhere, you might expect the seating at homecoming dinners to change. Even with a different table these days, the older siblings still dominate the "best chairs" making it necessary for others to pull up a folding chair! You may have always "slept on that side of the bed," "sat in this chair in the den," or "had the desk closest to the window." As a result, your tenure acts to prevent others from encroachment.

Source: Knapp, M. L. (1978). *Nonverbal communication in human interaction* (2nd ed., pp. 116–120). New York: Holt, Rinehart, Winston.

Touch

Closely related to the use of space in communicating is *touching* when it is used to transmit nonverbal messages. Touching is a far more flexible and meaningful form of nonverbal communication than most people realize. The study of touch as a means of nonverbal com-munication also has a special name. It is called **haptics** by scholars who study this form of nonverbal communication. In many ways, haptics is a logical extension of proxemics. That is, in order to touch people to convey meaning it is obviously necessary to be very *close* to them (that is, space is at a minimum). (See Figure 3.1.)

Handshake
agreement

Back-slap
approval

"High-five"
agreement

Forehead kiss
of fondness

Holding hands
in romance

Mutual back-slap
of greeting

Shoulder touch—
friendship

Cheek kiss
as greeting

Cheek pat—
fondness

Arm-in-arm
intimacy

FIGURE 3.1
Using Touch to Communicate
Human beings use touch in a variety of ways to transmit and express various kinds of meanings.

The importance of touching begins early in life. Classic research on animals shows us the importance of touch for infants. Psychologist Harry F. Harlow studied newborn monkeys that had been separated from their mothers and were kept in isolation—and consequently lacked being touched. While studies of monkeys do not provide sure indicators of what human beings will do, he discovered that the animals would cling for hours to a wire mesh surrogate (substitute) mother wrapped in soft cloth. Infant monkeys caged with other infant monkeys (who touched each other) survived as well as those that were exposed to the cloth surrogates. Still others, without either a cloth surrogate or other infant monkeys to touch, had clear problems. They developed socially maladaptive behaviors and became violent when caged later with the other monkeys.[40]

Whether or not Harlow's findings apply to human beings, there is evidence from human studies that touch does play a vital role in early childhood development.[41] During infancy, touching and stroking seem to satisfy important emotional requirements. In fact, if they are not touched at all, human babies may not even survive. A number of specialists who study early childhood have concluded that there is a relationship between extreme touch deprivation and mortality (chances of dying).[42] Evidence for this conclusion was also obtained from observations made many years ago of infants in orphanages. Some writers argue that the mortality rate of almost 100 percent of infants left in orphanages during the 1800s, and even the early 1900s, was due primarily to the lack of touch. In those institutions, infants were not picked up, talked to, or cradled. They were just cleaned, fed, and left by themselves. As a result, many died. Those who survived typically became maladjusted or retarded later.[43]

Infants who develop under normal family circumstances are touched very often until they are about two years old. Then, the frequency of touch begins to decrease. Thereafter, people are touched at a decreasing rate throughout life. In fact, senior citizens may be touched very little, or not at all.[44] Despite this withdrawal from touch, however, most people of all ages continue to enjoy both being touched and touching others.

What are the benefits of touch for adults? Perhaps some answers to that question can be seen if we ask, "What happens when we fail to get our needed quota of touch?" A number of correlational studies suggest that *health problems* often arise. For example, a variety of allergies and certain skin diseases are common among those who are deprived of touch.[45] Other research shows that normal speech development may be affected as well.[46] Most important, without the comfort of touch, all of us are likely to experience at least some stress in our daily lives.[47] In particular, during crises we feel greatly comforted and reassured when someone offers both verbal and nonverbal reassurance through touch.

Comfort and reassurance are not the only significant meanings communicated by touch. Depending on the kind of touch employed, such actions can communicate dislike or aggression. Poking someone on the chest while making a strong point can arouse hostility. More often than not, however, we consider touch to be positive because it usually communicates attraction or affection. We touch those we like and avoid touching or being touched by those we don't.

In summary, touching can transmit messages intended to arouse many kinds of meanings, ranging from the most tender and significant to those that are offensive or even repulsive. Some people are "touch avoiders" who would never touch a stranger and who feel very uncomfortable with gratuitous pokes, pats, hugs, or kisses. Others are "touch approachers" who just can't seem to wait to get their hands on people.[48]

Time

Have you ever noticed that some people are always late no matter how hard they try to be on time? By the same token, you may know others who are so punctual that they can be downright annoying. The study of the way in which people use time to transmit nonverbal messages is called **chronemics** by communication schlolars. Like other forms of nonverbal communication, it can be much more complex and subtle than people generally realize.

Populations in modern urban industrial societies depend greatly on clocks, watches, and reasonably accurate time in general. In more traditional societies, the position of the sun was the rough regulator of daily routines. Almost all aspects of life proceeded at a slower pace, and schedules were far less compelling. In contemporary societies, such as ours, almost all activities are rather closely regulated by the clock, and people have to be far more conscious of measured time. To appreciate our society's concern with time, count the number of clocks in your home, car, and office, and consider the number of watches you own (or would like to own!). Or, imagine how many times a day you glance at a timepiece. It is rare indeed to look at the sun to judge time. One of the first things we teach young children is what it means when the "big hand" is in one position and the "little hand" is in another.

There are remarkable individual differences in people's tolerances for early or late time schedules. These seem related to a person's biological clock, as is the case with jet lag, but on a more permanent basis. For example, those who are "owls" work best at night and drag around lethargically in the morning. They have difficulty relating to the "sparrows" who wake up early, even without an alarm.[49] Such early birds chatter their way through breakfast and continue to chatter cheerfully to teachers and friends as they arrive for an early morning class. Parking is rarely a problem for them; they are the first into the lot.

Conversely, owls sleep late in the morning if they possibly can. If they absolutely must get up, they may require both a snooze alarm and a wakeup call. Talking at breakfast is out of the question—they just sit glumly with a cup of coffee, trying slowly to get their act together.

(Owls never cite breakfast as their favorite meal.) However, owls become more and more functional as the day wears on. About the time the sparrows are at a low, say mid-afternoon, owls are starting to peak.

The study of chronemics encompasses not only our rules, ethical beliefs, and individual personality differences related to time, but also the study of how people actually schedule what they do. In particular, the focus is on what this means to others. For example, what does a host actually mean when he indicates that the party will begin at 7:00 p.m.? Most people understand an invitation to a 7:00 party to mean that it will begin some time between 7:30 and 8:00—a half-hour to an hour later. Their behavior reflects their understanding of that meaning, and they arrive within that time frame. Few hosts are offended if their guests do not arrive promptly at 7:00 p.m.

Consider this: What would be the implications if a guest used the rules of the work ethic and arrived early at the party, say at 6:30 p.m.? Or, what is the meaning if a guest arrives at 9:45 and then leaves at 10:00? Most people also understand that this informal time frame does not apply to a job interview scheduled precisely for 9:30 a.m. If the interviewee arrives late, as did Jerome in our opening vignette, what meaning does that communicate?

We also share a set of conventions that govern the meaning of time intervals. When friends call and claim they'll be along "in a minute," how long is that? How long is "a while," a "day or so," or "sometime soon"? Such informally specified intervals permit a wide range of actual behaviors—but there are limits. If "in a minute" stretches to several hours, it sends a message that is unlikely to be appreciated.

Misunderstandings concerning time intervals are commonplace because of such imprecise meanings and because of individual variations in actual behavior associated with them. Some people are punctual and take time literally. When they say a "minute" or an "hour," that's exactly what they mean. Others use time flexibly by expanding a second, minute, or hour well beyond limits of courtesy. Regardless of individual differences, however, we tend to judge others' punctuality by our own conception of and value for time. If we are punctual ourselves, we are likely to become upset, or at least concerned, when others fail to adhere to our expectations. If fuzzy definitions of time are more to our liking, we can be taken aback when someone arrives on time or early.

Time orientations are different in other cultures and societies, and this can pose problems in communication. For instance, some societies, like those of the Chinese and Native Americans, place great emphasis on the past. Such societies rely heavily on tradition, and respect the advice and wisdom advanced by their elderly. Present-oriented societies, like those found in the Philippines and many Latin American countries, are said to choose to live for today. In contrast to these past and present preoccupations, most people in the United States reflect a somewhat future-oriented society.[50] Consequently, many Americans share beliefs that tomorrow will bring us greater health, wealth, and happiness. Many middle-class Americans also subscribe to the idea of *postponement of gratification*. This is the idea of working hard today, putting off enjoyment, and saving up for later. This shared future orientation makes it difficult for us to understand those who fail to plan for their future in terms of their careers, family, education, and eventual retirement.

Communication as an Integrated Process

In previous sections of this chapter, the discussion of nonverbal communication has been *analytical*—that is, the process has been picked apart, element by element. The purpose was to explain how each nonverbal usage complements or modifies our verbal messages—showing how meanings are aroused through the "things" we use (our bodies, artifacts, clothing,

and so on). We also discussed how our actions (movements and gestures, voice, eyes, touch, and management of space and time) also send messages.

At this point, two notes of caution are warranted. The first is that the tendencies and generalizations that were pointed out are *just that*: That is, they are probabilities greater than chance that people will act in particular ways. They certainly are not ironclad or universal laws of behavior. Thus, even though some forms of nonverbal behavior we have discussed are supported by research, and most make intuitive sense to us, that does not mean everyone always behaves that way. Because this is the case, a particular generalization may fail to match up with our own personal observations or experiences.

The second note of caution is that all the nonverbal uses discussed so far need to be considered as a *system of factors* acting in a simultaneous transaction with one another. All must be considered as a part of the simultaneous transactions model set forth in Chapter 1. Thus, their influences on meanings of both senders and receivers are not element by element. More realistically, they are a kind of *integrated package*. What this means is that when people communicate, they do so as whole persons in a particular context. In a simultaneous way, then, as they transmit verbal messages to one another, they frame their messages by using artifacts, movements, gestures, their voices, and their eyes. While doing those things, they are also managing space and time. When these features of communication are added, the simultaneous transactions model is developed more fully. It is clear that it is *both* the verbal and the nonverbal systems we use that do the communicating, rather than either one alone. Finally, as we will see in chapters that follow, the additional and very important influences of the *context* will have to be added as an additional part of this holistic view. Considering all these features and aspects of human communication is necessary to understand the entire process.

The Importance of Nonverbal Immediacy

A practical note can be added to our discussion of nonverbal communication. Viewing human communication as a holistic or integrated process provides insight into ways in which we use nonverbal communication to get others to *like us*—to establish friendships or develop closer relationships with others. Verbal communication is clearly a very important part of that process. At the same time, however, we can achieve and manage our relationships by simultaneously using a number of nonverbal behaviors as part of an overall communication strategy aimed at developing positive relationships with others.[51]

Our use of nonverbal behaviors to get others to like us does not mean that we do so deliberately, in a calculated way or even consciously. Using nonverbal strategies to influence others to perceive us positively can be as unwitting and spontaneous as distancing ourselves from those we find unattractive or unappealing. Recognizing what we do to achieve those relational outcomes is an important part of development of an effective and practical communication strategy. Once we know how to initiate or promote positive outcomes, we are in a better position to exert at least some degree of control over our own behaviors and, eventually, over how others respond to us.

The use of nonverbal signals and other actions that promote physical and psychological closeness with others is called **nonverbal immediacy.**[52] The concept of immediacy is rather complex. It brings together a number of related behaviors that contribute to perceptions of closeness, liking—what psychologists call *affect*. According to Albert Mehrabian and others, the nonverbal immediacy behaviors that, when used together, communicate liking or closeness include smiling, head-nodding, forward-leaning, eye contact, touch, open gestures, and standing close to someone.[53]

Physical closeness with someone can be established using what we have called proxemic, kinesic, and haptic nonverbal behaviors. That is, by moving closer, leaning forward, and increasing our use of touch, we are effectively *decreasing the physical distance* between ourselves and another person.

Psychological closeness is more difficult to describe. Most of us have experienced that condition when we exchanged glances with someone even in the middle of a crowd. In other words, we need not be physically close to be psychologically close with another person. Instead, we might smile, nod our heads affirmatively, and maintain eye contact. Taken together, these particular nonverbal immediacy behaviors all contribute to perceptions of psychological or physical closeness or both.

To understand the importance of immediacy behaviors, we need to consider a modern version of what philosopher Jeremy Bentham (1789) called the "principle of utility." It is a simple idea: Specifically, it maintains that people approach things and others they like or prefer and avoid those they don't like or don't prefer.[54] Mehrabian has applied that principle to his concept of immediacy.[55] According to Bentham's principle, approach/avoidance implies physical as well as psychological and social distance. However, if we find ourselves with someone we dislike, we're not always able to put distance between ourselves and the offensive individual. In fact, we may be in the unenviable position of having to spend an entire evening sitting next to such a person. Unable to rearrange the seating, or otherwise move elsewhere, we are forced to rely on nonverbal behavior to increase (psychological) distance. We can do this by looking away, frowning, turning our body to the side, or leaning in the opposite direction. By such actions, we are able psychologically to reduce or even avoid contact.

In more positive circumstances we may find ourselves near, but unable to talk meaningfully with, someone we regard as special. The house may be full of guests, or the folks may be staying up late watching TV. In that case, we are likely to initiate or simulate psychological closeness by gazing longingly, sharing smiles, and "accidentally" touching one another.

One of the more fascinating results from research on nonverbal immediacy behaviors is that *immediacy often begets immediacy*. That is, when we engage in nonverbal immediacy behaviors with someone, the probability is high that our target will respond in kind. For example, some individuals laugh in such a contagious way that an entire room can become hysterical. There are some professors who smile, joke, and make eye contact to reduce distance. Usually, the class reciprocates in like manner.

We know that using nonverbal immediacy behaviors is an effective communication strategy in efforts to develop positive relationships with others. Basically, this strategy works because when people engage in immediacy behaviors with us, we often assume that they do so because they like us. When we see that a person apparently likes us, approves of us, and enjoys being with us, we feel like returning those feelings. Clearly, nonverbal immediacy behaviors are hard to resist. For example, even if you have had an argument with your best friend, it's extremely difficult to stay angry or aloof when he or she hugs you and tries to make you laugh.

Applying the Immediacy Principle

We suggested earlier that people usually do not deliberately try to develop nonverbal immediacy in a conscious way. However, there is no reason why that cannot be done. Should you discover that your supervisor or someone else who has authority over you is an ogre and picks on you, you might apply the immediacy principle. The next time you see him or her, go right up and shake hands. Initiate a conversation; smile a lot; give a lot of strokes, like nodding or laughing at jokes; and maintain eye contact. It probably will not have an effect right away, but keep it up and changes probably will occur. If all goes well, you may find the individual responding to you in a much friendlier way. If you're still not satisfied with the results, try

again; it is very likely that sooner or later the person will come around.

One of the more interesting side effects of this deliberate use of the immediacy principle may reside with you. Over and over, students who have used the strategy report confusion in their own feelings toward the targeted other. They begin to reevaluate their original assessment of the person and tentatively conclude that maybe, just maybe, he or she isn't all that bad.

Before you conclude that using the immediacy principle is the panacea for improving all bad relationships, or for getting everyone to like you, you need to understand the drawbacks of using immediacy behaviors.[56] All too often, people misunderstand nonverbal attempts aimed at eliciting psychological closeness. Some may misperceive our efforts as flirting or even a blatant sexual come-on. Liking is one thing; total intimacy obviously is another. As we saw earlier, if a sexual invitation or an advance is not welcome (as in the workplace), the consequences can be devastating to all parties concerned. Thus, under certain circumstances, attempts at too much immediacy may not be a good idea. Each situation must be assessed carefully.

Another potential problem is that immediacy often results in more, not less, communication with others. If that's what you want, fine. However, once you have initiated immediacy behaviors with someone, you may find it extremely difficult to limit or control the interaction. It is especially difficult if there is a need to terminate it gracefully. For example, it may be essential to initiate immediacy with a client in order to get a sale or close a deal. When the transaction is concluded, however, it's time to move on to other customers. At that point, the client may be unwilling to disengage from an interaction that was positive and reinforcing.

Generally, then, the principle of immediacy—and the nonverbal behaviors composing immediacy—are among the most effective strategies we can use to maximize our effectiveness as communicators. No other single aspect of nonverbal communication has been found to be

BOX 3.4   *Ethical Concerns*

USING NONVERBAL BEHAVIORS RESPONSIBLY

- If you know that by engaging in immediacy behaviors—eye contact, smiling, nodding, and leaning forward—you can get someone to like you, how ethical is it for you to be deliberately immediate with someone who is unaware of what you're doing?
- Could you honestly be immediate with someone you intensely dislike, knowing that you have to somehow get along with this person?

- Assume for a moment that you are the boss—the person with high status, position, and power. Would you require a dress code for your employees? Why or why not? What message does a dress code send?
- If someone compliments you on the cultured pearls you are wearing or the handsome ostrich leather briefcase you are carrying, would you admit that the necklace or briefcase is merely an imitation of the real thing? Why or why not?

more closely related to perceptions of liking and approval. When people engage in the immediacy behaviors of approach, they are perceived by others to be more popular, well liked, responsive, and sensitive. Those who behave in opposite ways are likely to be considered aloof, unresponsive, tense, awkward, and insensitive. At the same time, as noted, the principle of nonverbal immediacy has to be applied with careful anticipation of consequences. Box 3.4 discusses some of the ethical considerations involved with immediacy.

Overall, this chapter has shown that nonverbal communication is an extraordinarily complex process. It is not a separate language by which we can read the secret thoughts and intentions of people, but a part of the transaction processes by which people simultaneously arouse meanings in others. If techniques of nonverbal communication are well understood, we can use them responsibly to increase greatly our effectiveness as communicators.

Chapter Review

- Nonverbal communication refers to the deliberate or unintentional use of objects, actions, sounds, time, and space to arouse meanings in others. Nonverbal communication is used to complement our verbal meanings, regulate verbal interaction, and substitute actions for words; at times, it contradicts a person's spoken words.
- Our bodies communicate many kinds of messages, as do the artifacts we possess, including our dwellings and their contents, our cars, the glasses we wear,

and the purses or briefcases we carry. Clothing is one of the most meaningful of the artifacts we use to communicate nonverbally. We dress to communicate such meanings as status and power, social acceptability, occupational role, sexual attractiveness, and inner feelings.

- Sexual communication in the workplace has become a widely discussed problem in U.S. society. Some behavior by males is grossly offensive by anyone's interpretations. However, many common forms of nonverbal, or even verbal, communication may be defined as joking and harmless by men whereas they are interpreted as disgusting and sexually threatening by women.

- Actions themselves often communicate. Kinesics, vocalics, oculesics, proxemics, haptics, and chronemics all signal important meanings to others.

- Taken together, many of the actions that we use in nonverbal communication help to establish and maintain closeness with others. These immediacy behaviors include eye contact, touch, leaning forward, nodding, and smiling. In combination, these nonverbal behaviors of approach signal to others, "I like you and I care about you."

Key Terms

nonverbal communication	body language	proxemics	chronemics
frame	artifacts	territoriality	nonverbal immediacy
regulating	vocalics	personal space	
emblems	oculesics	haptics	

Notes

1. Fast, J. (1970). *Body language*. New York: Evans; Birdwhistell, R. (1955). Background to kinesics. *Etc., 13*, 10–18; Burgoon, J. K., & Walther, J. B. (1990). Nonverbal expectancies and the evaluative consequences of violations. *Human Communication Research, 17*, 232–265.

2. Mehrabian, A., & Farris, S. R. (1967). Influence of attitudes from nonverbal communication in two channels. *Journal of Consulting Psychology, 31*, 248–252.

3. Argyle, M., Alkema, F., & Gilmour, R. (1971). The communication of friendly and hostile attitudes by verbal and nonverbal signals. *European Journal of Social Psychology, 1*, 385–402; Argyle, M., Sater, V., Nicholson, H., Williams, M., & Burgess, P. (1970). The communication of inferior and superior attitudes by verbal and nonverbal signals. *British Journal of Social and Clinical Psychology, 9*, 221–231; Mehrabian, A., & Wiener, M. (1967). Decoding of inconsistent communications. *Journal of Personality and Social Psychology, 6*, 108–114; Burgoon, J. K., Manusov, V., Mineo, P., & Hale, J. L. (1985). Effects of gaze on hiring, credibility, attraction, and relational message interpretation. *Journal of Nonverbal Behavior, 9*, 133–146.

4. Dittman, A. T. (1987). The role of body movement in communication. In A. W. Siegman & S. Feldstein (Eds.), *Nonverbal communication and communication* (2nd ed., p. 37). Hillsdale, NJ: Lawrence Erlbaum.

5. Not all complementary framing is done with overt actions and gestures. Sometimes nonverbal cues are included in written or printed verbal messages. This is done not only by using phrasing that permits "reading between the lines" but also by including gesture-like cues. For example, we have all written and received letters with "Ha ha" or "Just kidding" inserted into the text.

6. Regulators are acts that maintain and regulate the back and forth nature of speaking and listening between two or more people communicating. Ekman, P., & Friesen, W. V. (1969). The repertoire of nonverbal behavior: Categories, origins, usage and coding. *Semiotica, 1*, 49–98.

7. Duncan, S. D., Jr. (1972). Some signals and rules for taking speaking turns in conversations. *Journal of Personality and Social Psychology, 23*, 283–292; Duncan, S. D., Jr. (1974). On the structure of speaker auditor interaction during speaking turns. *Language in Society, 2*, 161–180; Weimann, J. M., & Knapp, M. L.

(1975). Turn-taking in conversations. *Journal of Communication, 25,* 75–92.

8. Collier, G. (1985). *Emotional expression* (p. 95). Hillsdale, NJ: Lawrence Erlbaum; Kendon, A. (1967). Some functions of gaze-direction in social interaction. *Acta Psychologia, 26,* 22–63; Exiine, R. V. (1971). Visual inter-action: The glance of power and preference. Nebraska Symposium on Motivation (pp. 163–206). Lincoln: University of Nebraska Press; Burkhart, J. C., Weider-Hatfield, D., & Hocking, J. E. (1985). Eye contact contrast effects in the employment interview. *Communication Research Reports, 2,* 5–10.

9. Ekman, P., Friesen, W. V., & Bear, J. (1984). The international language of gestures. *Psychology Today, 18,* 64–69.

10. The use of the term *emblems* to describe nonverbal acts that have direct verbal translations was introduced by: Efron, D. (1941). *Gesture and environment.* New York: King's Crown Press. See also: Ekman, P., & Friesen, W. V. (1969). The repertoire of nonverbal behavior: Categories, origins, usage, and coding. *Semiotica, 1,* 49–98.

11. Riccillo, S. C. (1989). Physiological measurement. In P. Emmert & L. L. Barker (Eds.), *Measurement of communication behavior* (pp. 267–295). New York: Longman.

12. Knapp, M. L. (1978). *Nonverbal communication in human interaction* (2nd ed., pp. 21–22). New York: Holt.

13. Cameron, A., John, O. & Keltner, D. (2001). Who attains social status? Effects of personality and physical attractiveness in social groups. *Journal of Personality and Social Psychology, 81,* 1, 116–132. Berscheid, E., & Walster, E. (1972). Beauty and the best. *Psychology today, 5,* 42–46; Algozzine, R. (1976). What teachers perceive—children receive. *Communication Quarterly, 24,* 41–47; Dion, K., Berscheid, E., & Walster, E. (1972). What is beautiful is good. *Journal of Personality and Social Psychology, 24,* 285–290.

14. Social psychologists in the sociological tradition refer to this generalization as the basis of the "looking-glass self," whereby people develop beliefs about themselves on the basis of the reactions of others to them. It is a concept developed by Charles Horton Cooley early in the last century. See: Cooley, C. H. (1964). *Human nature and the social order* (p. 185). New York: Schocken Books. (First published 1909.)

15. Sybers, R., & Roach, M. E. (1962). Clothing and human behavior. *Journal of Home Economics, 54,* 184–187; Rosenfeld, L. B., & Plax, T. G. (1977). Clothing as communication. *Journal of Communication, 27,* 24–31; Taylor, L. C., & Compton, N. H. (1968). Personality correlates of dress conformity. *Journal of Home Economics, 60,* 653–656; and Molloy, J. T. (1975). *Dress for success.* New York: Warner Books.

16. Williams, M. C., & Eicher, J. B. (1966). Teenagers' appearance and social acceptance. *Journal of Home Economics, 58,* 457–461.

17. Lee, J. W., & Guerrero, L. K. (2001). Types of touch in cross-sex relationships between coworkers: Perceptions of relational and emotional messages, inappropriateness, and sexual harassment. *Journal of Applied Communication Research, 29,* 3, 197–220.

18. Interviews by one of the authors with recently arrived males who come to the United States to undertake graduate studies, and who can't wait to date American women, have shown that such first-date behavior is a common expectation, and also a constant source of disappointment when it proves to be untrue.

19. The study of the expression of emotion with the use of the face and other parts of the body is an ancient one. It goes back to the 1600s when artists were concerned with ways to capture human emotion on canvas. A classic work is: Darwin, C. (1965). *The expression of emotions in man and animals.* Chicago: University of Chicago Press. (First published in London 1872.)

20. Birdwhistell, R. L. (1970). *Kinesics and context: Essays in body motion communication.* Harmondsworth: Penguin.

21. Ekman, P., & Friesen, W. V. (1948). The repertoire of nonverbal behavior: Categories, origins, usage, and coding, *Semiotica, 1,* 49–98.

22. Ibid.

22. Addington, D. W. (1968). The relationship of selected vocal characteristics to personality perception. *Speech Monographs, 35,* 492–503; Addington, D. W. (1971). The effects

of vocal variations on ratings of source credibility. *Speech Monographs, 37,* 242–247.

23. Soskin, W. F. (1963). Some aspects of communication and interpretation in psychotherapy. Paper presented at the meetings of the American Psychological Association, Cleveland. Cited in Kramer, E. (1963). Judgments of personal characteristics and emotions from nonverbal properties of speech. *Psychological Bulletin, 60,* 408–420.

24. Scherer, K. R., & Oshinsky, J. S. (1977). Cue utilization in emotion attribution from auditory stimuli. *Motivation and Emotion, 1,* 331–346; Wiggets, M. (1982). Judgments of facial expressions of emotions predicted from facial behavior. *Journal of Nonverbal Behavior, 7,* 101–116; Manusov, V. (1990). An application of attribution principles of nonverbal behavior in romantic dyads. *Communication Monographs, 57,* 104–118.

25. Snyder, M. (1974). Self-monitoring of expressive behavior. *Journal of Personality and Social Psychology, 30,* 526–537.

26. Von Cranach, M. (1971). The role of orienting behavior in human interactions. In A. H. Esser (Ed.), *Behavior and environment: The use of space by animals and men* (pp. 217–237). New York: Plenum. Mazur, A., Rosa, E., Faupel, M., Heller, J., Leen, R., & Thurman, B. (1980). Physiological aspects of communication via mutual gaze. *American Journal of Sociology, 6,* 50–74.

27. Ekman, P., & Friesen, W. V. (1948). The repertoire of nonverbal behavior: Categories, origins, usage, and coding. *Semiotica, 1,* 118; Hocking, J. E., Bauchner, J., Kaminski, E. P., & Miller, G. R. (1979). Detecting deceptive communication from verbal, visual, and paralinguistic cues. *Human Communication Research, 6,* 36–46.

28. Vrij, A., Edward, K. & Bull, R. (2001). People's insight into their own behaviour and speech while lying. *British Journal of Psychology, 92,* 2, 373–389. See also: Vrij, A., Edward, K. & Bull, R. (2001). Stereotypical verbal and nonverbal responses while deceiving others. *Personality and Social Psychology Bulletin, 27,* 7, 899–909.

29. Navarro, J. & Schafer, J. (2001). Detecting deception. *FBI Law Enforcement Bulletin, 70,* 7, 9–13.

30. Ibid.

31. Costa, M., Dinsbach, W., & Manstead, A. (2001). Social presence, embarrassment, and nonverbal behavior. *Journal of Nonverbal Behavior, 25,* 4, 225–240.

32. For a detailed discussion of the concept of territoriality, see: Altman, I. (1975). *The environment and social behavior.* Monterey, CA: Brooks/Cole.

33. The classic discussion of the idea of personal space is that of: Hall, E. T. (1966). *The hidden dimension.* Garden City, NY: Doubleday.

34. Richmond, V. P., McCroskey, J. C., & Payne, S. K. (1987). *Nonverbal behavior in interpersonal relations* (pp. 118–128). Englewood Cliffs, NJ: Prentice-Hall.

35. Hall, E. T. (1959). *The silent language.* New York: Doubleday.

36. Watson, O. M. (1970). *Proxemic behavior: A cross-cultural study.* The Hague: Mouton.

37. Scherer, S. E. (1974). Proxemic behavior of primary school children as a function of their socioeconomic class and subculture. *Journal of Personality and Social Psychology, 29,* 800–805.

38. Sommer, R. (1969). *Personal space: The behavioral basis of design.* Englewood Cliffs, NJ: Prentice-Hall.

39. Ibid., p. 291.

40. Harlow, H. F. (1959). Love in monkeys. *Scientific American, 200,* 68–74.

41. Nguyen, T., Hesin, R., & Nguyen, M. (1975). The meanings of touch: Sex differences. *Journal of Communication, 3,* 92–103; Montagu, A. (1971). *Touching: The human significance of the skin.* New York, Harper & Row; Heslin, R., & Alper, T. (1983). Touch: A bonding gesture. In J. M. Wiemann & R. Harrison (Eds.), *Nonverbal Interaction* (pp. 47–75). Beverly Hills, CA: Sage. Thayer, S. (1986). History and strategies of research on social touch. *Journal of Nonverbal Behavior, 10,* 12–28; and Thayer, S. (1988). Close encounters. *Psychology Today, 22,* 30–36.

42. Montagu (1971), *Touching,* p. 75.

43. Adler, R. & Towne, N. (1990). *Looking out/looking in.* Fort Worth, TX: Holt, Rinehart and Winston; Burgoon, J. K., & Saine, T. (1978). *The unspoken dialogue: An introduction to nonverbal communication.* Boston: Houghton Mifflin.

44. Richmond, McCrosky, and Payne, *Non-verbal behavior,* p. 138. See also: Watson, W. H. (1975). The meanings of touch: Geriatic nursing. *Journal of Communication, 25,* 104–112. See also: Lavelli, M., & Fogel, A. (2002). Developmental changes in mother-infant face-to-face communication: Birth to 3 months. *Developmental Psychology, 38,* 2, 288–305.

45. Montagu, A. (1978). *Touching: The human significance of the skin* (2nd ed.). New York: Harper & Row; Fisher, J. D., Rytting, M., & Heslin, R. (1976). Hands touching hands: Affective and evaluative effects of an interpersonal touch. *Sociometry, 39,* 416–421.

46. Despert, J. L. (1941). Emotional aspects of speech and language development. *International Journal of Psychiatry and Neurology, 105,* 193–222; Hill, S. D., & Smith, J. M. (1984). Neonatal responsiveness as a function of maternal contact and obstetrical drugs. *Perceptual and Motor Skills, 58,* 859–866.

47. Richmond, McCroskey, & Payne, *Nonverbal behavior,* p. 141. See also: Montagu, (1971). *Touching.*

48. Andersen, P., & Liebowitz, K. (1978). The development and nature of the construct touch avoidance. *Environmental Psychology and Nonverbal Behavior, 3,* 89–106.

49. Richmond, McCroskey, & Payne, *Nonverbal behavior,* pp. 177–179.

50. Malendro, L. A., Barker, L., & Barker, D. A. (1989). *Nonverbal communication* (2nd ed.). New York: Random House.

51. See, for example: Rashotte, L. (2002). What does that smile mean? The meaning of nonverbal behavior in social interaction. *Social Psychology Quarterly, 65,* 1, 92–102.

52. Mehrabian, A. (1971). *Silent messages.* Belmont, CA: Wadsworth; Mehrabian, A. (1981). *Silent messages: Implicit communication of emotion and attitudes* (2nd ed.). Belmont, CA: Wadsworth.

53. Mehrabian, A. (1981). *Silent messages.* See also, Anderson, J. F. (1979). The relationship between teacher immediacy and teacher effectiveness. In D. Nimmo (Ed.), *Communication Yearbook, 3,* 543–560. New Brunswick, NJ: Transaction Books; Anderson, P., & Anderson, J. (1982). Nonverbal immediacy in instruction. In L. L. Barker, (Ed), *Communication in the classroom: Original essays* (pp. 98–102). Englewood Cliffs, NJ. Prentice-Hall.

54. See Bentham, J. (1823). *An introduction to the principles of morals and legislation* (rev. ed.). London: W. Pickering. (First published in 1798.)

55. Mehrabian (1981). *Silent messages,* p. 1.

56. Richmond, McCroskey, & Payne, *Nonverbal behavior,* pp. 203–204.

The Importance
of Listening

A hush fell over the conference room. No one was quite sure why Mike, the director in charge of the entire operation, had called this particular staff meeting. All his assistant directors were there. Everyone was a bit nervous. As soon as he sat down, Mike glared at everyone and then began by severely and publicly reprimanding Paul, who just sat there looking down at the table. The rebuke was highlighted by the fact that Paul was Mike's most important assistant director. Mike was upset because Paul "had not bothered to listen to what Mike was saying."

All the other assistant directors were stunned. They had always felt that Paul was Mike's favorite. None would have ever expected such open hostility during a staff meeting. Even more surprising was the fact that it was Paul's "lack of attention" that had aroused Mike's anger.

Although now calmer, Mike continued his point. His message was now more broadly targeted: "Every one of us at this table," Mike said pointedly, "is paid one hell of a lot of money to do an effective job of managing the operations of this corporation. Whether any of you like it or not, I am the vice-president here. This means I'm your boss and I'm in charge. It's my butt that ends up in a sling when any one of you screws up! So, when I'm talking I expect every one of you to listen very carefully to each and every word! It also means I had better be able to tell that you are listening to me when I look at you! Do you all understand me?"

All heads nodded vigorously. Mike once again focused his attention and concentrated his comments on Paul: "I don't know how many times I have had to tell you, Paul, that most of your mistakes around here follow directly from your not listening to what I am telling you. Now 'read my lips.' You are officially on notice. If I sense again that you're not listening, I am going to put a letter of reprimand in your personnel file. And any subsequent failure to listen to me will bring even more severe disciplinary actions! Do you understand me, Paul?"

By this time, Paul was sweating, and his back was pressed tight against his chair. The lines of tension on his face revealed the stress of the situation:

"Yeah Mike," Paul said shakily, "I understand—and I'm truly sorry. I guess I should have been more careful. It won't happen again. I promise that I will always listen when you are talking and I'll look like it as well."

Mike followed up with a number of routine issues that he wanted to discuss. It wasn't long, however, before he realized that his next meeting was due to begin and he had to leave. He ended the staff meeting, pulled himself up out of his chair, and said, "I'll see you guys later."

As soon as Mike had departed, Paul looked around and said apologetically, "Well guys, I feel pretty stupid. Mike was really mad, huh? I had no idea that it looked like I wasn't listening. The fact is, I wasn't, and I didn't realize it. I guess my mind just wanders sometimes. I'm really sorry to have put the rest of you in such a difficult situation and I apologize. I guess I did screw up, and I need to concentrate on what people say to me. I just had no idea that it was such a problem."[1]

———————————————————

Even though Mike's behavior as Paul's supervisor—correcting his subordinate in public—was not acceptable behavior, Paul's tendency not to listen to his boss is by no means unusual.[2] For example, one of the most frequent complaints people make about their physicians is that they don't listen to what they are saying. People sit down to talk with their doctor, expecting him or her to listen carefully to their explanation of what is troubling them and how they feel about the problem. Many times they find that the physician is not really listening but is mentally sorting through a number of standard symptoms that might indicate a particular problem, and a list of routine medications that might be prescribed to alleviate the condition. Such failures to listen are, of course, deplored by responsible medical authorities. For example, one distinguished physician, commenting on the importance of careful listening, puts it this way:

> I know from listening to patients, and my personal experience with illness, how important it is to be treated like a person and not an object. It's wonderful to have broken parts repaired by a competent fixer, but a person is more than the sum of her parts. True healing depends on the sense of trust that derives from being known as a person whose emotions, fears, beliefs and needs will be heard and considered.[3]

Failing to listen can create problems in many settings. A previous chapter explained that many men fail to listen to women in the workplace when the women object to the men's sexual messages; but inadequate listening is not restricted to the work environment. In fact, from time to time, all of us fail to take note of what people are saying, even when they are giv-

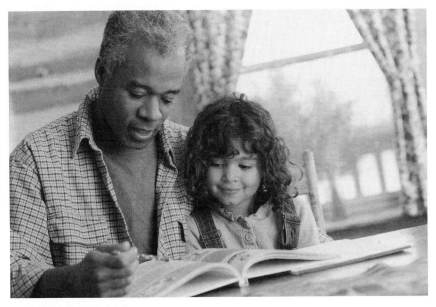

Listening is a critical and active part of the communication process. While listening, a receiver attends to and perceives information transmitted by a sender, and transforms it back into the message that was originally encoded.

ing us vital information. Some of us may be like Paul, a habitually poor listener, or we may be like some physicians, too busy to give people their full attention and not even be aware of it. In fact, when employees are asked why they are unhappy in their present positions, most say that they get no respect. They explain that upper-level managers are not listening to them, and that their suggestions and ideas do not seem to matter. Thus, they feel *ignored* and *unappreciated*.[4] (See Box 4.1.)

The fact is, few people are truly competent listeners who are able to grasp all the meanings intended by the source in every message they receive. At the same time, as discussed in both our linear model and the more comprehensive simultaneous transactions model, listening and making accurate interpretations of meanings intended by senders is an essential part of the communication process.

This chapter focuses on the *receiver*. It looks closely at listening as a central part of the human communication process. Not only is effective listening important in developing a the-

oretical understanding of the basic nature of human communication, but also it is one of the most fundamental, if often overlooked, communication skills.[5]

Why don't we listen to people effectively? At least part of the reason is that we take listening for granted. We assume that *we already know* what listening is all about, and, therefore, there is no need to learn anything more. We also assume that *it is easy* to be a good listener. In fact, like Paul, many of us probably believe we already have effective listening skills, even when we do not. Both of these assumptions are unwarranted: We cannot take it for granted that our listening skills are already at a maximum, and we certainly cannot assume that effective listening is simple or easy[6]

It is important to realize that listening is a skill and that, like any skill, it requires learning. What this means is that even someone like Paul can learn to become an effective listener. Further, if the foundations of listening skills are understood, anyone can improve his or her ability to sort out more fully the meanings of what is said.

BOX 4.1   *Workplace Perspective*

FIVE WAYS TO REALLY IRRITATE YOUR EMPLOYEES

Lou Hampton has described five irritating *listening habits* that can bother employees. It is a serious issue because when employees are unhappy they often seek jobs elsewhere. This can pose a real problem for a business because recruiting and training each new employee can cost as much as $13,000. Hampton notes, "A recent survey of 250 business professionals . . . uncovered the five most common listening habits that irritate employees."[1] A boss who employs these listening habits on a daily basis will see employee retention rates drop sharply and costs go up. The following quotations summarize what Hampton sees as the most irritating employer habits:

Irritating Habits

1. *Interrupt your employees when they speak.*
"When you interrupt an employee when he or she is speaking, you are taking the focus away from his or her message. Essentially you are telling the person that his or her ideas really don't matter. And there are more important ideas to deal with."

2. *Don't make eye contact with your employees.*
"Employees want the reassurance that when they are speaking, you are focusing on them and their ideas. Most people believe that if you are not focusing in a physical manner with eye contact, then there is a good chance that your mind is not focusing as well."

3. *Refuse to give your employees feedback.*
"When employees come to you with ideas or problems, they expect you to offer solutions, suggestions and guidance. When you don't respond to their requests or give them feedback in any way, they become confused as to whether you agree or disagree with what they've said."

4. *Ignore your employees to answer the phone.*
"Unfortunately, when the phone rings while they are speaking to their employees, the majority of people choose to answer the phone instead of letting their employees finish their thoughts. By doing this, you send your employees the message that the phone takes precedent over their ideas or concerns."

5. *Read the mail or newspaper when your employees are talking.* "[If] you read your mail or other papers while your employee is explaining something to you, you will be missing certain points of the conversation . . . and you [will] make him or her feel unappreciated and unimportant."

[1] Hampton, L. (2001). Five ways to really irritate your employees, *Business Credit, 103,* 5, 20–21.

As with many aspects of human communication, listening is a complex process, but, like the other stages in the linear and transactions models, listening is a process that can be analyzed in order to be better understood. Briefly stated, becoming a more effective listener requires us to understand our limitations. It also requires strategic planning for improvement and, above all, systematic practice.

In the sections that follow, we begin with a detailed analysis and description of the listening process. Next, we examine that process from the point of view of good and bad listening.[6]

Finally, in a step-by-step fashion, we discuss how each of us can plan to improve our listening skills.

The Listening Process

Social scientists have been attempting systematically to unravel the behaviors involved in the listening process since the 1920s.[7] A considerable body of evidence has accumulated showing the important aspects of that process. Over the past half-century, hundreds of investigators have proposed different definitions of listening. In fact, to list and discuss even the more popular among them would require at least an entire textbook. However, all that is needed for the present discussion is a basic definition that clearly identifies the factors that warrant discussion.

Listening as Behavior

An effective way of understanding listening is to view it as a form of behavior that is a part of the communication process. That implies that, like any form of behavior, it requires active efforts of attention and perception on the part of a person toward whom a message is being directed. In other words, listening is part of the transaction that takes place between people as they communicate. In more formal terms, *listening* can be defined as *an active form of behavior in which individuals attempt to maximize their attention to and comprehension of what is being communicated to them through the use of words, actions, and things by one or more people in their immediate environment.* That may seem to be an overly complex definition for something that, at first glance, looks so simple and elementary, but the definition includes all the essential features of the process that need to be understood to improve listening skills.

One of the problems many people have with listening is that they think of it mainly in terms of using the ears to attend closely to verbal messages. Of course, that is part of the process. In the present analysis, however, listening also refers to monitoring the *nonverbal* and *contextual* aspects of messages. As was discussed in Chapter 3, there is a great variety and subtlety of meanings that can be included in messages by nonverbal means. Thus, in the simultaneous transactions view of human communication, listening includes attending to and interpreting all the ways in which people use words, things, and actions to arouse meanings in their receivers. For this reason, listening is much more than just hearing spoken words.

In our discussions of communication models in Chapter 1, we explained the influence of different *contexts*. We explained that a variety of contexts can add to or modify meanings that are included in a source's verbal and nonverbal messages. For this reason, effective listening requires attention to the contextual aspects of a message as well as its verbal and nonverbal features. These contextual cues can be both complex and diverse and they can have significant influences on interpretation.[7] For example, what we interpret from what people are saying can be very different as we listen to them in familiar and unfamiliar places. This interpretation may vary, depending on whether they are people we know very well or strangers, or whether they are in group situations or are communicating with us one on one. Another kind of context is provided by different media that may be a part of the communication process—a written note, a memo or letter, a telephone call, an e-mail, a radio or TV program, and so on. Each of these constitutes a different context, a different communication environment, that has its own influences on the listening experience.[8]

It was also emphasized in previous chapters that what something means to us is based on the accumulation of both indirect and direct experiences we have had during our lifetime.[9] This provides a set of personal internal meaning responses for each of the huge number of symbols, gestures, rules, and so on that make up our language and nonverbal communication. Only when the sender's and the receiver's bases of experience are sufficiently similar can meanings of the parties involved be *parallel*, permitting individuals to share the same interpretations. Therefore, comprehension of a message we receive depends immediately and directly on the existence of parallel meaning experiences. The important point is that these can accurately be produced only by effective listening.

The preceding discussion implies that effective listening is *no accident*. It is not an automated form of behavior that we can engage in without thinking. Although it is true that some aspects of listening are habitual or reflexive, others certainly are not.[10] Therefore, we cannot simply stand when we talk to people and expect that high-quality listening is just going to "happen." To provide for accurate communication, both parties in the transaction need to be actively and consciously involved in attending to and comprehending what is being transmitted by the other, using all the means that we have discussed.

To be effective, then, listening is something that we must deliberately and consciously *manage*. In other words, successfully attending to and comprehending accurately what is communicated to us will be achieved only if it is deliberately set as a key objective—an objective we can achieve if we work hard and systematically. Furthermore, listening is not a part-time pursuit. We must set this objective whenever we communicate with other people.

At the same time, it is possible to listen too intently! It would be impulsive, unreasonable, and even impossible to give our total attention to what is being communicated to us at all times, in all situations, and via all media. This would engulf us in a tidal wave of information with which no normal person could cope. Furthermore, much of it would be either a ghastly bore or a total waste of time. We can all think of situations in which we wouldn't want to involve ourselves intensely in the task of attending to and comprehending whatever information was sent our way. For example, while viewing television, few of us need to focus our attention intensely on every commercial that is broadcast, nor, while reading a newspaper, do we devote highly focused attention to every advertisement. In other words, an important prerequisite to effective listening is acquiring the skills to be selective and to *discriminate* between what we should pay attention to and what we can safely ignore.[11] The importance of being able to listen selectively but effectively is closely linked to the essential objectives or goals of the process.

What We Gain from Effective Listening

Our listening activities serve at least four primary purposes.[12] One major reason we listen is *to acquire information*. Another is *to evalu-*

The Four Primary Purposes of Listening

1. *Acquire needed information.* In class, at work, or at home, we listen to messages to gain or acquire information we need. Moreover, even if we have been exposed to certain messages before, listening helps to reinforce that information.
2. *Evaluate and screen messages.* If we tried to actively listen to every message we were exposed to, we would certainly experience information overload! Instead, we pick and choose what is important or interesting to us.
3. *Recreation.* Listening can be recreational. Most of us enjoy listening to the radio or watching and listening to the television.
4. *Social efficacy.* In order to win friends and influence others, we need to listen well. It's our social responsibility to pay attention to what others say and participate actively in the conversation. In this way, we are able to better manage our relationships with others and get along at work, at home, and at play.

ate and screen information as it is being presented to us. Third, we often listen just *for recreation*. Finally, we listen because it's a requirement for **social efficacy** (competence in dealing with other people). (See Box 4.2.).

Acquire needed knowledge. Obviously, some message content is important and central to our well-being, whereas other content may be trivial. For example, when a person goes to the doctor to learn the results of a recent test for cancer, AIDS, or another serious illness, obviously the message content is extremely important. Even our friend Paul in our opening vignette would become a very effective listener in such a situation. In contrast, on hearing that a neighbor's cousin planned to visit, most of us might be more like Paul at his worst.

Most message content that we receive is somewhere between these extremes. Much of it has some importance to us. Every student knows, for example, that on those days when, for any number of reasons, it is necessary to miss a class, the lecture content presented will be essential to an upcoming test! When this situation occurs, most people seek out someone they know in the class to tell them what the professor presented. Here, they will be at the mercy of their informant's ability to listen to, comprehend, and record or remember the information that was discussed. In turn, their own ability to listen will dictate how well they acquire the needed material from their secondary source.

Screen and evaluate messages. At a low level of importance are all those daily messages that make up minor news and gossip about people, situations, conditions, or events of only limited significance to us. The key here is to develop the ability to monitor the ongoing flow of messages to which we are exposed. In that way, we can sort out that which has true significance in our lives. For the important ones we can raise our attention to a high level of intensity and listen very closely indeed. To a large extent, then, our ability to *discriminate,* to sort and choose, as we listen will determine the degree to which we can successfully screen what is important from what is trivial.

After screening out what we feel is not important, the second reason people listen is to *evaluate* messages. As previously noted, we are usually on the lookout for specific kinds of messages that are important to us, at least to some degree. However, most of us are exposed to so many people, and to such large numbers of messages every day, that the overload is too much to handle.[13] Indeed, information overload has been cited repeatedly as a major problem by employees in corporate surveys in recent years.[14] We must be able to sort through and evaluate quickly both the relevance and the accuracy of the messages we receive when interacting with others. As indicated earlier, we must be able to discriminate efficiently among the daily flood of transmissions we receive, and select for more intense listening that which is both trustworthy and important to us.

In order to select what is important effectively, we need a set of **criteria** according to which appropriate judgments can be made. These will permit us to evaluate the *source* of incoming messages and the *characteristics* of what is being said against whatever we have selected as standards for judgment. Such criteria are quite personal, but they are based on common sense and past experience, and are not difficult to formulate. Such criteria would normally include ways of deciding whether a source is *credible,* whether what the person is saying is *believable,* and whether what we are receiving is *important* to us in any way.

Such criteria for selective listening provide grounds for judging the degree to which what is being heard is accurate or inaccurate, and therefore unreliable. For example, when a used car salesman solemnly tells you, "This car has only been driven to church on Sundays by a little old lady," is he credible? Are his claims likely to be true? If you detect a faint, painted-out sign on the door that looks like "taxi," common sense suggests you should exercise caution. On the other hand, when the professor says, "We will have a test on Friday, and it will cover chapters 6 through 10 in the text, plus all the material covered in the lectures," common sense tells you to listen closely to this credible source, that the message is important, and that it can be believed.

In summary, effective listening for acquiring and evaluating messages does not occur in a passive or inactive manner. It takes place as we actively receive, interpret, and evaluate both the source and the message against those criteria that we believe to be adequate guides for accepting or rejecting what is said.

Recreation. A great deal of our listening comes under the headings of recreation, amusement, fun, and diversion. We engage in this form of listening when we socialize with relatives or friends, attend concerts, turn on our stereo, view television, or read a novel. In fact, we listen for recreation in most interpersonal situations that are not defined specifically by our need to acquire accurate message content. Recreational listening allows us to interact with people we like for the sole purpose of enjoying one another's company.

At the same time, all recreational listening may not be just fun and games. It all depends on how we define what we are doing. The way we classify a particular listening experience can have a significant influence on what we perceive and how we interpret the incoming message. It may be perfectly harmless just to enjoy much of whatever we are receiving. However, when we define certain types of listening as "simply recreation," it changes how we evaluate the importance and quality of the incoming messages.

In fact, classifying certain kinds of listening as recreational can be dangerous. That is, when we use the term *recreation* we normally think of parallel words like "amusement," "diversion," "entertainment" and "relaxation." Thus, if we are listening in the recreational mode it is unlikely that we will be attentive to certain kinds of information that might have real importance to us. For example, if a professor regularly provides a lot of entertaining jokes and interesting illustrations during a lecture, the important points of the presentation may well be lost on those students who have defined it as recreation. They will be able to remember the jokes and the amusing examples, but not the essential principles and concepts that were being illustrated. In fact, it is safe to conclude that a great deal of poor listening that goes on in the world results from the tendency to think of the process as recreational. Consequently, students flunk tests and can't figure out why.

Social efficacy. The term *social efficacy* means being able to form, manage, and maintain all kinds of social relationships in a positive man-

ner. This implies that success or failure in the vast majority of human encounters depends on how well we are able to listen to what people are communicating by verbal, nonverbal, and contextual means. Human encounters and relationships are found throughout all aspects of daily life—among friends and family, at school, at work, and so on. Learning to listen skillfully in each of these settings can spell the difference between a successful experience and a disappointing failure. In the workplace, for example, promotions and rewards for effective performance may be at stake. Ineffective listening can result in stagnation in a dead-end job.

Thus, in summary, good listening skills are practical tools for developing smooth and comfortable social relationships, including those on which professional success depends.[15] Research shows clearly that an important aspect of any form of work is just "getting along with the people you work around."[16] Outside the workplace, effective listening contributes to success in meeting people, enjoying the company of friends, maintaining family ties, initiating and maintaining a love relationship, and many other similar experiences. Indeed, all these activities depend largely on our ability to hear what people are telling us, to sort out the true meanings of their messages, and to respond in ways that meet their needs.

Actions Required of Effective Listeners

The word *active* was deliberately included in the earlier definition of listening because the degree to which we "actively" listen to someone directly influences our social efficacy.[17] Listening actively implies that we are deliberately aware of our listening behavior and choose listening strategies that make that behavior effective in the four ways described above.

Active versus passive reception.   Passive listening is receiving messages without exerting any effort, using any strategy or having any concern about what is being communicated. Depending on the circumstances, there are a number of reasons why some people are passive listeners. Obviously, the causes of passiveness can include complex problems associated with mental and physical illness, but these need not concern us here. Usually, passiveness stems from conditions as basic as boredom, fatigue, disinterest, and apathy. Of the four, the simple lack of interest is probably the most frequent.

Some people take great pride in their ability to avoid making an effort to listen. Some of these individuals can avoid listening while successfully remaining unnoticed for their lack of effort. This is not to say that it is always bad to act like we are listening when we are not. In fact, sometimes the reverse is the case. We need to appear as if we are not listening when we really are.

Commonly, people sending us messages are often absolutely sure that what they have to say is both profound and critical to our survival. They expect, and often demand, that we appear to be highly attentive. Typically, we give them what they want: We look and act like we are listening, even though we are not. We look observant, and perhaps nod wisely from time to time, but our minds can be miles away. In some cases, this listening mode is totally justified. The problem is that passive listening can become habitual. If it is used when information important to us is being transmitted, such passive message reception can result in a singularly unsuccessful listening experience.

Active listening, or the active reception of messages, occurs when the receiver makes a substantial effort to maximize attention to, and comprehension of, what is being communicated. As mentioned earlier, when the receiver exercises such effort, the likely result is not only greater attention and comprehension on the part of the receiver, but greater enthusiasm and appreciation on the part of the source. There simply is no better prerequisite to high-quality communication than the active reception of messages. It is almost impossible to listen closely without being actively involved in what is being communicated. That kind of feedback motivates the speaker and can make the entire transaction a far better experience than that which occurs when listeners are in a passive mode.

This notion of active listening applies even when a particular encounter ends in disagreement. Whatever the situation, if individuals listen actively, there is a very good chance they will have listened far more carefully to what the other has to say. Once understood, it may be that the differences between points of view are not as great as initially perceived. Effective listening, then, can be a beginning point for *conflict resolution*.[18]

The degree to which we find a person "interesting" will dictate how much effort we exert to listen to what that person has to say. We have a tendency to disregard individuals who, at first glance, appear to be dull or tedious. A major problem is that truly interesting people are in dreadfully short supply. Fortunately, however, almost every person is interesting in some way. One key to becoming an effective listener is to try to look for and isolate at least *one interesting thing* about each individual with whom we interact. In this way, individuals who initially appear terminally boring or totally tiresome can be redefined as worth listening to.

Listening as observable action. Effort and activity when listening are *internal* characteristics. That is, they are factors that operate "in our heads" to influence us as good listeners. Such subjective factors are not observable by others. However, the characteristics of an effective listener can also be inferred by others from observable actions that make us look the part. What are the external and recognizable actions, expressions, and other signs that enable someone to identify a person as a good listener? This is a very important consideration for understanding the relationship between a sender and a receiver.[19]

People easily recognize those who are actively listening to them—in contrast to those who are "tuning them out." They do this by noticing a variety of *signs* or *cues*. If you stop and think for a moment, you can almost close your eyes and see someone you know who is a good listener. He or she has a certain way of reacting to you as you talk. But what are these signs? It is not enough to just say that good listeners "look and act like good listeners."[20] For one thing, good listeners focus their *full concentration* on individuals to whom they are attending, and their bodies nonverbally communicate *receptivity* to what is being said. This is a very subtle nonverbal skill, but people who are concentrating on another's message tend to *lean forward* slightly, with *eyes fixed on the speaker*. Perhaps almost imperceptibly, they *nod in agreement* from time to time. The opposite is to stare off in the distance, with eyelids partially closed, perhaps arms crossed, leaning backward, and with a bored look or a slight frown. (See Box 4.3.)

Even a superficial examination of the face of a person engaged in active listening illustrates a variety of distinctive cues. Observable *eye contact*, an alert and *amiable expression*, and an obvious *focus on the source* are all typical of the look of a good listener. In this way, then, part of what it means to be an effective listener is being perceived and classified by others as a good listener on the basis of observable signs and behaviors.[21]

Looking like a good listener contributes to effective listening in at least two important ways: First, when someone is perceived to be a good listener, the person doing the communicating is likely to feel *sympathetic* toward that individual. Accordingly, the sender makes more of an effort to ensure that her or his message will be understood clearly. This is not easy. Making an effort to maximize understanding for the listener involves skill in **adaptation**, which is closely related to what was called "role-taking" in Chapter 1. Adaptation refers to various ways in which both senders and receivers independently *modify* how they think and behave toward one another. The results of this adjustment (adaptation) include a type of

Visible Characteristics of Good and Poor Listeners

Good Listeners

- Focus their full concentration on the individual to whom they are attending.
- Use their bodies to communicate receptivity to what is being said.
- Tend to lean forward slightly.
- Fix their eyes on the person to whom they are speaking.
- Nod in agreement from time to time.
- Visibly show an alert and amiable expression.

Poor Listeners

- Stare off in the distance, with partially closed eyelids.
- Cross their arms and lean backward.
- Look bored.
- Frown frequently.

joint posturing that contributes to the sharing of meaning.[22] This idea of adaptation will become more relevant in subsequent sections of this chapter. For now it is enough to say that a good listener can influence significantly the amount of effort exerted by a sender simply by *looking like* a good listener.

The second way that looking the part influences effectiveness occurs when a listener initiates a characteristic *pattern of responses* that others can identify. That is, conducting oneself in ways necessary to be seen by others as a good listener requires that certain standards of good listening conduct be met. To be viewed as a good listener, a person must exhibit a combination of activities that, taken together, are easily identified and associated with high effort and motivation. What is interesting about doing so is that performing these actions can actually change the listener's own habitual behavior.[23]

To illustrate, let's take the case of a below-average listener, like Paul, who was described at the beginning of the chapter. Such an individual would find it very difficult to behave in such a way as to be regarded by others as a good listener. In effect, it would involve changing deep-seated or habitual behavior patterns that have minimized Paul's listening effectiveness. However, such deliberate attempts are important keys to improvement. If a poor listener actually takes the appropriate kinds of actions, a real transformation can take place. New effective listening behaviors can displace the habitual poor ones. This means that if Paul, the ineffective listener, successfully exhibits the required look, two conditions will likely result: First, he not only will *appear* to be a good listener in his work situation, but he will, in fact, *be a good listener.* Second, if Paul's efforts to change continue successfully—in situations both within and outside work—the result will be a true transformation. Paul, the problem case, will become Paul, the good listener, not only to his boss but to everyone else as well.

The Listening Encounter

What should be clear by now is that listening involves behaviors on the part of both senders and receivers. In other words, as an important aspect of human communication, listening is a *transactional* process in which all parties are active. Receivers of messages, however, carry most of the burden in accomplishing the actual level of listening effectiveness. Nevertheless, if accuracy of communication is to be high, both senders and receivers participating in an encounter must adapt to one another.

Active attempts to adapt can produce a number of positive outcomes for listeners. For example, adaptation helps to promote and maintain *attention,* which in turn can improve message *comprehension.* When this happens, communication *accuracy* improves. Thus, the meanings encoded into the message by a source

are more likely to be interpreted as he or she intends.

Sender-Receiver Reciprocity

Senders and receivers adapt to one another in order to minimize the influence of various "noise" factors that can obstruct understanding of their messages. There are a host of such factors, including language limitations, personality differences, and membership in various social categories (defined by age, gender, race, education, and so on). Mutual adaptation is a means of getting around these potential barriers to accurate and easy communication. However, if this kind of adaptation is to occur, certain responsibilities must be met by both parties. By meeting these obligations, each will be able to communicate more accurately with the other. Thus, the responsibilities of being an adequate sender *merge* with those of performing as an effective listener, and only when these obligations are jointly met can communication accuracy be improved.

Successful adaptation to each other in a communication encounter, then, is a condition of what can be called **sender-receiver reciprocity.**[24] It is a process based on role-taking and feedback, both of which are basic to the simultaneous transactions model discussed in Chapter 1. Feedback, as you recall, provides messages from a receiver back to a source, revealing how the receiver is interpreting and responding to the message being transmitted. When each of the parties simultaneously engages in both role-taking and feedback, adapting their behavior to each other, they are engaging in sender-receiver reciprocity.

Simple illustrations of such reciprocity are the following: If I begin to talk, you start to listen, which makes me more systematic in my presentation. If you cup your hand behind your ear, I talk louder, which causes you to lower your hand, leading me to speak more softly. If I make a joke, you grin, which makes me smile. If I say something you like, you nod in agreement, which motivates me to provide more positive comments, which makes you blush. Or, at a somewhat more complex level, seeing that I am a woman, you avoid using certain four-letter words, which makes me feel that you are not being natural. Or, noting that you are a man, I refrain from comments that might suggest any form of sexual interest, which leads you to conclude that I am cold. At a very sophisticated level, you may mentally formulate a rebuttal to my argument even as I am presenting it, which leads me to anticipate just such a rebuttal, and, therefore, I systematically incorporate counter arguments into my message.

Such sender-receiver reciprocity can be analyzed by looking at the role-taking activities and feedback signals, and the consequent personal adaptations of each party (separately or jointly) as reciprocity. Reciprocity, in other words, is the combined influences of such behaviors on both parties as they adjust to each other.[25] Thus, adaptation and reciprocity are very similar ideas, but not exactly the same.

Understanding the need for reciprocity helps in understanding the listening responsibilities of both the source and the receiver. In the present analysis, the focus is on listening, so more attention is given to the responsibilities of receivers. At the same time, the behavior of listening is so closely linked to that of the sender (because of the need for reciprocity) that it is difficult to isolate the responsibilities of one party from the other. (See Box 4.4.)

Responsibilities of senders.   There are several listening responsibilities that are unique to the sources of messages:

1. Senders have a responsibility to understand *what content is to be communicated* before it is actually stated. Common observation indicates that much of the content that people communicate is not well thought out. In fact, poorly structured messages are frequent. This type of message confuses further the already difficult listening process. How can receivers ever be expected to listen effectively if senders

are careless in the formulation and preparation of the meanings they try to transmit?

2. Senders should consider carefully the *way a message is to be communicated* because this has a substantial effect on the way it is received. Should it be a formal statement, transmitted seriously, or should it be stated informally, with kidding and joking as a part of the transmission? Deciding how a message will be communicated is part of planning how it is to be received. Obviously, then, how a

message is sent will influence a receiver's ability to listen to it. There is no single or universal way to transmit messages effectively. It is the source's responsibility to select the way of sending a message that is most appropriate to his or her intended meanings and that assists the receiver in listening to the full implications and nuances of what is being said.

3. In deciding how a message can be most effectively articulated, senders should consider carefully the *importance of context*—meanings added because of contextual factors. The context can control both how a message is interpreted and whether listening occurs successfully. As discussed in Chapter 1, there are many kinds of contextual factors. However, the real issue of role-taking concerning the setting is to ensure that the context is appropriate for the message to be communicated.

4. Individuals sending messages to others should be certain that the *nature of the receiver,* that is, who is to receive the message, is considered when designing the message. Senders who either ignore or are insensitive to the characteristics of their audience use words that their receivers cannot understand, phrasings that are inappropriate, and even words that can arouse audience hostility. Insensitive phrasings and potentially offensive language significantly reduce listening effectiveness.[26]

5. Senders must consider the *consequences* of a message prior to its transmission. An old saying is that you "can't unring the bell." At one time or another, many of us regret having said the wrong thing, and it may not even have been something obviously inappropriate. Such troubling communication seriously limits a receiver's ability to listen.

Responsibilities of receivers. Just as senders have clear responsibilities, there are also a number of obligations unique to receivers.

1. Receivers should determine the *amount of effort* necessary for both maximum understanding and comprehension of what is communicated. Although effort is important in effective listening, not all messages are worth listening to, so receivers should be discriminating in their efforts to listen. Because we cannot listen with total effort to all the messages sent to us, we must determine from what is initially communicated how important it is for us to make the considerable effort required for effective listening. This type of decision involves discriminating carefully among the goals discussed earlier—information seeking, evaluation, and recreation.

2. Receivers should be able to *understand the reason or reasons* a particular message is being communicated. This responsibility is an extension of the previous one. That is, receivers need to be able to distinguish between important and unimportant message content. They also need to be able to identify content that is either relevant or irrelevant to them personally. The person who calls on the phone, unsolicited, with a sales pitch about why we should buy insurance against falling meteors may not have our best interests at heart. Good listeners ask themselves such questions as: Why is this individual sending this message to me? Is what is being said important? Is what this person is saying worth what it will cost me to listen? The simple act of asking these questions can alter significantly the way a message is received.

3. Receivers should always consider the *physical and social context* they are in when interpreting a given message. There are a number of obvious reasons why where a message is transmitted can shape the way it is received. The contexts within which messages are transmitted and received can alter the way receivers listen. For example, two workers at a job site discussing the solution to a problem will be more attentive listeners than if they were to discuss the same problem in a bar after work. Declarations of undying friendship after the consumption of large amounts of alcohol may not have the same level of accuracy as those made under more sober conditions. As with

the other receiver responsibilities, the issue of discrimination is important. To be effective listeners, we need to be able to discriminate competently among various communication contexts.[27]

4. Receivers should take into consideration *who* is communicating the message when interpreting it. There are a number of ways to explain this particular receiver responsibility. One is in terms of source credibility, or believability. Messages sent by trustworthy transmitters are almost universally listened to by receivers. Unfortunately, many of the people with whom we come into contact are not highly credible; how believable we perceive a sender to be can vary substantially. Moreover, in certain situations, even if we don't perceive an individual to be particularly trustworthy, what he or she has to say may have the ring of absolute truth. Who is speaking, as well as what that person says, can have an effect on the effort we are ready to expend to listen.

5. Receivers should make every attempt *not to overreact* to either what is being said or how it is being communicated. Often, receivers forget that an important and primary objective of all communication encounters is to come as close as possible to sharing meaning experiences. Failure to recognize this objective can arouse a variety of ill-advised responses to incoming messages. Inappropriate responses can decrease overall listening effectiveness. For example, if an individual compliments us on our appearance one day, it may be tempting to conclude that he is doing so because of a romantic interest. However, this may be far from the truth. Or, if on another occasion, an individual disagrees with our point of view, we might conclude that she "has it in for us" and is an enemy. Again, we may be way off target.

Sender-Receiver Similarity

In Chapter 2 it was explained that the use of language in communication is possible only because human beings have an enormous *mem-*

ory capacity. Each of us learns, organizes and stores personal meanings and shared symbol-referent customs in elaborate schemas. Thus, we are able to communicate as we do because we have such a high capacity for learning and remembering.

Effective listening depends partly on that same ability to recall previous experience. That is, our ability to listen is based on prior experiences we have had that parallel those of the source of the message. Listening cannot be effective unless we can experience some degree of shared meaning with the individual transmitting the message. This is what is meant by **sender-receiver similarity.** When we attend to and make an effort to comprehend what an individual is saying, we will succeed or fail, depending on whether we are able to construct meanings that are the same as, or at least very similar to, those intended by the source.

Efforts to increase accuracy in communication are widely used in business and industry where the bottom line is cost-effectiveness in the workplace. One corporation, a manufacturer of space satellites and vehicles, avoids the costs of hiring people by creating new work teams out of previously unacquainted employees.[28] Whenever a new item is being considered for inclusion into the company's product line, a group of current employees who have not worked together previously are assigned to the project. This can raise the level of accuracy in their communications about the new product, which can then increase their efficiency and productivity. In this way, the company has the advantage of having employees who are already knowledgeable about the work, even though they have not worked as a team previously.

Essentially, this is a problem in effective listening. Remember that shared experience is one important key to competency in this task. Effective listening skills are an important part of what enables people to work together efficiently and harmoniously as a team. Therefore, in forming such teams it is important to improve listening skills by providing opportunities for team members to share certain kinds of experiences. In particular, they need to get to know one another as individuals so that, in a team situation, they will be able to understand and anticipate how each of the others will assign meaning to the messages they send and receive.

Several approaches to getting employees acquainted very quickly have been tested. In one particular procedure, after the teams are created, provision is made for members to spend the time necessary to get to know one another well enough to be able to work together. This is done by providing for one-on-one interactions between all possible pairs in the team. After spending sufficient time in one encounter, individuals switch and pair up with another member of the team. This activity continues until each member of the work team has had a chance to get acquainted with every other member. Employees communicate with and listen to one another during all these encounters. Because these people have already worked with the company a while and know the general type of work they will be doing, each has had experiences that can contribute to their understanding of what other members will say. They are all members of the local community. They tend to be similar in terms of education; they have a similar income level; they tend to share a common lifestyle; and they have many other characteristics and experiences in common. In short, because of these similar stored experiences they quickly become able to listen effectively to one another.

How does this example from industry increase our understanding of listening skills in general? It shows that listening effectively is easy or difficult depending on the degree to which the sender and receiver *are similar*. For example, two college students can communicate and listen to each other with a relatively high level of accuracy. They can do so even if they are from different schools because they share many common experiences. However, a college student and a person of similar age who went directly from high school to work in a factory will have a much more difficult time listening effectively to each other. Thus, the ability of people sending and receiving messages to re-

call similar experiences (while listening) influences their understanding. Unfortunately, the listening problems of dissimilar people are not easily solved. Additional listening effort is needed to understand accurately what someone dissimilar to us is saying.

Misconceptions That Impair Listening

In addition to those already discussed, a number of other factors can reduce our listening effectiveness. These include making inaccurate assumptions about what listening requires, plus a number of physical, personal, and even cultural factors that can limit accuracy when listening.

Inaccurate Assumptions about Listening

Ineffective listening may result from having made inaccurate assumptions about the listening process.[29] There are at least four common misconceptions made by poor listeners. These include assuming that listening is *easy*, that it is just a matter of *intelligence*, that it requires *no planning*, and that one who *reads well* can automatically listen effectively.

Listening is easy. Our earlier discussion about recreational listening indicated that thinking about listening as fun or relaxation changes the way we attend to and understand what is being communicated. A common misconception related to this idea is that *all listening is easy.* Certainly, some of the listening we do is in fact easy, but most of it definitely is not. We have indicated repeatedly that effective listening is a complex activity that requires effort. Moreover, good listeners are not born; they are *made—* through hard work. Approaching listening with the assumption that it is effortless, amusement, play, or in any other way just easy is certain to lead to difficulties in interactions with others.

It's just a matter of intelligence. A second common misconception about listening is that all smart people listen well. The conclusion that seems to follow from such an assumption is that "I am smart; therefore, I am already a good listener." Unfortunately, this is not a logical conclusion. Recall the earlier example of Paul. He's no dummy, but he is not a good listener. This is not to say that dumb people make good listeners. More accurately, smart people, dumb people, and those in between can be either good or bad listeners,

Listening requires no planning. A popular belief is that because we engage in a great deal of listening every day, we need not plan so that we can do it more effectively. We assume that the large amount of listening we do as part of our routine automatically makes us good listeners. This is totally inaccurate. It is true that all of us engage in a multitude of communication interactions every day, and that whenever we assume the role of a receiver in an interaction, we do something that resembles listening. Unfortunately, most of us neither practice good listening skills nor have the ability to assess the effectiveness of our own listening behavior. What, then, do we actually learn from most of the listening we routinely do on a day-to-day basis? In fact, we learn almost nothing. Effective listening follows from having planned carefully, not just from sheer frequency of doing it.

Read better; listen better. A rather curious but misguided assumption is that by improving our reading ability, we will also improve our listening ability. This idea is founded on the belief that what is acquired in learning one skill automatically transfers to another, even though what is learned is different. This is an interesting idea, but no psychological or educational research has shown that this transfer actually occurs. Certain skills can generalize across a variety of activities, such as being able to run fast, which probably would help in making a touchdown at a football game or winning a foot race—but listening and reading are not based enough on common skills to allow for the same kind of transfer.

Five Barriers to Effective Listening

In addition to the incorrect assumptions just discussed, a number of different types of *barriers* to effective listening need to be considered.[30] The term *barrier* here refers to any condition that can reduce the accuracy in communication. Most of these barriers to effective listening can be grouped into five broad categories. These include *physical conditions* where the communication takes place, *personal problems* that the receiver may have, *cultural differences* between the parties, *prejudices* a listener may have toward the sender and misunderstanding of *connotative meanings*. Earlier, such conditions were referred to as "noise," and it was noted that there were a number of conditions that could reduce accuracy in communication.

Physical conditions. It is surprising how often physical noise can interfere with effective listening. Unfortunately many people tend to ignore such obstacles and assume that they have no influence on the accuracy of their communication. Nothing could be further from the truth. This type of noise interference can come from any number of causes which are often beyond their control. This includes sounds caused by printers, cars and trucks, lawn mowers, dishwashers, aircraft, and any other source that physically blocks our ability to hear. Another type of external barrier is loud voices in the background. These can either distract us or limit our ability to receive messages. Listening effort and concentration must be especially high when the location is noisy from any such physical sources.

Personal problems. The most obvious personal conditions that pose barriers to good listening are physical ones. Sickness, exhaustion, and discomfort caused by illness all limit our ability to listen effectively. Overindulgence in alcohol or even food can reduce our listening capacity. Also, if we have something on our minds that distract us, such as financial problems, a sick relative or friend, a stressful relationship with a loved one, or a preoccupation with a future event, our ability to listen is affected. We can also be so overextended at work or study that we are unable to concentrate effectively on the communication. Finally, one additional personal issue that can decrease listening effectiveness is *apprehension* about listening to others. Some people experience a high level of "receiver anxiety" when they try to process information from others, and this can interfere with their abilities to receive and interpret what is being said.

Cultural differences. Many of the problems of ineffective listening are brought about by differences in the cultural backgrounds of the communicating parties. This does not refer only to people from different countries trying to communicate, where languages and ways of life can pose barriers. For example, in Chapter 3 we noted that women in the workplace often find that men "just don't get it," even though women repeatedly tell men that sexual advances are inappropriate in that setting. This is a classic case of a cultural barrier to effective listening. In part, this communication failure occurs because of major differences in the cultural worlds of traditional men versus contemporary working women.

Differences in cultural beliefs of this kind occur widely. Individuals from low-income backgrounds may have difficulty in listening to the affluent and well-educated. Management may not listen carefully to the complaints of workers. Those from dominant groups in society may not hear what minority groups are saying. In any complex society with a diverse population, such cultural differences can pose problems. People from different backgrounds often define various features of reality in different ways, which can make it difficult to hear what is being said when communication crosses such lines.

Prejudices. A fourth set of barriers to effective listening is based on personal **prejudices.** These are a product of cultural differences

among various kinds of people in society. Thus, individuals may share with others like themselves negative attitudes toward another specific category of people. Commonly, these prejudices are based on unrealistic beliefs regarding that particular category of people. Common examples are anti-Semitism and prejudices against African-Americans, Hispanics, or even people who have wealth or power. The personal behavior resulting from such beliefs is a tendency to *prejudge* any member of the negatively defined category. Such prejudgments are usually based on **stereotypes**—assumptions that all people in a certain category are alike, regardless of their individual merits.

It is clear that such stereotypes can pose significant barriers to effective listening. They prevent us from perceiving and understanding the actual characteristics, abilities, or intentions of an individual simply because he or she is a member of the negatively defined category. Thus, it doesn't matter what that individual is actually saying; the message is perceived within the framework of the negative beliefs that are the basis of the shared prejudice.

Prejudices can truly mislead us. We may not realize that we judge people within stereotyped beliefs. For example, like the traditional men in the previous discussion of sexual harassment, we may believe that we know exactly what women want and like. They do not see their beliefs as a stereotyped view of women, or even a particular bias. Thus, such unthinking ways of judging people can influence how we listen, or fail to listen, without our actually realizing it.

The point here goes beyond common and well-documented prejudices, such as those focusing on race or ethnicity. Those are very obvious. More subtle is the fact that we may have a difficult time listening objectively to someone who is a member of virtually any category if we are convinced that such people lack good judgment or cannot perform effectively in some areas. For example, we may "tune out" individuals who do not have a college education, who have limited income; or who are older, or younger, than we are—assuming that they could not possibly appreciate our concerns and viewpoints. Particularly subtle are prejudices concerning physical attractiveness. We noted in Chapter 3 that many people tend to overrate the competence and capacities of men and women who are unusually handsome or beautiful while seriously underestimating the abilities of those who are unattractive or disabled.

Generally, then, prejudice against categories of people is an especially difficult problem in listening. We explained in Chapter 2 that in all acts of perception we rely on *labeled categories* of the features in our physical and social world. We use labels as concepts to make sense out of the world. We have to do this in order to cope efficiently with aspects of reality we encounter repetitively. However, if we are listening to a person representing a labeled category of people we judge to be negative, our listening is influenced by the schemas of beliefs we have constructed for that entire category. Like the mirrors in amusement parks that distort images, such prejudicial schemas twist the meanings we construct as we process the message. In other words, our beliefs about the entire category in which that person can be classified become part of her or his incoming message. In this way, we construct meanings and interpretations that were never intended by the source of the message.

Connotative meanings. A final category of barriers to effective listening is represented by the connotations we read into messages. Connotative meanings are those personal, subjective, and unshared interpretations we have for certain verbal and nonverbal symbols and signs. Obviously, these are not part of the meanings intended by the source, and when we build them into our interpretations of an incoming message, we impair our listening and reduce the accuracy of the communication. For example, you might remark to your friend, "Professor Jones is *such* an easy grader." Your friend, who knows Professor Jones only too well, recognizes immediately that your real

meaning is that the professor is anything but an easy grader.

The influence of connotative meanings on accuracy can be exasperating when either or both senders and receivers associate connotative meanings with the symbols used in a message. Senders may unintentionally use them in encoding messages, while receivers may use them in decoding and interpretation. It is an exasperating problem because it is so hard to detect. We have all come away from encounters feeling that we completely understood and totally agreed with someone, but then later discovered that the other person recalls a completely different version of what was said and what the agreements were. Often, we conclude that the person either has a faulty memory or is deliberately misrepresenting what was said. What we may be experiencing in this situation is an erosion of accuracy in communication due to the very different connotative meanings in the encoding-decoding processes of sender and receiver.

Very little can be done about this influence on listening. Usually, neither party realizes he or she is failing to separate connotative and denotative meanings. However, as listeners, we can be aware of the problem. If we find ourselves in that stressful situation of recalling a communication differently than the other person, we can then search for sources of confusion brought into the encounter by each individual. (See Figure 4.1.)

A Seven-Feature Plan For Strategic Listening

Any person can become a more effective listener by using a systematic plan.[31] This plan is not difficult to understand because its strategy can be based on the factors already discussed in this chapter. Such a plan can be viewed as a *series of steps* we can take to improve both our listening skills and our ability to interpret messages more accurately. The specific activi-

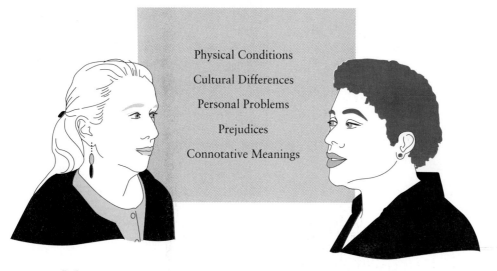

FIGURE 4.1

Barriers to Effective Listening
There are various barriers to effective listening, including personal issues with the listener
and context issues, such as where, when, and how the communication is taking place.

ties that can make up such a plan are described below.

Understand Your Current Listening Skills

The first step in assembling a strategic listening plan is to ensure that we clearly understand our present level of skills as listeners. Because each person has a unique personality, and because there are important individual differences (in attitudes, intelligence, interests, and many other factors) among people, each of us performs the role of listener in a particular way. Communication scholars designate these individual characteristics that influence our communication accuracy as **receiver eccentricities.** Simply put, they are those personal attributes and individual personality differences that either help or hinder our capacity to receive and interpret messages accurately.

Logically enough, before we can begin to refine our listening skills, we need to *identify* our current strengths and weaknesses as listeners

and our receiver eccentricities. These will provide the foundation on which to develop a plan to improve our skills. Remember, our overall objective is to sharpen our skills while minimizing our weaknesses.

Part of minimizing weaknesses involves the unlearning of poor listening habits and replacing them with good ones. To illustrate, we can ask ourselves several questions: Are there any *personal problems*, illnesses, or stressful conditions in our lives that will reduce our listening effectiveness? Can we understand people whose cultural characteristics are *different* from our own? Do we understand our *personal prejudices* well enough so that we can listen closely to what people of all kinds are really saying? Are we making *inaccurate assumptions* about the listening process of the kind we discussed earlier? Although we may not be able magically to set aside all of these problems, by becoming aware of them we take the first step toward minimizing their negative influence on our listening skills.

BOX 4.5   A *Closer Look*

Features of a Sound Listening Plan

1. *Understand your current listening skills.* Each of us is a unique individual who performs the task of listening in characteristic ways. The individual attributes that influence how well you listen are called your receiver eccentricities. You need to understand your eccentricities as a beginning point for an effective listening plan.
2. *Prepare to listen.* Prepare yourself to listen by understanding the concept of the sender–receiver reciprocity. This requires that you be open and sensitive to all kinds of sources and to the content of what they are saying.
3. *Control your concentration.* Learn to concentrate actively on what a person is saying. Such concentration rests on the distinction between active and passive listening. Such concentration must be selective, with the greatest effort focused on important messages and least attention on irrelevant ones.
4. *Show alertness and interest.* Appear to be listening even if your attention sometimes wanders from what a speaker is saying. The act of trying to show interest actually results in more effective attention to and understanding of a sender's message.
5. *Search actively for meaning.* Search actively for essential meanings in a sender's message, and summarize them in your own terms. Seek clues to take into account how the sender's background may influence what is being said.
6. *Keep active while listening.* Avoid slipping into a passive manner of receiving, with accompanying daydreaming and distraction. This may require changes in behavior, such as adjusting posture, more active breathing, or other shifts away from a relaxed mode.
7. *Suspend judgment about message and source.* Premature judgments about a person's intentions, qualifications, or actual positions can interfere with what is being said. Therefore, withhold early closure about the real meanings being transmitted, and wait until after the entire message has been heard.

Prepare Yourself to Listen

The second step of the planning process is preparing ourselves to listen. As discussed previously, effective listening is largely a product of the degree to which senders and receivers have *adapted* to one another to enhance their reciprocity. Preparing ourselves to listen, then, requires that we be sensitive in relating to others. We must be open to all kinds of sources and receptive to what they are saying.

One way of preparing ourselves for this type of receptivity is to guard against any hidden listening *barriers* and to fulfill those *receiver responsibilities* considered earlier. In effect, we have to be like a runner who is warming up and getting ready for a race. This means preparing ourselves to adapt to the speaker in order to achieve the required level of sender-receiver reciprocity. It also means anticipating the need to expend effort, to assess the intent of the person transmitting the message, and to understand the implications of the context, as well as recognizing the danger of overreacting.

Control Your Concentration

The third step of planning emphasizes controlling our *level of concentration*. Here we begin to expend the effort needed to be a good listener. This step addresses this question: How actively do we concentrate on what others say to us? This idea is related to the earlier discussion of active versus passive listening. Remember, this approach is based on the idea that effective listening is *no accident*. It requires that we deliberately and consciously attend to and try to comprehend what is being communicated to us. At the same time, a good listening plan allows us to maintain a reasonable amount of control over our concentration. As noted earlier, some messages need not be given the same level of attention as others. When a message seems important, however, the time has come to really concentrate.

Show Alertness and Interest

The fourth step in a good plan is to show or demonstrate alertness and interest to a sender when we listen. That was a problem with Paul in our opening vignette. He was reprimanded harshly by his boss for appearing to be not listening. What good listeners look like was described in earlier sections of this chapter—that is, how they engage in specific kinds of *overt behaviors* that lead senders to believe they are listening to them intently. This does not mean faking an attentive look. However, looking the part does, in fact, improve communication accuracy. Often, senders will try to communicate more effectively when they see that they have a good listener.

Search Actively for Meaning

The fifth step in a listening plan is to provide for *deliberate concentration* on the intended meaning of messages. In this step, we need to develop ways to construct for ourselves the meaning the source intends. This requires that we understand any significant cultural differences between ourselves and the source, as well as grasp how our personal prejudices may distort meanings of messages from people who are different from us. We can engage in a sort of reverse role-taking by trying to understand the purposes of the source's choice of symbols, nonverbal cues, and rules of syntax and grammar. This brings us back to our earlier notion of sender-receiver reciprocity. The point here is that if we are to comprehend messages accurately, we need to look for every clue to what the person is trying to say. Here we take into account the person's characteristics, possible

connotative meanings, and implications of the setting or context. If in doubt, we can ask questions, provide feedback, and follow up with requests for further details.

Keep Active while Listening

A sixth part of a good plan is to consider ways that will help us maintain a high level of activity during listening. Many people would like to be effective listeners but they can't seem to be active during the process. Some can't seem to exert any effort at all. Other individuals truly intend to listen actively, and they expend the necessary effort in the initial stages of an encounter, but as communication proceeds, their level of activity declines. Their motivation subsides; their degree of effort decreases; and they misinterpret the message. Most of us have experienced such decreases in activity. Consequently, this is a critical step in the formulation of a good listening plan. (See Box 4.6.)

Actively maintaining our determination to listen is a little like psyching ourselves up to run a race. Many competitors have lost races because they failed to develop the right mental outlook. Also, a runner must actually be the first to cross the finish line in order to be the winner, not just lead most of the way. In the context of listening, our efforts to attend to and comprehend messages need to last through the *entire encounter*. If listening deteriorates before our interaction is finished, we will likely miss something critical. There are no universally effective approaches to maintaining a high level of listening activity. Each person needs to use his or her own personal resources and determinations to continue listening until a sender has completed transmission of a message.

Suspend Judgment about Message and Source

The final aspect of a good listening plan is to avoid *prejudging* either the source person or the message. It is not easy to separate one's feelings about the person—and the labeled categories he or she represents—from the meanings of the person's message. However, if we can recognize our personal biases, we can take them into account in our listening plan. This kind of deliberate self-assessment helps to identify our problem areas. With this insight, we can limit their influences on our objectivity.

In overview, this seven-part plan may seem complex. Indeed, it may not be possible to start doing all the activities at the same time. A sensible way to start using the plan is to try to master one or two steps first, and incorporate additional parts later. As progress is made, adding activities will correspondingly improve your listening skills.

Chapter Review

- Effective listening is one of the most important of all communication skills. Fortunately, it is one that we acquire as a result of learning. This means that it can be analyzed, understood, and improved.

- Listening is the process in which individuals actively make the effort to maximize their attention to, and comprehension of, what is being communicated to them. People listen to acquire knowledge, to evaluate incoming messages, and for recreation.

- Learning to listen well is an important part of getting along with others, influencing people, and getting them to think of us in positive terms. Although passive listening is adequate for some recreational activities, a far more active effort is required in social and professional situations. Looking the part—through overt actions, expression, body posture, and eye contact—is an important strategy for becoming an effective listener.

- During the listening encounter, a reciprocity develops between source and listener. The source is responsible for formulating messages clearly, using an appropriate style of transmission, being aware of the influence of context, understanding the unique characteristics of the receiver, and assessing ahead of time the possible consequences of the content. The receiver, on the other hand, is responsible for determining how much effort is needed to listen, assessing the intent, appreciating the implications of the context, and avoiding overreaction. Listening effectiveness is reduced to the extent that people make erroneous assumptions about listening, including the assumption that listening is easy. Moreover, barriers to effective listening arise from five major sources: physical conditions, personal problems, cultural differences, prejudices, and connotative meanings.

- The seven-feature plan for strategic listening outlined in this chapter can help to improve our listening skills.

Key Terms

social efficacy	sender-receiver reciprocity	stereotype
criteria (in listening)	sender-receiver similarity	receiver eccentricities
adaptation	prejudice	

Notes

1. This account is based on an actual incident that occurred when one of the authors was serving in an executive role in a major corporation.

2. Listening problems are common in industry. In a recent survey of training directors in Fortune 500 industrial and Fortune 500 service corporations, 59 percent of those studied reported that they had formal training programs for employees to improve their listening skills. See: Wolvin, A. W., & Coakley, C. G. (1991). A survey of the status of listening training in some Fortune 500 corporations. *Communication Education, 40,* 152–164. See also: Cooper, L. O. (1997). Listening competency in the workplace; A model for training. *Business Communication Quarterly, 60,* 4, 75.

3. Clark, J. (July 7, 2002). A case study in learning to listen. *The Boston Globe,* p. D–8. Dr. Clark is the course administrator for the American Academy on Physician and Patient; Medical Director of the Addiction Resource Center Midcoast Hospital in Brunswick, Maine; and Lecturer in Medicine at Harvard Medical School.

4. Hampton, L. (2001). Five ways to really irritate your employees. *Business Credit, 103,* 20–22.

5. Bostrom, R. N., & Waldhart, E. S. (1988). Memory models and the measurement of listening. *Communication Education, 37,* 1.

6. Watson, K., & Barker, L. L. (1985). Listening behavior: Definition and measurement. In R. Bostrom (Ed.), *Communication yearbook 8* (pp. 178–197). Beverly Hills, CA: Sage.

7. Rankin, P. T. (1926). The measurement of the ability to understand spoken language. Unpublished doctoral dissertation, University of Michigan. University Microfilm Publication No. 4352, 1952.

8. Nichols, R. G. (1948). Factors in listening comprehension. *Communication Monographs, 15,* 154–163; and Nichols, R., & Stevens, L. (1957). *Are you listening?* New York: McGraw-Hill.

9. For complete discussions of the accumulation of experiences see: Baddeley, A. D. (1976). *The psychology of memory.* New York: Basic Books; and DeFleur, M. L., & Plax, T. G. (1980). Human communication as a biosocial process. Paper presented to the International Communication Association, Acapulco, Mexico.

10. Goss, B. (1982). Listening as information processing. *Communication Quarterly, 30,* 304–307.

11. Barker, L. L. (1971). *Listening behavior.* Englewood Cliffs, NJ: Prentice-Hall; Meyer, J., & Williams, F. (1965). Teaching listening at the secondary level: Some evaluations. *Speech Teacher, 15,* 299–304.

12. Brooks, W. D., & Heath, R. W. (1985). *Speech communication* (5th ed.) 89–90. Dubuque, IA: Brown, W. C. & Weaver, C. H. (1972). *Human listening: Processes and behavior.* Indianapolis: Bobbs-Merrill.

13. Hamilton, C., & Parker, C. (1987). *Communicating for results* (2nd ed. p. 20). Belmont, CA: Wadsworth.

14. Vander Houwen, B. A. (1997). Less talking, more listening. *HR Magazine, 42,* 8, 53.

15. Sarbin, T. R., & Allen, V. L. (1968). Role theory. In G. Lindzey, & E. Aronson, (Eds.), *The handbook of social psychology* (pp. 488–567). Reading, MA: Addison-Wesley.

16. Taylor, A., Rosegrant, T., Meyer, A., & Samples, B. T. (1986). *Communication* (4th ed., pp. 143–145). Englewood Cliffs, NJ: Prentice-Hall.

17. Pearson, J. C., & Nelson, P. E. (1985). *Understanding and sharing* (3rd ed., pp. 57–61). Dubuque, IA: William C. Brown.

18. Folger, J. P., Poole, M., & Stutman, R. (2001). *Working through conflict: Strategies for*

relationships, groups, and organizations (4th ed.). Boston: Addison Wesley Longman. See also: Cousins, R.B. (2000). Active listening is more than just hearing. *Supervision, 61, 9,* 14–15; Cohen, C. F. (1999). When managers mediate . . . stuck in the middle with you. *Dispute Resolution Journal. 54,* 3, 65–69.

19. Howell, W. S. (1982). *The empathic communicator.* Belmont, CA: Wadsworth.

20. Mehrabian, A. (1967). Orientation behaviors and nonverbal attitude communication. *Journal of Communication, 16,* 324–332.

21. Samovar, L. A., & Mills, J. (1986). *Oral communication: Messages and responses* (6th ed., pp. 84–85). Dubuque, IA: William C. Brown.

22. DeFleur & Plax, Human communication as a biosocial process.

23. Bandura, A. (1977). *Social learning theory.* Englewood Cliffs, NJ: Prentice-Hall.

24. *Sender-receiver reciprocity* is a contemporary term that communication scholars use for what George Herbert Mead called "interpersonal adjustment" early in this century. See: Mead, G. H. (1934). *Mind, self and society: From the standpoint of a behaviorist* (Charles W. Morris, Ed.). Chicago: University of Chicago Press. See the discussion of interpersonal "adjustment," p. 44.

25. This idea resembles what has been shown in research on how individuals vary in the degree to which they attend to others. This attentiveness has been studied as an aspect of "involvement," "perceptiveness," and "other-oriented perceptiveness." See: Cegala, D. (1981). Interaction involvement: A cognitive dimension of communicative competence. *Communication Education, 30,* 109–121; Cegala, D., Savage, B., Brunner, C., & Conrad, A. (1982). An elaboration of the meaning of interaction involvement: Toward the development of a theoretical concept. *Communication Monographs, 49,* 229–248.

26. For a discussion of which receiver characteristics can affect listening see: Plax, T. G., & Rosenfeld, L. B. (1979). Receiver differences and the comprehension of spoken messages. *Journal of Experimental Education, 48,* 23–28.

27. For a discussion of environmental characteristics that are thought to affect listening, see: Watson, K., & Barker, L. L. (1985). Listening behavior: Definition and measurement. In R. Bostrom (Ed.), *Communication yearbook 8* (p. 185). Beverly Hills, CA: Sage.

28. This example is drawn from the experience of one of the authors, who served as an executive in such a corporation for several years.

29. Brooks, W. D. (1974). *Speech communication* (2nd ed., pp. 80–84). Dubuque, IA: William C. Brown.

30. McIntyre-Birkner, R. & Birkner, L. R. (2001). Overcoming roadblocks to effective learning and communication. *Occupational Hazards, 63,* 4, 12–13; Hansford, B. (1988). *Teachers and classroom communication,* 43–46. Orlando, FL: Harcourt Brace Jovanovich; Watson & Barker, Listening behavior, pp.183–185.

31. Hagevik, S. (1999). Just listening. *Journal of Environmental Health, 62,* 2, 46.

Communicating Interpersonally

N o, it wasn't love at first sight. Even though Carmen found Philip attractive, she didn't think he was her type. In fact, it was quite some time before she really even noticed him. He was rather quiet and he seemed almost remote from all the others. They had first met at a party, where they had exchanged small talk. Later they were in a class together and they sometimes chatted briefly afterward. What he slowly began to reveal about himself began to intrigue her. She suspected that there must be much more to learn about this mysterious young man. As the semester went on, they had coffee after class. Eventually Philip asked her out for dinner and a movie. Carmen immediately accepted. Before long they were dating steadily and spending hours talking on the phone, and enjoying their time together.

As the relationship developed, Carmen also found herself disclosing more and more personal information to Philip. She knew that she could trust him to be sympathetic and kind to her about anything she shared with him. She even risked telling him about her fears that she would never be able to measure up to her father's demands and expectations. Always, Philip seemed to understand exactly how she felt about her dad, and about other things that mattered to her.

As time went by, Carmen and Philip began to refer to themselves not so much in terms of "you" and "I," but as "we." Their references to themselves changed to phrases like, "We need to go to the bookstore" and "We have to make plans for dinner." As this took place, their friends also began to see them as a couple. When Philip said something like "Jim and Mary invited us to have dinner with them," Carmen couldn't have been more delighted. She had come to believe that this relationship would move well beyond dating. In fact, she finally decided that she wanted to live her entire life with Philip—and even make babies with him!

It wasn't long after that when Philip asked her to marry him, and they became formally engaged. A bit later, they began to make plans for their marriage—who would be invited, who would be the best man, the bridesmaids, where they would go for their honeymoon, and all the rest. However, they both decided that it would be best to wait another year until each had finished college. At the height of their intimacy, it appeared to everyone who knew Carmen and Philip that they were a devoted couple. They seemed so happy together, so committed, and so loving. Surely these two would live happily ever after!

But something happened. The first sign was that Carmen couldn't get Philip to commit to a specific wedding date. This seemingly minor issue marked the point when their relationship began to erode just a bit. Even after they moved in together during their senior year, Philip would not agree on an exact date. Later, after they had finally graduated from college, there still was no wedding date on the calendar. It seemed that Philip always had some reason for putting off the wedding. He always had excuses. He pointed out that, after all, neither of them had yet found a permanent career path,

they still were in debt from student loans, and they had a number of problems with their future in-laws to work out. Carmen was becoming impatient.

Carmen remembers clearly the event that marked the real beginning of the end. That day, Carmen had prepared a surprise candlelight dinner for Philip, but her hopes for a romantic evening were dashed when Philip brought home some buddies from work to watch a football game on TV and drink beer. Carmen was furious. Why hadn't he called to check with her first? She strongly criticized him after his buddies left. Then Philip got mad and accused Carmen of trying to own him and control his life. That night they had a terrible fight. It was after midnight before they both calmed down.

After that, Carmen recalls, it was never the same. Both of them tried to repair the damage, but she was convinced that Philip never really wanted to make a commitment. She began to see him as immature and self-centered. He saw her as controlling and vindictive. Some time later, it was clear to both of them that the relationship was over. Philip stayed out later and later with his friends after work, and Carmen made herself scarce when Philip did come home. Finally, Carmen moved out. That was the end of their relationship. Now, they never even see or talk to each other.

The changing relationship between Carmen and Philip illustrates various phases that can characterize *interpersonal communication*, which is the focus of this chapter. The study of interpersonal communication looks at the kinds of messages people use in the stages of the gender relationship that Carmen and Philip passed through. At first, they made *an initial assessment of each other* in a casual encounter. They found each other attractive, and slowly developed an increasingly closer relationship. Then, over time, they *became a couple* by establishing more intimate ties to each other. Later, after they knew each other well, each saw that the relationship was less and less rewarding. It began to erode, leading them to *disengage*. Finally, they *separated permanently* and the relationship was totally finished.

Communicating in an Interpersonal Context

In a general sense, **interpersonal communication** is a process of using language and nonverbal cues to send and receive messages (between individuals) that are intended to arouse particular kinds of meanings. Thus, interpersonal communication incorporates all the verbal and nonverbal concepts and the principles of listening discussed in previous chapters. Although it is no different from other forms of human communication, it is set apart because it focuses specifically on interactions between two people.

This chapter examines interpersonal communication mainly within the context of establishing intimate gender relationships, which in some cases lead to permanent lives together, but in other cases end in separation. This focus on intimate gender relationships is deliberate. There are many other contexts in which interpersonal communication can be analyzed—relationships between friends; among family members; and, of course, at work. All are important. These other types are discussed in some detail in later chapters. However, the intimate ties that men and women develop are the basis of the most important and meaningful human experiences. Through such interpersonal communication, emotional relationships are established and maintained. If they work out, they may become the foundation for establishing families—the most basic of all social institutions. If they fail, both the individuals and

the society as a whole suffer a loss. For this reason, they are the focus of this chapter. As noted, communication in other types of interpersonal relationships will be discussed later.

As you will discover in this chapter, interpersonal relationships, good or bad, do not just happen: As they are being established and as they are failing, they are outcomes of communication exchanges. In both cases, these exchanges can be thoughtfully managed or awkwardly bungled. It is important to realize that such relationships are not static; they are constantly changing. As in the case of Carmen and Philip, they often move from lesser to greater levels of intimacy—or the reverse, from a deeply meaningful and rewarding relationship to one that satisfies neither party and is punishing.

The role of interpersonal communication in the development (or demise) of any given close relationship can be examined within the framework of (1) **engagement**—the process by which people try to move from an initial impersonal relationship to a more personal one, (2) **management**—using communication strategies to maintain valued interpersonal ties, and (3) **disengagement**—making use of communication strategies to withdraw gracefully (or not so gracefully) from a close association with another and remain apart permanently. We begin by discussing the process of interpersonal communication in a *general sense*. What are the major characteristics of this form of human communication, and what does it do for people as they develop close relationships with each other?

Characteristics of Interpersonal Communication

Some theorists argue that interpersonal communication is really a matter of degree and is not restricted by the number of people involved in the exchange.[1] In this book, however, the process of interpersonal communication is discussed in the context of two major background features: First, interpersonal communication takes place in the **dyad**, which is a technical term used by social scientists for *two people in*

Interpersonal communication is the foundation on which intimate human bonds are developed and maintained over long periods of time.

a relatively enduring social relationship.[2] Second, as the individuals involved come to know each other better, their relationship tends to move from *impersonal* to *personal;* that is, they become increasingly close and intimate. With these two features in mind, six key characteristics of interpersonal communication emerge.[3]

Interpersonal communication begins with the self. The term *self* is central to the process of communication.[4] **Self** (sometimes **self-image** or **self-concept**) is a complex idea, but it is not difficult to understand. It can be defined as *that pattern of beliefs, meanings, and understandings each individual develops concerning her or his own personal characteristics, capacities, limitations, and worth as a human being.* In other words, the self consists of our personal conceptions of *who* we are, *what* we are, and *where* we are in the social order. Our position in the social order within our society is determined by how we are classified into categories and on criteria judged broadly as important, such as age, gender, education, income, and ethnic identity.

Defined in this way, the self is our personal and subjective configuration of beliefs about how we are classified and evaluated, by ourselves and others, in terms of standards that most people feel are socially important.

The significance of the self-image or self-concept is that who, what, and where we think we are dictates to a large extent how we relate to and communicate with others. Considering our biological, psychological, and social makeup, we bring to our relationships with others complex beliefs about ourselves as human beings. Furthermore, when we communicate with others, we quickly form a set of beliefs (right or wrong) about who, what, and where *those persons* are in the social order. By the same token, those with whom we communicate bring to the process complex self-conceptions of who, what, and where *they themselves* are in terms of important categories and criteria. In addition, they quickly form an image *about us!* In a very real sense, then, we can recognize at least *four images at work* in the process of interpersonal communication. It is a crowded scene, consisting of my self-image, my image of the other, the other's self-image, and the other's image of me.[5]

These four patterns of belief about self and others truly can influence interpersonal relationships. For example, a young university professor may believe that she is attractive, hard-working, liberal, intelligent, independent, and a feminist. Another person, a young blue-collar worker who is a high school dropout, may consider himself clever, a bit reckless, hard working, a born gambler, irresistibly attractive, muscular, and committed to the notions of male dominance and superiority.

Suppose now that by an unusual set of circumstances these two individuals were brought together on a blind date. Although Hollywood might design a scenario whereby the pair overcome their differences and wind up romantically in each other's arms, in the real world these two would have a great deal of difficulty communicating in a way that would bring them closer together.

Previous chapters have shown that people who are very different may or may not have the same set of beliefs about each other that they entertain personally about themselves. These differences can serve as *serious barriers* to effective interpersonal communication. For example, the young woman in our imaginary blind date would be likely to form an image of the young man as a "dull, macho boor." He, in turn, would be likely to put together an image of her as "stuck-up, pushy, and hostile."

The selves or images of others that we construct, and that we project upon them as we engage in interpersonal communication, are what in ancient times were called **personae**, which means "masks." Masks were often used by actors to indicate the characters being portrayed. Today, we use the term *personality* for much the same purpose—to label the major psychological traits and social characteristics of an individual. Similarly, our "self" image is our imagined "personality."

Although you may never have realized that there can be as many as four distinct personalities or images involved in a conversation be-

tween two people, the situation is actually even more complex. After all, when you talk to someone, you cannot help but imagine what that person is thinking about you. Does he or she see you as gauche or sophisticated, as attractive or plain, as bright or stupid? Do you seem interesting or dull? Is what you are saying clear or confusing? How are your intentions being judged?[6] In much the same way, the other individual is doing exactly the same thing, putting together an image of what you are probably thinking about him or her. Thus, there are two additional images present during any interpersonal conversation: What you think your image is in the mind of the other person and what that person thinks is the image you have constructed about him or her.[7]

By now it may seem that there is almost an army of images that are present and playing a part in what initially seemed like a simple two-person exchange. It is true that all six personae are involved, and that these images of self and other help shape what is said and what is understood. Fortunately, the process of interpersonal communication takes place so rapidly that most of us ignore these complexities and simply carry on our conversations. At the same time, if you want to gain skill in interpersonal communication, you may want to think closely about these self and other images to help analyze your limitations and develop more effective strategies.

Interpersonal communication is fully transactional. More than in any other context, interpersonal communication is based on our simultaneous transactions model.[8] As communicators, each party uses verbal and nonverbal symbols and other signs to construct messages around his or her intended meanings. At the same time, the receiver brings similar, or possibly different, meanings to the task of receiving and interpreting that message. Information is returned in the form of feedback, and each communicator adjusts by role-taking for the next phase of the process. Thus, each party simultaneously influences the other's behavior while being influenced in return.

Interpersonal communicators share physical proximity. People have to be physically near each other to engage in interpersonal communication. They might talk on the telephone or exchange letters, but that is mediated communication, and it lacks important elements of the interpersonal process we are discussing. Interpersonal communication takes place with two individuals engaging in face-to-face interaction. This rules out all forms of impersonal exchanges or those in which interaction is conducted over longer distances. For example, we cannot have an interpersonal relationship with a rock star, movie actor, sports figure, or television personality who has no knowledge of our existence as we sit in the audience.

By being in physically close proximity, communicators are able to increase their chances for understanding each other accurately and efficiently. This is accomplished more easily with the accessibility of feedback. When we communicate one on one in physical proximity, we are able to recognize even the most subtle verbal and nonverbal cues that tell us whether or not we're being understood as intended. We can instantly detect eyebrows that suddenly go up, the hint of a frown, eyes that glaze over, tears beginning to form, a jaw that tightens or relaxes, a nose that turns up, a meaningful shift in body position, and other nonverbal cues that provide important feedback.

In interpersonal communication, such subtle and obvious reactions are immediate and frequent, but in other communication contexts, they may not be readily observed. As a result, in the face-to-face situation we are in a better position to adapt to each other's concerns. We can follow up with questions and comments, try to explain our position in another way, pause to let the other person talk, and appreciate the fact that we are able to interact flexibly and competently with one another.

Interpersonal communication is shaped by social roles. When people are engaging in interpersonal communication, what they are saying—that is, the content—can be interpreted only within the context of the roles that define their overall relationship.[9] For example, if we were to witness a man and a woman (whose role relationship is not known to us) arguing in the lobby of a hotel, we might attempt to analyze the situation by relying first on the content of the messages exchanged. The verbal content of the messages indicates that she wants some money from him and he's refusing to come up with it. Their nonverbal cues seem to indicate that their exchange is intense, serious, and evolving into an argument.

Without knowing anything else about the people involved, we could interpret their exchange as hostile or defensive, depending on the actual words employed by each party. However, to rely on what is said, verbally and nonverbally, is often insufficient for understanding the full meaning of such an argument. We have to understand the *nature of the social relationship* between the two people—the role that each is playing and how their roles are interrelated. For example, the woman and man could be married. The woman could be the man's daughter, or the man might be the woman's son. It is possible that the woman (or the man) works for the other person. The woman could be an undercover agent or police officer and the man a suspect. Or, the man might work for the hotel and the woman might be a guest. Notice how the interpretation of the underlying meaning of the argument changes from one set of such role relationships to another. Both content and relational messages, then, *interact* in determining the meaning of any interpersonal exchange.

Interpersonal communication is uniquely irreversible. There is no way to "erase" a regrettable message the way we erase a computer disc, unwanted sounds on an audiotape, or unwanted images on a video. All too often we find ourselves afflicted with "foot-in-mouth" disease, wishing we could take back the harsh words and labels that hurt someone in the heat of an argument. We can say we're sorry, but unfortunately we cannot make the person forget the unkind words. This "unerasable" feature of many kinds of communication is the case when a judge tells a jury, "You are instructed to disregard what this witness has just said." However, it is unlikely that the testimony will disappear entirely from their memories.

Interpersonal communication is not repeatable. We can all recall a special event with someone that we might wish we could experience again. You may have heard your parents talk sentimentally about how they first met and fell in love. What they said to each other, at least as they recall it, had such special meanings. Others are convinced that their high school or college years, when they communicated in rewarding ways with their friends, were the best times of their lives. Yet we all know that we cannot go back and relive the exact same communication experiences again. Even if we had one of those wonderful time machines, of which science fiction writers are so fond, we would find ourselves viewing it all with the changed perspectives, altered feelings, and new interpretations that come with later experience. Inevitably, we would communicate differently.

Overall, then, interpersonal communication is in one sense simply one form of the human communication process that was described in Chapter 1. However, it does have the above six characteristics that distinguish it from other forms. The characteristics of interpersonal communication are summarized in Box 5.1.

Reasons for Initiating and Maintaining Relationships

Missing from our analysis of interpersonal communication thus far are the reasons for which people initiate and try to maintain close relationships. Clearly, such relationships require a great deal of time and effort, and they are often accompanied by a great many stresses and emotional costs. Nevertheless, they can also yield very satisfying rewards. In this complex and uniquely human activity there is a kind of **cost–benefit ratio** that results when a person forms and maintains a close personal tie

---

BOX 5.1   *A Closer Look*

Characteristics of Interpersonal Communication

Interpersonal communication distinguishes itself from other forms of communication by two key features: (1) It takes place within the dyad, and (2) it is the means by which two people move their relationship from impersonal to personal. The following are characteristics of interpersonal communication.

- *Interpersonal communication begins with the self.* Our self-image influences how we relate to others.
- *Interpersonal communication is transactional.* Both individuals simultaneously influence each other's behavior, while being affected in return.
- *Interpersonal communicators share physical proximity.* By being close to each other physically, individuals increase their chances of understanding and being understood.
- *Interpersonal communication is shaped by social roles.* A written transcript of a dialogue is insufficient to show what is truly meant in an interpersonal conversation. Interpreting what each person means is determined in part by the context or the roles that define the relationship.
- *Interpersonal communication is irreversible.* No matter how much you may want to erase a regrettable message, you cannot. Once the message is sent, it's likely to be received and remembered!
- *Interpersonal communication is unrepeatable.* There is no way you can go back and experience the same interpersonal event in exactly the same way. Changed experiences, perceptions, and feelings alter the way we view past exchanges.

with another individual. For most people, the nature of this ratio influences both the formation and the stability of the relationship.

What are the costs and what are the benefits of this consequence of interpersonal communication? Perhaps the most important answer to this question is that human beings *want and truly need* close personal relationships. Indeed, life can be lonely and shallow without them. Thus, interpersonal communication is the foundation on which intimate human bonds are built. This is true of every kind of close personal relationship. Such interpersonal affiliations characterize the ties between devoted family members, trusting friends, and loving members of opposite-sex and same-sex relationships. There are many other kinds of one-on-one human bonds. Some are more intimate than others, but all are important. In each case, they are founded on effective interpersonal communication. In addition to those already discussed in detail, the list includes such ties as a mutually respectful relationship between employer and employee, professor and student, neighbors, and colleagues at work.

Three broad reasons can be identified for engaging in lasting interpersonal relationships. One is to obtain much needed information about *ourselves*. Another is more pragmatic: Friends, family members, and other intimate associates help us solve a long list of *problems of everyday living* that would be difficult to handle alone. Finally, in terms of *costs and benefits,* we develop close personal relationships with the people whose company and behavior are least costly compared to the benefits that they provide for us. Each of these reasons deserves to be understood in greater detail.

Constructing and maintaining a positive self image. Earlier in this chapter, we noted that one of the main characteristics of interpersonal communication is that it begins with the self. This was emphasized because it is one of the most significant of the benefits that are derived from interpersonal communication. For example, almost all of us love to tell others what a good person we are, and we especially enjoy hearing others say nice things about us. This may seem to be nothing more than a comment on egocentrism and human vanity. However, it points to deep psychological needs that we all have concerning the origins of the self-image and how it is maintained. As noted earlier, the self is a set of beliefs we entertain about who and what we think we are. As was explained, we learn answers to those questions when we observe the reactions of others toward us (i.e., the looking-glass self). What has not yet been explained, however, is why we urgently need *positive* responses from others, as we relate to them in hundreds of subtle ways through interpersonal communication.

Psychologists have understood for a very long time that every clinically normal person wants, needs, and enjoys a positive self-image. If we have to accept a negative one, even on a temporary basis, it is a difficult and miserable experience. To gain a positive self-image, we look early in life for people who will supply us with favorable evaluations of our behavior and characteristics. Although we cannot deliberately choose our family, we can respond coolly toward those family members who do not give us the responses we want and need, and warmly toward those who do. However, we can choose our close friends, and we screen them carefully, often without even thinking about it. That is, from the available pool of individuals we encounter, inevitably we find some who respond to us in a positive manner. They are the ones we value. They provide the *benefits*. Others, who are critical or negative can be rejected on the grounds that such unimaginative clods can be discounted as of little worth and deserve to be denied our friendship. Thus, by careful screening, selection, and recruiting of accommodating associates, we can build and maintain a satisfying self-image.

At the same time, our friends and associates need the same kind of positive feedback from us. They have their own self-images to construct and maintain. A part of the *cost* in the cost–benefit ratio, then, is that we must make continuing efforts that provide our valued family members, friends, or lovers with supportive and positive evaluations that will fulfill *their* needs.

Such considerations explain in large part why we find *ourselves* to be our favorite, our most engrossing, and our most completely captivating topic. We are anxious to share with others the details of our day—how we cleverly outwitted the professor, received approval from the boss, or put the clerk at the store in her place. We show what noble and long-suffering but clever persons we are when we describe the crowded subway, the unbearable freeway traffic, or the other pressures we have to endure. We offer personal testimony to our intelligence and good taste when we discuss the outstanding dinner we have planned for our date tonight, or our generous intention to take that date to a movie. We then look for self-image–fulfilling signs of approval and appreciation.

Of course, we like to hear what happened to the other person too, but if our friend, spouse, lover, or relative talks too long about his or her positive qualities and behavior, we are likely to become bored. We are willing to provide feedback that shows sympathy, approval, subtle applause, or commiseration as needed by the other—up to a point. After all, this is part of the cost we pay for the rewards of the relationship; but soon we will attempt to turn the conversation around again to those topics we feel reflect favorably on us—to those issues and events that best meet *our* needs as topics of discussion.

In summary, then, one of the most important reasons for entering into relationships with others is to learn more about how others perceive and feel about us. However, one of the built-in problems of constructing a self-concept on the basis of evaluations and assessments offered generously by mothers, sweethearts, or good friends is *validity*. That is, such intimate associates are unlikely to offer a dispassionate and balanced system of reality checks. They often lie! They tell us our new outfit "looks nice," when it is actually frumpy. They say we are "looking better," when we are obviously still suffering from an illness. Their reactions to us

are usually positive, and seldom negative. The consequence is that such feedback distorts the self-image we construct. Therefore, if we want to understand ourselves from a more objective perspective, we have to look beyond our immediate circle. The problem there is the reverse. Some whom we encounter will exaggerate our shortcomings or reject us on the basis of trivial criteria.

Either way, we are deeply dependent on the reactions and implied evaluations of others for constructing and maintaining our self-image. Anyone who wants to develop a realistic, if not always flattering, self-concept needs to rely on *many sources,* not just on those who provide positive responses.[10]

Coping with daily problems. Although we rely heavily on others to help with our self-image, we also need others for many practical reasons. Consider how difficult your life would be without the cooperation of others. If you have ever moved from one apartment to another, you may have counted on your friends' showing up to help pack, lift, and move. In the unlikely event that no one came, you might have found yourself unable to transfer the table from the kitchen onto the truck! Routinely, many of us rely on someone for assistance, such as taking the car in to get it worked on. Rather than waiting around at the shop for hours, we hope to have a friend or family member drive there with us and, when the car is ready, back again to pick it up. Individuals close to us supply information we need, work with us on projects, and even help with housework while we do the dishes. In short, we rely heavily on others to help us cope in a pragmatic manner with the realities of day-to-day life.

We are especially dependent on those close to us in times of stress or grief. Our friends and family members serve a **cushioning function.** They supply emotional support when we are anxious or afraid, when tragedy strikes, or even when we are just feeling down. They stand between us and an uncaring world, providing an emotionally safe haven when events beyond our control make life difficult. In many ways, then, both practical and emotional, we need and want their assistance in our efforts to control or adapt to the constraints of our environment.[11]

Maximizing benefits and minimizing costs. This is a very old but very valid idea. In 1789, the British philosopher Jeremy Bentham published *An Introduction to the Principles of Morals and Legislation* in which he developed a complete explanation of human political, social, and personal behavior, called **utilitarianism.**[12] Bentham claimed that people behave according to the *principle of utility,* which simply means that we choose to engage in those behaviors that maximize pleasure and avoid those that result in pain. This idea laid the foundation for more contemporary psychological theories of learning that stressed rewards (pleasure) and punishment (pain) as the basis for everyday, habitual behavior. Today, we no longer believe that Bentham's particular formulation of utilitarianism provides final answers, but it remains the basic framework for what psychologists call a cost–benefit ratio for those punishments and rewards that ultimately guide our actions.

Generally, then, the part played by rewards and punishments in shaping interpersonal relationships remains important. For example, spending a major holiday all alone can be a dismal (even punishing) experience. It is simply more fun, more rewarding, and more pleasurable to share such a time with those we love. Similarly, celebrating a new job, graduation from college, a birthday, winning big in the lottery—all these are events that few people want to experience alone.

For most of us, just being with certain people is rewarding in itself. We simply feel better when we are with those special friends or loved ones. By the same token, we all know people who make us feel bad about ourselves. Whenever we are with them, it turns out to be a punishing experience. In terms of maintaining a positive self-image, we actively avoid spending time with them if we possibly can. It stands to reason, then, that we do not associate frequently, if at all, with those who ridicule us, find us distasteful, or perceive us as unworthy of their affection or attention. A number of research studies support this modern form of utilitarianism.[13]

For all the above reasons—constructing a positive self-image, coping with daily problems, and maximizing pleasure while minimizing pain—we initiate or develop interpersonal relationships with others. We need and want others to like us, talk to us, and share life experiences with us. However, such benefits do not come without cost. Once you decide to enter into a relationship with another person, in order to obtain those advantages in the long run, you must pay a price. At least initially, you will need to follow a number of fairly rigid communication rules that provide self-image building responses for others.

Engagement: The Initial Encounter

What is the process by which two people first meet each other, begin to think that they have a basis for a closer relationship and then go on to develop one that increases to intimacy? Moving from the very first moments in the history of such an encounter to developing a devoted relationship involves a set of relatively regular stages. As this section will explain, the first stage is the *initial assessment* of the person on the basis of physical appearance and his or her opening remarks. Then, if the encounter survives those critical first moments, the next stage is likely to be characterized by **small talk.**

The Critical First Moments

Our first, even momentary, impressions of someone new can influence dramatically our decision to move forward into a relationship. Unfortunately, those initial impressions are often based on *trivial details* about the person we have just met. In fact, the first information we receive about a person usually consists of nonverbal cues—the person's overall physical appearance, clothing, and other "packaging." Yet, it is these initial data that will determine to a considerable degree whether we want to move on to any closer relationship.

If we do decide to continue, the next important information we receive about the candidate comes during the first few minutes of interpersonal exchange. Inevitably, it is based on a relatively superficial and nondisclosing kind of conversation. Nevertheless, both the first impressions we form and what immediately follows can be critical in establishing a new relationship.

When people strike up a conversation with someone new, they rely on well-established routines. These are often called **scripted conversations** because they are like lines rehearsed from a play. They can also be called **stereotypic** in that they are highly standardized and predictable.[14] Conversations can be classified as scripted or stereotypic if they follow clear, even rigid, rules in certain well-defined situations.

Exchanges of this type are easily illustrated by what we almost always say when we are introduced to someone we do not know. Our initial "Hello" is usually followed by their "How are you?" Most of us understand that we are not expected to answer such questions factually or at any length with a detailed health or personal problem report. The normative reply is "Fine." In reality, you may be feeling rather poorly because you had an accident an hour earlier, or you've been fired from your job, or your dog just died. Still, the expected and usually provided answer is "Fine. How are you?"

Why do this? Why shouldn't we just say whatever we want to say? There are very good reasons for not violating the norms of getting together. First, it is *customary*—meaning predictable and comfortable. Research shows that new acquaintances almost always exchange factual, nonopinionated, and relatively superficial information.[15] Second, few of us are willing to disclose to a new acquaintance any of our deep, personal feelings about sensitive issues. Not knowing the stranger, we cannot trust that she or he will interpret our disclosures in the right way.[16]

Generally, then, initial conversations with others almost always center on safe topics. It is for this reason that in such situations we often find ourselves discussing such trivia as the weather and sports, whereas we scrupulously avoid issues and topics that would disclose more significant attitudes and beliefs. Obviously, there are at least some interesting exceptions to this pattern. Under some circumstances, we may reveal our whole life story to people we have just met and whom we never expect to encounter again! This behavior was illustrated by sociologist Georg Simmel in 1908 in his classic essay, "The Stranger." He explained that when one is with a stranger, such as one sitting next to us on a train (or a plane in modern times), that person is both distant and near at the same time. Under these circumstances such a person can become an instant confidant. The reason is that the stranger is there and available, but at the same time, there is virtually no risk involved in disclosing personal information to a person whom we know we will never see again.[17]

Under most circumstances, however, after the very first moments, if the potential relationship survives beyond initial impressions and early assessments based on the scripted conversation of getting acquainted, it can move to a stage where the messages exchanged by the parties consist of small talk. These are discussions that focus on topics of general interest—ones that have little personal significance or emotional involvement. Although this may sound trivial, it can be a subtle and complex part of establishing a closer relationship. In fact, being able to manage small talk effectively may be one of the most important skills that an individual can develop.

It may seem strange to maintain that small talk may be the most important communication skill we can possibly master! We can say this in all honesty because every dyadic social relationship, to some degree, begins to develop during a stage of small talk. That is, after we form our earliest impressions of a person, we usually get to add additional assessments based on her or his initial small talk. This gives us a somewhat more fully developed image of what that person is like. Without this kind of exchange, we would have a difficult time moving on through the early stages of getting to know the other person. In fact, small talk can be so important in establishing a relationship with a new acquaintance that it should probably be called "big talk."[18]

Despite the importance of small talk, many people claim that they dislike it. We've all heard comments like "I hate small talk; it's so superficial" or "I went to the party and all they did was blab about trivialities." The final putdown of a person in the minds of many is something like "He can go for hours and not say a single meaningful thing!" We could find wide agreement that small talk consists of little more than meaningless chatter. What is missing from such negative interpretations is that small talk serves critical purposes. Beneath its apparent superficiality, small talk can be critical in the development of an interpersonal relationship that is destined to become more meaningful.

Auditioning for friendship.
One function of small talk is to provide what communication researcher Mark Knapp calls an "audition for friendship."[19] Individuals assess one another in an effort to determine whether or not a relationship is worth establishing. Obviously, not all new acquaintances audition well, and in many cases no relationship forms—or it remains purely at the level of small talk. Such an acquaintance-only relationship is likely to die on the vine later.

Controlling self-disclosure.
Small talk also allows us to reveal just a bit of who and what we are to others—in a cautious and safe way. We all have at our disposal a variety of *personae* that we can reveal to someone who hardly knows us. We can display our humorous side, our sensitive, or our highly critical side. At the same time, the other person in the interaction is providing us with similar information. In these early stages, we have little more to go on than superficial communication exchanges. Consequently, both individuals involved in the exchange are attempting to reveal limited personal information—while simultaneously struggling to decipher who and what the other really is!

Painless interaction.
One of the most useful features of small talk for many of us, when meeting another person for the first time, is that it is easy and relatively painless. It does not require a lot of brain power and it makes few stressful demands on new relationships. As such, small talk can provide a welcome alternative to discussions about more significant topics. This allows us to approach more meaningful dialogue and debates about complex and important themes at our own pace. Good manners dictate that we rarely leap right into heavy discussions with new acquaintances, or even those we know well but haven't encountered for a while. Think about it: The last time you called an old friend you probably initiated the conversation around light and effortless topics. Perhaps you followed the greeting with a brief discussion of the weather, a recent sports event, or a concert you just attended. All of this small talk may have served as a prelude to revealing information of a more important nature—your latest job prospects, progress in school, new friend, recent child, divorce, new car, or death in the family and so on.

The feeling-out period associated with small talk has been well documented. What researchers have identified from studies of conversations between new acquaintances is an exchange of very basic biographical data.[20] People in initial encounters tend to reveal simple demographic and biographical information, such as "My name is Dianne" and "I'm from St. Louis." They don't start out with "I'm involved in a messy divorce" or "I just got fired from my job." The simple disclosures are usually reciprocal. Dianne should be able to predict that a new acquaintance will reveal his or her name and hometown. If it is a former friend, he or she might provide basic data on life changes, such as a new child or new job. Importantly, both persons tend to avoid heavier topics because neither wants to risk disclosing their deep feelings about such matters as the abortion controversy or their troublesome health problems.

In summary, then, small talk makes it possible for each party to continue assessing the other, adding to initial impressions formed mainly on the basis of physical appearance. It enables each to begin developing a biographical database from which to round out their first impression of each other. In this way, small talk provides a basis for each person for determining whether or not they would like the relationship to continue. Because small talk serves these functions, it cannot be dismissed as trivial and superficial. For the analysis of interpersonal communication, it is a serious consideration deserving careful analysis. Indeed, when looked at in this way, it may be one of the most important communication skills a person can master.

The Skills of Small Talk

Perhaps one reason some people dislike small talk is simply that they lack the specific skills needed to handle this type of encounter well. Some people have no idea what to say after "hello." One source of worry is that what we say will be seen as trite and that others will find our attempts at conversation boring. Worse yet, we may be concerned that we will fail the "audition" and the interesting other will find us unworthy of further contact.

Unfortunately, in spite of its importance, researchers have not produced a body of systematic knowledge concerning the specific skills that comprise successful small talk. No book, chapter, or even single study has been published that addresses the details of verbal and nonverbal communication strategies that distinguish effective from ineffective small talk. Nevertheless, the sections below offer some helpful guidelines from the present authors that can be considered in your attempts to evaluate and improve your own small-talk skills.

Maintain eye contact. As in any form of interpersonal communication, eye contact is important. Indeed, it is mandatory for effectively initiating encounters with new people. As discussed in Chapter 3, eye contact is typically interpreted as a nonverbal sign of *interest*. Most people are pleased and appreciative when someone appears to take great interest in what they have to say. Eye contact provides a clear and standard nonverbal message communicating just that. Consequently, those who are successful at small talk rely heavily on *looking earnestly* at their partner. Note, however, that direct eye contact may be considered rude in some societies with different cultural rules. The Japanese, for example, are taught to avoid staring directly into someone's eyes. Instead, they concentrate on the lower part of the face during a direct conversation. This can pose problems for Americans who do not understand this norm. However, in this society, lack of eye contact may seem to signal a failure to listen closely, or even disinterest.

Be nonverbally immediate. Other nonverbal cues can signal interest as well. Recall from Chapter 3 that nodding, leaning forward, smiling, and open body positions all suggest interest and liking to the receiver. These actions were described earlier as signs of *nonverbal immediacy*. Using such techniques is one way of establishing physical and psychological *closeness* with your partner, and that is likely to lead to an interpretation of attraction on his or her part.

Remember the other person's name. This is really important, but it is sometimes difficult to do. Shakespeare got it wrong in *Romeo and Juliet,* when he had Juliet ask, "What's in a name?" She went on to claim that names have little importance because "that which we call a rose by any other name would smell as sweet." Maybe that's true with roses, but it does not work well with people. The significance of other persons is diminished if you can't remember their names—and they recognize that. Above all, then, and without fail, be sure to remember and use the other person's name! Our names are so important to us that they are the first pieces of information we deliver about ourselves. People quickly become offended when we misspell, mispronounce, or forget their names. This signals loudly and clearly that we regard them as not worth the effort.

Several strategies can help you remember someone's name. One is to rehearse it quickly several times in your head. Another is say it out loud right away, and frequently, if possible. Writing it down can also be very effective if the situation permits. If you are unable to catch the name when introduced, ask the person to repeat it, or even spell it. In fact, asking the person for the correct spelling can be a good strategy because it implies that the name is important to you. (If the name is Smith or Jones, skip this step!)

Draw out the other person. A great skill to develop in mastering in small talk is to get the other person to talk about himself or herself. People's favorite topic is *themselves*. Capitalize on that insight by asking your small-talk partners a lot of questions about themselves, such as "Where are you from?" "Do you follow sports?" "What brings you here to this event?" (Don't ask "Do you approve of abortion?" or "Do you approve of limiting welfare?")

Indicate further interest and *active listening* with follow-up questions. Pursue their responses with directed questions or comments. When your partner indicates that he is from Podunk, Nebraska, you can develop the conversation by asking, "What brings you all the way here?" or "Do you miss Podunk? I'll bet life was different there from how it is here." So as not to turn the conversation into an inquisition, you might comment, "I like small towns. In fact, I have grandparents who still live in a small community. I love to visit them because the people there are so friendly." Be sure that your comments and questions evolve either directly or indirectly from what the person just said. Try to avoid random topic switching. If

you try that, you'll probably end up talking about what *you're* interested in, as opposed to what the other person wants to talk about.

Keep the discussion light. As was implied earlier, an important rule is to keep the conversation *light*. Should you plunge too quickly into controversial issues early in the relationship, the other individual is likely to feel threatened. No one wants to reveal their deep-seated views on religion or politics, or hear about your latest scrap with your parents and your financial difficulties at this point.

Accentuate the positive. Finally, you are better off making most of your talk *positive*. That means avoiding complaints or criticisms. Even minor complaints—such as the weather is awful, your workload is too heavy, the professors are unfair, or the team is unsuccessful—are commonly perceived as "downers." In particular, commenting negatively about other people in the room, or a mutual acquaintance, can quickly lead to some rather destructive, disagreeable interactions—particularly if your partner finds those same individuals attractive.

Generally, then, mastering the skills of small talk is not all that difficult. (Box 5.2 summarizes the important guidelines.) Once a small-talk conversation has been managed successfully, the next stage in a developing relationship is likely to be more rewarding and more enjoyable.

Management: Moving Toward and Maintaining Intimacy

Movement toward greater intimacy—close friendship and more intensity in a relationship can be a complex process.[21] The term *intimacy* is often used to imply a sexual relationship. Indeed, many people think, "We have an intimate relationship" means the two are sleeping together. However, this is not always true. People can have sexual relationships without being intimate in the sense discussed in this chapter. A

BOX 5.2   A Closer Look

Guidelines for Successful Small Talk

What do you say after you say "Hello"? The following are six ways you can become more effective at small talk:

1. *Maintain eye contact.* Looking at the other signals interest.
2. *Be nonverbally immediate.* Look like you're listening. Lean forward, smile, nod your head, and uncross your arms.
3. *Remember the other person's name.* Some tips to help you do this are: Rehearse it several times mentally; use it right away in conversation; ask for the spelling if it's unusual; write it down.
4. *Draw out the other person.* Ask questions. Find out information about your partner. Get your partner to talk about himself or herself. Ask follow-up questions too, but try not to turn the conversation into an inquisition.
5. *Keep it light.* Avoid big talk about heavy issues like politics and religion. Talk about the weather, recent news, bulletins, sports, food, entertainment, and other topics unlikely to disturb, threaten or alienate the other.
6. *Accentuate the positive.* Talk about what you like as opposed to what you don't like. Avoid negative, "downer" talk. Talk about what you like about the food, (party, weather, movie) and avoid discussing what you don't like about it.

general meaning of the term *intimacy* is the implication of trust and open self-disclosure in communication.

As will be made clear, in the development of an intimate relationship (in the nonsexual sense) much depends on the *rewards* versus the *costs* we think we have gained, or suspect we will gain, from the affiliation.[22] Some theorists claim that we take a kind of mental inventory—perhaps at a less than conscious level—to determine the relative rewards and costs that we can potentially derive from a relationship before we commit ourselves to it. This interpretation is based on a very general sociological paradigm called **exchange theory,** which was originally developed by George Homans to try to explain all forms of human social interaction.[23]

Exchange theorists maintain that we implicitly "count up" the history of rewards received from interacting with a particular other person, weigh that against the history of costs, and then make an estimate of the *worth of the relationship to us.* According to this explanation, when the cost–benefit ratio has been calculated, we make our decision. That is, when the rewards for us outweigh the costs, then the relationship is likely to be continued. Conversely, if we conclude that the relationship is too costly, it is likely that we will not pursue it. That explanation works similarly for both partners. That is, for each the cost–benefit ratio must be favorable or the relationship will not be continued.

Many current theorists believe that this utilitarian, cost–benefit approach to relational development in its elementary form is oversimplified. That may be the case, but it still has something to offer. Granted, few of us are likely to take this type of systematic inventory regarding each and every person we meet. By the same token, however, we are not likely to be consciously aware that everything we do in a positive or negative way might influence the cost–benefit ratio for the other person. Yet, most of us can imagine at least some of the rewards versus costs that are derived from a particular relationship with another person. Furthermore, we can predict some idea of what that ratio might be for that relationship in the future.

Thus, the cost–benefit principle has at least some merit: We know for a fact that most of us prefer to be around individuals who make us feel good. We understand that such people provide us with rewarding experiences as we relate to them. Similarly, we know that we do not like to be around people who make us feel bad. That is pretty basic, but it does illustrate the idea of costs and benefits. Generally, then, the classic sociological idea of costs versus benefits—the balance of rewards and punishments in an exchange—is still a viable perspective that can predict the fate of a relationship.

Assessing Costs and Benefits

If the exchange concept has merit, it must be reflected in reality. For example, when you examine your current relationships, you should find that most of your good friends, over the long haul, have provided you with greater benefits and rewards than they have costs or punishments. It is not difficult to determine this. Benefits are fairly clear. Good friends probably tell you in many ways (both verbally and nonverbally) that they like you. They may laugh politely at your bad jokes, call you when you are sick or feeling depressed, lend you money when you're broke, and tell you what a great person you are even though others may feel quite differently. To be sure, these same individuals may be burdensome from time to time, and you may not like some of the things you have to do to retain them as friends. Over time, however, it should be clear that you *gain more from these relationships than you lose.* That is if the cost–benefit ratio is positive. (If that is not the case, you may be incorrectly formulating the exchange.)

The cost–benefit ratio is a long-term matter. That is, in lasting interpersonal relationships with friends or family, the individuals involved are likely to have accumulated a kind of *reservoir of rewards* that can be drawn upon in troubled times. It is these rewards that maintain the relationship. True, they have built up a reservoir of costs as well. But keep in mind that the rewards continue to outweigh the costs. This *accumulation process* is critical for managing a relationship. In times of temporary crisis, when costs can be very high, we can turn to that reservoir of rewards to help us through. If it does not exist, the relationship can be in big trouble.

There is, however, an important exception to the preceding principle: We can put up with an incredible amount of costs as long as we can also predict that significant rewards will follow. Social psychologists refer to this as the **principle of delayed gratification.**[24] It is a very significant idea that helps us understand many aspects of our behavior. For example, millions of college students keep their noses firmly pressed to the unpleasant grindstone of boring degree requirements in the expectation that all the work will pay off after graduation. Later, they will work hard in the labor force, anticipating that significant promotions and raises in income will follow.

Applying the principle of delayed gratification to interpersonal relationships, rewards that seem reasonably certain in the future allow us to endure the more immediate costs of continuing the bond with the other person. Such costs may involve financial strain, isolation, career interruptions, or even physical or psychological discomfort. On the other hand, there is no assurance that the principle will hold true over a long period. Consider the often-repeated story of the couple who married very young while they were both still in school. Alas, they couldn't make it financially, so the wife dropped out and took a full-time job. Her reasoning at the time was that her husband would get a good job after graduation and then it would be her turn to finish school. In the meantime, the wife accumulated a lot of costs, fully expecting the husband to deliver to her the rewards of financial solvency, loving gratitude, and other forms of interest on her investment.

In reality, many such couples do not live happily ever after when there is such a high level of balance due. Husbands may resent having to pay off the debt; wives may find that they cannot endure the costs. One party or the other may find another person more attractive. In such cases, the relationship will likely terminate (usually with considerable malice).

Overall, then, this process of assessing and cataloguing the ratio of rewards and costs in a relationship is important. The outcome appears to determine whether the relationship will move forward or backward—whether it will move toward greater or lesser intimacy. Two individuals moving from casual, impersonal contact to a more meaningful relationship are likely to put a lot of energy into filling each other's reward reservoirs. At the same time, they are likely to avoid adding to each other's costs. However, as the relationship continues, problems can arise that may have a significant influence on its future. One thing that can determine its fate is the degree to which the individuals involved put themselves *at risk* by revealing core information about themselves.

Revealing Core Information about Self

When a particular relationship is rewarding, that is, when the two parties seem to make each other feel good, they usually become more and more trusting. Soon, they find themselves sharing very private information with each other that is usually reserved for only a few individuals that they know very well. Such "core" information involves risks because it requires *disclosure of very personal matters.*[25] This can be a delicate process.

Testing the water with self-disclosure. As we begin this process of mutual **self-disclosure,** we may start cautiously by revealing something about our family or friends that affects us only indirectly. For instance, we might disclose the fact that we were once arrested for driving under the influence. We can dangle that personal skeleton and then wait to see what kind of reaction such a secret will provoke. If our partner responds sympathetically, we might conclude that he or she has passed our test, and perhaps we can reveal more sensitive information. However, if the response is criticism, our partner has failed.

Once a sensitive self-disclosure has been received negatively, we generally keep the other person at a safe distance. We choose not to expose further negative information about ourselves, or our family and friends, because we now have evidence that the person is unlikely to be understanding and supportive. However, if the person passed the test, we have at least an initial confirmation that it is safe to make a more significant self-disclosure or to expose even more sensitive information. Self-disclosure, then, is a key to the development of a relationship.[26]

It all comes down to *trust.* Can we trust the other to respond sensitively to our personal attributes, our secrets, and our deep feelings? Can we be confident that the other will continue to like us after we've disclosed such information about ourselves? If we can answer yes to all the above, with conviction, then we can assume that the relationship will move toward greater intimacy.

This movement toward greater intimacy generally occurs after the initial experimental or test phase of the relationship.[27] Satisfied that the other person will remain sympathetic and supportive, we begin to intensify the relationship. The new partner has similarly established trust; we have also been tested and have passed. In other words, this is a *reciprocal* process. The rule is that, for each party, self-disclosure increases as we tell each other more and more intimate details about ourselves. We begin to reveal not just more positive information, but also more negative information. In this way we risk disclosing information that few others may know. ("I was caught shoplifting when I was eight years old. I swiped a candy bar and my folks were really mad.")

Labeling the relationship and its consequences. Before long we begin to see that our relationship is taking on a life of its own. We provide many kinds of enduring relationships with labels. In heterosexual social settings, persons of the same sex call themselves "buddies," "pals," or "best friends." This labeling process is important because it attaches specific and culturally shared meanings to the relationship that it did not previously have. Labeling identifies the relationship as a specific instance of a generally understood concept (see Chapter 2). Once we have a symbol or label that is in use for a relationship between two people, it greatly changes their own self-conceptions. Suddenly the pronoun *we* becomes far more significant than either *me* or *you*.

In the man-woman case, this welding of two people into a single labeled entity—a *couple*—has significant implications. It brings with it a "baggage" of meanings that play a part in the *perception* and *interpretation* of the two individuals. That, in turn, alters our *responses* to them. They are no longer just two separate and unique persons. They are now a single entity that has to be thought about, responded to, and dealt with socially in a different way.

This change in meaning and behavior by friends, family, and others has many consequences. As noted, it brings different kinds of responses from others. As explained in the discussion of the "looking-glass self" theory, that brings about a reconstruction of the self-images of the individuals who make up the couple. This external social process, along with an increase in self-disclosure, reinforces the movement toward intimacy.

Another consequence is that as we become a two-person dyad, in the eyes of others as well as ourselves, we find that we have established mutually accepted expectations for *relating to each other*. All these new role expectations and normative rules for social relationships as a couple make up a fairly complex and mutually held conception of social organization with guidelines that define how each is supposed to communicate with the other.

At each stage in this movement toward intimacy, the two individuals employ "secret tests" to check out the level of commitment each feels toward the other and about the relationship.[28] For instance, we might test our new partner's commitment by suggesting that it's time to meet our parents—and we all know what that implies! Or, we might mention a chance meeting with a former boyfriend or girlfriend the other day (in hopes that our partner will act possessive and jealous!)[29]

Moving to full disclosure. Assuming that all goes well, the relationship moves on to greater

and greater levels of intimacy. Throughout this entire experimenting stage, we take risks by exposing more and more about ourselves. Then we observe carefully how our partner responds to that disclosure. The more consistently our partner responds in a supportive, understanding manner, the more likely we are to *trust* that person—gaining confidence that he or she won't hurt us, no matter what we do or say. In short, once the foundation of trust is established and we reach a state of full disclosure, we have become an *intimate pair*, who are seen as such by ourselves and others.[30]

Communicating with an Intimate Other

Once two individuals believe they are in an intimate relationship, a transformation takes place in the way they *talk* and *behave* toward each other. During the process of coming together, pairs develop norms for relating to each other in their friendship or marriage. Some of those normative rules are common to almost any set of intimate communicators. For example, in their study of intimate dyads, researchers Michael Argyle and Monika Henderson found that very good friends share several rules such as "Don't nag" and "Don't criticize a friend in public."[31] However, many of the communication norms that develop between intimates are unique to their specific relationship. For example, a couple may develop a communication norm that ensures an easy escape from tedious evening social events. They share an agreement that, when one or the other feels it's time to go home, that person signals the desire to the other by exclaiming, "Well, the kids sure get up early in the morning," or some other phrase serving the same goal. The other quickly agrees, and they then begin the process of leave-taking.

You probably can think of special understandings that you share with an intimate partner concerning what messages are or are not appropriate. Some couples have norms about fighting, such as that they agree never to call each other "ugly" names when they are angry.

BOX 5.3   *Ethical Concerns*

Is "Being Intimate" a Code Phrase for "Having Sex"?

All too often people make the mistake of equating intimacy with sexuality. In fact, people typically imply that they are having sex by instead saying, "We have an intimate relationship." Intimacy and sex are not the same thing! Intimacy involves communication: communicating about personal issues—like love, sex, fears, hopes, and dreams—and making yourself vulnerable to each other.

Are couples who are involved in a sexual relationship, then, necessarily *intimate?* Of course not; guppies can have sex! A better question would be to ask, "Are couples who can talk about having sex with each other necessarily intimate?" The answer is probably so!

Movement toward greater intimacy occurs when two individuals are able to communicate their deepest held beliefs, fears, attitudes, anxi-

eties, prejudices, and concerns. When couples are able to take risks and communicate about issues that don't particularly flatter them, that don't project them in the best possible light, they are being intimate. When couples *care* enough to criticize, argue, and share with each other, they are being intimate.

Now then, what does intimacy have to do with hopping into bed or shacking up? Nothing. For those fans of radio talk show psychotherapist Dr. Laura Schlessinger, if you really want to be intimate with someone special, "Why don't you talk first and have sex later?"

Source: Dr. Laura Schlessinger, a psychotherapist, hosts a nationally syndicated radio show and is the author of: (1994). *Ten stupid things women do to mess up their lives.* New York: Villard Books.

Others insist on discussing any conflicts before they go to bed at night. You may know couples who avoid any open communication of affection in public—even refusing to hold hands. Whatever they may be, norms tend to be both personal and private to the relationship. Some may be quite explicit and a consequence of negotiations between the partners. Others are implicit and are simply assumed by the two people.

Another characteristic of participants in close relationships is their use of "intimate idioms" and "inside" humor.[32] That is, special friends or lovers generally share words, nonverbal gestures, and private meanings for situations that others may not understand, recognize, or know about. You may have friends who talk *baby talk* to each other when they are alone. Should they slip and reveal that talk in public, others may laugh or feel embarrassed for them. You may know a couple in which one partner calls the other by a *pet name,* such as "Sweetie Pie" or "Honey Bunch," when they are

alone. Or, you and your best friend may use a *shared phrase,* such as "That's nice," to signal boredom when they are interacting with outsiders. Another example of an intimate and private dialogue is *inside humor,* in the form of private jokes. It is not uncommon to see a couple crack up over a remark, when no one else thinks it is funny.

In summary, this section traced how movement toward greater intimacy generally occurs. Obviously, although some relationships follow the stages just described, others do not. Some move forward quickly and almost overnight become intimate. Others may take years to reach that stage. Even less predictable is whether or not any given relationship is likely to be successful. Life would be far more comfortable if we could determine our probability of success or failure in the long run before developing an intimate relationship with another person. Unfortunately, many different factors, situations, and events may disrupt any human relationship.

Disengagement: Communicating When Relationships Erode

So far, the focus of this chapter has been relationships in which both partners choose to move toward greater intimacy, and eventually to a stable pattern of companionship or loving affiliation. Now it's time to look at the opposite process, in which the intimate qualities of the relationship deteriorate, become a problem, and are eventually so disrupted that one or both individuals decide to leave.

When the costs involved in a relationship seem to exceed the benefits, one or both of the partners may decide to disengage, or withdraw. The reasons for this vary widely, but one important factor is what each partner *believes* to be the problem. Some answers to what circumstances lead to disengagement can be found in the study of *alienation* (psychological disaffection) between husbands and wives. This condition often leads to the disruption of marriages: According to a *Redbook* (magazine) survey of marriage counselors, the 10 most common causes of marital breakup include (in order of frequency): (1) communication problems, (2) no longer sharing common interests or goals, (3) sexual incompatibility, (4) infidelity, (5) no more fun in the marriage, (6) money, (7) conflicts involving the children, (8) alcohol or drug abuse, (9) women's equality issues, and (10) the in-laws.[33]

Assuming that such a poll meets scientific standards, these are *what people say* were the reasons leading to their separation or divorce. It probably matters little whether the real causes of these disengagements were something else. Whatever the true reasons may be, the people in the survey thought their marital breakup was due to the problems they indicated in the above list.

A basic principle of social psychology is that what people *believe* guides what they *do*. Early in the 20th century, social psychologist W. I. Thomas developed the principle of the **definition of the situation**, which essentially states that *if people believe something to be real, they will act as though it were real.*[34] We saw earlier that people's beliefs, in turn, are developed in a process called "the social construction of reality"—that is, in a communication process with others (or today from mass media). This theory has ancient roots, extending back to Plato and other early philosophers.[35] Because of these basic principles, both members of a couple undergoing disengagement often go through a process of creating their individual interpretations—their own socially constructed realities—of what they believe to be the real causes of the disengagement. These define for them what went wrong, who is to blame, what they were justified in doing, and so forth. These meanings, then, as Thomas explained, become the basis for their subsequent actions.

Explaining the Reasons for Disengagement

Whenever we finally determine that a friendship, marriage, or any other type of serious intimate relationship is coming to an end, we need to *explain why*—both to ourselves and others. In particular, we feel a need to attribute *blame*. Blame is an important concept in our culture. It provides explanations of human behavior that are easy to understand and that seem to make sense. That is, most people interpret the causes of human behavior within a *good guy–bad guy framework*. It is simple to conclude that bad outcomes are due to bad people (and vice versa). It is too difficult for most people to probe more deeply and to try to understand how human decisions and actions are consequences of complex impersonal forces and factors.[36]

Handling the pressure for an explanation. Even if we try to avoid labeling the other person as the "bad actor," others invariably will ask, "So tell me, why did you two break up?" (Read: What bad things did he or she do?) We can be flippant in our response, but then people think we're being coldhearted and cruel.

They may speculate further that we were never really committed to the relationship in the first place. And so it goes. Friends and family need, want, and expect us to give them *an accounting of what went wrong.* Furthermore, not just any interpretation will do—only a certain kind of causal explanation will be met with their approval.[37]

In a plausible accounting there has to be blame. So, for the sake of others as well as ourselves, we have to create an explanation—a believable theory of what went wrong. It has to be one that our friends and family will find acceptable. Most of us do this by identifying the bad motives and misconduct of the other person that led to the problem.

Acceptable assignments of blame.   One of the first requirements of such a blame story is that our family and friends must believe that somehow, in some way, we were justified in leaving (and were not the guilty party). In other words, we need an explanation in which we are seen as occupying the *moral high ground.* For example, if we "got dumped," we must be careful to spin a tale that does not warrant the other person's leaving!

Ideally, the story we construct should lead us to believe in our own minds, and should compel the sympathetic listener to conclude: "You made a rational decision; and you are definitely better off without such a person!" In other words, we need to convince both ourselves and others that we are still worthy and acceptable candidates for future relational ties.[38] We could be greatly harmed, both personally and socially, if we gave a story in which we assumed blame and identified ourselves as the culprit. By the same token, it may be risky to create a version that blames our partner entirely, because our partner may be making us the villain in his or her version.

Another important requirement for a story explaining a disengagement is that it should reflect a sense of *emotional maturity* and recognition that it takes two to make and to break a relationship. Consequently, a well-crafted story that will be received sympathetically by those we care about ought to include just a little bit of self-blame. It can have a lot of "other-blame," as long as we indicate at least some degree of understanding of our partner's behavior.

Generally, then, a well-designed explanatory story provides an accounting that should satisfy the needs and expectations of others, and—if well constructed—it provides a "true" version of what happened for consumption by friends and family. Also, of course, it is one that we ourselves can firmly believe. Ideally, it lets us accept only a minor part of the blame, but it must assign the lion's share to the other so that we can feel better about our part in the disengagement.

Saying Goodbye

Just as the language of intimate communicators differs significantly from that of new acquaintances or strangers, the language of individuals involved in disengagement reflects a dramatic change. Obviously, couples going through disengagement are unlikely to call each other "sweetheart" or "honey." Commonly, they revert to first names, and once again use some of the more stylized, stereotypic language of strangers. Their conversations become hesitant and awkward as they hold back disclosure. They have trouble sharing their feelings because predictable responses of support are missing.

Couples begin to disengage by a twofold process called **distancing** and **disassociation**.[39] What this means is that in their interpersonal interactions they begin transmitting messages designed to *increase both physical and psychological distance* and to disassociate themselves from their partners.

Establishing social distance between self and other.   Messages designed to achieve the goal of distancing can take both verbal and nonverbal forms, but the goal is always the same. For example, one of the simplest and most obvious ways that a person can begin to disengage is by spending more and more time away from the other. He or she may work late at night, take weekend trips to visit friends or relatives without taking the partner along; or go to plays, concerts, or movies with friends. Increased physical distance can also be achieved at home. When one partner is in the living room watching television, the other reads alone in the kitchen. At some point, one partner may continue sleeping in their bedroom, while the other takes to the guest room or the couch.

Psychological distancing can be achieved in many subtle and indirect ways.[40] The partners may look at each other less, touch less, put up such barriers as folded arms, or experience more uncomfortable periods of silence, and they may employ colder vocal tones in exchanges. Psychological distancing can also be accomplished by close control over the content of their messages. That is, as disclosure begins to shut the relationship down, one partner may be unwilling to volunteer a lot of personal information to the other. When this happens, the responses become less supportive and less sympathetic. By any of these strategies and patterns, then, both physical and psychological distance replace the close association that had been developed and maintained earlier. Distancing is a very clear and necessary aspect of the disengagement process.

Disassociation by emphasizing differences. The term *disassociation* refers to reducing the use of the couple-implying pronoun *we* and reverting to the individualistic *you* and *I*. Unwilling or unable to invest any further interest into the relationship itself, couples are likely to become concerned with their own feelings, costs, and benefits rather than those they shared earlier. Typically, one begins to hear such messages as "You only care what happens to you. What about me?" Where they once referred to "our" furniture and "our" dishes, they now talk about "my" chair and "your" mother's china. Messages about the future become messages about the past.

Throughout the disassociation process, differences rather than similarities are emphasized. Even though such differences may have existed throughout the entire relationship, they are now seen as divisive—and the couple begin to communicate and complain openly, sometimes bitterly, about the differences. The other side of this coin is that discussions centered on common likes, dislikes, and mutual interests are now more limited, or are skipped altogether. Partners experiencing disassociation come to believe that they never really had anything in common with one another. They wonder why they failed to see this before, or, if they remember that they did have commonality earlier, each may conclude that he or she has "developed and grown," while the other has failed to change.

Obviously, neither distancing nor disassociation contributes to relational bonding. To some degree, however, even healthy intimate relationships occasionally experience both of these communication processes. We cannot (and probably should not) spend every waking and sleeping moment with our partner. All of us need personal space, independence, and time away from each other.[41] We cannot (and, again, probably should not) hide or suppress all our likes and dislikes either, simply because our attitudes and beliefs differ from our partner's. Unlike intimate communicators, though, disengagers spend an increasing amount of time and energy avoiding contact and stressing dissimilarities. Whereas intimates talk about togetherness, coupling, and attachment, disengagers frequently communicate separateness, autonomy, and detachment.

Dealing With Separation: When You Can't Go Home Again

There is no easy way. Most people find it awkward and difficult to make it through the final stage of complete separation.[42] What often happens is that the majority of attempts to disengage totally from relationships can be characterized as indirect. The reason is that people don't like to confront each other. It is stressful and they much prefer to just let the relationship pass away over time.

Common Strategies for Separation

In an effort to determine the most common strategies that people use to disengage from relationships, researcher Leslie Baxter had college students describe those termination attempts they had used in actual friendships.[43] She categorized their accounts into four main strategies: (1) **withdrawal and avoidance,** (2) **ending on a positive tone,** (3) **Machiavellianism,** and (4) **open confrontation.** The first two strategies are discussed in this section, the other two in the section immediately below.

Withdrawal and avoidance.   Rather than confront the partner with a direct statement such as "The relationship is over," individuals who use the withdrawal and avoidance strategy rely on a more *indirect* approach. They are likely to telephone less frequently, to be "too busy" to get together this weekend (or any weekend anytime soon!), and to avoid making any definite plans to spend time with the other person. This could be called the "Don't call me, I'll call you" approach. The outcome (if it works) is that the couple see less and less of each other without the strain of confrontation. Before long, the relationship simply fades away.

Obviously, this strategy may work well in terminating unwanted friendships, but it would be difficult to employ when you're married. For one thing, marriage is a relationship involving the community as well as the couple, and the legal constraints defining the relationship generally require that all loose ends be tied. The partners can't just drift apart and let the relationship fade. Nevertheless, we do know that some form of avoidance and withdrawal precedes almost all disengagement attempts.

Ending on a positive tone.   This strategy represents a socially appropriate means of ending relationships. Couples who use this strategy show concern and regard for each other. They try to avoid major conflict or attempts to malign or slander the relationship. In short, *they are nice* about the breakup! In rare instances, some of these couples may revert to a less intense relationship by remaining friends. There are couples who are divorced but still celebrate holidays together, and they may even attend each other's second weddings. Positive-tone strategies are strongly encouraged for couples with children. Divorced parents who are able to resolve their differences amicably may also be able to focus on providing their children with secure, stable (although separate) environments.

More Drastic Strategies

In some cases, achieving total separation becomes extremely painful and difficult. In such cases, where there is "no more Mr. (or Ms) nice guy," it may be necessary to resort to "hard-ball" measures. Among these are two that represent a kind of last resort. The first, *Machiavellianism,* derives its label from the Italian author Niccolò Machiavelli (1469–1527), whose work *The Prince* set forth a philosophy of amoral cynicism and advice to rulers by which they could use subtle and sneaky means to gain and retain political power.[44] The second more drastic strategy is *open confrontation.* It is seldom used, as it can result in an emotional uproar, with maximum stress on both parties. Nevertheless, these two strategies are available when all else fails.

Machiavellianism.   This is clearly the most unusual strategy. That is not to say it is infrequently used. Students in the Baxter study reported a variety of ways to use this technique. What makes Machiavellianism so unusual is the manipulation and deception involved. Specifically, the strategy is to seek to convince the unwitting partner that relational termination was his or her idea and *is in the partner's own best interest,* even though the person being convinced may not have wanted the relationship to end.

Machiavellianism incorporates the principle of the definition of the situation noted earlier.

If one partner can define the breakup as the preference of the other, and he or she believes it, then that other will act on the basis of the new definition. For instance, a woman may intentionally go out with the man's best friend, knowing that he will be angry. Then, when he does express his disapproval, she exclaims "Go ahead. Leave me. You deserve somebody better than me." Or a man may intentionally provoke his partner into a fight. At the height of the argument, she gets very angry and shouts, "Go ahead, just leave. See if I care!" When he quickly takes advantage of the situation and does leave, the woman is left wondering what happened.

Obviously, there are ethical questions involved in using a Machiavellian strategy. No one likes to be tricked or deceived. Yet we know that people justify their use of this technique by claiming their partners really are better off without them. Perhaps they are right. Furthermore, some who use the technique argue that because the partner initiates the disengagement, he or she may get over the relationship a little easier than if the tables were turned—it's more dignified to leave than to be left.

Open confrontation. This strategy contrasts sharply with Machiavellianism. It is, for understandable reasons, the least used way to say goodbye. As noted earlier, no one likes to face the partner, disclose that the relationship is over, explain why this is so, and cope with the emotional upheaval that ensues. First the partner expresses shock or disbelief, then anger, and finally hurt. Individuals using the open-confrontation approach should be prepared for an emotional roller-coaster.

In reality, the disengagement of a particular set of partners may involve more than one, or even all, of these strategies for termination. A partner who is seeking separation may try withdrawal and avoidance only to discover that this tactic doesn't work. Ending on a positive tone sounds nice, but there is no guarantee of success. Machiavelliansm may be distasteful, but it might prove effective. If all else fails, there is always open confrontation. In any case, breaking up a close relationship that started on a casual basis and then slowly, step by step, developed into a stable affiliation is never an easy process. The bonds of love, affection, and deep concern for the other, and the mutual attachments that were once in place, are not easily cast off. Disengagement leaves people drained, sad, and often bitter. At the same time, if the personal and emotional cost–benefit ratio has changed, parting may make it the only viable option.

Chapter Review

- The study of interpersonal communication looks at the kinds of messages people use when they want to develop close ties to others, when they try to keep valued relationships going, and when they seek to disconnect themselves from attachments that they no longer want.

- As individuals come to know one another better through interpersonal communication, their relationship tends to move from impersonal to personal. That is, they become increasingly close and intimate.

- There are six key characteristics of interpersonal communication: It begins with the "self," it is fully transactional, participants share physical proximity, their messages are shaped by social roles, interpersonal communication is irreversible, and it is unrepeatable.

- Patterns of interpersonal communication change during the different phases of relationship development. During the initial period, people rely on scripted and stereotypic conversational rules. Because all relationships begin with small talk, these communication skills are among the most important we can master.

- To the extent that we find our initial and subsequent encounters with another rewarding and interesting, we are likely to move toward greater intimacy. Much depends on the cost–benefit ratio of rewards versus punishments we think we will gain by going forward in the relationship.

- Communication during the management or intimacy phase of the relationship involves testing the degree to which the other person is open and supportive. This process requires disclosing selected sensitive information about ourselves and waiting to see how the other party responds. Assuming the partner responds positively, we increasingly engage in disclosure. Over time, we negotiate unique rules to govern our relationship, and we generate a unique, private language system for disclosure.

- In terminating a relationship, we have to construct an account of why it went wrong that will satisfy ourselves, our friends, and our relatives. It has to earn us some degree of social credit so that we are still perceived as having the potential for a good relationship in the future. We construct a plausible story that assigns blame to the "bad actor" and puts the best face on the relational disengagement.

- Breaking up a relationship that has yielded warm and satisfying rewards is never easy. Terminating the relationship generally involves both distancing and disassociation: We avoid spending time together and begin the uncoupling process. The strategies for saying goodbye and leaving include withdrawal and avoidance; showing concern for one another, the Machiavellian tactic of manipulating the partner into believing that the disengagement was his or her idea; and sudden, open confrontation.

Key Terms

interpersonal communication	small talk
engagement	scripted or stereotypic conversations
management (communication strategy)	exchange theory
disengagement	principle of delayed gratification
dyad	self-disclosure
self (self-image or self-concept)	definition of the situation
personae	distancing
cost–benefit ratio	disassociation
cushioning function	withdrawal and avoidance
utilitarianism	Machiavellianism

Notes

1. For a more extensive analysis of the distinctions between the situational and developmental perspectives, as well as in-depth discussion of impersonal and personal relationships, see: Miller, G. R., & Steinberg, M. (1975). *Between people* (pp. 7–29). Chicago: Science Research Associates; Miller, G. R. (1980). Interpersonal communication. In C. L. Bank, (Ed.), *Human communication principles, contexts and skills* (pp. 109–114). New York: St. Martin's.

2. Although it may seem a bit strange, this term specifies rather precisely the idea of two people in a system of repetitive social interaction. It was first brought into the study of human social behavior by the 19th century German sociologist Georg Simmel. See: Simmel, G. (1902). The number of members as determining the sociological form of the group (A. Small, Trans.). *American Journal of Sociology, 8,* 158–196. For a classic discussion of the dyad and dyadic communication see: Wilmot, W. W. (1979). *Dyadic communication* (2nd ed.). Reading, MA: Addison-Wesley.

3. Pearson, J. C. (1987). *Interpersonal communication: Clarity, confidence, concern* (pp. 7–14). Dubuque, IA: William C. Brown.

4. The term *self* derives from early-20th-century social psychology in which theorists were trying to understand how a person develops personal understandings of his or her social, psychological, and physical characteristics, and the value placed on them by the society. Generally, such understandings were said to be obtained in a process of social interaction with others. See Charles Horton Cooley's discussion of the "looking-glass self," in: Cooley, C. H. (1902). *Human nature and the social order* (pp. 81–263). New York: Charles Scribner's Sons. For a more recent discussion of the role of the self in interpersonal communication, see: Barnlund, D. C. (1970). A transactional model of communication. In K. K. Sereno & C. D. Mortenson (Eds.), *Foundations of communication theory* (pp. 98–101). New York: Harper & Row, 1970; and Pearson, *Interpersonal communication,* pp. 7–9.

5. This self-image and multi-image conception of interpersonal communication was first set forth by Cooley in *Human nature and the social order,* pp. 81–263.

6. Vangelisti, A. L., & Young, S. L. (2000). When words hurt: The effects of perceived intentionality on interpersonal relationships. *Journal of Social and Personal Relationships, 17,* 3, 393–424.

7. In a very general sense, the process of "reading" the reactions of the other was alluded to in Chapter 1 when we discussed role-taking and feedback. The same kind of activity has been called "taking the role of the other" by classic social psychologists in the symbolic interactionist tradition. See: Mead, G. H. (1934). *Mind, self and society: From the standpoint of a social behaviorist* (Charles W. Morris, Ed., p. 254). Chicago: University of Chicago Press.

8. Laing, R. D., Phillipson, H., & Lee, A. R. (1966). *Interpersonal perceptions.* Baltimore: Perennial Library; Wenberg, J., & Wilmot, W. (1973). *The personal communication process.* New York: Wiley; Wilmot, W. W. (1979). *Dyadic communication* (2nd ed., pp. 10–13). Reading, MA: Addison-Wesley; and Miller, G. R. (1990). Interpersonal communication. In G. L. Dahnke & G. W. Clatterbuck (Eds.), *Human communication: Theory and research* (pp. 91–122). Belmont, CA: Wadsworth.

9. Bateson, G. (1958). *Naven* (2nd ed.). Stanford, CA: Stanford University Press; Watzlawick, P., Beavin, J. H., & Jackson, D. D. (1967). *Pragmatics of human communication* (pp. 51–54). New York: Norton.

10. For a complete discussion of the importance of the family in interpersonal communication see: Fitzpatrick, M. A., & Badzinsk, D. M. (1985). All in the family: Interpersonal communication in kin relationships. In M. L. Knapp & G. R. Miller (Eds.), *Handbook of interpersonal communication* (pp. 687–736). Beverly Hills, CA: Sage.

11. Burke, R. J., & Weir, T. (1975). Giving and receiving help with work and non-work related problems. *Journal of Business Administration, 6,* 59–78; Roloff, M. E., Janiszewsk, C. A., McGrath, M. A., Burns, C. S., & Manrai, L. A. (1988). Acquiring resources from intimates: When obligation substitutes for persuasion. *Human Communication Research, 14,* 364–396.

12. For a summary of utilitarianism, see: (1954). Bentham: Principles of morals and legislation. In W. Ebenstein, *Great political thinkers* (chap. 19, pp. 484–499). New York: Rinehart and Company.

13. Byrne, D. (1971). *The attraction paradigm.* New York: Academic; Byrne, D., & Nelson, D. (1965). Attraction as a linear function of proportion of positive reinforcements. *Journal of Personality and Social Psychology, 1,* 659–663. For discussion of related research, see: Bowers, J. W., Metts, S. M., & Duncanson, W. T. (1985).

Emotion and interpersonal communication. In M. L. Knapp & G. R. Miller (Eds.), *Handbook of interpersonal communication* (pp. 500–550). Beverly Hills, CA: Sage.

14. Originally, a "stereotype" was a rigid cylinder of cast type that fit over a large roller in a newspaper press. Repeatedly, it turned out the same pages of print. Journalist Walter Lippman applied the idea to human thinking and behavior that is rigid and unchanging. See: Lippman, W. (1922). *Public opinion.* New York: Macmillan. The term *stereotype* has been widely used since the 1930s to identify rigid beliefs of a negative sort about a particular category of people. It can also be used to describe communication behavior. See: Knapp, M. L. (1984). *Human communication and human relationships* (pp. 149–176). Boston: Allyn & Bacon; Knapp, M. L. (1978). *Social intercourse: From greeting to goodbye* (pp. 105–124). Boston: Allyn & Bacon.

15. Berger, C. R., Gardner, R. R., Clatterbuck, G. W., & Schulman, L. S. (1976). Perceptions of information sequencing in relationship development. *Human Communication Research, 3,* 29–46; see also Knapp, *Social intercourse,* p. 116.

16. Rosenfeld, L. B. (1979). Self-disclosure avoidance: Why I am afraid to tell you who I am. *Communication Monographs, 45, 63–66.*

17. Georg Simmel's original essay is contained in: Simmel, G. (1908). *Soziologie.* Leipzig: Dunker and Humbolt. For a summary of the idea in English, see: (1950). The stranger. In K. H. Wolff (Ed. and Trans.), *The sociology of Georg Simmel* (pp. 402–408). New York: Free Press. See also: Miller, G. R., & Steinberg, M. (1975). *Between people* (p. 314). Chicago: Science Research Associates.

18. Knapp, *Social intercourse,* pp. 111–112, and Knapp, *Human communication,* pp. 166–169.

19. Ibid. p. 168

20. See, for example, ibid.; Berger et al., *Perceptions of information sequencing.*

21. See Schlessinger, L. (1994). *Ten stupid things women do to mess up their lives.* New York: Villard Books.

22. Altman, I., & Taylor, D. A. (1973). *Social penetration: The development of interpersonal relationships.* New York: Holt, Rinehart, and Winston.

23. Homans, G. C. (1961). *Social behavior in its elementary forms.* New York: Harcourt, Brace & World. Exchange theory itself was derived from Bentham's utilitarianism.

24. Homans, G. C. (1950). *The human group.* New York: Harcourt Brace Jovanovich; Thibaut, J., & Kelly, H. H. (1959). *The social psychology of groups.* New York: Wiley; Altman & Taylor, *Social penetration,* p. 33.

25. Altman & Taylor, *Social penetration,* 27–29; Knapp, *Human communication,* 208–215.

26. For a comprehensive review of research on self-disclosure, see Dindia, K. (2002). Self-disclosure research: Knowledge through meta-analysis. In Allen, M., et al. (eds.), *Interpersonal communication research: Advances through meta-analysis* (pp. 169–185). Mahwah, NJ: Lawrence Erlbaum Associates.

27. Knapp, *Human communication,* pp. 36–39.

28. Baxter, L. A., & Wilmot, W. W. (1984). Secret tests: Social strategies for acquiring information about the state of the relationship. *Human Communication Research,1,* 171–202; Duck, S. (1986). *Human relationships: An introduction to social psychology* (p. 50). Beverly Hills: Sage.

29. The use of "secret tests" is also employed in deteriorating relationships. See Chory-Assad, R. M., & Booth-Butterfield, M. (2001). Secret test use and self-esteem in deteriorating relationships. *Communication Research Reports, 18, 2,* 147–157.

30. Prager, K. J. (1989). Intimacy status and couple communication. *Journal of Social and Personal Relationships, 6, 435–449.*

31. Argyle, M., & Henderson, M. (1984). The rules of friendship. *Journal of social and personal relationships, 1,* 211–238; Duck, *Human relationships,* p. 96.

32. Ibid., p. 95; Knapp, *Human communication,* pp. 225–228.

33. Safran, C. (January, 1979). Troubles that pull couples apart: A Redbook report. *Redbook,* pp. 138–141.

34. See: Volkhart, E. H. (1951). *Social behavior and personality: Contributions of W. I. Thomas to theory and social research* (pp. 7–8). New York: Social Science Research Council;

also: Thomas, W. I., & Znaniecki, F. (1927). *The Polish peasant in Europe and America* (Vol. 1). New York: Knopf.

35. For an extended overview and summary of such social construction of reality theories, and how they are important in the study of all forms of human communication, see: DeFleur, M. L., & Rokeach, S. B. (1989). *Theories of mass communication* (5th ed., pp. 228–271). White Plains, NY: Longman.

36. For an examination of the descriptions people give of current and dissolved relationships see: Hortalsu, N. (1989). Current and dissolved relationships: Descriptive and attributional dimensions and predictors of involvement. *Journal of Social and Personal Relationships, 6,* 373–383.

37. Ibid.

38. La Gaipa, J. J. (1982). Rules and rituals in disengaging from relationships. In S. Duck (Ed.), *Personal relationships 4: Dissolving personal relationships* (pp. 189–210). London & New York: Academic.

39. Ibid.

40. Hess, J. A. (2000). Maintaining nonvoluntary relationships with disliked partners: An investigation into the use of distancing behaviors. *Human Communication Research,* 26, 3, 458–488.

41. Pearson, J. C. (2001). Conflict in our intimate relationships. In W. F. Eadie & P. E. Nelson, (Eds.) *The language of conflict and resolution.* (pp. 47–56) Thousand Oaks, CA: Sage

42. This analysis incorporates a number of the ideas of Knapp, *Human communication,* pp. 263–267, and Knapp, *Social intercourse,* pp. 189–193.

43. Baxter, L. A. (1982). Strategies for ending relationships: Two studies. *Western Journal of Speech Communication,* 46, 223–241; Cushman, D. P., & Kahn, D. D., Jr. (1985). *Communication in interpersonal relationships* (pp. 96–97). Albany: State University of New York Press.

44. Machiavelli, N. (1513). *The prince.* trans. Bergin, T. G. (1947). New York: Appleton-Century-Crofts.

Communicating in Small Groups

The three of them had been friends since they first met when they were 12 years old. Jimmy, Terry, and Bob had all been in Mrs. Ostrand's sixth-grade class. Tonight they were sitting in O'Leary's Pub, having a beer after their weekly bowling match. It was Bob who brought up Mrs. Ostrand and the way they had met 10 years earlier. When they were kids, Mrs. Ostrand had seemed forbidding. They called her "the Ostrich" because she had a skinny neck and round glasses that made her eyes look large. They didn't like her much, even though in later years they realized that she was actually a kindly and patient soul trying to keep discipline over the unruly boys they had been. Thinking back, they had to admit, it was an almost impossible task.

"When I first met both of you, I thought that you were a couple of stuck-up jerks," Bob said. "I knew that both of you were from wealthier families than mine, and I just knew that neither of you would want to have anything to do with me."

"Well you thought wrong, pal," Terry said. "Neither Jimmy nor I thought about that. We both liked you from the start. What was important to us was that you made us laugh a lot. You always seemed to be able to make a joke, or say something funny."

"Yeah," Jimmy added. "I remember how you told jokes. Even though most of them were totally stupid, you just had a way of holding our attention and keeping us in suspense till the punch line. You were just great."

"We had some bad times, too," Bob recalled. "I remembered when my sister was very sick, and I was afraid that she was going to die. Both of you were there for me and helped me deal with it. I'm still grateful. I was so relieved when she recovered."

"Do you remember when the Ostrich caught us with the dirty pictures?" Terry asked.

"Oh God!" Jimmy said. "We were so scared."

"I was terrified," Bob said, "when she told us she was going to tell the principal and our parents. Thank God she didn't. I would have really caught it."

"Where did you get them, anyway?" Bob asked.

"I tore them out of a magazine my older brother had hidden in a shoe box in the closet. I found it when he was away one day. When he discovered what I had done, I thought he was going to kill me. But when I told him I would tell Dad what he had hidden, he left me alone. I think he is still upset about that!" Terry replied.

"Well that was bad enough," Jimmy said, "But when you socked John in the nose and made it bleed, I thought the Ostrich was going to have a heart attack."

"Well," Terry replied, "You guys were great. I remember how both of you claimed that Johnny had started it by punching me in the stomach, and that I was just trying to defend myself. We all stuck to that story, even though Johnny said we were all liars."

As the three friends continued to remember their days in the sixth grade, they realized how close they had remained over the years. Each of them had gone on to a different college, but they had remained in touch. Then, when each had returned to work in the city, they had renewed their friendship almost immediately. They celebrated each other's birthdays, bowled together once a week, invited each other to their homes for dinner, and generally were as close as friends could get.

These three close friends are in a **peer group**—an important kind of small group that is based on close intimate communication and strong emotional ties among its members. Along with the *family*, sociologists refer to it as a **primary group**.[1] These two groups are "primary" in two ways. One is that they are of primary importance early in life, and the other is that they serve very basic needs. Both families and peer groups have existed since prehistoric times, when early human beings led a precarious life. Close bonding between people in families and as peers was essential to survival. They remain essential today. People can exist without corporations, government agencies, schools, factories, or other kinds of larger groups, but they cannot do so without primary groups.

Looking analytically at peer groups, such as the one which Bob, Terry, and Jimmy have formed, provides many insights into the importance of small group communication in human life.[2] For example, in the three-person peer group above, communication is completely open. Every member can communicate with every other member with complete *self-disclosure*.

Sociologists point out that peer groups in early life provide initial training for communication skills. For example, on the playground and among their young friends, children learn how to be polite, what verbal and nonverbal messages make people angry, what amuses them, and what makes them sad. These are valuable lessons in which children develop

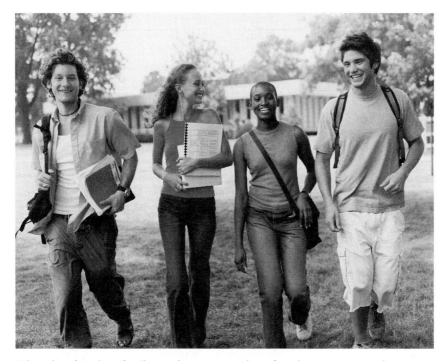

When close friends or family members interact, they often share experiences that are both unique to intimate groups and important to their development. For this reason, family and peer groups are often referred to as primary groups.

skills in role-taking and interpreting feedback. Children also develop these skills in the context of the family.

As the opening vignette illustrates, primary groups provide *sympathy and emotional support* in times of stress. Their members are *loyal to each other* in the face of outside threats. Over time they build up an accumulation of shared experiences that is the basis of the group's *social cohesion*—the ties members have to each other—the bonds that keep the group together. Both peer groups and the family, then, are primary to human development and human existence.

There are many other kinds of human groups that are very different in their goals and their rules for communication. Each is formed and carried out for different purposes. Whatever its nature and purposes, each type of group constitutes a different *context*. In the simultaneous transactions model developed in previous chapters, context was identified as an important feature that influences communication.

In many respects, human communication in any **group** is based on exactly the same concepts and principles examined in the dyadic contexts discussed in previous chapters. However, communicating with other people in any group is not the same experience as doing so in a face-to-face context consisting of only two persons. It requires different skills, follows different patterns, and has different consequences.

This chapter describes communication patterns and expectations within the context, not only of peers, but also within a variety of different types of small groups. It is important to understand the distinct rules and requirements for communication in each. These shared understandings define *who* can say *what* over *what channel* on *what occasion* for *what purpose*.

The Nature of Human Groups

Just what is a human group? This may seem to be an odd question because all of us have been members of many groups all our lives. Nevertheless, a definitive answer provides the basis for an analytical framework for discussing the communication system that people use in any human group.[3] So bear with us, and take a look at human groups in a more technical way.

Groups versus Social Categories

First of all, a human group is obviously more than one person. Also, the people involved are in some respects similar. However, that is not enough. There are many sets or collections of people who, using those two criteria alone, might seem to be groups—because either they are physically together or they are in some way alike. However, the mere fact that they are spatially near each other, or that they share some common characteristic, *is not a sufficient basis* for calling them a group.

Suppose, for example, that you came upon a dozen or more people who had gathered temporarily on a street corner to gape at an auto wreck that just happened. Later that day, you may have told a friend that you saw a "group" of people looking at an accident. However, in a strict sense, they did not make up a group. They were simply a number of people who happened to be there at the same time and engaged in similar behavior. In fact, they probably did not even know each other and probably dispersed within a few minutes. Strictly speaking, they were not a group, because they did not have any permanent basis for communicating in some regular way. Calling them a *crowd* would be more accurate.

Similarly, in everyday discussion we sometimes refer to some class of people in a population as a "group" because they all share some similar characteristic. An example would be an "ethnic group," such as Hispanics, who come from, or have ancestral origins in, a Spanish-speaking country. In a strict sense, they make up

what demographers call a "social category"—a number of people who can be *classified as similar* on the basis of some shared characteristic, in this case their (or their parents') countries of origin. Almost any shared characteristic or set of characteristics can provide the basis for identifying a social category. Wags who need to explain the basic idea of a social category sometimes use the example of "red-headed saxophone players who are left-handed and whose mothers were born in Lithuania." Yes, these people share four characteristics, but they are not a group! Nevertheless, the idea of social categories is an important one for *demographers*—social scientists who classify people using various criteria in order to study the composition of populations. They classify and analyze people in terms of age, gender, income, educational level, religious affiliation, occupation, and so on. Like the participants in a crowd, the members of such categories do not interact and communicate and probably do not even know each other. In short, they are not groups.

What, then, are the precise criteria or conditions that can be used to decide whether a set of people actually make up a group? The answer is not complicated. The first important consideration is whether the people are collectively pursuing a *common objective* by communicating and interacting together in some sort of coordinated way. People do not come together in groups for no purpose and then act randomly. They seek some goal by collective action that could not be achieved by each member acting alone as an individual.[4] For example, members of a peer group, such as Bob, Terry, and Jimmy, seek satisfactions that they obtain from each other's company. Those experiences would not be available to isolated individuals who do not communicate with each other. The satisfactions obtained in family life provide another example of a primary group objective. Larger and more complex groups—schools, factories, government agencies, and armed services—also have distinct objectives.

A second important criterion is whether the people in a group have worked out a *stable set of rules and expectations* that define how they are to communicate with each other and how to regulate their behavior to attain their goal. In seeking their shared objective, members of a group have to *coordinate* their actions within a set of understandings that define what is expected on the part of each member, what will not be tolerated, and what will be rewarded by the other members. These understandings define who is to do what; who will have more power, authority, prestige, and rewards; and what will happen to a member who does not do what the other members expect and want. This pattern of definitions and expectations is called the group's *pattern of social organization*. This is a critical feature for understanding communication within the context of any group, regardless of its size and objectives. With all the above in mind, then, a *group* can be defined as *three or more people who repeatedly interact to achieve a shared goal, regulating their conduct and communication within a pattern of social organization.*[5]

Obviously, some groups are small, intimate and informal. Others are the opposite—huge, organized in a very formal and impersonal way, and complex in the different rules for communication and behavior by their members. Nevertheless, each has its objective and each has its pattern of social organization. That pattern of mutual and shared expectations about who can communicate with whom under what circumstances, or behave in what way as a member, is an essential feature of any group that helps understand it as a context.

The Basics of Social Organization

The idea of social organization is essentially a simple and obvious one. At the same time, it can be difficult to "see" such a pattern without observing the members of a group over a period of time to see how they are relating to each other. If such observations can be made, at least four kinds of regularities can be detected in the way they communicate and relate to each other. In summary, these consist of the **norms**

that all members of the group are expected to follow; the **roles** or specialized parts that each member plays in the group; the **ranks** that they have worked out (understandings that some members have more of something than others); and the **controls** that members use to punish those who deviate negatively from the expected patterns, or to reward those who make positive contributions above and beyond those expectations. A group's pattern of social organization then—whatever its nature, size, and objectives—consists of its norms, roles, ranks, and controls.[6]

Norms. Rules that every member is expected to follow are called norms. These rules define such matters as when and where the members get together, what kinds of behaviors toward each other imply respect or disrespect, when humor is OK, when to be serious, and so on. In some groups there are dress codes, rules for intergender contacts, rules for use of space and equipment, and so on. In small groups norms are simply "understood." In large and formal ones, they may be written out in a formal way in handbooks or other official documents.

Roles. As in a play in the theater, people play different parts in a group. Mother and father act differently than brother and sister. In any group the members have to decide who does what in the group. In peer groups, all the members can act and communicate with the others in a similar way, but often even in this context some members play somewhat different roles from those played by others. In all but the most intimate and informal peer groups, the roles are different, but are linked together in such a way that each makes some contribution to the objectives of the group. This was clear in the older traditional family, where each person did different things for the group as a whole, and even the kids had their chores and obligations. In certain kinds of more formally organized small "task-oriented" groups (e.g., committees, task forces, juries, or boards) the roles are usually clearly defined. Someone serves as leader and others are members, who may perform different tasks.

Ranks. In virtually any group, large or small, formal or informal, intimate or impersonal, some members have "more" of something that is valued. They may have more power, authority, prestige, income, skills, education, or something else. This has to be accepted by the members. In groups where ranks exist, formally or informally, they are a part of the reality that each member must deal with. Acceptance may mean following orders from above, saluting (as in the military), using special titles, wearing different clothing, or just showing respect and deference to those higher in the group.

Controls. Once a group has worked out its pattern of social organization, the rules must be followed. If a member fails to meet the expectations of others, this deviance from the pattern makes it more difficult for the group to meet its goals. For example, in the peer group portrayed in the opening vignette, if Jimmy repeatedly failed to show up at the weekly bowling match, it would be a violation of the norms. If Bob had "ratted" on Terry when they were caught by the Ostrich with the dirty pictures, this would not have been consistent with the group's definition of the role of "friend." In either case, the objectives of the group would have been jeopardized. In such cases, some sort of punishment has to be administered to maintain the rules for communication and behavior. In the case of the peer group it might have consisted of nonverbal gestures, such as a frown, or verbal messages complaining about and denouncing the behavior. In other kinds of groups, negative sanctions can include a low grade, loss of pay, failure to be promoted, or being fired. In extreme situations it may mean life imprisonment or even the death penalty. On the other hand, if a member performs in some positive way above and beyond what members expect, verbal, nonverbal, or material rewards may be used to recognize that contribution. Social controls, then, consist of administration of positive or negative sanctions (rewards or punishments) that serve to maintain the pattern of social organization and ensure that the group can achieve its objectives.

What is it that transforms a number of individuals into a functioning group? Communication scholars have provided many answers to this deceptively simple question. Although most groups extend through time, certain groups meet only once to achieve the goal of orderly discussion or decision making. However, even these groups follow the rules and procedures of their pattern of social organization. (See Box 6.1.)

Informal versus Formal Communication

In our opening vignette illustrating the peer group, the patterns of communication between the three members was *informal*. That is, it was spontaneous, unplanned, and clearly not conducted according to any set of officially coded rules. Each member spoke to any other about any matter that concerned him at the moment, and self-disclosure was high. However, in every group, as we have explained, there is a pattern of social organization—a set of stable expectations that members have of each other. This pattern sets the rules and styles of communication within that group.

In following a pattern of **informal communication,** people feel relatively free to say what they want, and they do not constantly worry that their meanings will be misunderstood. This does not mean that there are no rules whatever regarding who can say what to whom on what occasion. Even in the most intimate groups there are understood prohibitions about certain topics or modes of communication. Name calling is out, and references to certain personal or family characteristics may not be acceptable.

When they participate in informal communication, people engage in role-taking and are aware of feedback, as is the case whenever people communicate face to face, but they seldom deliberate ahead of time to assess in detail what a person's response to a routine message is likely to be. Moreover, they do not scrutinize a

BOX 6.1   A *Closer Look*

Social Organization

All human groups have one thing in common. Whether the group is large or small, intimate or impersonal, formal or informal, it has what sociologists call a *pattern of social organization*. This pattern develops because people do not come together to form groups for no reason—or interact with each other randomly to carry on their activities. They do so to pursue collectively some *goal* or objective that they could not achieve while acting alone. To do this they need a shared set of mutual expectations that permit each member to *anticipate* how the others will communicate with and respond to them as they carry on the group's activities. That set of anticipations or expectations consists of four distinct types of rules that define what members are supposed to do and what they can expect of the others under a variety of circumstances. Thus, a human group is organized around its *norms, roles, ranks*, and *controls*.

Norms. All groups have *rules for behavior* that must be observed by every member. These dictate many of the ways all are expected to behave. (Examples are dress codes, time schedules, rules of politeness, modes of greeting, and use of company phones.)

Roles. Like actors in a play, each member of a group performs some *specialized activity* that complements the activities of others and helps achieve the objective. If each member's role is understood and accepted by the others, the members can act effectively as a team. (Examples are father, captain of the team, gang member, foreman, waiter, and supermarket clerk.)

Ranks. Some members play more critical or more honored roles. Others play less important roles. For this reason some members have more authority, power, and prestige, and get greater rewards. Members can be classified on these criteria into *strata* or *levels of ranks*. Those lower are often expected to show deference to, or follow instructions of, those in higher ranks.

Controls. If a member *fails to carry out*, or *deviates from*, the above expectations, the group's goal and stability are threatened and the person will be punished. However, if a member performs positively, above and beyond what is expected, that member will be rewarded. The negative and positive sanctions used constitute the group's system of social control. (Examples are smiles of approval, frowns, verbal compliments, pay raises, getting fired, advancement in rank, grades, fines, jail, and even the death penalty.)

---

receiver for subtle or minute feedback signals. They are "laid back" and comfortable with each other. Nevertheless, and in spite of the relaxed way that informal communication proceeds, it is patterned around the mutual expectations that members have of each other. In short, *informal communication* can be defined as *a spontaneous exchange of messages between individuals who feel free to engage in self-disclosure and to discuss whatever topic they wish, using mutually understood non-coded rules.*

In contrast, **formal communication** takes place within a set of official rules, often laid out very specifically in handbooks or other documents. Anyone familiar with life in one of the military services understands formal communication very well. Private Smith does not greet Major Jones, his or her company commander, with an informal, "Hey, how are you?" He or she stands at attention, salutes, and says something like, "Good morning, Sir (or Ma'am). Private Smith reporting as ordered." In such a formal system, messages must be couched in highly prescribed forms. Formal titles of address are compulsory. Nonverbal messages (salutes, standing at attention, eye contact) must communicate mutual respect. Slouching posture, sloppy salutes, rumpled clothing, and failure to listen carefully are major transgressions.

There are many systems of coded formal communication that are not as rigid as those used in the military. They are used in such settings as courtrooms, board meetings, and committee deliberations, as well as many other kinds of group settings where a set of coded rules for communicating set the pattern of social organization. The distinction between informal and formal communication is an important one for understanding how communication proceeds in a very large number of groups, both large and small. In this chapter, a number of examples of informal and formal communication in small groups will be discussed. In summary, then, *formal communication* can be defined as *controlled communication among parties who are allowed or required by the group's coded rules to transmit particular kinds of messages to specific receivers using officially designated rules and restrictions.*

The Consequences of Group Size

How is communication in a group influenced by the number of participants in the process? Communication in a small group is very different from that in a large organization. Even the addition of one person, such as an older adult parent, in a household that previously consisted of a husband and wife, can have a significant influence on the relationship.[7] To understand why communication is affected by the number of individuals involved, recall the linear and simultaneous transactions models, which analyzed the basic act of communication between two people in terms of a series of steps by which messages are organized, transmitted, and interpreted (Chapter 1).

The difference between dyadic and group communication is that in the latter a number of *pairs* of participants may be involved at the

same time. For example, consider a group with three members. At any given moment one sender may be transmitting a message to a maximum of two receivers. Although the other two may be simultaneously formulating their replies and providing ongoing feedback, the basic linear process is still there, taking place between what looks at first glance like two sender-receiver pairs who are involved in the exchange. However, if one looks more closely, *there are actually three pairs* involved. To be sure, only one person is talking and two listening, but another exchange of influences is taking place between the two receivers. Even though they are not talking to each other at the moment, they are influencing each other in subtle ways, through posture, facial expressions, and other nonverbal signs. In this sense, then, there are in fact three pairs to consider when one person talks to two others. A group of only three, then, has three possible pairs that are to be considered in any act of communication.

What happens when the number of participants is greater than three? How does this influence the communication processes that take place? To get an answer we can consider the number of possible pairs that can exist within groups of different sizes. As will be evident, as the number of such dyads (pairs) grows, it becomes more and more difficult to maintain a full flow of communication among all the members. For example, in our group with only three potential pairs, there would be little difficulty in turn-taking, in reading nonverbal cues, and in understanding potential nuances of connotative meanings. Role-taking would be more difficult than with a single receiver, but it would not be all that complex. Also, each member could recall fairly accurately who said what to whom in prior communication. Generally, then, with three members, even with relatively full participation by all members, achieving accuracy in any given exchange would not be difficult.

Now, consider larger groups. Adding only one more person to a group of three doubles the number of pairs to six. (Check it out, using either a diagram or high school algebra for combinations.)[8] This makes turn-taking, role-taking, keeping track of what each person has already said to each of the others, and so on considerably more difficult. A group of 10 has 45 possible pairs, and one with 20 members has a startling 190 potential pairings! Thus, as the number of group members grows, the number of potential pairs engaging in role-taking, feedback, turn-taking, prior communication, and nonverbal communication become geometrically more complicated as size increases linearly.

For these reasons, an optimal size for discussion and making decisions in a small group, with all members participating fully, is pretty small—something like five (with 10 pairs). This brings some diversity of views to the exchanges, but it still permits a relatively full flow of reasonably accurate communication. Although there are no hard-and-fast rules, when a group grows beyond five or so, the dynamics of communication begin to change dramatically.[9] Individual members have an increasingly difficult time communicating fully and accurately in face-to-face dyads to all the others. If the group gets up to, say, 20 or so, some members simply stop trying to participate and sit quietly on the sidelines. Others break up into small cliques, and a few talkers dominate the discussion. Thus, group size can be a critical factor in the way a group functions.

Stages in Group Development

In some groups, the rules for communicating can be designated before members are recruited (for example, formal **decision-making groups**, such as juries). However, many of the **task-oriented groups** discussed previously undergo a *series of stages* after the members first come together. During these stages the rules for communicating are developed by the members during their early encounters, and become stabilized only after a period.[10]

Sociologist Robert F. Bales has been one of the most influential researchers in the study of emerging group communication systems.[11] His classic experiments on "interaction process analysis," conducted during the late 1940s, broke new ground and showed that in an informal group discussion the members of small groups do achieve specialization in the kinds of messages they communicate.

Because there has been such a large amount of research devoted to the issue of stages of communication development, many labels have been applied to what takes place as participants come to know one another, confront various problems, and achieve the goals for which their group came together in the first place. Perhaps the easiest to remember of those labels were proposed by social psychologist Bruce Tuckman during the mid-1960s.[12] He came up with four distinct stages that he called *forming, storming, norming,* and *performing.* (See Box 6.2.)

Forming: The Stage of Initial Orientation

When people come together to confront a task or to solve a problem, they face many uncertainties. This is especially true if they do not know one another and are not able to predict how each will respond to what is said. Thus, there is a stage of *orientation,* both toward the task for which the group has been formed and toward one another. Sizing up one another is one of the first things that has to be done in such a task-oriented group. We discussed earlier the concept of *implicit personality*—the process by which individuals who do not really know each other use various salient and other visible characteristics to make judgments about what the others are like. This is exactly what happens in forming a task-oriented group in which the members are not well known to each other. A considerable amount of the early communication involves exchanges designed to determine who responds in what way to what kinds of messages. The forming stage, then, is one of uncertainty, probing, implicit personality formation, and trial.

It is in this stage that the rules that will govern communication—the *norms* of how ideas can be expressed and what can be said—begin to be defined. Will a sophisticated vocabulary

BOX 6.2   *A Closer Look*

Tuckman's Four Stages in Group Development

1. *Forming: The stage of initial orientation.* This is the stage of uncertainty: Rules governing communication are tested; norms and roles start to be defined; and members take on particular roles and communicate status, power, and control messages.
2. *Storming: The stage of emerging conflict.* During this stage, orientation activities transform into conflict: Members disagree about power, status, and control roles, and a leader emerges with a particular leadership style.
3. *Norming: The stage of stabilization.* During this stage, conflicts subside: Members finish sizing up one another, and they begin to operate as a group, turning to the task to be accomplished.
4. *Performing: The stage of task achievement.* During this stage, members address the task following a set of stabilizing rules for communicating: Various solutions are examined, and members come together in consensus about the best solution.

Source: Tuckman, B. W. (1950). Development sequences in small groups. *Psychological Bulletin, 63,* 384–399.

Status and power *ranks* within the group are also clarified during the forming stage. Some members transmit messages intended to define their special expertise. Some, with high status outside the group, will be seen as having more influence than others on what is said. These messages start to identify the levels of prestige that will exist within the group. If these definitions are accepted, the contributions by those group members awarded higher rank will be interpreted as having the most weight. Other group members may be intimidated by these emerging indicators of rank. They may see themselves as low in the system and having less to offer to the discussion.

Communication at this stage also begins to identify the signals of *social control.* Who will transmit messages of reward or punishment, and how will they do this? Will they use verbal ridicule or merely a nonverbal frown or raised eyebrow to transmit meanings of disapproval? Will the others reward a good comment with nonverbal immediacy—eye contact, a smile, a nod—or will they express their approval in verbal terms? Many messages of control are those used more generally by people communicating in other contexts, but some control system will characterize the group, and its dimensions are defined in the forming stage.

Storming: The Stage of Emerging Conflict

The orientation activities of the forming stage shift almost inevitably into one in which *conflict* emerges. Some participants may not accept certain individuals as qualified, of higher rank or competence. Others may construct a negative implicit personality and dislike one or more fellow members. Still others may not want to participate at all, or may want to shift topics, go about achieving the goal in a different way, and so on. Resentments may develop over perceived attempts at social control when negative feelings are aroused as controlling messages are transmitted. Of special importance at this stage is the emergence of a leader and a style of leadership.

be the norm? Is poor grammar acceptable? Will comments be expressed in a witty style or a serious style?

Depending on the nature of the group, communication *roles*—specialized parts to be performed by individual members—may also be defined in the forming stage. The need for a group leader may become clear, and some individuals may start to take on that role. Others may try out for the part of "group clown," offering funny anecdotes or jokes. Others may begin to play the part of mediator—the pourer-of-oil-on-troubled-waters—by specializing in the soothing of the feelings of others.

Norming: The Stage of Stabilization

After the group has worked its way through whatever conflicts arise, the members will have established the initial images—implicit personalities—they have developed for one another. In addition, they will have achieved definitions of self that are applicable within the group. This brings greater accuracy in role-taking and more predictability in interpreting feedback from verbal and nonverbal messages that are received and returned. At this point, members can move on from the process of sizing one another up and start resolving the conflicts that were generated in the earlier stages. Once they do this, they can deal with the group as a reasonably predictable pattern of social relationships and turn to their task.

Performing: The Stage of Task Achievement

With the group now stabilized, the task for which the participants came together can be addressed fully. Participants at this stage examine various proposed solutions, and they come together in consensus about the one they believe to be best. Not all groups go through these precise stages. Nevertheless, anticipating them can be particularly useful for understanding communication in small groups when participants do not know one another well and have been brought together to accomplish some purpose or goal. Many of the task-oriented groups described in this chapter will undergo some set of similar transitions, and these stages may be found to some degree, even in more formal decision-making groups where communication follows a more structured pattern of social organization.

Informal Communication in Small, Intimate Groups

Not all small groups are alike. We have already discussed the peer group, and we mentioned the family. We noted that both are critical in the lives of all of us and both are contexts in which intimate communication takes place. The factor of intimacy is critical to understanding human relationships within these primary groups and how they develop into intimacy over a period of time. Recall from Chapter 5 ("Communicating Interpersonally") that people sort out and select each other, and then become involved increasingly in self-disclosure and personal communication. In this chapter the approach is also *developmental,* looking at primary groups in terms of the rich functions they serve and the objectives they achieve for their participants.

The messages transmitted and received within both family and peer groups serve as critical sources that provide us with our deepest understandings of other human beings and how to relate to them.[13] It is not always easy to see that communication occurring in such groups has very basic goals. Most people simply carry on their activities within such groups without consciously thinking about them in terms of communication and its consequences. Nevertheless, those consequences are very real and very important—so important that we could not develop as fully functioning members of our community and society without deep involvement in small and intimate groups. More specifically, our family and our closest friends share the goal of shaping our psychological and social development in a variety of ways. In this sense, they are truly "cradles of human nature," and this can be identified as one of their most important purposes.

Communicating within the Family

The family is the most basic of all human groups. It is the context within which the first steps toward communication take place. The family is the great teacher of the symbols and rules of meaning that are the foundations of social life. Thus, the family has always been the principal source for learning vocabulary and linking symbols, meanings, and referents so that new members of society could take the first steps in communicating. Today, it is within the family that we sort out and learn the complexities of grammar and syntax.

The acquisition of language allows the child to begin participating in the mainstream culture of larger groups and to start internalizing the beliefs and understandings of the physical, spiritual, and social world. Language acquisition also allows the child to participate in specific specialized cultures with which the family identifies. Thus, the family functions as the primary group in our communication experience.

Learning language in family situations permits us to participate in the entire communication process of a society. Taken together, all these cultural and group influences, plus the learning experiences we acquire as we mature, can be discussed as **socialization.** The term *socialization* refers to those long-term processes of communication within which deliberate or unintended and indirect lessons are internalized, enabling the person to become a unique human being, a functioning member of society, and a participant in its general and unique cultures.[14]

Three aspects of human development are involved in this definition of the socialization process. These are that communication in family situations represents our initial sources of **personality, social expectations,** and **enculturation.** These terms are central to an understanding of both the process and the consequences of communication, especially in small and intimate groups.

Psychologists developed the term *personality* to refer to the individual's enduring organization of meanings, motivations, emotional patterns, orientations, skills, and all other personal attributes that give that individual a unique psychological makeup. Personality, in other words, is composed of *"the individual's distinctive, consistent, patterned methods of relating to the environment."*[15] What this implies is that each person has a unique psychological make-up. Some people are serious and others are happy-go-lucky. Some are driven to succeed and others are lazy. Some are smart and others are dense. In other words, there is an enormous list of psychological attributes or **personality**

traits on which people individually differ.[16] Long before there were psychologists, people commonly identified such individual differences with terms like *stingy, generous, smart,* and *lively,* to describe observable and predictable features of a person's behavior over time. Psychologists have developed many additional and more technical terms, such as *introverted, hyperactive,* and *anal-retentive,* but the idea is the same: People exhibit more or less enduring and predictable patterns of behavior as characteristics of their personalities.

As the above discussion of family communication suggests, personality is not inherited. We must acquire (that is, *learn*) it through our experiences in many kinds of social contexts and situations. The people around us, either directly or via various media, communicate (deliberately or not) a great variety of lessons about what we should think; how we should express our emotions; and what we should value, despise, accept, reject, understand, and so on. This process—including the presentation of lessons, their content, the act of learning, and our resulting personalities—is what is meant by *socialization.*

Socialization is also the source of *social expectations,* that is, our insights into how people expect us to behave in a pattern of social organization of a particular group. Through communicating in social situations, the individual comes to understand the norms, roles, ranks, and controls of various groups. This development of internalized social understandings is one way that socialization makes the individual similar to others. Although this seems contradictory, common sense tells us that all kinds of people, regardless of their individual personality differences, learn to conform to the everyday requirements of social life. By communicating in various social situations and contexts, we learn what others expect us to do in many kinds of groups, sports teams, families, friendship cliques, and so on. Thus, socialization produces both *uniqueness* and *similarity.*

Finally, enculturation also takes place in the socialization process, reducing individuality even further. To be accepted as members of their society, individuals must be keenly aware of that society's way of life—its general or mainstream culture. This includes not only language skills, but also the shared beliefs, emotional orientations, attitudes, values, and everything else that make people fit in socially. Overall, enculturation represents a very basic transformation of the individual. As anthropologist Ruth Benedict put it in her classic analysis *Patterns of Culture,*

> By the time [a child] can talk, he is the little creature of his culture, and by the time he is grown and able to take part in its activities, its habits are his habits, its beliefs are his beliefs, its impossibilities his impossibilities.[17]

By the same means, children learn the basics of unique specialized cultures in which their families participate. These may involve distinctive languages, values, styles of dress, diets, and many other practices that are different from those of the mainstream culture. These may be associated with race, religion, ethnicity, region, or even socioeconomic level in the society.

In short, the rich communication processes that take place within family situations provide the foundations for our developing mental processes, equipping us to engage in self-communication (thinking, recalling, and reasoning). They also provide our initial exposure to shared social understandings and cultural rules that enable us to engage in goal-oriented activities with other individuals.

Communicating with Peers

As discussed earlier, the family is not the only primary group. *Peer groups* also provide the individual with vital information about the physical and social world. Friends of the same general age and status give us an intimate primary group outside the family. This is very important during early childhood, and peer groups remain critical to our well-being throughout our lives. As mentioned earlier, through communication in peer groups, individuals improve

and maintain their role-taking skills and their ability to interpret feedback.

In the context of young children's groups on street corners, in schoolyards, and on playgrounds, individuals gain deeper understandings of how the messages they initiate influence others and what their friends' responses imply about the meanings they are reconstructing. Their critical skills in message construction, nonverbal communication, and understanding meanings intended by others are sharpened. Thus, by communicating in this peer "society-in-miniature," children learn what words, gestures, and actions make others angry, what causes them to smile or laugh; what brings respect or conveys dishonor; and what establishes one person as a leader or defines another as a follower. These are critical consequences of intimate communication in small groups.

The influence of peer groups does not stop with childhood. During the entire life cycle, people communicate in peer groups to achieve goals they seldom articulate and may never have tried to understand. If asked, their likely reply would be they simply want to enjoy their friends or have fun. Thus, members of such groups communicate among themselves simply for the pleasures that the process provides—the companionship and personal fulfillment that cannot be obtained in other ways. In such groups, communication provides a bonding among members that is its own reward.

Patterns of Communication in Small, Intimate Groups

This section describes the typical rules of informal communication that tend to develop within intimate groups. These rules guide and limit the spontaneous and unrestrained transmissions and receptions of messages that take place among members. The term *informal* means the absence of deliberately designed barriers or constraints—communication that is spontaneous and unrestrained. When they are communicating informally, people feel relatively free to say what they want and do not constantly worry that their meanings will be misunderstood or that they will arouse hostile responses. This is the kind of self-disclosing communication that takes place between good friends, family members on good terms, and friendly work associates.

The fact that informal communication is relatively uninhibited does not mean its social pathways are random. Even in the most intimate groups, rules dictate who can communicate to whom about what. There are always topics that are not to be discussed and times when certain issues are not to be brought up. However, those restraints are simply understood in an unspoken agreement; they are not deliberately designed prior to people entering the group. On the contrary, the members work them out as they go along and revise them as need be.

Communication *norms* are general rules that each member is expected to follow concerning what issues, topics, and modes of transmission are acceptable within the group. For example, few families or even peer groups permit members to discuss gross bodily functions at mealtimes. Sexual experiences and related topics may also be taboo. Even spontaneous and uninhibited primary groups impose a surprising number of limitations on what, how, when, and in what manner specific messages can be transmitted.

A second set of patterned expectations in intimate groups defines individual communication *roles*. That is, what specific person has the right to transmit particular kinds of messages, and who must pay attention to them. One person will usually talk and make decisions about certain areas of concern while another will initiate more messages about other issues. These areas may include such matters as automobiles, food, child rearing, income, and recreation. On the other hand, although one person may initiate more suggestions and proposals, another may be the one who gives final approval.

The roles of husband, wife, child, and even relatives in the contemporary family are more than simply a matter of agreements among members about who will be permitted or expected to say what to whom. Cultural traditions (backed by legal requirements) prepare people, long before marriage and parenthood, for the specialized parts they will be expected to play in the communication patterns of the family. No particular family fits the general model exactly. That is, when unique individuals come together to act out the parts of husband and wife to communicate about family matters, they modify the general model by developing consensus around their own definitions. These, then, become shared within the new group.

In many ways, the role expectations that develop among intimate friends follow parallel patterns to those that characterize the family. All cultures define how friends are expected to communicate with one another, and these serve as general guides for individuals in small groups of close associates. There is vast latitude in the way that one individual can communicate with another in intimate ways. Thus, peer roles have the most flexible of all communication rules found in intimate groups.

Many differences exist in the social *ranks* within intimate groups—hierarchies of authority, power, and privilege. Ranks may not always be easy to detect, but they clearly govern communication within families. Their nature depends on the specialized culture of the specific family involved. In one, the husband may be sternly dominant, constantly transmitting orders, with the wife meekly receiving them and feeding back messages of submissiveness. In another, the husband may be a hen-pecked wimp and the wife a blustering bully. In still another a true partnership may evolve, in which both husband and wife communicate fully and openly about sharing power, cooperating on domestic chores, and earning income.

An emerging general model in the United States is the *democratic* pattern, in which the ranks of husband and wife are the same and each has an equal voice. The children's position is less clear: In some cases they have considerable voice in family affairs; in others, they remain subordinate. In all families, however, some structure of rank has been established that governs their messages.

In friendship groups, the communication rules related to rank tend to be more subtle. People reject the idea that their close friends can order them around. Nevertheless, there is a ranking pattern in every group. This is the case because there is a need for ranks. Every group has a problem of coordination. Even close friends must make decisions—such as what to get involved in. For example, if all members decide to go to a football game, there is the problem of where they will meet, whose car they will drive, and what they will do afterward. Usually, one individual will suggest a plan and the others will agree to it. This is leadership (higher rank) in a very subtle form. If a party is to be held, there are the questions of location, who will bring what, at what time, and who will be invited. Again, one individual is likely to emerge as the person in control.

Ranking and power in the context of the intimate group of friends also illustrates the broader problem of *authority*. It is in miniature the same problem that Thomas Hobbes wrote about in his *Leviathan* centuries ago.[18] Essentially his idea was that someone has to be in charge. If members of a group refuse to accept the orders, commands, or even suggestions of another member, then chaos and anarchy prevail. It is more convenient to look to a particular individual, in whom the members have confidence, as a source for direction. If a particular individual holds such a position, he or she is informally vested by the members with authority (the principle developed by Hobbes).

The rules for communicating in intimate groups are maintained through process of *social control*. This takes place through the use of *sanctions*—rewards for compliance and punishments for deviance. Sanctions, or control messages, can range from nonverbal signals of approval or disapproval to verbal praise or abuse. Mainly, however, the communication of controls in intimate groups tends to be subtle.

Communicating to establish or maintain social control in the family can be a complex process. In the traditional family, if measures were needed to control the behavior of an er-rant child, the father got out the razor strap, took the offender by the ear to the woodshed, and soundly communicated a physical message to the child's posterior. In most families today, however, verbal and nonverbal messages are substituted for woodshed controls. It is generally not acceptable to use violence. Instead, parents may use frowns or smiles, scoldings or praise, "grounding," no TV, confinement to room, or other restrictions.

Adult members of families also use special communication categories as rewards and punishments. Simply ignoring another individual, or looking at the person with a stony stare, can arouse meaning. A raised eyebrow, or a glare, can speak volumes under some circumstances. On the other hand, such rewards as pats, strokes, hugs, flowers, candy, and many other kinds of nonverbal communication express approval and elicit emotional responses. Members of families develop sensitive skills at reading the intent and meanings of social control behind such transmissions.

Transmitting social control can be equally subtle in peer groups. Groups of friends do not resort to violence to enforce their rules. Most positive and negative sanctions are expressed in very subtle ways. Whatever modes of communication the group uses—verbal or nonverbal, violent or gentle, subtle or blatant—messages expressing approval and disapproval are the means used to stabilize its communication rules.

Communicating in Task-Oriented Discussion Groups

There is a large number of task-oriented groups in which people are brought together as participants to communicate and get something done. In each case, they seek to achieve some goal that has been deliberately set as an objective. Two main categories of such groups can be identified. One is the *informal group*. We have already discussed two informal groups— the family and the peer group—but there are many others, which do not have the same level of significance. Nevertheless, they are important for achieving the specific goal objectives for which their members participate. The other is the *formal discussion group*. There are many objectives that are sought in this context. These too are important for the specific goals that are sought.

Informal versus Formal Discussion Groups

Some task-oriented groups are devoted to *informal discussions* among people who know each other well. One example would be a group of friends who get together to discuss planning a surprise birthday party for a buddy. Another would be a group of friends who meet at one of their homes for coffee and goodies to try to work out some sort of plan to get the city to do something about the parking problem on their street. The pattern of social organization is not highly structured. The norms, roles, ranks, and controls are not rigid, and any member can chime in at any time with a suggestion or comment.

Other small task-oriented discussion groups are highly structured in that their communication follows a formal pattern of social organization. Examples here would be a jury, a **panel,** colloquium or a symposium. Such formal discussion groups can be private or public. A private group is illustrated by a business conference within a particular company, where systematic presentations and exchanges of comments take place about confidential policies and problems. In contrast, a public discussion group is a situation in which audiences observe proceedings, or perhaps even participate. Examples are scientific panels or symposia.

An important kind of task-oriented small group is devoted to *reaching consensus* so that a formal decision can be made. Here the pattern of social organization is often laid out in formal documents that prescribe procedures to be carefully followed. Examples are university committees, corporate boards of directors, courtroom trial juries, and permanent councils in religious groups. In this type of group, the goal is to arrive at orderly judgments on the basis of

well-regulated discussion. Many of these groups communicate privately, for the purpose of, say, allocating scarce resources, evaluating people's performance, and achieving consensus on the truth of a situation. They usually operate within some large organization or social system. Such groups usually have a highly formalized pattern of social organization, with norms, roles, ranks, and so forth specified in official documents.

Small, Task-Oriented Discussion Groups with Specific Objectives

There are a great many different types of small task-oriented groups that focus on some *specific objective*. Each is different in terms of the kinds of people involved, the goals its members seek to accomplish and the way in which communication proceeds among them. They can also differ in the degree to which their pattern of social organization is formal or informal. A number of different types can be identified. These are widely found in modern societies, and each is formed and conducted to accomplish a specific purpose that is important to their members.

A **round table** is a task-oriented small group in which diverse views on a topic or issue are discussed among a small group of participants. The members are typically experts or representatives of special interests. In the round table, there is no audience and the participants usually sit in a circle. Communication is usually informal, with limited rules and no formally designated leader.

Another small task-oriented discussion group is the *panel*. In many ways, it resembles the round table, but it is public rather than private. Panel participants tend to be experts or representatives of special interests. The panel is usually coordinated in a formal way by a moderator, and the discussion usually takes place before a live audience. Sometimes questions are taken from the audience after panel members have commented. Panels can be presented to audiences via radio and television, sometimes allowing questions to be called in. Panels seldom reach firm decisions, but they present alternative interpretations and insights, and their discussion may help audience members understand the issues.

A very formal and public small task-oriented group is the **symposium.** This is a discussion group only in a limited sense. Usually a symposium has some unifying theme—a problem or an issue that is being addressed. The participants are typically a small group of experts who are knowledgeable about the theme. They are introduced by a moderator, and each then makes a speech about the theme. The participants seldom talk with one another—even between presentations. Instead, they simply take their turn delivering their views. Sometimes the symposium takes questions from members of the audience afterward. Later, the presentations of the participants are often published as a set of proceedings or a book.

One of the oldest of all small task-oriented groups is the **seminar.** It originated with the ancient Greeks. Plato used this type of group as a teaching format. He and his students strolled through the grounds of his *Academy* and each student took a turn at addressing a central issue or question that was the focus of discussion.[19] The mentor then distilled the important lessons that could be derived from the body of the comments. Seminars remain an important teaching format in higher education, where candidates for doctoral degrees often participate in exchanges that are similar to those used by Plato. Seminars usually have regular meetings over a lengthy period of time, a clear organization, and an intellectual leader who coordinates the discussions of students.

Another small-group discussion format is the **forum.** It combines features of the round table, panel, and symposium. It is a one-time event and somewhat less formal than the panel, round table, or symposium. In the forum, there are usually brief presentations by a small group, each of whose members is introduced by a chairperson. Their presentations are followed by considerable audience participation, again coordinated by the chair. The forum is a favorite format on college campuses because it allows a great deal of audience participation.

A widely used small discussion group context is the **small group conference.** In typical small group conferences, several participants are brought together, usually privately. Their purpose is to share technical information or to discuss some problem in their area of expertise. Such conferences are common in corporations or agencies where solutions to problems can be worked out together. They are also common among professionals such as physicians, lawyers, and engineers. A rather unique feature of the conference is that the participants need not be together physically. Conferences can be held at long range, with some medium, such as television or even the Internet, linking the participants. Such conferences allow people to engage in reasonably full and accurate communication at a distance.

There are many additional types of specialized discussion groups that are task-oriented and they can be found in various settings. Most are conducted privately for confidential purposes. Some are called *buzz groups,* others *brainstorming sessions.* Here, the participants—often middle managers or supervisors—review a problem, issue, topic, plan, or policy to see whether the group can come up with a solution or improvement.

During the decades following World War II, in industrial settings, a favorite discussion group has been the *quality circle* (adopted from the Japanese). Here, employees get together periodically in small groups to discuss ways to improve their work. Their suggestions are passed on to management. In more recent times, other terms are sometimes used for this type of small discussion group. However, the goal and this type of employee discussion is still important and remains an effective tool for management.

Still another is the *focus group,* which is essentially a format in research—particularly of the kind done by the advertising and market research industries. Here, typically, a small group of typical consumers is brought together to discuss a new product, or proposed package design, so that the researchers can gain insight into ways to make the product more acceptable and more profitable.[20]

In the treatment of a variety of human problems, the **therapy group** is used by counseling psychologists and others who try to make people feel better through communication. The goal of the participants is to engage in self-disclosing discussions that will assist members who have personal problems. The discussion topic may be drug addiction, excessive gambling, alcoholism, smoking, loss of a loved one, or abuse of or by one's spouse, to name a few of many possibilities. Participants meet with a coordinator who usually has some special insight into the problem. The underlying assumption is that if people who share a common problem get together and disclose their experiences, thoughts, and feelings, it will help all of them feel better as they gain insight into their difficulty and learn to deal with it more effectively.

Similarly oriented toward making people feel better is the **encounter group.** More popular in earlier decades than they are now, encounter groups were organized for the purpose of identifying and coping with difficulties experienced in daily life. An example is the church-organized marriage retreat, in which couples spend a weekend away from the distractions of their daily environment. They tell one another about the problems they have faced in their marriages, the mistakes they have made, and the stresses they have had to manage. They learn from one another how to deal with such difficulties, and the experience is said to strengthen the marital bond.

Training goals are often sought in the small-group format. One example is the **assertiveness-training group,** in which participants learn how they can stand up for their rights and ensure that they are treated with dignity and respect. Other training-oriented groups seek applied skill development. In some, using the small group format, participants in training sessions learn a technical proficiency, such as word processing with computer software, or how to handle hazardous wastes.

Another type of training-oriented group that has been used to make participants who believe themselves to be disadvantaged feel better is the **consciousness-raising group.** Participants exchange views, listen to presentations, and gain insights into a topic of mutual concern. Typically, such groups focus on bringing awareness of significant issues to other people who seem to be the problem. The focus of these groups may be related to environmental issues, discrimination in the labor force, sexual harassment, or controversial issues such as capital punishment and sending military troops to a war zone. Participation in such groups is said to sharpen the thinking about the issue, raising the consciousness of those who take part.

In summary, a host of formats, goals, and patterns of social organization are used in small task-oriented groups to attain a great variety of goals. Some are formal and focused on reaching decisions important to larger groups or even the society as a whole. Others are informal and seek simpler objectives. Still others are conducted in such a way that members engage in self-disclosure in an effort to achieve a number of objectives. Whatever the goal or mode of communication, the small group format plays a key role in our society.

Patterns of Communication in Task-Oriented Groups

The rules for communicating in all types of task-oriented groups involve the same concepts of social organization previously identified—norms, roles, ranks, and controls. These take many variations in the different types and categories of such groups, but a number of general principles can be identified.

No single set of *communication norms* governs message transmission across the many kinds of task-oriented groups that exist. The rules for communicating in each context are set by the sociocultural situation—that is, rules are defined broadly by the goal or purpose of the group. In such forms as the round table, panel, and symposium, the norms are usually pre-designed, which means that their communication requirements are derived from traditions. When participants are recruited, they are expected to follow those traditional forms. However, each person will bring his or her own personal style and interpretations to those rules. One may joke and be lighthearted, whereas another will be subdued or serious.[21] Thus, the norms that are used will be some mix of the traditional patterns applicable to that type of group (panel, seminar, therapy group, or whatever) and the personal styles of each participant.

Many kinds of *communication roles* have been identified in task-oriented groups. A classic analysis of such roles is that of communication scholars Kenneth Benne and Paul Sheats.[22] They proposed three general categories, which depend on what members tend to do repetitively. Some are group *task-related* roles, such as "opinion seeker," "initiator," and "energizer." Others are concerned with *group building and maintenance,* such as "encourager," "harmonizer," and "gatekeeper." A third category concerns *individual* roles, such as "aggressor," "help-seeker," and "recognition-seeker."

Of particular interest to communication scholars is the role of *leader* in discussion groups. Typically, in the task-oriented type of groups listed above, a leader emerges to take charge and coordinate the group's activities. The questions of how leaders emerge, what kinds of characteristics they have, and what consequences result from their styles are of profound importance. These issues go beyond what happens in small groups. In fact, the question of how power is achieved and used to control the behavior of others has long been a critical issue in human civilization. It has been studied since the time of Confucius, and it came under special scrutiny by social scientists in the 20th century.

Interest in the relationship between communication and leadership heightened during World War II, when tyrants like Adolf Hitler, Benito Mussolini, and Hideki Tojo used propaganda and other persuasive techniques to gain popular support. Leadership remains a critical concern in government, the military, industry, and education. The exercise of leadership can have either very positive or very negative consequences. For example, researchers urgently seek answers to questions such as how a person like Shoko Asahara, the leader of the religious cult Aum Shinrikyo, could persuade followers to plant nerve gas in the Tokyo subway that killed 12 people and injured thousands in 1995.[23] Or how is it that Fidel Castro can control millions of Cuban citizens? Similarly, how did a dictator like Saddam Hussein rise to power in Iraq and lead a rich nation to devastation?

Obviously, answers to such questions are not found in the study of task-oriented discussion groups, but intriguing insights do emerge from looking at leadership in that context. For example, classic research suggests that three basic styles of leadership can be found in task-oriented discussion groups: *authoritarian, democratic,* and *laissez-faire.*[24]

In the *authoritarian style,* all goals, policies, and activities of the group are determined solely by the leader, including which members work together. She or he is personal in praise and criticism but tends to remain aloof. Other members are uncertain about future plans and steps. This type of leader sets the goal, decides who will do what to get there, and defines the techniques by which success will be achieved.

Where the *democratic style* is used by the leader, group members discuss prospective policies and then determine them by vote. The leader provides technical advice on how to proceed when needed, but members are free to divide themselves into work teams for specific tasks. The leader is balanced and objective in praise and criticism, tries to be like other members to some degree, but does not do much of the actual work. A democratic leader takes people where they already want to go: He or she helps them determine what that is, the best steps to take to get there, and then coordinates their efforts so that the goal will be achieved.

The leader using the *laissez-faire style* is "laid back" and does little to interfere with the choices or activities of members. He or she lets the group go whatever way it wishes, even if this leads to mistakes. Little visible authority or power is exercised, and the leader does not provide much criticism or reward. All the leader does is answer members' questions and give advice when asked.

In assessing the implications for these styles of leadership in small group discussions, real differences emerge.[25] The bonds between members tend to be stronger in the democratic group because the experience results in greater member satisfaction. On the other hand, there is typically less progress toward achieving solutions under this type of leadership. The authoritarian group accomplishes the most in the shortest time, but members tend to achieve their goals in a less original way, and they are less satisfied. The laissez-faire style is less efficient than either of the other two, and it tends to produce the lowest levels of member satisfaction.

What are some of the factors that result in a particular person becoming a leader? There are two answers: One is that the person has *special qualities* or leadership traits. These are personal characteristics that people admire and respect, attributes of personality that are the basis of leadership. This "trait theory" of leadership has been widely studied and seems to be true in many cases.[26] A second answer is that *situations,* rather than personal traits, determine leadership. If this is correct, different types of people (regardless of their individual traits) will be successful leaders in distinctive social circumstances. This interpretation also has merit.

A dramatic leader with a lot of *charisma* (attractive personal traits) may be just what is required in one situation, but entirely inappropriate in another. A different situation may best be served by a technically proficient but relatively inconspicuous individual. Thus, the best explanation for how and why some people become leaders seems to be that commanding personal characteristics do determine leadership in some situations, but in others, technical competence, insight into organizing work, and other factors are important.

Because there are so many types of task-oriented groups, one set of observations will not fit all in terms of how *social ranks* influence communication patterns.[27] In more formally organized groups, such as panels and symposia, members with formal roles of leadership and coordination are obviously in a position to control the flow of messages. Ranking is less clear in discussion groups in which members presumably start on an equal basis.

What often happens is that the person's social position and prestige *outside* the group play a significant part in determining rank within a discussion group. Thus, for example, a physician, a person in a high-prestige occupation, will almost automatically have greater authority in a small discussion group than, say, a dishwasher, or any other person in a low-prestige occupation. Much the same occurs with respect to personal attributes that are ranked by prestige in the community. Thus, in discussion groups, men sometimes appear to have an edge over women, and tall and imposing people may, at first, be listened to with greater conviction than short and small people. In addition, elderly people and people representing ethnic minorities may often be at a disadvantage. Finally, attractive people sometimes are afforded more authority than unattractive people.

In small discussion groups *social controls* take many forms. All the principles of communication set forth in earlier chapters govern the expectations of who can say what to whom in a task-oriented group. These expectations are enforced with feedback and with verbal comments and nonverbal signs, just as in any other type of communication. Nodding and smiling can encourage a person to keep talking, whereas sneers, eye rolling, frowns, and slumping can discourage comments. Thus, the group transmits various messages to control the topics of discussion, the performance of roles, and the rankings of the members.

Communicating in Formal Decision-Making Groups

One of the most important and useful small-group discussion formats in our society is that used for formal decision making. The goals of formal decision-making groups are easy to identify, define, and discuss. The manner in which this kind of small group is formed helps to identify its goals: Formal decision-making groups are deliberately constituted to serve decision-making needs of an organization, a community or even the larger society within which they operate.

The members of formal decision-making groups are not selected by chance or for convenience. Usually, their participation is requested, assigned, or even ordered after some sort of screening. More specifically, a board of directors, a jury, a committee, or a council is usually made up of members who have qualifications related to the goals for which the group is formed.

Anyone who has participated in the selection of the members of a jury knows the importance of specific personal and social characteristics as criteria of group membership. Potential jurors are questioned about various attributes that lawyers feel might influence their judgment. On the basis of such attributes, final selections are made. The same is true of the selection of participants for other important decision-making groups.

Goals Pursued in Formal Decision-Making Groups

What kinds of goals are pursued in the context of formal decision-making groups? Essentially, they are all related to making orderly judgments, which fall into four categories: *allocating scarce resources, evaluating performance, formulating or changing policies,* and *weighing evidence to reach the truth.* Each of these tasks is performed within the context of a small group.

Allocating scarce resources. Deciding on who should get resources that are in short supply is a thankless task. All large groups, such as corporations, communities, hospitals, and universities, have to determine who gets what share of their space, time, effort, money, or some other valued commodity. To handle such problems, committees are formed. These small, deliberately designed groups are formally charged with the goal of making recommendations, or reaching final decisions, regarding such matters as approving budget allocations, awarding research grants or prizes, approving loans, providing scholarships, and admitting students to educational programs.

A good example of a scarce resource is space. Not only do people require space in which to do their work, but space conveys nonverbal meanings of prestige and power within an organization. Far more people covet additional space than there is available square footage to be allocated.

In some organizations, one person is assigned the task of allocating space. In such a system, only a few individuals at the top can command the best, making life difficult for the single decision maker. A convenient solution is to appoint a committee to consider requests for more or better space. Although the decisions reached by such a committee may be identical with those of a single space master, at least the claimants can feel that their appeals were examined fairly by qualified individuals.

Such committees don't always achieve such an acceptable outcome. Some groups can act either stupidly or unfairly. However, decisions made by a group have a higher probability of being objective, fair, and intelligent than those made by a single individual. This is because it is difficult (but not impossible!) to assemble an entire group of truly stupid people or to have several individuals misuse their power in exactly the same way.

Evaluating performance. A very difficult task in large organizations is deciding who meets designated standards of performance and to what degree. No issue has more emotional significance than assessing merit—deciding whether people have been doing a good job or a poor job. Such judgments lead to the granting and withholding of salary raises, promotions, titles, or other rewards. In some cases, evaluations can lead to job terminations. Even awarding lesser perquisites—a desirable parking space, access to a special dining room, or a key to a restricted bathroom—can provoke emotional reactions.

Formulating or changing policy.   Establishing or changing the formal rules that guide how organizations do things is another task often assigned to a formal decision-making group. This may involve planning the objectives, strategies, and directions that an organization will take. Powerful policy groups of this type are almost always found at the top of the power structure within large organizations. For example, the armed services have the Joint Chiefs of Staff, and the president has his Cabinet and his White House staff of personal advisors. At local levels, every bank, agency, and corporation has a board of directors who are responsible for major decisions, new policies, and changes in direction. A local church will have a committee of lay people who advise the clergy. Even the smallest businesses, if they are incorporated under the laws of most states, must have boards of directors that hold annual meetings.

Weighing evidence to reach the truth.   Our society could not operate without groups that weigh facts in order to reach the truth. The trial jury is the most obvious example of a task-oriented group whose goal is to make orderly judgments about guilt or innocence, culpability or lack of responsibility. Coming from an ancient tradition, the use of a small group to weigh evidence and decide guilt or innocence has proved to be efficient over many centuries. Conveniently, truth becomes what a jury says it is—after discussion—even if it is wrong! The jury system is by no means foolproof. However, most people believe that it is the most acceptable of available alternatives. The organization of juries and selection of participants is well un-

derstood, but the communication processes by which they reach decisions are less so. Although there have been a few studies of actual juries in process, these are no longer permitted by the courts.[28] Researchers studying the jury process use simulated juries of volunteers selected in much the same way.

There are other kinds of fact-reviewing and truth-seeking small groups that are formally constituted to reach decisions. Examples are the federally operated Department of Transportation. If there is a major train wreck or an airplane crash, fact-finding experts are assembled. They sift through evidence and attempt to determine the cause of the accident. Other small groups, such as scientific panels, review information concerning new drugs, insecticides, and land use proposals.

Patterns of Communication in Formal Decision-Making Groups

Although there is great variation in the rules for communication in task-oriented discussion groups, the formal decision-making group is another matter. Key features characterize communication rules in this type of context. These features reflect the fact that such groups are typically formed within a larger organization, whose purposes they are designed to serve. As has been explained, small formal groups are necessary for reaching conclusions about resources, performance, policies, proposals, and other matters in all kinds of large contemporary organizations.

The most obvious feature of small decision-making groups is that they are deliberately formed and conducted in such a way that they use carefully defined codes as rules of communication. Thus, in such groups, communication is *formal*. The term *formal* itself implies "forms." These forms consist of the coded rules and definitions for communication that dictate who can communicate to whom about what topics in what way. Thus, the social pathways for the exchange of formal messages are confined by the group's pattern of social organization—its norms, roles, ranks, and systems of social controls.

There are several official versions of coded rules for formal communication, but the most widely used are those developed by Henry Marlyn Roberts, a 19th-century army engineer. Following the Civil War, Roberts was active in civic affairs and presided over debates in a number of nongovernmental groups. At the time, these debates were chaotic because there were no clear rules for discussion and collective decision making, other than those used by official governmental bodies.

Roberts studied the formalized rules for communication used in the British Parliament and the U.S. Congress. He simplified them and produced a short set of guidelines for conducting formal meetings. They seemed to work rather well, and he had them printed up in 1876 under the title *A Pocket Manual of Rules of Order for Deliberative Assemblies*. To meet the growing demand, Roberts sold the rights to a publisher, and it was first marketed in 1896 as *Robert's Rules of Order*. The book quickly became the world's standard, as the "official" rules to be followed in formal decision-making groups. Over more than a century, the work has been revised many times and has sold more than 3 million copies.[29] Essentially, what *Robert's Rules* provides is a clear pattern of social organization, with norms, roles, ranks, and controls.

Robert's Rules sets forth very clearly a number of *clearly codified norms* that any such group must follow.[30] Some have to do with what constitutes a *quorum*—a sufficient number of members present so that official business can be conducted. Others describe procedures for asking for the *floor,* ways to present proposals. One doesn't say to the group, "Hey, can I talk now?" *Robert's Rules* requires that a plea for the group's attention be phrased as a formal request to have the floor. A member can speak only if recognized by the *chair,* and while he or she speaks, others cannot simply blurt out casual remarks. If they do, they will be ruled *out of order* by the chair, and their comments will be disregarded when discussion of a proposal is allowed. Other norms specify how to call for a vote and ways in which a particular motion can be taken *off the table.*

In decision-making groups using formally coded rules for communicating, *roles* are clearly defined. For example, the role of leader is labeled "the chair." Others in the group can be *delegates* (of some other body) or *representatives* (of some constituency). If the group is very small, they are more likely to be called simply *members*. Formal terms of address related to these roles are deemed appropriate. The chair decides whether proposals for action, or possible solutions to problems, have been communicated to the group in the form of motions. Only after the motion is seconded and the chair indicates that discussion is appropriate can comments or discussion take place. The official rules, then, tightly control both the nature and the flow of messages among people in specific roles.

The *ranks* specifying a hierarchy of power in a formal decision-making group are well defined, and power in the group is not uniformly distributed. At the bottom, below the regular members, is a rank that may include nonvoting members, such as a secretary, who does not participate in debate but is responsible for keeping the *minutes* (an accurate record of all transactions). There may also be a sergeant at arms, whose duties are restricted to controlling unruly members if necessary, although this seldom exists in small groups.

Generally, the largest stratum or level of a group is made up of voting members, and they do have both power and authority. For example, they can offer motions, or amendments to motions, that are persuasive and that capture votes. Through effective presentation of arguments, they can create consensus or conflict regarding a particular issue.

The greatest power is vested in the chair. For example, under formal rules, the chair controls the *agenda*—the topics and issues that will be discussed. He or she can add items to the list, remove or keep off other items, move one item up the list for earlier consideration, or delay discussion or votes on others. Debate can be restricted or extended by the chair, remarks can be ruled out of order, and certain members can be recognized ahead of others. Finally, only the chair has the power to cast the deciding vote in the event of a tie.

Official codes provide ample means for exercising *social control* over members with the use of explicit messages. For example, if a member performs a task for the group particularly well, a *resolution* commending the member may be brought to a vote. If it passes, it is entered into the minutes. On the negative side, critical messages about a motion or a participant's conduct can be offered by an irate member. A member judged to be deviant may be criticized in a specifically worded *motion of censure,* which, if passed by vote, is placed in the official minutes. Beyond this, resignations are sometimes requested. If communication completely breaks down and, for example, a fistfight erupts, a sergeant at arms may have to eject the offenders physically from the meeting. It is not surprising that groups employing integrative conflict management styles tend to make more effective decisions than groups using confrontational methods.[31]

Group Cohesion and Disorganization

The final questions asked in this chapter are: What keeps groups together? What causes them to break down? In every kind of group there are factors that move the participants to maintain their membership and to perform the activities required of them. That binding condition, which is called *group cohesion,* can range from very strong to very weak. As long as the basis of that cohesion is present, members will maintain their memberships and try to achieve whatever goals they are collectively pursuing. If cohesion erodes, the group will begin to break down. Thus, group disorganization often stems from bad communication processes rather than from bad people.

Distinct Bases of Cohesion

Social scientists who study group organization and disorganization have identified four distinct bases of cohesion.[32] The one that is fundamental to intimate groups is **sentiment-based cohesion.** A second, which characterizes the small task-oriented group, is **reward-based cohesion.** A third, called **assignment-based cohesion,** is found in the formal decision-making group. Finally, a fourth variety is *dependency-based cohesion.* This type of cohesion is not typical of small groups but is a condition that is found in large impersonal organizations where a complex division of labor provides interdependency among the system of roles. For that reason, it will be not be discussed here, but will be explained in Chapter 7.[33]

Sentiment-based cohesion in intimate groups. This type of cohesion is based on bonds of affection generated within the group; it cannot be imposed from without. Thus, with sentiment-based cohesion, members of a group are tied to one another by their feelings. In a highly cohesive group, the members feel a deep sense of loyalty and obligation to one another. They willingly set aside their personal interests, modify their expectations for the welfare of the group, and are ready to make sacrifices for the other members.[34] In such groups each member is valued not just for a role that he or she can play but as a person. Disruption of the group by illness, death, or other circumstances is a matter of deep emotional concern. In such a group, commitment to the group's goals is very strong.

Such powerful cohesion is not universal in small intimate groups. In some, individuals can be tied less deeply to the other members. This can be true in either families or peer groups. In such cases, individuals may value their membership, but they do not feel their bonds so intensely. For this reason, the strength of sentiment-based cohesion varies.

Reward-based cohesion in discussion groups. Discussion groups are seldom held together because of the strong feelings participants have for one another. Here, member satisfaction of a personal nature provides reward-based cohesion. People continue in therapy or weight-loss groups, panel discussions, symposia, and consciousness-raising or encounter groups because they derive personal rewards by maintaining membership. By participating, they feel better, learn important information, or gain beneficial skills. If there are no such personal rewards, the participants will likely drop out of the group. If people do not want what the group is trying to achieve or if they are getting little out of membership, they will not remain.

Assignment-based cohesion in decision-making groups. People who wind up on the same committee or board of directors are not necessarily bound by strong feelings for one another. In fact, they may be relative strangers or may even actively despise one another. Furthermore, they may see no personal benefit in participation. Yet, it is possible for them to work together effectively to accomplish the group's goals. The reason for this is that these members participate because they have been assigned the task. That is, they have been asked (or ordered) to serve by some authority, they have been voted into membership by a valued constituency, or they must serve for some other valid reason.

Thus, member behavior in small decision-making groups is more likely to be cooperative than disruptive; their members seldom deliberately generate problems. The social control system of the larger organization served by the group carries into the smaller context with powerful influences on its members. People's careers, raises, promotions, and reputations are at stake. Assignment-based cohesion, then, is a condition binding a person to a group based on a willingness to work with others to accomplish goals because that has been defined as the person's duty. At the same time, people who have been assigned to work together in a decision-making group may genuinely come to like one

another, and some level of sentiment-based cohesion can develop in such a group. Thus, the two types of cohesion can coexist.

Communication Breakdown and Group Disorganization

The very same factors that produce cohesion in a group can sometimes be sources of confusion and disequilibrium. Whatever the type of group, a loss of cohesion can occur if members are *unclear about its communication norms*. If these have not been effectively understood and shared, or if consensus breaks down about what kinds of messages, topics, or issues are approved and disapproved, **normative confusion** is the result. This can be a serious condition, and it can quickly result in group disorganization. In such a case, individuals lose effective guidelines, conflicts arise, and group disintegration is likely.

Another source of potential disorganization is *unclear role definitions*. Like norms, consensus and shared understandings concerning the communication requirements of the various roles in a group are achieved when members agree on who can appropriately say what to whom in what manner. If these shared understandings are inadequate or unclear, confusion about who should transmit what kinds of messages to whom will result. Whatever the type of group, such role confusion can be a major factor leading to a loss of cohesion.

Failure to gain consensus about the *legitimacy of ranks* is another source of potential disorganization. **Rank ineffectiveness** will exist if members come to believe that the messages transmitted by those in positions of power and authority lack legitimacy or credibility. Under such a condition, group coordination is impossible.

In summary, the very basis of effective control over group communication behavior lies in shared beliefs accepted by group members. Deviating from its pattern of shared expectations—its social organization—will bring disapproval of actions and messages. This can result in hostilities, departures, or rejections. Conforming to the shared expectations will result

BOX 6.3 *Ethical Concerns*

GROUPTHINK AS GROUP BREAKDOWN

Group breakdown can also occur because of what the well-known social psychologist Irving Janis describes as *groupthink*. According to Janis, groupthink occurs when the members of a highly cohesive group reach an agreement around the dominant view that emerges during discussion; thus, they think alike, rather than reaching an agreement after members have objectively and honestly evaluated the alternative solutions to a problem. In other words, even though group members start out with different views, they quickly and rather mindlessly change their views so as to correspond with the dominant position that emerges in the group discussion. When this happens, group members are not fulfilling their responsibilities as participants; they are, in fact, behaving unethically.

Source: Janis, I. (1972). *Victims of groupthink.* Boston: Houghton Mifflin; Janis, I. (1982). *Groupthink* (2nd ed.). Boston: Houghton Mifflin.

in approval or even honor. Generally, then, communication breakdown in a group is the reverse side of cohesion. This is an important principle, and it clearly implies that when things go wrong one need not attribute group disorganization to "bad actors" with problem personalities. More likely is confusion in the components of social organization that define acceptable communication.

At the same time, when individual members conform too closely to the group's pattern of social organization and do not tolerate individual differences, it can lead to problems. Communication scholars refer to a phenomenon that they call "groupthink." Obviously, only individual human beings can "think," but the basic idea is that all members of a group may come to think in the same way. They become so much in agreement that they believe that they are always right about whatever issues come before them. This results in close agreement on issues, a belief in their own invulnerability and superiority. If this does happen, innovation in approaching problems may be lost and the ability of the group to address new problems may deteriorate. (See Box 6.3.)

Chapter Review

- Groups consist of three or more people who repeatedly interact, regulating their conduct within some set of rules for communication and social activity they mutually recognize and follow. People participate in groups in order to accomplish goals they could not achieve by acting alone. Different types of groups provide distinctive communication contexts with unique features.

- The study of groups is divided into two broad classes on the basis of size—small groups and (larger) organizations. Size is essential to understanding the dynamics of communication. As the number of pairs that can be formed in a group grows, it becomes difficult to maintain a full flow of communication. Many communication specialists assert that five members is the optimal size for a small group with all members participating fully.

- Intimate groups, both the family and peer groups of close friends, are sometimes called primary groups because they are earliest in the individual's experience, and they are critically involved in the individual's socialization, enculturation, and personality development.

- Social relationships among group members are controlled by the group's rules of communication. These relationships may be informal or may be formally specified as part of a deliberate design. In many kinds of discussion groups, the rules dictating who can transmit what kinds of messages when and to whom emerge through a series of stages.

- Classic research suggests that three basic styles of leadership can be found in task-oriented discussion groups: the authoritarian, democratic, and laissez-faire styles.

- There are two kinds of factors that result in a particular person becoming a leader.

One is that the person has personality characteristics (traits) that people admire and respect. Another is that the situation determines leadership and that different types of people will be successful leaders in distinctive social situations.

- In every kind of group, some set of factors motivates participants to maintain their membership and to perform the activities required of them. Such group cohesion can range from very strong to very weak. As long as cohesion is present, members will try to achieve the goals of the group. If cohesion erodes, the group will break down.

Key Terms

peer group	socialization	small group conference
primary group	personality	therapy group
group	social expectations	encounter group
norms	enculturation	assertiveness-training group
roles	personality trait	consciousness-raising group
ranks	panel	sentiment-based cohesion
controls	round table	reward-based cohesion
informal communication	symposium	assignment-based cohesion
formal communication	seminar	normative confusion
decision-making group	forum	rank ineffectiveness
task-oriented group		

Notes

1. The term *primary group* is an old one. It was introduced into the study of communication in groups by Cooley early in the last century. See: Cooley, C. H. (1909). *Social organization* (pp. 23–31). New York: Charles Scribner's.

2. For a classic statement of this function of small and intimate groups, see: Cooley, *Social organization* (pp. 23–31).

3. Homans, G. C. (1950). *The human group* (p. 1). New York: Harcourt, Brace & Jovanovich; Brilhart, J. K. (1978). *Effective group discussion* (pp. 20–21). Dubuque, IA: William C.

Brown; Shaw, M. E. (1981). *Group dynamics: The psychology of small group behavior* (3rd ed.). New York: McGraw-Hill; and Goodall, H. L. Jr. (1990). *Small group communication in organizations* (2nd ed.). Dubuque, IA: William C. Brown.

4. A number of explanations have been advanced for why people choose to become members of groups. For thoughtful reviews of theories and other relevant issues related to the determinants of such membership, see, Trenholm, S. (1991). *Human communication theory*

(pp. 188–191). Englewood Cliffs, NJ: Prentice-Hall; and Shaw, M. E., & Gouran, D. S. (1990). Group dynamics and communication. In G. L. Dahnke & G. W. Clatterbuck (Eds.), *Human communication: Theory and research* (pp. 123–155). Belmont, CA: Wadsworth.

5. Among communication scholars there is disagreement about whether it takes only two people to form a group, or whether it takes three or more. Sociologists point out that two people can share a common goal; can interact and communicate so as to develop distinct norms common to the two, different roles, different levels of prestige, power, or rewards; and can exercise social controls over each other to stabilize these expectations. Communication scholars prefer to call two people a *dyad,* and to reserve the term *group* for at least three people who engage in such a pattern of social organization.

6. For a detailed discussion of the nature and importance of norms, roles, ranks, and controls in the patterns of social organization in many types of groups, see: DeFleur, M. L., D'Antonio, W. V., & DeFleur, L. B. (1984) Social organization. In *Sociology: Human society.* N.Y.: Random House (pp. 72–104).

7. Bethea, L. S. (2002). The impact of an adult parent on communicative satisfaction and dyadic adjustment in the long-term marital relationship: Adult-children and spouses' retrospective accounts. *Journal of Applied Communication Research, 30,* 2, 107–125.

8. The number of pairs (*p*) in any group of people can be calculated as the number of twos that can be drawn from n (the number of members). The formula is [$n \times (n-1)/2$]. If we care to consider combinations of more than two, such as triads or even larger coalitions that can exist in a group, the numbers become astronomical. Here, the algebraic formula is that for combinations, which is typically given as:

$$n\,C\,r = \frac{n\,(n-1)(n-2)\ldots(n-r+1)}{r!}$$

where *n* = the number of people in the group; *r* the number of people in a given coalition of, say, 3, 4, etc.

9. Fay, N., Garrod, S., & Carletta, J. (2000). Group discussion as interactive dialogue or as serial monologue: The influence of group size. *Psychological Science, 11,* 6, 481–486.

10. A classic early study is that of Bales, R. F., & Strodtbeck, F. L. (1951). Phases in group problem-solving. *Journal of Abnormal and Social Psychology, 46,* 485–495. Notable research on group decision development includes: Fisher, B. A. (1970). Decision emergence: Phases in group decision making. *Speech Monographs, 37,* 53–66; Poole, M. S. (1981). Decision development in small groups I: A comparison of two models. *Communication Monographs, 48,* 1–24; Poole, M. S. (1983). Decision development in small groups II: A study of multiple sequences in decision making. *Communication Monographs, 50,* 206–232; Poole, M. S. (1983). Decision development in small groups III: A multiple sequence model of group decision development. *Communication Monographs, 50,* 321–341; Poole, M. S., & Roth, J. (1989). Decision development in small groups IV: A typology of group decision paths. *Human Communication Research, 15,* 323–356; and Poole, M. S., & Roth, J. (1989). Decision development in small groups V: Test of a contingency model. *Human Communication Research, 15,* 549–589.

11. Bales, R. F. (1950). *Interaction process analysis: A method for the study of small groups.* Cambridge, MA: Addison-Wesley.

12. Tuckman, B. W. (1965). Development sequences in small groups. *Psychological Bulletin, 63,* 384–399.

13. For introductory-level overviews of research on communication with family and friends and in close relationships see: Pearson, J. C., Galvin, K. M., & Brommel, B. J. (1982). *Family communication: Cohesion and change.* Glenview, IL: Scott, Foresman. For more advanced reviews of these literatures, see: Blumstein, P., & Kollock, P. (1988). Personal relationships. In W. R. Scott (Ed.), *Annual review of sociology,* (pp. 467–490). Palo Alto, CA: Annual Reviews; Clark, M. S., & Reis, H. T. (1988). Interpersonal processes in close relationships. In M. R. Rosenzweig & L. W. Porter (Eds.), *Annual review of psychology,* (pp. 609–672). Palo Alto, CA: Annual Reviews; and Perlman, D., & Duck, S. (Eds.) (1989). *Intimate relationships: Develop-*

ment, dynamics, and deterioration. Newbury Park, CA: Sage. For a classic theory on child-development within the family, see: Piaget, J. (1954). *The construction of reality in the child.* New York: Basic Books.

14. The term *socialization* was developed by sociologists to identify the process by which a person learns and incorporates into his or her behavior the patterns of social organization of groups in which he or she participates. These may be small and intimate groups, large and formal ones, or others in between. A related term is *enculturation,* which refers to the process by which a person understands, accepts, and incorporates into his or her behavior the features of a culture in which he or she is participating.

15. This is a typical definition. No single definition meets the approval of all social scientists and communication scholars. The present one was derived from a basic version in: Adorno, T. W., Frenkel-Brunswick, E. Levinson, D. J. & Sanford, R. N. (1950). *The authoritarian personality* (p. 5). New York: Harper & Row. See: Houston, J. B., Bee, H., & Rimm, D. C. (1983). *Invitation to psychology* (2nd ed. p. 490). New York: Academic Press. A variety of studies have been published over the years that suggest that an individual's personality influences behavior in groups. See, for example: Beckwith, J., Iverson, M. A., & Render, M. E. (1965). Test anxiety, task relevance of group experience, and change in level of aspiration. *Journal of Personality and Social Psychology, 1,* 579–588; Cartell, R. B., & Strice, G. F. (1960). *The dimensions of groups and their relations to the behavior of members.* Champaign, IL: Institute for Personality and Ability Testing; Haythorn, W. (1953). The influence of individual members on the characteristics of small groups. *Journal of Abnormal and Social Psychology, 48,* 276–284; Mann, R. D. (1959). A review of the relationships between personality and performance in small groups. *Psychological Bulletin, 56,* 241–270; and Plax, T. G., & Rosenfeld, L. B. (1976). Dogmatism and decisions involving risk. *Southern Speech Communication Journal, 41,* 266–277.

16. The seminal work on the nature and origins of personality traits is: Allport, G. W. (1937).

Personality: A psychological interpretation. New York: Henry Holt. See especially chap. 11, A theory of traits, and chap. 12, The nature of traits, pp. 286–342.

17. Benedict, R. (1934). *Patterns of culture* (pp. 2–3). Boston: Houghton Mifflin.

18. This is, of course, a miniature version of the social contract theory of the origins of roles for behavior (laws), discussed by Thomas Hobbes in the 17th century. See: Hobbes, T. (1950). *The leviathan.* London: J. M. Dent and Sons. (First published 1651.)

19. Plato. (1941). *The Republic of Plato* (F. M. Cornford, Trans.). London: Oxford University Press.

20. For a thorough discussion of focus-group communication, see: Plax, T. G., & Cecchi, L. F. (1989). Manager decisions based on communication facilitated in focus groups. *Management Communication Quarterly, 2,* 511–535.

21. Robinson, D. T., & Smith, L. (2001). Getting a laugh: Gender, status, and humor in task discussions. *Social Forces, 80,* 1, 123–158.

22. Benne, K. D., & Sheats, P. (1948). Functional roles of group members. *Journal of Social Issues, 4,* 41–49. For reviews of both classic and contemporary studies on group roles, see: Moreland, R. L., & Levine, J. M. (1989). Newcomers and old-timers in small groups. In P. B. Paulus (Ed.), *Psychology of group influence* (pp. 143–186). Hillsdale, NJ: Lawrence Erlbaum; Levine, J. M., & Moreland, R. L. (1990). Progress in small group research. In M. R. Rosenzweig & L. W. Porter (Eds.), *Annual review of psychology,* (pp. 585–634). Palo Alto, CA: Annual Reviews; Shaw & Gouran, *Human communication,* pp. 134–136.

23. Miller, J. (October 11, 1998). Some in Japan fear authors of subway attack are regaining ground. *The New York Times,* p. 12; Guest, R. (April 22, 1995). 24 poisoned in new gas attack in Yokohama. *The Daily Telegraph,* p. 15; Eckert, P. (April 25, 1996). Doomsday cult leader Asahara charged with sarin attack on Tokyo subway. *The Herald* (Glasgow), p. 11.

24. A classic small-groups study that focused on these styles was done in 1938 under the direction of Kurt Lewin. See: Lippit, R., &

White, R. K. (1958). An experimental study of leadership and group life. In E. E. Maccoby, T. M. Newcomb, & E. L. Hartley (Eds.), *Readings in social psychology* (3rd ed.). New York: Holt. pp. 137–152.

25. For example, see: Stogdill, R. M. (1974). *Handbook of leadership: A survey of theory and research*. New York: Free Press.

26. Fiedler, F. E. (1967). *A theory of leadership effectiveness*. New York: McGraw-Hill.

27. For an excellent review of the classic investigations of personal characteristics and attributes that influence perceptions of social ranking and leadership see: Gibb, C. A. (1969). Leadership. In G. Lindzey, G. & E. Aronson (Eds.), *The handbook of social psychology* (2nd ed., pp. 4, 216–228). Reading, MA: Addison-Wesley. Also, for an excellent discussion of research examining the relationship among physical attractiveness and various social rewards see: Schneider, D. J. (1976). *Social psychology*, (pp. 471–476). Reading, MA: Addison-Wesley.

28. One of the best known of such studies was reported before observation of actual juries in action was prohibited by courts. See: Strodtbeck, F. L., & Mann, R. D. (1956). Sex role differentiation in jury deliberations. *Sociometry, 19*, 3–11.

29. Historical details about this important work were supplied by editors at Scott Foresman and Company, of Glenview, Illinois, where *Robert's rules of order* has been published for many years.

30. See: Roberts, H. (1981). *Robert's rules of order* (rev. ed.). Glenview, IL: Scott, Foresman.

31. Kuhn, T., & Poole, M. S. (2000). Do conflict management styles affect group decision making? *Human Communication Research, 26,* 4, 558–590.

32. These four types of group cohesion were developed by the authors specifically for this chapter. These will not be commonly found in the communication literature.

33. The concept of dependency-based cohesion was derived by the authors from the underlying theory of mechanical versus organic solidarity set forth by Emile Durkheim for describing social solidarity in contrasting types of societies. Our application is not to societies as a whole but to the kinds of groups included in our analysis. See: Durkheim, E. (1947). *The division of labor in society* (G. Simpson, Trans.). New York: Free Press. (First published 1893). Sentiment-based dependency was derived from the contrast between two distinctive types of social bonds that bind people to simple and complex social systems. See: Tonnies, F. (1957). *Gemeinschaft und Gesellschaft* (C. P. Loomis, Trans.). East Lansing: Michigan State University Press. Reward-based and assignment-based cohesion were developed by the authors for this text.

34. The classic study of this type of cohesion was of common soldiers in units of the German army in World War II. The members of such groups were so intensely loyal to one another as peers (but not to Nazi political ideology or to the German high command) that they resisted surrender and fought on even when the odds became hopeless. See: Shills, E. A., & Janowitz, M. (1948). Cohesion and disintegration in the Wehrmacht in World War II. *Public Opinion Quarterly, 12,* 280–315.

Chapter 7

Communicating in Organizations

It was a bright fall day in Boston and Jeremy felt really fine as he got off the bus and entered the building where he worked. He really enjoyed working at KidsToys.com in Cambridge. It was just the kind of job that he had hoped to get when he had graduated, only a year and a half ago. His focus on computer skills as an undergraduate had really been a smart move. The pay was truly great and he was planning on buying a BMW convertible within a short time—as soon as he paid off his student loans. His boss, Lucas Berne, was a remarkable guy. He had started his dot-com "B2B" (business-to-business) company only two years earlier with a large amount of venture capital. Lucas had had plenty of funds to get KidsToys.com going. Its stock value had gone through the roof when it was initially offered to the public.

Jeremy spent his days programming to develop and maintain the website where the company sold the toys of various manufacturers online. He also developed and managed the administrative and inventory programs and systems for the company. The line of toy companies represented was constantly growing, as more and more manufacturers wanted to sell to both retailers and customers online. It was true that KidsToys.com had yet to make a profit, but Lucas had assured Jeremy that profits would come soon.

Among the things that Jeremy liked about working at KidsToys were the "perks."

There were so many. Lucas really looked after his employees. He knew how working on a computer hour after hour could stress the shoulder muscles, and he had a masseuse come in twice a week and give a great massage to the programmers—right there in their cubicles at their desk chairs. Jeremy never had to dress up to come to the office. Every day was "casual Friday." Then there was the Ping-Pong table in the back room. If programmers felt stressed they could play a game or two to loosen up their forearms. There were also the cold soft drinks that one of the interns brought them whenever they signaled that they wanted one. Why would someone with strong computer skills work anywhere else?

As he entered the office suite, Jeremy saw that Lucas was already there. He had a worried look on his face and he asked Jeremy to come into his office.

"Jeremy," Lucas said, "I guess there is no easy way to say this. The business is going under. KidsToys is broke. I don't have funds left to pay any of the employees beyond the end of the week. We have used up virtually all the initial venture capital that we had to get started. Now, our stock value has gone down the toilet."

"But," Jeremy said with disbelief, "You told me just a few months ago that we were about to turn a profit."

"I know, I know, and I hoped and prayed that we would. But it just never happened."

"Does this mean I am out of a job?"

"I'm afraid so. I suggest that you just clean out your cubicle by the end of the day. Take all your personal stuff, of course. I'll have to liquidate all the equipment and furniture right away

so I can pay as many of our debts as I can. I'm truly sorry, Jeremy. I never dreamed that it would turn out this way."

When the day ended, Jeremy left the office for good, carrying a few personal items in a cardboard box. He wondered what in the world he was going to do now. Goodbye, BMW convertible! Hello again, tuition loans! He wondered how in the world he would ever pay off his loans. Even paying his rent was going to become a problem. He hadn't saved much money, so he had to find another job right away.

Three weeks later, after he had responded to a number of ads and leads, Jeremy had still not found a job. At first, he couldn't figure out what was wrong. One thing was clear. He had quickly found that few dot-com companies were hiring. He had to try something else. Right away he had noticed that not many of the companies where he got interviews had much interest in his computer skills. Of course, he realized that things changed so quickly in the computer and software world that he was starting to fall behind. But that wasn't the problem he was encountering. The personnel directors at the firms where he applied seemed to want something quite different.

Jeremy had realized almost immediately that he would have to dress differently. His first interview had turned into a disaster when he showed up in his usual casual clothing. The interview was terminated in only 10 minutes. He quickly learned to wear a clean shirt, a tie, a suit, and shined shoes. He even got a haircut.

Clearly though, he would have to do even more. In several of the places where he interviewed he had been asked to take writing tests. Some were standard tests that focused on sentence structure, grammar, and vocabulary. In other places the interviewers sat him down in front of a computer and asked him to prepare a two-page essay. Each assigned him a somewhat different topic to write about, but it was clear that in each case they wanted to assess his writing skills. Jeremy had never been very good at writing. He had concentrated on computers and sports as an undergraduate, and his grades in classes where writing was important had not been all that great.

The other thing he began to notice was that interviewers asked him a lot of questions that seemed to focus on something like verbal communication skills. What would he say to a coworker or group in this circumstance? How would he respond if some said this or that? How would he feel about giving a brief presentation to a group of clients or a report to a committee? It wasn't computer competence that they seemed to want as much as the ability to communicate effectively.

Jeremy finally found another job. He is now working in a large real estate company where he manages computer systems—a job that doesn't involve much in the way of dealing with other people. Jeremy feels that it is essentially a dead-end job. While it pays the rent and allows him to make small payments on his tuition loans, it's just not the sort of job he had when he worked at KidsToys.com. There are no stock options, no masseuse, no ping-pong table, no intern with soft drinks, and not even a casual Friday.

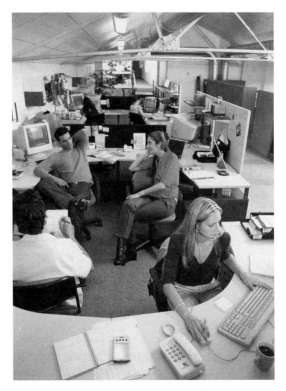

Communication within organizations follows both formal and informal channels. Formal channels specify rules for who can say what to whom on what topic. Informal channels, commonly called the "grapevine," include a complex set of passages through which people exchange gossip, rumors, or other unofficial messages by word of mouth.

In the late 1990s, the U.S. economy experienced rapid expansion and growth. Unemployment was low, and the Jeremys of the nation felt their futures were secure. However, the situation changed drastically in 2001. The tragic events of September 11, along with an economic recession and a drop in the stock market, resulted in the loss of jobs for large numbers of Americans in various sectors of the economy.

In spite of these changing conditions, it was clear that many available jobs were not being filled. Employers pointed to an increasing "skills gap" and described it as a long-term challenge facing the nation. The "new economy," they said, required an expanded list of capacities.

The employers also pointed to U.S. Department of Labor statistics showing that the typical person would now change careers about six times during his or her lifetime. What this indicates, they said, is the need for a workforce that does not have just one specific set of skills but the ability to learn new ones as well. Certainly, computer skills are crucial in the present and future workplace.

However, the employers also cited an increased need for "soft skills," such as *interpersonal communication, critical thinking,* and *problem solving.* In fact, a recent report by the Public Forum Institute concluded that these *"soft skills" were more sought after in candidates than were "hard skills," such as computer literacy and technical knowledge.*[1]

The reasons for this are many. First, employers say that it is essential that individuals entering the workforce be flexible and capable of adapting to new and changing work environments. However, employers also say that the explosive growth of technology in recent years has resulted in an environment where new software systems and applications are being introduced constantly. Knowledge gained before a person is graduated and obtains a first job quickly becomes outdated. Although employers feel that new hard skills can be taught on the job, they believe this is easier to accomplish when employees have the desired soft skills. In other words, it is important for job applicants to demonstrate the ability to learn, and one key indicator of this capacity is the *communication proficiency* of the applicant. Thus, communication has become increasingly important in the workplace and in **organizations.** (See Box 7.1.)

All modern urban-industrial societies, such as that of the United States and highly developed countries in other parts of the world, are highly dependent on large groups with complex patterns of social organization in which people work, study, or serve to carry on their activities. They can be found in business, industry, government, religion, education, the military, and virtually any other sphere of life where important objectives and goals are pursued.

Organizations have been studied for many decades—more than a century—by specialists in many disciplines, including management, economics, social psychology, sociology, and communication. The reason for such an intense focus by scholars is that organizations are critical to the prosperity; well-being; security; and, on occasion, even survival of modern societies.[2] Communication processes within organizations are different from those of other kinds of groups, and they are a critical part of the way that the groups function.[3] This chapter brings together in overview how designs for communication have been seen, not only by communication scholars but also by management and different types of social scientists over many decades. In particular, it focuses on both formal and informal communication processes within these important groups.

The Nature and Functions of Organizations

An organization is a human group in the same sense as discussed in the previous chapter. That is, it is a number of people who have come together to act collectively in order to achieve a goal that they could not attain acting alone as individuals. The term *organizations* is commonly used to label *large* groups that have carefully designed patterns of social organization. These are unlike the small spontaneous primary groups developed as members interact and communicate together.

In organizations the group's norms, roles, ranks, and controls have been thought out and planned deliberately before any people are brought in to carry on whatever activities are required to achieve its goals. That pre-designed pattern of social organization is *formal*—in the sense that it is set forth in documents, such as a table of organization, a reference book for rules and policies and written job descriptions. These provide "official" descriptions of the group's general norms, roles, and ranks, and of the controls that can be used to maintain the pattern.

BOX 7.1 *Workplace Perspective*

TEN COMMON WORKPLACE COMMUNICATION BLUNDERS

In a recent book, Stephen Viscusi has outlined a number of ways in which people in the workplace can make mistakes in both verbal and nonverbal communication—sending the wrong messages about themselves, providing meanings from which others can develop a negative image (implicit personality) of the sender that may be, shall we say, less than flattering. Here are some common blunders:

Blunder 1: *Do not share the intimate details of your life with your fellow workers.* Such sharing may make it difficult for them to see you as a competent professional.

Blunder 2: *If faced with a difficult confrontation, cool down and say little.* Walk away if you can and think everything over before responding.

Blunder 3: *Do not be a high-maintenance employee.* Avoid asking endless and pesky questions or frequently seeking unnecessary guidance.

Blunder 4: *Do not make a lot of noise.* This means not talking endlessly just for the sake of talking, humming, or even a lot of throat clearing. Such noise irritates people.

Blunder 5: *Get a good grasp on the meaning of "casual Friday."* Do not interpret it as "sloppy Friday." Check out your appearance carefully before going to work. Be casual but neat.

Blunder 6: *Do not engage in office gossip.* Listen to the grapevine to find out what people think is going on. You will learn a lot, but don't be an active gossip transmitter.

Blunder 7: *Do not mix romance and work.* People can find mates in the workplace, but if you do, do not communicate your relationship to fellow workers.

Blunder 8: *Choose e-mail words carefully and keep messages brief:* Long messages are a bore to read, and once the send key is pressed your emotional words cannot be taken back.

Blunder 9: *Remember that the boss is the boss, and that he or she has a boss.* The workplace is not a democracy. Know what your boss expects of you and be sure that you do it well.

Blunder 10: *Never put your résumé on your computer.* Someone will see it and assume that you are looking for another job.

Source: Based in part on: Stephen Viscusi, *On the Job: How to Make it in the Real World of Work* (2001). Three Rivers, MI: Three Rivers Press. See also a summary by Jaqueline Blais, (July 9, 2001) "On the job steers workers around blunders," *USA Today.*

However, there is a second organization to consider as well. It is the *de facto* one that emerges in practice once people are hired, or are otherwise recruited, to become actual members of the group. Then they have to carry out their day-to-day conduct and communicate with other members about the group's activities. When they do this, an *informal* pattern of social organization emerges. The reason is that people bring to the organization their own ways of doing things, their unique personalities—attitudes, values, opinions, understandings, and habits. These have profound consequences in shaping their behavior and bring participants to act out the group's pattern of social organization in unique and personal ways. Thus, there is both a *formal* plan for the group and an *informal* pattern of social organization in the conduct of the participants. Both play key parts in shaping communication within the organization.

As the organization's members engage in their activities, their communication patterns include all the verbal and nonverbal processes, both linear and transactional, that have already been discussed. Both within an organization and within the kinds of small group contexts that were described in the previous chapter, people communicate interpersonally, both formally and informally. However, an organization is *a distinctive communication context in its own right*. That is, it includes forms and processes of communication that are not found in the other contexts previously examined.[4]

As noted, an organization is a human group that has been deliberately designed to achieve a desired objective. Usually, it has a large number of participants, at least compared to the small groups discussed earlier. As indicated in the earlier discussion of the number of possible pairs in a group (Chapter 6, page 154), it is not possible for a large number of people to engage in interpersonal communication on a daily basis. Therefore a large group requires clear and complex rules that channel or restrict communication in such a way that the activities of its participants can be efficiently coordinated. This coordination is usually handled by a hierarchy of managers who transmit and receive various kinds of messages—upward and downward through the ranks; to and from the various participants; and, in a few situations, laterally from one part of the group to another.

There are many kinds of message transmissions that scholars in various disciplines call organizational communication. Some deal with ways in which the organization is related to outsiders—customers, clients, the general public, the political and legal systems, and so on. This chapter is primarily concerned with *internal* communication among workers, supervisors, and managers in the day-to-day operation of any kind of organization, whatever their goals and products happen to be. In this text, *organizational communication* is defined as *the transmission of messages, through both formal and informal channels, of a relatively large, deliberately designed group, resulting in the construction of meanings that influence its members, both as individuals and as a group.*

One way in which the goals of the thousands of large organizations existing in contemporary society can be understood is to view them within a framework of what a modern society needs. Those needs are different from those of more traditional societies. For example, as societies became more complex with the advance of the Industrial Revolution, more and more of the goods and services that their populations wanted and required had to be provided by organizations. The era of individual artisans, craftsworkers, and mom-and-pop operations as producers of goods declined sharply during the late 20th century. Larger and increasingly complex organizations were developed to produce and distribute consumer products and to satisfy growing markets for services.

Society's Need for Organizations

The basic needs of a population in any society are met by its social institutions. In this sense *institution* does not mean a particular group, like a college or hospital. It means a feature of a society that is "deeply established," or *institutionalized*. Within this meaning, a *social institution* within a society can be defined as *a broad arrangement of closely related cultural elements and organized social activities that are essential to fulfilling a perceived need of the social order.* Those cultural elements may be widely shared beliefs (e.g. "children are valued," "pursuit of profit is good," "democracy is best"). They may also be laws or other cultural rules, practices, values, or beliefs. They also include the groups that are necessary to carry on activities that fulfill the society's needs.

Although this definition may seem complex and technical, it can be illustrated easily. For example, the *educational* institution is one of the five basic ones that exist in every society—without exception. (Box 7.2 gives an overview of social institutions.) That is, organized social life requires that members born into the society be systematically introduced to its ways and requirements. In traditional societies, without formal schools, that task is usually assigned to parents or other relatives. These individuals are responsible for teaching children the skills they need as well as the rules for socially acceptable behavior. In our society today, some of those

BOX 7.2   A Closer Look

Basic Social Institutions

- *Educational institutions.* Introduce young people to and teach them about the ways and requirements of society.
- *Government institutions.* Render an order, predictability, and security in society.
- *Religious institutions.* Help people understand and try to influence the supernatural.
- *Economic institutions.* Handle the production and distribution of goods and services for a society.
- *The family.* The oldest and most fundamental institution, handles the bearing and rearing of children.

In modern urban societies, there are other institutions, such as medicine, science, spectator sports, and the mass media.

---

functions are still under the domain of the family, but many educational aspects are now handled by organizations, such as schools, churches, and even leisure organizations (such as the Girl Scouts and Boy Scouts).

In each institution a variety of groups may be developed to achieve the general goal of meeting a basic societal need. For example, in the religious institution there are many systems of beliefs, denominations, and so forth that serve this need. Some may involve great cathedrals or mosques, organized congregations, holy scriptures, and complex rituals. Others may include shamans, magic spells, the sacrifice of animals, or other designated procedures. Nevertheless, whatever their nature, they are part of the overall religious institution of their society.

All societies have five basic social institutions. In addition to the *educational* institution discussed above, the institution of *government* provides the order, predictability, and security that we need in social life. The *religious institution* meets our need to understand and try to influence the supernatural. The *economic institution* handles the production and distribution of goods and services. Finally, the *family*—the oldest and most fundamental institution of all—regulates the bearing and rearing of children within responsible and stable groups. In modern urban societies, there are many other institutions in addition to the basic five. Examples of today's newer institutions are medicine, science, spectator sports, and the mass media.

Against that background, the relationship among societal needs, social institutions, and organizations becomes clearer. It is easy to see this relationship with respect to the economic institution. Business enterprises, industries, banking, and commercial establishments that meet our economic needs are obviously structured around organizations. However, this is also true of other social institutions. Education, for example, is not just a matter of individuals learning how to read and the ways of their society. Our educational needs are satisfied by a complex list of beliefs, values, laws, groups, and their activities that provide educational services to millions of members of our society.

One reason for emphasizing the relationship between societal needs and social institutions is that scholars who specialize in the study of organizational communication typically have been more narrowly focused. They have been preoccupied with assisting management in solving problems of worker control and productivity in business and industrial environments.[5] Although this chapter addresses that issue because it is a traditional concern of the discipline, and is undoubtedly important, there is more involved in understanding organizational communication. Thus, several perspectives are presented that apply to all organizations, regardless of their location within a particular social institution.

Bureaucracy as a Theory of Formal Social Organization

The basic organizing theory of organizations is *bureaucracy.* It is a special way of defining the social organization of a complex group—such as the kinds of organizations discussed in this chapter. Unfortunately, the term has a number of negative connotations, such as red tape, mindless rules, and bumbling inefficiency. However, the technical meaning of bureaucracy is quite different and it is essential for understanding the link between an organization and the rules for communication that make it work. *Bureaucracy* in this technical sense, then, is defined as *a deliberately designed plan of the goals, norms, roles, ranks, and controls in an organization*. Simply put, it is these features that control an organization's patterns of formal communication, and they will provide a framework for the discussion in this chapter.

The need for bureaucratic organization arises for two reasons—group size and the complexity of the tasks a group must pursue to achieve its goals. Recall from Chapter 6 that as the number of members in a group increases, it rapidly becomes very difficult to maintain face-to-face communication. This means that frequent communication cannot take place among all members of a group larger than, say, about 20. Clearly specified and restricted channels of communication must be defined, if only to avoid having workers spend the entire day just trying to greet one another!

One of the critical features of a design for an effective organization, then, is provision for a formal communication network that will both *maintain cohesion* and make it possible for the group to *attain its goals*. In the sections that follow, we look closely at the nature of bureaucracy because in the sense defined it helps in understanding formal communication within a large and complex group.

Max Weber's Classical Theory of Bureaucracy

Although organizations have been with us since ancient times, the systematic study of the basic principles of their design did not begin until early in the twentieth century. A complex theory of bureaucratic organization was developed by Max

Weber's Four Principles of Bureaucracy

In articulating his theory of bureaucracy, the German born scientist Max Weber described four principles that should be inherent within a well-designed bureaucratic organization in a modern industrial society.

1. *Fixed rules.* Norms or rules within an organization should be grounded and concrete. These rules should be easy to follow and easy to learn. The rules should stay the same (remain fixed) for every individual within the organization.
2. *Division of labor.* Official rules and regulations concerning the duties of individuals holding various positions in an organization should be written out. These rules should be adhered to as a means of creating the most productive environment possible.
3. *Hierarchy of power and authority.* An established chain of command should be included in a well-run organization. Superior–subordinate relationships define who has power and authority over certain duties or individuals or both.
4. *Universal system of sanctions.* Workers' competence and performance levels in the organization should be the deciding factor as to whether they are promoted, demoted, given a raise, or fired. The criteria for this system should be fixed and applicable to all individuals within the organization.

Weber, a German social scientist.[6] (Box 7.3 describes Weber's four principles of bureaucracy.)

Weber developed his theory of bureaucracy to help clarify the broad societal changes that he saw resulting from the Industrial Revolution that had been taking place all during the 1800s. The underlying change was a movement away from traditional forms of society, in which relatively homogeneous and overwhelmingly rural societies were held together by cohesion based on sentiment, shared values, and beliefs.

The emerging urban-industrial society was quite different in that it was far more heterogeneous and impersonal; the new society was made up of many different kinds of people who did not have meaningful social ties to one another and who did not share the same set of values and beliefs. Nevertheless, they were able to live and work together in a coherent social order. Weber believed that one reason they were able to do so was that they made effective use of formal bureaucratic organization.

The Emergence of "Rational" Society

Weber began his analysis by asking an important question: If a population is heterogeneous and impersonal, how is the social order held together? That is, what is the basis of *social cohesion* in society itself? Weber believed that it was an outcome of the urban-industrial society's trend toward "rationality." Increasingly, he saw, the new society was developing around *thoughtfully designed organizations* that provided for the needs of their populations. He saw that there were two factors underlying this trend: society's increasing ability to design organizations along rational lines and an increasing understanding of the nature of the leadership that made such organizations work.

Weber wanted to understand the *basis of leadership* in the emerging rational order. This led him to an analysis of **authority** and the exercise of power in different types of societies. Understanding leadership in society as a whole and in its organizations, he felt, would provide an important clue to the basis of social cohesion. He saw that in earlier times, authority was often based on *tradition*. In some societies, it was based on *charisma*. In urban-industrial societies, however, authority tended to be based on *legal-rational organizational designs*. Each of these needs brief explanation.

The idea of tradition as a source for the leaders' authority is evident at almost all levels in many earlier societies. At the family level, the traditional power exercised by the father was virtually absolute. He had the undisputed, legitimate right to approve or disapprove of the actions of all family members. Similarly, the local lord of the manor had the (tradition-based) legitimate authority to assign work to serfs and peasants and to decide whether they could live on his lands. At the top of the society, the political sovereign's power was based solidly on tradition. An example is the Japanese society's traditional beliefs about the divine origins of the emperor. This was also the case among monarchies in other parts of the world.

A second source of legitimate power can come from **charismatic authority,** based on the personal qualities of the individual exercising power. Weber maintained that in such situations authority is grounded in charisma—a personal magnetism or charm that arouses feelings of loyalty or support in others.[7] For example, throughout history, strong personalities have emerged in many parts of the world. They brought together emotionally devoted followers into a remarkably cohesive whole. Powerful military leaders have often done this. To his followers, Genghis Khan seemed to possess extraordinary personal qualities. During World War II, this personal type of authority was characterized by Adolf Hitler in Germany and Benito Mussolini in Italy. Later, this type of charismatic leadership was characterized by Mahatma Gandhi in India and by the Ayatollah Khomeini in Iran.

Weber saw, however, that neither tradition nor charisma accounted for leadership legitimacy and authority in modern urban-industrial societies. Here, the exercise of power is far more likely to be based on what Weber called **legal-rational authority.** That is, leaders in the (bureaucratic) organizations that provide for institutional needs are usually selected or appointed not by tradition or for their charisma, but because they possess technical managerial skills, and they are permitted to exercise power within a limited sphere that is narrowly defined by official definitions and rulings.

Weber's Principles

Weber set forth a number of basic principles that should be present in the operation of a well-designed bureaucratic organization. Because his description is too complex to be presented in full, the focus here is on the central factors with which Weber was concerned. These help in understanding the nature of formalized channels of communication in bureaucratically organized groups.[8]

1. *Fixed rules.* This principle requires stable and explicit norms for all forms of behavior (including communication) that apply equally to everyone and that can be readily learned and followed. Today, such norms would include standards for relationships between male and female workers, between ethnic groups, and so forth.

2. *A rationally defined division of labor.* This principle requires that each position within the organization be mapped out in a formal (written) job description. The jurisdiction and official duties of the individual carrying out the specialized tasks of such positions should be set forth in official rules, laws, and regulations. These govern not only the exact activities to be performed but also what messages the person occupying the position can transmit to whom about what.

3. *A clear and graded hierarchy of power and authority.* This principle requires a chain of command in which the ranking system is formally set forth in an official plan. This shows that every worker has a supervisor, and every supervisor has specified subordinates. The official rules state who has authority to transmit what orders to whom, who must comply, who must communicate reports to whom, and so on.

4. *A fixed and universalistic system of sanctions.* This principle requires that workers be hired, promoted, rewarded, reprimanded, or fired solely on the basis of their competence and performance. The criteria should be made explicit and equally applicable to all (universalistic). That is, everyone should be judged by clear and uniform standards, and personal factors such as likes or dislikes, family ties, or, today, such factors as race, age, gender, and ethnicity should not influence the exercise of social controls. Such a system requires clear and accountable communication and records of all decisions concerning those rewarded or punished and the reasons on which such decisions were based.[9]

Although Weber was the pioneer in the systematic study of bureaucracy, scholars now publish thousands of research studies concerning many aspects of organizational design every year, especially from fields related to management.[10] As a result, a massive body of knowledge has accumulated about the relationship between types of organizations, various strategies of management, and the kinds of communication problems they engender.[11] In fact, so many different approaches, theories, and perspectives have been advanced that one scholar, Harold Koontz, has characterized the situation as the "management theory jungle."[12] Because it is impossible to cover such a body of knowledge in the present chapter, the next section provides a brief outline of several alternative ways of looking at organizations.

Management's Designs for Organizational Communication

As previously noted, the study of organizational communication today focuses heavily on problems of management and the design of production-oriented groups. This is perfectly understandable because factories, corporations, and other work-related organizations are at the heart of the economic institution in our industrial society. Communication within such groups has significant consequences for the society.

This section reviews four distinct theories of how communication is managed in work-related organizations. Each was originally developed as a means of promoting efficiency, raising productivity, and increasing output. Of course, these goals are critical to higher returns on investment—a deeply approved value in a capitalistic society. Thus, today's study of organizational communication is preoccupied with designs for the flow of messages and influences by which management can achieve more output from themselves and their employees.

The theories considered here were developed during the past two centuries. For simplicity, these can be called *human use theories* (developed between the early 1800s and the late 1920s), *human relations theories* (dominant from the early 1930s until the 1960s), and *human resources theories* (begun in the 1960s and still of interest today). More contemporary approaches such as *systems theories* are also included. Reviewing these theories provides an important foundation for studying communication patterns within organizations. Each of these theories reveals a different part of the organizational picture and the communication problems inherent in each.

Human Use Perspectives

In the first decades of the Industrial Revolution, those who established and managed factories or other organizations had little to guide their communication with employees but their intuition, prior experience, and common sense. They often made serious mistakes. They did not understand the social and psychological nature of workers or how workers could be motivated to produce more by effective messages. Additionally, managers did not view workers as sensitive human beings, but as *resources to be used,* along with machinery, and to be "exploited" much in the same way as are raw materials.

This kind of thinking was at the heart of the **human use perspective.** In fact, early in the 19th century, some owners and managers considered using slaves to work in the newly established factories, but public sentiment was against it. About the only other example of an efficient use of labor was the armed services. In the armed forces of the time, common soldiers or sailors were controlled in large part by violence; they could be flogged, clapped in irons, or even shot if they disobeyed orders, shirked on the job, or talked back to their superiors.

Communication within 19th-century organizations often seemed like military commands. Orders were given, and they were not to be questioned. Workers were often bullied into high levels of performance. Iron-fisted foremen drove them with blows and kicks. Low-performing workers were threatened with being fired. With no alternatives for earning a living, this meant disaster for their entire families.

A different way to communicate to workers the need for productivity was another human use perspective. It was based on what Weber referred to as "rationality." It focused exclusively on a *formula for wages.* In 1776, just as the Industrial Revolution was about to begin, Adam Smith published his *An Inquiry into the Nature and Causes of the Wealth of Nations*—one of the most influential books ever written and the foundation from which modern capitalism developed.[13]

During the early decades of the Industrial Revolution, Smith's ideas dominated thinking about management-worker communication. In particular, it was his ideas about the relationship between wages and the demand for labor that shaped the thinking of managers about the use and control of workers. Smith had maintained that if labor was scarce, higher wages would have to be paid—but a labor glut would permit them to be lower. Generally, he maintained, wages in balance with performance provide the proper return for work. Thus, wage level is not to be set based on humanitarian considerations, but solely on the demand for and the supply of labor, plus considerations of individual productivity. With little understanding of human nature as we know it today, wages were thought to be virtually the only means available to motivate employees. Thus, it was assumed that if ways to earn more money could be communicated to workers, they would rationally decide to work harder. It was an idea entirely consistent with the times.

Early in the 1800s, then, the major form by which managers communicated to motivate messages to workers was through **wage incentive systems.** Piecework formulas were developed so that wages were tied to personal output. That is, earnings for a worker in a production shop were determined by the number of units the individual produced in a given time period. Production norms (such as pieces produced by the worker per hour) were established for a standard day's work, and bonuses were added as motivating controls to stimulate workers to exceed those norms.

By the end of the 1800s, this approach to job design and to social control on the factory floor was in wide use. However, it had many problems. For one thing, workers hated it. They had discovered that if they increased the pace of their work—producing more per hour to receive bonuses—management would simply raise the norm to force their wages back down. Indeed that often happened. Then, they had to work harder than ever just to get the same wages as before. As a result, workers developed ways to undermine the piecework formulas to keep the norms down.

During the late part of the 1800s, Frederick W. Taylor developed a startling refinement of the human use approach for controlling workers. It came to be called **scientific management.** Taylor started his career as an apprentice patternmaker and machinist in a Philadelphia foundry. He gradually worked his way up and became a chief engineer in a large steel mill.[14] He began to make careful studies of conditions of work in the mill, and he was appalled at the inefficiency he found. Poorly qualified and ill-trained workers were left to figure out for themselves how to perform their jobs. The wage incentive formulas in use caused workers to restrict their output (which he called "systematic soldiering") to prevent management from raising workload norms.

Taylor decided to make detailed observations of how each worker actually performed his individual task in the mill. Taking careful notes and using a stopwatch, he painstakingly timed the various movements workers made while performing such mundane tasks as shoveling coal and lifting blocks of pig iron. As a result of his studies, Taylor was able to get workers to simplify, standardize, and control how they performed their tasks. Taylor rearranged work stations, controlled rest periods, and redesigned the flow of work through the mill. As a result of his innovations, the workers were less fatigued at the end of the day. In addition, they were able to increase their pay by an astonishing 60 percent! Furthermore, their increased efficiency raised the profit margins of the mill significantly.

It was with these *time and motion studies,* plus Taylor's other innovations, that "scientific management" was born. Essentially, it was a system for managing an organization by communicating rules to workers concerning how to perform their tasks, wage incentives, the flow of work, and patterns of authority. These ideas made Taylor famous.[15] He went on to develop his theories more elaborately, and by the beginnings of the 1900s, his principles of scientific management had been widely applied throughout the industrial world.

Unfortunately, Taylor's humane approach was not always followed by those who adopted his scientific management strategies for creating efficiency. Workers were often regarded as little more than mechanical cogs in the machine. Many were shamelessly manipulated and dehumanized as the drive to boost efficiency and maximize profits surged. During the Great Depression years, Taylor's open communication system between workers and managers was abandoned. However, even today, many of the innovations introduced by Taylor remain in use.

Still another important organizational design was embodied in what was later called the *universal principles of management.* These ideas were developed by theorist Henri Fayol, a French engineer and manager of a large mining enterprise. In 1919, Fayol published an important book setting forth his version of such universal principles.[16] He did not publish his book until he was 75 years old, and it reflects his many years as an experienced, practical administrator.

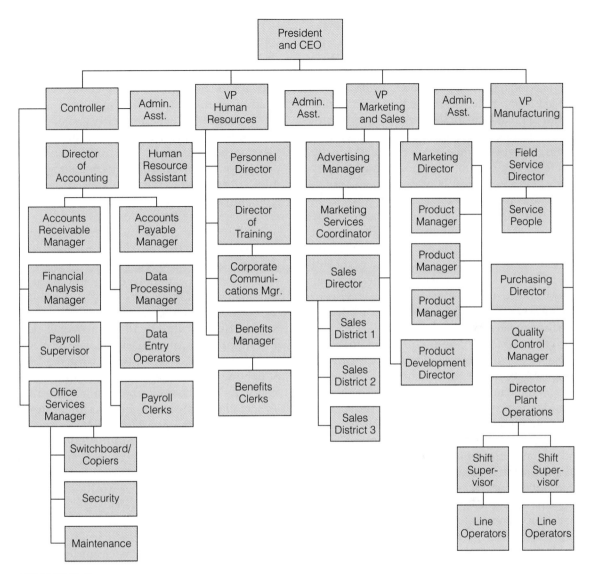

FIGURE 7.1

Organization Chart

An important feature of an organization chart is the graphic display of the links of power and authority in the group from top to bottom. It is also a map of the formal channels of communication, indicating clearly who must report to whom as well as who will give or receive orders from whom.

The most important contribution of Fayol was the *organization chart*. Such a chart communicates graphically the chain of authority and command and thereby the flow of formal messages. (Figure 7.1 illustrates such a chart.)

It is especially helpful in understanding the vertical flow of communication—up and down the organization. Fayol maintained that communication between supervisors and their subordinates should be easy and uninhibited, but it should also be restricted to the tasks or operations related to the work being done.

Furthermore, in normal operations, it was essential for communication to follow rigidly the channels mapped out in the organization chart. At the same time, he recognized that during times of crisis it might be necessary and helpful to "bridge" or bypass those formal channels. Thus, "Fayol's bridge" idea provided for the rapid transmission of vital messages when they were critically needed. However, this was necessarily an informal communication process. In recent times, this "bridging" process has recurred as an advocated idea in the federal government of the United States. A failure of communication by and between federal agencies, such as the FBI and CIA, was cited by some authorities as a critical factor that made it possible for terrorists to bring down the World Trade Center buildings on September 11, 2001.[17]

The work of Taylor and of Fayol added to Weber's classic bureaucratic theory in focusing attention on the essential nature of deliberate rational planning in the design of formal communication systems in organizations. Their norms, roles, ranking patterns, and systems of control (governing who should transmit what to whom) were not left to chance, spontaneous development, tradition, or common sense. People could work best in achieving their goals in organizations only if the activities and communication channels of every one of their members were deliberately defined. Few would quarrel with that generalization today.

Human Relations Perspectives

During the first two decades of the 1900s, American industry grew enormously. During the 1920s, for example, cheap immigrant labor, raw materials, abundant capital, weak unions, and seemingly insatiable markets brought manufacturers great prosperity. At that time, scientific management was in vogue. Business leaders were determined to maximize production by standardizing, organizing, and controlling all aspects of work—materials, space, pay incentives, and any other factor that would achieve top efficiency and profits.

The Hawthorne studies and their legacy. It was in the context of this search for ways to maximize production that a number of scientific management experiments began in 1924. They were conducted in Cicero, Illinois, at the Hawthorne Plant of the Western Electric Company.[18] These large-scale experiments were a joint effort between the huge Western Electric Company and the National Academy of Sciences. They have become classics in the study of organizational communication because they radically revised the thinking about how people communicate at work.[19]

One group of experiments in the series accidentally resulted in insights into the communication process. Researchers began by focusing on the effects of *illumination* on worker output. In the tradition of scientific management, their purpose was to see if some particular level of lighting would promote greater worker efficiency. As it turned out, the illumination studies serendipitously had significant implications for understanding important aspects of organizational communication, and they touched off a sweeping change in management philosophy. It was a shift from the perspectives of scientific management to what came to be called the **human relations perspective.**[20]

Strangely enough, the illumination experiments were total failures—at least from the point of view of scientific management experts. However, their seemingly inexplicable outcomes provided the major evidence that the personal and social characteristics of workers *as individual human beings* are often critical factors in the work process.

The scientific management perspective had regarded assembly-line workers as basically interchangeable—easily replaced parts or units that merely needed to be controlled and motivated by communicating to them simple economic incentives, or by other measurable factors. The illumination experiments were based on that perspective. The industrial engineers conducting the studies were convinced that output per worker was closely related to the *level of lighting* in the workplace—that is, the more light, the more work—at least within limits. They began by gathering *baseline data*. They recorded the output of three sections of women workers in the plant who were assembling telephone equipment. The women were fully aware of the nature of the experiments. They had been told that efforts were being made to find the best level of illumination to make their work easier and more efficient. Because pay was tied to productivity via a piece-rate system, this seemed fine to the workers.

After the initial baseline output levels were determined, the engineers began to vary systematically the level of lighting in the work areas, always keeping track of levels of worker output. During one week, they would increase the level of lighting slightly. The next week, they would lower it a bit or greatly increase the illumination. Finally, they would return to the very low level of lighting from which they had started. They maintained each of these conditions over a sufficient time period so that they were able to obtain accurate measures of per worker productivity. The engineers confidently expected that production per worker would increase with level of illumination, at least up to a point.

Oddly, however, every time the level of lighting was changed, *output per worker went up*—regardless of whether the illumination was increased or decreased. No matter what the condition, the workers just kept on getting more productive. Baffled by this, the engineers gradually lowered the lighting to a level where the workers could barely see what they were doing. Even this did not slow their productivity! At that point, the engineers threw up their hands and declared the experiments a total loss.

What they had failed to account for was that the workers had their *personal feelings and shared beliefs* about the experiments. The workers had informally discussed the situation among themselves, and generally they liked the idea that management was concerned about them.

They thought it was fine that management had sent the nice engineers to experiment and find the best level of illumination so that they could do their work better and make more money. They were happy that management was treating them in a special way and excited at being part of an important experiment. The women had talked it over and had decided to do a good job all the time, so that the experiments would be a success.[21] Those positive feelings motivated them to increase output, even when the lights were low.[22]

Given those understandings about human relations on the job, management set out to design new ways to increase worker efficiency. What they had to do now was to find messages that would motivate, encourage, and foster performance by taking advantage of factors in individual personality and human relationships.

This is the human relations perspective in a nutshell! Styles of supervision changed. New efforts were made to promote high morale and loyalty to the organization. Ways in which workers could obtain personal satisfaction and subjective fulfillment while working had to be built into the design of work organizations. Overall, the new gospel was that it was the responsibility of managers to design work environments in organizations that would produce high job satisfaction. (Remember the massages and the Ping-Pong table provided for Jeremy at KidsToys.com.) The assumption was that such satisfaction would lead to high work performance.

In reality, sometimes the human relations perspective worked and sometimes it didn't. Although it was more humane than earlier ones, the human relations approach to organizational management could not universally guarantee worker efficiency. However, the human relations theories did make it clear that social ties existing among workers and their patterns of informal communication were critical factors in tying the worker to the organization.

In summary, the early theories of Weber, Taylor, Fayol, and others were fine as far as they went. However, they were incomplete. They made it clear that the de facto organization was made up of some combination of the deliberately designed bureaucratic rules and the spontaneous peer group communication that emerged as people worked with one another on the job. Human beings at work develop complex networks of likes, dislikes, friendships, and animosities. These provide the basis of deeply established channels of informal communication that have nothing to do with the organization chart. The discovery of the importance of informal communication within the larger organization, then, was largely a result of the rather curious Hawthorne experiments. The study of informal networking and the kinds of communication that occur within this part of the organization thus came to be pursued with vigor by communication scientists and management specialists alike.

The decline of the human relations perspective. Overall, the human relations perspective remained the dominant one until the 1960s. However, managers slowly lost much of their initial enthusiasm for its principles because it was extremely hard to implement. Furthermore, in some cases it produced unforeseen and often undesirable consequences. For example, in practice it proved to be difficult to communicate freely with rank-and-file employees, and supervisors who tried to be caring and sympathetic to workers were sometimes seen as weak and indecisive by both workers and higher-level managers.

One requirement of the perspective—involving workers in decision making, policy formation, and power sharing—proved to be particularly difficult. People who lack expertise often make bad decisions. Effective policy making demands solid knowledge and experience, and it is not for amateurs. Furthermore, those who have status and power seldom want to share it with those lower in rank. These are central activities of management, jealously guarded by those with driving ambition. They are often the center of political upheavals in organizations, such as when competition for promotion be-

comes keen. Involving rank-and-file workers in such activities often created an uproar of unwanted tensions and conflicts.

In more recent years, still other perspectives have developed. Among them is the **human resources perspective,** which proved to be remarkably successful in at least some settings. The Japanese, in particular, used this approach in their organizational designs, and it helped their nation to become very productive.

Human Resources Perspectives

Although it is not widely known in the United States, some of the fundamental principles of industrial production that helped Japan to develop a strong economy following World War II were not invented by the Japanese. These principles were taught to the Japanese at the time by an American, W. Edwards Deming—a statistician and management consultant. Deming had developed a complex philosophy of industrial production that stressed *quality* above all else.

At the close of World War II, Japanese industries were in shambles—virtually bombed out of existence. But President Harry Truman and other American leaders decided that rather than punishing the nation for its misdeeds, they would develop a reliable ally against the Soviet Union that had emerged as a new threat. This was to be done by assisting the Japanese in rebuilding their lost industrial base. Deming was brought to Japan to help train postwar managers in techniques that would establish a solid manufacturing basis for the rebuilt economy.

Deming insisted that the best way to ensure a strong place for Japan in the postwar industrial world was get them to produce goods of maximum quality. That was a drastic change from prewar Japan, when the emphasis was on cheap goods of low quality. With his objective in mind, Deming taught Japanese industrialists to emphasize the production of goods manufactured *to the highest possible standards.* He provided them with a very clear program as to how to achieve this goal from a technical point of view. He believed fully that because they were, so to speak, starting from scratch, the Japanese could become a major industrial power within a relatively short time. To say that he was right is to understate the situation. By the 1960s, Japan was well on the way to becoming one of the world's foremost economic powers. Indeed, it remains second only to the United States today, even at a time of intense global competition.

Perhaps no one was more surprised at their success than the Japanese. They listened politely to Deming, and, equally politely, they followed his program. The end result was the incredible rise of postwar Japan as an industrial power producing goods known for their high quality. Today, Japanese automobiles, electronic consumer goods, and other products retain that reputation. As one Japanese executive wrote in his diary in 1950:

> Here was this tall American telling us that we would be an important force in five years if we listened to him. We really didn't believe him, but in order not to lose face, we did what he told us, *and it worked!*[23]

In terms of organizational communication, by 1970, it was clear that Japan was doing something different in its design of production-oriented organizations. The Japanese had not only adopted Deming's guidelines regarding statistical bases for quality control and management, but they had also developed production organizations with patterns of communication that were very different from those used in the Western world.[24]

Essentially, Japan had implemented a *human resources perspective* in their design of organizations. It was a management theory based on the belief that bonds of loyalty and attitudes of dedication to work can be created among employees by selective patterns of management–worker communication. The Japanese implemented this perspective in a way that was totally consistent with their culture and equally consistent with the principles of management brought to them by Deming. For example, until

recent times, many Japanese workers were virtually assured of lifetime employment in the same firm, and they were promoted solely on the basis of seniority. This was clearly contrary to Weber's principles, but it eliminated cutthroat competition among employees that could threaten the goals of the larger group. For example, in such a system, managers would have no reason to feel threatened by competent and successful subordinates. Those subordinates could communicate their ideas, which could then be incorporated into production processes.

Things have changed in Japan today. Lifetime employment in many organizations can no longer be counted on. Other nations have become industrialized, and an increase in the number of global multinational corporations has added to an intensely competitive environment. However, Japan's unique perspective on organizational communication and management style allowed it to overcome the devastated position in the industrial world that it started from at the close of World War II, and to do it swiftly and dramatically.

Even now, because Japan's population is racially and ethnically homogeneous, there are fewer barriers to communication than are typical in the multicultural United States. Senior members of a Japanese firm listen to and understand ideas suggested by those lower in the organization's hierarchy, which also makes training and indoctrination easier. Also, bonds are created between workers and management that would be more difficult to establish in a racially and culturally diverse labor force.

The Japanese realized that workers on the line have insights and a grasp of the production process that cannot be understood by executives far removed from day-to-day operations. For that reason, they created small groups of workers called *quality control circles*. These are composed of individuals from particular units right on the line whose members all face the same production task. In industries where they are used, they meet weekly as discussion groups and are coordinated by their supervisor. Their objective is to find ways in which their particular assembly work can be done more efficiently and at a higher level of quality. Their solutions are taken very seriously by management, and, if implemented, the group earns cash bonuses and awards.

The Japanese strategy was also tried in the United States, but was never particularly successful. It was quite different from the U.S. tradition, where jobs were usually designed by remote experts and where worker suggestions were often unwelcome. Under such conditions, workers seldom care about quality because they have no personal stake in the outcome. The Japanese quality control circles, on the other hand, effectively make use of human resources—the insights, talents, skills, and loyalties of workers—to improve efficiency of production and to maintain high standards in products. In other words, the channels of communication between workers and management are deliberately kept flexible and open, and workers' messages come through loud and clear.

In summary, the human resources approach is related to the human relations theory, but there are important differences. In particular, the human resources approach is more complex. Essentially, it sees employees as a major potential resource for the organization in terms of talent, energy, dedication, and pride in work. If the ideas of these human resources can be communicated effectively and incorporated into the manufacturing process, the result will be both efficiency in production and high quality in products. The task of management, then, is to design a system that minimizes communication barriers and leads to high performance by workers while maximizing factors that motivate them to work at a high level of quality.

Contemporary Perspectives

The search for models of organizational effectiveness did not end with human resources perspectives, however. Organizational theorists and practitioners recognized that classical and humanistic theories, such as those already described in this chapter, failed to consider the *effect of the environment* upon the organization. Thus, more contemporary perspectives such as *systems theory* were developed to acknowledge the interrelationship of different components, both within and outside, of the organization that have an impact on the organization.

Systems theory, derived in part from ideas developed in the field of botany, views the organization as similar to a living organism, composed of multiple subsystems working together to achieve balance or *homeostasis*. The subsystems of an organism, and the subsystems or parts of an organization, are related and function in similar ways. If one part of the organism breaks down, for example, the rest of the system is directly affected. In like manner, if one person in an organization fails to complete his or her work, the entire organization can suffer. Thus, the organization is a system of *mutually dependent parts*.

In addition to the interdependency of its parts, systems theorists emphasize the *synergy* of the organization. This means that the combined abilities and knowledge of organizational members is greater than the sum of the efforts of individuals working alone. In other words, members of the system who work together also learn together, and they are more effective and creative because of their interactions with each other.[25]

However, in order to maintain balance and "health," the organization must also consider the *outside environment*, which has a strong influence on its operation. This includes all political, economic, social, and legal or regulatory factors or institutions that may have a positive or negative impact upon the organization. Previous theories did not recognize the environment as a factor in the effectiveness of workers or the organization.

Finally, systems theory emphasizes the critical importance of *communication* within the organization. Communication is a central focus of the organization, rather than just a means for

BOX 7.4   *Workplace Perspective*

TEN EASY RULES FOR MANAGING YOUR MANAGER

The key to a successful working experience is to understand some basic rules for managing your manager better than he or she manages you. It is important to establish a relationship of mutual respect and confidence between you and your boss. He or she needs to know you as a decent and hard-working employee. Here are some basic rules offered by Guy Browning:

Rule 1: *Do your job without bothering him or her.* A good employee does not need to be managed. Develop your own solutions that get the job done the way the boss wants it.

Rule 2: *Inform the boss before doing it—not afterward.* Keep your boss "in the loop" by regular informal communication about what you are doing—but don't be pesky and overdo it.

Rule 3: *Unleash the power of gratuitous flattery.* Bosses are people and they like to be told what a good job they are doing. Flatter selectively. Do not overdo it or be too obvious.

Rule 4: *Ask the boss for his or her wisdom.* Ask bosses for specific advice and make them believe they have helped, even if you already know what they tell you. It makes a boss feel good.

Rule 5: *Help your boss to do his or her job.* Remember that someone is evaluating your boss

and that anything you do to make him or her look good will be appreciated.

Rule 6: *Go to your boss with solutions, not problems.* Do this and you will be seen as making positive contributions, not as a source of annoying problems to be solved.

Rule 7: *Do more than is required of you.* Relieving the boss of some task makes his or her life easier and expands your area of responsibility—and improves your evaluation.

Rule 8: *Treat the boss like a colleague and a sensitive human being.* This does not mean trying to become a pal, but it does mean making the boss feel better and less like a formal manager.

Rule 9: *Never undercut your boss with negative comments to fellow workers.* You may feel that such criticism is justified, but it is unwise and it may get back to him or her.

Rule 10: *Always invite your boss to office-related gatherings of fellow workers.* Bosses like to think they are appreciated and can mix easily with their employees, even if they can't.

Source: This list is based on Browning, G. (January 10, 2002). How to manage your manager, *People Management, 8,* 102.

---

controlling the behavior of workers. In other words, communication is the "glue" that holds all the subsystems together, enabling them to function in sync with each other and with the environment in which the organization operates.[26]

In recent years, managers and theorists have focused more closely on the degree of change in the modern workplace. With heavy reliance on computer systems and electronic methods for sending and retrieving information, organizations face more challenges as they seek ways to manage and process the massive amount of information they receive and process. Organizations must constantly adapt to changing technologies and global competition. It is not surprising, then, that newer theories that emphasize chaos and complexity are gaining support. Thus, it is clear that newer theories will continue to be developed to reflect the changing nature of the world in which people communicate and work together to achieve common goals. (See Box 7.4.)

The Flow of Messages in Large Organizations

One of the most important of all the kinds of behavior constrained by an organizational design is *formal communication*. That is, an important function of the social plan of any organization is to direct the way that messages flow through the system. As we have already noted, formal communication takes place only within a set of carefully defined rules between certain designated parties. Several other features could be added to that definition: Its messages concern only a range of topics *relevant* to the organization; they are transmitted and received via *prescribed media;* and their purpose is to *accomplish goals* set by the organizational design. That rules out all forms of personal messages transmitted for reasons other than the official business of the organization. A simple way of describing formal communication in an organization is to say that *the design for the content, transmission, and reception of messages dictates who can say what, to be received by whom, about specific kinds of topics, by communicating with what medium, in order to achieve specified types of goals.*

Because official channels of formal communication are so tightly controlled and restrained, and because they can be used for only a limited range of topics, more flexible and open channels for informal communication develop. People working in groups need to communicate in a variety of ways about a host of issues and topics. For that reason, the **grapevine** and other similar informal systems and networks also develop and are used to convey a great many messages to and among large numbers of people about a variety of topics without noticeable restrictions on their transmission.

Formal Communication through Official Channels

Four issues need to be considered in describing the flow of official messages through an orga-nization. One is the nature of the channels themselves—*who* is allowed or required to communicate *with whom.* The second concerns the kinds of *topics* that make up most of the message content. The third is the *quality* of communication. Finally, it is important to understand the *consequences* of both the restrictions and the limitations on accuracy produced by the formal communication system.

Vertical transmission. As can be seen in almost any organization chart, the hierarchical structure almost automatically implies **vertical transmission.** That is, in a group with clearly graded levels of power and authority, communication must by definition flow either up or down in the system. If messages follow the design, employees at the bottom in a given unit communicate formally only with their supervisors. Those supervisors, in turn, communicate formally only with the individuals who command their particular division, and so on up to higher-level officials and ultimately to the top. No one is supposed to short-circuit these channels and leak important messages between categories or across lines of authority.

Message content in formal communication. The message content that flows upward and downward through formal channels in almost all organizations is remarkably similar. What kinds of messages flow *upward* in a formal communication system? In most organizations, most messages deal with the following four categories of content:

1. *Routine operational messages.* A large part of the upward flow of messages consists of technical details about materials needed, inventory completed, personnel issues, accounting data, cost estimates, and the like. These provide the day-to-day data used by managers to make routine decisions.

2. *Assessments by experts.* These are messages regarding the best ways to accomplish certain kinds of goals or to do particular kinds of work. Employees at or near the bottom

often have precisely the skills, knowledge, and experience that supervisors need to understand when preparing proposals or designing work roles. Consequently, this type of content is sent up the line.

3. *Feedback on completion of tasks.* Reports on how well orders were carried out and on what results were obtained provide important insights needed at the top. Such details can be provided only in the form of reports that are initiated at the lower levels where the work is actually performed.

4. *Reports on problems.* Decision makers at the top must have full knowledge about problems encountered either within or outside the organization. These messages provide vital input so that policies can be changed to minimize such problems. Top management makes many decisions. The quality of those decisions depends on the accuracy and timeliness of the message content that moves up the system.

Looking at vertical transmission from the other direction, what are the categories of messages that flow *downward* in the formal system? Again, these messages generally fall into one of the following four basic categories of message content:

1. *Routine operational messages.* This is the counterpart to the first category of upward–flowing information.

2. *Specific orders and instructions.* These focus on particular individuals, concerning matters such as new job assignments, promotions, and staffing changes. They also include instructions concerning the production or processing of particular services or products (for example, how many are to be ready by what time).

3. *Operating guidelines.* These are generally messages on long-term matters. They may concern ways to perform particular kinds of work, how to allocate space for specific functions, means to incorporate certain materials, how to package finished products, or ways to handle the clients in a particular order.

4. *Policy-shift directives.* These messages usually concern relatively broad changes in the way of doing things. They represent shifts in the goals of an organization, in its organizational plan, or in the general way in which work will be handled. For example, a shift from a paper-based to a computerized accounting system, with consequent personnel changes, could be a policy-shift directive.

Messages moving within the formal channels are often critically important both to the people who send them and to those who receive them. People's jobs can depend on the kinds of messages they receive in the way of orders, assessments, reports, and instructions. Their rewards can be linked to how accurately they interpret the meanings that the messages are intended to convey. Indeed, improving such communication is a key factor in the motivation of employees.[27]

Given this high level of importance, it would seem to follow that people would make few mistakes, either as senders or as receivers, in constructing or interpreting official organizational communication; but the fact is that errors are common. What, then, are some of the factors that can contribute to a loss of accuracy, misunderstanding, and other limitations on the degree to which the meanings aroused by such formal communication are similar in senders and receivers?

Accuracy versus distortion up and down the line. As messages move upward and downward, a number of factors tend to distort the meanings that are encoded and decoded by those involved in the chain of transmission.

Viewed within both the linear and simultaneous transactions models (see Chapter 1), policymakers, managers, and supervisors at every level have the problem of *effective role-taking.* That is, they must encode their messages in such a way that, when they are transmitted downward, their content will be both understood as intended and influential in shaping the behavior of the persons they are supervising. If either of these goals is not achieved, the messages are ineffective. There are many reasons to anticipate that role-taking problems will be encountered. Furthermore, managers and supervisors face the challenge of effectively interpreting feedback—interpreting the real meanings of messages that originate with subordinates and that may have undergone change as they traveled upward.

To begin to understand how such a formal system can fail to provide for accurate communication, consider the fact that it is human beings who formulate the messages that move up and down the line and human beings who receive those transmissions and try to interpret their meanings. Unfortunately, no human being is a perfect sender or receiver, and many factors can distort and limit the paralleling of meaning between communicating parties. This is as true in the organizational setting as it is in any other communication context. In fact, given the significance of work and career to those involved, such factors may operate in this context with particular force!

Consider, for example, what can happen to formal messages that move up through an organization's hierarchy. (Box 7.5 summarizes how messages can be distorted as they move upward in an organization.) Such messages may not be interpreted correctly because they have been:

1. *Condensed.* Messages tend to grow shorter and more concise as they move up from one level to another. For example, a written report explaining a mechanical breakdown or a complex personnel matter is likely to be a much briefer version when it lands on the desk of the chief executive officer than it was when formulated several levels below by an immediate supervisor. Even the phrase *to brief* (an executive) implies that subordinates supply condensed versions of what has actually taken place.

2. *Simplified.* This is a counterpart to condensing a message. Details are selectively deleted from complex reports. They are then

organized around the most salient details. Often this transforms the content into simplified categories, such as "good," "bad," "all," or "none," whereas this was not the case in reality. This represents a loss of richness of detail that, although seeming to clarify the issue, actually deprives the original message of subtle interpretations. It may also exaggerate mild situations or conditions at the bottom into more glaring problems when they reach the top.

3. *Standardized.* Messages are couched in standard terms familiar within the organization's jargon. The original events may be of such a nature that the official language does not describe them accurately. For example, a soldier who, despite his or her best efforts, was unable to get back to base on time (for example, canceled flight) may be classified in official jargon as AWOL (absent without official leave). Unfortunately, this implies a deliberate moral transgression (which was not the intention) that should be punished. Thus, meaning is changed.

4. *Idealized.* A message transmitted to a higher level may be rephrased to cast the

sender in the best possible light. People want their supervisors to believe that they acted wisely and within organizational guidelines. Thus, they may leave out certain details and modify others almost unwittingly so as to idealize their own behavior.

5. *Synthesized.* The transmitted message may be combined with additional details to form a more understandable overall picture, even when the added meanings were never part of the original event. For example, a report on an individual who behaved unusually may have included a comment that the person was in the care of a psychiatrist several years earlier. This fact may have had no bearing on the incident, but it could obviously introduce distortions in the interpretations made by those above.

Messages coming *down* the line can also undergo characteristic changes, and their intentions may be undermined. The factors that may produce such a result are the same general communication factors that limit the degree to which senders and receivers achieve completely parallel meanings or the degree to which messages modify the behavior of receivers. (Box 7.6 lists these distortion factors.) Formal messages from supervisors may not be interpreted correctly for any of the following reasons:

1. *Selective exposure.* Messages may not be read or heard for a variety of reasons, including fatigue or just plain circumstance. Messages get misfiled, misplaced, and accidentally thrown away.

2. *Selective attention and listening.* Even if a person hears a message in full, attention may wander and listening may deteriorate. Busy people may be distracted by others, and attention to a formal communication may lapse. People are often surprised when they reread a message and find meanings in it that they simply did not notice the first time.

3. *Selective perception.* It has been shown repeatedly that the psychological process of organizing incoming message symbols into associated meanings is a complex activity that is

BOX 7.6   *A Closer Look*

Messages Can Be Distorted as They Move Down the Line

1. Messages may have *selective exposure* because receivers misplace them, lose them, or only read one part of the message.
2. Some messages receive *selective attention and listening*. They may be distorted because the receivers are distracted or their listening deteriorates for one reason or another.
3. Messages may be *selectively received* because receivers' physiological factors reshape what receivers hope for, want, fear, or like.
4. Messages may be *selectively retained and recalled* because receivers tend to remember what they want to remember and to repress what seems stressful, punishing, or difficult to interpret.
5. Messages may be processed with a degree of accuracy but they may be *selectively acted on*. The actions may be postponed for a variety of distorting circumstances.
6. Messages may be distorted because individuals at different points during transmission have *vocabulary differences;* they may not share the same meanings for important words or phrases.

fundamental to the communication process. Assigning meaning to formal messages in an organization follows the same general principles set forth in earlier chapters. In addition, formal messages coming down from high places are a particularly important kind of transmission that may have implications for a person's welfare. Therefore, perception and interpretation take place within a system of personal attitudes, beliefs, values, and expectations that may influence reconstructed meanings. To a considerable extent, those psychological factors may reshape the interpretation to fit with what the receiver hopes, wants, fears, or likes.

Along those lines, a message's meaning may be transformed by a receiver to minimize a potential threat; this is commonly referred to as a perceptual defense. Another transformation of meaning may occur because of perceptual set, whereby a receiver expects a particular meaning to be implied in a message. Although these are subtle psychological reactions, selective perception does operate to modify the meanings received, even via channels of formal communication that have been carefully designed to minimize misinterpretations.

4. *Selective retention and recall.* No one's memory is perfect. Receivers tend to remember complex meanings in important messages in very selective ways. This process involves reshaping message symbols to fit the interpretation of a particular receiver's hopes, wants, fears, or likes, in very selective ways. For example, people tend to remember good or rewarding parts of a message and to repress (unconsciously forget) those parts that seem stressful, punishing, or difficult. For this reason, a message coming down the line may be well understood at the time of reading, but later it may be remembered in a distorted way.

5. *Selective action.* Even if a message is perceived and interpreted accurately and remembered fully, it may not be acted on as requested or ordered. Circumstances may require that some of the ordered actions be postponed, modified, or ignored. Subordinates quickly learn how to sidestep or avoid difficult or unrewarding actions requested by supervisors, or how to develop logical reasons why the orders cannot be followed as specified.

6. *Vocabulary differences.* Well-educated managers and less educated employees may not have the same vocabulary, or they may not have the same meanings for words that they do share. Furthermore, in a multicultural society, language usages may vary among people who come from different social categories. These factors may distort interpretations of a message due to the different ways that people establish conventions linking words, realities, and subjective meanings.

Informal Communication in Organizational Contexts

Not only is the actual organization made up of its deliberately designed structure, but also it includes the social ties among the many small and intimate groups of peers found in any large group. Thus, messages flow not only through the official channels prescribed for formal communication but also through informal grapevines—complex social pathways in a network of intimate groups.

The use of the term *grapevine* can be traced back to the 1860s, during the Civil War. Because battle fronts moved frequently, the telegraph wires that were used by the army were loosely strung from tree to tree across battlefields, similar to grapevines. Because the wires needed to be hung quickly, and little effort was given to the care with which they were installed, the messages transmitted over them were often garbled, leading to misinterpretation and inaccurate communication. In time, rumors or unofficial commands were said to have been heard "via the grapevine." The grapevine has been part of organizational culture ever since.[28]

Social constructions of meaning. It is through such networks that rumors are passed on, gossip is exchanged, and word-of-mouth diffusion of important news is transmitted. In many ways, the fate of an organization may depend on message content within this network and how well it works. If communication through the grapevine continuously contains meanings defining management as negative, uncaring, callous, or exploitive to workers, then these are the socially constructed meanings about management that workers will share. This sharing validates such meanings—gives them social legitimacy. Individuals use these meanings to build or rebuild their personal beliefs about the organization. If this happens, a very different organizational culture may develop from the one desired by the organization. For such reasons, studies of informal communication within organizational grapevines can be very important.

Capacity, flexibility, and speed. Generally speaking, informal communication networks within an organization convey a great number and variety of messages on a day-to-day basis — possibly exceeding the number carried in the formal channels. These networks are very flexible, which is exactly the opposite of the channels for formal communication. In the informal process, messages flow by word of mouth, telephone, computer, and notes. They move without restriction, both up and down the ranks and horizontally within a given stratum. Certain centers for the exchange of messages facilitate the process. These include restrooms, coffee machines or water coolers, the cafeteria or lunchroom, and the parking lot. Indeed, any point or place where employees frequently encounter one another or get together can serve as a message center. Furthermore, people call one another at home and continue the process after working hours.

Because of these conditions of few barriers, many channels, and virtually no restrictions on content, informal communication can flow very swiftly to surprisingly large numbers of people. In this sense, it is a very efficient form of communication in that it can bring messages and meanings about a variety of topics to a large number of participants in a relatively short time. "Cybergossip" (gossip by computer) has made the grapevine an even faster means of communication.

The messages, rumors, and gossip that travel through the grapevine can have a dramatic impact upon the organization. However, these messages also have consequences for those who initiate them. Informal communication can enhance or detract from the influence an individual has in the workplace depending on the nature of the communication.[29]

Distortion of Messages in the "Grapevine"

The accuracy of an organizational grapevine can be very low. This is not always the case, however, especially with very short messages (such as "The boss has just quit" or "Jane has been promoted"). Nevertheless, for more complex messages, a number of specific patterns of distortion have been found by social scientists studying word-of-mouth communication as it occurs in a variety of contexts.

Two general patterns of distortion characterize the spread of rumors, the movement of news reports from one person to another, and almost any similar interpersonal transmissions of verbal messages. These two patterns will be described separately, but in reality they tend to occur together in the same setting when a particular message is transmitted by word of mouth along an interpersonal grapevine. The first is the **embedding pattern,** which has been widely studied by social scientists and communication specialists interested in the flow of messages through certain kinds of social pathways.[30] The second is the **compounding pattern,** which appears to characterize rumors transmitted within communities or large groups, such as military organizations.[31] Both are found in almost every organizational setting.

The embedding pattern. The embedding pattern refers to a particular set of distortions in a message that may occur when it is transmitted orally from one person to the next in a kind of serial pattern. That is, a person learns firsthand about some event or condition and then passes on a message about it by word of mouth. The receiver lacks access to whatever realities prompted the first person to formulate the story but passes on a new version of the message to a third. From there it continues in a chain of tellers and retellers, none of whom have actually seen or heard the facts that were the basis of the original account.

Such a system is typical of what often happens along a grapevine, and it invites several kinds of distortions. A considerable amount of research has identified three specific forms of distortion that often characterize the content of a message as it moves along a chain of tellers and retellers. These are **leveling, sharpening,** and **assimilation.**

Leveling refers to a general shortening of the original account, rumor, or story. As it travels from one person to the next, limitations of attention, perception, and memory (much like those discussed in distortions of formal communication) quickly reduce the message to fewer words and ideas. If the original account is relatively long, it can lose as much as half of its detail as it is retold by the first person in the chain. The second will forget additional details and pass on a still shorter account. The story or rumor continues to shrink in number of words and details as it passes on through additional individuals until only a short (leveled) version remains. This brief version is then passed along more or less intact as it continues to move from one person to another.

Sharpening is the counterpart of leveling. As the story or account shrinks, it becomes organized around its more central or salient details. The version becomes increasingly concise until it is only a summary of the original message. This is a result of the way human beings construct meanings and store them in memory. Inevitably, this results in loss of detail, and consequent distortions creep in as the message is successively repackaged into briefer and briefer versions.

Assimilation is a process by which the message is reshaped by the psychological characteristics and culturally learned habits of the person who hears it. This is what most people call distortion, in that meanings are changed and the story undergoes transformations in content. These transformations can be substantial. They occur because of selective perception, memory, and recall based on individual attitudes, values, and other personality factors. They also occur because of cultural tendencies to think about topics in characteristic ways. To illustrate, a man and a woman who are married, but not to each other, can be reported as having been seen in a lengthy and private conversation. The next person, with romantic orientations, may interpret this as a possibly passionate encounter. A third, using cultural definitions of male–female relationships as potentially implying intimacy, speaks of the couple as lovers, and a juicy scandal sweeps the organization.

Through leveling, sharpening, and assimilation, then, the embedding process can produce many unexpected and unusual changes in the content of a message as it moves by informal word-of-mouth communication through the grapevine of an organization.

The compounding pattern. The second major pattern of distortion is what DeFleur has called the compounding pattern.[32] When a message transmitted along a grapevine is of especially high interest to a group, it can move very swiftly and can undergo a pattern of distortion that is quite different from that described by the embedding process. A substantial body of research has revealed a pattern whereby an original message passed by informal communication in a grapevine gains additional details and interpretations that were never part of the original. This tends to happen under two conditions: first, if the original message is relatively brief and, second, if it is of a threatening or disturbing nature.

To illustrate, assume that a short rumor is transmitted along the grapevine to the effect that the factory will be closed and everyone will be laid off. Such a tension-producing message is likely to travel through the informal network very swiftly. However, as it moves along, individuals are likely to add elements that they believe are relevant and that help explain what is happening. One may have heard that some government agency was planning an investigation. Another may have heard that accountants were seen working overtime. These elements could be compounded into the idea that the factory was going to close and all would lose their jobs because the owners were going bankrupt as a result of someone mismanaging the funds. On this basis, the story could grow even more with the retelling. Speculation would arise as to who would be fired first, when the closing would take place, and what benefits would or would not be provided for those let go. Further, rumors could circulate about who mismanaged (embezzled?) the funds and who is being investigated.

In reality, the embedding and the compounding patterns tend to work together in the actual transmission of rumors through a grapevine. A story can grow one day and shrink the next. It can be shortened, assimilated, and compounded at the same time. No single pattern characterizes the flow of messages in a process of informal communication in an organizational grapevine. What can be said with certainty is that messages transmitted in this manner are very likely to result in reconstructions of meaning by receivers.

Implications for Managers

As the previous discussion indicates, the grapevine is not all *pinot noir*. Informal communication networks suffer many problems such as the inaccuracy of the content that is passed along and misinterpretation by those at the receiving end. Another potential problem is the threat of legal action arising from false information that is passed along in the workplace. In recent years, lawsuits for defamation, fraud, invasion of privacy, emotional distress, harassment, and discrimination have resulted from grapevine inaccuracies.

Yet, the grapevine can also be an asset to an organization. Although some managers try to silence the grapevine in order to avoid problems, management communication scholar Patricia Karathanos recommends instead that certain ground rules be followed to promote a "healthy" environment in which the grapevine operates. These include the following:

1. *Accept that the grapevine exists and don't try to eliminate it.* Although it has the potential to create problems, it can also be used to benefit the organization.

2. *Acknowledge the fact that the grapevine should generally remain unrestrained.* When managers try to systematically thwart or take control of it, the grapevine can loose its effectiveness.

3. *Do not underestimate the power of the grapevine or its importance to the organiza-*tion. Ignoring the grapevine can do more harm than good, as many managers have learned the hard way.

4. *Make use of the grapevine, rather than remaining a passive observer.* Monitor the content of the grapevine, so that false information can be corrected before damage is done. Used this way, it can serve as an early warning system for the organization. Indeed, managers often use the grapevine to send "trial baloons" or to test new plans or ideas and get employee reactions before final decisions are made.

5. *Maintain all formal communication channels in the organization.* The grapevine is not a substitute for formal communication; the idea here is to use the grapevine as an effective supplement.

6. *Remind and encourage organization members to question and assess the accuracy of grapevine messages before responding to them.* This will help keep the grapevine from becoming a facilitator of false rumors that can seriously damage the organization.[33]

Consequences of Organizational Communication

Communication processes in organizations are extraordinarily complex. Both formal and informal communication provide the basis for different forms of social organization and pathways for the flow of messages.[34] This rich flow has at least two major consequences: The first is the development of a unique or specialized organizational culture and the second is the development and maintenance of two kinds of cohesion that binds the members of the group to the whole.

Specialized organizational cultures. Every human group has a culture. As will be explained in Chapter 8, specialized cultures are those beliefs, attitudes, values, and patterns of behavior shared within some segment of a society that distinguish it from the general culture of the society. Within each organization, an internal culture develops that is unique to that particular group. Thus, IBM, your college or university, and the U.S. Army all have specialized internal cultures that are different from that of any other category or group. Similarly, each government agency, church, prison, and bank has its own specialized internal culture. It includes all the physical objects, attitudes, values, beliefs, sentiments, rules, and special language produced and shared by its members. In short, the internal culture makes the organization a unique context.

Moreover, within any organization, there are many mini- or microcultures. These are highly localized versions of unique cultures that are developed by particular branches or divisions— or even small groups of peers and friends.

Unique organizational cultures develop from two basic sources: One is the official organization as it functions with its carefully defined channels of formal communication; the other is the informal network from which many individual microcultures at all levels of the organization develop. In some organizations, the group's overall internal culture may support the organization and help it achieve its goals. In others, conflicting microcultures can become the basis of serious conflict. The next question to ask is, How are these unique cultures related to communication channels in the group?

Cultures in conflict. Recall the earlier discussion on the vertical nature of the formal channels of communication in large organizations. In a typical production-oriented industrial organization, then, within the engineering division, formal messages flow up and down the line. They do the same within the manufacturing division and within the sales division. However, few formal messages cross these boundaries. Engineers seldom communicate extensively with sales specialists, who in turn seldom communicate with those who manufacture the product. This results in three separate communication structures that foster unique cultures within the three divisions.

Thus, engineers, sales personnel, and manufacturing specialists develop and use their own languages and habits of perception. Within each of these separate cultures, people share distinctive attitudes, values, and beliefs that are not the same as those of the other divisions.

There is always a danger that these differences among unique cultures within a diverse organization will interfere with overall communication, that the language of one may become incomprehensible to the others. These are barriers to effective communication, even of the formal type, and the degree to which the group can achieve its goals is limited.

Such cultural differences can become a basis for *conflict*. Remember, even small groups of work associates can develop a microculture. A small group on the day shift, and an equally small group on the night shift, who do exactly the same work on the same machines, may have different microcultures. One may share favorable views toward management whereas the other views management negatively. In such circumstances, one group has been known to quietly sabotage the other.

Organizational cohesion. If some form of cohesion did not exist within an organization, there would be no way to keep its members performing the often unpleasant tasks needed to accomplish its goals. We saw earlier that various management-oriented approaches have tried to find policies and strategies to enhance motivation to keep workers performing at a high level of efficiency. These approaches were based on the necessity of providing personal goal satisfaction to maintain the loyalty and dedication of individual group members.

Organizational cohesion is different from personal satisfactions, such as one might derive from a good salary, a secure job, or high status. It is also different from that which keeps other kinds of groups together. For example, earlier it was discussed that it is sentiment-based cohesion that binds members to small intimate groups, such as families and peers. However, it is reward-based cohesion that characterizes discussion groups and assignment-based cohesion that operates in small, formal decision-making groups.

Cohesion in an organization is not easily explained by any of these types. Such a group is kept together as an organized whole by what is correctly called *dependency-based cohesion*.[35] This type of cohesion is a product of the complex division of labor that produces a strong pattern of dependencies among individuals (and even units) within an organization. To illustrate, workers on the assembly line depend on clerks in the payroll division who process their wages into a check. In turn, those clerks would have nothing to do if it were not for such workers. In the same manner, every person performing a task in the entire division of labor produces a product or service on which others depend. Such people may not even know each other— or if they do they may dislike each other. Nevertheless, they are in a relationship of mutual task dependency that holds the overall group together so that it can function as a unit.

What coordinates the activities within this division of interdependent labor is formal communication. For example, the payroll department would have no idea how much workers should be paid without formally communicated data regarding pay scale, hours worked, and so on, for each individual. Similarly, throughout the system, a flow of formal communication provides vital instructions that coordinate subgroups and individuals performing specialized tasks within the structure.

Generally, then, formal communication is the basis on which dependency-based cohesion is established and maintained. That was true at the time the pyramids were built, and it remains true today. If that formal communication becomes disrupted, distorted, or even delayed, serious consequences follow. Realistically, however, we must look at all four types of cohesion to explain fully what holds an organization together, enables individual members to satisfy their needs, and makes it possible for the group to attain its collective goals. That is, the bonds that link members to the whole in the de facto organization are based on a combination of sentiment-based cohesion within small groups of work associates, reward-based cohesion in more temporary groups, assignment-based cohesion among members of decision-making groups, and dependency-based cohesion that is a product of interrelated tasks in the overall structure. Throughout, however, communication in all its various forms holds the organizational system together.

Chapter Review

- An organization is a relatively large human group whose pattern of social organization has been rationally designed to achieve a desired objective. Any large group requires complex rules for communication so that the activities of its participants can be effectively coordinated. This is usually handled by a hierarchy of managers who transmit and receive messages, upward and downward, to and from the rank and file and, more rarely, laterally among themselves.

- Bureaucracy is a theory of social organization used in designing the goals, norms, roles, ranks, and controls in an organization. While some denounce its negative features, it is the impersonal rules of bureaucratic theory that define the basic ways in which people communicate and relate to each other in large groups with formal patterns of formal organization.

- Leadership in organizations is based on what Max Weber called legal-rational authority. Such leaders are usually selected because they possess technical managerial skills, and they are permitted to exercise power within a limited sphere that is narrowly defined by official definitions and rulings.

- Four general theories that focus on strategies of organizational design, management, and communication have been developed during the past two centuries: *human use, human relations,* and *human resources* and *systems theory.* Each incorporates very different systems of communication between workers and management in organization.

- Formal communication takes place only between clearly designated parties; it concerns a restricted range of organization-relevant topics; and messages are transmitted and received via prescribed media. In short, formal communication dictates *who* can say *what* to be received by *whom* about specific *topics* making use of what *medium.*

- Messages flow not only through the official channels prescribed for formal communication but through grapevines as well. Two general types of distortion have been found—the embedding pattern and the compounding pattern—that characterize the spread of informal messages through grapevines.

- A specialized internal culture can be found within any organization. Members of the group share language patterns, beliefs and orientations that set it apart from other similar groups. Furthermore, within the organization microcultures can develop in various units and divisions or even among small groups of work associates. These unique cultures can support an organization, or they can be the basis of serious conflicts.

- The bonds that link members in an organization are based on a combination of sentiment, reward, assignment, and dependency-based cohesion that is a product of task interdependencies in the overall structure.

Key Terms

organization	scientific management	compounding pattern
authority	human relations perspective	leveling
charismatic authority	human resources perspective	sharpening
legal-rational authority	grapevine	assimilation
human use perspective	vertical transmission	organizational cohesion
wage incentive system	embedding pattern	

Notes

1. *Help wanted: Workforce development and the new economy.* A report prepared by the Public Forum Institute, 2002. The report can be found at www.publicforuminstitute.com.

2. In earlier times of war, the survival of a society was largely a matter of the strength and bravery of individual armed men who fought each other in hand-to-hand combat. In modern times, individual bravery is still important, but wars are won or lost on the basis of production of military equipment, technology, and supplies that support armed forces. That was the case in World War I. It was true in World War II, when the Manhattan Project (a gigantic complex of organizations) provided the means to end the war with Japan. It clearly remains the case today as organizations produce the advanced technology that determines the outcome of conflicts.

3. For excellent elementary discussions of the importance of groups and communication in organizations, see: Goodall, H. L., Jr. (1990). *Small group communication in organizations* (2nd ed., pp. 1–21). Dubuque, IA: William C. Brown; Richmond, V. P., & McCroskey, J. C. (1990). *Communication in organizations* (pp. 1–10). Edina, MN: Bellwether. Also, for more advanced discussions see: Jablin, F. M., Putnam, L. L., Roberts, K. H., & Porter, L. W. (Eds.). (1987). *Handbook of organizational communication.* Newbury Park, CA: Sage; Jablin, F. M., & Sussman, L. (1983). Organizational group communication: A review of the literature and model of the process. In Greenbaum, H. H., Falcione, R. L., & Hellweg, S. A. (Eds.), *Organizational communication: Abstracts, analysis and overview* (Vol. 8, pp. 11–50). Beverly Hills, CA: Sage.

4. For excellent discussions of both the historical roots and the distinctive aspects of organizational communication, see: Jablin, F. M. (1990). Organizational communication. In G. L Dahnke, & G. W. Clatterbuck (Eds.), *Human communication: Theory and research* (pp. 156–182). Belmont, CA: Wadsworth; Redding, W. C. (1979). Organizational communication theory and ideology: An overview. In D. Nimmo (Ed.), *Communication yearbook 3* (pp. 309–342). New Brunswick, NJ: Transaction; Redding, W. C. (1985). Stumbling toward identity: The emergence of organizational communication as a field of study. In R. D. McPhee & P. K. Tompkins (Eds.), *Organizational communication: Traditional themes and new directions* (pp.15–54). Beverly Hills, CA: Sage.

5. Contemporary examples of research that have focused exclusively on assisting management in their control of workers include: Richmond, V. P., Davis, L. M., Saylor, K., & McCroskey, J. C. (1984). Power in organizations: Communication techniques and messages. *Human Communication Research, 11,* 85–108; Richmond, V. P., McCroskey, J. C., & Davis, L. M. (1986). The relationship of supervisor use of power and affinity-seeking strategies with subordinate satisfaction. *Communication Quarterly, 34,* 178–193; and Richmond, V. P., Wagner, J. P., & McCroskey, J. C. (1983). The impact of perceptions of leadership style, use of power, and conflict management style on organizational outcomes. *Communication Quarterly, 31,* 27–36.

6. See: Weber, M. (1947). Wirtschaft und gesellschaft, Part I of which has been translated by Henderson, A. M., & Parsons, T. (1947). *The theory of social and economic organization.* New York: Oxford University Press. A good secondary source is Gerth, H. H., & Mills, C. W. (Eds. and Trans.). (1946). *From Max Weber: Essays in sociology.* New York: Oxford University Press.

7. Perhaps an ultimate example of charismatic power in recent times was that of the Reverend Jim Jones, who in the 1960s established a religious group called the People's Temple. In the early 1970s, the group developed an agricultural community in Guyana in northeastern South America. In 1978 the Reverend Jones called on his more than 900 followers to join him in committing suicide. The world was horrified when these people unthinkingly followed his command.

8. Weber's analysis of the nature of bureaucracy was not focused exclusively on problems of communication. In fact, it dealt more centrally with components of formally prescribed social organization (which, of course, depend on well-defined channels of communication). For purposes of this text, we have adapted his analysis to emphasize communication issues.

9. This list is a composite drawn from: Henderson & Parsons, *Theory of social organization,* pp. 333–336. See also Gerth & Mills, *From Max Weber,* pp. 196–204.

10. Kreitner, R. (1983). *Management* (p. 38). Boston: Houghton Mifflin.

11. For representative reviews of the contemporary research on organizations and organizational behavior, see: O'Reilly, C. A., III (1991). Organizational behavior: Where we've been, where we're going. In M. R. Rosenzweig & L. W. Porter, (Eds.), *Annual Review of Psychology, 42,* 427–458. Palo Alto, CA: Annual Reviews; Ilgen, D. R., & Klein, H. J. (1989). Organizational behavior. In M. R. Rosenzweig & L. W. Porter (Eds.), *Annual Review of Psychology , 40,* 327–352. Palo Alto, CA: Annual Reviews; House, R. J., & Singh, J. V. (1987). Organization behavior: Some new directions for 1/0 psychology. In M. R. Rosenzweig & L. W. Porter (Eds.), *Annual review of psychology, 38,*

669–718. Palo Alto, CA: Annual Reviews; Rothschild, J., & Russell, R. (1986). Alternatives to bureaucracy: Democratic participation in the economy. In R. H. Turner & J. F. Short, Jr. (Eds.). *Annual Review of Sociology, 12,* 307–328. Palo Alto, CA: Annual Reviews.

12. Koontz, H. (1961). The management theory jungle. *Academy of Management Journal, 4,* 174–188.

13. Smith, A. (1976). *An inquiry into the nature and causes of the wealth of nations.* Chicago: University of Chicago Press. (First published 1776.)

14. Copely, F. B. (1923). *Frederick W. Taylor: Father of scientific management* (p. 3). New York: Harper & Brothers.

15. See: Taylor, F. W. (1919). *Principles of scientific management.* New York: Harper & Row.

16. Fayol, H. (1949). *Administration industrielle generale.* Translated by C. Storrs as: *General and industrial management.* London: Isaac Pitman & Sons.

17. Flynn, K. (January 30, 2002). A nation challenged: Emergency policy; a focus on communication failures. *The New York Times,* section A, p. 11; Downes, L. (June 4, 2002). Connect government stovepipes. *USA Today,* p. 13A.

18. Mayo, E. (1966). *Human problems of an industrial civilization.* New York: Viking. (First published 1933.)

19. The entire series of the Hawthorne studies are discussed in detail in: Roethlisberger, J., & Dickson, W. J. (1939). *Management and the worker.* Cambridge, MA: Harvard University Press.

20. For a concise overview of human relations theory and the human relations school, see: Pace, R. W., & Faules, D. F. (1989). *Organizational communication* (2nd ed., pp. 40–42). Englewood Cliffs, NJ: Prentice-Hall; Goldhaber, G. M. (1990). *Organizational communication* (5th ed., pp. 43–48). Dubuque, IA: William C. Brown.

21. This type of outcome, in which the experiment itself fosters motivations and behavior among subjects that can interfere with the results, came to be called the "Hawthorne effect." It is a standard research hazard to which social scientists are alert when they study human behavior in experimental settings.

22. Our account of these experiments is necessarily a simplified one. In later years they became more controversial than our discussion would make it seem. Various *post hoc* interpretations have been offered in later years about why the results were obtained and what they really mean. Some of these are quite different from those offered in the original reports. See, for example: Carey, A. (1967). The Hawthorne studies: A radical critique. *American Sociological Review, 32,* 403–416; Frank, R., Kaul, J. (1978). The Hawthorne experiments: First statistical interpretation. *American Sociological Review, 43,* 623–643.

23. Roth, J. (1985). The stuff that quality is made of. *Industrial Management, 9, 7,* 18–19.

24. McMillan, C. J. (Spring 1982). From quality control to quality management: Lessons from Japan. *Business Quarterly, 32.*

25. O'Hair, D., Friedrich, G. W. & Dixon, L. D. (2002). *Strategic communication in business and the professions,* 4th ed. Boston: Houghton Mifflin.

26. Byers, P. Y. (1997). *Organizational communication: Theory and behavior.* Boston: Allyn and Bacon.

27. Hymowitz, C. (May 28, 2002). Need to boost morale? Try good food, fitness and communication. *Wall Street Journal,* B1.

28. Karathanos, P., & Auriemmo, A. (1999). Care and feeding of the organizational grapevine. *Industrial Management, 41, 2,* 26–30.

29. Kurland, N. B., & Pelled, L. H. (2000). Passing the word: Toward a model of gossip and power in the workplace. *The Academy of Management Review, 25, 2,* 428–438.

30. The seminal study is that of: Allport, G. W., & Postman, I. (1947). *The psychology of rumor.* New York: Henry Holt.

31. For a summary of classic studies on these issues, see: DeFleur, M. L. (1962). Mass communication and the study of rumor. *Sociological Inquiry, 32, 1,* 51–70.

32. This concept as a description of message distortion in rumor transmission was introduced by DeFleur, M. L. (1962). Mass communication

and the study of rumor. *Sociological Inquiry, 33,* pp. 51–70.

33. Karathanos & Auriemmo, Care and feeding of the organizational grapevine.

34. For additional discussions of formal and informal communication see: Shockley-Zalabak, P. (1988). *Fundamentals of organizational communication: Knowledge, sensitivity, skills, values* (pp. 47–51). New York: Longman; Daniels, T. D., & Spiker, B. K. (1991). *Perspectives on organizational communication* (2nd ed., pp. 92–101). Dubuque, IA: William C. Brown; Kreps, G. I. (1990). *Organizational communication* (2nd ed., pp. 195–221). New York: Longman.

35. This is a version of what Emile Durkheim called "organic solidarity" in his classic analysis: (1947). *The division of labor in society* (G. Simpson, Trans.). New York: Free Press. (Originally published 1893.)

Chapter
8

Communicating Between Cultures

The Boeing 747 touched down at Chicago's O'Hare and slowly taxied to the gate to unload its passengers. It had been a long flight from Seoul, South Korea, and Yu-Jin Park was very glad that it was over. He waited patiently to get his small bag out of the overhead compartment. He had no other luggage with him. Everything he would need had been sent earlier to his cousin, who had an apartment in Chicago. He planned to live there, at least temporarily. Finally, it was his turn. He left the plane and walked through the long passage into the terminal.

Yu-Jin was really looking forward to his studies at Midwestern University, where he had been accepted as a graduate student. He planned to major in communication studies. He hoped that he would be able to work in either advertising or public relations when he returned to Korea.

He was very proud of his command of English. He had studied the complex language for a number of years—first at the high school level and then for four years at the university in Seoul. He and his friends had practiced English conversation, both among themselves and with the Korean English teachers at school. He had also seen a lot of American movies and television programs, so he felt that he understood the culture very well. He felt that he was ready to handle any kind of conversation, discussion, lecture, or book that he might encounter.

210

Yu-Jin knew that his Korean name might be difficult for native English speakers, so he had already chosen one with which they would be comfortable. He decided on "Eugene," because it sounded nice and was a lot like his real name.

Even though he was proud of his command of English, he knew that there would be at least some words with which he was not familiar. When he encountered them, he planned on using the really neat electronic gadget that he had recently purchased. It had been quite expensive, but it was wonderful. On the front it had a little computer screen and an array of keys. It worked on batteries. All he had to do to determine the Korean meaning of an English word was to type the term on the key pad, spelling it correctly, and then press the *Enter* button. The meaning of the English word in Korean would be instantly displayed on the screen. He decided that he would always carry this little gadget with him.

After clearing customs and immigration, where his passport and documents were carefully checked, he walked down a long passage and arrived in the main lobby area. Yu-Jin headed for the door marked "Ground Transportation." No problem there. He understood the meaning and knew that there would be taxies available—as there are at any airport in the world. All he had to do was tell the driver the address where he would be staying.

Yu-Jin entered the taxi and then politely asked the driver to take him to his cousin's address, which he carefully read from a card so he would say it right. The driver said nothing in reply. He just nodded and the taxi got under way.

For a long time the driver didn't say a word. Too bad, thought Yu-Jin, I would like to converse with an American worker. I need to practice my English as much as possible.

Finally, the driver turned to Yu-Jin and asked, "How do you like them Cubs?"

Yu-Jin was puzzled by the question. He was not quite sure of the meaning of "cubs." Whipping out his electronic translator, he quickly typed in "c-u-b-s." Instantly he saw the Korean translation on the screen: "The immature offspring of certain animals, such as lions and bears."

Ah, thought Yu-Jin, I can answer that question. "Oh yes," he replied, "they are animals. I like them," he replied.

"Yeah, you're right," said the driver. "They really are animals. I get disgusted with them sometimes, but at least most of the time they do it right. Just last night they were really hot."

Yu-Jin pondered that, and wondered why the little animals were overheated. "Perhaps," he said, "someone should take steps to cool them off."

"Don't worry," said the driver, "when they play tomorrow afternoon, the Reds are going to slaughter 'em."

Yu-Jin was not at all sure that he heard that right. He worried that perhaps he did not understand the term "reds." He thought it meant a color. To check he quickly used his translator and keyed in "r-e-d-s." The Korean meaning instantly came up: "A colloquial term often used to refer to communists." He knew a great deal about communists. They ruled North Korea.

Somewhat puzzled Yu-Jin replied, "Well, such a slaughter would be unfortunate. I hope that it can be prevented."

The driver nodded, relying, "Yeah, you're right. Let's hope that it isn't a real bloodbath."

As the cab pulled up in front of the apartment building, Yu-Jin felt that he had handled his first conversation with an ordinary working American quite well. Still, it did seem bizarre. He wondered why the Americans would allow such innocent animals at play to be killed by communists. Oh well, he thought, such animal sacrifices are probably just some sort of local custom. Maybe, he thought, there is still a lot that I have to learn about the American culture.

The cab driver thought, Nice kid. Seems to be from some foreign country, but he really knows a lot about American baseball.

The American society is a remarkable one.[1] One of the most important features is its great *diversity.* Not only are the cultures of nations from which people have immigrated represented, but also there is an almost unlimited number of **social categories** into which people in the population can be classified (see Chapter 7, pages 177–209). Each of these is are also characterized by its own **specialized culture.** Some social categories' cultures are based on age, gender, income, education and place of residence (e.g., rural versus urban). Others are defined by occupation, profession, or socioeconomic class. (See Box 8.1.)

A number of very important social categories will be the central focus of this chapter because they pose sensitive problems of **intercultural communication.** To be considered are communication patterns of people of a particular racial background as well as place of ancestral origin (e.g., African Americans or Japanese Americans). These categories, as well as males and females, all have somewhat distinctive styles of communication that will be discussed in detail in this chapter. It was the distinction between the culture of South Korea and the more specialized culture of a taxi driver from a particular social class level (defined by social scientists as people with a particular level of education,

income, and occupational status) that posed communication problems between Yu-Jin and the driver. Such intercultural communication difficulties are common in a multicultural society.

Why is intercultural communication important, and worthy of close study? A major reason is that the American society has greater diversity than virtually any other and it is very important that we all get along. Our society is one where, over nearly four centuries, starting in 1620, people came together from many places of origin and slowly had to learn to live together, even though they have always been of different religions, races, and specialized ways of life. In contrast, in many other parts of the world, people cannot seem to tolerate each other. They do not easily mix, or they even engage in massacres, holocausts, "ethnic cleansings," and endless wars against each other. In contrast, the United States remains a stable society in which many kinds of people coexist—with tensions and prejudices, to be sure, but with remarkable overall tolerance and accommodation in comparison with countries torn with hatred, brutality, and violence.

There is, of course, another reason intercultural communication is so important. Not only must we live and get along with many different kinds of people in the United States, but we, as a nation, must also understand, communicate with, and interact with those of other nations. The horrific events of September 11, 2001, are an indelible reminder of the importance of intercultural communication.

The chapter discusses the nature of **culture,** both in terms of *general culture* (sometimes called "mainstream culture"), such as the culture of an entire nation, and *specialized cultures,* such as the cultures that exist among different social categories of people in the society (important examples are people who share particular ethnic, racial, or religious backgrounds; people of male or female gender, distinctive socioeconomic classes, occupations, and sexual orientations; and people with physical impairment). In particular, this chapter analyzes the features of the *specialized cultures* among

BOX 8.1   ◯ *A Closer Look*

The Meaning of the Term *Culture*

Culture in a basic sense consists of the ways in which a society, group, or other category of people *solve problems* in approved and acceptable manners. Some problems are solved with tools and other forms of *material culture*. This began with the earliest human beings who made tools from stone. Later people developed clothing, shelters, pottery, and other artifacts. Eventually the need for reliable supplies of food was solved by the development of agriculture. Material culture accumulated over the course of eons; artifacts spread from one society to another and material culture became increasingly complex. This process continues today, as advanced societies develop more and more complex technologies (computers, aircraft, weapons, and objects of daily living) that solve problems.

Another category of culture is *symbolic*—that is, language-based. When the evolution of physical changes in the human body made speech possible, languages were developed to solve problems of communication. Language also made possible the accumulation, spread, and sharing of beliefs about the nature of social and physical reality. As advances were made through the development of writing, print, and eventually the complex media of today, the storing of ideas was freed from dependence on memory alone to pass on solutions from one generation to the next. Today the process continues with huge amounts of knowledge stored and accessible in many forms.

Finally, another category of culture is *normative*. This consists of a body of shared rules and beliefs about how people should behave as they relate to each other and conduct their daily activities. Such rules for behavior are embedded in a system of *values*, which are shared conceptions of what is right or wrong, permissible or not, punished or rewarded. Each society, category, or group may hold different versions of these norms and values.

---

examples of such categories that can pose barriers to effective interpersonal and group communication. It suggests guidelines as to how these can be dealt with in interpersonal and group contexts so that people who are different can relate to each other in more effective ways.

The Nature of Culture

The term *culture* was first introduced into the social sciences in 1871 by anthropologist Edward B. Tylor, who said, "Culture . . . is that complex whole which includes knowledge, belief, art, law, morals, custom, and any other habits acquired by man [and woman] as a member of society." Tylor's rather broad definition of culture is still basically correct today, but a more modern definition would be this: *Culture refers to the total of all material, social and symbolic creations that a society's members have incorporated into their overall design for living.*

One key to understanding the nature of culture is to emphasize the difference between a *society*—a large and complex group of people carrying on a common life—and their *culture*, which they produce and practice. In other words, a culture is not a group of people. It is the things they use, the beliefs they share, and the distinctive rules or patterns of behavior they follow. In this sense, culture is the social heritage of a society—all the solutions to problems of living that are handed down from one generation to the next.

Seen from this perspective, *culture* is an umbrella term—a very broad and inclusive concept covering many things that people use, say, think, and do. Two types or categories of culture fit under that umbrella here in the United States: The first is the *general* or mainstream

When people communicate interculturally, messages are exchanged between people of different cultures under conditions in which their backgrounds influence or change the process in a significant way.

culture, which brings a certain uniformity to the ways of life of people living in a diverse society. The second category is *specialized* cultures (sometimes called "co-cultures"), or the unique ways of life that characterize an enormous number of social categories within a complex society (such as ours).

General Culture

To the extent that people of a society share a more or less similar material culture and live together within a common set of major social institutions—even though there may be many diverse social categories among them—they participate in a *general* or mainstream culture. It is this basic culture that enables all of us to coexist within a larger, single society and to communicate with one another in relatively predictable ways. It holds society together in a functioning system regardless of where our parents or grandparents came from, the color of our skin, or the first or second language we speak.

In a diverse society, such as ours, **general culture** includes the basic design of what social scientists call the society's principal *social institutions* (family, economic, political, educational, and religious). There are also others, such as science, sports, and the military.[2] These institutions broadly define the ways such activities are carried on within the society, with many variations among specific segments of the population. The general culture also includes the principal *language* in use, widely shared *beliefs,* the material *artifacts* and *technologies* that people employ (airplanes, refrigerators, computers, spoons, wristwatches, and all the rest), plus the *values* to which most people subscribe. For example, almost all of us living by the rules of the American culture obey the nation's laws; rely on automobiles for transportation; buy things in supermarkets and shopping malls with U.S. currency; watch television; and live in homes furnished with tables, chairs, beds, and so on. As Americans, we also value children, condemn crime, wear customary clothing, and generally live out our lives in and around the major social institutions of our society.

Specialized Cultures

A second and equally important set of cultures are those that provide ways of life for members of social categories that are in some way unique or different from the general society. Examples would be those who are rich. Their way of life, artifacts, and shared beliefs, as well as many other features of what they own, do, and believe, is different from that of the poor. In each of these categories, people carry on *specialized cultures.*

These are "cultures within cultures."[3] They are unique ways of life, including material artifacts, language, values, shared beliefs, and ways of speaking that characterize people in particular social categories, such as those classified by occupation, racial, ethnic, and religious affiliations, social classes, regions of the country, and sexual orientation. Examples include Latinos, Muslims, the very wealthy, vegetarians, Midwesterners, lesbians, men, first-year college students, factory workers, marines, and prison inmates.

Actually, specialized cultures *in miniature* exist in every family, corporation, school, police department, hospital and other group within our society. In each the participants must learn how that specialized culture defines the social and behavioral expectations of the group—its way of life and the pattern of social organization discussed in earlier chapters.

In many ways this factor of specialization is the bottom line of diversity. It is a consequence of the fact that each social category—and even each small group—has its own different pattern of culture. Distinctive patterns of beliefs, attitudes, language, and norms for behavior set the members of each such group apart from others in society. At the same time, however, the group members all participate in the general culture along with everyone else.

It is socialization within the general culture—learning its ways and its requirements—that *makes all of us similar;* but it is socialization within the specialized and miniature cultures of the social categories and groups to which we each belong that *makes each of us different.* This is the source of the unique personality each person develops.[4] Unique socialization within a cluster of specialized cultures is what brings one individual to *think,* and on occasion, to *act* differently from another. For example, an individual might identify herself as an Asian American (one specialized culture), a woman (another specialized culture), an attorney (a third), a vegetarian (a fourth), and a Catholic (a fifth). The amount of influence those specialized cultures have on the individual depends on a number of factors. For example, being a woman may not be one of her more dominant identities for most of her interactions with others. However, being a woman may become an important part of how she thinks of herself and how others see her in many communication exchanges.

For some people, the general culture defines much of what they believe, think, and do—especially among those whose families have been in the society for generations. Others, whose ancestral origins in another society are more recent, may enjoy retaining distinct identities of a specialized ethnic culture. Importantly, the general culture ensures that all the various categories and groups with specialized cultures in the United States are not completely separate entities. They interact and overlap. With disparate specialized cultures in contact with one another, some assimilation and accommodation is inevitable. Consequently, we have learned to borrow from or imitate one another; to observe one another's holidays and eat one another's foods, to adopt one another's specific words and phrases, and to adjust to one another's customs and traditions. The result is a mix and match of diversity coming together.[5] Things that were originally unique to one specialized culture (tacos, sushi, soccer, specific fashions) may, over time, become part of the ever-evolving general culture.

Our cultural diversity is greater than that of any other nation in history. People from every nation on earth have immigrated to this country. No other nation can boast of the special contributions that each of our immigrant categories brought to this country. However, even though we are a nation of diversity, and a nation striving for justice, equality, and harmony among all people, we often fall short of that goal.

In the year 2000, the number of foreign-born residents in the United States reached the *highest level in history*.[6] According to the results of the 2000 census, the estimated foreign-born population climbed to 28.4 million, a 44 percent increase since the 1990 census. An additional 27.5 million Americans reported that they had at least one parent who was born in another country. Thus, a total of 56 million Americans, or 20 percent of the population, had either been born in a foreign country or had at least one parent who was.

The 2000 census results also showed that half of the foreign-born residents were from Latin America, especially Mexico. Many others came from Cuba, the Dominican Republic, and El Salvador. Another 26 percent came from Asia, especially from China, India, Vietnam, and Korea. Only 15 percent came from Europe—a significant change from many previous decades when the majority of immigrants listed a European country as their place of birth.[7]

These recent arrivals settled mainly in California, New York, Florida, Texas, New Jersey, and Illinois. These states combined accounted for 70 percent of the total. However, California led the nation with 26 percent of foreign-born residents. Indeed, by the year 2005, the majority of California's population is expected to be nonwhite, a demographic event that signals a dramatic change in the cultural composition of the nation's most populated state.[8]

States in which so-called minorities have become, or will become, majorities are not confined to California, as is evident when one considers cities like Miami, Atlanta, San Antonio, Chicago,

Baltimore, Houston, New York, and Memphis.[9] In these census data, the lines between majority and minority blur.

Importantly, the immigrant cultures brought to the United States remain with us. Even third and fourth generations can find influences on their lives that are derived from the ethnic, religious, or racial origins of their ancestors. Thus, although we in the United States are Americans, we are not all alike. We truly live in a multicultural society where cultural divisions often create special problems in communicating accurately and effectively. To assume, then, that all people will, and should, behave and communicate in the same way ignores our rich cultural mix. This chapter attempts to sensitize us to unique demands of specialized cultures that make a difference in how we communicate.

Dealing with Diversity

How has the United States coped with the diversity of its population? Initially, our country was committed to a **melting pot policy**—an attempt to reduce cultural differences between people as quickly as possible and to assimilate them into the general culture. The logic behind that policy was that, if strong "tribal"-type groups developed in the country, they would soon make efforts to separate themselves into politically independent entities. That was, in fact, a real and understandable risk. It had happened earlier, in the South during the Civil War and in Louisiana and Texas, where separate governments came into existence. More recently there is the example of the struggle in Canada with many in its French-speaking population seeking independence from the country.

It was the schools that led the melting pot effort. They were used to transform the children of immigrants from "foreigners" to "Americans" as fully and as soon as possible. In the early part of the twentieth century, the nation's goal was to *eradicate the differences* among people and thereby to eliminate language, social, political, and economic problems. Everyone was required to learn English and adopt the basic general American culture.

It worked! The nation remained together even though millions of people from other countries poured in during the 1800s and the early 1900s. Later, and in more recent times, the melting pot policy has come under criticism on the grounds that it did not respect people's ways of life. Furthermore, it often produced many problems for immigrant families—especially between children, who assimilated rapidly, and their parents, who retained their culture of origin.

The melting pot policy has also been criticized for producing a majority-is-superior viewpoint. That is, any culture outside the majority was expected to assimilate or conform to the majority—certainly not the other way around. A quick look at the numbers of each ethnic category in the United States reveals that the majority who immigrated were primarily from European countries. It is for this reason that most white Americans in the United States are called *European Americans* by some scholars (as opposed to African Americans, Native Americans, etc.).

Originally, the word **majority** was intended to refer to the actual numbers of those most numerous in the population. Later it came to have connotations, including dominant, superior, and more powerful. In comparison with the majority, then, all so-called **minority** cultures were regarded as somehow less significant, less dominant, and less important. This view has by no means vanished. It may not be acceptable to many, but in a factual sense, there has been a long tradition, which remains an ethnocentric tendency today, for some people in the United States to regard themselves and their way of life as superior, while looking down on that of others.[10]

While the melting pot policy did prevent political breaks from the union, and it did very effectively help develop a general American culture, it did not completely eradicate cultural differences among immigrant people. In communities across our country, people whose ancestors came from one "old country" or another continue to keep alive many of the traditions and feelings of identity that the policy was intended to remove. Even people who are several generations removed from their immigrant ancestors still feel the influences of their cultural roots.

On the other hand, it is also true that after several generations have passed, many Americans no longer feel a connection to the land of their ancestors. On the 2000 census, for example, the number of people who wrote in the word *American* in the "other" category, when asked for their ancestry, increased to 20 million from 13 million in 1990. At the same time, the number who claimed European ancestry decreased significantly.[11] In other words, with the passage of time and increased assimilation into the general American culture, many believe that they and their families have "become" American.

In addition, many of the specialized cultures of those groups who came to this nation earlier have disappeared or are doing so now. For example, a study of 80 older Issei women (Japanese women who had immigrated from Japan to the United States) was completed back in 1957. It showed that the women of the immigrant generation maintained an essentially Japanese way of life—in language, relating to their husbands and children, diet, recreation, religion, and many other ways. About half of their Nissei daughters (second generation) had married men outside their ethnic group (mainly white Americans). Additional studies showed that by the third generation, the Japanese language was no longer in use by such women. Their daily routines were typically American. Their physical characteristics had changed due to the biological mixing. In every other respect they had both amalgamated (biologically) and assimilated (culturally) into the mainstream of American culture. Much the same process is occurring among those who came to the United States from Cuba, Mexico, the Caribbean, and elsewhere in recent decades. As each generation matures, then, features of their original immigrant culture disappear to be replaced by those more common in the general American culture.[12]

Today, our nation embraces a policy of **cultural pluralism,** which means that we try to tolerate and accept our differences; maintain a strong sense of diversity; and, at the same time, remain a unified nation committed to similar democratic ideals. Within the context of cultural pluralism, we recognize that although we remain diverse, citizens of all backgrounds share a general American culture that enables us to carry on our day-to-day activities and relate to one another in fairly predictable ways. In a mature multicultural society with a strong political system, complete assimilation is no longer needed.

Excessive Ethnocentrism

Regardless of how long they or their ancestors have been living in the United States, most U.S. citizens are proud to be Americans. When faced with outside threats or aggression, Americans are very patriotic and loyal to their country. Indeed, many have died defending their country against brutal aggressors who were bent on destroying it. There is no doubt that pride in country, loyalty, and patriotism are beneficial. Still, in the extreme, such beliefs can be problematic if they are used to exclude or dominate others' valued cultural orientations. The sense of pride that teaches us to value our way of life can also teach us that we are somehow superior to all others. The point is that cultural pluralism depends on **cultural inclusion**—a commitment to acknowledge, respect, and (when possible) defer to others who may think, feel, and behave differently from ourselves. In contrast, **cultural exclusion** is a condition that ignores our inherent diversity and imposes a singular view of all other people—one that insists that there is only one right way to think and act.

A term for such an attitude is **ethnocentrism**—from the Greek word *ethnos,* meaning "the people." This attitude is often at the root of cultural exclusion. People like to think of their particular group as the "insiders," and everyone else as "outsiders," who are not as acceptable. Such distinctions between "in-groups" and "out-groups" are sometimes harmless.[13] Indeed, some level of ethnocentrism can be helpful to a society or to a particular group if patriotism or pride is needed to meet an emergency.

But rampant ethnocentrism is sometimes found in a more troublesome and exaggerated form called **chauvinism,** which can be defined as a condition of "boastful and truculent group self-assertion."[14] Chauvinism has in some cases in the past been particularly ugly and dangerous when people came to believe not only that their group is superior but also that they had a right to exploit, suppress, or even eliminate others whom they defined as less worthy. Such self-righteous and exaggerated ethnocentrism has been at the heart of many forms of truly dreadful human abuse throughout the world.[15] These include religious and ethnic wars, slavery, forcing women to serve as sexual servers for an army, and the concentration camps of World War II.

Cultural Relativity

An important way to view cultures without being judgmental is to use the principle of **cultural relativity,** a perspective that recognizes and accepts the idea that other people do things differently. This principle embodies the idea that what works for a group is right and correct from their point of view—even though it may be different from our own. For example, many of us would enthusiastically endorse the general American way of life as the most desirable, but if we were to ask people living in, say, South Korea, Iceland, or Maylasia, we would find that they do not agree and would argue that their own ways are just as desirable. Similarly, we might find people practicing different specialized cultures within the United States disagreeing over standards to live by; for example, consider some of the different attitudes of Catholics and Protestants, women and men, teenagers and senior citizens, and rural farmers and city dwellers. Looking at other groups of people within the perspective of relativity can help us understand how people can approach specific aspects of life in very different ways. Such understanding is the foundation for accepting them as people like ourselves.

At the same time, common sense must prevail. Few in the United States would have been willing to accept with comfort the culture of the Taliban, the Muslim fundamentalists who took power in Afghanistan in 1996 after the Soviets left. While they brought a rigid sense of order to that war-devastated country, their beliefs and practices were brutal. Ritual punishments and arbitrary, immediate flogging and other measures administered by gun- and whip-wielding youths were commonplace. Scholars have described the treatment of women by the Taliban as "the most systematic repression of women in history."[16] Special laws against women left them destitute, terrorized, without medical care, and physically and mentally ill. In addition, no woman could leave her home without the company of a male relative. Every woman had to wear a *burka* (a sacklike garment that covers the entire body, with only a small screen in front of the face out of which the woman can peer). No girl was allowed to go to school. Punishments for transgressions were severe. The Taliban "moral police" beat women with sticks in public for minor transgressions such as showing an ankle. All males were forbidden to shave. Listening to popular music, watching TV, and going to the movies were strictly forbidden. Finally, when the Taliban were found to support terrorist groups, such as the ones that attacked the World Trade Center on September 11, 2001, Americans had had enough. Cultural relativism did not prevail and armed forces were sent to root them out.

In a similar way, contemporary neo-Nazis, wanting to restore a society like that of Hitler, would not be acceptable to Americans. Or, a group like the Ku Klux Klan—with its negative definitions of African Americans, and its cultural practices of intimidating victims, burning crosses, and wearing white robes and hoods—would be difficult to accept using the principle of cultural relativity. Nevertheless, and again within a perspective of common sense, differences in cultural practices and beliefs that do not harm people need to be interpreted within that principle. Thus, cultural relativity does not mean that one must accept *any* form of behavior simply because some group practices it. The excesses of pogroms, "ethnic cleansing," and oppression that exist in many societies could never, and should never, be acceptable to us.

The Influence of Culture on Communication

Culture and communication are inseparable. Anthropologist Edward T. Hall argues that *culture is communication and that communication is culture.*[17] He explains that the way we communicate—how our beliefs influence what we say, the language system we use, and the gestures we employ—are all preset for us by the culture we acquire. In other words, how we relate verbally and nonverbally to others is learned from the culture in which we grow up. In the same way, how we dress; our use of time; the odors we savor (and the ones we abhor); the distances we use to interact with others; and when, where, and with whom we maintain eye contact all are dictated, to a large extent, by the culture of our particular society or group.

In other ways, communication style speaks volumes about a person's specialized cultures. For example, Chinese Americans tend to be indirect and to understate their own accomplishments and successes. They learn to speak "humbly." European Americans, in contrast, learn to be "assertive" and to show pride in what they are able to do. Nonverbally, we might find some Latinos and Latinas and some African

Americans associating direct and prolonged eye contact with status and power. Among them, looking directly and steadily at the eyes of someone of higher status is a sign of disrespect. It is not difficult to understand, then, that communication and culture are inseparable.

Intercultural Communication Defined

In recent years, no single area of interest has commanded the attention of communication theorists, researchers, teachers, and practitioners more than the study of intercultural communication. This increasing awareness that cultural backgrounds are central to understanding communication has been coupled with dramatic economic, political, and social needs to communicate internationally. Thus, researchers have urgently tried to discover those factors that "make a difference" in our efforts to communicate accurately and efficiently with others who are different.

Probably the single most significant lesson learned so far is that knowing someone's language *does not* ensure understanding. In fact, effective intercultural communication requires much more than learning, say, how to speak Spanish, French, German, Russian, or any other language. It requires an understanding and appreciation of the cultures that permeate the interaction. We all know of foreign visitors who are quite competent English speakers (some understand our grammar better than we do!) who violate our culturally defined norms dramatically. They may "invade our space" or arrive inexcusably late for an appointment or a dinner engagement—the sort of deviation that speaks volumes about their lack of understanding.

Similarly, some Americans traveling abroad have earned a reputation for being boorish because they did not recognize; accommodate to; and, at times, respect the rules of other people's cultures. For example, Americans sometimes blunder when they jump too quickly to a first-name basis with the English or French, ignore the strict dietary rules of a devout Hindu, or heartily slap a Taiwanese business person on the back.[18] Similar problems occur here in the United States when we violate one of the norms defined by a person's specialized culture.

More specifically, what do we mean when we speak of intercultural communication? We can define *intercultural communication* as *an exchange of messages that takes place between people of different social categories under conditions in which the cultures of those categories influence or change the process in some significant way.* In other words, a transaction classified as intercultural communication takes place between people whose culture-based perceptions and interpretations of verbal and nonverbal symbols are different enough to influence in different ways the meanings involved in the communication event.

In spite of these problems and considerations, the need to practice cultural relativism, to try to get along with other kinds of people within our own society, and to accept them fully even though they are different from ourselves has never been more important. Following the end of the Cold War, the United States became locked in intense international competition in world markets, which has a powerful effect on us all. If we cannot meet that competition, our standard of living and general way of life will deteriorate.

Principles of Intercultural Communication

What do we need to know about intercultural communication that will help us relate to one another better? (Figure 8.1 illustrates the factors involved in intercultural communication.)

At least five factors should be acknowledged: First, *a person can belong to several specialized cultures, and the number of such affiliations can vary for an individual.* A man might identify himself as a business executive, a member of the upper middle class, and a Vietnam War veteran. He might further identify himself as a New Yorker and a Mormon. Each of these terms is a label for his participation in specific specialized cultures.

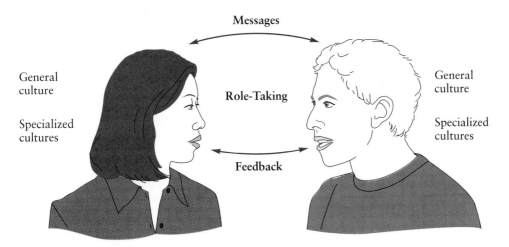

FIGURE 8.1

Intercultural Communication

Intercultural communication involves all of the factors of communication, with the influence of general cultures and specialized cultures that communicators bring to the exchange.

Second, *being a participant in a specific culture is both self and other defined.* Others may not know of, or may refuse to recognize, your identification with a particular culture. By the same token, they may assume incorrectly that, and act as though, you are a part of others. That is, you may think of yourself as independent politically, but others may regard you as a liberal Democrat or a conservative Republican. Or, consider a woman who denies the charge that she is a feminist, but others continue to claim that she is, and further, they respond to her as if she were. Remember the principle of the social construction of reality and W. I. Thomas's dictum: *If people believe something to be true they will act as though it is true.*

Third, *any given specific culture can emerge to dominate a person's beliefs sufficiently to influence or alter a message exchange.* Whether or not a particular culture emerges and dominates the interaction depends primarily on the context and the parties involved. For example, being a male may not be one of your more dominant identities during most of your interactions with others. However, there are occasions, and there are individuals, who can trigger

that identification. If this happens, being a male can substantially change an ongoing interaction. For example, your male cultural identification may not be important to you when you are discussing the weather, your workload, or your reading preferences—particularly in your interactions with good friends, other men, and so on; but you probably will discover very quickly the special meaning of that identity when you have conversations with guys who are fans of particular sports teams, or when you find yourself among a group of mothers discussing problems of infant and child care.

Fourth, *the greater the number of similar cultures an individual brings to a conversation with others in an exchange, the higher the potential for accurate communication.* Recall that we expect others who share our background and cultural experiences to think as we do; behave as we do; and more important, construct meanings as we do. If this is indeed the case, people can communicate more accurately. Sometimes this does not work because we can have mistaken interpretations of cultural overlap. For example, just because two individuals are of a particular racial origin does not necessarily mean that both identify themselves as partici-pating in the same specialized culture. Some may reject such a self-identity, preferring to dis-tance themselves from the category, particularly if membership is associated with negative stereotypes and prejudice.

Fifth, *the greater the number of shared cultures individuals bring to a conversation, the greater their feelings of attraction and comfort while communicating.* We know that persons who think of themselves as holding similar be-liefs, attitudes, and values are likely to find each other compatible and even attractive. The old saying "Opposites attract" has been overshad-owed by a greater traditional saying: "Birds of a feather flock together." Recognizing that culture has a dramatic influence on the way we think and act, we are likely to welcome those who share some features of our identity. Discovering that another person you have just met grew up in your hometown, is of the same religion, and has ancestors who immigrated from the same coun-try increases your attraction toward that person significantly. These shared backgrounds, and the shared specialized cultures they imply, reduce your uncertainty about initiating a relationship.

These principles of intercultural communi-cation, then, emphasize the importance of searching for shared identities we can use in communication with others. But what happens when there is no such overlap, and two people have virtually nothing in common? Obviously, disparate cultural backgrounds might interfere with efficient and accurate interaction; but, given the multiculturalism of the United States, we need to know how to communicate inter-culturally with people in our own backyards—whether they are like us or not.

Features of Culture that Make a Difference

The need to get along with people of all special-ized cultures within our own society, to accept them fully, and to be able to communicate with them with a high degree of accuracy has never been more important. There is an abundance of different specialized cultures in our society of great diversity. Obviously, we all live within the general American culture prevailing in the United States. However, if we think about our own gender, profession, and family history for a moment, most of us can clearly identify with several specialized cultures that influence in some fashion how we communicate with oth-ers. In this way, we all bring something differ-ent to our multicultural society and to the communication situations we face.

What we bring from our specialized cultures are different (and sometimes opposing) values or ways of viewing the world that can influence how we construct, transmit, receive and inter-pret messages. Researchers have found four cultural features that make a difference in how we relate to one another. They refer to these as: (1) **individualism** *and* **collectivism**, (2) *high and low* **context**, (3) *high and low* **power distance**, and (4) **masculinity** *and* **femininity**. Each of these terms represents extreme ends of a con-tinuum that illustrates different values or ways of viewing the world. As you will see, no cul-tural group or individual actually is at those extremes—most are somewhere in between. Each of these continua need explanation.

Individualism and Collectivism

The first of these continua—a cultural feature that seems to make a difference in how we com-municate—indicates whether a particular cul-ture views the world from an individualistic or a collectivistic orientation. To clarify, a culture with an orientation toward *individualism* places a high value on people who can speak or stand up for themselves and not have to depend on others beyond their immediate family. Peo-ple who view the world this way like to think of themselves as "rugged individualists" who can "stand on their own two feet" and take care of themselves. Such people work hard to remain emotionally independent of any partic-ular social, organizational, or institutional af-filiation. Individualists emphasize the "I" when they speak, not the "we." This type of culture promotes personal initiative, independence, individual expression, and privacy.[19] General cultures of societies around the world that can be described as highly individualistic include Australia, Great Britain, New Zealand, and Canada. In the United States, African Americans and European Americans (in particular, male European Americans) tend to represent such an individualistic orientation.

At the other extreme of this value continuum is *collectivism*. This cultural feature is characterized by close-knit and familylike groups of people who clearly define themselves as part of a particular in-group. Others are considered outsiders. Individuals belonging to the in-group (relatives, clans, organizations) are required to look after one another in virtually every situation and context. In-group membership means not competing with others in the in-group. Collaboration and respect are required. In exchange for such loyalty, the group offers support, care, and protection. Collectivists emphasize the "we" when speaking, rather than the "I." Predominantly collectivistic cultures are Japan, Pakistan, Colombia, Venezuela, Taiwan, and Peru. In the United States, Middle Eastern Americans, Latinos and Latinas, Asian Americans, Native Americans, and many females in other specialized cultures tend to value this orientation over individualism.

High and Low Context

A second world view that governs how people from different cultures relate to one another is context.[20] In this continuum, *context* has to do with whether what is communicated is inherent in the setting and simply "understood" by the people involved (high context) or whether the bulk of information must be communicated *overtly* through the spoken exchange of messages (low context). In contrast, *low context* implies that individuals tend to be verbally explicit, precise, and accurate. They do not assume that others will be able to figure out what they mean without a lot of help.

To illustrate by analogy, low-context communication can be seen in the way people interact with computers. For computers to "understand" a message, every statement must be very precise. Computers simply do not understand instructions that do not have every space, period, letter, and number in precisely the right location. The message must be overt and very explicit.[21]

In a parallel way, people communicating in a low-context culture have trouble understanding one another unless every effort is made to be as explicit and clear as possible. When relating a story or explaining how to do something, low-context communicators are likely to provide a lot of background information, nonessential details, examples, and other data. If insufficient information is provided, low-context receivers will ask questions and demand even more details. Vagueness and ambiguity are simply not tolerated.

High-context cultural groups, on the other hand, are more verbally *implicit*. They don't need to be so explicit because much is taken for granted or assumed. High-context cultural groups tend to be more indirect and subtle, and to rely more on nonverbal cues in communicating with one another. Interactions between two people who have been married for a long time provide an example. Over the years, they have come to know each other so well that they sometimes complete each other's sentences. They "just know" how the other will respond in a given situation; and they do not always feel a pressing need to talk in order to understand each other.

In other words, high-context cultures rely a great deal on *what is not said* and depend less on what is actually said in the explicit message. They look for meaning from the physical setting itself, or from the implied demands of the situation. As a result, they often talk in "verbal shorthand" simply because they already have a good idea of what each means. Recognizing that not everything needs to be spelled out in conversation, high-context speakers rely more on innuendo, ambiguity, equivocal

Individualistic	◄──────────────────────────────►	Collectivistic
African Americans Euroamericans		Asian Americans Latinos/Latinas Middle Eastern Americans Native Americans
Males		Females

Low context	Moderate context ◄──────────────────────────────►		High context
Euroamericans	African Americans Latinos/Latinas		Asian Americans Middle Eastern Americans Native Americans
Males			Females

Low power distance	◄──────────────────────────────►	High power distance
African Americans Euroamericans		Asian Americans Latinos/Latinas Middle Eastern Americans Native Americans
Females		Males

Masculine	◄──────────────────────────────►	Feminine

African Americans
Asian Americans (Japanese Americans)
Euroamericans
Latinos/Latinas (Mexican Americans)
		Asian Americans
		  (Chinese Americans and
		  Taiwanese Americans)
		Latinos/Latinas
		  (Chilean Americans,
		  Peruvian Americans, and
		  Spanish Americans)
		Middle Eastern Americans
		Native Americans
		Scandinavian Americans

Males		Females

FIGURE 8.2

Value Orientations of U.S. Ethnic and Gender Cultures

Each of the ethnic and gender cultures described in this chapter can be placed on continua representing the four different cultural features. An individual's ethnic and gender cultures may differ in their orientations. The amount of influence a particular orientation has depends on the individual and the context: In some situations, ethnic background may be the dominant factor influencing communication style; in others, gender or another cultural identity may be the more important factor.

messages, and implication. Rather than on telling someone what and how to think, high-context communicators merely suggest or offer alternatives.

Societies around the world that are more low context in their cultural orientation are Germany, Sweden, and England. High-context cultures include Japan, China, and Korea.[22] Here in the United States, Asian Americans, Native Americans, and Middle Eastern Americans can be characterized as high context. Latinos and Latinas and African Americans tend to be more moderate in their contextual orientation, with European Americans characterized by the lowest context.

High and Low Power Distance

How societies with different cultures distribute power, rank, and status among their members—their power-distance preference—is a third factor that influences the way people communicate. Although some cultures allow for, encourage, and even legislate as much equal status, rank, and power among individuals as possible, others greatly value status differences and social hierarchies.

As a feature of their general culture, Americans tend to value equality as a way of life. In the official and widely accepted view, no one is inherently superior or inferior to anyone else. Most Americans believe they can speak to virtually whomever they want, about almost any topic, in practically any style of delivery, and in any public or private situation without having to consider very carefully the other person's power, rank, or status. Americans believe that they can call in to radio and television talk shows and ask questions directly—even of the president, or other prominent people. Such familiar interactions would be unheard of in other parts of the world! In fact, outside of showing a minimum level of respect for others, Americans have few cultural restrictions or sanctions on the way they communicate with other people. Similar cultures with regard to low power-distance preferences are Austria, Denmark, Israel, New Zealand, and Ireland.[23]

Other cultures, such as those of Mexico, the Philippines, Venezuela, and India, place a high value on social status, birth order, and occupational and political rankings.[24] In these societies with high power-distance cultures, people tend to have less access to and less direct communication with individuals of higher status, and they are less likely to question authority figures. They tend to accept the actions of high-ranking individuals, often without question or justification. Vietnamese-American children, for instance, are expected to obey their parents without question or debate. In contrast, African American children are often rewarded for being assertive and challenging their parents' points of view. Your own culture's view toward power and status may similarly influence how willing or reluctant you are to engage in the following:

1. Disagree with a professor during class (even when you know the professor is wrong).
2. Ask questions in class.
3. Interrupt your boss at work.
4. Call your instructor by her or his first name.
5. Question your boss's evaluation of your performance.
6. File a grievance at work.
7. Marry someone of whom your parents disapprove.
8. Drop by your professor's office just to say hello.
9. Report your boss to a higher authority if you feel he or she has done something unethical or illegal.

In the United States, specialized cultures that are likely to represent a high power-distance orientation can be found among Asian Americans; Latinos; Native Americans; and, to a lesser extent, Middle Eastern Americans. A low power-distance preference is more characteristic of African American and European Americans (especially females).

Masculinity and Femininity

The fourth discriminating cultural factor is a continuum that concerns the extent to which cultures are traditionally more masculine or more feminine in their orientation. *Masculinity* in this regard refers to the degree to which a culture values and encourages assertiveness—sometimes illustrated as achievement, success, ambition, and competitiveness. *Femininity*, on the other hand, is evident in a peoples' preference for nurturance—often defined as friendliness, affection, compassion, and general social support.[25]

In more masculine-dominated cultures, sex roles are clearly differentiated; males are supposed to be aggressive and females passive. Personal achievement and competitiveness is highly valued in masculine cultures; relational concerns are secondary. Winning is more important than how you play the game. Ambition is a highly desirable personal quality; so is being a good provider for the family. At the other extreme, more feminine-dominated cultures deemphasize strictly defined role definitions. Sex roles are more flexible, and equality between the sexes is likely.

In feminine cultures, social and personal relationships are highly valued; being a good father and mother, husband and wife, sister and brother, and son and daughter are very important relational roles. More than achieving, winning, or accomplishing some instrumental goal, getting along, cooperating, and collaborating are more likely to be recognized and rewarded. Being a good person and showing sympathy and concern for unfortunate others are culturally valued qualities. Feminine cultures emphasize the more intrinsic, almost altruistic aspects of life.

Masculine and feminine orientations permeate how we communicate. Highly masculine communicators are likely to emphasize their credibility and expertise, to prefer objective facts and data, and to come across forcefully and directly. At the other extreme, highly feminine communicators strive to connect with their receivers by building rapport and empathy, seeking support for their views, and appealing to others' feelings and personal experiences.

Countries identified as masculine in their cultural orientation are Austria, Italy, Japan, and Mexico. Included among the more feminine cultures are Chile, Norway, Portugal, and Thailand.[26] In comparison to others, the general culture prevailing in the United States tends to be slightly more masculine than feminine in its orientation. Within the United States there are many specialized cultures representing the more masculine orientation. These include a number of specific Asian American cultures (particularly among Japanese Americans), African Americans, some Latino groups (especially Mexican Americans), and European Americans (particularly males). Feminine cultures in the United States can be found among Native Americans, certain Scandinavian-American groups, Middle Eastern Americans, and some Latino groups (especially those of Chilean, Peruvian, and Spanish ancestry). Box 8.2 summarizes the cultural features that make a difference in how we communicate.

Unique Styles of Communication Common in Specialized Cultures

Each of the four cultural features discussed in the previous section influences how people from different specialized cultures relate to one another. Each feature makes a difference in how we communicate with people from our own cultural background as well as react to others whose cultures are different from our own. When we understand why other people communicate or behave as they do, we can begin to accept and understand our own pluralistic society.

The discussion that follows focuses on the specialized cultures of six racial and ethnic categories—European Americans, African Americans, Latinos and Latinas, Asian Americans,

Native Americans, Middle Eastern Americans—and two gender categories (males and females). These are, of course, very important in a culturally diverse society that constantly seeks to improve the meaning of democracy, and it is for this reason that they are analyzed in some detail. At the same time, it must be kept in mind that the term *diversity* also refers to specialized cultures that can be found within occupations; social classes; regions of the country; organizations like corporations, universities, and churches; and many more. These too are important in an analysis of intercultural communication, and when people from these distinct categories or human groups communicate, many of the same problems arise as have been discussed.

People in the United States have come to take pride in their specialized cultural identities and to accept the importance of all such cultural groups. However, coexisting and communicating comfortably within that cultural diversity is not easy. The challenge, then, is to acquire enough information about other people's specialized cultures to be able to communicate in ways that show respect for them and to adapt to their differences. To accomplish that goal, this section describes major communication styles of some of the principal specialized cultures present in American society.

Before turning to a discussion of particular styles, however, there are two cautionary notes to keep in mind: First, we must *never* assume that just because a person is a member of a given social category, he or she will necessarily assume all its cultural characteristics. In other words, the danger of identifying patterns of unique cultural characteristics is the very human tendency of *stereotyping* all individuals who affiliate with that pattern. For example, just because Cuban Americans tend to value social contact with friends and family more than with others, we cannot assume that all people of this background share this equally. In other words, there is diversity *within* social categories of similar people as well as *between* them. So, we must be open to exceptions and individual variations at all times.

Second, we need to keep in mind our almost inescapable tendency to be ethnocentric. As the unique characteristics of each specialized culture are described, we need to keep in mind the principle of cultural relativity: We all do things differently. What works for another group is all right for them (within the commonsense limits we have discussed)—even if it differs from our way.

To illustrate how even sophisticated people can be surprisingly ethnocentric, one of the authors of this text had the following experience. Pat Kearney comes from a small farming community in the Midwest. Its specialized culture actively promotes hunting for game birds, rabbits, and, occasionally, deer. Currently, she lives in a very urban environment in southern California, but her family continues to send as special delicacies pheasants and wild rabbits they have hunted themselves. On one very special occasion, Pat invited her city friends (a different specialized culture with different values and views) to a dinner of baked rabbit. Much to her dismay, they refused to eat the "little bunnies" that had been hunted down, terrorized, and murdered!

The point is, our own cultural background may bring many surprises when we spend time with people unlike ourselves. To prevent problems, we must recognize that we are all ethnocentric to some degree and inclined to judge people by our own cultural standards. We should also remember that our goal is to communicate accurately and efficiently with others who are not like us. Consequently, we need to try to understand why other groups of people behave as they do.

The results of the 2000 census showed that the population of the United States has grown to almost 274 million. Furthermore, the largest category of people in the United States is composed of those of European ancestry. Of these, the most frequently reported ancestry is German. A total of 46 million Americans reported that they were of German or part-German ancestry. The next largest ethnic groups are Irish and English.

BOX 8.2 ☌ *A Closer Look*

Cultural Features Affecting Communication

Individualism

Place high value on those who stand up for themselves.

Rugged individualists who stand alone and do not depend on others.

Work hard to be emotionally independent.

Emphasize "I" when they speak.

Promote individual initiative, achievement, competition.

High Context

What is communicated is implied or simply understood.

Nonverbal communication is more important than verbal.

Information is indirect and subtle.

Communicators rely on innuendo and implication—suggest rather than demand.

High Power Distance

Value status differences and social hierarchies.

Less access to and communication with those of higher status.

Expected to obey parents and leaders without question.

More formal and distant.

Avoid confrontation; listen agreeably.

Masculinity

Value assertiveness, competitiveness, and success.

Ambition an important personal quality.

Winning is more important than how you play the game.

Emphasize personal credibility and expertise.

Important to be forceful and direct.

In addition, 34 million Americans stated their ancestry was of Hispanic or Latino origin; 32 million reported they were African American; 10 million reported they were Asian; more than two million stated they were Native Americans. Many other ethnic groups and races were represented in the census, and large numbers reported that they were of mixed ancestry.[27]

As the following discussion will show, each specialized culture has unique styles of communication.

European Americans

This chapter uses the label "European American" to refer to individuals residing in the United States whose common cultural heritage comes primarily from a European country. Ad-

mittedly, that is not very specific. Some came from England on the Mayflower. Others came over a three-hundred-year period in various ways. Some came on the Queen Mary—an elegant passenger liner. Others came packed in steerage on rusting ships to pass through Ellis Island. More recently, some came by jet airliner. During different periods, the majority of newcomers were from northern Europe, southern Europe, or eastern Europe. It is clear that all these countries have very distinct cultures. There is no European American source of common origin. The primary shared characteristic of such people is that they are *Caucasians*—commonly referred to as "white." (Other labels, such as "Anglos"—implying English origin—are in use, but they are misrepresentations. A person whose grandparents came from Ger-

Collectivism

Define themselves as members of a group.

Members of the in-group take care of one another.

Virtues are collaboration, respect, and loyalty.

In exchange for loyalty, group offers support and protection.

Emphasize "we" when they speak.

Low Context

What is communicated is explicit and overt.

Verbal communication more important than nonverbal.

Word choice is important—must be precise and accurate.

Communicators spell out everything, including what to think and how to feel.

Low Power Distance

Value equality; no one inherently superior or inferior.

Speak to whomever they want about almost any topic.

Children are encouraged to question and challenge authority.

Considered a "right" to confront, ask questions, or disagree.

Accessible, approachable, and unassuming.

Femininity

Value interpersonal connections and nurturance.

Sex roles are more flexible; equality between sexes is preferred.

Getting along, cooperating, and collaborating are important communication skills.

Strive to build support through empathy and rapport.

Valued qualities are being a good person and showing concern and sympathy for unfortunate others.

---

many, Sicily, or Poland is scarcely an "Anglo.") Other than their skin color, then, those societies of origin actually share little in the way of language or common culture.

Clearly, then, so-called European Americans are a large, diverse, and frequently misrepresented category of people. However, as they either helped develop, or over succeeding family generations become *enculturated* into, the general culture patterns of the majority in the society, they came to share a number of unique communication features that distinguish them from other categories. Admittedly, it is difficult to separate out those that are unique to this broad category from those that are part of specialized cultures practiced within other categories, such as various professions, socioeconomic classes, and religions. Even so, at

least some common characteristics do exist among those who can be identified as European Americans.

So, what are the common characteristics that distinguish the communication styles of this large and heterogeneous category from other kinds of communicators in the United States? According to Gary Althen, there are several.[28] These are summarized in the paragraphs below. To begin with, he claims that European Americans tend not to communicate readily about highly personal topics—they simply do not disclose a lot of personal information. Although this tendency may be more descriptive of males rather than females, it is often illustrated in conversations between strangers, casual acquaintances, or business associates. That is, when European Americans first meet someone, they normally engage in a period of small talk about uneventful or unimportant issues, such as the weather, sports, a TV program, a type of automobile, a particular restaurant, or a product in the grocery store. They avoid discussions about more substantive topics, such as financial matters, personal earnings, religion, politics, and sexual behavior.

The nature of communication exchanges between European Americans also distinguishes them from people with other specialized cultures. European Americans do not tend to speak with one another for a very long time. Their public presentations are generally short, and they tend to be impatient with people who "talk too much or too long."[29] There is little formalized ceremony or ritual in exchanges between European Americans. Because equality is valued, they are careful to take turns when they talk. They also tend to avoid arguing in public when they communicate with one another. For the most part, they believe that intense arguments in public are rude. When they do argue in public, they strive to remain noticeably calm, objective, and unemotional or rational.[30]

European Americans tend not to get very involved with one another when they communicate. Once again, this is probably more true of men than women. Also, European Americans tend to avoid close involvement with a lot of different people, reserving their involvement with a few close friends and family. Most of their initial interactions with strangers, acquaintances, or business associates occur on a surface level. When they do communicate with one another, they often want to know what the objective of the conversation is and how long it will take.

In terms of the cultural features that were discussed earlier, European Americans rank high in individualism, low in context and power, and high in masculinity. Based on these features, then, we can assume that they tend to be ambitious and competitive, and that they value and appreciate assertive, outspoken communication behavior. Althen believes that this is particularly the case with European American men in that they generally value individual

over group achievement, believe in equality, and minimize status differences. Such Americans also rely more on explicit than implicit information when they communicate. That is, they rely more on verbal than nonverbal messages. This overwhelming preference for verbal communication is revealed in their preoccupation with *facts* and *evidence* as opposed to emotional appeals. They tend to distrust people who are emotional in an argument or a message.[31] Composure is a sign of credibility, they believe. Losing control of emotion and extreme displays of emotion are signs of weakness.

Overall, then, according to Althen, a large number of European Americans can be characterized as communicators who are self-oriented and who may appear to be cold, distant, impatient, unemotional, rational, exact, nondisclosive, and uninvolved. Obviously, there are many individual differences and not every European American fits these descriptions exactly. Similarly, not every African American or Latino and Latina will fit the descriptions to be developed below either. However, it is also important to note that each of us is typically the last to know what we are like as communicators—especially in terms of how we appear to others from different cultural groups.

African Americans

Citizens whose ancestral origins were in Africa represent the second largest category of people in the United States. The designation "African American" acknowledges both their ancestral origins and the influence of African societies on their cultural heritage. Although it has become popular, generally replacing racial epithets and other labels with negative connotations, the term *African American* is not accepted by the entire membership of this social category.[32] A significant number still refer to themselves as "blacks," or sometimes as "people of color." Still another term preferred by some is *Afro-American*.[33] In a recent opinion poll, however, respondents identifying with this social category expressed a clear preference for the label

"African American," and for that reason it is used in this book.[34]

African American communication behaviors, like those that characterize other specialized cultures, are unique enough to differentiate them from others. Few people who are not themselves African Americans appear to understand the African American style of communicating—and how much there is to appreciate. For many African Americans, how individuals package themselves—dress, act, walk, and even talk—is almost as important as what they say! How people connect and share with one another—how they use wit, humor, intelligence, touch, and other personal characteristics—is of primary importance.[35] African Americans often project and emphasize their own *individual styles* of communicating: They like to communicate a uniquely assertive and powerful self-image.[36] For example, some people might walk across a room; African Americans "move." For many African Americans, clothing not only provides a functional purpose but it also doubles as a *costume.* Hats and sunglasses worn indoors may be part of the overall look—items that others might expect to be removed.

The African American style of communicating tends to be highly *intense*—expressive, distinctive, forceful, assertive, and openly emotional—which is easily misinterpreted by people in other social categories. European Americans and Asian Americans, for instance, may perceive African Americans as being loud, laughing too heartily in public, and even acting out of control.[37] To others, African Americans can seem to call far too much attention to themselves—to "showboat"—that is, they may seem "immodest, unrestrained, and self-congratulatory."[38] In return, African Americans are likely to perceive European Americans, as well as Asian Americans, as being cold, overly objective, stodgy, and stiff. African Americans sometimes use the phrase "acting white" to describe a person who appears to be unemotional and undemonstrative.

The African American style of communicating can be illustrated by a European American university professor's story about her early experiences in teaching an introductory communication course that enrolled over 500 students. The entire first two rows of the huge classroom were populated by African American students. The rest of the class consisted of individuals from a variety of other backgrounds. During peak moments of her presentation to the class, when most students were attentive, quietly polite, and interested in what she was saying, some of the African American students would interrupt and say things like "I hear you!" or "Damn straight!"

If she had not understood the communication style of typical African American young people responding with approval, she might have interpreted such "interruptions" as rude, mean, or even vulgar. She might even have concluded that her African American students did not like her, or disapproved of what she had to say. She understood, however, that these "call-response patterns" are employed by African American audiences as positive feedback to public speakers. African Americans are open and expressive and let speakers know that they are actively listening and giving their approval and support.[39]

In summary, with reference to those cultural factors that make a difference, African Americans tend to be individualistic, more moderate in context, low in power distance, and high in masculinity. In other words, most value competition and personal distinctiveness, and trust their emotions and feelings—but also appreciate the power of the spoken word. They also tend to be highly intense and assertive. African Americans appreciate the use of examples and personal testimony or stories when arguing a point, and they have a keen sense of justice.[40] The style of speaking and communicating more generally of a large number of African Americans can be characterized as active; expressive; colorful; emotional; often humorous; nonverbal (as opposed to verbal); and, overall, positive in outlook. Once again, "one size does not fit all." It would be a mistake to assume that all African Americans communicate in these ways at all times. As with the European Americans described previously, and all the others that follow, there are many individual differences among African Americans and by no means will all follow the patterns of communication described.

Latinos and Latinas

The third largest ethnic category in the United States is made up of people whose surnames or cultural origins can be traced through their family background to a Spanish-speaking Latin American country or to Spain itself.[41] A number of designations are used to identify people in this social category, including Hispanic, Chicano or Chicana, Mexican American, and Latino (or, for females, Latina). All are regularly used synonymously in the United States. As is the case when referring to any of the categories of people described in this chapter, we must be able to distinguish among these labels if we are to communicate respect and adjust to the unique characteristics associated with this specialized culture. Researchers Ron Lustig and Jolene Koester effectively distinguish among these alternative labels:

> *Hispanic* derives from the prevalent use of the Spanish language, but many shy away from this term because it tends to homogenize all groups of people who have Spanish surnames and who use the Spanish language. *Chicano* (or *Chicana*) refers to the "multiple-heritage experience of Mexicans in the United States" and speaks to a political and social consciousness of the Mexican American. Specific terms such as *Mexican American* or *Cuban American* are preferred by those who *wish* to acknowledge their cultural roots in a particular national heritage while simultaneously emphasizing their pride in being U.S. Americans. Finally, *Latino* (or *Latina*) is a cultural and linguistic term. As Juan Gonzales, Jr., suggests, *Latino* includes "all groups in the Americas that share the Spanish language, culture and traditions."[42]

Taking the lead from Lustig and Koester, this text refers to this broad and varied category of people as *Latinos and Latinas*. The different endings in these two labels—the "o" and the "a"—are required in the Spanish language to identify men and women, and in that language one term is not used for both. In the present chapter, however, because English does not follow that language structure, the term *Latino* is sometimes used for both categories, for convenience—with the clear implication that it refers to both males and females.

Like the African American specialized culture, Latinos show a great deal of expression when they communicate. To the Latino, a person's manner of expression is often more important than what the person says. Latinos value *elegant speech*—often using words and phrases in ways that others might consider flowery. To people who value quiet or understated communication, Latinos may sometimes appear flamboyant or dramatic.[43] For instance, a Latino youth may declare his love for a young woman by saying, "Her eyes sparkle like the stars," or he may lament the loss of a loved one by explaining that "My heart is in my hands." To members of other cultural groups, such ways of speaking may seem overly emotional or passionate.

Socializing and being friendly are very important to typical Latinos.[44] Arguing or disagreeing in public is considered rude and disrespectful. Instead, Latinos like to appear agreeable and courteous. They like to talk; visit; and establish an amiable, cheerful climate or speaking environment. These characteristic communication styles may (and often do) frustrate traditional European American businesspeople who are often preoccupied with *time;* that is, they want their Latino or Latina associate to get down to business. For Latinos, however, showing concern for one another and chatting to show that they care are precursors to doing business. Demonstrating diplomacy, tact, and respect for one another is essential.

As communicators, Latinos are highly expressive, compelling, and intense. Similar to African Americans, they enjoy telling a good story, often relying on metaphors or parables. More important than the story itself, however, is the telling of it, using graphic, vivid expressions. Latinos are likely to be responsive and agreeable when others talk. They are unlikely to challenge an individual publicly, even when they think she or he is wrong; instead, they prefer to show respect.

In terms of world view orientation, the Latino culture is collectivistic, moderate in context, and very high in power distance. Some Latino cultures are highly masculine in orientation (Mexican American), whereas others are more feminine (Chilean American, Peruvian American and Spanish American). Consequently, Latinos prefer relating with in-groups, are very loyal to family and friends, place a high premium on smooth and pleasant social and business relationships, avoid conflict, and enjoy small talk. Moreover, they value conformity, obedience, and respect for authority. Latinos are a "contact culture"; that is, they stand closer to one another and engage in more physical contact than others might find comfortable. Even though the stereotyped perceptions of male "machismo" have not been fully documented, traditional sex roles are strongly encouraged. Whereas men are expected to be husbands, fathers, and providers and to be responsible and brave, women are expected to be protected, to stay closer to home, and to nurture and support their families.[45]

From this profile, we can summarize the Latino communication style as amiable, expressive, dramatic, friendly, cheerful, and extroverted. Once again, we caution against assuming that all Latinos behave according to these generalizations. These characterizations are merely guidelines for the decisions we make in our attempts to relate effectively with one another.

Asian Americans

The label "Asian American" is another broad label for a category of citizens that includes a number of very different specialized cultures. These consist of people whose ancestral and cultural roots are in China, Japan, Taiwan, Korea, Singapore, Thailand, and Vietnam or in other countries with predominantly Asian populations. Thus, whenever we draw conclusions about Asian Americans, we must be careful not to assume that all have similar cultural backgrounds or communicate in the same style. However, despite substantial differences among their cultures of origin, research shows that, in a broad sense, Asian Americans do tend to share certain communication patterns that differ from those of others we have discussed.

More than any other cultural feature, *collectivism* dominates the world view of Asian Americans.[46] First-generation Asian Americans—more than those of second and third generations—are likely to value collaboration, conformity, loyalty, and acceptance of, acquiescence to, or even deference to *authority*. Power, rank, and status differentials are valued and highly respected. These cultural values contrast sharply with the dominant values of the African American and European American cultures we examined. In those, the values emphasized are personal achievement; resistance or even rejection of authority; disapproval of status differences; and approval of competition, independence, freedom, and individual thought and opinions. Not coincidentally, then, we find that with increased contact with the general American culture, all specialized cultures derived from immigration become less extreme as each generation passes.

Even so, many Japanese Americans may hesitate to voice their opinions or express what they truly think, simply because it is customary to show deference to persons of authority, higher status, or greater age.[47] Moreover, Asian Americans as a group tend to be more sensitive to the feelings of others and, thus, unwilling to directly challenge a person's beliefs or attitudes or give unsolicited advice. Instead, they may be more likely to disagree or offer advice in some indirect and highly tactful manner.[48] Engaging in assertive behavior or self-disclosure with people outside their family is unlikely. Self-restraint is important to Asian Americans. Thus, being polite and tactful is a key characteristic of these communicators.

As members of a high-context culture, Asian Americans tend to mask their emotions nonverbally when they communicate. Intercultural communication scholar Don Klopf notes that "in Japan, looking someone in the eye, whether talking or listening, is not common and when it occurs it makes people uneasy and uncomfortable."[49] Instances of similar nonverbal behaviors are found among the other Asian American cultures here in the United States; many of their participants are also restrained in their nonverbal behavior. They usually do not engage in direct eye contact, nodding, smiling, or gesturing when making public presentations. It is easy for others, who use openly expressive communication styles—African Americans and Latinos for instance—to misinterpret the reserved manner of Japanese or Chinese Americans as signs of boredom, inattentiveness, or even passive aggressiveness.

As an illustration of how confusion can occur, one sensitive student of intercultural communication related the following incident: While at work, he observed his European American supervisor become increasingly frustrated toward an Asian American employee. The problem arose during an information-giving session in which the supervisor was explaining to the employee how to proceed on a particular job. Instead of looking directly at the supervisor and occasionally providing some nonverbal feedback (a nod, a smile, or an "Uh huh"), she continued to look down and away, waiting respectfully for the supervisor to finish his "lecture." The supervisor totally misinterpreted her response. If the student observer hadn't interfered and explained to the supervisor the communication style the employee was bringing to the encounter from her cultural community, she might have lost her job.

Family honor is another important part of the Asian American collectivistic orientation. Whereas many people are concerned about family honor and reputation, Asian Americans tend to be even more so. One's personal achievements bring honor to the entire family, while one's failures bring shame and dishonor. Evidence of this orientation can sometimes be seen in the classroom. Asian American students have a reputation for working hard to achieve high grades. They do so not just for self-satisfaction but, importantly, for the honor of their family. To fail a course can mean letting one's family down, and bringing disgrace. Among European Americans, on the other hand, the individual is likely to take (or be granted) personal credit for her or his successes and, at the same time, be forced to take responsibility for personal failures as well.

As communicators, we might expect Asian Americans to be much less flamboyant and outgoing than either Latinos or African Americans. Compared to the others that have been discussed so far, Asian Americans are likely to be constrained in both their manner and their words. Their communication style is simple and restrained, with little or no dramatic, illustrative facial expressions or gestures. They tend to be more indirect in their approach, preferring their listeners to provide their own interpretations and draw their own conclusions. Asian Americans often come across as *good listeners:* In public situations, they can be counted on to be quietly reserved, polite, and pleasant. They are unlikely to ask questions or publicly to challenge another's point of view.

In summary, Asian Americans are highly collectivistic and high in both power and context. However, they are not easily classified on the masculinity-femininity continuum. Japanese Americans tend to be high in masculinity (assertive, ambitious, achievement oriented), but other Asian Americans tend to be much less so—particularly Chinese and Taiwanese Americans. All of these cultural orientations influence the way the broad category of Asian Americans communicate. As a result, they can be characterized as implicit, understated, deferential, quiet and somewhat withdrawn, sincere, and always respectful.

Native Americans

Ambiguity has long surrounded both what constitutes *membership* and what is the most appropriate *label* to use in talking about this complex category of Americans. Locke effectively explains the chronology or these ambiguities and provides the rationale for the appropriateness of the label "Native American" as used in this book.

> Historically, the name *Indian* was used, followed by *American Indian* and, more recently, *Native American*. The Bureau of Indian Affairs (BIA) (1988) defines a Native American as one who is a registered or enrolled member of a tribe or whose blood quantum is one-fourth or more, genealogically derived. Hirschfelder (1982) reports that one Native American law center has assembled 52 legal definitions of Native Americans. The U.S. Census Bureau, on the other hand, records anyone who claims native identity as Native American. Although there appears to be no consensus as to the most appropriate term, *Native American* is used here because it connotes both the heritage of the original inhabitants of this continent and the group's status as United States citizens.[50]

Native Americans, like the other categories of citizens described in this chapter, represent a number of tribes, nations, pueblos, and unique individuals that are not easily classified or characterized. Although they are diverse, Native Americans use a number of identifiable cultural patterns. As in the Asian American specialized culture, collectivism is highly valued; cooperation, harmony, and getting along are the expectations in interactions with one another. Unless personal competition benefits the entire group, and the situation is clearly defined as competitive (as in an athletic event), it is an undesirable human characteristic.[51] Among the Pueblo nations, such as the Zuni of New Mexico, the traditional culture restricts anyone who tries to outdo others by striving for personal power or success.[52] This restriction on competition can pose significant problems for Native Americans who attempt to assimilate into other specialized cultures. In a competitive business world, for example, traditional Native Americans may have a hard time competing for jobs, dollars,

and power. On the other hand, they may be successful working in businesses that depend on team players who can work harmoniously to get the job done.

Given the high-context nature of their cultures, Native Americans also avoid sustained and direct eye contact when speaking. Both the Hopi and the Navajo define direct eye contact as offensive. In fact, staring can be interpreted as a form of aggression.[53] Moreover, the Hopi tend to be restrained in their nonverbal facial expressiveness; their communication exchanges tend to be more implicit than explicit. Compared to other moderate- or low-context cultures (such as Latinos, European Americans, and African Americans), Native Americans are observably less dramatic and less animated in the way they normally communicate with others.[54]

Although their nonverbal behaviors may not be all that expressive and obvious to others outside their specialized culture, these cues are a vital means for relating. With the exception of Cherokee, written language was virtually nonexistent before Native Americans were forced to interact with White settlers. Over the years, Native Americans have taken pride in passing on their traditions and customs through oral myths, legends, and stories. "One can learn much by 'listening' to what Native Americans are expressing through body language, eye movements, silence, and tone of voice."[55]

Characteristic of high-context cultures, Native Americans learn from early childhood to communicate in more indirect ways. To illustrate, let's look for a moment at the Laguna, another Pueblo people of central New Mexico, whose children enjoy a rather unique relationship with their parents.[56] When Laguna children misbehave, their parents seldom punish them—and they seldom need to. When a child does misbehave, the parents turn to a unique and indirect way of communicating social control. They instruct the child that the *cha-be-u* (chah-bey-oo)—dreadful beings said to come from Mexico—will come for them.

Actually, the *cha-be-u* are enacted by two members of the tribe, who dress in fearsome costumes and ride into the village on horses for the occasion. Their task is to punish those children who have seriously misbehaved—or at least to scare them so that their behavior will improve. In the case of younger children, the *cha-be-u* appear at the door of the home and ask whether a naughty child lives there. The parents admit that their child has misbehaved and will not obey them. The *cha-be-u* then say that they are going to take the child with them, away from the parents and the village, to a very bad place. The child, of course, is terrified. The parents then have a change of heart and plead with the *cha-be-u* to leave the child with them.[57]

Not only does the *cha-be-u* method of communicating discipline result in well-behaved children for the most part, it also preserves a warm parent-child relationship. Laguna children fail to associate punishment with their parents; instead, they see their parents pleading on their behalf. In other cultures, parents *are* the punishers in that they communicate discipline directly. Indeed, a conversation among European American parents about disciplining children ("Spare the rod; spoil the child") and the associative guilt after applying punishment ("It hurts me more than it hurts you") would probably shock and repel a Laguna parent.

The analysis of cultural features that influence the way Native Americans communicate suggests that they can be characterized as a high-context culture and are, thus, indirect, quiet, understated, inexpressive, nonassertive, and even somewhat withdrawn. Also, because they are collectivistic, Native Americans are group- and family-oriented, noncompetitive (except under special circumstances), publicly agreeable (privately, they may disagree), and cooperative. In terms of power distance orientation, Native Americans respect the elderly: With age comes experience; with experience comes knowledge. They also believe in harmony and balance with nature—showing great respect for all living things. Finally, Native Americans can be characterized as more feminine than masculine in their value orientation. The family is of utmost importance, and inter-

personal relationships are more valued than personal success or ambition. Native Americans also tend to be wary of material wealth and the collection of material possessions.[58]

In summary, as communicators, Native Americans tend to express themselves similarly to the way Asian Americans do. Their nonverbal gestures and body movements are likely to be restrained or subdued. They appreciate a good story, relying heavily on myths and legends that have been passed on for generations. They are likely to suggest rather than insist on a particular way of thinking or behaving. Native Americans often appear agreeable and accommodating. Saving face or maintaining the dignity of self and others is important to them. They "are keenly sensitive to being singled out for public disapproval, laughter, or ostracism."[59] Consequently, Native Americans are likely to be publicly polite and receptive to other communicators—whether or not they agree with or like them.

Middle Eastern Americans

Middle Eastern Americans form another category of citizens that has substantial representation in the United States. People from Egypt, Lebanon, Jordan, Armenia, Iran, Iraq, Syria, and numerous other Middle Eastern countries have long made the United States their home. Although these Americans operate in every social, political, and industrial sector of our society, they maintain many traditional aspects of their cultures as well. Despite their assimilation into the general culture, some of their behaviors continue to differ noticeably from the social and cultural practices of the majority. Similar to the traditions of Native Americans, they communicate as a predominantly oral culture. For centuries in the Middle East, people relied on tribal storytellers to serve as the record keepers of significant events, recording history and passing it on orally generation after generation.[60]

Today in the Middle East, this oral tradition continues, but the storytellers are now called "poets." Poetry is an essential part of contemporary Middle Eastern culture. Poets often interpret political and social events; thus, poets influence what opinions people hold and how they respond to events.[61]Because of this, poets are held in very high esteem in Middle Eastern countries.[62]

The oral tradition of the Middle East has influenced the way people from this part of the world define public discourse more generally. Middle Easterners view public speaking as a highly valued activity. Much of their public discourse relies heavily on religious references; it's not at all unusual for Muslims to quote extensively from the Koran or for Jews to quote from the Torah.[63] Their style of speaking is highly emotional, and they rely heavily on the rhythm of language and the sounds of words as they compose their messages. Both the content and the logical presentation of ideas is secondary. In her handbook for Westerners, Margaret Nydell sums up the speech mannerisms of Arab communicators:

> Arabs talk a lot, repeat themselves, shout when excited, and make extensive use of gestures. They punctuate their conversations with oaths (such as "I swear by God") to emphasize what they say, and they exaggerate for effect. Foreigners sometimes wonder if they are involved in a discussion or an argument. If you speak softly and make your statements only once, Arabs may wonder if you really mean what you are saying. People will ask, "Do you really mean that?" or "Is that true?" —not that they do not believe you, but they need repetition and a few emphatic "yeses" to be reassured.[64]

Middle Eastern Americans are less likely than European Americans to believe that the future can be controlled. Because they tend to be more retrospective than prospective about life, what happens in the past concerns them more than what will happen in the future. Thus, Middle Eastern Americans view speaking primarily as a way of relating, rather than controlling. Speaking eloquently holds particular appeal to them. They might communicate to express formal generosity to someone or to maintain their cultural pride, honor, and personal self-respect.[65]

Like African Americans and Latinos, then, Middle Eastern Americans tend to be dramatic, demonstrative communicators. They frequently speak to evoke an emotional effect as opposed to communicating a specific message. In other words, they don't always say exactly what they mean. When communicating within their high-context culture, Middle Eastern Americans insinuate or imply, expecting others to know or understand what they mean. Their arguments rely more on subjective personal experience than on objective data. Middle Eastern Americans also tend to be collectivistic, somewhat high in power distance, and marginally feminine in their value orientations. They are very sensitive to others' perceptions of them. As a proud people, they make every effort to be perceived positively in all social and political situations.[66]

Females and Males

Whether we belong to one of the foregoing specialized cultures or not, we all identify with a particular *gender category*. That is, we are either male or female. Being either male or female is more than a biological condition of the body. It also means that, as a product of socialization into our society, enculturation into its general culture, plus into the specialized cultures characteristic of our particular gender, we hold unique world views directly related to our sexual classification. Whatever their conditions during childhood or adolescence, females and males learn during their entire lives to think and behave in particular ways. If you are a male, you have learned in a variety of ways to act the way males in our society are expected to act. The same is true for females. When males and females do not behave in expected gender-appropriate ways, they are responded to negatively. Growing up as a male implies being a member of the male culture, and growing up as a female means being a member of the female culture. The question here is: How does membership in a particular gender culture influence how we communicate?

The same four cultural features we have already discussed, which significantly influence how different categories of people communicate, can help us understand the communication styles of females and males. Across the many cultures present in the United States, certain tendencies define women's value orientations that differ from men's. Obviously, these value orientations are dominated or mediated in part by each individual's other memberships and affiliations, along with other factors.

Even so, when compared to men, women tend to be different in how they communicate. They tend to be collectivistic, high context, low power, and feminine in their orientation. As a result, we might expect women to place a high priority on personal relationships, particularly family and friends. Providing support, showing compassion, and nurturing others are important personal and social qualities. To achieve symmetry or equality, "women often match experiences"[67] to show others "I felt that way, too" or "The same thing happened to me." Moreover, because they value being polite and showing respect and courtesy toward others, they "avoid criticizing, outdoing, or putting others down."[68]

Women also tend to be sensitive and indirect in their communication transactions. In contrast, men tend to be individualistic, low context, high power, and masculine. Consequently, we might expect men to prioritize individual success and achievements, to appreciate competition, to assert themselves and challenge others, and to control or dominate interactions.

To some extent, research findings support the influence of such value preferences.[69] Women's talk is perceived as being deferential and polite; men's speech as forceful and assertive. Women use more qualifiers than men, words such as maybe and perhaps. They introduce their questions with phrases such as "This may be trivial to ask, but. . . ." Women further rely on verbal fillers during silent, awkward moments: "OK," "Well," "Sure," and "You know." Women use tag questions two to three times more often than men: "It's a beautiful day, *isn't it?*" Women are also more likely than men to insert intensifiers into their speech; instead of "That's pretty," women are more likely to say, "That's so pretty."

Nonverbally, women use more facial expressions than men, and they initiate and return smiles more often (even when they're not happy). They also rely on more eye contact to communicate. Men tend to talk more loudly than women, at a lower pitch, and with less tonal variation. Men also use more sweeping hand and arm gestures when they speak, tap their feet more than women, and take up more physical space. Whereas men usually sit with their legs apart and seem to expand when they sit on a chair, women hold their knees together and seem to contract.[70]

One of the myths that is often perpetuated between the genders is that women talk more than men. Contrary to popular belief, no single study supports that claim.[71] In fact, there appears to be no difference between how much females and males talk; however, in most contexts (but particularly so in male-female conversations), males are more likely to decide what is talked about and for how long! Also, when men talk, they tend to be more absolute, directive, and authoritative than women.[72]

These differences between male and female communication styles have led some researchers to label men's talk as "powerful" and female talk as "powerless."[73]Unfortunately, such nonegalitarian labels can have devastating effects on women in politics, at work, at home, and in virtually any social context. For example, research indicates that women communicators who use numerous intensifiers, qualifiers, verbal fillers, and tag questions are often perceived negatively—by both men and women.[74] Listeners tend to interpret such verbal cues as indicators of uncertainty, a lack of knowledge (or intelligence), and a limited ability to influence others. Alternatively, it has been suggested that the tentative quality of female speech reflects women's desire to create equality and to invite others to participate in conversation.[75]

What is also disturbing for many women is that research finds that women are negatively perceived when they use these verbal cues, but that men (when they use the same tag questions and qualifiers) are often perceived as polite and receiver oriented.[76] At the same time, however, women's communication style is also rated as more attractive, more polite, and closer to the ideal than men's.[77] Although the female communication style is preferred, a double standard is applied when it is used by women; that is, women who use this style are less likely than men to be seen having authority, credibility, and control.

Communicating Successfully in Intercultural Contexts

Even in the best of circumstances, most of us are not completely successful multicultural communicators. The success of our multicultural encounters depends to a large extent on our approach. What follows is a set of guidelines for achieving or maximizing our success.

1. *Recognize that every individual has emotions, needs, and feelings that are as sensitive as yours.* Never make the mistake of believing that people who differ from you, in one or in many ways, are less sensitive or even less worthy of your respect. Their eyes look out on the same reality as yours, and although their particular culture may cause them to respond to it differently, their perceptions and interpretations are as valuable as yours.

2. *Try to understand the cultural norms of the person with whom you communicate.* Recall that culture, by definition, prescribes rules not only for communicating but also for virtually all human behaviors. To maximize the success of our multicultural communication, then, we need as much understanding of their culture as possible when we interact with people from backgrounds and orientations that are different from our own.

3. *Respect the customs and traditions of others.* Remember the principle of cultural relativity, which asserts that people practicing every specialized culture we have discussed in detail in this chapter have worked out solutions for the problems encountered in day-to-day living. For these people, their solutions define the correct ways of thinking, believing, and behaving. Although certain behavior may seem unrealistic, inappropriate, or even unappealing, we can appreciate that it is proper and satisfying to other kinds of people. Every effort should be made, therefore, to respect the customs and traditions of others.

4. *Listen actively in a communication encounter with others from a different culture.* Effective listening is crucial to the success of any communication encounter and even more so when the exchange involves more than one culture. In fact, multicultural differences only further confound the difficulty of achieving fidelity in communication. The skills of effective listening are more important than ever in multicultural exchanges (see Chapter 4).

5. *Learn to cope with uncertainty.* A predictable and normal response to encountering people from different cultures is uncertainty.[78] As a result, our level of anxiety is aroused. How we handle such uncertainty and the associated anxiety is crucial to determining the relative success of our multicultural communication experiences. The key is to monitor and control our overt reactions. By accepting that we are going to experience some degree of uncertainty, we can more easily suspend judgment and thereby open ourselves to accepting and understanding differences between ourselves and others.

6. *Avoid stereotyping people who are different from you.* Negative labeling and stereotyping not only have long histories but also are alive and well in today's multicultural society. Unfortunately, the meanings aroused by such labels strongly influence the way individuals in different social categories are perceived, understood, evaluated, accepted, or rejected. Stereotyping people who are culturally different from

us in negative ways obviously exacerbates our efforts to communicate. To avoid this, we should check very carefully all labels we use to designate others. Are the labels derogatory? Do they in any way humiliate or belittle others? Then, determine what labels (if any) the people use to describe themselves; that is, discover what labels, if any, are acceptable from their perspective. Finally, make every effort to avoid negative sterotypic thinking; instead, seek understanding beyond simple and obvious categories.

7. *Be aware of your own ethnocentrism.* Most Americans would state with conviction that their way of life is the best. That may be true—for us. We tend to be ethnocentric in much the same way as we label and stereotype. Excessive ethnocentrism can be both dangerous and counterproductive to communicating multiculturally. Accept that we are all ethnocentric to some extent—and that this can be positive—but recognize that ethnocentrism in multicultural communication can at times significantly reduce the chances of successful interaction.

Overall, these seven guidelines (summarized in Box 8.3) offer practical advice with which to approach multicultural communication. Viewing them as a set of interrelated suggestions is the most productive way to consider their application, as the issues they address overlap in one or more ways.

BOX 8.3 *A Closer Look*

Tips for Successful Intercultural Communication

Successful multicultural communication results when all individuals involved are satisfied with the process and the consequences of their encounter. How do you know when successful communication occurs? Briefly, all communicators will want to pursue their conversation further. Also, they will seek future opportunities to interact with one another. And, when asked, communicators will report positive, satisfied feelings about their exchange. But this is no simple task. How do we go about becoming a successful multicultural communicator?

1. Recognize that every individual has emotions, needs, and feelings that are as sensitive as yours.
2. Try to understand the cultural norms of the person with whom you communicate.
3. Respect the customs and traditions of others.
4. Listen actively in a co-cultural communication encounter.
5. Learn to cope with uncertainty.
6. Avoid stereotyping people who are different from you.
7. Be aware of your own ethnocentrism.

Chapter Review

- Culture influences how we think, feel, and behave. Because of the cultural diversity of the United States, nowhere is there a greater potential for inaccurate communication and misunderstanding. Cultural pluralism depends on cultural inclusion—a commitment to acknowledge, respect, and adapt to others who are different from us.

- Culture and communication are inseparable. The way we communicate, what we believe, what we say, the language choices we use, and the nonverbal signals we employ are all a function of the culture we acquire. How we speak and relate nonverbally to others is learned from the culture in which we grow up.

- Some cultural identities are more important than others. In a communication encounter, the greater the number of cultures the participants share, the greater the accuracy of their messages and the more satisfied they are with their exchange.

- Researchers have found four cultural features that make a difference in how we relate with one another: individualism and collectivism, high and low context, high and low power distance, and masculinity and femininity. Each of these cultural features represents different values or ways of viewing the world.

- This chapter reviews the cultural orientations and communication styles of the six largest ethnic and racial categories in the United States—European Americans, African Americans, Latinos, Asian Americans, Native Americans, and Middle Eastern Americans—as well as the important differences between the communication styles used by women and men.

- Successful intercultural communication is an exchange of messages in which all individuals in an encounter are satisfied with the process and the consequences. This chapter offers guidelines to help you communicate interculturally.

Key Terms

social category	melting pot policy	cultural exclusion	collectivism
specialized culture	majority	ethnocentrism	context
intercultural communication	minority	chauvinism	power distance
culture	cultural inclusion	cultural relativity	masculinity
general culture	cultural pluralism	individualism	femininity

Notes

1. There is a debate among some scholars and others about whether citizens of the United States can legitimately be the only ones in the Western Hemisphere to call themselves "Americans." Other countries, particularly in Latin America, point out that they too are "Americans" in the sense that they live on a continent named after the Italian explorer Amerigo Vespucci—who (on behalf of Spain) in 1499–1500 voyaged to the new world encountered earlier by Columbus. Vespucci became convinced that it was a separate land, and not China, as Columbus had concluded. When this was confirmed, both continents of the Western Hemisphere were named after him (North and South America). However, today and historically, few in other countries on these continents use the label "Americans" to identify themselves. Canadians call themselves "Canadians" (not Canadian Americans). Mexicans refer to themselves as "Mexicans." Only Mexicans living in the United States are commonly called "Mexican Americans." Similarly, there is no United States of Bolivia, Peru, Uruguay, or Argentina. Citizens of those countries call themselves "Bolivians," "Argentines," and so on. On the other hand, historically, for more than two centuries of cultural practice, citizens of the United States have called themselves "Americans," not "United Statesians." The term *America* is in the official name of the country, on the currency, and in countless official documents. For those reasons the term is used in the traditional way in this text.

2. Generally, these are a set of broad and complex patterns of deeply established beliefs, practices, traditions, customs and other social forms within the culture by which a society achieves important goals (e.g., economic activity,

family relationships, political systems, religious beliefs, and the education of the young). Complex societies also have a number of other goals—military, scientific, welfare, and so on.

3. There is a lively debate among communication scholars about what such specialized cultures should be called. The name *subcultures* (meaning a culture within a larger culture) was the term used initially by anthropologists and sociologists when, many years ago, they began to study different lifestyles that existed among unique social categories in the society—such as among convicts in prison, those practicing specific occupations, prostitutes, confidence men, college and university professors, commercial fishermen, and police officers (among many others). Later, some scholars worried that the prefix "sub" implied inferiority, especially when racial and ethnic categories were the focus. They advocated the use of *co-cultures* instead. A problem with using *co-culture* is that it is hard for many ordinary people to regard professional criminals, the drug trade, prostitutes, and others who are held in legitimate disrespect as having cultures (beliefs and practices) that are "equal" in value and in their contribution to society, to the cultures of law-abiding groups. To avoid this problem, the nonjudgmental term *specialized cultures* is used throughout this book.

4. See, for example: Triandis, H. C., & Suh, E. M. (2002). Cultural influences on personality. *Annual Review of Psychology, 53,* 133–160.

5. Samovar, L. A., & Porter, R. E. (1995). *Communication between cultures* (2nd ed., p. 60). Belmont, CA: Wadsworth; Dasenbrock, R. W. (1992). The multicultural West. In P. Aufderheide (Ed.), *Beyond PC: Towards a politics of understanding* (pp. 201–211). St. Paul, MN: Graywolf Press.

6. Although the number of foreign-born residents and their children is at its highest level, their percentage in the population is not. In the 1910 census, for example, this group represented 35 percent of the population, compared to 20 percent in the year 2000. See: Scott, J. (February 7, 2002). Foreign born in U.S. at record high. *The New York Times,* p. A26.

7. U.S. Census Bureau (2000). *Coming to America: A profile of the Nation's foreign born (2000 Update).* www.census.gov/population.

8. Lustig, M. W., & Koester, J. (1993). *Intercultural competence: Interpersonal communication across cultures* (p. 9). New York: HarperCollins.

9. Ibid.

10. Sumner, W. G. (1906). *Folkways* (pp. 28–30). Boston: Ginn.

11. El Nasser, H., & Overberg, P. (June 5, 2002). More people identify themselves as simply "American." *USA Today,* p. 1A; Census finds "American" identity rising in U.S. (June 9, 2002). *The New York Times,* p. 27; U.S. Census Bureau (2000). *Profile of selected social characteristics: 2000* (QT-02). www.census.gov.

12. DeFleur, M. L., & Cho, C. S. (1957). Assimilation of Japanese women in an American city. *Social Problems, 4,* 3, 244–257.

13. Sumner, *Folkways,* p. 27. See also: Brewer, M. B. (1999). The psychology of prejudice: Ingroup love or outgroup hate? *The Journal of Social Issues, 55,* 3, 429–444.

14. p. 30

15. See, for example: Okafor, T. (2001). Ethnocentrism in Africa. *UN Chronicle, 38,* 2, 30–31.

16. Schulz, J. J., & Schulz, L. (1999). The darkest of ages: Afghan women under the Taliban. *Journal of Peace Psychology, 5,* 3, 237–254.

17. Hall, E. T. (1959). *The silent language.* New York: Doubleday, p. 37.

18. Axtell, R. E. (1990). *Do's and taboos of hosting international visitors* (pp. 6–7). New York: Wiley.

19. Samovar & Porter, *Communication between cultures,* p. 85.

20. Hall, E. T. (1976). *Beyond culture.* New York: Anchor Books/Doubleday.

21. Lustig & Koester, *Intercultural competence,* pp. 131–132.

22. Samovar & Porter, *Communication between cultures,* p. 104.

23. Hofstede, G. (1984). *Culture's consequences: International differences in work-related values.* Beverly Hills, CA: Sage. See also: Samovar & Porter, *Communication between cultures,* p. 93.

24. Hofstede, G. (1984). *Culture's consequences: International differences in work-related values.* Beverly Hills, CA: Sage.

25. Dodd, C. H. (1991). *Dynamics of intercultural communication.* (3rd ed., pp. 73–74). Dubuque, IA: William C. Brown. See also: Hofstede, *Culture's consequences,* pp. 89–191.

26. Samovar & Porter, *Communication between cultures,* p. 95.

27. U.S. Census Bureau (2000). *Profile of general demographic characteristics: 2000. (QT-01); Profile of selected social characteristics: 2000* (QT-02). www.census.gov.

28. Athen, G. (1988). *American ways: A guide for foreigners in the United States.* Yarmouth, ME: Intercultural Press.

29. Ibid., pp. 21–20.

30. Ibid., pp. 23–25.

31. Ibid., pp. 27–28.

32. Hecht, M. L., Collier, M. J., & Ribeau, S. A. (1993). *African American communication: Ethnic identity and cultural interpretation* (p. 74). Newbury Park, CA: Sage.

33. Lustwig & Koester, *Intercultural competence,* p. 21.

34. Vox pop (1994). *Time,* p. 12.

35. Hecht, Collier, & Ribeau, *African American communication,* p. 97.

36. Ibid., pp. 104–106. See also: Kochman, T. (1981). *Black and white styles in conflict* (pp. 130–132). Chicago: University of Chicago Press.

37. Hecht, Collier, & Ribeau. *African American communication,* p. 98; Kochman, *Black and white styles,* pp. 106–108.

38. Kochman, *Black and white styles,* p. 147.

39. Hecht, Collier, & Ribeau, *African American communication,* pp. 102–103; Kochman, *Black and white styles,* pp. 111–113.

40. Locke, D. C. (1992). *Increasing multicultural understanding: A comprehensive model* (p. 26). Newbury Park, CA: Sage.

41. Marin, G., & Marin, B. V. (1991). *Research with Hispanic populations: Increasing multicultural understanding* (p. 21). Newbury Park, CA: Sage.

42. Lustig & Koester, *Intercultural competence,* p. 21.

43. Klopf, D. W. (1991). *Intercultural encounters: The fundamentals of intercultural communication* (2nd ed., p. 183). Englewood, CO: Morton.

44. Collier, M. J. (1988). A comparison of conversations among and between domestic cultural groups: How intra-and intercultural competencies vary. *Communication Quarterly, 36,* 122–144.

45. Marin & Marin, *Research with Hispanic populations.*

46. Gudykunst, W. B. (1991). *Bridging differences: Effective intergroup communication* (pp. 45–49). Newbury Park, CA: Sage. See also: Hofstede, *Culture's consequences;* Hofstede, G., & Bond, J. (1984). Hofstede's culture dimensions. *Journal of Cross-Cultural Psychology, 1, 15,* 417–433.

47. Locke, *Increasing multicultural understanding.*

48. Ting-Toomey, S. (1988). Intercultural conflict styles: A face-negotiation theory. In Y.Y. Kim & W. B. Gudykunst (Eds.), *Theories of intercultural communication* (pp. 213–235). Newbury Park, CA; Sage.

49. Klopf, *Intercultural encounters,* p. 11.

50. Locke, *Increasing multicultural understanding,* pp. 46–47. See also: Bureau of Indian Affairs. (1988). *American Indians today.* Washington, DC: Author; Hirschfelder, A. (1982). *Happy may I work: American Indians and Alaska natives today.* New York: Scribner's.

51. Bennett, C. I. (1990). *Comprehensive multicultural education* (2nd ed., pp. 164–165). Boston: MA: Allyn & Bacon.

52. DeFleur, M. L., D'Antonio, W. V., & DeFleur, L. B. (1981). *Sociology: Human society* (3rd ed., p. 92). Glenview, IL: Scott, Foresman.

53. Samovar & Porter, *Communication between cultures,* p. 195.

54. Ibid., p. 193.

55. Locke, *Increasing multicultural understanding,* p. 50.

56. DeFleur, D'Antonio, & DeFleur, *Sociology,* pp. 146–147.

57. Ibid, p. 147.

58. Locke, *Increasing multicultural understanding.*

59. Dutton, B. P. (1983). *American Indians of the Southwest* (p. 13). Albuquerque: University of New Mexico Press.

60. Hamod, H. S. (1963). Arab and Moslem rhetorical theory. *Central States Speech Journal, 14,* 97–102.

61. Almaney, A. J., & Alwan, A. J. (1982). *Communicating with the Arabs: A handbook for the business executive*. Prospect Heights, IL: Waveland.

62. Anderson, J. W. (1991). A comparison of Arab and American conceptions of "effective persuasion." In Samovar, L. A., & Porter, R. E. (Eds.), *Intercultural communication: A reader* (6th ed.), pp. 96–106. Belmont, CA: Wadsworth.

63. Ibid., p. 98.

64. Nydell, M. K. (1987). *Understanding Arabs: A guide for Westerners* (p. 104). Yarmouth, ME: Intercultural Press.

65. Ibid.

66. Condon, J. C., & Yousef, F. S. (1975). *An introduction to intercultural communication* (pp. 159–162). New York: Macmillan.

67. Wood, J. T. (1994). *Gendered lives: Communication, gender, and culture* (p. 141). Belmont, CA: Wadsworth.

68. Ibid., p. 140.

69. For a review of that research, see: Mulac, A., Bradac, J. J., & Gibbons, P. (2001). Empirical support for the gender-as-culture hypothesis: An intercultural analysis of male/female language differences. *Human Communication Research, 27,* 1, 121–152; Ivy, D. K., & Backlund, P. (1994). *Exploring gender speak: Personal effectiveness in gender communication.* New York: McGraw-Hill; Pearson, J. C., Turner, L. H., & Todd-Mancillas, W. (1991). *Gender and communication* (pp. 111–115). Dubuque, IA: William C. Brown; and Wood, *Gendered lives.*

70. Pearson, Turner, & Todd-Mancillas, *Gender and communication;* Wood, *Gendered lives.*

71. Ibid., pp. 134–146.

72. Pearson, Turner, & Todd-Mancillas, *Gender and communication;* Wood, *Gendered lives.*

73. Lakoff, R. (1975). *Language and women's place.* New York: Harper & Row; and Lakoff, R. (1973). Language and woman's place. *Language in Society, 2,* 45–80.

74. Bradley, P. H. (1981). The folk-linguistics of women's speech: An empirical examination. *Communication Monographs, 48,* 73–90.

75. Wood, *Gendered lives,* p. 143.

76. Bradley, The folk-linguistics of women's speech.

77. Mulac, A., & Lundell, T. L. (1986). Linguistic contributors to the gender-linked language effect. *Journal of Language and Social Psychology, 5,* 81–101.

78. Gudykunst, W. B. (1985). The influence of cultural similarity, type of relationship, and self-monitoring on uncertainty reduction processes. *Communication Monographs, 52,* 203–217; see also: Gudykunst, *Bridging differences.*

Presenting Yourself Effectively

J im was nervous about meeting Maria's parents. Ever since they had become a serious couple, and especially after he proposed, Jim knew that this day would come. All during the three-hour drive from the city, Jim thought about what kind of impression he was going to make. Were they going to see him as a decent guy, worthy of their daughter? Or would they see him in negative ways and counsel her to dump him? He was very anxious to make a good first impression and he knew how important it was. He understood completely that what he looked like, how he acted, and what he had to say in the first few minutes of this important meeting were likely to influence her parents' judgment of their future son-in-law. He also knew that this first impression would last for a long time.

In planning his strategy for the meeting, Jim had considered a number of factors that could influence the impression he would make. For one thing, he anticipated (correctly as it turned out) that Maria's parents would be different from most of the people they knew in the city, and that their ideas about language, dress, and appropriate behavior between men and women would be conservative. Jim did not want to misrepresent anything, but he agreed with Maria that they should not disclose that they had had premarital sexual intimacy: He would occupy a guest bedroom and Maria would sleep in her old room.

From what Maria had told him about her parents, they were quite religious and conservative in their political views. Jim decided to be cautious about discussing both his own rather thin religious background and his liberal political beliefs. The best strategy, he decided, was to avoid too much *self-disclosure* along those lines.

Jim knew also that physical appearance was going to be important, so he had made sure that his hair was neatly trimmed. He had dressed carefully for this first meeting. His clothes were casual, but pressed. His shoes were shined and indeed everything about him looked very clean and neat.

Suddenly they were there. As they got out of the car, Maria introduced him to her smiling parents. Still, Jim felt that they were examining him closely. He started with a broad smile, telling them how much he had been looking forward to meeting them. He could see right away that they were assessing his every feature. However, he sensed that he was over those first moments when initial impressions first were formed and that things were positive. They seemed to have formed at least an initially favorable impression. After they went inside and sat down, they talked a while about the drive from the city. Jim said how pleased he had been when they invited him. For a while it was just small talk—about how nice the weather was, the traffic on the roads, and where they had stopped for lunch. After a few minutes, he and Maria took their luggage to their separate rooms. Then lunch was ready, and they all sat down together as a family for the first time.

As it turned out, the conversation at lunch went well. Maria and her parents had a lot of catching up to do and that took a while. At first, Jim did not have to carry much of the conversation. When it was his turn, he was able to explain clearly the kind of work he did and how he and Maria had met. Then they discussed their future plans. Both parents smiled a lot, and seemed happy.

That night, when he and Maria were alone briefly on the porch swing, she told him that he had been a big hit with her parents and that they were both delighted they were going to have such a nice son-in-law. Her mom had even mentioned grandchildren.

In today's diverse society, the meeting between Jim and Maria's parents is hardly a unique situation. Regardless of our backgrounds, we all face the problem of communicating a positive first impression when we meet someone unlike ourselves with whom we might want to have more than a passing relationship. This happens a lot. First impressions are important when you meet someone you might want to date, when you make a presentation in class or at work, when you give a speech to a group of strangers, and when you interview for a new job.

Although initial encounters proceed within the frame of reference of the simultaneous transactions model that was discussed in Chapter 1, they also have a number of unique other important features that need more discussion. Therefore, this chapter will answer four major questions: First, *how* do people form impressions of others when they are meeting them for the first time? Second, how can you influence the first impressions others form *about you?* Third, what specifically can be communicated, both verbally and nonverbally to make the impressions others form about you *more favorable?* Finally, what can be done to change *unfavorable impressions* that people already have about you? A good place to begin is with a review of what has been learned from communication research that has examined the general process of getting to know others and forming initial impressions.

The Impressions You Make in Initial Encounters

It is very important to understand every feature of the process by which people get to know one another. Such an understanding provides a solid basis for developing skills that are needed for effective self-presentation. It is not a simple process, and it involves a number of considerations. Fortunately, scholars have spent decades studying what is involved when people undergo the process of getting to know one another.

The Process of Self-Presentation

The term *person peception* is used to refer to the broad area of investigation that focuses on the stages people pass through when they first meet and develop initial assessments of one another. A simple definition of the concept, advanced by Renato Tagiuri, states that **person perception** refers to *"the processes by which a person comes to know and to think about other persons, their characteristics, qualities, and inner states."*[1] This chapter focuses specifically on the steps involved in what has been called **presentation of self.**

The fact is that each of us makes a presentation of self whenever we meet someone new. The term *self* was explained in Chapter 5. As explained, it refers to the pattern of beliefs, meanings, and understandings each of us has developed through communicating with others concerning our own nature and worth as a human being. The idea of *presentation* of self refers to *formulating and transmitting verbal and nonverbal messages to other people about the kind of person you are.* It is in every respect an interpersonal communication process that proceeds according to the linear and simultaneous transactions models set forth in Chapter 1.

As you talk, dress, or act in various ways, you communicate meanings about your personal qualities. In doing so, you present descriptions and definitions about your inner nature to others. From these messages, others construct interpretations, understandings, and impressions about what you are really like. It works both ways, of course. As others form impressions about you during your initial encounters with them, you will be doing the same about them. It is, as you will see, an inescapable form of human behavior.

In your initial encounters, you do not always try or plan to get other individuals to evaluate you in some particular way. However, if you want to do so, it is certainly possible. You can plan a communication strategy and transmit verbal and nonverbal messages that are deliberately designed to create a particular set of impressions. Sociologist Erving Goffman referred to this process as **impression management.**[2] In this chapter, impression management refers to *effective* self-presentation. Messages can be said to be "effective" insofar as they cause others to evaluate you in ways you desire.

There is little doubt that what an individual says and does during an initial encounter leaves lasting impressions in the minds of others. In other words, the verbal and nonverbal messages you transmit as you are getting to know someone can strongly influence what that person comes to believe about you. Those early impressions may be very difficult to change. For these reasons, presentation of self can be a serious business on which both personal and social success can depend.

What Research Tells Us about Initial Impressions

To develop a greater understanding of the relationship between initial encounters and person perception, some of the classic experiments on how people form impressions of others provide important insights. A brief review of the principles discovered in early research can show you how to improve your ability to manage your impressions—that is, to present yourself effectively to others.

The principle of rapid impression formation. Of the pioneering research on impression formation, the work of Solomon Asch in the 1940s was the most significant.[3] At the time, Asch was conducting experiments to try to find out how a person quickly infers personality traits and attributes concerning another individual when all he or she has is a limited amount of known characteristics. (Obviously, this is related to the idea of forming impressions of a person one has just met.) The point here is this: You must make some sort of assessment—even though these are guesses or assumptions—about people you have just met if you want to talk to them. You can't relate to another human being where everything about that person is just a *blank*. Each new person has some things you notice right away, and you use these to make assumptions about what that person is like, and how she or he will respond to what you say.

It was this issue that prompted Asch to conduct his classic experiments focused directly on the problem of examining how a person forms first impressions of other people. They were simple experiments but they revealed provocative findings. In the typical investigation he conducted, each participant or subject received a list of descriptive words said to characterize a target person—an individual whom the subject had never actually met. All the subject had about that person was the list of words said to describe the otherwise unknown individual. Then, after reviewing the words, each subject was asked to write a paragraph describing her or his first impressions of what that person was like. Following that, each subject was given a second list of descriptive terms and asked to indicate those terms each felt would *also* be likely to characterize the person each had already described in the previous paragraph. Each did so, thereby revealing in greater detail the overall impressions of the new person.

Thus, in this second step, Asch was able to gather each subject's early impressions of the target person formed on the basis of the very limited descriptions (by the words) supplied in the first step. Because early impressions in real life are formulated during initial meetings, this simple experiment was like the real impression-forming process. Asch found that subjects quickly formed surprisingly elaborate impressions of the target person after receiving only very limited descriptions of that individual.

In another of Asch's classic experiments, additional aspects of the process were shown. Again, subjects were provided with lists of descriptive terms and asked to form an impression of a target person. This time, however, the list of words described the unknown person quite positively as intelligent, skillful, industrious, determined, practical, and cautious. Next, each of the subjects was asked to write a paragraph describing the target person. After these paragraphs were completed, the subjects were again asked to assess that same individual, but in terms of four additional attributes: generous, happy, good-natured, and important. The results of this experiment were striking. Table 9.1 provides the findings. Look at the column titled "Trait List A." The point is that if the target was thought to have one set of favorable qualities, subjects believed that he or she had other favorable ones, too.

The principle of the salient characteristic. In a similar experiment, Asch inserted the descriptive word *warm* in the middle of his first list of characteristics—the words used by the subjects to write their descriptive paragraphs. What happened was that the subjects' initial impressions of the target person were *favorably influenced* by the word *warm*. This is shown in Table 9.1 under the column labeled "Trait List B." Clearly, adding a single known **salient characteristic**—a feature of the person that "stands out" ("warm" in this case) sharply altered initial impressions of the target person.

Asch was interested in whether this substantial change in impressions would occur with an emotionally negative quality as well. Therefore, he did still another experiment using the same

TABLE 9.1	Impression Formation in Asch's Experiments		
	Trait List A	**Trait List B**	**Trait List C**
	Intelligent	Intelligent	Intelligent
	Skillful	Skillful	Skillful
	Industrious	Industrious	Industrious
		Warm	*Cold*
	Determined	Determined	Determined
	Practical	Practical	Practical
	Cautious	Cautious	Cautious
Attribute	**Percentage of Subjects Indicating That Attribute Is Characteristic of Person Described by Trait List**		
Generous	55%	91%	8%
Happy	71	90	34
Good-natured	69	94	17
Important	88	88	99

Source: Asch, S. E. (1946). Forming impressions of personalities. *Journal of Personality and Social Psychology, 41,* 258–290.

procedures, but this time he substituted the unfavorable word *cold* in place of *warm*. What happened was that the favorability of the final ratings of the target dropped sharply. This can be seen in Table 9.1 under the column labeled "Trait List C." Thus, this final experiment strongly confirmed the principle of the salient characteristic.

Asch concluded that the words *warm* and *cold* had served as strong focuses of attention for the subjects. That is, these emotionally meaningful terms did indeed become **salient characteristics** around which the subjects organized their overall impressions of the target person. The more neutral words, used in the first step to describe target persons, implied a positive general impression of temperament and social acceptability; but when the more powerful words *warm* and *cold* were introduced, the resulting impressions were restructured considerably.

Although these were experiments in an artificial setting, the results of Asch's research provided guidelines that could be studied in more realistic settings. In that way, they provided valuable insights into how people seemed to form impressions of others. The findings implied that when individuals meet a stranger they quickly bring together a kind of initial configuration of impressions of that person on the basis of what limited characteristics they can observe. In addition, a single bit of significant information—a salient characteristic—can alter that impression considerably.

Asch's ideas were followed up by many scholars and it became clear that the principles of rapid formation and salient characteristics operate in real life. When we meet someone who seems to have many attractive qualities, our initial pattern of impressions is positive. Then, a single additional revelation suddenly changes the picture drastically. Such a salient characteristic might be that the person is an ex-convict, uses drugs, or was fired from his or her job for sexual misconduct. Upon fitting that into the configuration, our impressions may switch immediately to a negative or less favorable pattern.

The principle of labels as shaping perception. Those who study various kinds of deviant behavior—activities that depart from the norms of society—have extensively discussed the salient characteristic phenomenon. They have observed it not just through experiments with words but also through observations of the way people in real life respond to individuals who break accepted moral norms. They call this principle **labeling theory**.[4] It is in many ways an extension of the Asch principle. For example, if you learn that your neighbor's child, little Johnny, who is your son Eddie's friend, was brought home by the police after a local merchant complained that he had swiped candy bars in his store, Johnny has suddenly become a "problem child," or worse, maybe even a "juvenile delinquent." Such labels identify new salient characteristics that bring with them emotionally charged meanings.[5]

In our language culture, labels such as "juvenile delinquent" or "thief" are associated with switchblade knives, mugging old people, early drug and alcohol use, and the like. Perhaps little Johnny had never done anything bad before, and never will again. However, his 10-second act of shoplifting has now labeled him in a very serious way. Although this is no doubt unfair, after hearing that Johnny has become a "juvenile delinquent," you forbid your son Eddie to play with him ever again.

The basic idea, then, is that one critical piece of information about a person can communicate a powerful message. Labels are often the means that communicates such messages, regardless of whether the interpretation they bring is right or wrong. Any negative label—such as "former mental patient," "suspected sex offender," "unfair professor," "cheater," or "plagiarist"—can have a dramatic influence on the impressions people form. The label is like a magnet: It brings a baggage of cultural meanings commonly associated with it, whether deserved or not.

The principle of implicit personality formation. During the 1950s and 1960s, social scientists continued to use the investigative methods developed by Asch. They followed up on his study of the strong influence of a salient characteristic on people's overall impressions of others.[6] In a line of investigation called **implicit personality theory**, researchers tried to determine just how people combine different kinds of visible features attributed to a person into an overall configuration of beliefs about that person. They were concerned with how people put together their early patterns of impressions about a person, quickly making a set of assumptions about the nature of the person on the basis of what they know up to that point. They were also concerned with the way in which some readily observable (salient) characteristic comes to be seen as more important or central and how other attributes are interpreted as less essential. In other words, how do people construct an assumed personality for someone they have just met, and, on the basis of limited data, project it onto a person to form a pattern of initial impressions?

Recall that the general meaning of the term *personality* was discussed in Chapter 7. The term refers to a pattern of psychological attributes that makes each individual different and that those traits are thought to shape the individual's responses to his or her physical and social world. Thus, the reason we form impressions of another person, constructing our interpretations of his or her implicit personality, is that we are trying to predict in our own minds how that person will behave toward us and others. As noted earlier, we literally *have to do this*. We cannot communicate with a total blank.

An investigation by John Wishner clearly illustrates implicit personality research.[7] He reasoned that when we are responding to a target person, the central characteristics "warm" and "cold" would have the greatest influence on those personal characteristics that were most related to the personality traits they imply. It is a complex idea, but to illustrate, the characteristic "strong" is not particularly related to either "warm" or "cold." In contrast, the attribute "friendly" is definitely related to "warm." That is, "warm" and "friendly" as attributes of a person fit together very well, but "cold" and "friendly" do not. Thus, adding "warm" to the list of terms describing a person should raise estimates of *friendliness*, whereas adding "cold" could be expected to reduce them.

Wishner tested this reasoning by having a group of college students rate their professors on a list of personal characteristics. Then the terms *warm* and *cold* were added, as in the Asch experiments. An examination of the students' evaluations of their professors showed that the characteristics that were most strongly affected when "warm" or "cold" was added were those traits in the list that the students perceived to be *most highly related* to the general ideas of "warm" and "cold." Also important, the results indicated that for characteristics that were not related, impressions of the target person were not influenced.

What Wishner's results imply is that the overall pattern of impressions of a particular individual can be *predicted* from the relationship between the list of characteristics that the target person is first thought to possess. What this means is that people construct a relatively *well-organized* pattern of what they think is important about someone on the basis of very few facts. Furthermore, certain kinds of characteristics have a truly powerful influence on the implicit personality that is projected onto the target person. This is important because that quickly constructed personality will strongly influence both the subsequent evaluations of and the actions toward that person.

Is what has been found in these experiments closely related to what happens in reality? The answer is yes. The findings of studies like those of Asch and Wishner are consistent with extensive observations of people in everyday life. It may not be particularly comforting to realize that certain of your own personal salient characteristics will be observed very quickly by people when they first meet you. They will then use these characteristics as the central features of a rather elaborate set of assumptions about your nature and probable behavior. Those salient characteristics may be visible indicators of racial, ethnic, or cultural differences. Or they may be mannerisms, speech patterns, labels,

modes of dress, hair length, or some other prominent and visible feature.[8] Salient characteristics may also include the firmness of a handshake during a job interview,[9] or any attractive or unattractive features that you possess.[10] According to a recent study, such characteristics may even include whether or not you exercise regularly.[11]

You might wonder what your salient characteristics are. Are they flattering or demeaning? Furthermore, what kind of implicit personality do others project onto you on the basis of a few central attributes? Is it one that truly represents you, or is it some grossly distorted image of you? Above all, can you control or manage the kind of personality assumptions that others make about you?

Before turning directly to specific ways in which self-presentation can be managed more effectively, we need to review several additional features of initial encounters that can pose problems when meeting people for the first time.

Problems in Initial Encounters

It is important to look closely at three additional considerations that influence the process of getting to know one another. The first consideration is the *difficulties* inherent in meeting someone for the first time; these are likely to influence the presentation of self. Some difficulties are obvious and widely understood, whereas others are so subtle that the participants may not even be aware they exist, let alone that such problems are influencing the encounter. Second, the *number of people* present in an initial encounter can be an important consideration. Whether we meet one person or several changes the factors that can make first meetings more or less difficult to handle. Finally, the context or setting in which people meet can play a significant role in determining people's success in their presentations of self and the impressions they make in initial encounters.

Common difficulties when meeting people for the first time. If you were to worry about all the potential problems that can come up when you initially meet someone you might never want to go through it again.[12] More realistically, it is possible to learn to handle effectively the most common difficulties associated with initial encounters. Consider the following list of common problems that are encountered when people meet for the first time:

- Finding things in common with strangers.
- Finding things to say to strangers.
- Not knowing how to say things appropriately.
- Meeting people you just don't like.
- Meeting people who just don't like you.
- Adjusting to language differences.
- Adjusting to different backgrounds or experiences.
- One- or two-way communication apprehension.
- Feeling generally awkward.
- Feeling self-conscious.
- Feeling alienated from others.
- Worrying about saying the wrong thing.

Suppose these potential difficulties arise in the context of a worst case first meeting. The scene is a party: Cynthia and Bill have just been introduced. Bill is from a small town in Texas, and Cynthia comes from Chicago. Both are new to the area, and both really want to make some friends. Each is anxious to make a positive first impression. During the first few moments of their meeting, they both react positively and are even physically attracted to each other. Each sees the other as about the same age, obviously intelligent, and about right in height; and they even have the same hair and skin color. Neither has bad breath, dirty fingernails, a detectable body odor, or any other salient characteristic around which an unfavorable implicit personality can be instantly organized. So far, so good! All things considered, Cynthia and Bill should be able to get along just fine. So, rather than politely disengaging and moving on, each decides to try to carry on a friendly conversation—engaging in effective self-presentation and hoping that it might lead to a pleasant outcome.

Unfortunately, as the conversation begins, things begin to go downhill. The first problem they encounter is that they actually don't seem to have much of anything in common. They really do come from very different cultural backgrounds—rural Texas versus big-city Chicago. They have difficulty in finding things to say to each other, and there are a lot of long and noticeable pauses in their conversation. The more difficult the meeting becomes for each, the more frustrated they are by the whole situation. Yet they do not give up. Each continues to try to find out things about the other. Both ask questions and probe as best they can, but it doesn't work. The encounter is falling on its face.

After a few more uncomfortable moments, it becomes apparent that they are both being very careful about how they are communicating with each other for fear of saying the wrong thing and being misunderstood. Neither Cynthia nor Bill wants to prejudge the other—and each is obviously trying to avoid not being liked.

The more they talk, the more they discover that they come from very different worlds and have had totally different experiences. They even seem to be using language differently. It sounds as if they are both speaking English, but the words that each is using appear to be arousing different meanings for the other. Each has to explain and apologize for meanings that were not intended. Cynthia's language was acquired both in her family and in schools typical of a sophisticated and well-educated urban class. Bill's language is from a ranch culture in rural Texas.

By this time, each has constructed a pattern of impressions about the other. This now strongly influences how they speak and act. To Bill, Cynthia seems to be a sophisticated city girl—maybe "stuck up"—and accustomed to having a lot of boyfriends. He is afraid she will think he is just a dull country boy. To Cynthia, Bill seems very polite and sincere but a bit old-fashioned and shy. She is afraid to say anything that will seem like she is putting him down.

It has become clear that both are apprehensive. Moreover, their apprehensiveness seems to be accentuated by having to communicate with a total stranger. In other words, each feels awkward and self-conscious. So, the more they try to talk to each other, and the harder they try to get together, the worse they feel.

At this point, things are not looking good. It is obvious to each that there will be no lasting relationship between them. In fact, after about 20 minutes both Cynthia and Bill decide to give up. Their conversation just sort of dries up, and the noisy confusion of the party allows them to drift apart physically. It should be obvious from this vignette that Cynthia's and Bill's chances for a second meeting, let alone a lasting relationship, are near zero. In fact, nearly every problem in the list of difficulties occurred. At the same time, both had very good intentions; both sincerely wanted to make an effective and positive presentation of self; however, things just happened that derailed what started as a promising encounter.

Often, things "just happen" in many of our sincere efforts to communicate a good first impression to others. The bottom line of all this is that presenting ourselves effectively is a difficult job. It is not easy to communicate our preferred pattern of positive first impressions.

Returning to Cynthia and Bill, a fair question to ask about this first meeting would be, What (if anything) would have been different if more than the two of them had been present? That is, what happens to the process of getting to know others when more than two individuals are involved in an initial encounter? In particular, how would this influence both the presentation of self and the resulting formation of impressions? Would it have helped the situation or made things worse?

The effects of meeting one person or several. Many initial encounters involve more than two people. Examples are students and teachers walking into their classroom for the first time, a new employee going into an office full of people on the first day of work, or indeed any situation where people meet in groups.

The influence of group size was discussed in Chapters 6 and 7. As opposed to two-person dynamics, what happens in a group situation is very different. Additional potential difficulties are typically involved.[13] This is not to say that all group encounters are negative; in some ways, they can be easier. However, the inclusion of additional individuals can influence perceptions, evaluations, and the exchange of messages.[14]

First, consider some of the typical problems that arise when more than two people meet:

- Fragmenting participation and focuses of attention.
- The problem of "you can't please everybody."
- Individual differences that create difficulties.
- Perceptions of favoritism.
- Speaking generally versus specifically to one person.
- Coalitions among pairs.
- Conversational intrusions and interruptions.

With this list in mind, reconsider the scene with Cynthia and Bill. This time assume that they encounter each other not alone but in a trio that includes Peggy. They have all just been introduced at the party. In such a situation, the energies and focuses of attention will be spread across three people rather than just two.

In the new scene, Cynthia and Bill are introduced along with Peggy, who is about the same age. During the first moments of appraisal, all three look each other over and reach the same conclusions. Initially, each is impressed favorably, and all is "go" for trying to get to know one another better. Therefore, each thinks that it is a good idea to try to engage in favorable presentations of self, just on the chance that a meaningful, long-term, friendly relationship might develop.

So, there they stand in a trio, surrounded by other people at the party. Just as Bill begins to open the conversation by asking Cynthia where she is from, Peggy interrupts and asks Bill's opinion about last night's football game, a topic about which she seems quite enthusiastic. After they spend a few moments listening to his negative opinions about spectator sports, Cynthia tries to present a positive self-image to Bill by telling him of her impressions of a recent symphony performance she attended.

Before Bill can explain that he isn't into classical music, but likes country and western, Peggy begins explaining her devotion to a local rock group. It is clear that Peggy's tastes are quite different. Both Bill and Cynthia now seem somewhat bored. They begin looking around the room to see what other possibly interesting people there might be at the party. However, they decide to try once again to learn more about each other. They begin discussing what restaurants each knows in the area. Peggy, who was initially somewhat taken with Bill, now senses that he has less interest in her than in Cynthia. She feels a bit slighted, with just a twinge of jealousy. At this point, she asks Bill if he would mind getting her a fresh drink. Bill, whose mother tried to teach him to be a gentleman, agrees to do so. He leaves the trio to go to the bar. When he returns with the drink, Cynthia is gone. She is now talking animatedly with another guy in the far corner of the room. Bill is disappointed and feels that he has been rejected. He decides he doesn't like the party and soon leaves.

This account illustrates several of the limitations inherent in trying to communicate positive impressions of self in conversations that involve more than two people. First, it is difficult to maintain a central focus on getting to know someone when a third person introduces topics that derail such an effort. In Bill's case, with two individuals interested in him, he could not be equally pleasing to both. Furthermore, it seemed that none of them had the same tastes. In such a situation, Cynthia and Bill could not concentrate fully on personal matters but had to discuss general topics (football, restaurants, music), rather than each other. In spite of all these difficulties, there was at least the beginnings of a dyad within the trio, sometimes called a "coalition of the triad" into an obvi-

ous pair interested in each other.[15] Peggy, who was left out, perceived that to be favoritism and took action to disrupt it. Thus, with all the interruptions and intrusions, Bill and Cynthia never did get to know each other, and each went their separate ways.

Could anything have been done to improve the chances that what took place between Bill and Cynthia would have resulted in a more positive outcome? For example, if they had met in a different place, would the dynamics of the initial meeting have been altered and would the outcome of their encounter have been different?

Meeting in familiar versus unfamiliar places. The idea that where you meet people can influence the outcome of a meeting is scarcely new.[16] However, when this idea is linked to implicit personality theory, it becomes meaningful in terms of understanding what factors influence effective self-presentation.

Generally, people are more at ease in familiar surroundings.[17] The importance of location is that the physical surroundings where a person meets others can have a dramatic effect on how capable and *confident* the person feels during that meeting. When manifested in behavior, those feelings can serve as salient characteristics that help observers organize the pattern of personality traits they project onto the individual. Thus, persons who are seen as at ease, capable, and confident are also perceived more positively overall than those who are thought to be inept and nervous. In addition, observers may make judgments about the personality of an individual they are meeting based on the physical environment or setting—a room or office, for example—that the individual occupies.[18] In these direct ways, then, physical settings can help or hinder the outcome of self-presentation.

To illustrate this principle, consider once again the initial encounter between Cynthia and Bill, but this time in terms of a different location and without the troublesome Peggy present. Previously, the initial meeting occurred in the unfamiliar context of a party—a place in which neither was particularly at ease. Suppose now that Cynthia and Bill had just met in a quiet lounge at the dorm where both were living. In such familiar physical surroundings, they would have had something in common from the very start of their encounter. Clearly, this would have made it easier for them to find out the many other things they had in common. In this way, their concern about liking or not being liked by the other would have been far less significant. In all likelihood, neither would have been as guarded, and they would have had a basis for more easily dealing with their differences. Factors like their regionally associated languages would have become less central.

Unfortunately, people cannot always count on meeting others on familiar ground. When they do, however, it provides a sense of assurance about having successfully negotiated a complex social context. In other words, a familiar meeting place often has associated memories of previously successful self-presentations. The lessons learned from those efforts greatly aid communicating favorable impressions in the same surroundings the next time the need arises.

Presenting Yourself in Encounters That Really Matter

Thus far, this chapter has highlighted factors that are pertinent to getting to know other people and forming first impressions. It has concentrated on essential issues that can enhance or limit the effectiveness of a person's presentation of self to others. From what has been discussed, it is safe to assume that people tend quickly to form impressions of others based on a limited amount of information. Moreover, some salient characteristic often has a strong influence on that overall pattern of impressions. Also, the number of people present can make a difference, and, finally, physical settings are another factor in the formation of first impressions.

These principles provide a good basis from which to develop practical strategies for the effective presentation of self. The next task, therefore, is to move from a review of what researchers have concluded from experiments and real-life observations to a consideration of what is actually needed on an everyday basis to achieve the goal of managing people's impressions.

Goals in Initial Encounters

Meetings can be either intentional or accidental. They can be organized as either very structured or completely open-ended. As discussed previously, the social situation that you happen to be in defines the purpose of meeting people for the first time. That purpose might be a job interview, getting to know someone that you have just noticed in a crowded room, getting acquainted with the parents of a close friend, or giving a talk before a group. Whatever the nature of the encounter, having a clear idea of why the meeting has been initiated can help in the selection of strategies, content, and style of delivery. In particular, in those meetings that can have an effect on your future, understanding every aspect of impression management in self-presentation can be truly important.

Many people fail to realize how important it is to map out a *deliberate strategy of self-presentation* before an important meeting. Others sense the value of planning but feel that first meetings should be spontaneous and fall together naturally. However, if the encounter is a critical one, planning in advance for self-presentation can lead to a more favorable outcome.

Obviously, in many social situations where you meet people little is at stake. Going to the supermarket and meeting the checkout clerk or dealing with a server in a restaurant is hardly an occasion that calls for strategic consideration of effective self-presentation. Similarly, when you are among people close to you—peers and family—you can indeed just be yourself and let it all fall together as it will. However, it is crucial to approach those encounters that really count with a thoughtfully formulated plan.

Developing a strategy for initiating and engaging in a social encounter is not as difficult as it may sound: First, before the encounter takes place, you must clarify for yourself the *goals* to be achieved as a result of your presentation of self. Second, you must focus attention on setting the stage to accomplish those goals. This means selecting strategies of self-presentation ahead of time that are most likely to accomplish those objectives.

What are the goals to be achieved in an important encounter? If you want the outcome to be favorable, there are three. Each is an important part of the self-presentation process, and the strategies you use to achieve them are all related to gaining greater control over the outcome. You plan ahead to achieve effective control over at least three outcomes:

1. The *earliest impressions* formed during initial moments of the contact. Recall the previous discussion of the critical nature of the first qualities others attribute to you. You need to ensure that some salient characteristic that can turn people off right away does not immediately spoil your identity.

2. The *expanding configuration* of impressions organized as your presentation of self unfolds. This is a result of systematic impression management, and it needs to be done with grace and style so as to produce a positive image of your qualities in the minds of observers.

3. The *lasting pattern* of impressions that the other party takes away. This is the bottom line—the fairly permanent implicit personality that observers attribute to you. It is the most important goal of all.

A very effective way to gain control over these outcomes is to know your objective ahead of time. Simply ask yourself, "What is it that I really want out of this meeting?" The answer may be obvious, like getting the job. Or it may be something very different, such as entry into a particular social group, an experience with a member of the opposite sex, wanting to be assertive, or perhaps even getting paroled.[19] In any case, knowing clearly what you want in the first step makes that goal easier to attain.

Defining the goal of an encounter ahead of time contributes to the design of the self-presentation strategy needed to attain it. Goal clarification, in other words, helps you identify the impressions that are most likely to contribute to success. Stated more simply, knowing what you want helps identify what it is that people need to believe about you.

Preselecting the Impressions You Want to Make

In some first meetings, what you really want and how you want to be perceived may be virtually the same thing. For example, if you are running for public office and will be speaking to groups of potential voters, you will want the audience to feel positively enough about you to cast their vote in your direction, and to convince others to do the same. As you can see, what you really want (to get elected) and how you want to be perceived (to be liked) are closely linked.

It is important, then, to communicate those *characteristics that count* in the situation so that they will be quickly and unmistakably perceived and understood by those on the receiving end. We see politicians do this all the time. A candidate will don a farmer's cap and an informal jacket and use a country folks speech style when addressing a rural audience. The next day, when speaking to a group of bankers, the same candidate will be dressed in a conservative suit and will use a different vocabulary. Still later it will be hard hat, blue shirt, and macho talk when making a speech to factory hands.

Few of us need to go to such lengths in our personal presentations of self, but the principle is there. Strategies can be used in a more subtle way to preselect certain kinds of impressions that we want to create so as to achieve our goals. As discussed later, this can be done through selection of clothing, vocabulary, message content, demeanor, and many other alternatives.

There are two major reasons why preselection of qualities that can create positive impressions is not particularly difficult. The first is that *everyone has many positive qualities.* Each of us—no matter what our gender, race, ethnic identity, cultural background, age, body shape, educational background, and so on—has a long list of favorable characteristics that will be of genuine interest to others. The real task is to understand those attributes and to demonstrate them in appropriate ways through verbal and nonverbal communication. At the same time, pitfalls do exist. All of us have dull, unimportant, and undistinguished characteristics that if arbitrarily communicated in the wrong situation can be boring or interpreted negatively. An important part of the task of effective self-presentation is to minimize such potentially negative influences.

The second feature of the process of meeting someone for the first time that works in favor of creating positive impressions is the fact that most people *tend to like* other people. Unless there is something obvious that quickly turns them off, the cards are stacked for, rather than against us, and a favorable impression is likely at the outset in most encounters. The real trick is to identify and maximize the influence of your positive features and to minimize those potentially troublesome salient characteristics that are so important in initial impression formation.

From the principles of salient characteristics and implicit personality we know that first impressions tend to be lasting. However, lasting or not, it is difficult to explain just how people immediately pick out some particular characteristic from an individual's presentation of self that they decide is salient and then organize other attributes or qualities around that factor. It is this, the universal tendency to perceive selectively, that is at the heart of impression formation.

The significance of selective perception. The term *perception,* explained in Chapters 1 and 2, refers to making sense of, that is attaching meaning to, some aspect of reality that has been apprehended by the senses. Perception is an important part of forming impressions of other people, and there are easily understood reasons why it is inevitably a selective activity. We all have different memories of meanings linked to signs, signals, and symbols, and even to human characteristics stored in our memories from our lifetime of experience. No one's associated meanings for those stimuli are exactly like those of anyone else. Thus, no one's stored meanings used to interpret a particular thing or event are an exact duplicate of those of others. What happens is that when you search your memory traces and schemas for an interpretation of something you see or hear, you cannot avoid putting your own personal stamp of meaning on it. This is the basis of **selective perception.**

Selective perception is heavily influenced by what we like and dislike. This occurs because people have a stable organization of **predispositions**—probabilities of behavior that lead us to approve of some things and disapprove of others. These are shaped by our attitudes, values, opinions, preferences, and so on. These predispositions modify our perceptions and interpretations of things that we experience, because they lead us to like some stimuli and dislike others.

Even our ever-changing emotions and needs can alter the way we interpret something we see or hear at a particular moment. For example, when you are angry or afraid, things don't seem the same as they do when you are happy and relaxed. Or you see some things differently when you are hungry, like a big juicy piece of apple pie, as compared to seeing the same piece just after having finished a huge Thanksgiving dinner. Thus, people perceive and experience the world through their own internalized meanings, dispositions, emotional states, and needs. *Selective perception,* then, refers to *the unique way people interpret and assign meaning to what they observe.*

The importance of selective perception for present purposes is that it will always happen. It is a fundamental part of person perception that always takes place in initial encounters. It is also the basis for the selection of a salient characteristic around which an observer can create a complex initial set of impressions about what another person is really like. It may not be easy to detect when another person is perceiving you in some selective way, but you can be totally certain that it will take place.

Knowing the consequences of selective perception, and that it is inevitable, it is obviously very important to try to control it. This may be easier said than done. However, one good way to influence the way others perceive you is to *plan ahead* by organizing a flexible preliminary game plan. This will go a long way toward limiting a display of negative salient characteristics. By the same token, presenting positive ones is an obvious part of such a strategy.

Developing a preliminary plan. Strategies of effective self-presentation are not hard to identify. They consist of using such nonverbal forms of communication as clothing, mannerisms, gestures, posture, and demeanor, plus verbal messages with specific content delivered with a particular style and level of vocabulary. The problem here is that the best combination can be difficult to identify. Furthermore, you can never be sure exactly what people might pick out as salient characteristics. In one context, shaggy hair, sloppy clothing, and scruffy shoes, plus a laid-back speaking style sprinkled with four-letter words, might be a basis for negative selective perception (as in a group of conservative business people). In another context, a tailored suit, neatly trimmed hair, well-polished shoes, plus a sophisticated vocabulary and a well-organized speaking style, might make exactly the wrong impression (for example, among a group of construction workers).

Clearly, clothing plays an important role in impression formation and can affect one's ability to obtain a good job. Clothing worn by a job applicant may be an indicator of status, power, and ability, and may determine the outcome of the interview. As a recent study indicates, clothing is especially critical for poor women who lack the financial resources necessary to enhance their appearance with appropriate job-related clothing. In the past few years, a number of programs have been designed to provide clothing to poor women entering the workforce and to recognize the unique challenges they face.[20]

How do you know in a general way which strategies to use so that personal characteristics might be perceived selectively in ways you desire? Perhaps the best guide is common sense. Do not do, say, or otherwise communicate, either verbally or nonverbally, anything that those whom you are meeting might perceive selectively and use as the basis of their negative implicit personality for you.

Although one single checklist cannot be used as a game plan for all people in all situations, certain principles can be used in preselecting the kind of impression that you want to create during a particular initial encounter. For example, examine the following guidelines. (Box 9.1 overviews these principles also.)

BOX 9.1   🔍 *A Closer Look*

Principles for Preselecting Initial Impressions

1. Analyze the people to whom you are making a self-presentation. Understand the standards they will probably use in judging you.
2. Analyze the physical setting where the encounter will take place. Understand the factors in that environment that might be important in your self-presentation.
3. Never intentionally misrepresent yourself. People can spot a snow job very quickly. The discovery of even a minor untruth will backfire into a negative salient characteristic!
4. Use all available communication channels to get your positive qualities across. This means both verbal and nonverbal messages that communicate your positive characteristics.
5. Analyze feedback messages of a subtle nature. Use them to shift strategies if necessary or to follow up on ones that seem successful.

1. Assess carefully the people to whom you are making a self-presentation. Who are they? What criteria will they probably use in judging you? This is another way of saying that you should engage in accurate role-taking.

2. Appraise the physical setting carefully. Where will the encounter take place? What factors in that environment might be important in your self-presentation?

3. Above all, do not try to misrepresent yourself. People can spot a snow job very quickly. Even the discovery of a minor falsehood will backfire into a negative salient characteristic!

4. Use all communication channels open to you to get your positive qualities across. This means both verbal and nonverbal messages that communicate your positive characteristics.

5. Look very closely for subtle feedback messages. Use them to shift strategies if necessary or to follow up ones that seem successful.

You need to be very deliberate in your preencounter planning—specific in the selection of the self—defining characteristics you decide to present and intentional in the strategies you plan to use. Your presentation must be honestly communicated, while focusing attention away from anything that might result in negative evaluations. Careful assessment of the people, the situation, the available channels of communication, and the nature of feedback transmitted during the encounter is far more likely to result in an effective self-presentation than a strategy that consists of just letting things proceed naturally.

Assessing the People You Meet

The central factor in any encounter is the *people*. All the planning in the world will make no difference unless it is done in conjunction with an understanding of the individuals to whom you will be presenting yourself. You must have enough knowledge about them to engage in effective role-taking and to have a pretty good idea about how they are going to interpret your presentation and how they are likely to respond to you.

Fortunately, there are many role-taking guidelines that have emerged from research and common experience for making educated guesses about people. Furthermore, most of us have already learned to make certain assumptions about how and why people from different categories in society will think and behave. Although these can sometimes prove to be wrong, they are certainly better than mere guesses. Nevertheless, social scientists have studied not only how people think others are likely to behave in certain situations but also the causes to which they attribute such behavior.

Attributing motives to others. An important part of the study of person perception is what social scientists call the **attribution process.** This process refers to *the selection and assignment to another person of various personal qualities, conditions, or dispositions that we believe are the causes of or influences on some aspect of that person's behavior.*[21] The attribution process is explained most clearly in what is called "attribution theory." According to attribution theory, making assumptions about other people's behavior is a normal human process—people do it all the time. That is, people make attributions whenever they try to understand why someone is behaving in a particular way. According to the eminent psychologist Fritz Heider, people act like naive psychologists when trying to figure out why someone acted in a specific way. They draw inferences about the cause of someone's actions. Moreover, the inclination to draw inferences about others' behavior involves several steps (described in Box 9.2).

Some attributed causes or influences are seen as *internal* to the person (for example, attitudes, values, and motivations). Other influences are seen as *external* to the person (such

BOX 9.2   A Closer Look

The Attribution Process

When you first meet someone, you experience a certain degree of uncertainty about that individual. In order to reduce that uncertainty, you tend to categorize or stereotype that person. In this way, you create an environment that offers you some degree of predictability concerning the other person's behavior. Your categorizing involves attributing the causes of a person's behavior to internal and external factors. By attributing causes in this way, you feel that you can anticipate how and why that person is likely to react to you. The attribution process can be summed up as follows:

1. You meet someone new and face some degree of uncertainty regarding how the person will behave.
2. In an attempt to establish some degree of predictability concerning the person's behavior, you place the person in social categories or stereotypes.
3. The categories in which you place the person are based on internal and external clues. Internal clues are those within the person, such as their attitudes and beliefs. External clues are based on circumstances outside the person, such as social norms and rules.
4. In order to predict how a person will behave and understand that behavior, you attribute their behavior to salient internal or external clues.

As an example of the attribution process, suppose you work at a retail store and have mistakenly given a customer too much change. The woman who made the purchase realizes she is holding more money than she should be and gives the excess change back. Based on external clues—such as her clothing and the context of the situation—and internal clues—such as her honesty—you attribute her behavior of returning the money to her being a nice, caring, and honest person.

---

as requirements of norms or roles or other aspects of group organization).[22]

The attribution process is related to the idea of implicit personality discussed earlier. The difference is that, in an encounter in which attributions are made about causes of a particular form of behavior, you are not considering the entire personality. You are concerned only with selective characteristics that can explain why you think a person will engage in a particular action. For example, you may assign (attribute to) the other person the specific traits of being mean and malicious if you believe the individual will be likely to refuse you a raise or a promotion.

Thus, when you assess people, you are making inferences about them in two ways: (1) how they are likely to react to you and (2) why that probably will be the case. In so doing, you base your predictions on either *internal factors* that you believe will influence their action (personality traits) or *external conditions* (norms, roles, social controls) that you see as limiting or shaping what they will do. Either way makes you feel better because it makes their behavior more predictable.

Remember the earlier discussion of the ways in which personality traits are attributed to others in initial encounters. Recall that as part of the communication transaction, others form their assumptions about what we are like during the early part of an encounter. The point now is that, in an additional transaction, you also form impressions of what they are like—all before anything happens. But how can you make judgments about either internal personality traits or external influences on action? One way is to examine the **social categories** to which the individuals belong; another is to grasp the social constraints (norms, roles, and so on) within which they are performing.

Typical behavior as a basis for attribution. You cannot invent attributions about probable behavior or its causes out of thin air. One source of information that can be used for attributions about other people is their *membership in significant social categories* (such as males, children, educated people, working class, farmers). Often, people in such categories are said to be characterized by certain predictable *regularities* in their behavior. These are generalizations about behavior considered typical of people from particular walks of life. For example, if you want to make a good impression on an elderly person who has little schooling and a low income, your initial small talk with that individual probably would not be based on the merits of the local symphony orchestra or a particularly good year for French wines. You could be wrong, of course, but it would seem safer to discuss alarming increases in the cost of medical services or possibly the local baseball team.

As a normal part of living in a complex society, people learn to make such predictions on the basis of typical interests of people in specific social categories. However, there are certain dangers in such forecasts. As discussed in Chapter 2, rigidly held assumptions, categorical attributions, and unfounded forecasts become *stereotypes*—especially if they attribute socially undesirable qualities to the target category. Still, there are topics of interest typically associated with people of a particular age, occupation, gender, region, social class, religion, ethnic and racial identity, and so on. Knowing the category memberships of individuals to whom you will make a presentation of self, then, provides at least some information for making attributions about their tastes, beliefs, values, attitudes—and therefore their probable behavior.

Socially imposed conditions as a basis for attribution. External to the individual, but very influential on behavior, are social norms, roles, and ranks that dictate at particular times how the individual has to evaluate and respond to your self-presentation, regardless of inner feelings and attitudes. For example, a person who is acting as a recruiter for a company may be all business in such an encounter. The same person would be different at a cocktail party with peers or at home with the family. Similarly, people in positions of power and authority have to think and act according to the mandates of those positions at times. If they did not, they would lose their jobs. Response to your self-presentation, then, may be strongly influenced by social organization factors, stemming from the demands of externally imposed constraints, as well as by a person's inner psychological traits.

What, then, are some practical techniques for assessing others so that you can understand how and why they will respond to your verbal and nonverbal communication? The following list includes seven simple and effective steps to help you gather personal information about others and to reduce uncertainties about their probable reactions and behavior:

- Observe people to identify any obvious verbal or nonverbal behavior that communicates psychological characteristics (attitudes, intelligence, emotions).
- Observe people interacting to see how they respond to one another (aggressively, politely, formally, warmly).
- Ask questions about your potential audience in advance if possible, to understand as much as you can about who they are and where they come from, both geographically and socially.
- Compare the people with individuals you know. If they seem alike, they may think and behave similarly.
- Gather information about social category membership (education, occupation, age, race, ethnicity, religion) that can provide clues to probable normative behavior.

- Review the social constraints on these people at the time of the encounter, or other requirements they have to meet, and assess what they require them to do.
- Review everything you have learned and try to put together a composite—an organized prediction—of how they will respond to various aspects of your self-presentation and why.

In review, note that there are several steps in the development of a sound design for self-presentation. First, consider carefully what you want to achieve in a first meeting. Second, you must preselect the impressions you want people to perceive. Third, you need to analyze the information you have about the individuals to whom you will be presenting yourself. Fourth, anticipate how they will react to verbal and non-verbal messages that communicate your characteristics. The final step is to consider, choose, and incorporate the actual techniques and strategies that you will use to create the impressions you prefer. A successful plan means that you communicate well-designed messages through all available channels in such a way that the people receiving them immediately begin to like you.

Getting People to Like You

In recent years, social scientists have done extensive research on strategies that people use to try to get others to like them. A more precise and widely used term for that process is **affinity seeking**.[23] A number of affinity-seeking strategies have been reported by researchers. For example, students often use specific strategies to get their teachers to like them, such as observing the rules of conversation in a classroom or completing additional course requirements. Teachers, on the other hand, also use affinity-seeking strategies, such as listening closely, treating a student with equality or trustworthiness.[24]

Affinity-seeking strategies. The search for effective affinity-seeking strategies has turned out to be unbelievably complex. The problem is that there are literally dozens of strategies that seem to work, at least sometimes. To provide an idea of how complex this process can be, Box 9.3 identifies 25 affinity-seeking strategies.[25]

Although this may seem like a large number of possible strategies for getting people to like you, the situation gets much more complex because each participant can use more than one strategy from the list. Two, three, or more strategies may be combined. If so, the number of available patterns of strategies has to be added to the original 25. Taking each of these two at a time, and then three at a time, then four, and so on, the number of all possible combinations adds up to a staggering number—over 40 million combinations. This is the same issue of combinations of two taken from a larger number that we discussed in Chapter 7—where organizations include huge numbers of pairs of people.

It is clear, then, that there is no shortage of strategies and huge numbers of combinations of strategies can be used to get people to like you. The question is, in the face of this abundance, which strategy to select.

Selecting strategies to use. It is not possible to set forth a simple set of rules for the selection of strategies. Certainly, no single strategy is appropriate for everyone. A particular person's selection of a strategy, or some combination of strategies, must be based in part on that person's gender, cultural identity, personal preferences, and familiarity with the situation, plus a combination of personality characteristics. Your own selection and eventual use of any of the available strategies needs to occur in combination with all the other issues relevant to planning for self-presentation. That is, the effectiveness of a decision to employ a particular strategy or set of strategies within a unique social context depends in large part on your knowing what you want, how you want to be perceived, and as much as possible about the people to whom you will be presenting yourself.

For example, assume that Linda, a local real estate agent, has several houses to sell. She has scheduled a meeting this afternoon at the local real estate office with a young married couple interested in purchasing their first home. Linda's objective for this first meeting is the successful initiation of a relationship with the couple that will lead to their purchase of a house. After assessing the situation, she believes that the best way to maximize the chances of meeting her objective is to communicate as quickly as possible the impression to the couple that she is a very honest and credible business person.

Considering the time available, Linda has gathered as much information about the couple's social categories as possible. She knows that the young man and woman (1) are in their mid-20s, (2) both have college degrees, (3) do not have children, and (4) together make just over $60,000 a year. With this information, Linda can choose from the impressive number of available affinity-seeking strategies listed in Box 9.3. To be realistic, she needs to consider whether she can reasonably employ some of them in this particular context. Additionally, she must consider whether she has the ability to communicate a given strategy effectively.

After evaluating all these issues, Linda decides that her best alternative is to go with a combination of five strategies from the box. Her selections are *nonverbal immediacy, reward association, similarity, supportiveness,* and *trustworthiness.* There are, of course, others that might work. However, she has concluded from her planning and evaluation activities that she might risk reducing her chances of communicating a positive impression if she attempts to employ too many.

Deciding What to Say

At this point, the time for background data-gathering and preliminary planning is over. Now you must decide very specifically what you intend to say in your self-presentation. This is in many ways the most critical point of any encounter. It is here that sitting and thinking about what you want to do stops and actual performance begins. You need to move easily from plan to performance without a hitch. What are some of the guidelines for making this transition?

One pitfall to avoid is getting to the point of communicating with someone for the first time and then saying nothing like what you had intended to say. A very effective way to minimize either having nothing to say or saying the wrong thing in initial encounters is to begin with a topic that you know a lot about. In fact, it is a good idea to select a subject that you know better than anyone else. What is that topic? What you are most qualified to talk about (are you ready for this?) is *yourself!* Furthermore, it is a most suitable subject matter for beginning a self-presentation. Almost by definition **self-disclosure** (revealing information about yourself) is an important part of what goes on in any self-presentation. Let's look at this idea more closely.

Self-Disclosure in Initial Encounters

The issue here is the idea that disclosure of information about yourself dictates both how others will perceive you initially and how they will formulate impressions about you. However, self-disclosure does not mean gushing on about intimate details about your life. That is not an effective strategy.

The actual content of your self-disclosure will depend on both the depth and the breadth of what you communicate about yourself.[26] The *depth* of self-disclosure refers to the degree of intimacy of what you say about yourself. *Breadth* refers to the amount of personal information you communicate. Appropriately, deciding what to say about yourself in a particular situation is tied to all your planning decisions and, in that way, to the overall development of your design for self-presentation.

BOX 9.3 🔍 *A Closer Look*

Affinity-Seeking Strategies

- *Altruism.* The affinity-seeker strives to be of assistance to the target in whatever she or he is currently doing. Example: The affinity-seeker is generally available to run errands for the target.
- *Assume control.* The affinity-seeker presents him- or herself as someone who is in control over whatever is going on. Example: The affinity-seeker takes charge of the activities engaged in by the target and her- or himself.
- *Assume equality.* The affinity-seeker strikes a posture of social equality with the target. Example: The affinity-seeker avoids one-up games and behaving snobbishly.
- *Comfortable self.* The affinity-seeker acts comfortable and relaxed in settings shared with the target. Example: The affinity-seeker ignores annoying environmental distractions, seeking to convey a "nothing bothers me" impression.
- *Concede control.* The affinity-seeker allows the target to assume control over relational activities. Example: The affinity-seeker permits the target to plan a weekend the two will share.
- *Conversational rule-keeping.* The affinity-seeker adheres closely to cultural rules for polite, cooperative interaction with the target. Example: The affinity-seeker acts interested and involved in conversations with the target.
- *Dynamism.* The affinity-seeker presents her- or himself as an active, enthusiastic person. Example: The affinity-seeker is lively and animated in the presence of the target.
- *Elicit other's disclosure.* The affinity-seeker encourages the target to talk by reinforcing the target's conversational contributions. Example: The affinity-seeker queries the target about the target's opinions regarding a significant personal issue.
- *Facilitate enjoyment.* The affinity-seeker tries to maximize the positiveness of relational encounters with the target. Example: The affinity-seeker enthusiastically participates in an activity that the target is known to enjoy.
- *Inclusion of other.* The affinity-seeker includes the target in the affinity-seeker's social group. Example: The affinity-seeker plans a party for the target at which numbers of the affinity-seeker's friends are guests.
- *Influence perceptions of closeness.* The affinity-seeker engages in behaviors that cause the target to perceive the relationship as closer than it actually has been. Example: The affinity-seeker uses nicknames and talks about "we," rather than "you and I," when discussing their relationship with the target.
- *Listening.* The affinity-seeker listens actively and attentively to the target. Example: The affinity-seeker asks the target for frequent clarification and elaboration and verbally recalls the things the target has said.
- *Nonverbal immediacy.* The affinity-seeker signals interests in the target through various nonverbal cues. Example: The affinity-seeker smiles frequently at the target.

That is, as you consider what it is about yourself that you should incorporate into your presentation, you must keep in mind your objective for the meeting, how you want others to perceive you, what you know about the individuals with whom you will be communicating, and what you have selected as your affinity-seeking strategies.

In light of the above, let's go back to the real estate example to illustrate what is involved in appropriate self-disclosure. Because Linda—the agent—and the young couple had never met be-

- *Openness.* The affinity-seeker discloses personal information to the target. Example: The affinity-seeker reveals the some social insecurity or fear to the target.
- *Optimism.* The affinity-seeker presents him- or herself to the target as a positive person. Example: The affinity-seeker focuses on positive comments and favorable evaluations when discussing mutual acquaintances with the target.
- *Personal autonomy.* The affinity-seeker presents her- or himself to the target as an independent, free-thinking person. Example: The affinity-seeker demonstrates a willingness to express disagreement with the target about personal and social attitudes.
- *Physical attractiveness.* The affinity-seeker tries to look and dress as attractively as possible in the presence of the target. Example: The affinity-seeker always engages in careful grooming before interacting with the target.
- *Present interesting self.* The affinity-seeker presents her- or himself to the target as someone who would be interesting to know. Example: The affinity-seeker discreetly drops the names of impressive interesting acquaintances in the presence of the target.
- *Reward association.* The affinity-seeker presents her- or himself in such a way that the target perceives the affinity-seeker can reward the target for associating with him or her. Example: The affinity-seeker showers the target with gifts.
- *Self-concept confirmation.* The affinity-seeker demonstrates respect for the target and helps the target to feel good about her- or himself. Example: The affinity-seeker compliments the target frequently.
- *Self-inclusion.* The affinity-seeker arranges the environment so as to come into frequent contact with the target. Example: The affinity-seeker plans to have afternoon cocktails at the same time and place as the target.
- *Sensitivity.* The affinity-seeker acts in a warm, empathic manner toward the target. Example: The affinity-seeker sympathizes with the target regarding a personal problem the target is experiencing.
- *Similarity.* The affinity-seeker seeks to convince the target that the two of them share many similar tastes and attitudes. Example: The affinity-seeker often points out things to the target that the two of them have in common.
- *Supportiveness.* The affinity-seeker supports the target in the latter's social encounters. Example: The affinity-seeker sides with the target in a disagreement the target is having with a third party.
- *Trustworthiness.* The affinity-seeker presents her- or himself to the target as an honest, reliable person. Example: The affinity-seeker consistently fulfills commitments made to the target.

Source: This information was originally reported in Bell, R. A., & Daly, J. A. (1984). The affinity-seeking function of communication. *Communication and Monographs, 51,* 91–115.

fore, it would be inappropriate for the realtor to present either intimate details or vast amounts of personal information in this initial encounter. When strangers provide intense self-disclosure, it tends to make their listeners feel very uncomfortable. Consider for a moment how you would feel if a real estate agent you had never met before disclosed a lot of intimate information, such as personal finances, sexual interests, and life history. Obviously, disclosures of such breadth and depth would be inappropriate.

BOX 9.4   *A Closer Look*

Why Tony Soprano Seems So Likable

The basic idea that there are specific strategies that can be used to get people to like you has not escaped the world of television entertainment. For example, the writers who prepare the popular TV show *The Sopranos* faced a difficult job. A major character in the show is Tony Soprano—who by any set of rational criteria is not a nice man. He arranges murders for hire; distributes drugs; profits from prostitution; practices extortion; and engages in a number of other "mob" activities that can only be objectively described as despicable, immoral, unethical, and illegal. Yet, somehow, the writers for the program have made this gangster character seem human and congenial. How did they do it? Essentially, they have "Tony" act out a number of impression-management techniques, such as those listed in Box 9.3 (Affinity-Seeking Strategies). To many in the audience he comes across as a likable and accessible character who takes charge of every situation. In many ways, he appears to be a decent man who is loyal to his friends, supportive of his family, concerned about his children, and rewarding to his associates. Indeed, those affinity-seeking depictions in his on-screen behavior may be an important element in making the show so popular.

Tony Soprano (actor James Gandolfini) from HBO's *The Sopranos*.

Source: See: Barretta, A.G. (2000). Tony Soprano as post-modern gangster: controlling identities and managing self-disclosure, *New Jersey Journal of Communication, 8,* 2, pp. 211–220.

What would be more acceptable in Linda's situation would be the disclosure that she and her spouse, Ed, had made a similar choice when they purchased their first home. Then she could further indicate that they had felt terribly uneasy with this first purchase, but that later they saw it had been a wise decision. In other words, two additional admissions of personal information would appropriately follow from the disclosure of the agent's similar family decision. First, information about the uneasy feelings could be disclosed—obviously similar to what had been disclosed by the young couple. Second, information about the long-term wisdom of the choice could be disclosed. This definitely would be perceived as supportive of the clients' decision to buy a house. Any other topics would need to be carefully prescreened before being disclosed.

There are good reasons for being cautious what you say about yourself during self-disclosure in an initial encounter. Because of the factor of selective perception, early disclosures communicated to strangers are highly susceptible to misinterpretation. Also, elaborate attributions are made to people on the basis of very limited information. Thus, the risks are especially high during the early phases of an encounter. Putting this idea a little differently, it should be remembered that self-disclosing information that is other than what is obvious, likely to be misinterpreted, or too intense and revealing for strangers is both undesirable and highly risky. For these reasons, effective self-disclosure aimed at creating positive impressions must be provided carefully, gradually, and systematically.

Talking with People You Have Just Met

Looking at the process more specifically, there are several kinds of messages that offer opportunities for self-disclosure in initial encounters.[27] They are divided here into *greetings, small talk,* and a broad category referred to as the *main topic* of the encounter.

Greetings. These messages include all the salutations that are employed when individuals recognize and acknowledge one another. They can be verbal, nonverbal, or both. Regardless of which of these you employ, the specific salutation you communicate to others at a first meeting can have important implications for how you are perceived from that point on. Thus, even your greeting can influence receptivity to what you say later.[28]

For example, assume that you are going to meet for the first time a group of individuals with whom you hope to maintain a very formal and long-term professional relationship. Greeting this group with a "Hi there. How ya doin?" is likely to be less helpful than a simple "Good morning." In fact, employing the "Hi there. How ya doin?" salutation with such a group would almost certainly lead them to form a negative impression of you. As a general rule, then, initial salutations must be considered very carefully.

Small talk. In addition to choosing a greeting, small talk, which was discussed in Chapter 5, typically has an important place in your presentation of self. Remember that what makes small talk important is that individuals getting together for the first time can maintain distance and do not have to discuss immediately topics that they are not ready to talk about.

Consider the possible small talk that could have occurred between Linda, the realtor, and the young couple to whom she was showing a house. In addition to the self-disclosure that Linda engaged in, a number of totally unimportant topics could have been introduced and discussed. Engaging in small talk while showing the couple neighborhoods and homes would create a more relaxed climate. Moreover, such small talk could contribute to the impression that Linda was a nice person from whom to buy a home.

Generally, then, introducing small talk on such casual topics as the weather, the quality of a local restaurant, the recent football game, or whatever fits the occasion can stimulate relaxed discussion. Important business issues can be inserted gradually and naturally into the encounter. The only caution is that small talk must be perceived as sincere and believable as well as spontaneous.

Changing to the main topic. If the occasion is informal, there will be no main topic to discuss. That is, when people are at parties or in other social gatherings, self-presentations typically do not extend beyond greetings, small talk, and perhaps a limited amount of self-disclosure. In contrast, in a formal encounter (such as an interview, a sales presentation, or a committee meeting), the stages are different. After greetings and a certain amount of small talk, the participants must get down to business and communicate about the subject matter that brought them together in the first place.

However, there are several kinds of formal situations, and the stages of the encounter differ in each. For example, one common situation is the initial meeting with the primary objective of presenting information to an audience.

Although the individual delivering the information does make a presentation of self to members of the audience, it occurs as a secondary activity. Examples of this type of situation include lectures, informative talks, narrations, and public reading of factual material. In these situations, audience attention may be devoted more to the specific subject matter than to the individual presenting the information.

Another common situation occurs when an individual is presenting a message to one or more others and it is that person's specific interpretation of a situation that is the concern of the audience. Examples would be a witness giving testimony at a trial, a job applicant responding to questions during an interview, an expert presenting a personal analysis to a decision-making group, or a student explaining to a professor why he missed the final examination and should be excused. In these situations, almost everything that is transmitted is used to assess the presenter. In other words, the presentation of self is much more relevant to the audience than are the specifics of the message. It is not uncommon for the members of an audience in this type of situation to hang on every word of the speaker. Here, **credibility** can be a critical factor. That is, the information that is communicated may be judged within a framework of important dimensions—as valuable or worthless, critical or trivial, true or false—depending on the presenter's perceived sincerity and honesty as evaluated by the audience. Thus, perceived personal credibility can have a strong influence on the interpretation of the main topic under discussion.

In overview, whatever the specifics of the situation, an effective strategy for talking with new people begins with a greeting that is appropriate to the situation and the audience. Next, the right amount and kind of small talk is used to put people at ease. This provides an opportunity for beginning a planned, subtle self-presentation. Above all, personal credibility must remain high or subsequent efforts to present ideas about the main topic will be discounted and the entire encounter will fail.

Changing Negative Impressions

There is one additional issue to consider before bringing this chapter to a close. Sooner or later, you will have to confront someone's old and lingering impression of you, which unfortunately may be based on earlier unfavorable attributions. In other words, someone may still be evaluating you in a negative way from an earlier encounter. How can the strategies, techniques, and analyses described in this chapter be used to change such old impressions?

Changing someone's entrenched convictions about a person is a formidable task. However, there are a number of similarities between the steps needed to do this and those required to communicate a new impression. Even so, working back through each of the areas discussed so far would only partially undo someone's negative impression of you.

It is much more difficult to change a person's previously formed impression because there are more steps involved in changing an impression than in creating a new one. The individual has to *erase the existing impression* and then *recreate a new one* by effective communication of fresh messages while disregarding older, well-remembered, and entirely workable views of you as a person. That is a complex task.

To aid in understanding why it is difficult to make the transition, recall two principles learned earlier in this chapter from the Asch experiments on person perception: (1) People quickly form impressions of others when they meet them for the first time; (2) people formulate those impressions on the basis of a limited amount of data.

It should not be surprising that these two principles are so important. People have to adapt to those they have just met in these ways. That is, when you encounter someone new, you must immediately use a kind of filter for selectively perceiving the target person. You must be ready to respond to that person in an appropriate way from the beginning. Therefore, you have to make quick attributions and assumptions about the individual. However, in doing so, errors are likely. Because each human being is immensely complex, it is not possible to take in and understand every aspect of a person all at once. You have to work first with incomplete data (which can lead to inaccurate impressions). Nevertheless, you project onto that person a general framework of attributions as quickly as possible. These enable you to respond in what you think is an appropriate manner.

Thus, right or wrong, you quickly form impressions on the basis of the first indicators that you perceive. These tend to become entrenched right away because once you have formed an initial impression about a particular person, you have reduced your uncertainty regarding how you should relate to that person. Reducing uncertainty makes you feel more comfortable. From then on, any attempt to change your framework for selective perception will threaten to bring back that uncertainty and resulting discomfort. Therefore, the energy and inconvenience required to abandon an existing impression and create a very different one will be resisted. Nevertheless, people who entertain older negative impressions about you can be retrained, although it is not easy.

The Inflexible Nature of Preexisting Impressions

A plan to extinguish a preexisting impression begins with an understanding of the way that people make attributions about themselves. This process differs from the way other people attribute personality characteristics to you. Specifically, conclusions derived from research indicate that when you engage in an activity you perceive as unacceptable to others, you tend to attribute the causes of that behavior to external forces beyond your control, rather than to your own internal preferences and desires, which you can control. However, when other people observe you engaging in that unacceptable activity, they make just the opposite attribution: They tend to believe that you have deliberately chosen this course of action because of internal motivations. In other words,

in interpreting the causes of your own behavior that is judged unacceptable by others, you feel you are driven by outside forces, but others believe you deliberately choose to be bad.

This fascinating difference between how you see yourself and how others see you is particularly relevant to attempts to change the impressions others have of you. For example, if you meet someone who has been told by another person (who claims to know you) that you are untrustworthy, then your new acquaintance will have a preexisting negative impression of you coming into a first encounter. In fact, that person is very likely to perceive you negatively and to make biased and unfavorable attributions about the causes of your actions. In short, you have a problem.

What can you do to change such an impression? The first thing would be to begin planning what you are going to say and how you are going to say it. The basic goal is to suppress the existing impression and help the target individual in rebuilding a new one that includes greater credibility and more favorable attributions to you. Objectively speaking, your preparation in this instance would follow the same sequence of activities that was described for all self-presentations. However, because the purpose of the presentation would be to change rather than to create an impression, the specifics of your plan would have to be different.

Important guidelines can be drawn from researchers who study the attribution process. According to one well-known investigator, attributions concerning behavior are a function of three factors: the distinctiveness of the behavior, its consistency over time, and the consensus regarding the behavior among attending persons.[29] Research done on such factors has uncovered what is called the *principle of covarying attribution*. This is a kind of general rule, and it goes like this: If a person engages in a repetitive pattern of behavior, observers will attribute the behavior to either an internal or an external cause with which it seems to be consistently related over time. For example, suppose you are excited about having been accepted at a particular university (distinctive behavior) and you continue to be so over a period of time (consistency). Now assume that all your friends are not the least bit positive about that university; in fact, they are uniformly negative (consensus). Under these conditions, an attribution concerning the causes of your behavior is likely, and it will be made directly to you. That is, you probably would be perceived as *lacking good judgment*—an internal cause. If, however, under different circumstances, where you are fascinated with the idea of attending this particular university and all your friends believe it to be a good one, an attribution probably would be made to a different cause of your behavior, namely, to *the high quality of the university*— an external cause.

These conclusions offer a possible strategy for attempting to change the impressions people have of you by altering their attributions. Let's return to the problem of the person who has a preexisting impression of you as *untrustworthy*. You now design a strategy that will communicate effectively to that person that your behavior was, in fact, acceptable to many people (consensus); that such acceptance has been in effect for a long period of time (consistency); and that such a behavior pattern (distinctive) is typically expected of people in similar circumstances; that is, it is externally caused. If the self-presentation is effective, the initial unfavorable impression of you might begin to change.

Overcoming Resistance to Change

It was suggested earlier that people tend to resist attempts to modify existing impressions of an individual. In fact, it is difficult for people who have constructed internal meanings for almost any object or situation to shift to new ones. There are clear reasons why this is the case, and they are embedded deeply in the psychological processes people use to cope with the complexities of their physical and social environment.

Specifically, all people, everywhere, construct "pictures in their heads"—meanings for various aspects of the world they live in. They do this in a process of communication with others.[30] Those constructions include their meanings, impressions, and interpretations not only of physical objects and situations but of specific individuals as well, such as each of us. Chapter 2 showed how meanings are shaped and how they help people interpret and adapt to their environment. Meanings, then, are tools of perception and adjustment by which people negotiate through the daily world of stimuli that they encounter or that are thrust upon them. Because meanings serve such essential purposes, attempts to change them will be resisted.

Generally, then, attempts aimed at restructuring constructed realities of others will inevitably be resisted. One typical situation in which there is likely to be strong resistance to change is when a person has privately formed a negative first impression of you. Another case would be a long-term negative impression passed on by a trusted third party. The outcome of either of these situations is that you will be consistently and selectively perceived negatively. What do you do?

Because long-term habits of meaning can be so deeply established, the first question to consider is whether it is realistically possible to change another's impression of you. Second, is it worth the effort? Here you have to consider what was referred to in Chapter 5 as an assessment of *costs versus benefits*. There are going to be situations where the effort involved in changing someone's impression greatly outweighs the value associated with any change. If that seems to be the case, don't even try! In addition, there will be occasions when a negative impression is so sturdy that it is virtually impossible to change. Again, don't even try. Part of being successful at presenting self is learning to evaluate effectively such costs versus benefits.

Constructing New Realities

Let's assume that you feel change is possible and worth the considerable effort. You have decided to move ahead. The process of reconstructing a person's impressions and attributions by self-presentation should begin by careful consideration of the objectives. Obviously, if you are being perceived in a negative way, your overall goal is to change it to a positive one. But what beyond that? Do you have specific kinds of personal qualities of which you want that person to be aware? Furthermore, what are effective strategies for successfully communicating them so as to alter the person's existing impression?

Remember from Chapter 2 that the specific reality people perceive for any particular object is made up of subjective or internal meanings aroused by the perception of that object (or by a symbol that stands for that object). In the case of human beings, such realities are constructed from the variety of experiences the person has with the other individual. Finally, this present chapter shows that early experiences are especially influential in forming that construction of reality.

Given all of that, the task of restructuring is to communicate unmistakably favorable (distinctive) meanings that are shared by others (consensus). This needs to be done *over and over* (consistency) without belaboring the message. By actions and comments, skillfully communicated, you can show that others regard you favorably, respect your judgment, believe you to be trustworthy, and so on.

In addition, another person's impression of you may lack depth. You may have additional distinctive characteristics that can simply be added to what that person already thinks he or she knows. For example, if you are active in charities, play an instrument, have a special hobby, own an interesting pet, or have other positive qualities, communicating this new knowledge may improve the impression another entertains. If such information can be linked to the interests of the target person, so much the better; it may open new channels of communication that can be used to displace or at least minimize the unfavorable impressions that already exist.

To achieve such change, you have both verbal and nonverbal communication at your disposal. The meanings associated with words, gestures, and actions are the bricks and boards with which you can assist people in constructing new realities. The use of verbal and nonverbal communication for the restructuring of realities to achieve a positive impression follows the same general sequence of design activities outlined in previous sections. Note again that self-presentations must not be false or misleading. Phony presentations are a sure route to disaster. Being perceived as honest and truthful in self-presentation contributes to being perceived as ethical and having personal credibility.

The final caution regarding the effective use of verbal and nonverbal symbols and signs when presenting self to others is to communicate only that which contributes to the creation of a supportive climate for interaction. In many ways, that is the most important principle and the hardest lesson of all. Because you are human, you are emotional; when people make you mad, you feel a normal need to express your feelings in no uncertain terms. However, it is a losing game that can bring only unfavorable consequences. Defensive or hostile words and phrases fired off in the heat of the moment cannot be withdrawn or erased. They do not contribute to either a positive impression or a supportive communication climate. Achieving thoughtful control over emotional responses is the factor that most clearly sets apart the person who is in complete control of self-presentation from those who are content to just let it fall together naturally.

Chapter Review

- The process of presenting yourself effectively is based on communicating, verbally and nonverbally, favorable meanings of your personal qualities. The goal is to help others form as positive an impression of you as you can.

- People make elaborate inferences about others on the basis of relatively little information. Salient characteristics become particularly important in constructing an impression of what another individual is really like. In fact, with limited data, you put together an organized implicit personality that you think can predict the behavior of the individual you have just met.

- Labels are an important part of implicit personality construction. If you have a convenient label—"nerd," "sexpot," "jock," or whatever—you will load onto the person all the meanings such terms carry. These meanings may be incorrect

and quite unfair, but they provide guidelines for action that may seem at the time to be based on realities.

- One of the problems in self-presentation is selective perception. People tend to attribute unacceptable behavior to your personal shortcomings and praiseworthy behavior to causes beyond your control. Thus, it's important to plan ahead—to decide what to say and how much to self-disclose. Saying too much too quickly may be counterproductive.

- Changing impressions that people already have of you is very difficult. It is possible to change their impressions, but at times it may not be worth the effort. If such a change is necessary, you must first deal with people's natural resistance to change. This means being prepared to keep your emotions under control and carefully constructing the new impression you wish to create.

Key Terms

person perception	implicit personality theory	social categories
presentation of self	selective perception	affinity-seeking
impression management	predispositions	self-disclosure
salient characteristic	attribution process	credibility
labeling theory		

Notes

1. Tagiuri, R. (1969). Person perception. In G. E. Lindsey & E. Aronson (Eds.), *The handbook of social psychology*, (2nd ed., pp. 3, 395–449). Reading, MA: Addison-Wesley. For several excellent examples of contemporary communication research on initial encounters, see: Beinstein, J. (1975). Conversations in public places. *Journal of Communication, 25*, 85–95; Berger, C. R., & Calabrese, R. J. (1975). Some explorations in initial interaction and beyond: Toward a theory of interpersonal communication. *Human Communication Research, 1*, 99–112; Berger, C. R. (1975). Proactive and retroactive attribution processes in interpersonal communications. *Human Communication Research, 2*, 33–50; Berger, C. R., Gardner, R. R., Clatterbuck, G. W., & Shulman, L. S. (1976). Perceptions of information sequencing in relationship development. *Human Communication Research, 3*, 29–46.

2. Goffman, E. (1956). *The presentation of self in everyday life*. Edinburgh: Social Sciences Research Centre. For an excellent discussion of impression management, see: Giles, H., & Street, R. L., Jr. (1985). Communication characteristics and behavior. In M. L. Knapp & G. R. Miller (Eds.). *Handbook of interpersonal communication* (pp. 205–262). Beverly Hills, CA: Sage.

3. Asch, S. E. (1946). Forming impressions of personalities. *Journal of Personality and Social Psychology, 41,* 258–290.

4. See: Becker, H. S. (1973). Labeling theory reconsidered. In H. S. Becker (Ed.), *Outsiders: Studies in the sociology of deviance* (2nd ed.). New York: Free Press. A classic in this field is: Goffman, E. (1963). *Stigma: Notes on the management of spoiled identity.* Englewood Cliffs, NJ: Prentice-Hall.

5. The salient characteristic and the labeling principles are also closely related to the concept of *stereotype.* Insensitive people still use pejorative labels to "keep down" categories of people, some of whom have a salient characteristic, such as skin color or some other visible feature. Prejudiced people try to dominate such a category of people by using a slang label in such a way that negative meanings are uniformly associated with all its members of the category.

6. Hays, W. L. (1958). An approach to the study of trait implication and trait similarity. In R. Tagiuri & L. Petrullo (Eds.), *Person perception and interpersonal behavior.* Stanford, CA: Stanford University Press; Bruner, J. S., Shapiro, D., & Tagiuri, R. (1958). The meaning of traits in isolation and in combination. In Tagiuri & Petrullo (Eds.), *Person perception;* Wishner, J. (1960). Reanalysis of impressions of personality. *Psychological Review, 67,* 96–112; and Crockett, W. H., & Friedman, P. (1986). Theoretical explorations of the processes of initial interactions. *Western Journal of Speech Communication, 44,* 86–92.

7. Wishner, *Reanalysis.*

8. Diabase, W., & Hjelle, L. (1968). Body-image stereotypes and body-type preferences among male college students. *Perceptual and Motor Skills, 27,* 1143–1146; Secord, P. (1958). Facial features and inference processes in interpersonal perception. In Tagiuri & Petrullo, *Person perception, p. 300–315;* Verinis, J., Roll, S. (1970). Primary and secondary male characteristics; the hairiness and large penis stereotypes. *Psychological Reports, 26,* 123–126. For an excellent general discussion of the characteristics influencing impression formation, see: Burgeon, J. K., Buller, D. B., & Woodall, W. G. (1989). *Nonverbal communication: The unspoken dialogue* (pp. 219–259). New York: Harper & Row.

9. Chaplin, W. F., Phillips, J. B., & Brown, J. D. (2000). Handshaking, gender, personality, and first impressions. *Journal of Personality and Social Psychology, 79,* 1, 110–117.

10. Jackson, L. A., Hunter, J. E., & Hodge, C. N. (1995). Physical attractiveness and intellectual competence: A meta-analytic review. *Social Psychology Quarterly, 58,* 108–122.

11. Martin, K. A., Sinden, A. R., & Fleming, J. C. (2000). Inactivity may be hazardous to your image: The effects of exercise participation on impression formation. *Journal of Sport and Exercise Psychology, 22,* 4, 283–291.

12. For a complete discussion of the many difficulties of getting to know others, see: Duck, S. (1987). *Human relationships: An introduction to social psychology* (pp. 155–186). Beverly Hills, CA: Sage.

13. Wilmot, W. W. (1975). *Dyadic communication* (2nd ed.). Reading, MA: Addison-Wesley.

14. Ibid., pp. 20–33.

15. Ibid.

16. Goffman. *Stigma,* pp.106–140.

17. Knapp, M. L. (1978). *Social intercourse: From greeting to goodbye.* Boston: Allyn & Bacon.

18. Gosling, S. D., Ko, S. J., & Mannarelli, T. (2002). A room with a cue: Personality judgments based on offices and bedrooms. *Journal of Personality and Social Psychology, 82,* 3, 379–398.

19. Ibid., 84–87.

20. Turner Bowkar, D. M. (2001). How can you pull yourself up by your bootstraps, if you don't have boots? Work-related clothing for poor women. *The Journal of Social Issues, 57,* 2, 311–322.

21. An excellent introduction to this area of study is provided by: Shaver, K. G. (1975). *An introduction to attribution processes.* Cambridge, MA: Winthrop.

22. Attribution theory was originally proposed in: Heider, F. (1958). *The psychology of interpersonal relations.* New York: Wiley. It was refined by: Kelley, H. H. (1973). The process of causal attribution. *American Psychologist, 28,* 107–128. For reviews of the accumulated research, see: Kelley, H. H., & Michela, J. L. (1980). Attribution theory and research. *Annual Review of Psychology, 31,* 457–503. Also, see: Harvey, J. H., & Weary, G. (1984). Current issues in attribution theory and research. *Annual Review of Psychology, 35,* 427–460.

23. Bell, R. A., & Daly, J. A. (1984). The affinity-seeking function of communication. *Communication Monographs, 51,* 91–115.

24. Wanzer, M. B. (1998). An exploratory investigation of student and teacher perceptions of student-generated affinity-seeking behaviors. *Communication Education, 47,* 4, 373–382; Prisbell, M. (1994). Students' perceptions of teachers' use of affinity-seeking and its relationship to teachers' competence. *Perceptual and Motor Skills, 78,* 641–642.

25. Ibid.

26. For several excellent examples of contemporary research and writing on self-disclosure, see: Bochner, A. P. (1982). On the efficacy of openness in close relationships. In M. Burgoon (Ed.), *Communication yearbook 5* (pp. 109–124). New Brunswick, NJ: Transaction; Bradac, J.J., Tardy, C. H., & Hosman, L. A. (1980). Disclosure styles and a hint at their genesis. *Human Communication Research, 6,* 228–238; Pearce, W. B., & Sharp, S. M. (1973). Self-disclosing communication. *Journal of Communication, 23,* 409–425; Rosenfeld, L. B. (1979). Self-disclosure avoidance: Why I am afraid to tell you who I am. *Communication Monographs, 46,* 63–74; Wheeless, L. R. (1978). A follow-up study of the relationship among trust, disclosure, and interpersonal solidarity. *Human Communication Research, 4,* 143–157.

27. Dindia, K. (2002). Self-disclosure research: Knowledge through meta-analysis. In M. Allen et al., eds., *Interpersonal communication research: Advances through meta-analysis* (pp. 169–185). Mahwah, NJ: Lawrence Erlbaum; Goldsmith, D. J., & Baxter, L. A. (1996). Constituting relationships in talk: A taxonomy of speech events in social and personal relationships. *Human Communication Research, 23,* 87–114.

28. Krivnos, P. D., & Knapp, M. L. (1975). Initiating communication: What do you say when you say hello? *Central States Speech Journal, 26,* 115–125; Nofsinger, R. E. (1975). The demand ticket: A conversational device for getting the floor. *Speech Monographs, 42,* 1–9; Schegloff, E. A. (1972). Sequencing in conversational openings. In E. J. Gumperz & D. Hymes (Eds.), *Sociolinguistics: The ethnography of communication* (pp. 346–380). New York: Holt, Rinehart, and Winston.

29. Kelley, H. H. (1973). *Causal schemata and the attribution process.* Morristown, NJ: General Learning Press; also: Kelley, H. H. (1973). The processes of causal attribution. *American Psychologist, 28,* 102–128; Kelley & Michela, Attribution theory, pp. 457–503; and Harvey & Weary, Current issues, pp. 427–460.

30. For a detailed review of scholarly writings (from Plato to the present) and various contemporary theories about the process by which people construct meaningful and shared interpretations of reality, see: DeFleur, M. L., & Rokeach, S. B. (1989). Mass communication and the construction of meaning. In DeFleur, M. L., & Rokeach, S. B. *Theories of mass communication* (5th ed., pp. 228–271). White Plains, NY: Longman.

Overcoming Communication Apprehension

Katherine sat outside the paneled boardroom waiting for her turn to make a presentation. Having just been promoted to assistant manager of the transportation department, she knew that she had a lot riding on the report she was about to make. In her previous position, she had never been invited to make a presentation to the board of directors, and she was very nervous. She felt especially apprehensive about her ability to speak fluently before the important and powerful board. She knew that they would be evaluating her and, if she blew it, her career might well be over before it really got started.

Her anxiety had been growing over the last few weeks. It began when her boss had first asked her to make the presentation. Since that moment she had spent every night and weekend preparing. She just knew that she might make mistakes. She had gathered all the information that she would need and had outlined her presentation in at least five different ways. She had tried to practice it more than 10 times. Her poor husband Alvin was nearly bored to death.

This was the moment of truth. Despite all her preparations, Katherine began to experience a sense of panic as she sat waiting. She began to feel a hard knot in the pit of her stomach. Her hands started to tremble and her mouth was dry. She felt a sudden urge to bite her fingernails.

Suddenly, she heard laughter coming through the door of the boardroom. Oh no, she thought, are they laughing at me? The very thought made her feel like she was going to throw up. Why did she ever consent to do this? She had always dreaded the idea of getting up and talking in front of a group. When she was in college, she had avoided any kind of public speaking class. Now she knew that she had to master her anxieties, but she just didn't know what to do.

Then, the door opened and one of the men asked her to come in. She suddenly felt like running away, but she knew she had to face them. She began to sweat and wanted to cry. As she walked into the board room, she was afraid that her legs would give way under her.

At some point in our lives, most of us have had a counterpart of Katherine's experience. Even polished and accomplished communicators never quite get over a sense of nervousness and *communication apprehension* about getting up to speak in front of a bunch of strangers. Anxiety and nervousness about communicating in a public setting are common and unavoidable; in fact, they are the primary factors that interfere with effective public speaking performances.

Note that it was not that Katherine lacked the necessary skills. She had a good report prepared and she knew her subject well. She was an intelligent woman and was carefully groomed and had dressed well for the occasion. She had never had any formal training in public speaking, but contrary to popular opinion, research reveals that all the skills training in the world may contribute only minimally to effectiveness as a speaker.[1] Furthermore, practice does not always make perfect. Performing over and over again may help some to communicate more effectively, but others may actually get worse.

What is important is one's emotional state before and during a presentation. This may have little to do with training or skills. In fact, the results of over 200 separate studies reveal that a person's ability to perform well while speaking to a group is closely related to a condition called **communication apprehension.**[2] This condition—its causes, its consequences, and how to cope with it in various contexts—is the central topic of this chapter.

Communication apprehension is a condition closely associated with *public communication,* such as presenting a talk to a group. However, it can occur under other conditions, such as when it is necessary to talk to strangers. In contrast, communicating within intimate groups—among family members and close friends—is seldom a problem for people. After all, those people are safe. As discussed in earlier chapters, we trust our friends and family to support us, encourage us, and generally make us feel good about ourselves. We don't share that same trust with people we do not know. We have no reason to believe that an audience of strangers will understand and sympathize if we forget part of what we were going to say, generally look stupid, and are forced to sit down in embarrassment. We have no reason to believe that any audience will easily overlook our "uhs" and "ums" and "you knows" as we stumble through our presentation. Clearly, then, we have *very good reason to feel apprehensive* whenever we consider communicating to an audience of strangers.

Many people—far too many—are convinced that competent communicators are just born with the right performance skills, or that speaking is just naturally easy for some. There are no grounds for such a belief. A large body of research underscores the need to reduce people's fears of addressing audiences.[3] For example, skills training is likely to aggravate some people's anxieties and actually make their condition worse.[4] These people, unable to perform competently in front of a group, are exposed over and over again to their own failures. It doesn't take too many trials before they learn to *expect* failure. This expectation only increases their fears about trying to do it again. Even if such people are able to acquire all the necessary skills to give a good talk, anxieties about communicating before an audience can continue to interfere with competent performance.

This chapter has been designed to help you cope with the communication apprehension and anxieties we all feel under a variety of circumstances. For example, apprehension can arise when we interact with people we don't know very well, or when we have to engage in small talk, handle conflict, justify our employment in an interview, work productively in a small group, give a briefing, or simply participate in class discussions. All these situations can provoke anxiety.

Communication Apprehension as a Common Reaction

Because apprehension is such a widely occurring condition, no other aspect of communication has received more attention from scholars and researchers over the past decades. But more precisely, what are we referring to here? Defined simply, communication apprehension refers to *fear or anxiety associated with either real or anticipated communication encounters.*[5]

Note that communication apprehension does not have to coincide with the actual speaking encounter; it can occur ahead of time, simply in anticipation of having to speak. Take yourself, for example. Your grade in a course may be contingent, in part, on your participation in class discussion. Just knowing that you will have to talk before the group may trigger enough anxiety to inhibit your ability to ask or answer questions. Similarly, anticipating the social demands of a dinner at the home of your new boss may stimulate communication apprehension long before you arrive. In other words, anxiety about communicating is a condition that can occur either prior to or during any particular encounter.

Some specialists regard communication apprehension as a special kind of shyness.[6] However, the two are not really the same. Reasons for shyness can vary greatly. Some shy people may lack communication skills. Others may have the necessary skills to communicate effectively, but may simply enjoy being unobtrusive or reflective. Certainly it is not true that all shy individuals experience communication apprehension. Looking at the population as a whole, about 40 percent report being shy, whereas only a little over 20 percent experience a truly significant degree of communication apprehension.[7] Therefore, about half of the people who are shy appear to be satisfied with avoiding interaction with others. The remainder, however, are probably shy because of some degree of fear about communicating. This is especially likely among those who lack communication skills. A kind of circular pattern can often be seen in the behavior of many shy people. It begins with a person being shy, which creates anxiety, which reduces communication skills, which results in increased shyness, and so on.

The circular link between shyness and apprehension can manifest itself in many ways: Because such individuals are not good at small talk, they become anxious about engaging in it. Also, because they are not skilled at speaking eloquently in front of a group, they become fearful of doing it. Similarly, because they are not good at asking for dates, they become apprehensive about that. Then, because of limited experience, they become even more shy as time goes on.

Others just dread communicating, not because of any skill deficiency, but simply because they are afraid of the act itself. Even thinking about it ahead of time brings on fear.[8] People who are afraid to communicate may actually avoid interacting, even when it's in their own best interest to do so. For example, they are unlikely to approach a boss to ask for a raise, although they know they deserve more money. They may avoid answering a professor's question in class even when they know the answer. In both instances, such individuals may know how to perform the required behavior—that is, they can utter the words necessary to request the raise, or they can comprehend and respond to the professor's demand; however, their emotional reactions to the situation often prevent them from doing so.

To understand further the nature of communication apprehension, it is necessary to differentiate between two categories of people in which this condition is present. The first is *apprehensive individuals* who, regardless of the situation, almost always feel anxious about relating to others. The second is people who have had *apprehensive experiences* that have incited fears about communicating. Both categories are widely found. But, although apprehensive people are troubled with a continual and pervasive condition, individuals who have had apprehensive experiences often suffer more temporary anxieties.

Individuals High and Low in Apprehension

Apprehensive people fear communicating with almost anyone in any kind of situation. McCroskey labels this type of relatively stable and predictable fear "traitlike."[9] Recall that the term **trait** refers broadly to *"any [personality] characteristic in which one individual differs from another in a relatively permanent and consistent way."*[10] Each of us has literally thousands of personality traits—such as stingy, sweet, creative, loyal, and humorous. Evidence of such traits is observable in a person's patterns of behavior over time. Similarly, over time, individuals can acquire a trait of being *highly apprehensive about communicating* across situations.

Social scientists do not assume that personality traits have genetic origins. That is, we do not *inherit* traits, we *acquire* (learn) them over a long period of time.[11] In terms of the trait of communication apprehension, then, we learn from our past experiences to be generally anxious (or nonanxious) while communicating. Because of its learned nature, such trait apprehension can be reduced by training.[12]

Personality traits are not rigid. Individuals characterized by a particular trait may or may not exhibit the behavior in every instance. For example, a person who is generally honest or jovial may not be like that in every circumstance. The same is true of people with the communication apprehension trait. Much depends on the *context* and the nature of the *other party*. For example, individuals who are high in communication apprehension report little or no anxiety in the context of interacting with their best friends or with family. They may even be comfortable communicating with a specific professor or employer. Thus, they are fully aware that they experience anxiety under some circumstances. Overall, however, persons high in the apprehension trait usually try to avoid most communication situations.[13]

At the other extreme are people who actively seek out others and talk easily and sometimes endlessly. Some talk so much that it is hard to get a word in edgewise. These individuals are classified as *very low* in the apprehension trait. In our society, being low in communication apprehension can have great advantages—as long as it is not too low. For the most part, we tend to approve of those who can give a good interview, entertain a crowd, or meet new acquaintances with finesse and charm. In contrast to the chronically apprehensive, who avoid communication encounters, those low in the trait seek them out. For example, a person low in communication apprehension will look forward to attending a party where he or she may not know anyone. On the other hand, a person high in this trait would dread such a situation.

A number of studies reveal that persons with little fear of communication tend to talk more, to date a greater variety of individuals, to choose occupations that demand more social contact, to communicate more assertively, and to engage in more self-disclosure than do those who are more fearful.[14] In contrast, the accumulated research shows that apprehensive people tend to be withdrawn, to engage in steady dating (versus playing the field), to select careers that allow them to work apart from others, to agree with the opinions of others (rather than express a dissenting point of view), and to be reluctant to reveal much information about themselves.

Although people who are high or low in communication apprehension represent the ends of the continuum, most people can be categorized as *moderately apprehensive.* In other words, having some fear of communicating is normal. About 20 percent of the population fall into the high category, and roughly the same percent are at the other end of the scale. This means that the remaining 60 percent—the majority—is in between.[15]

This in-between category experiences apprehension only when a particular situation arouses discomfort. For example, it is normal for most people to experience some level of apprehension in situations where their behavior is being *evaluated.* When people recognize that what they say and how they say it will make a difference in how some significant person (such as a prospective employer) views them, it is entirely normal for them to feel some anxiety or fear. Furthermore, it is highly likely that everyone experiences some *stage fright* before or during any kind of presentation. If a speaker is ill prepared, or believes that the audience will be hostile, this fear probably will (and should) increase.

Experiencing Communication Apprehension

There is probably no one who has not at one time or another temporarily experienced communication apprehension. The situations that trigger it vary greatly. Some people feel anxious even when they have to talk into a tape recorder or leave a message on an answering machine. Suddenly, they can think of nothing intelligent to say! For others, it is particular individuals who trigger apprehension, such as a person conducting a job or promotion interview—or a special friend's parents. If you take your pulse and it is rapid when you approach your boss for a raise, meet your future in-laws,

ask someone special for a first date, or sign for a telegram, you may be such a person.

When people's apprehensions are temporarily provoked (even for low or moderately apprehensive individuals), they are likely to respond just as high apprehensives do—they will avoid apprehension-producing situations. Thus, whether apprehension is a function of some enduring personality trait, or is based on an experience producing temporary apprehension, the ability to communicate suffers in similar ways. People become avoiders, or they become incapacitated—unable to either send or receive messages adequately. They may forget what they were planning to say, stammer in embarrassment, or clam up just when they need to perform their best.

Causes of Communication Apprehension

Trying to explain why we develop fears that interfere with our ability to communicate competently is no simple task. Sometimes we improperly blame the other individual with whom we are in a social relationship. Such interpretations are usually wrong, and we have to look further for answers. Sometimes those answers can be found *within the immediate context* of communication, and other times they are deeply ingrained *within the individual* who continuously experiences communication apprehension.

Contextual Sources of Anxiety

Certain situations as well as certain individuals can lead us to be apprehensive. Sometimes there are good and logical reasons for concern. For example, if we are driving at 70 miles per hour in a 45-miles-per-hour zone and a police car with flashing red and blue lights and a siren pulls up quickly behind us, adrenaline will undoubtedly flow! In such a situation, we have real cause for anxiety.

At other times, however, we feel distress even when the situation does not realistically call for such feelings. Also, we often misinterpret the context: We believe there's reason for concern when, in fact, there really are no objective grounds for worry. An example of how our imagination can mislead us is provided by the following (actual) experience of a former student.

Terry developed a severe case of communication apprehension when his girlfriend Jill announced that she had planned for him to meet her parents. Jill explained that her mom and dad were looking forward to meeting him. She knew that her parents were loving, sensitive, and warm individuals. Clearly, Terry had no basis in reality for fearing a meeting with Jill's folks. However, even though Terry was normally a personable and outgoing young man, his initial meeting with Jill's mom and dad revealed quite another side to his character. It was almost like a Dr. Jekyll and Mr. Hyde situation. At their first encounter, he seemed withdrawn; he mumbled responses to their questions; he spilled coffee on his pants and then retreated to the bathroom where he stayed for a long time. Jill was embarrassed (and furious). Afterward, Terry justified his behavior by arguing that he suffered great apprehension about the whole encounter. However, Jill contended that he distorted the situation and misread the entire context.

Both were correct. Understandably, Terry and Jill interpreted the situation differently. Each defined the meeting with Jill's parents from her or his own perspective. Jill believed that a meeting with her parents would be enjoyable. Terry, however, believed there was good reason to be nervous because he worried that they might judge him unworthy of their daughter.

Whatever the contextual cues, factual or imaginary, a major principle of human behavior is that people behave according to their own personal and subjective *definition of the situation* That is, they react to *what they believe is real*.[16] And what people believe about the context influences how they communicate. Researchers have identified a number of contextual factors that heighten our apprehension and affect our ability to communicate effectively.[17] Included in the list are: *unfamiliar or dissimilar others, novel or formal occasions, subordinate status*, conspicuousness or excessive *attention from others*, undergoing *evaluation*, and previous repeated *failure*.[18] (Box 10.1 overviews these contextual causes of communication apprehension.)

Communicating with people you don't know or who are not like you. It is always easier to talk to people you know as opposed to those who are unfamiliar. Initiating conversation with strangers can in itself be anxiety-producing. In such an encounter, where do you start? What do you say to people you don't know?

Correspondingly, people who are different from you may generate anxious moments. If you have ever interacted with someone who dropped out of high school and who resents college students as "smart alecks" who always "look down" on others, then you know how difficult it can be to try to communicate. Or imagine a conversation between two people who hold opposing views on a controversial and emotional topic like abortion, gun control, or capital punishment. These individuals are likely to be hard pressed to find common ground in order to communicate constructively with each other about such topics.

Communicating in formal or unfamiliar situations. Novel, formal, or unfamiliar occasions tend to trigger communication apprehension because they are filled with uncertainty. Predictability is a very important factor in social interaction. The nature of your relationship and the context itself allow you to anticipate correctly what people will say, do, and expect of you. This helps you to know what to say and do. When you can't make such predictions, you begin to worry. A good example of the consequences of an unfamiliar situation was your very first date. No doubt, you felt much anxiety about what to say, what to wear, and what to do (or not do). Similarly, your first day at

BOX 10.1   A Closer Look

Contextual Causes of Communication Apprehension

Sometimes there are good reasons for us to be apprehensive. The context or situation itself may cause us to feel tense and anxious. Consider the following factors:

- *Communicating with unfamiliar or dissimilar others.* Strangers or mere acquaintances may cause us to feel some uncertainty and anxiety. At the same time, people who seem different from us, who don't share our beliefs and attitudes, are likely to make us feel a little anxious.
- *Novel or formal situations.* It's difficult to predict what to say or how to behave in new circumstances or in situations that require following a particular set of rules.
- *Subordinate rank.* People of higher status may make us feel nervous and self-conscious when we try to speak.
- *Conspicuous and excessive attention.* If we feel that we have become the center of attention, we are likely to be anxious when its our turn to talk.
- *Undergoing evaluation.* If we feel that someone is scrutinizing us, evaluating our performance, we typically feel anxious when we try to present our point of view.
- *Repeated failure.* If we know that we have performed poorly in the past, we will be worried that we will fail again the next time we try to do it—whether its giving a speech, relating a story, telling a joke, or giving a toast.

important ceremonies—are also likely to induce uncertainty and apprehension. Recognizing that such events require you to behave correctly, you may feel uncomfortable because you are not familiar with the etiquette others expect you to follow. Or, you may not know how to behave casually in a rented tuxedo or a long formal gown. Again, the factor of unpredictability raises apprehension.

Communicating with people of higher status or rank. Certain kinds of situations define people's status and rank. Many of those situations underscore your own lower status compared to others. For example, attending a dinner party at your boss's home may remind you of where you fit into the power structure—making you self-conscious about your behavior in the presence of those who control your destiny. Communication apprehension is likely to follow.

Communicating when you are suddenly the center of attention. In any context in which you are suddenly singled out, with everyone's attention directly on you, can be a source of intense communication anxiety. More than any other aspect of a public speaking situation, *conspicuousness*—the belief that all eyes are riveted on you, scrutinizing everything about you—can induce communication apprehension. This can happen in any occasion when you become the center of attention. Perhaps you've felt self-conscious when a professor used your work as an example to the class of what to do, or worse, what not to do!

Similarly, *excessive* attention from others may give rise to communication apprehension. For example, you are likely to feel uncomfortable when a counselor seems determined to have you reveal private and confidential information. You may find it difficult to communicate in such circumstances. Another example is the discomfort you feel when someone *monopolizes all of your time* at a party. You may wish the person would go away or that you were somewhere else. Most of us like *some* moderate

college, the first day on your new job, or the first visit to your future in-laws all presented you with uncertainty. Communication apprehension tends to be very high in such unfamiliar and relatively unpredictable situations.

Truly formal situations—such as elegant dinners, elaborate weddings, and funerals, or other level of attention from others but are ill at ease when someone wants to peer at us through a microscope.

Communicating when you are being evaluated. Being evaluated is almost certain to bring on communication anxiety. In situations where you know that your supervisor at work—or your professor in class—is appraising you on the basis of an oral performance, you are likely to become anxious. Even though you might do well without the scrutiny, the idea that you're being evaluated heightens apprehension about what you say or do. Students often report that when they practice their speeches at home, they experience no problems. However, as soon as they see the professor with that grade book, they get nervous, forget their lines, and generally perform poorly.

Communicating when you have repeatedly failed before. Finally, memories of previous failures in identical or similar situations are a common source of apprehension. For instance, if the last 12 times you tried to arrange a date with someone attractive, only to be repeatedly turned down, it may be distressing to ask for the 13th time, to say the least. Or, if you know from past experience that every time you have asked for a raise, the boss has listened impatiently and then flatly denied your request, you might well be nervous and reluctant about going in and asking one more time.

Most of us can readily identify with such contextual sources of communication distress. We all have found ourselves in circumstances that seemed to provoke a degree of temporary or transitory apprehension. They are relatively easy to understand and explain. However, the problem becomes more complex when one attempts to identify causes of communication apprehension as *a persistent personality trait*.[19]

Learning to Be Apprehensive

People whose apprehension is a stable personality trait tend to distort their interpretations of the contextual factors discussed above. They selectively perceive events around them and interpret them differently from the ways those who are not usually apprehensive interpret similar events. For example, those high in apprehension sometimes perceive a situation to be more novel or more formal than it really is; or they may feel very conspicuous and feel convinced that everyone noticed a mistake they made and is laughing at them. Even if we try to persuade them otherwise, they don't buy it. Unfortunately, those with a high apprehension trait engage in so much self-monitoring that they can be oblivious to reality or to the way other people interpret the context.

Where does such a personal condition come from? The answer is that a person who is high in the trait of communication apprehension has acquired that condition through a process of learning.[20] Social scientists refer to the process of learning some condition of personality within a social and cultural environment as *socialization*. There are two related ideas that must be understood. One is *learning*—a process by which a person's behavior and knowledge is shaped by experience. Learning can take place with no one around. People have personal experiences from which they acquire a greater understanding of their environment, even though no one else is present. Such learning can also occur through observation of other people doing something. The term *socialization* refers more specifically to a particular kind of learning that takes place within a social and cultural environment, such as a family, peer group, society, workplace, or school. Here, the expectations of those in that environment shape what the person learns.

Long-term socialization. Trait apprehension is a function of long-term socialization. To illustrate, it will help to compare the socialization process that produces communication apprehension to that which produces fear of going to the dentist. In our society, fear and dread—supposedly caused by pain and suffering—are indelibly associated with dentists.

Children understand this early and well—even if they have never gone to a dentist. Any child can tell you that it is a dreadful experience to be avoided! They have learned this from cartoons, old movies, lore in the street, jokes heard from others, and tales told by earlier generations. The fact is, however, that going to the dentist today is virtually painless. It may be inconvenient, perhaps uncomfortable, and certainly expensive, but it is hardly an experience that leaves every person visiting a dentist racked with pain and suffering. In short, this is a culturally shared construction of meaning that people learn for "going to the dentist" through a process of socialization, rather than from personal experience with objective reality. In a similar way, some people acquire convictions about the terrors of "speaking before a group," even if they have never done so.

The importance of learning and unlearning. The good news about the socialization process through which communication apprehension is acquired is this: Anything that is learned can be unlearned. Although there may be little hope that people's apprehension can be totally eliminated, with systematic training they may be able to unlearn *at least some* of the negative beliefs that promote communication anxiety. In other words, with adequate training, new beliefs, attitudes, meanings, and behaviors can be acquired that will make it easier for shy and apprehensive people to communicate more comfortably. Such approaches to relearning have been successful in reducing fear of flying, improving sexual adequacy, reducing smoking, and minimizing fear of snakes.

To gain a perspective that may help reduce excessive fears of communicating, it will be useful to examine the process of learning. It is a complex topic. Social scientists have developed many theories of how learning takes place. In this chapter we will consider only two of the theories of learning. These are particularly relevant to learning communication apprehension: One is **social learning theory** and the other is **reinforcement learning theory.**[21]

Learning to fear by observing others. Acquiring a habit, idea or trait or some other pattern of behavior by seeing it performed by others is often explained by *social learning theory* (sometimes called "observational" learning theory). This theory was developed originally by psychologist Albert Bandura.[22] As the name suggests, this theory explains how individuals learn, not by performing actions themselves, but by observing how other people cope with similar problems. This idea may be applied to communication apprehension.

Essentially, social learning theory explains that we begin learning to be high or low in communication apprehension by observing the behavior of people who are important as *models* in our lives. When we were young children, our parents and siblings served as our primary models of how to behave. When we entered school, friends and teachers probably became significant models as well. As Bandura and others have illustrated, we often learn how to do something by seeing how others do it. We watch another person perform an activity—such as smoking—and then, under certain circumstances, we imitate that performance. We do this all the time with many forms of behavior. For example, from our earliest years, we learn to talk and respond to others appropriately by copying many of the verbal and nonverbal patterns of others—especially those we admire and want to emulate. Looking to the behavior of other people is the main source from which we find out what our family, friends, and society at large expect of us. From the beginning, they serve as our models, and we emulate them.

The key to this modeling approach is trying out the observed behavior. We're more likely to do that when we perceive that the model is *rewarded* for engaging in that behavior. In other words, it is not enough just to imitate. Any new form of behavior copied from another has to be *useful* to us in some way. If it seems so, we may try it out. Then, as a result of such trials we may or may not adopt the new behavior as part of our own habit patterns. What leads us to adopt it more permanently is when the modeled behavior does actually help us cope with a problem. If it does so successfully, we experience a personal reward (that is, "it worked, and the problem was handled"). Removing a problem and feeling relief can in itself be a reward.

Learning specialists refer broadly to the consequences of such rewarding experiences as *reinforcement,* which can be defined as an increase in the probability that we will respond in that particular way again when confronted with the same circumstances. By this means, the response is learned—it becomes "habitual"—a lasting part of our overall behavioral patterns. On the other hand, if adopting the modeled behavior results in a bad or punishing experience, it is very unlikely we will make it a permanent part of our behavior.

Not only do we copy actual or overt behaviors in this manner, we are also good imitators of our models' fears and anxieties. Some people learn to fear spiders, snakes, or mice simply by observing the anxiety of a parent shrieking at the sight of them. For example, an actual instance of such modeling occurred in the following way. When Kerry was in third grade, her teacher owned a pet tarantula named Precious. The pet became Kerry's favorite. Despite that early positive experience with Precious, Kerry, now a young woman, shakes in fear every time she faces even the tiniest spider. What happened? Observational learning played a key part. Over the years, she was exposed to the repeated hysterics of her mother every time an uninvited spider, or any bug, entered the house. Her parent served as a model, and, in spite of her earlier comfort with the creatures, Kerry acquired her pattern of reacting with fear to the stimulus of a spider. Her mother was someone she wanted to be like, and emulating her was rewarding. That reward "reinforced" the bug-fear connection.

Similarly, children pick up on the subtle and obvious cues of their parents', siblings', or peers' anxieties about communicating.[23] Exposed at an early age to a number of important models who appear to be uncomfortable in communica-tion situations, any of us might have been unintentionally socialized to be high in apprehension.

Learning as a consequence of rewards and punishments. While social learning theory is an attractive explanation that seems to make sense, it fails in one important respect: It does not explain fully why one individual raised in a particular set of circumstances acquires a communication apprehension trait whereas another, reared in exactly those same circumstances, does not. We know, for instance, that a child who is high in communication apprehension may grow up in the same family that also produces another child who is low in such anxiety. Presumably each has been exposed to the same behavioral models by the parents. Therefore, social learning theory may explain the problems of one but not the other. Furthermore, we know that children can be low in apprehension about communicating even when both parents (as models) are highly apprehensive. The same is true in reverse. Thus, whereas the modeling perspective may provide a reasonable account of why apprehension results in some people, it fails in others.

An alternative explanation that does not have the preceding shortcoming is *reinforcement learning theory.* (See Box 10.2.) According to this explanation, individuals try out a number of behaviors by chance in some cases, or in others for some different reason. These initial trials are followed by some sort of *consequence.* If the consequence is positive, that is rewarding (and thereby reinforcing), then the behavior has a chance of becoming part of the individual's more permanent repertoire, to be repeated in similar circumstances.[24] If this happens over and over, a connection is established—that is, learning has occurred. Should the initial consequence be punishing, however, the behavior is likely to be dropped and replaced with some other response. Assuming that we prefer positive consequences to our behavior, reinforcement learning theory explains why some of us enjoy social situations that re-

BOX 10.2   A Closer Look

Social Learning Theory versus Reinforcement Theory

Communication scholars explain how individuals acquire communication apprehension with one of two theories. These theories are reviewed here.

Social Learning Theory

This theory, originally developed by Albert Bandura, was first used to explain how children learn, based on observing other people's behaviors, fears, and anxieties. Here, it is used to explain how we learn to be more or less apprehensive when we communicate.

1. We begin by observing how our role models (parents, siblings, teachers) respond to communication situations. For example, is our role model assertive or passive? Does she appear tense or relaxed? Does he apparently enjoy talking or not?
2. If our role model is rewarded for communicating and if we determine that what our role model does is useful to us in some way, then we will try it out ourselves. For example, is she rewarded for communicating that way? Does he get punished?
3. When we try out the new behavior ourselves, we are more likely to adopt it as our own if we get rewarded. If punished, however, we will likely discontinue that behavior. For example, if we try to be assertive ourselves (a rewarded behavior for the role model), and we find that we get what we want as a result (a reward), we will continue to be assertive. On the other hand, if we are punished for our attempts to be assertive, we will abandon it and opt for another way.

Reinforcement Theory

This theory is based on the notion of trial and error. That is, we try out a number of different behaviors (not just those we've observed our role models use) in response to particular situations.

1. We begin by encountering a novel situation. We're not sure what to do or how to act. For example, we see an attractive individual that we would like to ask out for a date. What do we say? What do we do?
2. So, we try out different responses to the situation. To continue with our dating example, we have a number of options available: We could wait to see if the person asks us out; we could see if the person is available Saturday night; or we could simply ask the person to go out for a date.
3. If we are rewarded for our trial (received reinforcement), then it's likely we'll adopt this behavior and use it again. Let's assume then, that our dating target decides to accept our direct invitation to go out. Thus, we'll try that particular approach again the next time we see an attractive individual we want to date.
4. However, if we are either punished or ignored for our trial, then it's likely we'll drop this behavior and, thus, try out an alternative response. In our dating example, we could have received a punishing response ("Are you kidding? I wouldn't go out with you!") or the individual could have ignored our request altogether and kept walking. Either response is sufficient to keep us from trying the direct approach the next time.

quire communication, whereas others avoid them. More than any other explanation of communication apprehension, this perspective has been fairly consistently confirmed by research.[25] Basically, then, reinforcement theory can be used to explain how people high in com-

munication apprehension have been punished for their communication, whereas those low in apprehension have been rewarded.

However, an important question is this: Why does the individual try out a new response in the first place? One answer to that question is provided by what are called *operant* versions of reinforcement theory. Essentially, this view holds that *chance* plays a part. The individual may need to cope with some sort of problem. To do so, he or she randomly tries out many potential solutions—similar to trial and error—and finally gets it right. In fact, hitting on a form of behavior that reduces the problem and thereby produces rewards need not be the result of a conscious decision. The individual may simply have unwittingly engaged in a form of activity that produced a rewarding experience. That response pattern then is reinforced and has a higher probability of being repeated. If rewards continue when the behavior takes place, it becomes a permanent habit pattern, perhaps without the individual even realizing what has happened.[26]

The resiliency factor.   Despite our learning histories, many of us have encountered negative consequences to our communication behavior at one time or another, and yet, we have not become crippled by communication apprehension. Fortunately, most of us are psychologically *resilient* enough to not let a failure or two shape our behavior permanently. We simply try again to gain positive consequences. This **resiliency factor** is a product of our socialization and reinforcement history, which suggests that we can usually expect our communication to be well received. As a result, when an occasional performances goes wrong, we are able to chalk it up as an unusual event—a mistake.

Those already high in apprehension do not share this resiliency. For them, success is not expected. Failure or punishment is. Such individuals have learned to expect failure or punishment when they talk. A history of punishment for talking prompts those high in apprehension to avoid the behavior that typically results in negative consequences. Thus, fear of communicating and the expectation of negative consequences have become a deeply established personality trait.

The consequences of inconsistency.   A follow-up of reinforcement theory suggests that some

individuals may experience inconsistent consequences to their behavior. If a youngster is rewarded for talking *sometimes,* but punished at *other* times, the child is likely to develop high communication apprehension. Irregular or inconsistent consequences for behavior over time can induce a condition of **personal anomie**—a feeling of anxiety or distress arising from confusion concerning the social expectations of others. This can be a serious condition, and it has even been linked to increased probability of suicide.[27] In the present discussion of communication apprehension, if we cannot accurately make reliable predictions about what will happen to us—whether we will be rewarded or punished when we communicate—we probably will develop fears and anxieties about it and stop communicating altogether.

Another source of anxiety is the *no-win situation.* For instance, we may always say the wrong thing. Suppose we greet the next-door neighbor saying, "Good morning," and then she grumbles and claims that it isn't. Then, the next morning, we change strategy and declare, "We've seen better days than this one." She then argues that we should appreciate what we have. After a few such attempts we choose to ignore her altogether. She then tells other neighbors that we are cold and unfriendly. This no-win situation, like the repeated-failures condition, is likely to make us feel very apprehensive in subsequent encounters with that neighbor. We are helpless to initiate a successful communication. Should this experience occur often in other contexts and with other individuals, it becomes apparent that **learned helplessness** would be aroused in almost all of our attempts to communicate with others.[28]

By the time we are adults, we have confronted and learned from a number of communication experiences that eventually result in different levels of communication apprehension. Those of us who share a history of positive reinforcement for communicating are probably moderate to low in our apprehensions. Although we may occasionally suffer from anxiety in a specific situation, as a rule we tend to be comfortable with people and enjoy talking with them and to them. Conversely, those who have experienced a very different history of socialization—with punishment or unpredictable consequences tied to attempts to communicate—are likely to be chronically apprehensive about approaching any communication task.

Consequences of High and Low Communication Apprehension

Suffering from high anxiety about public speaking is not the only consequence of being chronically apprehensive. Over 100 research studies demonstrate that individuals high in apprehension are evaluated differently by others than those low in apprehension.[29] The consequences of these assessments can be seen throughout the subjects' lives. Those who are low in apprehension are evaluated positively, whereas those who are high are regarded negatively in a variety of ways.[30] These assessments can have profound and long-term consequences. One of the earliest arenas for such evaluation occurs in the classroom and on the school playground.

In the Classroom

The social dynamics of the classroom (in all school levels) have been intensively studied in the search for understanding of the causes and consequences of communication apprehension.[31] One important aspect of the classroom context is the way in which teachers evaluate individuals. The consequences of evaluations in the classroom can be illustrated by comparing two boys: Jerry, who is low in communication apprehension, and Richard, who is high in communication apprehension. We will assume that the two are actually twins, who were separated at birth and raised in similar middle-class homes in different cities. Neither is aware of the other. While these are two fictional people, they represent composites of individuals whose experiences have been closely studied.[32] These composites will seem familiar because we all know people who fit each of these profiles.

Jerry and Richard are both 14 years of age, and are both healthy and active. They both like sports, girls, pizza, and rock stars (not necessarily in that order). Jerry is outgoing and popular, and is captain of the soccer team. Richard is more of a loner. He reads a lot, and checks his e-mail on the computer before school every morning. Jerry is rarely, if ever, apprehensive about talking to anyone about anything. Richard seldom initiates conversations with others at school.

There is a striking difference in the ways teachers respond to Jerry and Richard. Their responses favor Jerry, who is low in communication apprehension. Teachers perceive Jerry to be a better student than Richard, even though the two are intellectual equals and have identical grades and IQ scores.

The patterns of communication affect the ways teachers respond to Jerry and Richard. In class, Jerry raises his hand and volunteers to talk frequently. Teachers call on Jerry more often than on Richard. Teachers also initiate informal conversations with Jerry much more often than with Richard.

When teachers ask Jerry a question and he doesn't know the answer, they assume the question is too hard or unclear and give hints to assist him. When the same thing happens with Richard, teachers assume that he doesn't know the answer because he's not too bright, and they move on to another student. Teachers interpret Jerry's ease in communicating as a sign of an enthused, dedicated, and delightful student. Richard's quietness is construed as detachment, indifference, or even apathy toward school.

Clearly, students like Jerry, who are low in communication apprehension, are more likely to be seen as ones who do well in school, despite the fact that teachers often give them extra help and attention. Students like Richard, who are high in communication apprehension, have their work cut out for them. Teachers regularly underestimate their intelligence and misinterpret their quietness as an attitude problem. This discriminatory behavior magnifies communication apprehension by punishing or ignoring students high in apprehension.

In Social Encounters

Richard and Jerry are now 19 years old and both are in college. Richard and Jerry's differing levels of communication apprehension continue to affect their lives, both in the college classroom and in interpersonal relationships. For example, Jerry dates more than once a week, and he enjoys seeing a number of different young women. Most women he meets find him attractive, affable, and exciting. Richard's experience in intergender relationships is quite different. Few women notice him when he's in the same room with them. Like most people high in apprehension, Richard appears to hide or physically contract when others are around. He does date one person somewhat regularly, but he would like to date others. Unfortunately, he seldom has the opportunity because people interpret his high-apprehension behavior to mean that he is cold and distant.

Interpersonal opportunities are much greater for individuals like Jerry, who are low in communication apprehension. Such individuals seem approachable and fun to be with. They are affinity-seekers and give the appearance of being good listeners in conversations. They ask and answer questions; and they are generally perceived as being friendly and personable. People with high communication apprehension, like Richard, give off the wrong signals. They send a clear message of avoidance: They look away, respond only when spoken to, and rarely ask questions about another person with whom they may be talking. As a result, people with high apprehension are perceived as being disinterested and unfriendly—even though they may really want companionship.

At Work

After graduating from college, both Richard and Jerry looked for jobs. Jerry applied for career opportunities in public relations (his major), whereas Richard considered jobs in data analysis and computer software development (he majored in computer information systems). Obviously, the communication demands of these career paths differ dramatically: Jerry's choice required him to interact regularly with corporate clients, whereas Richard will have limited interaction with others.

When you consider your own major and the career decisions you have made thus far, do these decisions reflect positive or negative feelings about communication? People low in communication apprehension are more likely to choose careers in speech communication, theater, journalism, advertising, and public relations. Those high in communication apprehension are more likely to choose careers in accounting, computer science, pharmacy, and engineering.

The situation of applying for a job clearly illustrates how communication apprehension can affect the impressions people form in the workplace.[33] All things being equal, those who communicate easily generally make a better first impression in job interviews than those who are more anxious. Employers would be more likely to perceive Jerry as being sociable, competent, responsible, and having leadership potential. Richard would more likely be perceived as being uncommunicative, restrained, aloof, and tense. At the extreme, potential employers might conclude that Richard isn't really interested in working for them!

In Lifelong Careers

If we look in on Richard and Jerry seven years after graduation, we find Jerry in management and Richard still working at a lower career level. Those low in communication apprehension are promoted significantly more often than those who continue to be fearful and nervous about communicating. Those who communicate comfortably are apparently able to alert their bosses to their achievements and to assert their needs. Those reluctant to communicate may hesitate to tell others about their successes; they are more likely to wait for a promotion to come to them.

In terms of job satisfaction, Jerry is more satisfied with his work than Richard.[34] This may be a reflection of reality—that is, those low in apprehension report significantly more satisfaction than their high-apprehension counterparts simply because their jobs are more rewarding. After all, Jerry's job probably pays more, includes greater work variety, and provides more flexibility than Richard's lower-ranking position.

To summarize, the selective, distorted impressions that people construct on the basis of someone's apprehension about communicating can easily lead us to conclude that the world of the "easy talker" is much more positive than that of the person who is shy and timid. In some ways it is. Overall, people who are more or less permanently apprehensive about communicating appear to be less likely to succeed in academic pursuits, social relationships, and career opportunities. In contrast, those who are not troubled by such anxieties seem to get more of what they want because they are perceived as being competent, sociable, popular, hardworking, attractive, responsible, and more qualified for leadership roles.

Remember, however, that the descriptions of Richard and Jerry represent tendencies documented by research, not ironclad laws. In other words, they are *generalizations* with many exceptions. There are children high in communication apprehension who do well academically. As adults, many such people establish long-term successful marriages and friendships and have rewarding and high-paying jobs. In contrast, there are people with low communication apprehension who have trouble finishing college, getting a date, or holding down a job for long. Thus, no one needs to feel doomed simply because of being shy and somewhat uncommunicative. For one thing is possible to change if desired. However, the majority of people who are apprehensive about communicating have learned to live with this tendency and see no need to change.

Dealing with Stage Fright

At one time or another, everyone has to make a presentation before a group. A common form of communication apprehension is what is commonly called **stage fright**. In fact, few people have never experienced it.[35] This section looks at stage fright to understand its nature and suggest ways of coping with it.

First, stage fright is *normal*. In fact, it is even routine for those who repeatedly perform before audiences. Almost all professional performers complain about feeling nervous before they address an audience. It's no simple feat to march up onto a stage with all eyes on us, and then to speak fluently and meaningfully.

To understand stage fright, two of its potential causes need to be examined: the *apprehension-producing event* itself and *your own level of communication apprehension*. Contrary to what you might think, it's not a good idea to rid yourself completely of stage fright. Like unpleasant medicine, in limited doses it can serve you well! Because stage fright is often a necessary condition for expert performances, you need to understand why you suffer from it and how it can help or hurt your performance.

The Contributions of the Context

To discuss stage fright, the focus here is more narrowly on public speaking rather than on communicating in general. Thus, this section concentrates on those specific occasions when we have to make a report, address an assembly, or speak to a group or audience.

Like other aspects of communication, stage fright is partially a product of the context in which the activity takes place; public speaking is done in a *physical place*, in a *social setting*, and among people in particular *social relationships*. Each of these contextual factors can contribute to the speaker's temporary communication apprehension. In addition, speaking before a group is characterized by the contextual sources of anxiety as noted earlier such as *unfamiliar*

As an example of the apprehension many people feel about speaking in public, consider the sitcom *Seinfeld*, where the main character says: "The number one fear is public speaking. The number two fear is death. This means that if you have to go to a funeral, you'd feel better off in the casket than delivering the eulogy."

others, formal occasions, conspicuousness, and *evaluations*. It is little wonder, then, that this kind of communication generates anxiety.

Are these sources of apprehension real or only imagined? They are very real! Giving a talk places us in a formal situation with unfamiliar others where we are conspicuous and being evaluated. Every audience rates a public speaking event much the same way they judge ball games, soap operas, or movies. Because most public events are culturally defined as entertainment, people expect speakers to be amusing or at least informative and interesting. The audience's expectations seem to increase as a function of how much money, time, and effort is involved in attending the presentation—making everyone a critic.

The Contributions of the Speaker

Recall that people with high communication apprehension are likely to magnify the stress factors in almost any situation. Even though we all recognize the conspicuous situation of the public speaker and the evaluation involved in the event, people who are chronically apprehensive negatively interpret the situation, perceiving that the people in the audience are strangers and that their presentation will be judged harshly.

As much as possible, those high in communication apprehension avoid speaking before an audience. Such people would not voluntarily enroll in anything like a public speaking class. If their university requires such a class, these students may enroll, drop the class, and enroll again. Sometimes they do not muster the courage to enroll in the class until the last term of their final year in college, and, in fact, there are students who have never graduated simply because they were unable to complete that one required course.

In contrast, easy talkers typically enjoy public speaking courses, and, despite stage fright, they learn to perform quite well. For such individuals, and indeed for those who are moderately apprehensive, stage fright can be controlled. By practicing skills, they learn to channel their apprehension toward the event in productive ways. For these people, a certain amount of stage fright generates motivation—enough drive so that they can excel on stage.

Unfortunately, many novice speakers—along with those who are highly apprehensive—fail to manage their stage fright productively. Rather than using their anxiety to stimulate motivation, they allow it to inhibit their abilities. They don't act on their fears; they give in to them. As a result, these speakers cannot perform competently, and they exhibit observable signs of defeat. For instance, their palms become sweaty, and their hands and knees shake. Their skin may develop blotches, and they may even get stomach cramps. On stage, they may stutter and forget what they need to say. For these people, the expectation of failure causes failure. However, even speakers who are very anxious can break this pattern.

Reducing Communication Apprehension

No one has to go through life avoiding events that require him or her to communicate. Anyone can learn to cope with stage fright and even modify a communication apprehension trait. Strong evidence indicates that even those who are truly anxious can be moved to a moderate level where their apprehensions can be managed. If so, they can gain enough confidence to communicate with others effectively in both public and private settings.

A number of methods have been touted as potential cures for communication anxieties. This chapter considers only three that appear to be effective. These are *systematic desensitization, cognitive restructuring,* and *skills training.* There are many other techniques in use, such as hypnosis, group counseling, and psychoanalysis. Although these may have merit, they can be very costly, and none is as successful as the three discussed here. Today, most col-

leges and universities offer at least two of these techniques as part of training in public speaking. After reviewing each, you may want to consider examining one that is available to you.

Systematic Desensitization

The process of **systematic desensitization (SD)** is the most widely used of all treatment programs for communication apprehension because it has one of the highest success rates.[36] Systematic desensitization, developed in the early 1950s, is a form of treatment used to reduce many kinds of fears, including fears of flying, heights, driving, and so on, as well as communication apprehension.

In the mid-1960s, research began on the effects of SD on public speaking anxiety. Experimenters repeatedly found that the procedure significantly reduced students' fears about communicating. In 1972, a SD program was initiated for students at Illinois State University. It included published guidelines that others have used to initiate similar treatment programs at universities and high schools across the country.[37]

Systematic desensitization focuses on *physical responses* to apprehension. We all become tense and tighten our muscles when we are anxious. It is an involuntary response.[38] If we have reason to be fearful, our bodies automatically react to prepare for action—whether or not physical action is required to deal with the source of the anxiety. Systematic desensitization works on the principle that if an alternative response—muscle relaxation—can be substituted for tension and stress, then people can learn to cope with anxiety-producing situations, including communication situations.

So, the big message of SD is *relax!* "Well," you say, "that's easier said than done. How can anyone ease back and relax when they have a speech to perform?" The fact is, it can't be done without learning how to do it. In SD treatment programs, individuals are actually taught *how* to relax. They learn to tense and then relax each of their muscles and to control their breathing

FIGURE 10.1

Sequence of Commu-
nication Situations
for Systematic
Desensitization
In systematic desensitization, the individual learns
to associate relaxation ,
rather than tension, with
increasingly stressful
speaking situations.

High Apprehension

Giving a speech
Participating in a class discussion
Standing in front of class without talking
Asking a question during class
Working on a group project
Talking with an instructor after class
Talking with a friend

Low Apprehension

so that, on cue, they can let go as they exhale. In this treatment program, then, the trainee becomes conscious of physical tensions and practices releasing that tension on command.

The next phase of SD introduces the anxiety-producing conditions for which the training is all about. In the case of communication apprehension, students are exposed gradually to a sequence of communication situations. Figure 10.1 illustrates a hierarchy of communication situations commonly used in SD training, ranging from most apprehensive (giving a speech) to least apprehensive (talking with a friend).

At first, situations are presented that arouse relatively little apprehension. For example, while in a relaxed state, subjects are asked to imagine themselves talking on the telephone to their best friend. Next, to increase the level of potential stress, they may be asked to visualize themselves working on a group project or going on a blind date. In later stages of the program, subjects are asked to visualize situations that would have produced a lot of stress before the therapy began, such as presenting a speech or being interviewed on television. By the time they get to this level, subjects have developed their relaxation techniques to a point where they can handle the situation. Over time, individuals learn to associate *relaxation,* not *tension,* with the increasing demands of each successive communication situation.

In addition to its obvious success rate, SD is cost effective. Each session lasts about an hour, and the entire program only requires about five to seven sessions. Research shows that if students are exposed to SD at the same time they are enrolled in public speaking classes where they learn specific skills, they are more likely to finish the course, perform competently, and report feeling less apprehensive about communicating.

Cognitive Restructuring

An interesting alternative to SD is **cognitive restructuring.** Whereas systematic desensitization focuses on muscle tension—the physiological effects of our apprehension—cognitive restructuring centers on (as the name suggests) our *thought processes.* It examines the individual's *interpretations* of the anxiety-producing situation itself. Again, this is a general therapy system and is not restricted to communication anxieties. Nevertheless, it is used to reduce temporary or chronic communication apprehension.

Proponents of this method argue that people label certain situations inappropriately and that they often evaluate events as being more negative than they actually are.[39] These negative evaluations are based primarily on specific irrational beliefs that underlie a lot of their emotions.[40] Three irrational beliefs that individuals commonly entertain can be summed up in the following statements:

- Everyone must love me all the time or I am a bad person.
- I must be competent or successful in all situations or I am a bad person.
- When life is not the way I want, it is awful and upsetting.

Cognitive restructuring focuses on changing these kinds of beliefs. The role of the therapist is to help individuals understand the basis for their anxieties. When irrational beliefs are exposed, the therapist challenges them, questioning each and arguing logically against them all. Then the therapist offers rational alternatives to replace those that have been discredited. In this way, troublesome beliefs are restructured or removed, and new convictions are established.

When cognitive restructuring is applied to communication apprehension, five major steps are involved. Let's look at how each of these steps is applied to fears about public speaking.

In the *first* step in cognitive restructuring, called the "introduction," the basic principles involved in cognitive restructuring are explained. The trainer (or therapist) explains that apprehension about public speaking is learned and that anything that has been learned can be unlearned and replaced with new ideas and behavior. Apprehension can be reduced significantly when people become aware of their irrational beliefs or negative thoughts about public speaking.

The *second* step requires that subjects identify negative self-statements that inhibit their speaking performances. These are derogatory convictions that anxious people often say (to themselves) about the situation or their activities in that situation. Subjects are asked to consider three separate occasions for saying (silently) those negative statements—before, during, and after the speech. Step 2 in Box 10.3 lists some sample negative self-statements. Do you recognize any that you might use? What are others you may have said to yourself?

In the *third* step, each of these statements is then analyzed for errors in logic. (Notice the logic errors in step 3 in Box 10.3 that undermine or disable each negative self-statement identified.) Cognitive restructuring aims to show individuals that they have been rehearsing an entire monologue of irrational negative self statements that typically form the basis for a kind of self-fulfilling prophecy: Believing that they are failing, they wind up doing so. It is no wonder their attempts at public speaking have been so frightening and frustrating up to this point.

In the *fourth* step, individuals learn a new set of coping statements to communicate to themselves. The therapist helps them generate these alternative statements and substitute them for the previous list of negative ones. Once again, the coping statements are generated for use before, during, and after the communication event (see step 4 of Box 10.3). The trainer encourages everyone to replace their entire repertoire of negative expectancies and evaluations with positive, self-directed statements. Rather than emphasizing the negative aspects of their performances, they learn to attend to the positives.

Finally, the *fifth* step of cognitive restructuring requires that individuals practice the new coping statements. The trainer points out that given the number of years the subjects have been rehearsing negative self-statements, they should not realistically expect to replace them immediately with positive ones. Old habits are hard to break. A whole new tool kit of coping statements has to be developed, memorized, and made available for immediate recall when the occasion demands. Eventually, these coping statements become automatic and help subjects reduce communication anxieties. This kind of automated behavior is common in such physical tasks as driving, typing, reading, and playing tennis, in which, over time, we have learned not to monitor every move we make. Our responses to communication situations can also be reduced to this level by appropriate cognitive restructuring.

Like SD, cognitive restructuring has a record of success in dealing with communication

BOX 10.3   *A Closer Look*

Cognitive Restructuring

What are the steps in cognitive restructuring? These four steps are outlined here:

Step 1: Introduction

The principles of cognitive restructuring are explained to subjects. The trainer explains that subjects' apprehensions and fears about public speaking are learned and can be unlearned.

Step 2: Identify Negative Self-Statements

Before Speech

- My topic is so boring. Why did I pick it?

- I know I'll forget my second major point.

- No one will like me or my speech.

During Speech

- I can see that no one likes what I'm saying.

- My hands are all sweaty. Everyone can see how nervous I am.
- They don't think I'm funny. I'm doomed!

After Speech

- I blew it.

- I can't do it again.

- I was as bad as I thought I was going to be.

Step 3: Identify Errors in Logic

- Topics are inherently boring. I will make this one interesting.
- I have a notecard with all my major points listed.

- People generally like me; they'll like what I have to say, too.

- I'm overgeneralizing; of course, someone will like it.
- Sure, they're sweating, but no one will even notice.

- Not everyone will die of laughter, but I'm sure I can get most of them to smile.

- I did it, didn't it? I gave my speech.
- Of course I can. That's why I'm taking this course—to learn how to give a speech.
- The truth is, I'm never as bad as I imagine I'm going to be. I didn't throw up; I didn't fall down; and I'm still alive.

Step 4: Learn New Coping Statements

- I chose my topic carefully. People in my audience will be interested in it.
- I've rehearsed my speech over and over. I'll remember all my main points.
- My audience will love me—and they'll love my speech, too.

- Most of my audience is interested; they appreciate what I'm saying.
- I am a little nervous: no one seems to notice it but me.
- Nearly everyone in the audience laughed or grinned when I delivered that funny line.

- I did a good job. I did a great job!
- I'm looking forward to my next speech so I can do an even better job.
- I did very well—better than I expected.

Step 5: Practice

This final step is often overlooked, and yet it can't be more important! Subjects must rehearse over and over the positive self-statements that they generated in step 4. In this way, subjects are more likely to recall positive rather than negative statements when they need them most—during apprehensive moments.

apprehension. Over and over again, we find that people's apprehensions toward communicating are reduced significantly with this technique. The emphasis of the treatment program, however, should be on the coping statements themselves and the practice of those statements, rather than understanding the principles. Mere insight into the negative self-statements is insufficient and can even serve to increase anxieties simply by giving excessive attention to the problem rather than to the solution.

Skills Training

The third and final method of reducing communication apprehension is **skills training.** It differs sharply from the other treatment techniques. The major difference is in the assumptions underlying the procedure. Rather than assuming our apprehensions lead to problems in communicating successfully with others, skills training reverses the causal sequence. It assumes that people's skills limitations in communicating influence their apprehension levels. That is, proponents of this technique argue that a primary cause of fears of communicating is a deficit in skills. Gerald Phillips, the leading spokesperson for this mode of treatment, reasons that some people develop apprehensions partly because they find themselves inept in communication situations.[41] In other words, they have good and sufficient reasons for feeling anxious: They just do not know how to communicate effectively. Once they learn how to perform successfully, their apprehensions will be reduced. Thus, training programs based on these assumptions are designed to teach appropriate and effective communication skills.

When skills training is used to help reduce public speaking anxieties, the usual approach is to expose speakers first to lectures, readings, and discussions of important public speaking concepts and principles. This exposure is typically followed by some form of rehearsal or performance of the principles studied. Speakers are encouraged to practice their new communi-

cation behaviors in front of an audience. Practice is seen as the key to success.

Early in this chapter it was maintained that practice does not always make perfect, yet the popular skills training method holds that it does. There is little doubt that training in skills can result in learning more effective techniques and strategies for communicating in various settings. However, the degree to which it specifically reduces apprehension is another matter. The fact is, there is less agreement on this issue, and research evidence on the effects of skills training on apprehension remains equivocal. There are many clear instances where, with specific training, amateur speakers have learned the requisite communication skills to become effective—and thus less anxious—public speakers.[42] If your own anxiety about public speaking stems from not knowing how to prepare and deliver a speech, skills training should help reduce your apprehension a great deal.

Nevertheless, there are people who have learned exactly how to perform the necessary public speaking skills, but whose apprehension continues to interfere with their ability to give a talk. The source of their apprehension, then, is not a deficit in skills but some other anxiety producing cause. In other words, skills training sometimes reduces apprehension and sometimes it doesn't. Compared to SD and cognitive restructuring, skills training alone is probably the least effective approach to reducing apprehension. A recent evaluation of all of these methods reveals that a combination of all three is more effective than any single treatment.[43]

Chapter Review

- Some individuals suffer from a chronic communication apprehension trait; others tend to be low in that apprehension. Those high in apprehension are often shy and withdrawn; they seek occupations that demand little interaction with others, and they prefer quiet evenings at home with family and friends. In contrast, people who are low in communication apprehension are likely to be open and talkative, to choose careers that require interaction with the public, and to look forward to parties and large get-togethers.

- For many people, apprehension is only temporary. Contextual factors that can temporarily affect our ability to communicate include unfamiliarity, dissimilarity, novelty, formality, subordinate status, conspicuousness, excessive attention from others, evaluation, and previous failure.

- Those who are chronically apprehensive differ in their socialization and learning histories from those who are not. According to social learning theory, individuals who are truly apprehensive acquired their anxieties by adopting the fears and behaviors of models that were significant to them in their early social development. Reinforcement theory explains apprehension by suggesting that those high in the trait may have tried a variety of responses in social encounters that failed or were not reinforced.

- People respond differently to individuals who are characteristically high in communication apprehension. Apprehensive people are often regarded as aloof, disinterested, and uncaring. These negative impressions influence their experiences in academic, social, and work situations. In contrast, people low in communication anxiety are perceived as friendly, industrious, and warm, which gives them advantages in the classroom, at work, and in social life.

- A number of treatment programs are available to reduce communication apprehension. The most successful programs include systematic desensitization (SD), cognitive restructuring, and skills training. The SD method reduces communication apprehension through muscle relaxation techniques. Cognitive restructuring changes or modifies beliefs about the particular communication event and substitutes positive self-statements for negative ones. Skills training recommends instruction and practice in communication skills.

Key Terms

communication apprehension

trait (personality)

social learning theory

reinforcement learning theory

resiliency factor

anomie (personal)

learned helplessness

stage fright

skills training

systematic desensitization (SD)

cognitive restructuring

Notes

1. A number of studies indicate that skills training alone fails to reduce fears about communicating. If these fears aren't addressed and alleviated, performance may continue to suffer. See: Dwyer, K. K. (2000). The multidimensional model: Teaching students to self-manage high communication apprehension by self-selecting treatments. *Communication education, 49*, 72–71. For a more detailed review of relevant research, see: Allen, M., Hunter, J. E., & Donahue, W. A. (1989). Meta-analysis of self-report data on the effectiveness of public speaking anxiety treatment techniques. *Communication education, 38*, 54–76.

2. For a comprehensive review of studies, see: Daly, J. A., & McCroskey, J. C. (Eds.). (1997). *Avoiding communication: Shyness, reticence and communication apprehension*, 2nd ed. Cresskill, NJ: Hampton Press.

3. Ibid.

4. Ibid., pp. 13–38.

5. McCroskey, J. C. (1977). Oral communication apprehension: A summary of recent theory and research. *Human communication research, 4*, 78–96; McCroskey, J. C. (1982). Oral communication apprehension: A reconceptualization. In M. Burgoon (Ed.), *Communication yearbook 6* (pp. 136–170). Beverly Hills, CA: Sage.

6. McCroskey, 1982, Oral communication, pp. 142–143; McCroskey, J. C., Richmond, V.P., & Stewart, R. A. (1986). *One on one: The foundations of interpersonal communication* (pp. 41–42). Englewood Cliffs, NJ: Prentice-Hall.

7. Duck, S. (1986). *Human relations: An introduction to social psychology* (p. 19). Beverly Hills, CA: Sage; McCroskey, Richmond, & Stewart, *One on one*, pp. 41, 48.

8. McCroskey makes a distinction between communication competence (knowing and understanding the appropriate behaviors to engage in) and communication performance or skill (being able to adequately perform those behaviors). He argues that even competent communicators can be apprehensive about interacting with others. For a more intensive explanation of this distinction, see: McCroskey, J. C. (1984). The communication apprehension perspective. In Daly & McCroskey, *Avoiding communication*, pp. 13–38.

9. Ibid., pp. 14–22; McCroskey, Richmond, Stewart, *One on one*, pp. 49–58.

10. Hilgard, E. R., Atkinson, R. C., & Atkinson, R. L. (1975). *Introduction to psychology*, 6th ed., p. 368. New York: Harcourt Brace Jovanovich.

11. The seminal work on the nature and origins of personality traits is: Allport, G. W. (1937). *Personality: A psychological interpretation*. New York: Henry Holt. See especially chap. 11, A theory of traits, and chap. 12, The nature of traits, pp. 286–342.

12. See, for example: Rumbough, T.B. (2000). The effects of impromptu speech exercises in reducing trait and situational communication apprehension. *New Jersey Journal of Communication 7*, 2, 206–215.

13. McCroskey, 1982, Oral communication, p. 164; McCroskey, Richmond, & Stewart, *One on one*, pp. 58–63.

14. Between 1970 and 1980 alone, over 200 reported studies examined the causes and effects of communication apprehension and related constructs. For extensive reviews of these, see: McCroskey, 1982, Oral communication, pp. 136–170; Richmond, V. P. (1984). Implications of quietness: Some facts and speculations.

In Daly & McCroskey, *Avoiding communication*, pp. 145–156. In addition, a complete bibliographic listing of relevant studies is available in: Payne, S. K., & Richmond, V. P. (1984). A bibliography of related research and theory. In Daly & McCroskey, *Avoiding communication*, pp. 247–294.

15. McCroskey, Richmond, & Stewart, *One on one*, pp. 49–50.

16. This concept had its roots more than two millennia ago in Plato's "Allegory of the Cave," set forth in his *Republic*. In more modern form it was developed as a specific principle of human behavior by W. I. Thomas (1923) in *The unadjusted girl*. New York: The Social Science Research Council. A summary can be found in Coser, L. A., and Rosenberg, B. (1964) *Sociological theory: A book of readings* (2nd ed., pp. 233–235). New York: Macmillan.

17. For a discussion of alternative interpretations of the causes of communication apprehension, see: Beatty, M. J., & Friedland, M. H. (1990). Public speaking state anxiety as a function of selected situational and dispositional variables. *Communication Education, 38*, 142–147; and Beatty, M. J., Balfantz, G. L., & Kuwabara, A. Y. (1989). Trait-like qualities of selected variables assumed to be transient causes of performance state anxiety. *Communication Education, 38*, 277–289.

18. Buss, A. H. (1980). *Self-consciousness and social anxiety.* San Francisco: Freeman; McCroskey, Richmond, & Stewart, *One on one*, pp. 56–58.

19. Many approaches and explanations have been advanced to account for the origin of communicator traits. This focus of research has produced a number of models of the origins of communication apprehension. For example, see: Beatty, M. J., & Valencic, K. M. (2000). Context-based apprehension versus planning demands: A communibiological analysis of anticipatory public speaking anxiety. *Communication Education, 49*, 1, 58–71.

20. For a general explanation of the principles of operant conditioning or reinforcement theory, see: Skinner, B. F. (1957). *Verbal behavior.* New York: Appleton, Century Crofts.

21. For a brief but comprehensive review of the origins and nature of learning theories and their relationship to both socialization and communication, see: DeFleur, M. L., & Ball-Rokeach, S. (1989). *Theories of mass communication* (5th ed., pp. 174–181, 212–219). White Plains, NY: Longman.

22. Bandura, A. (1977). *Social learning theory.* Englewood Cliffs, NJ: Prentice-Hall.

23. Beatty, M. J., Plax, T. G., & Kearney, P. (1985). Reinforcement vs. modeling theory in the development of communication apprehension: A retrospective analysis. *Communication Research Reports, 2,* 80–85.

24. For a general explanation of the principles of operant conditioning or reinforcement theory, see: Skinner, B. F. (1957). *Verbal behavior.* New York: Appleton-Century-Crofts. For a discussion linking reinforcement theory to the development of communication apprehension more specifically, see: McCroskey, *Communication apprehension perspective*, pp. 22–30; McCroskey, 1982, *Oral communication*, pp. 153–155.

25. Beatty, Plax, & Kearney, Reinforcement vs. modeling, pp. 80–85; Daly, J. A., & Friedrich, G. (1981). The development of communication apprehension: A retrospective analysis of contributory correlations. *Communication Quarterly, 29,* 243–255.

26. One of the problems of such operant explanations is that they give little credit to the rational abilities of human beings to engage in analysis, planning, insight, and other thought processes. As we have explained in earlier chapters, human beings are able to use language as a basis for such rational and analytic mental activity. Psychologists, seeking universal laws of learning that apply to all organisms, have generally been reluctant to bring uniquely human mental processes into their learning theories.

27. The term *anomie* was first introduced into the analysis of social life by Emile Durkheim at the end of the 19th century. See: Durkheim, E. (1951). *Suicide: A study of sociology* (J. A. Spaulding, Trans., and G. Simpson, Eds.). New York: Free Press. (First published in French in 1897.)

28. Early research on learned helplessness examined dogs' responses after inconsistent or ran-

dom rewards and punishments were applied to their behaviors. After trying out a variety of behaviors, the dogs eventually gave up responding altogether and, instead, retreated to a corner. See: Seligman, M. F. (1975). *Helplessness: On depression, development and death*. San Francisco: Freeman. For a more intensive application of learned helplessness to communicate apprehension development, see: McCroskey, Communication apprehension perspective, pp. 26–30.

29. Daly, J. A., & Stafford, L. (1984). Correlates and consequences of social communicative anxiety. In Daly & McCroskey, *Avoiding communication*, pp. 125–144; Payne & Richmond, *A bibliography*, pp. 247–294; Richmond, Communication apprehension perspective, pp. 145–156.

30. McCroskey, Richmond, & Stewart, *One on one*, pp. 63–66.

31. See, for example: Myers, S.A., & Rocca, K. A. (2001). Perceived instructor argumentativeness and verbal aggressiveness in the college classroom: Effects on student perceptions of climate, apprehension and state motivation. *Western Journal of Communication, 65*, 2, 113–137.

32. Payne & Richmond, *A bibliography*, pp. 297–294.

33. Ayers, J., et al, (1998). Communication apprehension and employment interviews. *Communication Education, 47*, 1, 1–17.

34. For a review of the research that examines the impact of communication apprehension on job satisfaction and other work-related variables, see: Richmond, V. P. (1984). Implications of quietness: Some facts and speculations. In Daly & McCroskey, *Avoiding communication*, pp. 153–155.

35. Bippus, A. M., & Daly, J. A. (1999). What do people think causes stage fright? Naive attributions about the reasons for public speaking anxiety, *Communication Education, 48*, 1, 63–72.

36. Friedrich, G., & Goss, B. (1984). Systematic desensitization. In Daly & McCroskey, *Avoid-*

ing communication, pp. 173–187; McCroskey, J. C. (1970). The effect of systematic desensitization on speech anxiety. *Speech Teacher, 19*, 32–36.

37. McCroskey, J. C. (1972). The implementation of a large-scale program of systematic desensitization for communication apprehension. *Speech teacher, 21*, 255–264.

38. Kelly, L. & Keaton, J. A. (2000). Treating communication anxiety: Implications of the communibiological paradigm. *Communication Education, 49*, 1, 45–57.

39. Fremouw, W. J. (1984). Cognitive-behavioral therapies for modification of communication apprehension. In Daly & McCroskey, *Avoiding communication*, p. 210. For a more detailed description of the steps involved in cognitive restructuring, see: Fremouw, W. J., & Scott, M. D. (1979). Cognitive restructuring: An alternative method for the treatment of communication apprehension. *Communication Education, 28*, 129–133.

40. See, for example: Messman, S. J. & Jones-Corley, J. (2001). Effects of communication environment, immediacy, and communication apprehension on cognitive and affective learning. *Communication Monographs, 68*, 2, 184–200.

41. Phillips, G. M. (1977). Rhetoritherapy versus the medical model: Dealing with reticence. *Communication Education, 26*, 34–43; see also the review by: Kelly, L. (1984). Social skills training as a mode of treatment for social communication problems. In Daly & McCroskey, *Avoiding communication*, pp.189–207.

42. Kelly, Social skills, pp. 201–205.

43. A recent analysis comparing the effectiveness of the three methods in treating public speaking anxiety reveals the relative superiority of both SD and cognitive restructuring over the more popular (but also effective) skills training. For further information, see: Allen, Hunter, & Donahue, Meta-analysis on public speaking anxiety treatment.

Influencing Others

At first, defense attorney Elva Garcia had been hesitant to represent Martin Symington because his situation looked like an open-and-shut case. Finally, she had agreed to do so, and as the trial approached, she had been working on her presentation of evidence to the jury for days. From the outset she was determined to get a "not guilty" verdict if it was at all possible.

Martin was charged with driving while intoxicated and with leaving the scene of an accident after injuring a child—a serious felony. The tough part of the case was that Martin had clearly been drunk when the police arrested him about two hours after the accident and several miles away. Not only had someone written down his license number as he left the scene, but the prosecution had the evidence of the breath test. It showed a level of alcohol well over the legal limit.

Martin claimed that he was not drunk when it happened and that he thought he had hit a dog. It was a tough neighborhood, he said, and he was afraid of what might happen if he stopped. He had no idea, he claimed, that he had hit a child. His story was that he had been so shaken by the idea of hurting someone's pet, like his own dog George, that he had stopped for drinks, a couple of miles farther on, to calm his nerves before driving home. He claimed the police had arrested him just as he was unlocking the car door after he left the bar.

Elva knew it was going to be difficult to sell that whole line of defense to the jury. It would seem like a phony story he had cooked up. Even though she believed Martin, when she had checked it out no one at the bar could remember him, and the bartender had left town. It did not look very promising.

Step by step, however, Elva questioned the witnesses as the trial began. She got the police officer to admit that the blood alcohol test had not been completed until more than two hours had passed after the accident. The fact that he was drunk at the time of the test, Elva told the jury, did not mean he had been intoxicated at the time of the accident. Furthermore, leaving the scene after striking someone's dog in a tough neighborhood, she argued, was an understandable, and even rational, decision. She skillfully reminded the jury of the principle of innocent until proved guilty; of the legal concept of criminal intent (which was absent in this case); and that proof could not be based on guesses, assumptions, or mere conjunction of circumstances advanced by the prosecutor.

After two hours of deliberation, the jury filed back into the courtroom. The judge asked the jury if they had reached a verdict. Then he asked Martin to stand. Both Elva and Martin nervously faced the jury box. "We the jury," declared the foreman, "find the defendant, Martin Robert Symington, not guilty!"

Few of us will have to persuade a jury that a defendant is innocent or guilty of a serious crime. Yet, the process of getting other people to accept our ideas and conclusions, or get them to reach decisions and take actions that we desire is something central to all of our lives. Obviously, it is very important to understand this kind of communication. Sometimes we are like Elva Garcia, the lawyer, trying to influence others whose decisions are important to us. At other times, we are like members of the jury, being bombarded by claims and counterclaims as we try to sort out the truth. In both cases, whether we like it or not, we are participants in the process of *persuasion*.

This chapter examines that process—influencing others using various strategies of communication. It discusses how such influence takes place; the various kinds of messages that can be used to try to modify how people think, feel, or act; and some of the barriers encountered in persuading others to change. It also discusses strategies for resistance. As you will see, the basic principles on which persuasive communication is based are those that were outlined in Chapter 1 (in the linear and transactions models) and in discussions in other chapters.

The Importance of Persuasion in Everyday Life

One of the most frequent tasks we all face daily is to try to influence people's ideas, feelings, or actions—either by trying to get others to make a change in their thinking that seems desirable, or by influencing their actions in some way. In addition, we constantly receive other peoples' messages aimed at modifying our thinking or conduct. It is something with which all of us are only too familiar. Almost from the time we get up in the morning until we retire at night, various kinds of people, groups, and agencies try to get us to attend to messages urging us to buy some commercial product, favor a particular political candidate, support a cause, modify our health practices, donate to a charity, or change some other way that we think and act. Such efforts impinge on us from the worlds of advertising, politics, education, religion, and health care, to mention only a few sources.

In other words, persuasion is one of the most ubiquitous communication processes in modern life—so pervasive, in fact, that people have to develop "mental calluses"—to learn how to ignore and resist most such efforts. But some forms of such communication are beneficial. Persuasion for a variety of purposes is so critical to many of our social institutions that we could not continue our contemporary way of life without it. For instance, it is a basic part of government. Politicians use it in their campaigns for reelection and to establish support for legislative policies. Persuasion also plays a key role in religion, education, and public health. In short, it is widely found in virtually every aspect of life where someone wants to shape or modify the ideas, feelings, or actions of someone else in a specific way.

Many persuasive processes are associated with mass communications. Such efforts make use of intentionally constructed messages designed to influence people to modify their ideas or actions. We encounter them every time we view TV, listen to the radio, surf the Internet, read a newspaper, or glance through a magazine. However, there is another, less obvious kind of persuasion that is even more important in our society, and it is one that each of us must deal with directly every day. In almost every significant face-to-face human encounter, people initiate communication for the purpose of modifying the beliefs, attitudes, or behavior of someone else. The individual toward whom persuasive messages are directed may be a friend, neighbor, boss, professor, or family member. This kind of persuasion is attempted and accomplished, almost unnoticed, in many kinds of situations by individuals in all walks of life as they construct and present messages to one another for the purpose of influencing someone in some way. This chapter will focus on that type of persuasion.

Person-to-Person Persuasion

The persuasion that occurs in everyday social interaction is a complex communication process. For example, in a single day, we might need to coax a friend into loaning us a few dollars, convince our parents that they should not be concerned with our low grade in chemistry, talk our way out of a speeding ticket, and persuade an instructor to let us into a closed class. At first glance, the goals involved in these influence attempts, and the persuasive communication process required to achieve them, all seem quite different, and, in fact, there are differences. However, on closer analysis, it becomes clear that they all have a great deal in common.

To look more closely at person-to-person persuasion, let's examine a situation in which an individual constructs and presents messages to another person in an attempt to achieve influence, and in which the second party responds by changing views, feelings, or actions.

Tony was upset with the D he got on his history test. He knew that he didn't do well on essay exams. However, he felt that his answer to the question about the factors that brought about World War I contained all the major points Professor Cheng had presented in her lectures and had mentioned when she discussed the test in class. If he could talk her into just a few more points for that answer, he thought to himself, his test grade would become a C. Then he would not have an overall D going into the final. (Moreover, it would be worth the effort to avoid having to explain such a low grade to his parents.) He decided to make an appointment to try to persuade Professor Cheng. He knew he could be pretty convincing and felt it was worth a try.

Tony appeared at Professor Cheng's office at the appointed time. He was dressed neatly and had rehearsed all the points and arguments he was going to use to present his case. He felt he had a good chance. When she smiled and invited him to sit down and explain what he had in mind, his spirits rose.

He began his presentation by claiming that she really had not read his answer to the one question carefully enough. (He knew this was a form of aggression but thought it would place him in a strong position and her on the defensive.) Then, to soften the attack, Tony outlined how really interested he was in the subject matter of her course and how much he enjoyed her lectures. (This, he knew, was flattery, but he thought most people liked it.) He then explained with great sincerity how hard he had studied for the examination. (This, he believed, would arouse her sympathy.) Tony concluded by explaining to Professor Cheng how badly he needed the grade. He pointed out that, because of personal problems he had earlier, his overall GPA was quite low and that he was working hard to raise it. If she did not give him a C for the course, he might have to leave school. (This, Tony felt, would make her feel guilty.)

Professor Cheng listened carefully and then went over his written answer to the test question. She asked him to show her how he had addressed each of the major issues. She also asked a few questions, all of which were about the specific content of his answers. Then, for a time, she just sat there, looking at him a little strangely and drumming her fingers on her desk. Tony felt a growing fear that his effort to persuade her had bombed. But then, to his surprise, she said, "Well, Tony, I see that you really did include all five of the major points in your answer. I think that you have a good case, and I will give you an additional five points on your grade for the examination."

Tony could hardly contain himself; he left her office grinning. "It worked," he said to himself. "She really is a sucker for a sob story. I laid on aggression, flattery, sympathy, and guilt and got her to change the grade. Wow, what a tear-jerker! I should have gotten an Academy Award."

As Tony was leaving, Professor Cheng thought, "What a con artist! He thought I would fall for his baloney about his burning interest in the course and how much he enjoys my lectures. His heart-wrenching story about how hard he had studied and how he might have to leave school was too much. I really had to try not to laugh." Professor Cheng smiled to herself and thought, "In spite of all his B.S., the fact is that his answer really was more complete than I first thought, and it did merit an additional five points."

Did persuasion take place? Clearly, the grade was changed, and Tony's effort was successful in that sense. Yet, somehow it doesn't seem that Tony's messages really *caused* Professor Cheng to comply with his goal. There are, in fact, two different interpretations of what actually happened during the encounter: One is that Tony's cleverly constructed appeals based on interest, admiration, hard work, and deep need swayed Professor Cheng to comply. The other is that she was unmoved by Tony's appeals and that she had actually persuaded herself to make the change because of the factual content of his test answer. Which of these interpretations is correct *depends on how one defines persuasion*. In fact, the major lesson to be derived from the little drama is that there are two ways to go in formulating a definition. Persuasion can be viewed either as a one-way, that is linear, process or as an interactive exchange between the parties.

Linear versus Transactional Views of Persuasion

Earlier in this century, when research on the process first started, persuasion was something that one person "did to" another. That is, a person wanting to persuade another took an active role and used "tools of persuasion"—messages expressing *appeals* that could modify the thinking or action of a passive receiver. Later, researchers began to realize that every person brings to every act of communication (whether persuasive or not) all the personal attributes that were described in previous chapters. They saw that these attributes play a critical part in forming the meanings people construct in response to an incoming message. These two views of the persuasion process are obviously very different: One is a kind of linear "magic bullet" interpretation, whereas the other is consistent with the simultaneous transactions model.

Persuasive messages as "magic bullets." In this view, the message transmitted by the sender

An older method of persuasion used simple messages that worked like "magic bullets." Their appeals were designed to capture attention by arousing significant and persuasive meanings that would then trigger direct action. This poster, from World War I, was thought to be very effective in persuading young men and women to volunteer for military service.

in the persuasion process is seen as "aimed at" the person selected as the "target." The components of the message are designed as persuasive verbal projectiles—striking the receiver and having an effect. That is, a source organizes a message with clever words, arguments, and appeals, then aims these at the person to be persuaded. Once the bullets arrive, the receiver undergoes the alterations desired by the source. Thus, the message organization and appeals are what cause a change of belief, attitude, or behavior. In this perspective, the change of grade made by Professor Cheng would be seen as a direct result of Tony's clever transmission of messages with meanings of aggression, flattery, sympathy, and guilt.

Persuasion as transactional communication. A second interpretation of the way in which persuasion works, and thus the manner in which it needs to be defined, is based on the other view of what happened between Tony and Professor Cheng. That is, he presented his messages, including all his carefully constructed appeals and arguments, and she listened carefully to what he was saying. However, in the end, she herself decided to make the change that Tony desired. She did not do so because of his clever magic bullets but because of her own decisions about the meaning of the situation and the response she should give.

This interpretation of persuasion indicates that the receiver of the message plays as active a part in achieving whatever changes take place as does the source or sender. It requires that persuasion be defined as a *transaction* that occurs between two parties, rather than simply as a one-way action of one individual firing verbal bullets at another so as to achieve desired change. This interpretation does not mean that the organization, appeals, images, and other features of persuasive messages are unimportant—indeed, they may have a significant influence on the transaction.

Most communication scholars now subscribe to this transactional view of the persuasion process. Because of the importance of persuasion, and the power inherent in the ability to influence others, researchers continue to search for understanding as to how the process takes place. Every aspect or factor in the process has been considered, even such things as the nasality of a voice and how it affects persuasion.[1] Other studies have investigated the "third-person" effect, or the degree to which an individual believes that he or she is less susceptible to persuasive communications than other people.[2] However, the heaviest emphasis in the search remains on the so-called tools of persuasion—just the right kinds of symbols, images, and combinations of words that can arouse emotions, shape beliefs, sway attitudes, and change actions as the receivers of the message play their part in the transaction.

The fact is, this kind of persuasion can work! Messages have been designed to which people have responded with great enthusiasm. This persuasion strategy has led large numbers of people at various times to buy things, vote for people, or take other actions that someone has wanted.[3] Sometimes, however, the strategy fails, and when it does no one is quite sure why. Nevertheless, given the potential power at stake, it is little wonder the search for the "magic bullets" that will work—the effective appeals, message organizations, and other persuasive tactics continues with great enthusiasm.

A Formal Definition of Persuasion

In bringing these many ideas together, persuasion can be defined in a way that is entirely consistent with the two models of human communication set forth in previous chapters; that is, although linear processes are involved, both parties engage in simultaneous transactions and play active parts.

What makes persuasion distinct from other communication transactions is that change takes place in the person interpreting the message. That change may be precisely what the originator of the message intended, or it may not, depending on the way the interpretation is constructed. However, if the desired change is in fact achieved, **persuasion** can be defined as *a communicative transaction in which a source constructs and transmits messages designed to influence a receiver's constructions of meanings in ways that will lead to change (desired by the source) in the receiver's beliefs, attitudes, or behavior*. If the attempt fails, the message is then just another piece of the vast communication clutter all of us experience every day.

As this definition implies, messages from a source can be very important, even though persuasion is a transactional process. A sender's messages can bring facts, arouse feelings, and present logical arguments that lead receivers to form new conclusions. Sometimes they do not, and even if they do, they may not do so in ways intended by the sender. However, if no transaction takes place, no change will occur. In the example of Tony and Professor Cheng, a transaction did take place that resulted in a change. Without a visit from Tony, she never would have awarded him additional points. Even though his linear-type message structure and appeals fell flat, she did review the situation and raise his grade, and in that limited sense it was a consequence of the transaction.

Alternative Methods for Achieving Influence

It is not difficult to understand why people try to persuade others: They want them to comply with or conform to some desired change that is the objective of the persuasive attempt. Achieving compliance or conformity means getting someone to hold certain beliefs, have particular feelings, or engage in specific actions that seem desirable to the person originating the message. By looking at several important kinds of situations, it is possible to see how people modify their ideas, feelings, or actual behavior as a result of persuasive communication. (Box 11.1 overviews reasons for people's compliance with persuasion.)

One kind of compliance results from *coercive* messages, in which people may have little choice but to change their behavior. A second and very different basis for compliance occurs because messages arouse meanings of *sociocultural expectation*. That is a fancy way of saying that people will change in order to conform to some sort of group norm or standard and behave in ways expected of them. A third kind of change comes about because of *cognitive reorganization*. What this means is that those receiving the message change their way of thinking about the topic of the persuasion.

Coercion

The term **coercion** refers to compelling others to do something, or restraining them from action, by threatening them with undesirable

BOX 11.1　　🔍　*A Closer Look*

Why People Comply with Persuasive Messages

- People comply because a coercive message forces compliance.
- People comply because group expectations influence compliance.
- People comply because a persuasive message changes the way people think.

consequences. Many kinds of goals are pursued by using the threat of force and bodily harm to alter behavior. At one extreme is the threatening statement of the mugger, who, with knife at throat, simply says, "Give me what I want or I will kill you!" That message, of course, can be very persuasive! In fact, this type of persuasion fits the magic bullet definition very well. The statements of the sending person directly and immediately cause the receiver to behave in the manner demanded.

At the same time, coercive messages that threaten force or bodily harm to modify another's behavior do not really fit with most people's idea of persuasion. The process implies a much more subtle communication in which the individual is led to make changes by some kind of clever message. For that reason, no further discussion is included regarding physical coercion as a form of persuasion by which one person controls another's behavior.

Social Expectations

The organizing factors of all kinds of human social behavior (including communication) in group settings are the kinds of shared rules referred to in Chapter 8 as norms, roles, ranks, and controls. These general concepts are the heart of the sociocultural persuasion that is based on clarifying **social expectations.** (Simply put, group members are expected to follow the rules.) The key here is that persuasive messages can define the kind of behavior that is permit-

ted and expected, or discouraged and even punished, by members of a group. Such messages can be very effective in getting people to conform. This social expectations approach to persuasion is widely used in our multicultural society for the purpose of getting people from all backgrounds to behave according to some set of social rules.

Of particular importance is that such sociocultural persuasion can be an effective strategy in getting people to change their behavior in relatively difficult ways. People value their memberships in groups and want to be accepted by others. For this reason, the compelling nature of social expectations can sometimes bring about changes in people's behavior that probably would not occur as a result of lectures, pleas, appeals, or other conventional persuasive strategies. For example, people who urgently feel the need to lose weight often go to commercial groups that specialize in persuading people to drop pounds. Part of their process is to get such individuals on a weight-reduction diet and perhaps into some form of exercise. These are truly difficult goals. The task of convincing them to follow such rules is a classic exercise in sociocultural persuasion. It works something like the following:

> Lois has been seriously overweight for a number of years. She hates being fat and has tried many kinds of exercises and diets. Most importantly, she understands that being overweight can have serious consequences for her health. Numerous people have lectured her about her weight and have tried to get her to reduce. Over the years she lost a few pounds from time to time, but they always seemed to come back. As something of a last resort, Lois decided to go to Pounds Ltd., an organization specializing in helping people with weight reduction. She listened to their sales pitch, read their literature, and with the tantalizing vision of a slim figure to come, she paid her (rather substantial) fee. She started preparing her meals according to the plan and ate them without cheating, even though at first they left her hungry and unsatisfied.

A few days later, at her first Pounds Ltd. group meeting, Lois had to get on a scale and be weighed by one of the counselors. She was embarrassed when the trim young counselor said that she tipped the scales at 183 pounds. She was told that her weight would be recorded again next week. Then the counselors and clients held a group discussion of different problems people were having in managing their eating. As part of the meeting, each person's weight was revealed to the others. For each participant, a history of where they had started was summarized along with details about their present weight. Those who were success stories were vigorously applauded. Even those who were still new to the program but who had lost a pound or two were given a round of applause. Those who had gained were given encouragement and sympathy—along with looks of pity, she thought.

In the weeks that followed, Lois had mixed feelings about the program. She did meet some nice people who were struggling with her same problems. She also admired those who had been fat and were now trim. It gave her hope. However, it was humiliating to have her weight revealed publicly. Most of all, she was in constant fear that she would not lose weight during the week and that she would be the object of pity when her weekly weigh-in was announced.

As the weeks turned to months, however, Lois did lose weight. Within four weeks she was down to 170; in six months she weighed 150. She stayed with the program and finally broke the 130 mark in 16 months. She began to feel better and be asked out on dates. She had become accustomed to the smaller meals and felt that she soon would get down to a normal weight for her height. Perhaps the most helpful thing about the program was the people she had met and their joint determination to get rid of their excess pounds.

What are the factors of persuasion here? Clearly, losing a lot of weight is a difficult goal and a long-range process. Equally clearly, motivating a person to do that takes far more than persuasive pep talks or lecturing by those in charge of the program. One key factor in this situation is the negative evaluation (norm) existing in society concerning being fat. That shared belief in its negative assessment was most significant in getting Lois into Pounds Ltd. in the first place. Once she was participating, however, the functioning of the group itself played a central part in persuading her to continue. One factor was the *norm* constantly apparent within the group—defining weight loss as beneficial and approved, and weight gain as harmful and deviant.

In addition, messages concerning *role definitions* within the group centered on personal responsibility for adherence to the diet and on continued weight reduction. When this role is played according to expectation, the applause received from the others is a well-appreciated social reward—a form of *social control*. Another social control is that failing to lose, or gaining on the weekly weight report, results in a significant negative sanction. Those who have achieved substantial weight loss are *ranked* much higher in prestige within the group than those who have yet to do so. They receive messages of deference and are envied for their accomplishment. Along with all these factors, there is the additional reward of forming friendships with others who are trying to cope with a similar problem.

Thus, the process of sociocultural persuasion based on social expectations is far more than simply a sender formulating a persuasive message and a receiver constructing some kind of meaning that will influence action. It is a complex process in which norms, roles, ranks, and social controls all play a part in defining what is acceptable versus what is deviant behavior.

Cognitive Reorganization

The commonsense view of how behavior is determined and how it can be changed goes something like this: We all have a mental organization of understandings, attitudes, feelings, beliefs, and preferences. This cognitive organization is what guides our decisions about acting. In other words, it is commonly assumed that mind controls action. From this assumption it follows that if mental organization (feelings, attitudes, and beliefs) can be changed—by gaining the attention of receivers to persuasive messages—then overt behavior will correspondingly be changed.

Although that is not a bad way of thinking about certain kinds of persuasion, the language is old-fashioned. Today these "mental" phenomena are discussed with greater precision in terms of *cognitive functioning*. This term broadly refers to what used to be called thinking, interpreting, and knowing. The related term, *cognitive organization,* refers to the structure or patterning of one's beliefs, attitudes, and values, as they exist "in our heads," so to speak. A third term, *cognitive processing,* refers to the way we perceive, interpret, remember, and recall some event, message, or situation as we observe it. These terms will be used in this chapter.

Cognitive organization (or structure) is important in discussing persuasion because many communication scholars assume that persuasive messages can alter the components of that organization. That is, they believe that carefully designed messages can change the way people think, believe, or feel about a topic. They assume that if such changes are achieved, they will alter the way they act toward the object of the communication. This has also long been an assumption made by advertisers.[4] Stated simply, this approach, which can be called the **psychodynamic strategy**, rests on the assumption that the route to achieving behavioral change lies in achieving **cognitive reorganization**. Sometimes it works, but sometimes it does not.

Constructing or reconstructing meanings. One important way in which cognitive organization can be influenced is by providing people with meanings for objects, situations, and events that they have to interpret and to which they must react or respond. This is most easily accomplished when the phenomena are unfamiliar. Through the clever use of symbols, message senders can sometimes get receivers to accept their desired meanings. Then, when those same receivers are called on to act toward whatever is at stake, those meanings can have an influence in determining what they will do.

The nature of meaning was discussed in Chapter 1 and is important in understanding the dynamics of influence, compliance, and change as these are achieved through the transmission of persuasive messages. The discussion of the meaning triangle in Chapter 2 showed that every symbol used in communication has associated with it, by conventional rules, both denotative meanings for the referent and a number of connotative meanings that are sometimes aroused. The important point here is that people trying to persuade others often make use of such connotative meanings to influence the interpretations that receivers make of a particular message.

In that way, a sender can control to some degree the constructions of meaning that will take place as receivers of a message take part in the communicative transaction. Just how cleverly people can influence the meanings of others can be illustrated by referencing an important historical event that took place back in 1989. It was a year of political turmoil and upheaval all over the world, but some of the most remarkable episodes were the massive demonstrations that occurred in the People's Republic of China as many thousands of people congregated and demonstrated in Tiananmen Square in Beijing.

Those demonstrations were protests over corruption and misconduct by officials in the Chinese government. The students who led the protests were demanding certain reforms of the existing system. They were certainly not advocating that the existing Chinese government based on communism be replaced by democratic institutions, modeled by the United States. At the same time, those student leaders urgently wanted international attention focused on their cause—particularly U.S. attention. They were afraid (with ample justification) that without this scrutiny from abroad the Chinese leadership would put down their demonstrations with military force, which has long been a traditional Chinese solution.

What did they do? Because leaders among the Chinese students understood very well the cognitive organization of the average U.S. citizen, they supplied the American public with a substantial number of televised symbols and images. They wanted to make sure that what the Americans saw on their TV sets would be completely familiar and acceptable. What they did was use a meaning-construction strategy designed to attract and hold the attention of Americans and to gain their sympathetic support.

To understand the strategy they used more fully, it must be kept in mind that the entire upheaval was, as previously indicated, a *Chinese* event. Its causes and solutions were firmly rooted in the problems and the system of that country. However, by carefully selecting and presenting symbols that had *powerful connotative meanings* for Americans, they were able to redefine it into terms that had special significance for the people of the United States.

How did they do this? They accomplished this goal by focusing on slogans, sayings, expressions, and symbols that are at the heart of American democratic values. Then they made sure these were presented to the American public by television, newspapers, and magazines that were trying to show what was going on in Beijing. For example, many signs and banners with slogans in English were paraded before television cameras, who obligingly focused on them. These placards and banners displayed messages with which Americans are deeply familiar—such as "Give me liberty or give me death!"—which is not exactly an ancient Chinese saying. Students were shown reciting the Declaration of Independence, or talking about the importance of "freedom of the press," along with other American favorites. A big statue was built—called the Goddess of Democracy. It was carefully modeled after the Statue of Liberty and it was conveniently located where the television cameras couldn't miss it. Thus, a barrage of Fourth of July Americanisms were used to give the events in Tiananmen Square a special connotative meaning for Americans who tuned in.

The fact is that those American icons have little meaning for the average Chinese citizen. Indeed, the vast majority neither understand English nor know anything about the history of the American Revolution. Few would recognize the Declaration of Independence if they heard it in their own language. These *Americana* had little to do with the cause of eliminating corruption in the Chinese government or the proposed reforms in the communist system—the issues that actually brought on the demonstrations in the first place.[5]

Although the demonstrations in Beijing ended in tragedy, crushed by the Chinese military, the purpose in using this example is not intended to be a criticism of either the demonstrations or the Chinese students involved. It was a very clever thing to do, and it clearly accomplished its objectives. Americans were genuinely sympathetic with those who led the protests and were deeply disturbed when they were put down by the Chinese authorities with a great deal of bloodshed. The purpose in citing the events at Tiananmen Square is simply that it provides a clear example of the meaning-construction strategy for redefining an event in terms that can be understood and approved by those to whom the messages were directed.

These same strategies of meaning construction and redefinition can be very effective at any level of communication and within and across different cultural groups. Watching commercials on TV can show how a mechanical object (an automobile) can be given new meanings of glamor, power, and sexiness by persuasive advertising. Observation of the tactics of an effective trial lawyer can show how a body of factual evidence can be given new meanings by questioning selectively, raising doubts, suggesting alternative interpretations, and so on. This is not to imply here that this strategy is based on untruths or deception. Rather, it is a process of establishing, extending, substituting, and stabilizing *meanings* that are associated with particular words, concepts, events, or situations.[6] (Box 11.2 reviews the process of cognitive reorganization.)

BOX 11.2 $\wp$ *A Closer Look*

The Process of Cognitive Reorganization

- Establish new meanings for particular objects, situations, and events.
- Extend old meanings for particular objects, situations, and events.
- Substitute new meanings for currently held meanings.
- Stabilize (or reinforce) currently held meanings.

Shaping or altering beliefs.   One of the most important parts of our cognitive structure (the way things are organized in our heads) are our beliefs. The term **beliefs** is so fundamental that it is not easily defined. In terms of the present discussion, a belief is a kind of statement of truth that an individual accepts about some object, situation, or event.

Each of us has thousands of such truth statements in memory, such as "the world is round," "the sun rises in the east," and "water runs downhill." But, for many objects or situations we have no statements. One strategy that is widely used in persuasion is to provide people with *preshaped* beliefs about events, issues, or situations where they have not yet formed any. Or, if they have, the strategy focuses on *modifying* the beliefs they already have but hold only slightly.

Some beliefs are simply factual—like the three examples listed above. They do not involve any kind of judgment (positive or negative) or imply any kind of emotional orientation on the part of the person holding the belief. Other beliefs are affectual. That is, they do have an evaluative or emotional quality that implies such feelings as like, dislike, acceptance, rejection, approval, or disapproval. For example, it is one thing to believe that San Francisco is a *large* city. It is and that is factually correct. Such a statement of truth about San Francisco

implies no evaluative judgment. However, it is quite another thing to believe that San Francisco is a *beautiful* city. This kind of belief does have an affective component. It is a statement of truth, to be sure, at least for the person holding the belief. More important, it reveals a positive affective orientation toward that particular city.

The psychodynamic strategy of shaping or altering beliefs focuses mainly on affective truth statements because they are closely linked to the kinds of actions often sought in persuasion—that is, accepting or rejecting something or acting positively or negatively toward it in some other way. Note that people who hold beliefs rarely make the distinction between factual and affective beliefs in their own minds. For a person who truly believes that Detroit is a mean city, the negative character of that belief is for that person simply a part of the statement of truth about that particular community. For him or her, it seems as correct as the belief that Detroit is a large city. In other words, our affective beliefs seem as valid and compelling to us as do those that incorporate only emotionally neutral facts.

The reason that altering beliefs is so often sought as a goal of psychodynamic persuasion is that beliefs—both factual and affective—are fundamental to us as guides to our actions. More than 2,000 years ago, Plato, in his "Allegory of the Cave," showed that if people believe a situation to be real, they will act as though it is real.[7] In the 1920s, Walter Lippman stated the principle in a much simpler way: The "pictures in our heads," he said, guide our actions toward things in "the world outside."[8]

That principle—that beliefs are guides to action—is amply illustrated thousands of times every day. People regularly punish others whom they believe to have violated the acceptable norms. Fistfights break out when one individual believes that another has insulted or ridiculed him, even if that was not the other's intent. Even more serious, every year some police officer regularly shoots an innocent person when he or she believes that the individual is going for a gun. In each of these cases, reality is not the basis of action; it is their *beliefs about reality*.

This link between beliefs and behavior provides the foundation for one of the most important assumptions underlying the entire field of persuasive communication: It is assumed that *persuasive messages can be designed to alter people's beliefs*—factual or affective—at least under some circumstances. If the messages do indeed achieve that objective, and people do modify their beliefs, then it follows that their actions may also change.

This assumption of a dynamic relationship between beliefs and action is the guiding principle of the psychodynamic strategies for influencing changes through cognitive reorganization. Stated in the simplest terms, messages that change beliefs, will then (presumably) serve to modify behavior.

Does such a persuasion strategy work? The answer is a hesitant yes, but only sometimes. Successful persuasion can often be an indirect, cumulative process that occurs over a long period of time. It seldom works dramatically in a quick and immediate sense (like a magic bullet). Many research studies have focused on this issue. How do people change beliefs through the use of persuasive message content? Traditionally, in the social sciences, changing people's beliefs has been seen as a *learning process*. Thus, belief changes have been brought about by lectures and exposure to training films, by group discussions, by asking people to read different kinds of materials, by having them listen to radio presentations, or by viewing material on videotape. Through any of these forms of communication, beliefs can be changed, but not easily. Relevant research on these issues will be reviewed in a later section.[9]

Creating or modifying attitudes. Most research on persuasion has focused not on beliefs, in the basic sense discussed previously, but on configurations or structures of beliefs that are called **attitudes**. The term *attitude* is very old, and it predates all the social sciences. It was adopted about a century ago by the social sciences from previous meanings. The word came into the English language during the early

1700s. Originally, it derived from the Latin words *aptitudinem* and *aptus*. When it became a part of both French and Italian during the 15th century, it was as an important term in the world of art and design meaning the *physical positioning* of an object in space. In England, in the 1830s, it became associated with the positioning of the mind. However, it did not become an important concept in the behavioral sciences until 1918, when it was used in its present form by W. I. Thomas and Florian Znaniecki to denote a person's affective or emotional beliefs about an object that bring about particular forms of action toward that same object.[10]

Today, the term *attitude* is perhaps the most widely used concept in the social sciences, and it has been studied in research for nearly a century. Unfortunately, during that long period it has been defined in dozens of different ways, providing many different interpretations of the term's meaning.[11] However, these controversies can be avoided by dealing with it in a way that is completely consistent with the previous discussion of beliefs and their relationship to behavior.

First, reject the notion that an attitude is some mysterious force that lies latent in your psyche and that becomes activated only when forming intentions to act. That is too complicated. A much simpler approach is to view attitudes as an extension of what has already been analyzed in the way of *beliefs*. That is, an attitude can be thought of as a package or configuration of beliefs of an evaluative or affective nature that a person has about some "object."

An attitude may be held about many kinds of "objects." An example would be a particular category of people. These evaluative beliefs about that object will be related to one another. For example, if a person believes certain people to be undesirable, he or she probably will also think that they are stupid, cruel, lazy, and immoral. Alternatively, if the person believes that category of people are attractive, he or she probably would also believe that they were smart, virtuous, hard-working, and trustworthy. Thus, the person has an interrelated set of affective beliefs about the attitude "object." When confronted with individual members of that category of people, either directly or indirectly, the person uses those affective beliefs to shape his or her thoughts or actions toward them.

How closely do people's actions match their beliefs? If one has a negative attitude toward some category of people, will that person act unfavorably toward the individuals in the category? The answer is "not always"! Common sense tells us that our behavior seldom takes place in a social vacuum. Furthermore, whatever or whoever is present in a situation of action can influence our behavior, regardless of our inner feelings. For example, we may feel negatively toward some topic. Perhaps we have a negative attitude toward dogs; but if we are among friends who own and love dogs, we may refrain from saying or doing anything that we know they would resent. Thus, although our negative attitude can increase the probability (the chances) that we will act negatively toward the object, various factors in our immediate situation of action can greatly reduce that probability.

Although this discussion gives a kind of commonsense explanation of what is meant by attitude, and the relationship of attitude to behavior, it is such an important term that it is necessary to set forth a carefully formulated definition. In this way, the part that attitudes can play in cognitive reorganization and behavioral change—using the pychodynamic strategy of persuasion—can be better understood.

Reaffirming that an attitude is a configuration of affective beliefs about an object is a good place to start. In the previous section, careful attention was given to the meaning of the term *belief* because it is so central to the meaning of attitude. Affective beliefs, as explained, are "truths" that people embrace—implying such feelings as good/bad, like/dislike, acceptance/avoidance, and approval/disapproval.

The attitude object (that we think about, evaluate, and respond to) can be almost anything. However, it is usually thought of as *general* rather than specific. That is, it is a broad topic or issue, as opposed to a narrowly focused concern. Examples are categories of people (like those who are addicted to drugs or those who litter beaches), policies (capital punishment or disarmament), practices (abortion or child abuse), or issues (animal rights or welfare reform). Social scientists do not normally use the term *attitude* for people's affective beliefs about very specific objects (like left-handed saxophone players who have blue eyes, or brown dogs with long ears).

Two additional features of an attitude must be a part of a formal definition. One of them is that attitudes are presumed to be a *relatively enduring* (long-lasting) part of a person's cognitive structure. Many are learned early in life, and they remain as a permanent part of the individual's psychological makeup. What this implies, of course, is that they are not easy to change. The second feature of attitudes is the assumption that they play a significant part in *shaping or determining actions* toward whatever is the object. This follows logically from the widely accepted principle that was set forth earlier—that beliefs shape actions. That is, if attitudes are interrelated organizations of beliefs, they should also provide a basis for influencing the ways we act—in a manner consistent with those beliefs. With these features in mind, *attitude* can be defined in a more formal way as *a relatively enduring organization of affective beliefs about some broad object (such as a policy, social category of people, or situation) that increases the probability that an individual will respond to that object in a manner consistent with those beliefs.*[12]

Where do attitudes come from? They are learned. Like beliefs of any kind, our attitudes are developed through experience. From the experiences we have with objects, people, and situations, we acquire complex patterns of interrelated affective beliefs that define our liking or disliking of those things. For example, we can develop a negative attitude toward the elderly by having a number of negative experiences with older people. These can then influence our behavior toward senior citizens.

As was suggested, when people talk about influencing others by using persuasive communication, they are typically talking about changing attitudes. It seems self-evident to many people that if a person's attitude toward a particular topic or object is changed, then corresponding changes in behavior will also take place. This is a very important issue.

The relationship between attitudes and behavior. Research on the relationship between attitudes and behaviors has been extensive.[13] For decades, researchers have continued to probe the question of whether or not attitudes are related to behavior.[14] Although there is a substantial controversy among researchers who continue to study this issue, there is general agreement that, in fact, there is often little direct association between attitudes and behavior in most real-life situations.[15]

Why, then, does such strong interest in this particular psychodynamic strategy continue? The answer is that the relationship between attitudes and behavior is not yet fully understood, and it is far too early to dismiss changing attitudes as a means of bringing about changes in behavior. A far better alternative is to ask what are the conditions under which attitudes and behavior are related, and what factors in a situation of action can either reduce or enhance this relationship? Social scientists first faced the reality of inconsistencies between attitudes and behaviors in the 1930s when an early study challenged the assumption of a direct relationship.[16] Prior to that a direct relationship was almost universally assumed.[17] However, investigations of the degree of correspondence between attitudes and behavior have shown that any number of situations can have an influence on that relationship. That is, if some factors are present, the link between attitudes and behavior may be strong indeed. If other factors are in the situation, the relationship may be weak or even nonexistent. What these statements imply is that the probability of acting in accord with one's attitude depends on the presence or absence of several limiting and facilitating factors.

Therefore, it is critical to have a solid understanding of such factors when attempting to manipulate behavior by changing attitudes.

There are three considerations that must be understood about the relationship between attitudes toward a topic and the probability of consistent behavior toward that same topic. Each must be considered in any communication strategy designed to change people's attitudes when making the assumption that their behavior will then be changed in a parallel way. These three considerations are topic importance, *social pressures*, and action constraints.[18] (See Box 11.3.)

One reason that attitude change may not necessarily lead directly to corresponding behavior change is that the topic may not be important to the person. Some topics for which we hold attitudes simply have very little influence on what we actually do. If a topic is not of much importance to us, our attitude toward it is not likely to be strongly held. In other words, it is relatively easy for someone to get us to change our attitudes toward topics that have no real consequences in our lives. Such topics could include political issues like programs for farm parity supports, campaign finance reform, or federal regulation regarding steel tariffs. Typically, young adults do not hold deeply entrenched views about such issues, and they seldom resist changing attitudes toward them. Furthermore, whatever their attitudes on such topics, they may have no relationship to their behavior if ever confronted with a need to act in some relevant way.

On the other hand, a variety of topics can be truly significant and consequential for a person. It is unlikely that behavior toward them will be easily changed by exposure to a few persuasive messages. For example, people are often deeply committed to their positions on such matters as abortion, genetically modified foods, capital punishment, using animals in experiments, and smoking.

For many people, the beliefs they hold about such topics are deeply entrenched. If this is the case, both their attitudes and behavior toward such topics are very difficult to change by any means. People work out their configuration of affective beliefs about such matters after long experience, and those patterns of convictions remain very durable. Having a firm attitudinal position on a controversial issue makes life easier. This is because decisions concerning the topic are uncomplicated. When such topics come up, people can simply respond with behavior consistent with their strongly held attitudes. There is no need to work it all out over and over again, with endless considerations of new facts and new appeals for change. In that sense, then, an entrenched and well-defined attitude toward a personally significant topic is efficient in providing immediate guidelines for action.

Another critical factor in shaping our overt and visible behavior is the pattern of **social pressures** we encounter in the situation of action. These are our needs and desires to comply with social rules for behavior that are expected

by others whose approval we seek. As indicated throughout this text, action and communication always take place in a context that includes a sociocultural situation and human relationships. Thus, what we say and what we do are usually observable by other people. The context of our actions then almost always includes rules for social behavior. (Remember how that worked in the example about overweight Lois and Pounds Ltd.) Thus, while attitudes are invisible inside heads, overt behavior is visible and therefore subject to scrutiny by others. This poses a set of social pressures on us that can cause attitudes and behavior toward the same topic to be very different (inconsistent).

Generally, then, the relationship between attitudes and behavior is unpredictable if that action takes place in a group context. If we know that the people in that context hold the same attitude and expect corresponding behavior, then there probably will be a close relationship. However, if people whose opinions we value would be appalled by our behavior if it were consistent with our privately held (but contrary) attitude, then it is entirely unlikely that the two will correspond.

To take a simple example, suppose that Jim, a college senior, came from a conservative business-owning family in which there has been a longstanding anti-union tradition. As a result of family discussions at home, Jim has held anti-union attitudes since childhood. At the home of Sandra, Jim's fiancée, however, her parents are not only union members, but her father is an officer in a large local union. Jim is really taken with Sandra, and he has visited with her parents several times. They like him. He certainly wants to be on their good side. Now suppose that Sandra's father invites Jim to accompany him to the union meeting one evening. What will happen? One scenario would be that Jim's attitude would guide his behavior and he would decline. Another would be that social pressures would prevail and Jim would accept the invitation so as to please Sandra and avoid a strained relationship with her parents. In other words, it would be difficult to predict whether his attitude and behavior would be consistent.

Each of us faces a diversity of such social pressures daily. They come from social expectations at work, at school, in family relationships, and so on. Regardless of our feelings, we may or may not act in accordance with our attitudes. The importance of the topic may carry the day, but social pressures in the context of action can have a strong influence on our behavior.

There are also many **nonsocial constraints** on our actions. That is, there can be occasions when people are inclined to act in accordance with their attitudes, and there are no social pressures to inhibit such behavior, but their actions do not correspond with their attitudes. One simple reason is that a number of physical and personal difficulties interfere with the action. They may be too busy or too lazy. Or, the act may be inconvenient, perhaps requiring traveling a long distance to perform it. The behavior may involve potential financial loss. There may be risks or unwanted trade-offs. The act may be physically difficult to perform. There may be no real opportunity, or the person may lack competence to engage in the behavior. Action constraints of this type can sharply reduce the consistency between attitude and action.

Understanding Resistance and Yielding

Attempts to change our beliefs, our attitudes, or our actions are everywhere. We live in a society in which we are constantly the targets of an almost unlimited number of message sources who seek to control our behavior in some way. Think about it. Every day we face an army of persuaders who are determined to alter our lives. They include public health officials encouraging individuals to stop smoking, get more exercise, eat more nutritious foods, and adopt a healthy lifestyle. The persuaders also include advertisers seeking to change the products we buy, politicians trying to shape our voting intentions, charities soliciting contributions

to worthy causes, professors trying to improve our minds, and religious leaders wanting to shape the ways we believe about and relate to the supernatural. It would be totally impossible to comply to everything they want us to believe or do. We absolutely must develop personal strategies that enable us to *resist change*.

Resistance as Reaction to Persuasion Attempts

How do we go about resisting change? In spite of the importance of the topic, published research focusing directly on resistance to change is limited. Furthermore, the information that is available explaining people's universal tendency to resist change is only indirectly related to the issue of persuasion. One particular perspective, however, is Jack Brehm's theory of **psychological reactance.** This theory does provide valuable insights into the universal inclination to resist change.[19] (See Box 11.4.)

Psychological reactance occurs when people are motivated to rebel when their established beliefs, attitudes, or habits of behavior are threatened by persuasion. Consequently, those who demand compliance from us may actually increase our determination to resist persuasion—causing a reaction against the attempt. Brehm expresses this idea by suggesting that the person who is the target of the influence attempt feels that "he can do what he wants, that he does not have to do what he doesn't want, and that at least in regard to the freedom in question, he is the sole director of his own behavior."[20]

Thus, our need to be in control, plus our strong desire for a stable and balanced life, provides the foundation for reactance. As adults, we expect and like the freedom to choose what we think and to control most of our own behaviors. This expectation of freedom, the importance of that freedom, and many other closely related issues all motivate us to resist particular influence attempts.[21]

Brehm's perspective is a useful one for several reasons. First, it makes intuitive sense. Think about how you react to the endless flow

BOX 11.4 🔍 *A Closer Look*

Brehm's Theory of Psychological Reactance

When someone tries to persuade us to do something, or to change our attitudes and beliefs, we are resistant to that change. Our resistance to change follows from our desire to remain in control over the way we think and the way we act. If someone tries to persuade us differently, we are likely to tune that person out or to develop a strong negative feeling for the person. Social psychologist Jack Brehm calls this type of resistance to change psychological reactance. Brehm's theory of psychological reactance can be summed up as follows:

1. Throughout the course of our life, we develop various attitudes and beliefs.
2. Because we like to be in control of our lives, we are resistant to attempts to change us. We do not like others telling us what to do or what to think.
3. When someone tries to convince us to change our beliefs, or tries to alter our behavior, we are likely to resist that person and his or her message.
4. The overall resistance to change is known as psychological reactance.

of commercials on TV, pushing products that advertisers want you to buy. You probably click the sound off or try not to look and listen. We do generally react negatively to people who openly attempt to get us to do things we don't want to do. We don't like to believe that we are being talked into doing something against our better judgment. Moreover, because we are bombarded with such a daily barrage of messages attempting to change us, we have to develop a "thick skin"—a strong tendency to resist—just to get through the day.

A second reason why Brehm's explanation has merit is that it complements our previous explanations of the nature of beliefs and attitudes, including the position of the relatively unpredictable relationship between attitudes and behavior. Brehm's perspective strengthens an important part of that discussion. Although the previous explanation focused on social and nonsocial factors, Brehm's theory adds a psychological perspective to our understanding of attitude and behavior inconsistency by noting people's *universal tendency to resist changing their behavior* as a result of exposure to persuasive communication.

Finally, Brehm's explanation serves as a useful point of departure for discussing additional areas that are important in learning how to communicate in ways that will influence people. Specifically, before considering how a variety of available communication strategies can be used, it is necessary to consider the nature of resistance to change through persuasion.

Types of Resistance

Discussions of resistance to persuasion often characterize any kind of opposition to persuasion as negative or even destructive.[22] Furthermore, the idea of people resisting to only a limited degree has seldom been addressed. This is unfortunate because viewing resistance as essentially "destructive" limits our ability to understand those who resist to some degree, but who do not entirely reject, influence attempts. Obviously, some kinds of resistance are entirely justified and serve constructive purposes. Thus, it is more realistic to maintain that there are essentially two types of resistance—*destructive* and *constructive*—and to assume that people resist in *varying degrees*.[23]

Destructive resistance. In its maximum form, **destructive resistance** is characterized as disagreeable, negative, subversive, or rebellious behavior. From this perspective, resistance is *misbehavior*—disobedience or corruption of authority. This type of resistance clearly illustrates contempt for an authority figure or for authority itself. That is, people who resist the requests and influence attempts of legitimate authorities, for no other reason than that they are authorities, are, in fact, destructive.

For example, if a manager directs an employee to engage in a legitimate work task (that does not involve immoral or illegitimate behavior) and the employee refuses to comply, the employee is being *destructively resistant*. In this situation, the employee is being openly disobedient and is undermining the manager's rational-legal authority. The fact that it is a designated superior who is making the assignment legitimizes the request and requires the employee to comply. In such a case, the employee's destructive resistance contributes nothing to a situation.

Constructive resistance. There are numerous ways in which **constructive resistance**—refusing to comply when the behavior being solicited is against ethical norms—can contribute to a situation. For example, in the well-known psychological experiments of Stanley Milgram, subjects were ordered to administer what they thought were dangerous levels of electric shocks to other individuals. (The subjects believed that were administering strong shocks to others, but the people being "shocked" were pretending to be in pain by shouting and screaming.) Many who read the reports of these experiments were surprised that only a few subjects resisted their orders.[24] Similar real-life situations arise on some occasions in the armed forces during wartime, when soldiers are unethically ordered to kill civilians. Some refuse. Unfortunately some do not. Refusing to engage in such behavior, despite orders to comply, provides an example of constructive resistance.

In normal daily activities, the boundaries between constructive and destructive resistance can be very murky indeed. What seems constructive to one group may be interpreted as destructive by another. For example, members of certain fundamentalist religious groups refuse to consult physicians when a family member becomes ill. They hold deep convictions that prayer will provide healing and that turning to conventional medicine amounts to a rejection of their faith. From a legal standpoint, such resistance can be a violation of law. Some see such resistance as destructive and unacceptable when lives are at stake. Others, however, see that society needs to respect religious convictions and make provision for such resistance.

The debate about what is constructive or destructive may never be settled. Today, some people feel morally compelled to resist laws supported by the majority of society that they deem improper. One example is the animal rights groups that throw blood on women wearing fur coats or break into laboratories to free animals used in medical research. Another example is activists who block the entrances of abortion clinics even though they know they will be arrested for their resistance. These individuals believe they are engaging in constructive resistance. Others in society see their behavior as destructive resistance to legitimate norms and laws.

Two important implications follow from the previous discussion: *First,* and most obvious, is that when trying to persuade people to change their views or behavior, it is almost certain that resistance will be encountered. This implies that provision must be made for reducing that resistance if at all possible. *Second,* to develop a strategy for reducing resistance, it is important to understand whether, from the resister's standpoint, it is seen as constructive. If this is the case, persuasion may be difficult or virtually impossible because constructive resistance is often based on deep commitments to ethical, moral, and culturally based positions. Such beliefs are particularly difficult to overcome. For example, it would not be an easy task to persuade an animal rights advocate that wearing fur coats is a positive form of behavior, or an anti-abortion advocate that undergoing the procedure is acceptable for any reason. Thus, viewing resistance as constructive *from the subjective viewpoint of the person to be persuaded* changes the way we think about it, and it certainly has a bearing on the strategies that might be used to circumvent it.

Types of Yielding

There are many occasions when people either consciously or unconsciously need to submit to influence. That is, there are a variety of circumstances in which we might want to yield in a particular situation when someone is attempting to influence our beliefs, attitudes, and behaviors. In a now-classic article, the social psychologist Herbert Kelman described three common and frequently overlapping types of yielding.[25] These are what he calls *compliance, identification,* and *internalization.*

Compliance. Kelman's first type of yielding is consistent with the previous discussion of compliance. It refers to yielding publicly or observably to an influence attempt—but, in this case, privately refusing to accept the change. A number of questions arise in discussions of this kind of **compliance.** First, why would anyone publicly *appear* to change while not having some corresponding private change in his or her own mind? The answer is that we frequently find ourselves in situations in which it is better to "go along to get along." That is, it is more expedient or useful not to challenge what is being said by an individual or a group than it is to speak out in opposition or to resist.

It is for that reason that many people simply comply in situations like this, either to receive a reward or to avoid being punished. For example, suppose you are driving on the highway and a police officer drives up alongside and directs you to slow down. Even though you are not exceeding the posted speed limit, you slow down. The issue here is that you accept being influenced because this individual controls certain punishments that can be imposed (such as a ticket). When the police officer is down the road and out of sight, however, you are likely to resume your original speed. Compliance in this situation is solely public or observable; it lasts only as long as the influencing agent is visibly present. Compliance as a form of yielding, then, is based on our expectation of *gaining rewards or avoiding punishment.*[26]

Identification. Kelman's second type of yielding to influence occurs because of our desire to emulate or imitate a particular individual or group. Yielding of this type is based on our wish to gain satisfaction in *being like* some individual or group that we want to imitate or that we admire. For example, suppose that you became acquainted with a man you would like to have as a close friend. The primary reasons you like this individual include that you feel good about yourself when you are around him and that he has a positive influence on your behavior in ways that please you very much. In other words, you admire, and want to be like (identify with) this individual.

Now suppose that this person you admire is zealously committed to an antinuclear power position—an issue that you find boring or even feel the opposite about. Your new friend frequently attempts to get you to accept his position. Although your natural inclination is to resist change, based on what has been described, it is likely that you will yield to his attempts to influence you. You will become more negative toward nuclear power. This probably would not come all at once, but if your relationship with this individual continued to develop in a rewarding way, you probably would eventually yield. Why do you end up yielding in these kinds of circumstances? The answer is that there are *rewards* in having this individual as your close friend and in feeling that you are like this person. He makes you feel good about yourself, and that, in itself, is very rewarding.

Internalization. Kelman's third type of yielding indicates that we do so because it is personally rewarding or useful. But more important, people yield in this manner so as to be *consistent with their values.* The term *value* refers to whatever an individual deeply believes to be important in life. Thus, values (like attitudes) are configurations or interrelated sets of affective beliefs. Unlike attitudes, however, they do not have clear-cut objects. Furthermore, they are much more general because they are goals or end-states that people seek, rather than objects. To illustrate, a person may value (seek as a major goal) such end-states as a moral life, happiness, freedom, service to others, power, or even wealth. Such broad and general objectives help to determine many of an individual's attitudes and beliefs as well as actions.[27]

The basis of Kelman's **internalization** as a type of yielding is how much intrinsic value a specific change actually provides for the person. It is no simple task to influence people to internalize a change. They must have an incentive; that is, making the change must be worthwhile for them. This type of yielding is the result of a rational decision to do so because the change fits into the individual's system of values. In this way, such change is interpreted as consistent with the person's innermost convictions of what is important in life.

Traditional Communication Strategies for Influencing People

The result of most of our attempts to influence people won't extend over a long period. However, even immediate or short-term influence encounters can and should be handled as if we intend to develop a long-term relationship. That is, to make any influence attempt successful, we must approach the encounter as we would approach the development of a lasting relationship.

This long-term perspective is critical. Regardless of the cultural or ethnic groups to which we belong, all of us like to feel special, attended to, and cared about. It is impossible to create the impression that you care about people you want to influence unless you sincerely approach your encounters with them as if you would like to develop a lasting relationship. Convincing people that you care in this way contributes to the style and affect of your influence attempt.

In addition to the influence processes and changes already discussed, several specific communication strategies can contribute to the success of attempts to influence people. This use of the term *communication strategy* refers to a specific message technique, or a series of such techniques, for influencing change. These strategies, which have been researched for many years, focus on characteristics of *receivers, messages,* and *sources* of persuasive messages.

Understanding Characteristics of Receivers

Persuasion strategies require some knowledge of the receiver targeted for change. If an individual is identified as possessing a particular attribute or a set of characteristics, then that knowledge can be part of a planned communication strategy. There are a variety of ways we can acquire information about people we want to influence. (Recall the discussion in Chapter 9 on assessing people's characteristics.)

The focus here is on areas that are relevant to the use of persuasion strategies. The first of these is *receiver susceptibility.* This refers to the degree to which people's personal characteristics make them either more or less easily influenced by others. Such attributes are important in deciding the best ways to influence receivers. Any person in the role of receiver possesses a number of identifiable attributes that make them more or less susceptible to influence attempts. These include *gender differences* and certain *personality characteristics.*

Gender differences. One of the more widely investigated (and most controversial) of the attributes related to susceptibility is whether a person is male or female. Investigators have studied the effect of gender on susceptibility for many years. Early studies supported the assumption that females were more easily influenced than males.[28] By the late 1970s, however, researchers had concluded that there probably are no major gender differences in susceptibility to persuasion. Contemporary investigations indicate that certain features of traditional male and female specialized cultures probably do affect the degree to which they are susceptible to influence. Attributes like emotionalism, expressiveness, and assertiveness that were part of the definitions of traditional male and female roles in decades past do seem to be related to susceptibility to persuasion. Overall, however, no assumption should be made that either males or females are easier to persuade.

Personality characteristics. Many researchers have investigated whether differences in personality characteristics are related to susceptibility to persuasion. One particular study provides insights into the specific receiver personality characteristics that should be considered in the selection of communication strategies. This study examined a number of *receiver attributes* as a way of determining susceptibility to certain topics of influence.[29]

As an initial step in the research, college students completed an extensive battery of personality tests. Their attitudes toward several topics of communication were also assessed. Later, on a different occasion, the investigators asked randomly selected groups of these same students to engage in a "counter-attitudinal activity." This required them to act as if they actually believed in one or more of the originally assessed communication topics. Attitudes toward these topics were assessed again at the end of this second session. Analyses of the results enabled the researchers to define *receiver personality profiles* of students who showed high and low levels of yielding. The results indicated that high and low amounts of change were clearly tied to particular receiver personality profiles. Specifically, large amounts of change occurred with receivers who were *obliging, changeable, dependent, and unstable.* Minimum change occurred among those who were *aggressive, unchanging, forceful, efficient, and well informed.*

What is the importance of these findings? If the person seeking to persuade another understands the personality structure of the target individual, and if it includes the first list above, persuasion may succeed. If the target person is like the second list, success is less likely.

Features of Effective Messages

As noted earlier, for decades researchers have tried to discover the *magic keys* (words, appeals, message structures) that can be used to influence people. Of all the potential keys examined in thousands of studies, only a few come even close to working that way, and few universal prescriptions exist for influencing people with messages.

With this caveat in mind, there are several keys to changing people that have shown at least some results in research. These keys are more accurately called *features of effective messages* that have persuaded people, at least in experiments and other kinds of studies. Keep in mind that the degree to which these can be incorporated into real-life influence attempts outside experimental settings is not clear.

Message "sidedness." Some of the earliest and most meaningful examinations of communication strategies were conducted in the 1950s by social psychologists Carl Hovland, Irving Janis, and Harold Kelley.[30] One of the factors they studied was called **message sidedness.** Specifically, this concerns whether to use a message that presents *only one side* of a persuasive argument, to *include both sides,* or to use both sides and *refute the opposing arguments* as well. Results from a number of studies seemed to show that the strategy of using the two-sided message, which refutes the other's position, worked best.[31]

Message order of presentation. A substantial amount of research has examined whether the first side of an argument that is presented, or the most recent side, carries the most influence. This is often referred to as **message ordering,** or the *primacy-recency* question. That is, is it more persuasive to put the arguments favoring a position early in a message, or does more change result when arguments are inserted at the end of the message? The safest recommendation concerning this persuasion strategy is that no universal law of primacy-recency has been uncovered, and one's choice should depend on the conditions that exist at the time of the influence attempt.[32]

Fear appeals. One of the more intriguing communication strategies involves the use of fear-arousing appeals to influence change. Results of many studies remain contradictory. The original research examining the effectiveness of this strategy indicated that large amounts of change are produced with *weak* fear appeals and that little or no change results from *strong* appeals that arouse high levels of fear.[33] More recent fear-appeal studies suggest that the opposite is the case.[34] That is, strong fear appeals do work, producing more persuasive influences than weak appeals. The explanation of this seeming contradiction may be that there is a point at which too much fear in a message causes people to avoid or disregard the message, or to do both.[35] As with the other strategies described, the only safe recommendation is to consider both the target and the situation carefully prior to trying this strategy.

Behavior-alteration techniques. This refers not to a single persuasion strategy, but to a set of message techniques. Each of these techniques is represented by a set of messages of a particular kind. For example, one of these techniques is called "reward from behavior." It includes messages such as "You will enjoy it," "You will get a reward if you do," "It will make you happy," "It will help you," and "You will benefit if you do it." Investigations of these techniques indicate that using several behavior-alteration procedures may sometimes be effective in motivating a person to yield in a particular influence attempt.[36]

Recent research indicates that the **behavior-alteration techniques** are more appropriately categorized into two general types—*prosocial* and *antisocial*. For example, the "reward for behavior" technique is an example of the prosocial type. A technique called "punishment from behavior" is a good illustration of the antisocial type. Messages using this antisocial type include "You will lose if you don't," "You will be punished if you don't," "You will be unhappy if you don't," and "You will be hurt if you don't." Again, there are no solid rules to use as guidelines concerning which of these techniques will succeed or fail in a given persuasion attempt.

Nonverbal cues. In Chapter 3, the nature of nonverbal cues in messages was discussed in detail. One of the principles from that discussion that is extremely important in trying to influence people with persuasive messages is *nonverbal immediacy*. This can be the basis of an integrated verbal and nonverbal persuasion strategy, especially in cases in which the goal of the persuasion is to create a lasting relationship.

Recall that nonverbal immediacy refers to such behaviors as smiling, nodding, leaning forward, eye contact, and standing close to someone. Also recall that the effects of immediacy are based on the *principle of utility*. In brief, we tend to approach people we like both physically and psychologically, and we tend to avoid behaving in these ways toward people we don't like. People understand this, and, therefore, signals of nonverbal immediacy can be an effective form of persuasive communication. Clearly, nonverbal messages of all kinds can exert significant influence on the persuasive process.[37]

Credibility of the Source

The issue of how trustworthy or credible the sender seems to the receiver can be discussed separately because it is not always seen as a feature of an effective message. However, it is treated as such in this chapter. It is also set apart because it requires detailed explanation.

In its simplest form, **credibility** refers to "how believable a person believes a message source to be."[38] This simple definition says two very important things: First and most critical, credibility is something that is *perceived*—that is, it is in the eye of the beholder. Thus, a man may think that he is a highly credible person, but if others don't think so, he is not.

The second issue implied by the definition is that to be credible we must be *believable*. This looks like the two concepts are defined in terms of each other. However, both credibility and believability mean several things. After many years of investigating source credibility, researchers have come to define it as a combination of five separate dimensions: *competence, trustworthiness, extroversion, composure, and sociability.* For us to get people to perceive us as credible sources, and thus use it as a communication strategy, we need to understand each of these dimensions and how they fit together.

The five dimensions of credibility can be explained very simply. The first, competence, refers to how *knowledgeable* or expert a source is thought to be in a given content area. The second, *trustworthiness*, refers to whether people believe us to be honest: To be credible we need to be perceived as honest. (See Box 11.5.)

The third dimension of credibility is *extroversion*. This refers to the degree to which we are believed to be talkative, bold, dynamic, and outgoing. Interestingly, if we are not perceived this way to some degree, we tend to be perceived as untrustworthy. The fourth dimension is *composure*. To be composed is to be in control of one's emotions. That is, reasonably composed people tend to be perceived as poised, relaxed, and confident. The fifth and final dimension is *sociability,* which refers to how likable and friendly we seem. If people interpret us in this way, they perceive us as the kind of person with whom others would want to socialize.

Taken together, these five dimensions influence people's perceptions of credibility. Note that too much extroversion can be perceived as oppressive, too much composure can be perceived as uncaring, and so on. The best combination is to try to control how you are perceived so as to possess moderate to high levels of each of the five dimensions. If you are successful at getting people to see you in these ways, you will

likely be seen as a *believable* person. If that can be done, you might be effective at changing a person's beliefs, attitudes or behavior.[39] In fact, that conclusion has been suggested by a considerable body of research.[40]

The Elaboration Likelihood Model of Persuasion

Psychologists Richard Petty and John Cacioppo, who have studied the process of persuasion extensively, have developed a complex theory that brings together many of the factors and considerations that have been discussed in this chapter. They have labeled their theory the "Elaboration Likelihood Model of Persuasion (ELM)."[41] The term *elaboration* refers to the perceptual and cognitive processes by which a person receives and carefully considers the meaning of a persuasive message, the appeals for change that it contains and other features of its content. The idea of *likelihood* refers to the chances or probability that some change will take place in a person's attitude (and related behavior) as a result of receiving, considering and understanding the persuasive message.

Essentially, the ELM theory consists of a number of "postulates" (propositions or statements that are to be considered as "correct" for the purposes of the theory). In the section that follows, and in Figure 11.1, the basic ideas of the ELM model are summarized, but because of space limitations simplified versions are presented.[42] The basic features of the process can be described as follows:

The theory begins with the proposition that people are motivated to hold "correct" attitudes. That is, attitudes that are consistent with those held by people they regard as important in their social environment. For example, if our peers, other friends, and family all hold negative attitudes toward the death penalty, it is unlikely that we will have positive attitudes toward that form of punishment. A second proposition states that if a person receives a message designed to persuade him or her to hold a particular or different view about some issue or topic, the amount of "issue-relevant elaboration"—defined as the extent to which a person thinks about or considers the relevant arguments or appeals in the message—will vary with the message and the situation.

The next consideration is whether the message and topic are "relevant" to the person. Many of the persuasive messages we all receive are not. For example, we constantly see advertisements about products that have no place in our lives, or attempts to convert our views to positions on topics we have no interest in. These are not relevant. On the other hand, if our col-lege administration tries to persuade us that a huge increase in tuition is a really great idea, we would probably see that as very relevant. We would be strongly motivated to try and understand why they are saying that, and what the consequences to us might be (in ELM terms, we would engage in "issue-relevant elaboration").

Assuming that the individual finds a persuasive message both relevant to his or her interests and is motivated to consider it carefully, close attention will then be paid to whatever "appeals" or persuasive arguments have been placed within it. On the other hand, if the message is about something not relevant, the person is less likely to "process" or think carefully about it. Instead, the receiver will use a variety of "cues" as guides to making a quick decision to accept or reject the message. Such cues may include the credibility, attractiveness, or status of the speaker, or the number (rather than the type) of arguments presented. Even if the message is accepted, any attitude change that may take place is likely to be weak and temporary. (This is the "peripheral route" to persuasion indicated in Figure 11.1.)

However, if a person does indeed have the capacity and interest to process the message carefully, considering the appeals in some detail, and if a good case is made for a change in thinking, he or she may be persuaded to alter his or her attitude toward the position advocated in the message. (This is the "central route" shown in Figure 11.1.) Indeed, if that is the case, and if the appeals have an influence on the person's thinking, an enduring change in attitude toward the topic or issue is likely to be the result. This change may be in a positive or a negative direction, depending on the topic and the appeals. That is, as a result of exposure to the persuasive message, and the mental "elaborations" described, the person may now have a favorable or an unfavorable attitude toward the topic or issue at stake.

The model also assumes that if a person undergoes a change in attitude as a result of receiving a persuasive message (the central route),

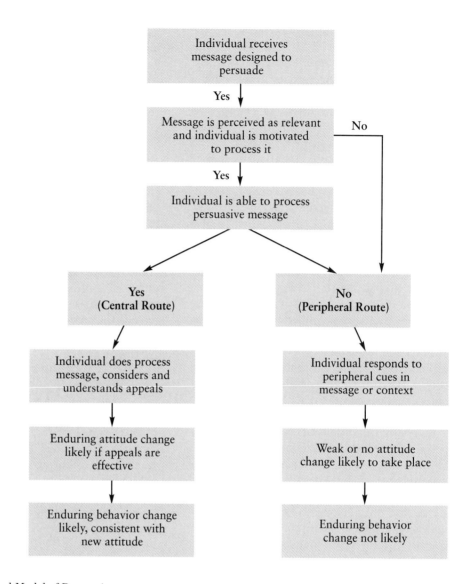

FIGURE 11.1
Elaboration Likelihood Model of Persuasion

then it is likely that his or her behavior will undergo a corresponding change (which is an assumption not always supported by empirical evidence).

Thus, the model emphasizes two distinct types of persuasion. For those messages that are relevant and important to us, we will be motivated to think about the issues involved, and we will consider the merits and the strength of the arguments or appeals (the central route). Under these circumstances, the theory predicts, the attitude change that may result is likely to be strong, enduring, and predictive of behavior.

However, we can't scrutinize in depth every message that is presented to us. So we often use a "mental filter" to allow messages that aren't significant to us to pass through with little processing or consideration (elaboration). Instead, we will use simple cues to make a decision, rather than analyze the information that is presented (the peripheral route). Under these circumstances, any attitude change that may result is likely to be weak, temporary, and less predictive of behavior.

The ELM model, then, is an attempt to bring together a number of the complex factors, considerations and psychological processes that are involved in achieving attitude change through the use of persuasive messages. In that sense, it represents another way of understanding how people can be influenced through communication.

Chapter Review

- In modern society, numerous individuals, groups, and agencies constantly try to influence people's ideas, feelings, or actions. At one time, persuasion was seen as something that one person "did to" another, following the linear magic bullet model. Now we know that influence is determined by both sources and receivers, following the simultaneous transactions model.

- Compliance falls into three categories: coercion, in which people may have little choice but to change their behavior; sociocultural expectations, using persuasive messages; and cognitive reorganization, in which people change the way they think or feel about the topic of persuasive messages.

- The attitudes we hold and the actions we engage in are seldom consistent. Although an attitude can increase the probability that we will act consistently, other more immediate social factors can greatly reduce that probability.

- Human beings are universally resistant to change, making persuasion especially difficult. Psychological reactance to persuasion occurs because of our need to be in control, plus our strong desire for a stable and balanced life. As adults we expect and like the freedom to choose and control most of our own behaviors. Desire for this freedom, and many other closely related issues, motivate us to resist influence.

- There are two types of resistance—destructive and constructive. Extreme destructive resistance is characterized as disagreeable, negative, subversive, or rebellious behavior, clearly illustrating contempt for authority. In contrast, constructive resistance can be positive, especially when the behavior solicited is against ethical norms.

- There are three types of yielding: compliance, identification, and internalization. Compliance refers to yielding publicly to an influence attempt, but without actually changing privately. *Identification* is yielding to the influence of another due to desire to emulate a particular individual or group. Internalization is yielding because it is personally rewarding or useful.

- All persuasion strategies require knowledge of the receiver, including receiver susceptibility, gender, and other personal characteristics that make people either more or less easily influenced by others.

- Five features of messages have been widely studied as possible keys to persuasion: message sidedness, message ordering, fear appeals, behavior-alteration techniques, and nonverbal cues of immediacy.

- Source credibility refers to whether a receiver believes the originator of the message can be trusted or believed. Researchers define credibility as a combination of five dimensions: competence, trustworthiness, extroversion, composure, and sociability.

- The Elaboration Likelihood Model (ELM) represents an attempt to bring together a complex set of factors and variables that explain how a person may or may not be influenced to change his or her attitude toward a topic or issue. If the topic is relevant, and the appeals effective, such change will take place as a result of "elaboration"—and will presumably be followed by corresponding behavior change. If these factors are different, enduring behavior change is unlikely.

Key Terms

persuasion	social pressures	identification
coercion	nonsocial constraints	internalization
social expectations	psychological reactance	message sidedness
cognitive reorganization	destructive resistance	message ordering
psychodynamic strategy	constructive resistance	behavior-alteration techniques
belief	compliance	credibility (of a source)
attitude		

Notes

1. Bloom, K., Zajac, D. J., & Titus, J. (1999). The influence of nasality of voice on sex-stereotyped perceptions. *Journal of Nonverbal Behavior, 23, 4, 271–281.*

2. See, for example: Henriksen, L., & Flora, J. A. (1999). Third-person perception and children: Perceived impact of pro- and anti-smoking ads. *Communication Research, 26, 6, 643–665.*

3. A classic example is the case of Kate Smith, a popular singer and radio personality of the 1940s, who sold $39 million worth of war bonds during an 18-hour marathon radio broadcast. See: Merton, R. K. (1946). *Mass persuasion: The social psychology of a war bond drive.* New York: Harper & Brothers.

4. Advertisers who strive to sell products with the use of persuasion communications mastered this formula decades ago. They call it the "learn, feel, do" approach. As far as they are concerned, it is not particularly effective. See: Jones, J. P. (1986). *What's in a name? Advertising and the concept of brands* (p. 141). Lexington, MA: Heath.

5. This example was drawn from a seminar paper: Ordman, L. (Fall 1989). On money and meaning in the popular press. Prepared for a graduate course, Syracuse University, Syracuse, NY.

6. Originally formulated by Melvin DeFleur and Timothy Plax as an explanation of certain kinds of effects of mass communication, meaning theory is equally applicable to persuasion at an interpersonal and group level. See: Lowery, S., & DeFleur, M. (1983). *Milestones in mass communication research* (pp. 28–30, 383–385). New York: Longman.

7. Cornford, F. M. (Trans. and Ed.). (1941). *The Republic of Plato* (pp. 227–231). London: Oxford University Press.

8. Lippmann, W. (1922). The world outside and the pictures in our heads. *Public opinion* (chap. 1, pp. 1–19). New York: Macmillan.

9. A large earlier literature is summarized in: Hovland, C. I., Janis, I., & Kelley, H. H. (1953). *Communication and persuasion.* New Haven, CT: Yale University Press.

10. Thomas, W. I., & Znaniecki, F. F. (1927). *The Polish peasant in Europe and America* (Vol. 1). New York: Knopf. (First published in 1918.)

11. DeFleur, M. L., & Westie, F. R. (1963). Attitude as a scientific concept. *Social Forces, 42,* 17–31. See also: Fishbein, M., & Azien, O. (1975). *Belief, attitude, intention, and behavior*

(pp. 5–13). Reading, MA: Addison-Wesley; Bettinghaus, F. P., & Cody, M. J. (1987). *Persuasive communication* (4th ed., pp. 6–10). New York: Holt, Rinehart, and Winston.

12. This definition is derived from: Rokeach, M. (1973). *Beliefs, attitudes and values* (p. 122). San Francisco: Jossey-Bass.

13. Seibold, D. R. (1975). Communication research and the attitude-verbal report-overt behavior relationship: A critique and theoretic reformulation. *Human Communication Research, 2,* 3–32; Cushman, D. P., & McPhee, R. D., eds. (1980). *Message-attitude-behavior relationship: Theory, methodology, and application.* New York: Academic; Cooper, J., & Croyle, R.T. (1984). Attitudes and attitude change. In Rosenzweig, M. R., & Porter, L. W. (Eds.), *Annual review of psychology* (Vol. 35, pp. 395–460). Palo Alto, CA: Annual Reviews.

14. Ibid.

15. Ibid.

16. LaPiere, R. T. (1934). Attitudes versus actions. *Social Forces, 13,* 230–237.

17. DeFleur, M. L., & Westie, F. R. (1958). Attitudes and overt acts. *American Sociological Review, 23,* 667–673.

18. Plax, T. G., & DeFleur, M. L. (1980). *Communication, attitudes, and behavior: An axiomatic theory with implications for persuasion research.* Paper presented to the Western Speech Communication Association, Portland, OR.

19. Brehm, J. W. (1966). *A theory of psychological reactance.* New York: Academic.

20. Ibid., p. 9.

21. Most explanations of why people resist change follow from discussions of the human need for a comfortable, stable, and balanced life. In U.S. society, middle-class children are told from early childhood that if they engage in the right forms of preparation, a comfortable lifestyle will follow. In other words, if they work hard, go to school, get good grades, get a good job, and save their money, they will have stability, balance, and thus happiness in their lives; they will achieve the American Dream. We are taught to make achieving this lifestyle one of our highest priorities, and to do so we must attain control across a diversity of activities. Our natural and common reaction to threats to such control, with their possible suspensions of personal freedom, is to resist both change and attempts to get us to comply.

22. Burroughs, N. F., Kearney, P., & Plax, T. G. (1989). Compliance-resistance in the college classroom. *Communication Education, 38,* 214–229.

23. Ibid.

24. Milgram, S. (1963). Behavioral study of obedience. *Journal of Abnormal and Social Psychology, 67,* 371–378.

25. Kelman, H. C. (1961). Processes of opinion change. *Public Opinion Quarterly, 25,* 58–78.

26. Wood, W. (2000). Attitude change: Persuasion and social influence. Rosenzweig, M. R., & Porter, L. W. (Eds.), *Annual review of psychology* (Vol. 51, pp. 539–570). Palo Alto, CA: Annual Review.

27. The most frequently cited treatment of values is Rokeach, *Beliefs.* For other interesting discussions of values see: Oskamp, S. (1977). *Attitudes and opinions* (p. 13). Englewood Cliffs, NJ: Prentice-Hall; Simmons, H. W. (1976). *Persuasion: Understanding, practice, and analysis* (p. 20). Reading, MA: Addison-Wesley.

28. For a discussion of the early research on this topic see: Cronkhite, G. (1969). *Persuasion: Speech and behavioral exchange.* Indianapolis: Bobbs-Merrill. A large number of subsequent research studies have probed this issue, but the findings have been inconsistent. Some studies indicate that women are more susceptible; other studies suggest that men are more susceptible; and yet other research reveals no differences between the two.

29. Plax, T. G., & Rosenfeld, L. B. (1977). Antecedent of change in males and females. *Psychological Reports, 41,* 811–824. For additional examples of research examining personal characteristics and persuasion see: Boster, F. J., & Stiff, J. B. (1984). Compliance-gaining message selection behavior. *Human Communication Research, 10,* 539–556; Hunter, J. H., Gerbing, D. W., & Boster, F J. (1982). Machiavellian beliefs and personality: Construct invalidity of the Machiavellian dimension. *Journal of Personality and Social Psychology, 43,* 1293–1305. Also, for a review of research on locus of control and

persuasion, see: Cody, M. J., & McLaughlin, M. L. (1985). The situation as a construct in communication research. In M. L. Knapp & G. R. Miller (Eds.), *Handbook of interpersonal communication* (pp. 263–312). Beverly Hills, CA: Sage.

30. Hovland, C. I., Janis, I. L., & Kelley, H. H. (1953). *Communication and persuasion.* New Haven, CT: Yale University Press.

31. Allen, M., Hale, J., Mongeau, P., Berkowitz-Stafford, S., Stafford, S., Shanahan, W., Agee, P., Dillon, K., Dickson, R., & Ray, C. (1990). Testing a model of message-sidedness: Three replications. *Communication Monographs, 57,* 275–291.

32. Hovland, C. I., Mandel, W., Campbell, E. H., Brock, T., Luchins, A. S., Cohen, A. E., McGuire, W. J., Janis, I. L., Feierabend, R. L., & Anderson, N. H. (1957). *The order of presentation in persuasion.* New Haven, CT: Yale University Press.

33. Janis, I. L., & Feshbach, S. (1953). Effects of fear arousing communications. *Journal of Abnormal and Social Psychology, 48,* 78–92.

34. See, for example: Kraus, S., El-assal, E., and DeFleur, M. L. (1966). Fear-threat appeals in mass communication: An apparent contradiction. *Speech Monographs, 23,* 23–29. Also: Higbee, K. L. (1969). Fifteen years of fear arousal: Research on threat appeals: 1953–1968. *Psychological Bulletin, 72,* 426–444.

35. McGuire, W., J. (1968). Personality and susceptibility to social influence. In E. E. Borgatta & W. W. Lambert (Eds.), *Handbook of personality theory and research* (pp. 1130–1187). Chicago: Rand McNally.

36. Kearney, P., Plax, T. G., Richmond, V. P., & McCroskey, J. C. (1984). Power in the classroom IV; Teacher communication techniques as alternatives to discipline. In R. Bostrom (Ed.), *Communication yearbook 8* (pp. 724–746). Beverly Hills, CA: Sage. For an excellent review of the research on compliance-gaining in other contexts, see: Seibold, D. R., Cantrill, J. G., & Meyers, R. A. (1985). Communication and interpersonal influence. In M. L. Knapp & G. R. Miller (Eds.), *Handbook of interpersonal communication* (pp. 551–614). Beverly Hills, CA: Sage.

37. Ifert, D. E., & Gibbons, C. A. (1999). Look at me when I'm influencing you: Nonverbal messages and persuasion. *New Jersey Journal of Communication, 7,* 2, 171–179.

38. McCrosky, J. C., Richmond, V. P., & Stewart, R. S., *One on one: The foundations of interpersonal communication* (p. 73). Englewood Cliffs, NJ: Prentice-Hall.

39. Plax, T. G., & Rosenfeld, L. B. (1980). Individual differences in the credibility and attitude change relationship. *Journal of Social Psychology, 111,* 79–89.

40. Bettinghaus & Cody, *Persuasive communication,* pp. 84–94.

41. Petty, R.E., & Cacioppo, J. T. (1986). The elaboration likelihood model of persuasion. In L. Berkowitz (Ed.), *Advances in experimental social psychology* (Vol. 19, pp. 123–205).

42. Note that Figure 11.1 is a simplified version based on, but not identical to, the much more complex original diagram presented by Petty and Cacioppo, the elaboration likelihood model of persuasion. P. 131.

Coping with Conflict

J ohn and Loretta both work in the personnel unit of a large computer manufacturer. They have the same boss. They had always worked well together, but then things changed. Unfortunately, they are currently in serious disagreement over a specific assignment their boss gave Loretta that John thought should have been given to him. In fact, they are now engaged in a heated conflict that is keeping them from communicating rationally with each other about their work. Not only that, but they no longer trust or even like each other.[1]

Their mutual dislike has become obvious to everyone around them. In fact, it has gotten to a point where each seems to take pleasure in finding ways to undermine the other. By now, other people try to avoid talking with them about this dispute. In fact, it has become difficult to talk to them at all, and this situation is hurting everyone's morale and productivity.

The problem started when Loretta was assigned a task that would normally have been John's responsibility. What happened was that she was asked to evaluate the success of the company's program for recruiting and training new workers. This was a program that John had originally developed. To her benefit, Loretta didn't really want to make this evaluation because she knew that John would be upset. In fact, she tried to explain John's probable reaction to their boss. It was to no avail. Her boss's response was simple: "Loretta, I gave you an assignment and I expect you to get it done. I couldn't care less what John thinks. Just do it—understand?"

Loretta understood. On the one hand, she knew that she was competent to handle the assignment. On the other hand, staffing plans were John's responsibility, and she knew how possessive he was about his work. Nevertheless, she realized that she really had no alternative. She could not defy her boss, so she went ahead with the evaluation.

Loretta tried to tell John that it wasn't her fault. Again and again she tried to explain to him that she had no choice and that she felt uncomfortable, but he became more hostile each time she approached him. Finally, Loretta began to get angry. The madder she got, the more hostile he became toward her. Finally, she became furious. Resolving their conflict just seemed impossible.

After several weeks, the boss called both of them into her office to try to settle the dispute, and moved right to the point: "You two people have wasted a lot of this company's time over the last several weeks," she said, "Your uproar over this evaluation is costing a great deal of money. It is interfering with your work and everyone else's. I want both of you to put a stop to this nonsense. So listen to me very carefully! Your conflict is officially over. Got that? Stop dreaming up ways to convince me and the rest of us here that the other person is in the wrong, and stop bad-mouthing each other. Quit screwing up our work.

"I am giving you two the rest of the day to get your act together," she continued. "I don't care how you do it, but just do it! Tomorrow morning I expect you two to be talking to each other just like old buddies. Let me remind both of you that no one—I mean no one—in this organization is indispensable. Neither of you is going to waste one more minute of this company's time. Do you two get the drift of what I am saying?"

John and Loretta both gulped, and reluctantly nodded yes to their boss. They got "the drift" loud and clear. It was time to resolve their differences.

Perhaps the conflict between John and Loretta sounds unusual—the kind of thing that rarely occurs between intelligent people. After all, employees are adults, and they must surely think and act like mature individuals. Almost anyone can disagree from time to time, but intelligent people control themselves. Responsible human beings don't act in irrational and vicious ways, trying to destroy each other's careers over some issue as insignificant as who evaluates a staffing plan. In fact, people who would purposely go out of their way to behave like John and Loretta may be emotionally unstable. Perhaps what they really need is psychiatric counseling, right?

Wrong! Given the right set of circumstances, almost any one of us is likely to behave just the way John and Loretta did. No one is immune. We all get angry when we perceive a threat to something we value. We try to protect ourselves and to stop the person who is representing the threat. We feel it is natural to get back at anyone who tries to take something away from us that we feel is ours. The result is often an *unresolvable conflict*.

Why does this happen? For one thing, it is a standard psychological principle that, regardless of what is at stake, we all respond to frustration with *aggression*.[2] Hostility between people can occur anywhere, and for a variety of reasons. *Conflict* occurs between people in all sorts of relationships—between strangers, friends, and lovers; between employees and employers; between spouses, and relatives; be-

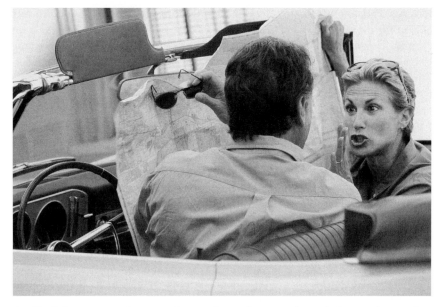

Conflict is just as normal as any other routine exchange, and people frequently experience disagreements over many issues. Conflict can also produce positive consequences as people understand ways to handle their differences and make compromises.

tween teachers and students; between parents and children; and so on. Conflict is as common among highly educated people as among high school dropouts, as characteristic of highly intelligent people as of the mentally challenged. Conflict is both widespread and normal. Sooner or later, we all get mad at someone.

Conflict can develop between people in almost any relationship. In fact, the scenario of John and Loretta as employees could be rewritten into a description of John and Loretta as husband and wife, as close friends, as landlord and tenant, or as professor and student. Perhaps the only unique aspect of the conflict as written above is that they had a boss who forced them (rather clumsily) to do something about their confrontation. Most people involved in conflict don't have the luxury of a built-in controlling agent. They have to either negotiate their conflict themselves or seek the help of some type of referee or mediator. The latter seldom happens, because in most cases it is either inconvenient or impossible to find a suitable mediator. Therefore, the majority of

the conflicts that we face in life have to be resolved by each of us as best we can.

The Major Characteristics of Conflict

One of the first characteristics of conflict to recognize is that it can range from trivial to brutal. However, this chapter is not concerned with violent conflicts, such as gang wars, police shoot-outs, or barroom brawls. The concern here is with people's everyday conflicts, such as occur in the family, at work, among neighbors, or at school—the type illustrated by what happened between John and Loretta.

These kinds of conflicts are normal and as typically American as apple pie, motherhood, and the flag. Actually, certain forms of conflict are an established and approved part of our culture. That is not to say that as a general culture we blindly approve of violent or destructive behavior. However, ours is a complex society made up of many groups and categories, with distinctive specialized cultures and agendas. People are often in competition for power, privilege, and other scarce resources. This inevitably generates struggles—conflicts—among various segments of the society. Thus, Americans often see themselves in a "we versus they" perspective. Examples are management versus labor, rich versus poor, males versus females, one racial or ethnic group versus another, farmers versus city dwellers, or old versus young.[3]

A second major characteristic of conflict can best be understood within this cultural perspective: That is, within limits, to be a fighter is commonly regarded as a good thing by U.S. standards. To shrink from conflict is widely regarded as bad. People who typically go out of their way to dodge conflicts are sometimes described with pejorative terms, such as wimpy, spineless, yellow, and soft. The mainstream U.S. culture, then, often supports a culturally approved readiness to engage in conflict, as long as it does not escalate to physical violence.[4]

There are other cultural roots of our readiness to engage in conflict. In many ways, this orientation is an extension of our cultural mandates to *succeed in life*. Middle-class children in both the dominant and many minority groups are taught early on that, to be happy and, above all, worthwhile, they must be successful. In childhood this means winning in various settings, ranging from sports contests to spelling bees. Later, it means making it by acquiring impressive material possessions and achieving upward mobility in a career. Thus, getting ahead is a very important value to many Americans, particularly among the middle class and perhaps the majority.

Getting ahead inescapably means getting ahead of *someone else*. Thus, we share a conflict perspective on the so-called American Dream (of upward mobility). To act in ways consistent with this aspect of our culture, then, we literally must engage in a lifetime of competitive conflicts. To please ourselves and others, we compete at home, at school, on the job, and in any other situation that lends itself to rivalry. Thus, our tendencies to be competitive and to

engage in conflict are deeply embedded in our way of life. They are part of our mainstream cultural traditions, and they inevitably become a central part of our personalities as we participate and are socialized within that culture.

Formulating a More Precise Definition

Although the idea of conflict may seem simple enough in a commonsense way, there is surprising disagreement among experts about exactly what kinds of states, situations, and behaviors should be called conflict. Consequently there are a variety of definitions of conflict, each stressing a different meaning. Unfortunately, most are either narrowly linked to a specific scientific research project or quite complicated and technical. Thus, few existing definitions fit the present general discussion. For the purposes of this text, then, **conflict** is defined as *a dispute in which different values result in claims to rewards or resources that are in limited supply, and in which the main objective of the people engaged in the process is either to neutralize or to eliminate their opponent's prospects to win what is at stake.*[5]

This definition may seem complex, but it systematically sets forth the essential features of conflict: It notes the *object* around which conflict develops, the *goals* of the participants (to win, and to keep the other from doing so), and the *nature of their relationship* (as one of controversy). These are important features that need to be included in a workable definition.

In many ways, this definition asserts a kind of *economic model* of the causes of conflict. This is only one way to look at the causes of conflict, but it does provide a good beginning because it shows that conflicts develop over some *commodity* (reward or resource) that all the participants desire but that not all can have. If a commodity is valued, and if it is possible for only a few people to have it, the commodity will appear to them to have *great worth*. This sets the stage for strong competition to attain it. The struggle can be over any commodity—anything people want: money, power, authority, prestige, immediate access to the boss, or an office with a nice view. The scarcity of the reward or resource valued in the specific situation serves as an important beginning point for the development of conflict.

These principles are inherent in the John and Loretta example. Their conflict represents one of the most common types found in the workplace—competition for rewards and resources such as status or power positions. Thus, the conflict began when part of what normally was John's authority became an object of competition—or at least he believed that to be the case. He felt that he had worked long and hard for the right to assess programs—after all, that fell within his job description. In his mind, that authority belonged to him as part of the status rewards of his job. John felt threatened because he thought that Loretta was attempting to seize some of his status and power. It didn't really matter whether Loretta or his boss initiated Loretta's actions. To John, she was the direct and visible competitor.

Was John's interpretation irrational? Perhaps. But we each define our own interpretations, of reality, and as explained in previous chapters, they become the facts on which we base our actions and decisions.

For Loretta, a very different set of facts was operating. She knew that she did not ask for the assignment. Indeed, she tried to avoid it; and she tried to explain to John that she had no intention of usurping his authority. When he was inflexible, however, she came to believe that he wanted to fight. When that happens, our general culture instructs us that only spineless wimps let others walk all over them! That, then, becomes a compelling guide for behavior. Thus, if John wanted a fight, it was OK with Loretta. She could give back whatever he "dished out," and then some. After all, career issues and getting ahead were at stake.

As indicated in the definition of conflict, the main objective of individuals in conflict is to either neutralize or eliminate the prospects of their opponent. Because middle-class Americans have a strong culturally based need to succeed, it makes sense that beating the opponent is a primary goal in all types of conflicts. If we neutralize our opponent's efforts, we get what we want. If we eliminate his or her prospects altogether, we guarantee that we get what we want. Either way, we win the struggle and capture the valued commodity.

There are, however, other cultural norms surrounding the goals and objectives of those in conflict. Specifically, they define limits on how we go about winning—that is, neutralizing or even eliminating the chances of the opponent to capture the commodity. It is not acceptable in our society to damage, destroy, or discredit our opponent in a destructive way. Our mainstream culture requires that we follow certain ethical standards.

These seemingly conflicting cultural definitions are not incompatible. There are ways to neutralize one's competition in a conflict while remaining ethical and constructive. That is, the opponent does not have to be destroyed and end up with absolutely nothing. In some situations, and ideally in *all* situations, each of the parties in a process of conflict can and should benefit in some way when it is resolved.

Getting what we want, then, simply means that in a conflict we compete with someone in an ethical manner—and in the end gain at least some advantage (from our perspective). This implies getting a share of whatever value, reward, or resource is at stake, but in a way that allows both parties to gain something through the resolution of the conflict.[6]

These points about the process and meaning of "winning" are extremely important. Opponents in a conflict need not even be cold and distant; in fact, they can compete vigorously and remain friends. For example, friends and family members frequently train for and compete in activities ranging from athletic events to courtroom trials. Co-workers often spend time in conflicts that lead to formulating the best approach to such activities as marketing, employee relations, labor negotiations, hiring, and so on. Viewed in these ways, conflicts are not inherently negative or adverse. In fact, conflicts can range along a continuum from positive to neutral to negative.

Consequences of Conflict

Conflicts are not, inherently, either productive or destructive. What is important is *how people behave* during a conflict and especially the specific *consequences* of the process. Moreover, it is the people who initiate and engage in a conflict who determine whether it will ultimately be productive or destructive; their specific personalities influence the kinds of outcomes that result from all forms of human interaction. Conflict is no exception.

Conflicts produce unproductive, negative, or even destructive outcomes when the participants enter the process with negative attitudes or hostile feelings toward their opponent. As previously noted, these directly arouse needs for *aggression*. Therefore, as one might expect, conflicts that start on a negative note often end up that way. Fortunately, most of us are not normally antagonistic toward other people. Unless provoked, we seldom go out of our way to be hostile toward one another. Because we aren't naturally antagonistic, most of our conflicts start out innocently. In some cases, however, things "just happen" and a conflict begins and escalates.

Conflicts that produce bad feelings and destructive results tend to be those that get out of hand. One of the opponents gets hot under the collar, or the other gets angry, and the encounter deteriorates into ugliness and hostility. The case of John and Loretta provides an example. If it had been handled properly from the beginning, it might have had productive consequences. However, having a third party end the situation was one of the few options remaining.

Examples of conflicts that often end unproductively are those centering on divorce, child custody, job termination, disputes between family members over an inheritance, and union-management impasses. These frequently lead to bitterness; alienation; sabotage on the job; or even, in some cases, physical violence.

In these kinds of cases, all the parties involved lose even if they win, because of the negative consequences they face, whatever the outcome.

Conflicts that have bad or unproductive consequences for the people involved seldom start out in a dramatically negative way. Often, the initial events are minor, and the early exchanges seem little more than mild disagreements. In fact, what occurs between people during the early stages of a conflict can, and often does, dictate what happens later in the encounter, as well as its ultimate consequences. In particular, what happens initially usually determines whether a conflict will escalate or deescalate, becoming unproductive or productive for the people involved.

It is important to keep in mind that the uncontrolled escalation of a competitive encounter can change an apparently minor disagreement into something resembling World War III. Part of learning to handle confrontations effectively is acquiring the ability to distinguish between potentially good and bad conflicts *during their early stages*. Thus, we need to learn to recognize the symptoms of disagreements that potentially lead to escalating and unproductive conflicts. This is not always easy, but there are several obvious identifiers of potentially good and bad conflicts. One class of such identifiers is the characteristics of the people in the encounter. People who are likely to engage in unproductive conflicts are the easiest to spot. (See Box 12.1)

Specifically, individuals likely to escalate a conflict and cause it to have unproductive outcomes often show signs of stress, even during the early stages. Such signs can include a conspicuous loss of energy or dedication; rapid conversation; noticeable anxiety; and various forms of compulsive behavior, such as overeating, excessive consumption of alcohol, or drug abuse. If an unproductive conflict persists over a long period, other symptoms are likely to be evident. These might include spending inappropriate amounts of time and resources to undermine an opponent at the expense of getting important work done.[7] Many of the behaviors of John and Loretta fell into this category.

BOX 12.1   🔍 *A Closer Look*

Observable Indicators of Unproductive and Productive Conflict

Unproductive Indicators

Decrease in dedication.

Anxiety and energy loss.

Rapid speech or conversation.

Excessive or compulsive behaviors.

Attempts to sabotage or undermine.

Productive Indicators

Friendly conversation.

Open discussion and deliberation.

Productive problem solving.

Creativity and innovation.

Careful and critical analysis.

There are a variety of additional identifiable indicators of unproductive conflicts as well. The effects of conflict on individuals tend to vary, both by person and by particular situation. It is important to be able to recognize the negative signs of either a useful and positive conflict or one leading to counterproductivity. If we recognize these signs in time, it may be possible to redirect a degenerating communication encounter into one that yields productive consequences.

Productive conflicts can be identified by a different set of signs. The most important are the participants' characteristics and actions. The most obvious include friendly conversation between the opponents. At the nonverbal level, the signs are smiles versus frowns, friendly versus threatening gestures, and the distance at which the opponents have positioned themselves during their encounter.

Most of the constructive signs are very obvious. Yet, typically, people who witness a productive conflict tend to see the encounter as negative

because people are committed to the idea that all conflicts are somehow destructive. As explained earlier, such a narrow interpretation is both incorrect and unfortunate. Certain types of conflicts can result in positive consequences that far outweigh the potential drawbacks.

For example, two individuals working together on the design for a product's sales campaign with a profit potential are likely to engage in conflicts. Disagreements will inevitably occur over issues pertinent to the potential effectiveness of the campaign. These may focus on which media to use, how to phrase the advertising copy, what colors are best, what meanings to imply, whether personal endorsements are worthwhile, and so on. In such a case, some level of disagreement is a normal part of a productive working relationship.

Conflicts of this kind amount to a forum for deliberating on and discussing important professional ideas. Depending on the profession, the result of such a conflict can be a thorough and critical analysis leading to a variety of ways to solve problems more effectively. Those solutions may be innovative legal strategies, more accurate medical diagnoses, more efficient production techniques, or (among students) more effective presentations in classes. Constructive conflicts of this type are common in almost all educational, professional, and business environments.

Conflicts can be productive in *any* setting where people communicate with one another. For example, conflicts of varying intensity constantly arise between husbands and wives. Most couples find some mutually acceptable means of dealing with such disputes—they have to if they are to continue their relationship over time. These solutions range from the congenial settlement of long-term disagreements to the mutual definition of acceptable ways to communicate during heated discussions over sensitive issues. Thus, constructive conflict and negotiation can be beneficial for couples because it signals a commitment to the relationship.[8] To illustrate this point, consider some typical and potentially productive conflicts that were observed between a husband and wife.

Marla and Tom spent many years dating before they were married. Afterward, they found that living together involved a variety of problems, which, if not handled constructively, could affect the stability of their relationship. They hadn't anticipated having conflicts over such issues as money, domestic chores, disciplining children, relating to friends, privacy, or pets—to list just a few of the issues that caused trouble during the early years of their marriage. During the first year, especially, it seemed as if almost every issue they dealt with provided a basis for disagreement. They often didn't understand why they were so frequently at odds with each other.

Ironically, when Marla and Tom were dating they seemed to agree on almost everything of importance. They truly believed that they had considered and worked through all the potentially rough spots in their relationship. They were so sure that they were completely compatible, and that they agreed on everything important, that marriage seemed the natural next step.

Clearly, any number of things happen to people when they marry that can contribute to the occurrence of conflict. For example, research has identified three primary tensions that can lead to conflict for such couples. First, they will experience differing needs for *independence,* and changes in these needs are highly likely to produce conflict. Another source of potential conflict is each individual's need for *expression.* Each must learn to balance the need to state personal views with remaining open to the other's views. Finally, *change* is also a source of tension, as the couple balances the need for predictability and novelty in their relationship.[9]

Thus, it is in the first few years of marriage that people are particularly likely to experience conflicts. During this period, failures to resolve conflicts often have negative outcomes. Statistics on divorce show that breakups are most likely within the first 10 years. If the marriage survives this critical early period, it is likely to last much longer.[10]

There is no way to simulate and work through the problems of marriage before the relationship becomes a fact. Marriage means forming a family in a legal sense, merging resources into a single economic unit, changing relationships with friends, renting or buying a home, carrying on domestic activities, earning a steady income, and relating to in-laws. Living together can provide at least some indications of potential sources of conflict, but the marriage and family relationship is far more complex. Moreover, many issues that new couples face after marriage are poorly understood beforehand, or they seemed insignificant during the periods of dating and engagement. At that time, love and romance were the priorities in their lives.

Generally, then, the single most important issue for newlyweds is not where and how they will live, or even when they will have children and how they will raise them. The truly critical issue is how they will handle their conflicts. In large part, the success or failure of their marriage hangs on that issue. If they allow minor disagreements over the problems that arise to escalate into negative and unproductive conflicts, they will soon be making arrangements with divorce lawyers. If they can deal with their disagreements, and keep their conflicts from escalating, they are more likely to continue their married life together.

Fortunately, when conflicts occur, many couples try to direct their discussions toward productive outcomes, which is just what is required. Obviously, the actual nature of the effort depends largely on the specific causes of each conflict; however, it also depends greatly on the probable reactions of the people involved in the encounter. It is important, then, to consider the common ways in which people deal with conflict.

Common Causes of Conflict

It is important to understand some of the common *causes* of conflicts. Recall that conflict was defined earlier within an economic perspective. The definition stressed that conflicts arise when there is a scarcity of some reward over which competition has developed. This is still a good explanation, but two other major causes can also play a part in generating conflicts between people. One is obvious, consisting of the *meanings* constructed by each party for the messages transmitted and received during a process of communication. The other cause is more subtle. It consists of *contextual factors*—physical settings, sociocultural situations, and social relationships in which people communicate.

Misunderstood Meanings as a Primary Cause

To say that the meanings people construct during processes of communication can be a primary cause of conflict is to state the obvious. Unless people communicate with each other, there is no way for them either to initiate or to engage in conflict. In this sense, the meanings aroused as people disagree, become competitive, or get angry are—as logicians say—a "necessary" but not "sufficient" condition. Conflicts of all types are in some way an outgrowth of human communication.[11] By the same reasoning, it is our ability to communicate fully and effectively that enables us to resolve conflicts. Ironically, then, although communication skills enable us to show aggression and hostility toward each other, it is precisely these same skills that provide the foundation for peaceful resolution of conflicts.

Returning to the opening discussion of what happened between John and Loretta, their conflict started with a work assignment communicated by their boss. Loretta communicated her concerns to their boss about John's probable interpretations of the meaning of the assignment when it was given to her, but the boss ignored these messages. Then, every time Loretta attempted to clarify the meaning of the assignment for John, he became increasingly hostile. Eventually, what John provided in the way of feedback to Loretta made her change from a patient compromiser to a hostile competitor. When that happened, both John and Loretta

began communicating messages with negative, malicious, and hateful meanings about each other to other employees and to their boss. The meeting at which the boss demanded an end to the conflict also depended on communication. Thus, from the beginning, the meanings constructed by each party from the messages transmitted served to define, maintain, and escalate their conflict.

Generally, then, problems of meaning are at the heart of virtually any conflict. Stated more systematically, the *constructions of meaning* by communicating parties assume a primary instrumental role in generating and escalating conflicts. Also, messages transmitted and interpreted by senders and receivers who are in the process of conflict development are likely to be of *low accuracy*. These two conditions work together as central causal factors in producing and intensifying controversies.

Contextual Factors That Can Generate Conflict

Although, as the previous section indicates, misinterpretations of meanings may be primary causes of conflicts between people, other conditions typically seem to the participants to be the real causes. In particular, many people in a conflict come to believe that their opponent's flawed personality is responsible for what occurs. In fact, this is almost universal. To the participants in a conflict, it seems obvious that bad people cause bad relationships.

To those outside the conflict, this is not at all obvious. It usually seems to observers that both parties are decent people and that their conflict must be the result of other factors. In most cases, this is far closer to the truth. The flawed-personality explanation seldom holds up.

A very different set of factors that contribute to the generation of conflict can be found in the *context* within which communication takes place. Here, as the general transactions model suggests, both the sociocultural situation in which the communicators are involved and the social relationships that exist between them play parts in shaping the meanings they construct as they communicate. The physical setting may also play a part, but it is these two contextual features that contribute most significantly to the generation or escalation of a conflict, regardless of the personalities involved.

The sociocultural situation.   It is not difficult to see how the sociocultural situation in which people pursue goals can be a factor in generating conflict. In the conflict that developed and escalated between John and Loretta, both parties were in a work situation. In that feature of their context, both were dedicated to the same overall group goals: doing a good job in carrying out the assignments of the personnel unit. However, each had very different personal goals. One party (John) believed strongly that the goals of the unit could best be accomplished by having him pursue his personal goal: conducting all evaluations of new programs for recruiting and training. He felt strongly that it was his legitimate right to do so. The boss had another view, and she gave the assignment to Loretta. Although Loretta sympathized with John's position, she had her own personal career goals to think of, and she wanted the boss's approval. This kind of situation—where all the parties are basically good people, but all are convinced that they are in the right in pursuing their own goals—is almost certain to generate conflict.

Counterparts to John and Loretta's situation are common in daily life. Every family in which a husband and wife both have jobs to which each is dedicated has many potential sources of conflict. Personal goals, work goals, and family goals can produce an unstable mix. Two common goal conflicts come easily to mind: (1) If either the husband or the wife has a great opportunity for advancement, but it requires moving to another city, which partner should sacrifice his or her career goals? (2) If the husband's or the wife's job requires evening and weekend work to be successful, should the partner complain or make sacrifices to help achieve that goal?

Even achieving the routine domestic goal of living together as a family provides bases for conflict. For example, whose job is it to do the shopping, run the vacuum cleaner, look after the cars, make the beds in the morning, do the laundry, feed the cat, cook the meals, clean up the kitchen, and take out the garbage (to mention only a few domestic tasks)? Each of these may seem to be a minor assignment, but each poses the potential for a disagreement that can escalate into conflict.

Social expectations.   The way in which expected patterns of social relationships are a basic feature of a communication context was discussed at length in Chapter 5. It was pointed out that the basic social rules for behavior in human groups—norms, roles, ranks, and controls—provide powerful definitions concerning who can legitimately communicate what kinds of messages to whom within a particular social situation. The discussion in Chapter 7 focused on how misunderstandings or misinterpretations of those social expectations are often at the heart of breakdowns and difficulties in groups; serious problems of group disintegration can develop when there is confusion concerning any of those rules and expectations.

In precisely the same way, conflicts can arise. That is, conflicts among members of a group tend to occur when inaccuracies in communication lead to normative confusion, unclear definitions of roles, inadequate understanding of the rules of power and authority (social ranks), and ineffective messages of social control.

How difficulties with such rules can contribute to a conflict can be illustrated by referring again to John and Loretta's case. The social relationships between them in the workplace were defined by a large number of norms, role definitions, considerations of social ranking, and social controls. These placed many demands on them—dictating both their overall behavior in the group and the kinds of messages each could transmit to others. These rules were shaped by a number of policies, decisions, practices, and company politics.[12] Like all employees, John and Loretta constantly had to deal with these complexities and consider them when formulating messages and making decisions.

Looking more closely, a number of norms common to almost any work group were openly violated by both John and Loretta. For example, the boss pointed out that they had been wasting time—absolutely unacceptable in work settings. They had also been interfering with the work of others—again, a violation of norms and unacceptable. Each apparently had been bad-mouthing and acting viciously to hurt the career chances of the other—serious transgressions. Although these deviations of norms may have come about because each of the parties deliberately chose to behave in that way, other normative problems were not under their control. For example, Loretta had to follow a compelling norm demanding that she satisfy the boss by doing a good job. At the same time, she had to cope with a different norm that required her to avoid hurting the feelings of her friend John. It was not possible to comply with both norms–a situation of *anomie,* a contradiction and confusion of norms.

Another confusion in social relationships that contributed to their conflict was the conflicting role definitions that prevailed. Specifically, John was convinced that he was supposed to do what his job description stated. Such descriptions communicate clear, formal definitions of an employee's rights, duties, and responsibilities. However, the boss confused the situation by assigning the evaluation to Loretta—communicating a different set of rights, duties, and responsibilities to both parties. Job descriptions (and even temporary assignments) of work roles indicate what employees are supposed to do (or not do) if they are to perform their work satisfactorily. Workers can experience confusion when their roles are not clear or when they conflict with those of others.

In many respects, then, the social expectations prevailing in John and Loretta's work situation forced both of them into a no-win situation. Both may have behaved badly, but they were caught in a turmoil of confusing and even conflicting definitions of norms and roles created by the boss.

In the situation that developed, therefore, the boss must bear a special responsibility. An effective leader understands social expectations defining relationships and takes steps to head off conflicts before they begin by appropriate communication. Instead of explaining to John ahead of time her valid reasons for assigning the evaluation to Loretta, and gaining his approval and support, the boss let a serious conflict develop. Only after it escalated did she step in and forcefully exercise social control by communicating her power and authority in strong terms. Gentler controls communicated earlier would have been far more effective. Therefore, if anyone was most responsible for the messy situation that developed, it was neither John nor Loretta. It was the boss.

Generally, then, the social settings within which people communicate can be major factors in generating or escalating conflicts. Potentials for their development arise out of the general sociocultural situation (work, family, and so on) within which people interact, and especially when confusions and contradictions exist in the rules and expectations defining their social relationships. Although conflicts can arise because of personality clashes, few are due solely to the bad actions of bad people.

Personal Styles of Coping with Conflict

Much human behavior is relatively predictable because it follows patterns of action and reaction deeply established by the rules and expectations of our culture. This is certainly true of reactions to conflict. That is, it is possible to predict with some degree of accuracy how people will try to deal with various kinds of conflict situations. These can be described in terms of what communication researchers refer to as *personal conflict styles.*[13]

Although the idea of common coping styles to deal with conflict has been examined in a number of ways, the discussion here will focus on an assessment and classification system devised by Ralph Kilmann and Kenneth Thomas.[14] According to these investigators, one's personal style of handling conflicts is based on the need to meet two interconnected yet competing objectives: *concern for self* and *concern for the opponent*. Although these appear to be different goals, they actually overlap in terms of the way we make decisions about coping with confrontations. Kilmann and Thomas maintain that this struggle over goals is a reflection of our underlying desire to be either competitive or cooperative in dealing with opponents in a conflict situation.

Our resolution of these two interdependent goals in a specific situation represents our predictable style of reacting to all kinds of conflicts. This formulation allows for the assessment of five distinct **conflict styles** based on competition, collaboration, compromise, avoidance, and accommodation. These five coping strategies point directly to alternative ways in which conflicts are typically handled. (See Box 12.2.)

The Competitive Style

Although the term *conflict* is generally defined to mean some sort of competition over something of importance, certain people are so predictably and strongly competitive that they can be described as fitting this style. What are such people like? Strongly competitive people narrowly view all conflicts as win-lose events. They believe that winning is their only goal and that having a concern for their opponent is both unnecessary and unimportant. Highly competitive people would agree with statements like "Once I get going in a heated discussion, I am unable to stop" and "I like the exhilaration of engaging in disagreements and conflicts." In short, such people are commonly very aggressive in the way they react to conflicts.[15]

Individuals who clearly illustrate a **competitive style** are often found in jobs or professions where this style may be an advantage, such as courtroom lawyers, police interrogators, labor

Kilmann and Thomas's Coping Strategies for Conflict

1. *The competitive style.* Characteristic of strongly competitive people who view all conflicts as win-lose events; they believe that winning is their only goal and that having a concern for their opponent is both unnecessary and unimportant.
2. *The collaborative style.* Characteristics of individuals who not only are seeking personal goals in a conflict situation but also care about their opponents' objectives.
3. *The compromising style.* Characteristic of people who fall somewhere between the competitive and cooperative styles. Their behavior in conflicts is sometimes incorrectly interpreted as giving in.
4. *The avoidance style.* People with this style do not expect to attain personal goals, nor are they sympathetic to their opponents' goals. They refuse to engage in conflict. Avoiders stay away from situations where conflicts are likely to arise.
5. *The accommodating style.* This is the opposite of the competitive style. Such individuals are passive; they forgo trying to reach their personal goal, opting to let their opponents reach their goals.

leaders, salespeople, or people doing other types of work in which conflicts are defined as strictly win-lose encounters. For example, in labor-management negotiation meetings, where demands are being made by representatives from both sides, every issue is defined as a win-lose conflict. Opponents on both sides predictably act as if they are doing battle to their last breath. In some respects, such competitive behavior is often seen as acceptable in negotiation sessions for union contracts because they have become a tradition, but these same behaviors can be far less productive in other conflict situations. However, they are typical of highly competitive individuals who tend to use this style as a means of resolving their disputes.

The Collaborative Style

Another common style of coping with conflict is based on collaboration, which literally means working jointly or willingly in cooperation with an opponent. The **collaborative style** is characteristic of people who not only are seeking their own goals in a conflict situation but also have a sincere concern for their opponents. People who use this style would endorse statements like "When I get in a conflict with someone, I try very hard to find mutually acceptable solutions," or "I like to assert myself, but I also like to cooperate with others." These kinds of statements communicate that the person is trying to find alternative solutions to conflict that will maximize reaching goals for both participants.

An example of collaborative styles of conflict would be two members of a study group who have a conflict over whether each chapter in their textbook should be outlined and summarized as a study aid. Each disagrees with the other's position on the need for the outline. However, both parties feel that their personal objective in studying together is to get a better grade on the next test (self-goal). At the same time, they believe that by working together both parties can score higher than by studying alone (opponent's goals). Thus, in an attempt to maintain a productive relationship, they resolve their disagreements and work collaboratively toward a shared interpretation of what should be done.

The Compromising Style

A third common and predictable way of coping with conflict is based on compromise. this means reaching agreement by making mutual concessions. People who use a **compromising style** fall between competitive and cooperative styles on the coping strategies continuum. The behavior of compromisers in conflicts is sometimes incorrectly interpreted by observers as "giving in."[16] Individuals using this style would agree with statements like "I accept the fact that I can't always get my way," "I am thankful to get part of what I asked for," and "I know I am going into a conflict where I will have to give a little."

An example of a person using this style would be an individual who is brought in as a third party to help resolve a conflict. Neither of the protagonists is willing to reach an agreement, and all efforts to resolve their differences thus far have resulted in increased hostility. Finally, they agree to seek help. Typically, third parties in such mediation efforts try to get the participants to compromise. There really are no alternatives to getting each party to move toward a middle-ground position so that each of the opponents makes equal compromises.

The Avoidance Style

The typical coping style of individuals who are passive, subservient, and acquiescent in conflicts is avoidance. People using an *avoidance style* do not expect to attain personal goals from the conflict, and they are not sympathetic to their opponents' goals. They just want to escape from the whole confrontation. Thus, they generally remain idle and refuse to engage in what we would normally expect from people in a conflict. Avoiders simply stay away from situations where conflicts are likely to occur. If they are in a conversation that is beginning to sound like a disagreement that might lead to a conflict, they find some way to remove themselves from confrontation.

Conflict avoiders are easily recognized. Many are highly apprehensive individuals. Some are even reclusive people who fear all interaction with others. For example, people with high levels of communication apprehension experience fear and anxiety when they have to talk with others in a variety of social contexts. If they are communicating in a situation that might lead to conflict, they will either excuse themselves or find some reason to change the topic of discussion. They will not make any effort to pursue their side of a position on an issue.

At the same time, people use avoidance for other reasons. Many times conflicts break out among one's fellow workers, associates, relatives, or friends. Often, taking part in such confrontations has no payoff for an individual. Indeed, it can easily result in significant losses. It may be far better to stand on the sidelines and watch the fight, rather than join the fray for no personal benefit. Although this is also a form of avoidance, it is a mature and thoughtful strategy that does not imply negative, apprehensive personality characteristics.

The Accommodating Style

The last style of coping with conflict in the Kilmann and Thomas category system is based on accommodation. People who use an **accommodating style** give in to their opponents. Thus, accommodators are the opposite of competitors. They tend to be passive in that they forgo trying to reach their personal goal, preferring to let their opponents reach their objectives. Moreover, accommodators typically go along with the position argued by the majority of the individuals in the conflict. In other words, they exhibit no resistance and make every effort to yield to their opponents' decisions.

Examples of accommodators in conflicts are those who never want to be the leader of a group, those who commonly defer to authority, and those who place a higher value on relationships than on being decision makers. Arguing with accommodators is very difficult: They simply will not engage in much disagreement over anything. Even if they initially take a position on a particular issue, they will push the point only to a limited extent. Their primary objective in all conflict situations is to conform to the majority position of their opponents.

Although each of the above styles may be used exclusively by some people, it is more likely that a particular person will *shift among these various styles*, depending on the nature of the conflict and the characteristics of the people involved. On any given day, an individual may choose to compete vigorously with one person, collaborate with someone else, and compromise with still a third. The same individual may avoid a particular conflict but accommodate in another. It all depends on the circumstances and on whether the conflict is with a loved one, a stranger, a person in a subservient position, a boss, or a child.

These conflict styles offer different models for us to apply to try to defuse, escalate, or ignore a particular conflict. This implies, of course, that we are capable of shifting from one style to another. If this is not the case, and if we do tend to use one strategy to the exclusion of the others, at least understanding our likely reaction to conflict situations can be helpful. Specifically, such understanding provides us with important information about ourselves that can help us in selecting conflicts in which we really want to engage. In this way, we can better assess which conflicts are likely to be productive for us and which strategy we want to use in managing our conflict relationships.

Successful Conflict Negotiation

Now that we have seen some of the more salient causes of conflicts and the different strategies people use to cope with them, the remaining question in this chapter is, How do people successfully negotiate conflicts when they occur? Answering this question begins by defining the term **negotiation**. Then, clear-cut principles and guidelines for negotiating many kinds of conflicts will be presented.[17]

Understanding Negotiation

In a basic sense, *negotiation* refers to *a continuing set of transactions in which proposed solutions are communicated back and forth between opponents for the goal of reaching agreement on ways to resolve a conflict.* A principle that is evident in this definition is that the basis of negotiation is carefully planned communication with the goal of the mutual construction of similar meanings between opponents. Thus, communication plays two parts in conflicts: Just as it is a primary cause of conflict, it is also the principal means by which opponents negotiate conflicts.

The effective resolution of a conflict cannot begin until all the individuals involved start to explore ways in which they can seriously propose and consider *alternative solutions* to their disagreement. This may seem like a strange way to explain such a process, because it says that the people involved need to settle on the rules for resolving their differences before they actually begin the process itself. Moreover, for negotiation to get off to a good start, the primary objective of the discussions that are to take place between opponents must be agreed upon. This primary objective is to reach an agreement as an end-product of the negotiations. In other words, if people agree that they want to agree, and then set up rules for proceeding, they can then begin the process of working out the specifics. After that, discussions continue until communication between opponents results in an arrangement that is acceptable to everyone involved.

As implied earlier, equally critical to being able to negotiate a conflict successfully is that opponents agree to communicate about *potential solutions*. Without sincere agreement to communicate by all opponents, efforts to negotiate will prove unprofitable. All the discussion in the world will not result in a successful resolution if the people involved do not agree that they want to air their grievances and try to resolve their differences. In fact, what usually occurs when opponents in a conflict are not serious about negotiating is further escalation of the controversy.

Guidelines for Negotiation

Over several decades, a group of researchers at Harvard University studied extensively the process of conflict negotiation. The result of these efforts has been the identification of a number of specific guidelines concerning *the most feasible way to negotiate conflicts through the use of carefully planned communication.*[18] Their program has been widely recognized as one of the most effective approaches to conflict resolution. The section that follows is directly derived from that program, with a review of the basic features of the researchers' suggested guidelines and illustrations for using them. The objective is to present ways in which individuals can better understand the process of successful negotiation and negotiate their own conflicts.

Part of the popularity of this approach has to do with its demonstrated applicability. That is, it provides a practical and effective way to negotiate conflicts by using a specific set of guidelines for planned communication. The method, called *principled negotiation,* is designed to help people get what they want from others in every conceivable type of conflict—from the simplest to the most complex—and to do so within an ethical framework, which is very important. For example, principled negotiation has been used successfully in a variety of legal situations (including sticky divorce cases), union contracts, and a host of political and organizational conflicts, from local to international levels.

These recommendations boil down to eight points, which, if applied correctly, lead to successful negotiation and thus conflict resolution. (See Box 12.3.) Each point is a kind of rule of thumb as to what should and should not be done. Each guideline is discussed and then applied to John and Loretta's case.

Don't bargain over positions.   People trying to negotiate should not attempt to bargain over, to explain, or to justify the different positions they hold on the issue of disagreement. Conflicts are seldom if ever negotiated when people try to bargain solely over their opinions on a particular issue. If each party in a conflict takes a strong position on an issue, and if the positions are far apart, there is simply no way for negotiation to occur. People are never going to reach

BOX 12.3 ⚲ *A Closer Look*

Eight Recommendations for Principled Negotiation

1. *Don't bargain over positions.* Never bargain over the different positions people hold on the issue of disagreement. Trying to defend different positions contributes to more disagreement.
2. *Separate the people from the problem.* Look beyond the personal characteristics and suspected motives of the people involved to what actually led up to the conflict.
3. *Focus on interests, not positions.* Look beyond individual positions to the goals and needs of each of the participants.
4. *Invent options for mutual gain.* It is not true that there is only room for one winner. Opponents should try to invent options of mutual gain.
5. *Insist on using objective criteria.* Begin negotiation by setting mutually agreed-upon rules within which to discuss potential solutions.
6. *Develop the best alternative.* Know ahead of time exactly what the bottom line will be to resolve the conflict.
7. *Cope with resistance to negotiation.* Don't attack the position the resistant opponents are advocating. Deal with what is compelling them to be resistant. Minimize the time spent defending ideas; ask for criticism and advice from opponents. Ask questions and pause for answers.
8. *Deflect dirty tricks.* Recognize a dirty trick; raise the issue candidly, question the appropriateness of using the trick, and negotiate over it.

Recall a similar stalemate over positions in John and Loretta's case. Loretta approached John several times in an attempt to explain and justify her position regarding the work assignment. She wanted to stress that it wasn't her fault and that she was simply acting under orders. John, on the other hand, wasn't buying that interpretation, and he wanted to defend his position that evaluations were his turf.

The result was an early collapse of the relationship. Her bargaining attempts increased John's hostility toward her. Moreover, because Loretta was frustrated in her bargaining effort, she ended up as antagonistic toward John as he was toward her. They held very different positions on the issue of who should be evaluating the staffing operation. It was not a viable issue for bargaining. It didn't even matter that Loretta's position was the result of their boss having directed her to do the assignment. As long as they narrowly stuck to their initial positions, no concessions could be made.

Separate the people from the problem. This rule stresses the need to get the participants to look beyond personal characteristics and suspected motives to see the nature of the problem itself. That is, what led up to the conflict? What is at stake for both parties? How might it have happened to anyone in the same social situation and set of relationships? This makes a great deal of sense. Individuals engaged in conflicts often tend to build up more and more antagonism toward each other. The results of such antagonism typically include rampant misunderstanding, counterproductive communication, and irrational or overly emotional reactions.

This was clearly the case between John and Loretta. Each of them failed to separate the person they were dealing with from the problem. In fact, John and Loretta saw each other as the problem. As long as they continued to approach their conflict in this fashion, no negotiation could occur. The more John and Loretta associated the issue of their conflict with their beliefs about the personal motives and characteristics of the other, the more they became each other's

an agreement over an issue if they stubbornly maintain very different views. Moreover, trying to defend very different positions on an issue can only contribute to opponents' greater and more heated separation on that issue.

enemy. They forgot that they were working in the same organization; they forgot that they shared the same basic business goals. Their conflict became a personal vendetta—a search for ways to punish the other as a bad person.

Separating people and their personalities from the problems that cause conflicts reinforces that it is the relationships between the people that are most important. If people take the position that their relationships must remain constructive if at all possible, their opponents will change how they perceive, think about, and communicate with them. Thus, the participants are less likely to overreact emotionally to what they say and do to each other. What occurs when opponents separate people from problems is an increased willingness to negotiate compromises and solutions that may be acceptable to all.

Focus on interests, not positions. This guideline recalls the first principle: the recommendation that opponents refrain from bargaining over positions. Instead, opponents should focus on interests, looking beyond their positions to the personal goals and needs that must be served for each party. That is, in all conflicts, opponents take positions because of the personal interests at stake. In John and Loretta's case, John's primary concern was to protect all the rights, duties, and obligations associated with his job. Loretta's primary interest was to do what her boss directed her to do, so as to remain a valued employee.

If John and Loretta had focused on their primary interests and dealt directly with what was at stake, they could have negotiated their conflict themselves. There would have been no need to involve their boss. They could have explained their interests, discussed alternative ways to solve their dilemma, and still found ways to satisfy their boss. For example, John could have worked with Loretta on the evaluation, which would have avoided the negative consequences of their extended conflict.

Invent options for mutual gain. An important part of resolving a conflict is to get to a

point where each party gets something he or she values out of the process. One of the many incorrect assumptions that we make that can lead to an escalating conflict is that there is room for only one winner. This is by no means always true; as indicated earlier in the chapter, people engaged in conflict do not have to be enemies. Remember also that conflicts, if handled properly, can actually be beneficial to everyone involved.

To illustrate, if John and Loretta had not acted as if there was only one solution to their disagreement, a variety of other possible outcomes could have been considered. From the start, the position of each was "It's my way or no way." Making the assumption that there is only one possible solution precludes negotiation.[19] The opposite is assuming that there are alternative ways to resolve the problem so that everyone can gain. This is an important foundation for successful negotiation. If both John and Loretta had been open to communicating about options for mutual gain, they would have been able to negotiate their conflict without intervention by their boss.

Insist on using objective criteria. Remember that, in negotiation, it is important to have mutually agreed-upon rules within which to communicate about potential solutions. Establishing shared criteria for evaluating proposals from one side or the other is part of that process. If this is not done, opponents in the heat of an intense conflict typically impose subjective criteria when they are evaluating proposed solutions. The phrase *subjective criteria* refers to personal or private standards for making such evaluations—standards not necessarily shared by others.

Subjective criteria seem fair *only to the person using them.* Objective criteria seem appropriate to *most people.* When subjective criteria are used, conflicts escalate because they often seem unfair to the other party. Employing an agreed-upon set of objective criteria that both parties regard as fair provides an important basis for successful negotiation.

Using subjective standards will almost always lead to such evaluations as "Your proposal is totally unfair to me" and, in response, "You are unwilling to make any concessions." These judgments are oriented toward only one side's feelings and interests. A more effective approach is for opponents to develop a mutually agreed-upon set of objective criteria before negotiation even starts.

Neither John nor Loretta even considered employing objective criteria for evaluating their positions in the conflict. If they had mutually generated a set of objective criteria when their conflict first started, they could have handled the disagreement much more rationally. Also, if they had taken the time to do this, they would have been able to reach an agreement long before their boss called them into her office.

Develop the best alternative. Even when people follow the five previous guidelines, things can go wrong. In this case, several other strategies need to be addressed to reach a successful negotiation. One important strategy is for each person to develop an acceptable fallback position in case the negotiated outcome is not entirely satisfactory. In other words, it is wise to have in mind an acceptable alternative to what is considered the most desirable negotiated agreement.

This alternative refers to knowing ahead of time exactly what is acceptable as a resolution to a particular conflict. It is the bottom line by which a particular conflict can be resolved. It has to be a realistic position. It may not be the most desirable option, but one that could be agreed to if all else fails. When a party to a conflict has such a position already in mind, he or she is in a much better position to ask for concessions from the opponent.

If both John and Loretta had gone into their disagreement with a solid grasp of their own best alternative to a negotiated resolution, the composition of their conflict would have been very different. For example, although John normally had the power position in the staffing area, Loretta had more power because their boss had given her the assignment. John was

taking a no-win position when he expected her to back away from that assignment. However, he could have developed an acceptable alternative that would have allowed him to gain at least some concessions from Loretta. For example, he could have agreed to assist her, which would have permitted him to provide input into the assessment of the staffing plan he had originally developed. This would not have been difficult because Loretta was initially open to communicating with John about the assignment and at that point would have accepted his help. Thus, John lost out completely by not having considered an acceptable alternative.

Cope with resistance to negotiation. Like Loretta, we all run into people who simply stonewall all attempts to negotiate a conflict. This can bring things to a permanent halt. We must be prepared to cope with such a situation without abandoning the negotiation process. Fortunately, most people, even when in a resistant mood, can be persuaded to communicate and even to negotiate if it is done in the right way. It can be a complex and difficult task, but there are several ways it can be approached.

First, never attack the position a resistant opponent is advocating.[20] Look beyond the position to the personal values and interests that are motivating the individual on the issue. It is these that are leading to his or her unwillingness to change. By dealing directly with what is driving the resistance, it is much easier to weaken it. Proposed solutions can be based on those same values and interests. People have a difficult time resisting proposed solutions that are consistent with their own needs and orientations.

Second, minimize the time spent defending your own ideas during conflict, and solicit criticism and counsel from your opponent. This disarming tactic seems to work especially well. When given the opportunity, people can rarely resist the chance to criticize and give advice. This, of course, changes their perspectives on the issues at stake.

Third, ask questions and pause for answers. This promotes a transactional process—a rather simple and obvious idea based on the analyses of verbal and nonverbal communication in the early chapters. It is an important tactic for lowering resistance to negotiation because it opens and promotes communication, which in turn provides a basis for proposing mutually acceptable criteria, different perspectives, alternative solutions, and so forth.

Promoting a transactional process would have helped greatly in John and Loretta's conflict. Specifically, if during Loretta's initial attempts to communicate with John she had backed off and asked him a few simple questions, he might have responded differently. This is not to say that Loretta was at fault for John's early resistance; but if she had advanced questions respectfully, with each followed by a period of silence, John might have responded in a positive way. Creating the need for someone to answer a question sometimes brings him or her to do so.

Deflect dirty tricks.   Many conflicts are characterized by dirty tricks that opponents often play on each other.[21] These can include using deception, inventing phony facts, invoking ambiguous authority, creating stress, employing retribution, and making personal attacks. (See Box 12.4.) This final guideline is based on three steps

to follow when an opponent appears to be employing a dirty trick: (1) "Recognize the tactic," (2) "Raise the issue explicitly," and (3) "Question the tactic's legitimacy and desirability—negotiate over it."[22] These three steps can sometimes deflect further dirty tricks.

Chapter Review

- Every human conflict represents a unique and complex process. However, each of us can determine the kinds of outcomes we get from the conflicts in our lives.

- Conflict is a large part of our culture. Many conflicts result from our shared cultural orientations regarding competition and getting ahead.

- Conflicts are not inherently negative; many can have positive consequences. People determine how productive or unproductive their conflicts will be. Some people tend to be highly competitive; others are collaborative. Some are com-

promising or accommodating; others attempt to avoid conflict at any cost. Finally, some people shift from one style to another as the occasion demands.

- The primary cause of conflict is problems in communication. However, context can serve as the basis of conflict as well. Both the specific situation in which we pursue goals and the social relationships that prevail in that situation can cause conflicts between people.

- The Harvard group's recommendations for negotiating conflict include suggestions concerning bargaining over positions, separating people from the problem, focusing on interests rather than positions, inventing options for mutual gain, using objective criteria for assessing issues, developing a bottom-line position for settling a conflict, coping with resistance to negotiation, and handling dirty tricks.

Key Terms

| conflict | competitive style | compromising style | accommodating style |
| conflict style | collaborative style | avoidance style | negotiation |

Notes

1. This is a real case drawn from the experience of one of the authors who served for several years as an executive in a large corporation. The names are fictitious but not the situation.

2. Berkowitz, L. (1964). Aggressive cues in aggressive behavior and hostility catharsis. *Psychological Review, 71,* 104–122; Berkowitz, L. (1965). The concept of aggressive drive: Some additional considerations. In L. Berkowitz (Ed.), *Advances in experimental social psychology* (vol. 2, pp. 301–329). New York: Academic.

3. DeFleur, M. L., D'Antonio, W. V., & DeFleur, L. B. (1981). *Sociology: Human society* (3rd ed., pp. 93–94). Glenview, IL: Scott, Foresman.

4. At least some Americans stress the opposite—to avoid standing out or being pushy. Native American groups, such as the Hopi and the Pueblo groups of New Mexico, share a strong orientation toward maintaining harmony and avoiding actions that imply one is trying to rise above others.

5. This definition is similar to Lewis Coser's. See: Coser, L. (1956). *The functions of social conflict* (p. 8). New York: Free Press.

6. A similar discussion of conflict is offered in: Jandt, F. E. (1985). *Win-win negotiating: Turning conflict into agreement.* New York: Wiley.

7. Ibid., p. 101.

8. Booth, A., Crouter, A. C., & Clements, M. (Eds.). (2001). *Couples in conflict.* Mahwah, NJ: Lawrence Erlbaum.

9. Pearson, J. C. (2001). Conflict in our intimate relationships. In W. F. Eadie, & P. E. Nelson, (Eds.). *The language of conflict and resolution* (pp. 47–56). Thousand Oaks, CA: Sage.

10. Rollins, B. C., & Feldman, H. (1970). Marital satisfaction over the life cycle. *Journal of Marriage and the Family, 32,* 20–28.

11. Ibid., p. 10.

12. Koehler, J. W., Anatol, K. W. E. & Appelbaum, R. L. (1976). *Organizational communication: Behavioral perspectives* (p. 241). New York: Holt, Rinehart, and Winston.

13. Frost, J. H., & Wilmot, W. W. (1991). *Interpersonal conflict* (3rd ed.). Dubuque, IA: William C. Brown; Cai, D. A., & Fink, E. L. (2002). Conflict style differences between individuals and collectivists. *Communication Monographs, 69,* 1, 67–87.

14. Kilmann, R., & Thomas, K. (1975). Interpersonal conflict-handling behavior as reflections of Jungian personality dimensions. *Psychological Reports, 37,* 971–980.

15. Frost & Wilmot, *Interpersonal conflict,* p. 29.

16. Ibid., p. 31.

17. Fisher, R., & Ury, W. (1987). *Getting to yes: Negotiating agreement without giving in* (p. 33). New York: Penguin.

18. This definition is similar to Fisher and Ury's position. See: Fisher & Ury, *Getting to yes,* p. 33.

19. Ibid., p. 61.

20. Ibid., p. 114.

21. Ibid., pp. 136–138; For the indirect and informal ways subordinates use to "get even," see: Fortado, B. (2001). The metamorphosis of workplace conflict. *Human Relations, 54,* 9, 1189–1221.

22. Ibid., p. 135.

Chapter 13

Using Media to Communicate Interpersonally

Margaret knew that it was going to be a busy day. She was Vice President of Human Resources for Grover Industries, and an important part of her job was to oversee all personnel actions. In plain English, this meant making final decisions regarding hiring, firing, and promoting for her division, as well as representing the corporation in settling grievances with the union and so on. Grover Industries was a large organization, with over 8,000 employees. Her job was to hire well-qualified team-oriented supervisory people; to terminate problem people; and to move the right ones up the ladder.

She began with the stack of memoranda on her desk from supervisors who had interviewed prospective applicants. Each had been screened by the personnel office as well, and their cases had been passed on to her for final approval. The cover memorandum for the first application was from Phyllis, a mid-level manager in accounting. It explained the qualifications of the applicant, where and why the person was needed, and why the manager thought this was a good choice. Margaret was annoyed that the memo from Phyllis rambled on for three and a half pages. She did not have time for long-winded and poorly organized memos, and she also noted with disgust that this one had a number of spelling and grammatical errors. As she turned to the next application, Margaret wrote a note to herself,

"Take another look at Phyllis—maybe we should deny her recent request for promotion."

After making decisions about each new applicant, Margaret carefully composed letters offering positions to those who had been selected. She usually had her assistants use "boilerplate" to write routine correspondence, but she always used her word processor to write letters offering employment. Such letters had to be done carefully, with accurate details of the salary and benefits and a clear explanation of the nature of the position and the duties for which the new hire would be responsible. In the past she had allowed her staff to write such letters, but some such letters had been inaccurate, with poor organization and bad spelling. The staff members who had written these letters were no longer with Grover Industries.

Once the letters were completed, Margaret turned to the long list of telephone calls she had to make. Even though she made dozens of phone calls a day, she did not think the telephone was an effective medium for explaining important ideas or complex situations. Role-taking by phone was impossible with strangers, and feedback was very limited. Moreover, many people used the phone thoughtlessly, such as those who called and just started talking without identifying themselves, leaving her to guess who was on the other end. Margaret thought, "There ought to be some way of training people to deal with the phone more effectively and more confidently."

After lunch, she turned to her e-mail. She screened the list of incoming messages and answered those she felt were most important, leaving the rest for an assistant to deal with.

She shook her head when she saw some of the messages, with poor composition and errors in spelling and grammar. Others appeared to have been dashed off without much thought. "People should learn," Margaret said to herself, "to prepare their messages more clearly when using this medium."

Late that afternoon, when things had quieted down, she used her computer to go on to the Internet. She logged onto a website and learned about an important upcoming meeting of human resource professionals. "Great," she thought, "I'll mark my calendar." She then reviewed Grover's website and updated some information. Previously, that would have been done by a technical expert, but new software made it easy for Margaret to do.

Before wrapping things up for the day, Margaret used the computer for a prearranged conference with the four personnel managers in the other cities with Grover Industries plants. The managers spoke with one another using the voice facility of their computers and saw a small video of each person on the screen. Margaret downloaded some documents and graphics from the conference for later study. "This is really an effective way to discuss common problems," Margaret thought. "Just a few years ago, we would have had to travel to some centrally located city and take a whole day to get done what we just accomplished via the Internet in a computer video-conference of less than an hour."

Using media to communicate directly and effectively with other people may seem simple and easy. However, there are a great many ways that mistakes and unwanted negative impressions can be made.[1] Computers, telephones and all the rest are great, but effective writing and speaking skills when using media are still essential. Such skills are critical for landing a good job and then advancing up the ranks. People with poor spelling and incorrect grammar are easily spotted, as are poor speaking styles. Such individuals are the least likely to be hired, are the most likely to be stuck in dead-end jobs, and are among the first to be fired.

People who work in business, government, education, and elsewhere must initiate written messages and send them via postal or express services, e-mail, fax machines, or other communication media. Although the new technologies make moving messages across space much easier and faster, they are likely to expose people whose writing skills are limited.

A mere 15 years ago, it was easy to correct mistakes in grammar and spelling. Virtually all business letters and memos were dictated to secretaries, who took down messages in shorthand. Many secretaries were able to correct problems of grammar, syntax, or overall message composition before they prepared final copies. They would type a draft and submit it to the originator for approval and signature, along with suggestions for change. Those days are gone. Today, nearly all businesspeople type their own messages on a computer and send them by e-mail, fax, or traditional letter composed with word-processing software. Only a few Neanderthals still use typewriters. Carbon paper has all but disappeared, and secretaries who know how to take shorthand are becoming an extinct species.

This chapter examines the interpersonal communication process as it takes place using a number of different media, from traditional written letters and memos to electronic systems that instantly move information. Significant differences exist between face-to-face communication and mediated communication. The chapter also shows that the widespread adoption of any new communication technology affects the social, economic, and cultural lives of those using it.

Face-to-Face versus Mediated Communication

Chapter 1 discusses human communication as a process that may be conceptualized in both linear and transactional terms. As explained, the linear model indicates that a source person begins with some purpose or goal that can be achieved with a message. The source then selects a pattern of symbols to represent intended meanings. Those same initial stages characterize any linear form of communication, whether media are involved or not. Once the message has been formulated, the transmission stage requires that the distance (and in some cases time) between the message sender and the intended receiver be overcome. Obviously, media are used both to increase the distance the message can travel and reduce the amount of time the transmission requires.

What do such media actually do? In terms of the analysis in Chapter 1, they simply transport "information" from one place to another. Examples of *information* are the sound waves produced by human vocal cords or the variations in light patterns that travel between a person sending a written message and a receiver who reads and interprets the symbols. Information, then, is a set of physical events. It can range from simple agitations of air molecules, or variations in light patterns, to high-frequency radio waves relayed through space by satellites.

Whatever the means of information transmission, in the final stages of the communicative act the physical stimuli are perceived by a human being and reconstructed into symbols. That is, one or more receivers interpret them within their own frameworks of meaning. Those interpretations may or may not match those hoped for by the sender. Accuracy in communication is attained only if the decoded meanings of the receiver correspond to those

Computer technology has become the mainstay for rapid transmission and reception of information all over the world. However, effective writing and speaking skills are still essential to good communication.

intended by the sender. It is with those functions in mind that the actual role of media and the difference they make in the communication process will be examined.

Why Media Matter

A **medium** can be defined simply. It is *a device that moves information over distance (or through time) so that people who are apart can communicate.* The simplest medium that might be imagined is a children's toy, consisting of a wire stretched between two tin cans. When the message sender shouts into his or her tin can, the can's bottom acts as a diaphragm and sends vibrations (information) along the wire. The bottom of the can at the other end vibrates sympathetically and reproduces the sound, which is then interpreted by the receiver. Although it doesn't really work all that well, the communication principles are there. Like the tin cans and the wire, all the media that are used today are designed to move information

across distance, whether they are traditional handwritten letters or sophisticated microchip technologies.

A key question to ask is whether the process of moving information across distance by using a medium *alters the correspondence* in some way between the meanings intended by the sender and those constructed by the receiver. As this section will indicate, the answer is a definite yes. Each medium places its own demands on both the sender and the receiver. As will be seen, mediated communication is both similar to, but different from, face-to-face communication. Some media alter the process greatly. Others do so only minimally.

The major similarity between mediated and face-to-face communication is that there are people at each end—just as in the example of the tin cans and the wire. There is a *source* person transmitting. That source has to formulate a message at one end so that a *receiver* (or receivers) can interpret it at the other. If the medium requires writing, the process is complicated by the rules, skills, and requirements of written expression. So it is with other media. Each has its own requirements. Thus, contemporary media systems—such as cellular telephones, answering machines, facsimile, and computers linked by satellite relays—continue to make use of the basic features of human communication—verbal and written symbols based on language, nonverbal cues and signals, transactional constructions of meaning, and all the rest, but they add additional features as well. Thus, despite the similarities in the underlying principles of all forms of human communication, there are also important differences. Some involve the social relationships that link face-to-face senders and receivers versus mediated communicators. Others involve the technical features of the media themselves.

Media limit effective role-taking. One difference in the social relationship between sender and receiver when media are used is the limit on role-taking. This activity on the part of the message sender is especially critical in face-to-face communication. As explained in Chapter 1, the sender mentally plays the part of the receiver (assuming his or her role) to try to predict how that person will interpret and respond to particular kinds of messages. If the sender knows the receiver well and can anticipate subtle ways in which he or she will interpret a given message, there can be very effective role-taking.

Role-taking can be accomplished reasonably well with some media, such as private and confidential letters between people who know each other intimately. However, it is far less possible to anticipate others' responses in many of the communication contexts where media are used. For example, when a typical internal memo goes out to a number of readers in an organization, it is simply not possible to forecast the potential reactions of each person reading the message. Even when friends talk on the telephone, role-taking can be less than complete. One cannot forecast for sure whether the person at the other end will be bored or excited.

The same is true when drafting an e-mail message to another person. The sender cannot anticipate exactly how the receiver will react as the message is read.[2]

Media limit the adequacy of feedback. A second problem in using media centers on the process of feedback. Here, more depends on the nature of the medium than on the existing relationship between the communicating parties. For example, in a telephone conversation, at least some immediate feedback is possible. Nonverbal cues such as voice tones, long pauses, audible yawns, or laughing convey to the speaker the manner in which his or her message is being received. However, some cues that would be visible in a face-to-face situation cannot be observed. One never knows in a telephone conversation—even one with an intimate friend—whether that person is smiling, frowning, slumped down looking bored, or listening intently with an enthusiastic expression. Thus, a conversation via telephone is not as rich in nonverbal feedback as one in which the two parties can see each other.

Thus, accuracy in communication is automatically reduced by limitations imposed by the use of a medium. For this reason, face-to-face communication is the mode of choice for those who want to get a valid understanding of others' feelings or views or who are trying to gain their cooperation, sell them something, or otherwise influence them. Nothing beats face-to-face communication when accuracy is desired or influence is an important goal. That is true whether it is a conversation among peers, an interview, a personally presented sales pitch, or a talk before a group.

Despite these disadvantages, mediated communication is critical to us all and has long been a part of civilized life. Throughout history, increasingly sophisticated media have been used —from carvings on stone to systems using computers and satellites—to preserve information over time or to send it over longer distances at an ever-faster pace.

How Communication Technologies Change Our Lives

The current so-called revolution in communication processes is more than a change in the gadgets we use or the speed of transmission of messages. Throughout human existence, new media have always altered people's personal and social lives. When papyrus replaced stone, the portability of the new medium allowed empires to extend their boundaries. When Johannes Gutenberg's press made hand-copied manuscripts obsolete, large-scale production of books resulted in the rapid spread of new ideas in science, religion, economics, and politics. Those ideas altered the entire nature of society. Thus, the transition to new communication technologies has always had both personal and social consequences.

The reason for these changes is that new technologies alter the communication process itself. This is because each new medium (1) imposes its own special requirements on the ways in which messages are formulated, (2) governs the speed and convenience with which message transmission takes place, and (3) influences the ways in which receivers reconstruct meaning from what is sent to them.

The ways in which new communication technologies influence both the communication process and the people who use them can be well illustrated by noting the changes that took place during the 19th century after the introduction of the now-venerable telegraph. That new technology (at the time) made it possible to send words at a mind-boggling 186,000 miles per second—literally the speed of light. Before 1844, when practical telegraphy started, the fastest way of moving a message was by swift horse or by train, which could reach the then-frightening speed of about 40 miles per hour.

The telegraph was adopted very rapidly. The first message, "What hath God wrought?" was sent in 1844 along a copper wire between Washington, DC, and Baltimore. Within a mere three years, New York had been linked by wire to New Orleans, nearly 2,000 miles away, and a network of the magic wires connected every major city in the United States.[3]

How did this new medium change the communication process? For one thing, a message via telegram took on distinctive meanings for both sender and receiver that other forms of communication did not have. The implication was one of *urgency* and *importance*. When families received a message sent to them via the wires, they knew that it probably meant emergency or crisis. Telegrams brought news of illness or death, making the opening of the envelope a stressful event. For business and commerce, the great increase in speed provided by the wires enabled the stock market to develop, and the nation's economic activity accelerated greatly. Changes also took place in communication within the military as well as in the government as a whole.

Communicating by wire had broad and subtle effects on the entire society. For one thing, it greatly expanded the consciousness of U.S. citizens concerning events far away. Prior to the telegraph, newspapers concentrated mainly on events in local communities. There was some national and international coverage, but it was often delayed and limited. In the spring of 1848, the Associated Press (AP) was formed for the purpose of transmitting news stories over the magnetic wires.[4] A single reporter could send copy to many papers on the system at the same time. Within a decade the AP had expanded nationwide, and even the smallest newspapers got a daily flood of wire stories from outside their local area, reporting relatively trivial happenings such as fires, robberies, and murders.

When local papers published these accounts, many critics were offended; they thought the press was encouraging crime and should serve a more noble purpose. (Many still think this today.) Moreover, the wire services provided stories for both liberal and conservative newspapers. Reporters had to develop a style that was not supposed to be rejected by either group. It was out of this requirement that *objective journalism* developed—a way of reporting that did not editorialize (take sides) in its stories.

Thus, the introduction of the telegraph as a new medium of communication was far more than just a technological advance. It brought about significant changes in both interpersonal and mass communication that touched the lives of every citizen. It altered the functioning of our most basic institutions and changed the way people thought about their society.

What lessons can be drawn by this brief look at the development of the telegraph as a new medium? We are now living in a period of accelerating change in communication media that will bring about consequences even more sweeping than those of the 19th century. During the 21st century, our ability to communicate with one another will grow to a degree that has never before been experienced. We already have satellite-based digital phones that can be carried in our pockets—phones that can contact anyone in the world who also has a telephone. Hundreds of television channels are now available and more will come. More sophisticated computers and networks will expand the offerings on the Internet. Although it is difficult to forecast the specific ways in which these media will influence us, both individually and collectively, it is certain that our ways of communicating will become different from the way they are now. Inevitably, these changes will influence us personally, socially, and culturally.

Communicating Using Traditional Written Media

Written communication has been around for thousands of years and will continue to be used in both traditional and innovative media that will be developed in the future. The present chapter does not address such traditional print media as books, magazines, and newspapers. These are very complex and worthy of intensive study in their own right (they will be discussed in the next chapter). The focus here is on *written communications* that originate with a single individual who wants to transmit a message to one other person, a small group, or even a larger number of people. In particular, this kind of written communication takes place when people write personal or business letters or send memoranda in the workplace. Later sections include written communication that makes use of technologically sophisticated media such as facsimile and e-mail.

Letters

Writing effectively is a complex skill that can be acquired only by experience.[5] Nevertheless, letters remain the medium of choice for many kinds of message transmissions. These include private correspondence between friends or family members as well as various messages from individuals to organizations, between officials in different organizations, and from organizations to outsiders.

In an organizational context, letters remain of critical importance. Composing a concise and readable letter is *one of the most important job skills that one can master.* Letters are sent for a host of purposes including to advise customers and clients, request donations, solicit business, ask for voters' support, respond to specific inquiries, provide notification, build goodwill, and accept or reject applicants.

People have been exchanging letters since writing began, and until very recently, this was the only way that people could communicate at a distance. Letter writing as we know it began with the development of portable media. Earlier media were either slabs or walls of stone which, to say the least, were difficult to move around—or a bit later, clay tablets—which were somewhat easier but still cumbersome. However, as papyrus, parchment, vellum, and paper became available, it became much easier to transport written documents over large distances.

The great problem of letters in earlier times was, of course, just getting them to their destinations. The process was neither reliable nor cheap. Mainly it was the rich and powerful who sent letters. In the United States until about 1850 it was very costly to use the mails, and they were dreadfully undependable. Although

Congress established an official postal service as early as 1790, it was not until the mid-19th century that a reliable and inexpensive system became fully operational, making use of improved roads, trains, and steamship lines.

Even today, the mail can be relatively slow. For example, the consulting firm Price Waterhouse recently tested the system by sending 425,000 pieces of mail to 5,000 recipients in 286 zip codes. Fewer than three-quarters arrived within the number of days claimed by the U.S. Post Office.[6] For such reasons, a number of private and public ("express") services have developed over the last decade so that a letter or parcel from virtually any city in the United States can get to any other city overnight.

How well can letters achieve that complete and accurate communication discussed at a theoretical level in Chapter 1? What factors reduce accuracy conveyed in a letter, compared to one transmitted face-to-face in a verbal and nonverbal context? On the other hand, are there features of this medium that give it an edge in certain situations? (See Box 13.1.)

Advantages. One nice feature of letters is that they are not based on a complex technology, and they are truly portable. All the letter sender needs is a pen or pencil, writing paper, an envelope, and a stamp. After delivery, letters can be carried easily and read almost anywhere. Letters do not have to be plugged into an outlet, and they do not require that either party use a complex machine demanding technical skills.

Another distinct advantage of letters is that they are "hard copy." This is especially important in work settings, because letters can be placed in a file—as official documents. In business correspondence, a distinct advantage of letters over either conversations or phone calls is that they imply the recipient should *do something*—make a decision, take some action, or at least send a written reply. Oral communication often lacks this implication of required action. Conversations can accidentally—or conveniently—be forgotten. The same is true

of the content of phone calls, which leave no permanent trace. Letters, however, are physical objects, and they sit there on the desk of the receiver, reminding the receiver that they need to be dealt with.

Another positive feature of letters is that they can be composed thoughtfully at the writer's own convenience and pace. In writing to a loved one, words and phrases can be selected with care. The same is true of business or official communication, where the words used can have significant legal implications. In private exchanges, a letter can be carried in a pocket, saved as a treasured memento, and read or reread at one's own pace. In these ways, letters as a medium share a distinct advantage over face-to-face communication, in which one can regret irretrievable messages formulated and transmitted in haste.

Finally, letters sent through the U.S. mails have one clear advantage not found in other written media. They are *private*. Strict federal laws forbid tampering with a person's mail or even the mailbox. Although these laws do not totally deter a highly motivated snoop, they certainly reduce people's temptation to take a quick look at another person's letters. As will be explained, other written media—such as memoranda and especially *e-mail*—lack these legal protections. Publicized messages sent by unprotected media can be embarrassing and sometimes disastrous.

Disadvantages. The disadvantages of letters are their inconvenience, limitations on length, and slowness. Composing a letter thoughtfully—getting each phrase and sentence in a logical sequence and spelling every word correctly—can be a demanding task. In addition to composition, one has to locate stationery, something to write with, an envelope, and a stamp. Furthermore, the letter has to be taken to a mailbox. For many people, these steps seem like a lot of bother, and it is far easier just to pick up the phone and call or quickly knock out an e-mail message.

There is no doubt that writing a good letter requires skill with word selection, spelling, syntax, and grammar. Even if the intended receiver is a loved one or close friend, drafting a letter requires *creative composition*. Many of today's students and employees lack these skills, which is a significant handicap.

Although there are complex rules for good letter writing that cannot be reviewed adequately here, some basic guidelines can help in the preparation of any business letter:

- *General features.* Business correspondence requires *meticulously correct grammar, spelling, and punctuation.* Such letters must meet the highest possible standards of neatness, and most should be written on formal letterhead stationery that identifies the source of the communication.
- *Format.* There are a variety of acceptable business letter formats for positioning the address, the salutation, the body of the letter, and the signature. To some degree, these are a matter of personal preference, although many organizations insist on a common style. A host of manuals and style-books set forth various business letter formats in use today.[7]
- *Appropriate message.* A vast number of considerations are involved in formulating effective messages for business and professional purposes. The appropriate strategy depends above all on the writer's goal. Such goals can range from applying for a job to persuading a receiver to buy a product. Some letters bring happy news about promotions and raises; others bring unwelcome news about denials, refusals, and unfavorable decisions.

Whatever their purpose, effective letters express sincerity and concern, and they are readable and concise. They not only emphasize the main points in the message, but also have some pleasantries. Letters, especially those bringing bad news, must be couched in diplomatic terms. Finally, they must never contain discriminatory language. The inappropriate use of masculine pronouns (for instance, using *he* and *him* but not *she* or *her*) is perhaps the most frequent error made in business letters today. After all, women make up half of our labor force.

Memoranda

A **memorandum** is similar to a letter in that it is a written document sent to one or more receivers. However, it has important features that are different from those of letters. For one thing, it serves a relatively restricted purpose.[8] The memorandum (or "memo" for short) is a widely used medium for written communication among members of an organization, particularly when a permanent record is desired. There are some organizations that use memos to communicate with people outside the group, but memos are seldom used for communication between friends, family members, or other private parties.

```
                    Memorandum

  TO:         (receiver's name)
  FROM:       (sender's name)
  DATE:       (month, day, and year)
  SUBJECT:    (concise statement of topic)



        (The body of the message goes here,
        seldom exceeding one or possibly two
              8 ½ × 11-inch pages.)
```

FIGURE 13.1

Memorandum Format
The typical memorandum format includes "To,"
"From," "Date," and "Subject" headings, as well as
the body of the message.

The memorandum is a very "stylized" medium. That means it follows a very standardized form that has evolved for internal organizational communication over many decades. Some organizations even supply preprinted forms for convenience, and users can just enter the information on the form that they want to transmit. Minor variations exist, but generally a memorandum follows the form shown in Figure 13.1.

Within organizations, this medium is used for a number of purposes. One is *vertical communication*—up and down the levels in an organization. Supervisors send messages to subordinates. Subordinates use memos to transmit requests or to send reports up the line. Memoranda also flow between divisions in an organization. At times the CEO will send a memo to everyone in the entire organization if the message is important to all.

Advantages. As the Latin origins of the name suggest, one of the most important features of memoranda is that they *leave a memory,* that is, a "paper trail," in an organization. Memoranda, like letters, are hard copy that can be placed in a file. Such files often develop around sensitive transactions. (An example would be performance evaluations of specific individuals for purposes of granting or withholding salary or promotion.) Memos are the proof that certain communications took place, such as warnings about incompetence or sexual harassment. Thus, memoranda are often used later, in hearings or legal cases, when there are disputes about what happened earlier. For this reason, even though it is quicker and more convenient to call or to send a quick note via e-mail, the memorandum effectively preserves messages through time.

Most memoranda are concise. This makes them convenient for both senders, who need not compose a long message, and receivers, who do not have to plow through long documents. A rule of thumb is that the memo's message should fit on a single page; if this is not possible, the rule says, send the message another way.

Disadvantages. Although memoranda serve important purposes in an organization, they do have a number of limitations. For one thing, they lack legal protection. In addition, they can be interpreted as trivial or unimportant. Further, they suffer from the same limitations on role-taking and immediate feedback as do other media.

Even if memoranda are marked "Secret" and "Confidential," there are no legal sanctions to protect their privacy. In other words, memoranda lack the official protections and deterrents applicable to letters sent through the U.S. mails.

As noted, certain kinds of memoranda tend to be given little attention or ignored. This can be particularly true for those that are addressed to collective receivers like "Staff," or "All Personnel." They may actually contain very important information. However, this address is so impersonal that the memos may be seen as another form of junk mail, and receivers may either throw them away after a quick glance or not read them at all.

To try to bring more attention to the message, some organizations use computers to generate personal labels for each staff member. However, once people recognize the automated labels, they once more classify the communication as unimportant, which obviously reduces the accuracy of the transmission.

Finally, memoranda suffer from numerous role-taking and feedback limitations. Because they need to be concise and to be formulated in official language, memos may contain unnatural and sometimes awkward wordings. This is especially true of memoranda that are sent to many people at different levels and in different areas in an organization. The differing abilities and resources with which receivers bring to the task of constructing interpretations of the memo's meaning can significantly reduce the accuracy of the communication.

Despite these disadvantages, however, the memorandum remains an important medium in organizational communication. In particular, because it has the advantage of being a memory record, it will not be easily replaced. In recent years, however, newer media have reduced the need for many paper-based memoranda with messages that are not truly important.

Communicating by Telephone and Related Media

The basic instrument and technology by which we telephone one another was invented in 1875 (and patented the following year) by Alexander Graham Bell.[9] And, despite the incredible growth and remarkable changes in telephone technology, when we use this medium we still use the basic principles that he developed. The telephone, like the telegraph before it, had a powerful influence on the communication process during the 19th century and introduced great changes in our culture.[10] Today, not only are we very frequent telephone talkers, but our worldwide system has made other media possible. Long-distance and oceanic telephone lines and satellite-based systems carry media, such as facsimile, computer networks, and teleconferencing worldwide.[11]

Telephone

By 2002, there were approximately 500 million telephones (also referred to as "fixed" or "land" phones) in use worldwide, with nearly 200 million in the United States alone.[12] In addition, the use of mobile or cell phones has increased dramatically. More than 50 percent of American households now have cell phones, and each year the number of minutes used on cell phones increases by 20 percent. The rate of growth for cell phone adoption and use is estimated to be the fastest of any electronic medium in history, including radio, television, VCRs and compact disc players.[13] Indeed, it is expected that the number of mobile or cell phones in use worldwide will very soon exceed the number of "fixed" telephones.[14] (See Figure 13.2.)

We can dial directly to virtually any phone in the world. Today, cellular phones do so without being connected to a traditional wire system. Smaller, very portable phones can transmit to each other directly via satellite. As this system develops, direct-wire long-distance lines will no longer be needed, and every phone in the world may be on one gigantic system.[15] Thus, telephones continue to be, and will remain, one of our most important interpersonal communication media.

We all use telephones so often that they are taken for granted. Americans make in excess of an astonishing 800 million telephone calls a day. This means more than three calls per day for each member of our population. One of the unique features of this type of interpersonal communication is that we seldom take the time

The triumph of mobles

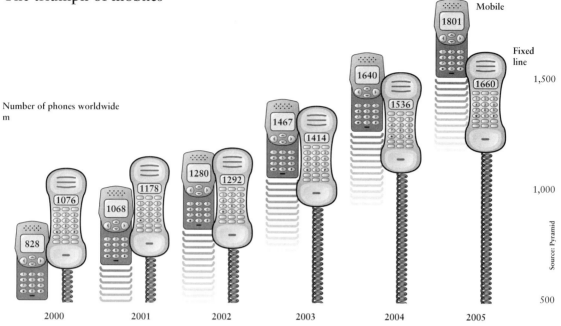

Number of phones worldwide
m

FIGURE 13.2
The Triumph of Mobiles
Source: The world in 2003. *The Economist*, p. 104.

to plan a telephone message before we start talking. We simply grab the phone, dial the number, and begin. However, there is a reasonably well-understood etiquette used by thoughtful senders and receivers. These are rules for effectively using the phone, as outlined in Box 13.2.

Telephone norms. Telephone calls can be divided into two general categories—*business* calls and *personal* calls. Sometimes the lines between the two become blurred when people who work together become good friends, but it is still a useful distinction.

What are some of the norms of telephone etiquette that separate the thoughtful business call from the rude and objectionable call?

- *Make business calls during business hours.* Many people are annoyed when they are called at home for business purposes, even

though they may say it is all right. Such calls interrupt other important activities.

- *Avoid calling during mealtime.* It is one thing when friends do this; it is annoying when aggressive salespeople try to catch people during this period. Evening mealtime is a favorite for hucksters who want to sell insurance, photo portraits, or other goods and services over the phone. Some pretend to be taking some sort of survey, so as to gain the receiver's attention and cooperation. For many people, such intrusive phone solicitations rank near the top of their list of annoyances.

- *Calls should not take priority over more important activities.* In some business settings, the telephone seems to take precedence over any other form of communication. We have all been in an office or waiting in line to conduct business, or even in a meeting,

BOX 13.2 *Workplace Perspective*

THE ETIQUETTE OF BUSINESS AND PERSONAL TELEPHONE CALLS

Business Calls
- Make business calls during business hours.
- Never make a call that interrupts a meal.
- Calls should not take priority over more important activities.
- Return calls as promptly as possible.
- Callers should quickly identify themselves and the purpose of the call. Receivers should also identify themselves.
- Callers should ask whether receivers have time if they want to chat.
- Assume that business calls are not private and that someone else may be listening.

Personal Calls
- Avoid letting young children answer the phone.
- Callers should be sensitive to the time when placing calls.
- When appropriate, callers should apply the suggestions for business calls.

should also identify themselves. Some people call and just start talking, assuming that the listener will instantly recognize their voice. People make mistakes, and telephones distort voices. A caller can simply say, "This is Mary Jane," or a receiver can say, "Ed Stevens here."

- *Callers should ask if receivers have time if they want to chat.* Time is a precious commodity to nearly everyone. People may continue to be polite to the person who extends a conversation after the business has been conducted, but they may be thinking of how to get off the phone so they can get back to work.

- *Assume that business phones are not private and that someone else may be listening.* Someone may be in the receiving person's office, or the phone may be located where others can hear one side of the conversation. When in doubt, ask whether others can hear.

There are also telephone norms that apply to personal calls. For example:

- *Avoid letting very young children answer the phone.* It is exasperating for some callers to have to ask, "Is your mommy or daddy at home?" This can be especially annoying if it is a business or long-distance call.

- *Callers should be sensitive to the time when placing calls.* Phone calls before 8:00 a.m. or after about 9:00 p.m. can be considered rude. Pay particular attention to time zones. A call initiated at 8:00 a.m. in New York will be received in California at 5:00 a.m.

- *When appropriate, apply the suggestions for business calls.* For example, even friends should identify themselves. It is not always easy to recognize a voice over the telephone.

As it was true of the telephone more than a century ago, the explosion in cell phone use is having both personal and social consequences. For example, some experts claim, "downtime" is becoming a thing of the past. Air travelers kill

when the phone rings. Everything comes to a halt while the call is answered. Such calls should not be allowed to intrude, or systems for handling such calls must be in place to limit the intrusiveness and inconvenience to others.

- *Return calls as promptly as possible.* If people are unable to return a call promptly, they should have someone else call and indicate that they will personally call back as soon as possible. Of course, failing to return a call or extensively delaying a callback is a message in itself, which may be the meaning that is intended.

- *Callers should quickly identify themselves and the purpose of the call.* Receivers time between flights dialing business contacts and friends. Commuters caught in traffic make office calls from behind the wheel. Parents can keep a tighter "leash" on the whereabouts of their children. The use of cell phones is pervasive; on the street, at the theater, during meetings, in restaurants, at the mall—even in restrooms. Emergencies can be reported in seconds rather than minutes, potentially saving lives. At the same time, however, studies have linked cell phone use by motorists to as many as 1.5 million accidents every year. One state has banned motorists from using handheld cell phones except in emergencies, and other states are considering similar legislation. More and more businesses are fighting lawsuits filed by those who claim they were injured in accidents caused by employees talking on company cell phones.[16]

Clearly, cell phones have erased communication boundaries to enable conversation anywhere and anytime. According to many people, however, they have created a new problem: *wireless boorishness.*[17] Complaints and anger over the inappropriate or discourteous use of cell phones by others are increasing. In addition, the growing use of cell phones with built-in digital cameras has created unique problems. These devices are triggering fears that they can be widely abused as "spy cams," causing some health clubs to ban these camera phones from locker rooms where voyeurs can snap compromising photos of patrons.[18] However, along with the complaints of inappropriate use of cell phones comes a plea for the development of an etiquette for cell phone use. (See Box 13.3.) Norms of behavior include the following:

- *Don't be a cell phone "hotshot."* No one is impressed with how many calls you receive, the number of calls that are interrupted by call waiting, or your personal (and loud) ring tone. Just because it is possible to receive a call anywhere doesn't mean you should. No one wants to hear the intimate details of your conversations; this can be a problem, especially for people who are seated next to you. Whenever possible, move away from others to answer your calls.

- *Don't yell.* Using a cell phone like a megaphone is distracting and annoying to others.

- *Accept the limits of the technology.* When cell connections disintegrate, call back after finding a stronger signal or a land line. Shouting over the static will not improve the reception.

- *Avoid answering a cell phone during a business meeting.* It sends the message that the intruder on the cell phone is more important than the client next to you. It may also cost you business. Turn your cell phone off *before* the meeting, or switch it to "vibrate" mode. If you know a call is coming, and it is absolutely *necessary* to take the call, forewarn others of the call and the fact that you must take it. Even then, take the phone outside the meeting to someplace private and quiet.

- *Do not answer a cell phone, or even allow one to ring, during public events.* This includes religious ceremonies, concerts, symphonies, speeches, or other presentations. Always exercise good judgment and consideration of others.

Answering machines. These devices are increasingly prevalent, for both business and home use, to record messages so that calls can be returned. Many people also use them to screen calls, listening to determine who is on the line before they pick up the receiver.

People use a great variety of recordings on their home telephone answering machines. The simplest message is—"You have reached [the phone number]. Please leave a message at the sound of the beep." This provides some security in that the caller is given only minimal information. Some people like to tell a little more, such as "The Smiths are not home right now" (or "can't come to the phone") and "they will return your call as soon as possible." Some owners try to entertain their callers by using well-known voices (such as Donald Duck), or

A Closer Look

Do's and Don'ts for Cell Phone Users

Always do the following:

- Turn off the phone before entering such settings as a movie theater, classroom, or concert hall.
- If you forget to do this, turn it off instantly if it rings in such a setting.
- Turn off the ringer and keep the phone on vibrate mode when you are in crowded public areas.
- Speak as softly as possible when others are present so that they need not share your call.
- Show respect for others near you by limiting the length of your call.

Never do the following:

- Display your cell phone conspicuously to impress other people.
- Take your phone to a setting where it can be a problem—such as a funeral or a church service.
- Place your phone between you and someone else when dining or doing business. To do so implies that any caller is more important than the person you are with.
- Discuss private and personal issues in public settings where others can hear.
- Approach a rude cell phone user with anger. Don't respond to rudeness with rudeness.

Source: Based on the recommendations of Carol Page, a promoter of cell phone etiquette. *The Boston Globe,* July 26, 2003.

musical greetings. Such curiosities send their own nonverbal messages.

Voice mail. An elaborate extension of the answering machine is **voice mail.** Although voice mail is used primarily in organizations, it is popular for personal use as well. In an organi-

zation, the caller dials the number of another person in the organization; a machine answers if the person is not there or is on the line. By pressing appropriate keys, a voice message can be left, which the person can retrieve by calling a central answering machine. Messages can be archived on the system for later reference or simply erased. Users can call the system from elsewhere and hear their messages, leave messages for others, or dictate self-directed reminders.

Facsimile

A telephone-based medium of significance is *facsimile,* or **fax,** as it is more popularly called. Like many other electronic devices, it is an American invention. As a technology, it has been available since the late 1940s, but in recent times it has come into very wide use both in business and in homes with the development of small and relatively inexpensive machines.

Fax is a telecommunication system by which exact copies of a document or photograph can be sent via phone lines. Fax machines in business or other organizations usually have their own phone numbers. The user simply feeds documents (typewriter size) into the machine, dials the fax number of the party to whom the material is to be sent, and presses the transmit button. The machine quickly scans the document, using an array of photodiodes that convert it into very fine horizontal lines of electronic picture elements (pixels). These are transmitted in the form of digital pulses via the phone lines to the receiving machine, where a reverse transformation takes place and a copy of the document is printed out. This sophisticated technology can even reproduce photographs with impressive accuracy.

Like other forms of telecommunication, fax has advantages and disadvantages. The advantages are, as has already been suggested, speed and cost. Fax is remarkably cheap to operate, once the machine has been purchased. Sending a typed page by fax from New York to Los Angeles, for example, would require from 15 to 20 seconds on a long-distance line. Depending on the machine, a two- or three-page document can be transmitted in less than a minute. That is even less than first-class postage, and it arrives immediately. By regular mail, the document would arrive three to five days later. Sending it by a private express service would cost more, and it would get there the next day at best. Because of these speed and cost advantages, fax is an effective way of transmitting printed messages that need to arrive quickly.

One of the limitations of fax is that in many cases, it may not be private. Usually, the fax machine at the receiving end is operated by a secretary or someone in the mail room, who can read any of the documents that come off the machine (although some can be programmed for security). Also, it is cumbersome to send long documents.

A fax transmission should always include a *cover sheet,* which indicates the number of pages being sent, the originator of the transmission, the addressee, and the telephone number of the sending fax machine. Above all, it is essential to indicate the *full identification of the intended receiver* because a single machine may serve a number of users and the receiving operator may not know to whom the message should be delivered.

For a while, fax systems were plagued by unsolicited messages. Everything from restaurant menus to jokes and advertisements were sent to networks of fax machines. It became such a problem that an appeal was made to Congress to bar unsolicited messages on fax networks. The lesson here is that fax machines should not be tied up with unsolicited transmissions or otherwise improperly used.

If Alexander Graham Bell were alive today, he would be astonished at how his invention is being used. Millions of conversations crisscross the nation daily, along with an increasing number of digital signals related to facsimile and other telecommunication systems. Thus, the telephone and other media using its lines are indeed among our most important media.

Communicating by Computer

Much as the telegraph and then the telephone have had dramatic impacts on our society, today's computers have in many ways revolutionized communication. This revolution, which is still taking place with breathtaking speed, has already brought about remarkable modifications in the ways people relate to one another.

Background

Communication by computer in homes and businesses is a comparatively recent development. The machines began as esoteric devices that could be used only by highly trained technicians. Today, even children can use them effectively. Yet the transition has been so painless that few people realize how remarkable it is. Thus, today, the widespread use of computers is influencing the way we work, the way we communicate with others, and the way we spend our leisure hours.

Although early forms were used as far back as World War II, computers before about 1960 were large, difficult to use, very expensive, and (by today's standards) severely limited in capacity. A large computer in the 1950s might have had as much 4K RAM (random access memory). That means a temporary working memory of only about 4,000 letters, numbers, or other characters. Also, before 1960 there was nothing like the word-processing software we know today. A computer accepted only cumbersome decks of cards with holes punched in them, which the machine read one by one. It then processed the information and printed out the results on paper, because there was no monitor on which to view information. Although such machines represented a great leap forward, and calculated numerical data swiftly, each could be used by only one person at a time. Because they were not connected to any other computers, they had no communication applications.

In 1960 Digital Equipment Corporation made a significant advance in computer hardware by developing the first commercially available *interactive* computer. This meant that it allowed what a person was typing on a keyboard to be displayed on a screen as it entered the computer's working memory. Then a software program written by Dan Murphy at Massachusetts Institute of Technology (MIT) allowed people to write and edit programs on a screen *before* they were run. This was truly a great advance. Murphy's program was the forerunner of today's screen-displayed word-processing software.[19] Soon, scientists and engineers began working on the idea of *linking* several computers in different locations (via long-distance telephone lines).

Out of this need to transmit information to others effectively via computer came the first **computer network.** By the late 1960s, a small community of computer scientists—backed by the U.S. Defense Department's Advanced Research Projects Agency (ARPA)—came together to determine how scientists and engineers could communicate and share technical data quickly and easily, even if they were widely dispersed.[20] They designed a system by which computers could be linked by long-distance phone lines. With several universities linked in this way—via a computer network—rapid communication between researchers became possible, allowing faster scientific advances.

Only one additional step was needed to create a new medium of communication: This was how to *package* information electronically for efficient transmission. Paul Baron of the Rand Corporation found the solution. He realized that digital messages (where each letter or character is coded into a distinct pattern of electronic impulses) could be sent in "packets" over phone lines by one computer to another. In this way, the network would be an efficient communication medium. In 1968 a group of scientists began to design the network.

The original ARPA net was very slow by today's standards, but at the time it seemed blazingly fast and a marvel of technology. It was designed to use smaller computers to handle the phone connections and larger, more sophisticated ones to pass along the messages. All were linked through a network of dedicated phone lines. In 1969 the first ARPA net site was installed at UCLA. By 1970, facilities were completed at Harvard and MIT in Boston.

Today people use a vast system of computer networks to communicate back and forth across the nation at speeds vastly faster than the original system. They can transmit complex information in a few seconds that would have taken days or even weeks in the pre-computer-network age. Furthermore, people do not have to be sophisticated about computers to use such systems. As already mentioned, even children can use them.

Of significance to most people using computers for communication purposes is the Internet. It was originally designed during the Cold War as a secure system of communication for military and government purposes. Even in the event of an attack on key U.S. cities, military and government officials could still communicate because the system could not easily be damaged. The reason was that it was like a spiderweb. It was a network of networks. Connecting links among the networks form a web-like system, and although large parts of the system might be destroyed, messages could still get through, following the remaining connected lines.

Today's Internet has expanded enormously. No one owns the Internet. It is a huge cooperative venture that links millions of host computers in local networks around the world. The Internet's size is difficult to specify as it continues to grow at a rapid rate. Sometimes called the *information superhighway,* this vast system of linked smaller networks provides worldwide access to e-mail, surfing, topical searches, information websites, databases, and many other information resources. On the World Wide Web (www), a special application of the Internet, can be found an almost unlimited number of interactive multimedia displays with graphics in color, audio and video messages, advertisements, and entertainment. Many thousands of websites display information—websites ranging from simple home pages of individuals to sophisticated presentations by corporations, government agencies, colleges and universities, charitable groups, and virtually any other source imaginable.

In a somewhat different way, many corporations and other groups have developed *intranets*—local area networks (LANs) that function like the Internet but that only serve their members. These networks, which are not open to the public, are used to distribute e-mail and other information to those within the system. Intranets usually consist of a set of linked desktop computers and a *server*—a mainframe (large) computer that coordinates them. Intranet systems allow individuals at work stations to send and receive e-mail and to share programs, software, data files, storage space, and expensive equipment. Composing and sending e-mail on an intranet is no different from doing the same on the larger Internet.

The following sections briefly review three specific functions for communicating by computers: using e-mail, accessing sites on the World Wide Web, and *teleconferencing*. Although there are many other uses for computers, these require the user's active involvement. These computer communication functions represent mediated interpersonal communication in that the individual plays a significant role as a sender—deciding what a message should contain, designing its style, assessing its likely influence on its receiver, and so on. Thus, the same steps that were outlined in Chapter 1 in the discussion of the basic linear model are followed when communicating by computer.

E-Mail

Although networks originated to make it easier for scientists to communicate, they are now almost universally used for business and personal correspondence. One of the most commonly used applications is **e-mail** (electronic mail)—messages sent from one person's computer to another's by combining word-processing software with nearly instantaneous transmission.

Advantages. E-mail allows people to send print messages. In earlier times each such message was sent as a paper document, and the sender had to stuff and address an envelope and wait several days for delivery. Instead, the e-mail message is typed on a keyboard to be seen on a computer screen and transmitted almost instantly to the receiver's electronic address. The source's computer sends electronically coded "information" along the network directly to the recipient's computer. The receiver can see the message on the screen and respond immediately if he or she is "online." If not, the message is stored in the receiving computer's memory so that it can be called up later. E-mail is sent directly to the intended receiver, without having to be filtered through secretaries and mail rooms. Copies of a message can be sent instantly to a single receiver, to several receivers, or to an entire local area network. E-mail can be sent through gateways to receivers in other networks or to receivers in other countries via international connections.

E-mail maintains its own archives. Almost all systems have two files: a temporary reader file for recent messages that have not yet been read by their recipients and a "notebook" file that contains all past messages. If needed, these can be permanently stored on disk or tape. These storage systems replace file cabinets filled with folders of paper correspondence. If "hard copy" of a message is needed, it can easily be printed out.

Obviously, e-mail has great advantages. It is incredibly fast and efficient, which by itself justifies its cost for many organizations. E-mail can significantly reduce the time required to make decisions, which can increase profits and efficiency in operations. And, although computers and software are not cheap, network e-mail saves labor costs because organizational e-mail does not require a large typing pool, filing clerks, and secretaries. In addition, once the staff has learned to use the hardware and soft-room. This allows relatively effective role-taking, feedback, and the use of nonverbal cues. Another advantage of videoconferencing is that people can see various graphics, film clips, or displays of physical objects. For example, if a new product is under discussion, it can be shown on screen. In medical videoconferencing, delicate surgery can be shown in a way that may be even more visible to viewers, because of special camera effects, than if they were right in the operating room. The video conference, then, is an effective system when the issues under discussion are time sensitive, when interaction is important, and when the discussion can be significantly enhanced by the video.

On the other hand, videoconferencing is very expensive. Equipment—including special cameras, satellite modems plus uplinks and downlinks, special rooms, lights, complex receivers, and transmitters—and trained technicians are needed. In some cases, it is necessary to scramble and unscramble the signals, especially in legal, military, and industrial uses. That adds greatly to the cost of equipment and services.

In addition, seeing another person on a TV screen is not the same as face-to-face contact. Immediately after the terrorist attack on the World Trade Center on September 11, 2001, the use of video teleconferencing spiked upward. It seemed like a safe alternative to bringing executives and specialists together by flying them to face-to-face meetings. Indeed, the *Boston Globe* reported that by the beginning of 2002 the stocks of companies like ACT, Polycom, and WebEx, which make the necessary equipment, surged up on Wall Street as a result of the terrorist event.[24] More recently, however, the spike in the use of videoconferencing had sagged back down. The increased use of videoconferences was a "bubble." The reason was (according to a number of business executives) that clients and colleagues who need to get together want face-to-face contact. Seeing and listening to each other via a two-dimensional screen is just not the same. The bottom line here is that new technologies, like e-mail, voice mail, computer contact, and other

media for message exchanges, are useful and often efficient. However, they do not replace the firm handshake, the direct eye contact, and the warm smile that are so important in many kinds of business activities that require interpersonal communication.

Computer Conferencing

A quick, simple, but limited form of teleconferencing can be based on e-mail exchanges through computer networks. If the software and the equipment are suitable, two or more people can communicate with each other in a kind of conference. That is, by prior arrangement, they can all be at their computers at a particular time. Each participant can type and send messages to all the others. This is cumbersome in many systems because e-mail messages are routed to each receiver for later retrieval. In some systems, however, short messages can be coded and transmitted so that they immediately appear on all the receiving screens at the same time, allowing people to communicate more or less interactively.

Computer conferencing of this type would be unsuitable when sensitive discussions are needed and when consensus must be reached through subtle arguments. Examples of efficient and effective use of computer teleconferences include occasions when a quick vote needs to be taken, rapid solicitations of opinions are needed, or an immediate short report is required from various locations. Not only can participants provide whatever information is requested, but the system stores a record that can be printed later if hard copy is required. Furthermore, computer conferences can be arranged with very little lead time and the participants can remain at their regular work stations. In addition, e-mail-based computer conferencing is inexpensive.

By far the most efficient form of computer conferencing today is accomplished through the use of desktop computers linked to the Internet and using special software. Participants sitting at their desktop computers hear one another as they speak and see small videos of one another on their screen. This is the least costly form of teleconferencing—with the possible exception of simple audioconferencing (which provides no video of the other people).

Using the voice and video capacities of modern computers has simplified the teleconference greatly. The older televised version required participants to convene in special studios. Sensitive and complex cameras, satellites, and so forth were required, along with technicians to operate them. The computer teleconference requires little or no advance preparation, no technicians to operate complex equipment, and no need for people to leave their offices or workstations.

There are limitations to the computer conference using the Internet for video, with the main problem being in the technology itself. At this point, telephone lines can carry only so much information at high speeds (limited "bandwidth"). This restricts the number of video frames per second that can be transmitted and downloaded to the host computer. As a result, the video seen on a computer screen may be small, jerky, or fuzzy. Sometimes audio transmissions are downloaded slowly. Nevertheless, for many applications, Internet teleconferencing may be entirely suitable.

Whatever the limitations, however, one thing is clear: Internet teleconferencing technology is undergoing rapid development. Just as with the telephone, radio, and television, the original versions were crude by later standards. In the years ahead, as computers continue to develop, to be more affordable, and to be increasingly purchased for home use—and as the software for Internet conferencing evolves—this technology will have profound consequences for the way people relate to one another in American society. In the decades ahead, the audio-only telephone will likely be replaced by a computer-based system in which anyone, *anywhere in the world,* will be able to talk to another person while seeing a video image of that individual as the conversation takes place. At that point, the distinction between direct face-to-face and mediated interpersonal communication will no longer be important and the two forms will merge.

Chapter Review

- We are living in an age of swiftly changing and developing communication technology. Mediated communication differs from face-to-face communication. Some elements of the communication process are absent or severely curtailed when people use media, including opportunities for role-taking and the availability of feedback.

- Each new medium alters the communication process itself—by imposing special requirements on the ways in which messages are formulated, by controlling the speed and convenience with which messages are transmitted or recorded, and by influencing the ways in which receivers reconstruct meanings from the messages they receive.

- Letters and memoranda are the traditional media for many communication needs. Letters are simple and portable; their messages can be carefully formulated and read at the receiver's convenience. Memos are mainly used in organizations, where a permanent record is desirable. Both letters and memos have specific advantages and disadvantages.

- Telephones, along with answering machines and voice-mail networks, continue to be among the most widely used media in our society.

- Fax is now an accepted means for transmitting written messages quickly and inexpensively.

- Increasingly, people are relying on computer networks to transmit information. Electronic e-mail is typed into the sender's computer, sent over a network, and recorded by the receiver's computer to be read on screen later. E-mail is rapidly replacing slower paper media. Over the Internet, people can now exchange written messages rapidly worldwide.

- New norms are developing for designing and transmitting messages over computer networks.

- Teleconferencing helps to overcome distance and link people in ways that approximate face-to-face meetings. There are audioconferences with telephone systems and videoconferences that closely approximate the conditions of a face-to-face meeting.

- A newer form of teleconferencing makes use of desktop computers, specialized software, and the Internet. Without leaving their offices or workstations, people can use their computers for voice and video transmissions, allowing them to see one another on screen while conducting a conversation.

Key Terms

medium	computer network	audioconferencing
memorandum	e-mail	videoconferencing
voice mail	teleconferencing	computer conferencing
fax(facsimile)		

Notes

1. Ramirez, A., Jr. (2002). Information-seeking strategies, uncertainty and computer-mediated communication. *Human Communication Research, 28,* 2, 213–228.

2. Hancock, J. T., & Dunham, P. J. (2001). Impression formation in computer-mediated communication revisited: an analysis of the breadth and intensity of impressions. *Communication Research, 28,* 3, 325–347.

3. Czitron, D. J. (1982). *Media and the American mind* (p. 6). Chapel Hill: University of North Carolina Press. This book offers valuable insights into the social and cultural impact of three new media after they arrived: the telegraph, motion pictures, and radio.

4. Stephens, M. (1988). *History of news* (p. 259). New York: Viking.

5. Chenoweth, N. A., & Hayes, J. R. (2001). Fluency in writing: Generating text in L1 and L2. *Written Communication, 18,* 1, 80–98.

6. In New York City, overnight deliveries arrived on time in only a dismal 46.94 percent of cases. For the whole Northeast, it was 71.12 percent. Nationwide, the figure for all categories of delivery was 80.61 percent.

7. For an extended treatment of the art of writing effective business and professional letters, see: Treece, M. (1986). *Communication for business and the professions* (pp. 50–101). Boston: Allyn & Bacon.

8. The word *memorandum* derives from the Latin *memor,* which means "with a good memory." Two spellings for the plural of *memorandum* are widely used. One is the Latin *memoranda* and the other is an English-language version, formed by simply adding an "s" to make *memorandums.*

9. For a detailed history of the early years of the telephone see: Casson, H. N. (1910). *The history of the telephone.* Chicago: McClurg & Co.

10. de Sola Pool, L. (1977). *The social impact of the telephone.* Cambridge, MA: MIT Press.

11. Increasingly such systems are based on wireless technologies. The use of traditional long-distance lines will be declining sharply in the decades ahead. See: Vanston, L. K., & Hodges, R. I. (1998). *Wireless vs wireline for voice services: Forecasts and impacts* (3rd ed.). Austin, TX: Technology Futures.

12. Access to telephones worldwide has increased sharply in recent times, even in rural areas in developing countries. For example, as a result of governmental policies, the percentage of residents who had no access to a telephone in rural areas of Chile decreased from 15 percent to only 1 percent in 2002. See: Wellenius, B. (2002). Closing the gap in access to rural communication: Chile 1995–2002. *The Journal of Policy, Regulation and Strategy for Telecommunications, 4,* 3, 29–41.

13. Lollar, M. (September 15, 2002). Is it time to cell out? For many, wireless service replacing old land phones altogether. *The Commercial Appeal* (Memphis, TN), p. D1.

14. Standage, T. (2003). The triumph of mobiles. (Special issue: The world in 2003.) *The Economist,* p. 104.

15. Einhorn, M. A. (2002). International telephony: A review of the literature. *Information Economics and Policy, 14,* 1, 51–74.

16. McDonald, J., & Davies, J. (December 20, 2002). Talk culture. *The San Diego Union-Tribune,* p. A–1.

17. Crowley, M.. (December 20, 2002). Experts say cell phone users must relearn manners. *Las Vegas Review-Journal.*

18. Howe, P. (November 8, 2003). Camera phones roiling gyms. *The Boston Globe,* p. A1.

19. Markoff, J. (December 16, 1990). Digital fetes the "germ" that began a revolution. *The New York Times,* p. 11.

20. This brief history of the development of networks is based on: Markoff, J. (September 2, 1990). Creating a giant computer highway. *The New York Times,* sec. 3, p. 1.

21. Anderson, A. (1988). The etiquette of electronic mail. *Perspective, 12,* 3, 1–5.

22. See: Young, J. R. (June 11, 2002). Online education's drawbacks include misunderstood e-mail messages, panelists say. *The Chronicle of Higher Education.* Available: http://chronicle.com/free/2002/06/2002061101u.htm.

23. Waldeck, J. H., Kearney, P., & Plax, T. G. (2001). Teacher e-mail message strategies and students' willingness to communicate online. *Journal of Applied Communication Research, 29,* 1, 54–70.

24. Howe, P. (September 16, 2002). Farewell to face-to-face. *The Boston Globe,* p. C-1.

Understanding Mass Communication

Emily reached over to shut off the radio alarm. The music was hard rock, which she basically disliked, but it did wake her up! She didn't feel like facing the rat race this Monday morning, and it was going to be a busy day. After her shower, she clicked on the TV to catch *The Morning Show* while she dressed. She followed the chatter and the commercials as she fixed a light breakfast. Then she turned to the cable weather channel to see what Mother Nature had planned for the day. Rain was predicted, so she took her umbrella.

Driving to work wasn't too bad. Emily tuned to a local radio news station to find out about any traffic tie-ups, and then changed to her favorite FM station that played classical music. That was just the thing to ease the stress of driving—even the ads were subdued.

As she passed through the lobby of her office building, Emily picked up the morning paper at the newsstand. She enjoyed reading about the love problems of others, so during her coffee break she would read her favorite advice column. She also read at least some of the news and did the crossword puzzle. She also needed to look at the classified ads to see if she could find an apartment closer to work. Sometimes she read the comics too—a habit left over from childhood.

On her way to lunch, Emily bought her favorite fashion magazine; she liked being up on the latest styles, cosmetics, and diet plans. She would glance through it during her afternoon break and then take it home to read. Also she had seen a very attractive actress on TV, in one of the soap operas, wearing a pants suit she liked; and she wanted to buy one just like it.

During the drive home, she listened to a radio talk show on which a political candidate discussed the merits of her new plan for improving health insurance in the country. Emily liked what she heard and decided to vote for the politican. A bit later, she changed to a Golden Oldies station that played a lot of her favorite music from the late 1970s. She made a brief stop at the supermarket for a loaf of bread and some cereal. While passing through the checkout line, she picked up a tabloid. The sensational headline ("84-Year-Old Grandmother Gives Birth to Two-Headed Baby Gorilla") was hard to resist. She knew it was nonsense, but it was fun to read.

Emily ate her dinner while she watched the local and network television news. She found the stories about crime, sexual misconduct, and auto wrecks and house fires interesting. However, she didn't have much time because her boyfriend, Everett, was picking her up at 7:45. She had picked out a movie she wanted to see from the advertisements in the paper.

After the movie and a snack, Everett drove her home. They talked about the movie, which had included a lot of graphic sex scenes, violence, and curse words. This bothered both of them.

Before going to bed, even though it was getting late, Emily decided to do some surfing on the Internet. Using her laptop, she found what she was looking for—a website that offered an interesting vacation package in Cancun, Mexico. After requesting mailed information, she

went to bed. She wasn't really sleepy, so she read her paperback romance novel for a while.

Finally, she turned on the TV with the remote and caught the last few minutes of a talk show. A bespectacled communication professor was claiming that we have become a media-saturated society and that all of us are heavily *dependent* on mass communications. "What a nerd," Emily thought. "Media dependent, indeed!" As she reached over to set the radio alarm, she muttered, "I'm completely independent, and I'm not influenced by mass communications."

Like Emily, we all live in a society saturated by mass communications. We seldom realize how dependent we actually are on mass media. Yet, because of this **dependency,** the media influence our decisions and actions on a daily basis.[1] Many discussions of the effects of the media focus on violence and sexual depictions, but media influences extend far beyond these two issues.[2]

Obviously, our contemporary media did not just appear overnight in our society. They developed over a very long period to become part of the complex set of communication processes—verbal, nonverbal, and mediated—that we all make use of constantly. In order to understand how they are organized, how they operate to present the content that they deliver, and how that content has influences on us as individuals and as a society, we need to begin with a brief overview of their past.

Before mass media became common, people got the information they needed from their families, friends, neighbors, local leaders, and the occasional stranger. Today, we are bombarded almost constantly by messages aimed at influencing what we do or think about. We are targets for mass communicators who want us to purchase, vote, donate, adopt, support, or otherwise behave in ways they desire. Even the entertainment offered by media poses unintended lessons about what we should look like, how we should live, what we should like and dislike, and how we should relate to other people.

The question is, where did all these media come from, and why do we allow them to operate as they do? How do people cope with this daily tidal wave of mass media messages? Do the media directly influence us or do they affect us in ways that are unintended and maybe even unnoticed? These are some of the questions that will be addressed in this chapter.

In order to understand these issues, then, the chapter begins its analysis of mass communications by tracing briefly the development of each major medium in our society—print, broadcast, film, and digital. The section that follows will provide an overall view of mass communication as a *process*. This will help to explain why our media continuously deliver the kinds of messages that they do. The chapter also examines how people cope with their daily deluge of information. It shows that, as the 21st century began, American media were serving a multitude of purposes for a multitude of different kinds of audiences, and, in turn, were having a multitude of influences.

Social and Cultural Factors That Have Shaped Our Media

What is mass communication and what are mass media? Where did they come from? What was there about the American society that shaped their technologies, their present patterns of ownership, their audiences, and their ways of operating? To answer these questions, a necessary first step is to review the accumulation of communication technologies and the cultural heritage that have influenced the ways in which our media have evolved in the setting of the United States.

We will offer a formal definition in a later section, but simply put, mass communication can be thought of as a *process* that in many respects is similar to the one described by the analytical linear model discussed in Chapter 1.

That is, sources (professional communicators) select and encode messages that are transmitted widely and rapidly over distance (by media) to arouse intended meanings in large numbers of people who receive them.

Our mass media came into being only as new technologies for communicating over time and distance allowed them to develop. While the technologies of print, broadcast, computer networks, and film are basically the same for the media used in many countries, each system of mass communication came to be organized and regulated in different ways. These technologies changed cultures as they came to be used in different systems of mass communication. It is important, then, to look briefly at the development of media technologies and the influences on social life that they produced.

The Influences of New Communication Technologies

At various points in time—some of them in the distant past—new technologies of communication were developed. These developments were the foundation of *drastic changes in human culture*. An illustration is the beginnings of writing. Human beings began to be able to speak and use language, much as we know it today, somewhere around 45,000 years ago. However, a new technology began to arrive about 15,000 years back when ancient people (the Cro-Magnon) painted beautiful representations of animals on the ceilings and walls of caves.[3] Such representations were the only way they had to preserve ideas graphically over time. Not much changed for thousands of years. Then, about 7,000 to 6,000 years ago (between 5000 and 4000 B.C.) people in various regions of what we now call the Middle East began to record messages by scratching crude pictures of ideas on rock slabs.[4] Rock was the only medium that they had at the time. Crude though it was, making marks on rocks to express meanings was a new technology. Those who saw these simple *pictographs* were supposed to be able to interpret the intended meanings of the person who made them. Sometimes it worked—but not always. Within a few centuries, however, hundreds of *stylized* (that is, simplified) **pictographs,** with specific meanings for each, were *standardized* to form the earliest writing systems.[5] Independently, the Chinese and (later) the Mayans of Central America also developed complex systems of writing.

With this new technology available, people could record and later recover ideas without relying on human memory. It was even possible to understand ideas from people who were dead—which gave writing a special significance. When true writing began, it had profound consequences for human civilization. Recorded speech was a great advance over mere talking and gesturing. One of its consequences was that writing made possible great advances in science, medicine, law, philosophy, and many other forms of knowledge. Early on, it was used mainly by the political and religious elite. This was another factor that gave writing a special significance.

About 1700 B.C., another great advance was made in communication technology. Alphabetic writing began. The basic idea was that very simple symbols were developed to represent *sounds* rather than whole ideas.[6] This greatly simplified writing and made it possible for much larger numbers of people to master its skills. Although alphabets were developed in many regions, the system currently taught in the United States was first standardized by the Ionian Greeks about 500 B.C. It was then refined by the Romans, from whom it passed to Europeans and eventually to settlers of the New World. As you read this text, you are using a communication technology that was first developed nearly 4,000 years ago.

The term *medium* (plural *media*) refers to any system of surfaces or devices that is used to transport some form of stimulus (that can be detected by human senses) over distance. For example, we project our human voice by noises we make. These move across space to our listener in the form of physical *information*—in this case sound waves. Print relies on variations

and patterns in light waves that we receive and recognize as letters and words. Other forms of information conquer space and distance as electrical impulses along a wire, or electromagnetic pulses, such as those in radio and television broadcasts. All move or store information that human beings can detect and then interpret within their learned language or visual cultures.

As noted, the first medium was stone. It was very effective for preserving messages through time, but it was not easy to move around. Later, clay tablets baked in fire were used—a little easier to move, but still cumbersome. In time, *portable* media were developed to overcome this problem. Early ones were **parchment, vellum,** and **papyrus.** Papyrus was made by the Egyptians from interwoven slices of a tall reed growing along the Nile. When squashed together, pressed, and dried, it produced a paper-like surface. Papyrus was an excellent medium and it made possible long and complex documents. Because papyrus was scarce, the skins of sheep (parchment) and calves (vellum) also came into use.

Such portable media made it possible to transmit messages swiftly by horsemen and boats, permitting military and political leaders to administer large territories much more effectively. Indeed, some scholars maintain that great empires, such as those of China and Rome, could never have been established and maintained without portable media.[7]

As empires and other complex religious and political systems developed, archives and libraries of "books" (rolled-up scrolls of papyrus and parchment) became increasingly important. These were developed to standardize systems of law, disseminate religious interpretations, preserve government records, foster commerce, and accumulate knowledge. The Romans developed the book in the form we know today, with cut pages bound at the left, writing on both sides of the page, and thin boards on the ends. They also standardized sentence structure, paragraphs, and punctuation. Books in this form, then, became an established idea well over 2000 years ago.[8] Again, new communication technologies advanced the human condition.

During the fifth century, a major setback took place. Rome was destroyed and its dozens of libraries burned by the invading Vandals and Visigoths. Writing and book production skills were almost lost. Fortunately for us, however, the basic skills were preserved by members of religious orders during the Dark Ages. Skilled specialists in Latin copied books by hand, producing **manu-scripti** for use by the Church.[9] This continued for hundreds of years.

Eventually, stationers—secular merchants—began to produce hand-copied books as well. By about the 13th century, they were producing many kinds of books on portable media for sale to scholars and students in the new universities, and for others who were literate. By this time, paper was used to supplement parchment and vellum. Papermaking from rags had been invented by the Chinese; the process was adopted by the Arabs shortly after 700 A.D., and the Moors brought papermaking to Spain. After about 1200 A.D., it had spread throughout Europe.[10] It was a great new medium. Once more, a new technology added to ways in which human beings could communicate.

In 1455, Johannes Gutenberg, an obscure goldsmith in Mainz (Germany) was able to print 200 elegant and identical copies of the Bible. He had experimented for more than 20 years with ways to cast letters in metal, arrange them line by line in trays, and use a special press to imprint multiple copies of a page. But before Gutenberg could get the pages of his Bible bound and sold, he was taken to court over a loan. He was stripped of the completed pages of his Bible, his inventions, and his shop; his work was sold and the profits were confiscated. He died blind and in poverty a few years later.[11]

The printing press was an astounding new technology that brought a great revolution in human communication. At the time, Gutenberg feared that his new system would not catch on because book buyers would prefer *manu-scripti*. However, by the time Columbus reached the New World, only 37 years later, the printing press and movable type had spread throughout Europe and millions of copies of books had been printed.[12]

The importance of the press was that it made books widely available to people in their own languages. No longer did people have to read Latin to have access to significant ideas. Printed books spread religious interpretations, new ideas about government, scientific discoveries, and many other topics throughout the world. Those ideas changed the course of history. The great Protestant Reformation, the rise of democracy, and the development of modern science were made possible because books became available in languages many people could read.

It is clear, then, that human communication—beyond the spoken word—is tightly linked to *technology*. As new media and related technologies come into use, patterns of communication change. More and more people are able to communicate with greater and greater ease and efficiency to ever larger numbers of others. This makes communication—and especially mediated communication—more central to their lives. Thus, as the future unfolds, this relationship between technology and communication will continue to be important. Mass media will become increasingly sophisticated and available. Devices for interpersonal communication (phones, faxes, and whatever new gadgets are in the works) will continue the process of transforming human life. Whether this improves the human condition significantly or creates harm remains to be seen.

The Development of Media in the United States

Today, the mass media in the United States reach large and diverse audiences through point-to-multipoint dissemination of messages. Traditionally included among these media are books, newspapers, magazines, film (and videotape or DVD extensions), radio, and television (either network or cable and satellite). Today,

FIGURE 14.1

Numbers of Book Titles Published per Year in the United States, 1900–2000

Source: U.S. Census Bureau, *Statistical Abstracts of the United States.*

the Internet, with its World Wide Web, is also a mass medium in some applications.

Books. The first book printed in the American colonies was a religious work called *The Whole Book of Psalms.* It came off a press at Harvard College in 1640, the first to operate in the colonies.[13] (However, a press was established in Mexico in 1539, and books were being produced there almost a century before the Pilgrims arrived in the New World in 1620.)

By the 1840s, statewide mandatory and free (tax-supported) *public education* began in the 1830s. After Massachusetts established such a system, other states soon followed. Publishing centers were established in Boston, New York, and Philadelphia. By 1855 more books were being published, purchased, and read in the United States than in England, and they were making a great influence on public opinion. Henry Wadsworth Longfellow's *The Song of Hiawatha* enriched people's ideas about Native Americans. Harriet Beecher Stowe's *Uncle Tom's Cabin* shaped the ideas of American abolitionists. Thus, as the century progressed, and especially after the Civil War, books became a major mass medium. Libraries were established in virtually every community; books were the foundation of education, and the ideas expressed in them shaped the culture.

Today, books are still our most respected medium. Despite complaints about reading skills among American children, book reading is more popular than at any time since World War II. Publishing is a growing industry, and more books have been printed and sold in recent years than during any period of our history. (See Figure 14.1.)

Books are a unique medium in American life. Many have relatively small audiences, selling only a few thousand copies. Moreover, even when a given book reaches beyond its original purchasers through libraries, used book sources, and borrowing, its audience usually pales by comparison with the millions who watch a Super Bowl game or a single episode of a soap opera on TV. Yet a book's influence may far exceed that of even the most wildly successful television broadcast. College textbooks pass on our cultural heritage in the arts, sciences, and humanities. Novels entertain us and provide sources of stories for films and television. Technical books provide references for critical technologies.

Many books have had a powerful influence on history. Obvious examples are Adam Smith's *The Nature and Causes of the Wealth of Nations* (1776), providing the foundation of modern capitalism, and Karl Marx's *Das Kapital* (1844), which became the intellectual base of

20th-century communism. The influence of books continued. After World War II, Rachel Carson's *Silent Spring* was a source for the early environmental movement, Michael Harrington's *The Other Americans* stimulated efforts to redress the problems of our nation's elderly poor, and Betty Friedan's *The Feminine Mystique* played a key role in establishing the feminist movement. In short, books have long been and will remain a major medium in our culture.

Newspapers. The earliest versions of newspapers were the *corantos* that appeared in England early in the 1600s. They provided mainly commercial information. By 1665, a regularly published newspaper, *The Oxford Gazette* (later published as *The London Gazette*), was established, and it survived into the present century. Like virtually all newspapers of the time, *The Gazette* was controlled by the Crown, but it had the characteristics of a true newspaper: It was published regularly (twice a week) and was produced by a mechanical printing press. Available to the public (for a price), it contained news of general interest (as opposed to specialized topics, such as religion or commerce) and was readable by those with ordinary literacy. Its reports were timely, and it was stable over time.[14]

The development of the American **colonial press** was influenced by a number of social and cultural factors, including the nature and distribution of the population, the growth of commerce (creating a need for news of shipping and advertising), and increasingly strained relationships with England.

Because of low literacy, uncertain financing, and suppression by the Crown, newspapers were difficult to establish and maintain in the Colonies. In 1690 Benjamin Harris published a four-page paper called *Publik Occurances Both Foreign and Domestick*. It caused an uproar, and its first issue was also its last! Harris succeeded in insulting the King of France, Native American allies of the British, and the governor of Massachusetts. The paper was immediately banned.

A number of other printers tried newspaper publishing in the early decades of the 1700s with mixed success. Most ran into the problem of "prior restraint," meaning that the Crown's representatives insisted on approving the content of the papers before publication. A number of printers refused and wound up in jail. It was this policy that instigated the belief in **freedom of the press** among American colonists.

One of the most significant events in the long struggle to establish freedom of the press began in 1733. John Peter Zenger published the first issue of the *New York Weekly Journal*. He ran articles that were openly critical of Governor William Cosby. Soon he was sent to jail and charged with "seditious libel" (inciting people to rebel against authority by publishing false statements). He was clearly guilty under existing British law.

Zenger was brought to trial in 1734, where he was defended by Andrew Hamilton, a distinguished lawyer. In a stunning upset, a jury acquitted Zenger—even though he had clearly violated the Crown's laws. The trial strengthened the people's belief that the press should be allowed to criticize government. A few decades later, that principle would be incorporated in the first of the amendments to our Constitution that make up the Bill of Rights.

Newspapers before 1800 were very different from those we know today. They were smaller (about 10 by 14 inches) and shorter—on average only about four pages. They were very expensive: A year's subscription cost today's equivalent of $200 to $300. Their content was designed for well-educated readers, and they were usually highly partisan (advocating a particular political point of view).

Early in the 1800s, the new technology of steam was applied to printing. The Hoe rotary press of 1830 could produce an astonishing 4,000 sheets an hour, printed on both sides. That invention made modern newspapers possible in the sense of large numbers of copies printed cheaply. In September 1833, a curious little newspaper called the *New York Sun* appeared on the streets of New York. Its publisher, Benjamin Day, was experimenting with a totally new approach. The Sun offered exciting stories of local events, with an emphasis on crime, human interest, accidents, and humorous happenings (real or otherwise).

There were three major differences between the *Sun* and earlier papers. The first was that it was aimed at ordinary people, not an educated elite. The second was that Day's plan was to recover his costs and make a profit by selling his newspaper for only a penny. By this means, he hoped to boost circulation hugely, which Day knew would appeal to advertisers who wanted to get their messages to the largest number of readers possible. Because he had so many readers, Day was able to charge very high rates for advertising space. He was able to recover the cost of production and make a substantial profit.

The third difference between the *Sun* and earlier papers was in the *system for distribution.* Instead of mailing his paper, Day devised a system for selling copies to newsboys for 67 cents per 100. They could hawk them in the streets to make 33 cents per 100 sold. Regular routes were soon established, and the system worked.

The New York Sun was an instant success, launching the era of the **penny press.** Within weeks, it was selling 8,000 copies a day. Within three years, its daily circulation was over 30,000. Day's experiment resulted in the newspaper as we know it today.

With the invention of the telegraph, another new communication technology, the Associated Press began distributing stories by wire to subscribing papers in 1848. By the time of the Civil War, railroads and regularly scheduled steamboat service on inland waters made it possible for large numbers of citizens to receive a daily newspaper. Daily newspaper usage grew steadily from the mid-19th century until the early decades of the 1900s. They reached their peak about the time of World War 1. (Figure 14.2 shows the newspaper subscription rate from 1850 to 2000.)

A major trend in modern newspapers is in *patterns of ownership*. Mainly as a result of declining circulations, more than 80 percent of newspapers in the United States are now owned by chains. In 1920, a mere 31 chains owned an average of 5 newspapers each. Today, Gannett, the largest chain, owns well over 130 dailies. Concentration of ownership had reduced the number of dailies from a high of about 2,400 in 1910 to slightly less than 1,500 by 2000.[15]

Another major trend is that on a per capita basis *newspaper use is now declining*. In 1910, households in the United States subscribed on average to some 1.36 newspapers per day (many received both a morning and an afternoon paper). Today, that has dropped to 0.62 per household. Still, newspapers remain a substantial mass medium. More than 63 million copies are sold every day, and newspaper publishing is the nation's 10th largest industry.

One of the reasons for the survival of newspapers is that they serve a variety of functions not served by other media. These include detailed analyses of local news and in-depth coverage of national and international events. However, only about 20 percent of space in a typical newspaper is devoted to actual news. The remaining 80 percent consists of comics, stock market reports, classified ads, supermarket sales, gossip, advice, puzzles, editorials, and so on. Because they serve so many functions, newspapers are very likely to remain with us for a long time. Although they may continue to decline in terms of circulation per capita, it would be hard to imagine contemporary life without them.

Magazines. Magazine publication began in Europe, where concentrations of literate, urbane, and affluent people took a keen interest in social and political affairs. Thus, magazines started as *media of politics*. The first magazine to be published in English was *The Review,* which appeared in London in 1704. Its publisher was Daniel Defoe (who later wrote *Robinson Crusoe*). It contained essays on politics, manners, and morals intended to influence

FIGURE 14.2

Subscriptions to Daily Newspapers per Household in the United States, 1850–2000

Source: U.S. Census Bureau, *Statistical Abstracts of the United States.*

the opinions of its readers. It caught on quickly and soon had imitators.[16] By the mid-1700s, the magazine was an established medium. It made a profit from subscriptions and advertising, and its readers were well educated and affluent. It was not a medium for the masses.

Experiments with magazines in the United States were unsuccessful at first.[17] Unlike Europe, with its great urban concentrations of elites, the United States had only a few small cities and a widely dispersed population, most of whom were poor and had limited reading skills. Even more of a problem for early magazines was the quality of postal services: Until the 1850s, mail delivery was uncertain and very expensive. After that, the postal system in the United States provided relatively cheap and reliable delivery of magazines. Once those barriers were removed, the magazine industry began to flourish: The American population was expanding and becoming increasingly urbanized. More people were literate, subscription costs dropped, and magazines for virtually every interest and taste became available.

During the early 20th century, general interest magazines had circulations in the millions. Their readers were like contemporary television audiences in that they were from diverse social classes and backgrounds. Some magazines—such as *The Saturday Evening Post, Colliers,* and the *Ladies Home Journal*—came out monthly; oth-

ers were weeklies. All carried a mixture of short stories, serious articles, humorous pieces, and serialized fiction. They were an ideal medium for advertisers who wanted to reach a broad spectrum of consumers across the nation to promote mass-produced products like cosmetics, automobiles, patent medicines, and soft drinks.

After about 1960, when television had become almost universally adopted, virtually all of the great general circulation magazines *began to fail* as the new medium took away their advertising income. Television could reach more people more rapidly than magazines, and on the basis of per-person exposure to an advertising message, TV was far cheaper. One by one, the magazines that had been so successful stopped publication.

For a time it appeared that the magazine was finished as a mass medium. Then, magazines found a new format and new audiences to serve and came back stronger than ever. The key was *content specialization*. Although there are still several very popular general interest magazines with circulations over 10 million a month (*Reader's Digest, National Geographic,* and *TV Guide*), most are much smaller and aimed at specific categories of consumers.

Today, thousands of small magazines are published for readers with some *specialized interest*—for instance, photography, home decorating, boating, painting, cooking, horses or any one of literally hundreds of other topics. These specialized publications are an effective medium for advertisers with products that relate to a particular age category, hobby, or other topic. In fact, there are over 15,000 periodicals of different kinds currently in circulation, catering to everyone from Bible buffs to pornography fans.

Magazines remain a major mass medium. They survey the political and economic landscape, often delivering *information and analyses* ahead of other media. They *correlate* events in society by interpreting trends and movements and linking isolated facts and events. They also serve many other information and entertainment needs.

Motion pictures.   Two of our modern media provide what we commonly think of as motion pictures—film and television (including cable, VCRs and DVDs). The Internet may also be included in this category insofar as it distributes video entertainment.

The first form of motion pictures was what has now become the traditional movie—a film produced for screening in theaters. This section is mainly concerned with this form. Although, as a mass medium, the movies were a 20th century phenomenon, they have a long technological history.[18] Even the first motion pictures required an understanding of optical principles of *lenses*; techniques for *projection of shadow images*; the functioning of *human vision*, which perceives an illusion of motion from a series of still pictures; the *chemistry of photography*; and mechanical techniques for photographing and projecting *rapid sequences of still pictures*.[19] Other matters involved in making the movies a mass medium included paying for and making a *profit* from their production and distribution, and defining *limits* on what they could portray to the public.

The movies became a mass medium to entertain the public during the first decade of the 20th century.[20] Inexpensive and crude movie houses (called nickelodeons) were established in cities to exhibit to unsophisticated audiences the short films produced by the fledgling industry. They were very successful, and by 1910 they had spread to most major U.S. cities and were grossing more than $90 million a year.

Beginning in the 1920s, movie theaters became more elaborate. Films became longer and more sophisticated as producers and exhibitors sought larger markets among the middle class. One factor boosting films produced in the United States was that World War I shut down the movie industry in Europe. This gave American films a global marketing advantage that they still enjoy. In 1927 sound was added to the film, and movies emerged as one of the nation's leading forms of recreation. Figure 14.3 shows the pattern of motion picture attendance per household in the United States from 1920 to 2000.

In terms of box office receipts, movies had a *Golden Age* during the 1930s. One reason was that they had no competitors. For a modest ticket price, an entire family could go to the movies and see a relatively wholesome film about 90 minutes in length, along with special features, like a newsreel and a cartoon. The movies were made to order for the difficult economic times of the 1930s, and motion picture attendance reached all-time highs during the Great Depression (see Figure 14.3).

By 1950, theater attendance began to drop. As the decade increased, box office receipts plunged. The problem was that television was gaining acceptance, and people were simply staying home to view whatever came on their sets. Slowly, the deeply established habit of going to the movies often declined. Neighborhood theaters closed, drive-ins disappeared, and exhibitors shifted to malls where they could operate multiple screens. The number of films produced dropped sharply from over 300 per year between 1931 and 1942 to less than 150 per year since 1980.

In recent decades, movie audiences have changed as well. They are now mainly teenagers with leisure time, plus some young dating couples. Few people today attend movies as a family. Older people seldom go to the movies. To adapt to their tastes, films now emphasize

FIGURE 14.3

Weekly Purchase of Tickets to Motion Pictures per Household in the United States, 1920–2000

Source: Motion Picture Association of America.

themes that appeal to younger age groups—fast action, vulgar language, and sexual depictions. Although Americans are now spending more dollars than ever to attend films, this trend mainly reflects the increasing cost of admission. Thus, films shown in theaters are attracting a smaller proportion of the household entertainment dollar than ever before.

Are movies headed for oblivion? Not at all. Although the traditional form of viewing movies in theaters has obviously declined greatly, more and more motion pictures are being seen via videotape, DVD rentals, and cable television. The industry labor force is actually growing overall, even though the number who work in traditional motion picture theaters is declining.[21]

These trends are the result of many more motion picture products being made for television and video industries, with fewer products strictly for theaters. Foreign markets continue to be a very important source of revenue. People in Nigeria, Iran, Pakistan, and Taiwan see the same movies that are available to American audiences—often with dubbed-in local languages. Even if their governments try to prevent such imports, pirated copies are available on the streets. Most countries in the world lack local production facilities and import their films. Thus, motion pictures as a medium will continue to be financially healthy.

Radio and television. Although radio and television are very different media, they share a history of technological, social, and economic development.[22] Television is a child of radio in many respects. As it emerged as a separate household medium, many program formats and stars of the radio industry were simply adopted into television. These included the basic legal provisions of the Federal Communications Act and related legislation, advertising support, regular programming, a star system, and many categories of content (sports, daytime serials, evening drama). For that reason it is possible to discuss these media together from a common technological, economic, and cultural base and then to indicate how they developed into two distinct media.

With the arrival of the telegraph, incredibly swift, long-distance communication became possible. Prior to the development of the telegraph, the fastest a message could be moved was at the speed of a train (about 45 miles per hour at the time) or at the speed of a pigeon, which was not much faster. With Samuel Morse's invention, all that changed.

In 1887 a German scientist, Heinrich Hertz, developed devices that could generate and detect curious *invisible magnetic waves* (what Hertz called "radiations") that traveled through the air from one side of his laboratory to the other. Within a few years many people were experimenting with these curious phenomena. Guglielmo Marconi, a wealthy young man in Italy, succeeded in turning the radiated waves on and off to produce the *dots and dashes of Morse code*. This allowed him to send and receive messages by a wireless telegraph. Marconi patented his device and improved it to the point where it could span huge distances. By the beginning of the 1900s he had sent a signal across the Atlantic Ocean.

A number of important inventions followed quickly—the vacuum tube, systems for transmitting and receiving on specific frequencies, and circuits that greatly increased the quality of performance. By 1906, the *radio telephone* became a reality when the human voice was first heard over the airwaves on ships along the Atlantic seaboard.

Despite these impressive inventions, radio did not become a household medium until the early 1920s. By then its technology was developed sufficiently that simple sets for home use were being manufactured and eagerly bought by the public—even though there were no regularly scheduled programs for them to listen to.

Radio station KDKA in Pittsburgh was the first to begin regularly scheduled broadcasting.[23] It went on the air on November 2, 1920, with a historic broadcast of the returns of the Warren Harding presidential election (with information from a nearby newspaper received by telephone).

The early 1920s were a chaotic time for the new medium. People eagerly bought sets, and hundreds of unregulated new transmitters went on the air, often broadcasting on the same frequencies as existing stations. It was a chaos of sound. Both the public and the new industry cried out for help from a reluctant federal government. Temporary measures were taken, but it was not until Congress passed the *Federal Communications Act of 1934* that the frequency assignments and power levels of transmitters were finally controlled by licenses. This legislation established the principle that *the airwaves belong to the people* and that they can be used only with their government's permission.

Meanwhile, radio became a mass medium delivering regular broadcasts into American homes. Financing the transmissions was accomplished with advertising. Time was sold to those who wanted to publicize their products over the airwaves. Although people resisted this at first, the money made it possible to hire popular performers and to transmit plays, sports, religious programs, concerts, dance music, and other content that would have been impossible without such funds.

Radio quickly became a truly massive medium. By 1935, set ownership in American homes was at the saturation level. By 1970 it exceeded an impressive five sets per household, where it has remained. Figure 14.4 shows the growth of radio ownership from 1920 to 2000.

Radio prospered from the mid-1930s to about the mid-1950s, largely because it had no rival on the airwaves. Major networks brought an enormous variety of programming to the nation. Radio became a much-appreciated source of free home entertainment, especially during the Depression, when a third of the labor force was unemployed.

Radio served well as a news source, and by 1940 worldwide systems permitted direct broadcasts from virtually every part of the globe. After World War II broke out in Europe, dramatic broadcasts were received from London. Then, on Sunday, December 7, 1941, the nation learned that the Japanese had bombed Pearl Harbor. It was radio's single most dramatic day, and its messages unified what had been a divided United States. (On September 11, 2001, television played a similar dramatic role.)

Meanwhile, in 1933, a new kind of radio was patented by Edwin Armstrong. He termed it FM, for *frequency modulation*. Unlike the prevailing *amplitude modulation (AM)* systems, it was virtually static-free. Ultimately, it came into use for radio stations specializing in music and for carrying the audio signals of television. Today, more than three-fourths of radio listeners tune into FM stations, and the use of AM system is in slow decline.

FIGURE 14.4

Ownership of Home Radio Receivers per Household in the United States, 1920–2000

Source: Census Bureau, *Statistical Abstracts of the United States.*

Television is an extension of the technology of radio. It began with experiments on ways to send pictures over the air via radio waves. The basic technology of television was being developed during the time that radio was becoming a mass medium.[24] At first, mechanical systems of whirling (Nipkow) disks seemed promising. The disks had little holes punched in them that let through lines of reflected light as they swept across a surface. Sensitive receivers detected the light and transformed it into radio transmissions. In a reverse system, a picture could be crudely reproduced at the receiving end.

In 1922, far more efficient electronic circuits were designed, based on a cathode ray tube oscilloscope and electronic sweeping. The first to be patented was the work of Philo Farnsworth, an unusual high school boy who lived in remote Rigsby, Idaho. Farnsworth astounded his high school teacher with sophisticated diagrams for an electronic system of television transmission and reception. In 1927 he moved to California and succeeded in transmitting and receiving moving pictures.

Early TV broadcasts began before World War II. A transmitter had been built on top of the Empire State Building, and a few broadcasts had begun, but the war intervened. Once the war was over, television stations went on the air in a number of cities. The Federal Communications Commission (FCC) slowed down television's growth between 1948 and 1952. No new transmitters were licensed during those years so as to allow the development of a system of frequency and power allocations that would avoid the chaos of early radio. After the "freeze" was lifted, the sale of sets and the construction of transmitters soared. Within a decade, 90 percent of U.S. homes had a television receiver. As Figure 14.5 shows, the new medium was adopted very rapidly, and within only a few years most of the families in the U.S. had a TV set at home.

For over four decades, television has been the dominant medium in American society. Cable systems now deliver TV signals to well over two-thirds of the nation's households. About three-fourths of those households now have a videocassette recorder (VCR) and the use of DVD systems is growing.

New ways of delivering television signals and programming grew rapidly. Systems for receiving direct broadcasts from satellites (DBS) are actively being marketed and adopted. Such

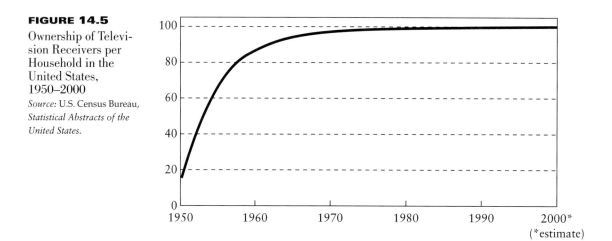

FIGURE 14.5

Ownership of Television Receivers per Household in the United States, 1950–2000

Source: U.S. Census Bureau, *Statistical Abstracts of the United States.*

signals now reach virtually every part of the country to be received via a small dish about the size of a dinner plate in the attic or on the roof. Another delivery system rapidly developing uses fiberoptic cable instead of copper wire to deliver signals to homes.

Computers are playing an increasing role in what we receive on our television sets. Interactive systems, on which movies and other programming can be received on demand, are under development. Soon, Internet delivery will become increasingly common. A home computer can now download a movie (for a fee). With the computer hooked to a TV set, the movie can be seen at home. Such systems are being tried now, in selected areas, and are likely to become more common in the years ahead. Other new technologies are being developed almost daily. These, too, will alter how people use communications systems.

However dazzling the new technologies, in some ways *not much will change*. What comes over the new systems will be basically what we have today—spectator sports, formula serials, staged wrestling, old movies, cartoons, soap operas, news, religious broadcasts, home shopping, and all the rest—and, of course, advertising. The problem is content tailored to the tastes of the audience from which profit can be derived. That is unlikely to change greatly.

One major change in television viewing has resulted from the same competitive forces that brought intense specialization to the magazine industry. "Splintering" or "narrowcasting" has become clearly established as an increasing number of new television delivery systems have been developed. Early televison had only a few over-the-air channels—so programs had to appeal to more general audiences. Now, with literally hundreds of channels from which to choose, the number of general interest shows has declined and highly specialized channels have sharply increased. In the future there may be special channels devoted solely to baking cherry pies, repairing lawn mowers, knitting, or other highly specialized interests.

Will the new systems dominate our lives to a greater extent? Not really. Americans now have their sets on more than seven hours a day in one mode or another (cable, video, direct broadcast, etc.). Overall viewing time probably will not increase because there are only so many hours in a day. Thus, the trend toward specialization of content around focused audience interests may not result in more viewing time but in an alteration in what content is viewed.

The Internet and the World Wide Web.   It was not until after World War II that computers began to be routinely used in science, education,

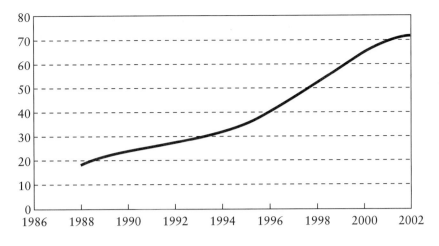

FIGURE 14.6

Percent of Households in the United States Who Go Online, 1998–2002

Source: Veronis Suhler Communications Industry Forecast, 2000.

business, and government. By comparison with what we have today, they were large, difficult to use, and intimidating to nontechnical people. However, they were extremely efficient, at least compared to anything available earlier, as a means to store vast amounts of information or to analyze complex mathematical problems.

The arrival of the desktop computer in the early 1980s changed all that. Today, with computer use becoming common, small desktop, laptop, and even hand-held machines are not only in virtually every workplace but also in an ever-increasing percent of American homes.

The Internet—initially developed during the 1960s by the federal government for scientific and military uses—is now used by millions of citizens for a remarkable array of purposes. This technology is not technically a mass medium in the same sense as radio, television, movies, and newspapers. True, it can provide point-to-multipoint transmission in terms of some content. However, it is also a medium by which people contact one another with millions of email messages every hour, or search for recorded information in databases. Thus, it combines features of both mass, interpersonal and reference media.

Despite these differences, the Internet—and especially its World Wide Web (the part that can carry multimedia content)—has developed many of the characteristics of traditional mass media:

advertising, entertainment and educational content, federal regulation, and so forth. Therefore, business, government, and the public are increasingly using computers to communicate.

At present, those using the Internet tend to be somewhat better educated and more affluent than the majority. As the system was developing, more men used it than women. That began to change as more women acquired computer skills. As prices for computers continue to drop, as technological advances allow simpler machines to be hooked to the Internet, and as software makes the system easier to use, larger and larger proportions of the population will use them. Figure 14.6 shows the pattern of the increasing number of U.S. households going online between 1988 and 2002.

How will computers and the Internet affect the mass media that have been described in preceding sections? It is difficult to predict, but it does seem clear that the Internet and the computer *will not displace our traditional media,* although they will increasingly alter their mix and use. There may be increasing convergence (as explained above with movies on the Internet). Today's computers are still expensive, complex, and not particularly easy to use. The screens are still relatively small. Moreover, for the most part, the Internet does not have regular "programming" as do radio and television.

Smaller, less expensive, and simpler computers will make the Internet more user-friendly, but no truly major change is foreseen in the near future.

Most likely, computers and the Internet will have an increasing influence on the business community in such areas as advertising goods and services and direct-market retailing. That could take advertising revenue away from other media, which would force them into a more competitive situation.

At present it appears that using the Internet will become increasingly important for a number of reasons. Many people already use the Internet for e-mail and to find news and information. The system is very useful for such purposes as contacting government officials, locating information in libraries, scheduling travel, chatting with like-minded people, and exchanging ideas with other professionals. Those uses are likely to grow.

Mass Communication as a Process

Like other forms of communication, **mass communication** is a *process* that depends on verbal and nonverbal uses of symbols and language—including the factors of context that have been discussed in earlier chapters. However, there are also significant features of mass communication that set it apart. The stages in the process can be summarized as follows:

1. Messages are formulated and encoded into standardized formats by *professional communicators* for specific goals and purposes.

2. These messages are *widely disseminated rapidly over distance* through the use of point-to-multipoint media.

3. The messages are available to *large and diverse populations*, who attend to them selectively.

4. Individual audience members *construct interpretations*—experience meanings—that to at least some degree parallel those intended by professional communicators.

5. As a result of experiencing these meanings, individuals' feelings, beliefs, attitudes, and behaviors are influenced. That is, the communication *has some effect*.

These stages provide not only a definition of mass communication but also a set of criteria by which mass media can be distinguished from other types. In summary,

> **Mass communication** is a process by which professional communicators use media to disseminate messages widely and rapidly over distance to arouse intended meanings in large and diverse audiences who are influenced in various ways.

By this definition, the media reviewed earlier (print, film, and broadcasting) are mass media engaged in mass communication. Excluded would be a long list of point-to-point media, such as the telephone, and all of those that do not involve professional communicators, large audiences, transmission over distance, and regular dissemination. The Internet is a special mixed case.

Notably missing from this description of mass communication are two critical factors that were central in the interactional and simultaneous transactions models: *role-taking* and *feedback*. Recall that these factors are also not involved when people communicate with several other kinds of point-to-point media.

The absence of role-taking and feedback is particularly critical in mass communication because senders using, say, a newspaper, a film, or a television broadcast have no way of knowing specifically who will be reading or viewing. For example, they do not even know that you exist. Thus, there is no way that their message can be altered *during delivery to you* on the basis of perceived feedback from you—as is the case with interpersonal communication. For example, when Peter Jennings, or his counterpart, delivers the evening network news, he has no way of knowing that you personally are among the audience, and certainly no way of altering the message if you fail to understand, disagree with, or express anger about something he has said. Mass communication, therefore, is a *rigidly linear process*. The messages move from sender to multiple receivers without the simultaneous role-taking and feedback features of the interactive model.

One might argue that letters to the editor, formal protests filed with the FCC, boycotts of the box office, or complaints via telephone calls to the broadcasting station are feedback. They are, in a delayed sense. However, such after-the-fact reactions provide no opportunity for professional communicators to modify their delivery *during dissemination*. As such, these reactions do not play a part in shaping the ongoing encoding of messages, as is the case of immediate verbal and nonverbal feedback cues in face-to-face communication.

The same can be said about role-taking. Mass communicators often benefit from research on their audience's composition, interests, and tastes. However, such statistical data are not the same as knowing the personal characteristics of an individual receiver in a face-to-face situation.

The Great Debate over the Influence of Mass Communication

All during the 1800s there was an enormous outpouring of complaints about the effects of mass newspapers. These complaints were based on the widely held assumption that newspapers had powerful influences on individuals in unwholesome ways. Similarly, all during the 1900s, people were deeply concerned about negative influences created by the newer media—movies, radio, and television. Recently, complaints about pornography on the Internet have resulted in similar complaints and restrictive legislation. Throughout these controversies, each of these media has been popularly assumed to have *great power*. These views result in a troubling conflict in our society and a great debate: People love the media, but there is also a **legacy of fear** that our mass media have widespread, unwanted and harmful effects.

If the media do indeed have great power to influence us individually and collectively, and if they have bad influences on us, we might be justified in controlling them far more than we do. It may not be in the best interests of our social and mental well-being to allow mass communicators to print, broadcast, or display whatever content they wish. However, censorship of media raises a very troublesome political issue. It goes to the very heart of our freedoms of speech and expression as guaranteed by the First Amendment to the U.S. Constitution.

How do we determine whether a particular form of mass communication content has antisocial or prosocial effects? Numerous critics of the media are convinced that their personal views provide answers. However, most contemporary communication scholars and social scientists think that *scientific research* is the best way to obtain answers. Understanding the nature of science and what it has revealed about the effects of the media is necessary for anyone who speaks out on the issue of the influence of the media. (For that reason, the nature of the scientific perspective and the methods by which communication research is conducted are discussed in Chapter 16.)

Early Research and the Magic Bullet Theory

Scientific research on the effects of mass communication began long after the media were well established. This was because the statistics and designs for surveys and experiments that are required for such research were not developed until the late 1920s. Well-conducted research begins with a theory, which in communication studies is often stated as a set of *propositions*. These propositions (statements) set forth what consequences are expected to occur if certain prior conditions are present. Thus, a theory is an *explanation* that indicates what *causes* some behavior, in the sense that it is a consequence of certain messages that have been received and understood by a person or audience.

Theories have to be tested against carefully assembled observations, and they must be abandoned or revised as necessary if they do not seem to get it right. Generally, then, the search for theories to explain the influences on audiences of mass media messages has been the guiding framework of scientific research on the process and effects of mass communication for many decades.

The earliest theory about the influences of mass communication—commonly called the **magic bullet theory**—stated that mass media messages: (1) reach virtually every member of an audience; (2) penetrate every mind equally; and (3) influence everyone's ideas and conduct, both uniformly and powerfully. Thus, message content—crime stories in newspapers or portrayals of sexual conduct in the movies—was thought to penetrate all persons' psyches and influence all persons' behavior in uniform ways.

This theory, which was accepted beginning in the early decades of the 1900s, now seems naive. At the time, the theory was based on what were thought to be correct assumptions about the nature of human nature. These were Darwinian-based assumptions that stressed biology and the inheritance of instincts that were said to control human conduct in uniform ways. Influenced by this genetic perspective, scientists of the time expected human beings to react to their environment instinctively, unconsciously, and uniformly.

This view of human nature led media scholars of the time to *fear* the power of mass communications. They assumed audiences could easily be controlled by demagogues through the clever use of the media.[25] Furthermore, startling influences, such as media advertising and wartime propaganda, seemed to confirm the worst fears of media critics, and they alarmed the public.

When research began, then, the magic bullet interpretation of media power still seemed logical. Eventually, however, communication scientists conducting empirical research found that it was seriously flawed. Indeed, it came to be totally abandoned by communication scholars.

The public, on the other hand, in some ways still embraces this kind of thinking about the effects of mass communication.

Ironically, the first major research project on the effects of mass communication seemed to *support* the magic bullet theory! In the late 1920s, a group of social scientists investigated the influence of the movies on children. It was a massive project aimed at uncovering the influences of motion pictures on youth called the Payne Fund Studies.[26] The results seemed to indicate that children imitated forms of behavior, became sexually excited, and learned about crime and alcohol from these movies. Horror movies seemed to disturb their sleep, and attitudes about minority groups reflected in the movies seemed to have parallel influences on the children's attitudes. As research continued, however, those findings were not supported and a new general theory of media influences was needed.

Evidence of selective influences. It did not take long for the magic bullet theory to be questioned, as new evidence indicated that mass communications might have **selective influences**—that is, effects on some people but not on others. For example, in October 1938, a dramatic radio broadcast based on H. G. Wells's *War of the Worlds* (about a Martian invasion) panicked millions. Many people heard the broadcast and thought that creatures from Mars actually were invading. However, research right after the program showed that many others did not panic and were able to determine that it was only a radio play.[27] Thus the effects were selective. Those who panicked tended to be less educated and less able to make critical decisions. In addition, those with strong religious beliefs were especially likely to have panicked. This research refuted the claim that everyone is similarly influenced by the media.

Evidence of limited influences. Additional evidence of nonuniform effects, and new evidence of weak effects, came from impressive studies conducted during World War II. The goal was to determine the influence of films on *attitudes*. A now-famous series of films (*Why We Fight*) was prepared to teach army recruits about the enemy and the reasons for the war. The films were then evaluated to assess their influences on the soldiers, in meticulously planned and highly controlled experiments. The results were clear: Exposure to the films did little more than enable some subjects to *learn more facts* and modify a few *minor opinions* about the enemy and the war. Exposure to the films did almost nothing to change their attitudes in any deeper sense.[28] Clearly, there were no magic bullets at work here. At this point, the magic bullet theory was essentially dead.

A Theory of Selective and Minimal Influences

The studies of the *Why We Fight* films also were important because they showed that soldiers with higher educational levels learned more from the films than did those with less schooling. This led to an interpretation that *individual differences* in personal ability and social background made a difference in determining influence from mass communication.

Another famous study (*The People's Choice*) contributed historically to theories about the effects of mass communication.[29] The results of this remarkable research project, conducted in Erie County, Ohio, investigated how people make up their minds when voting in a presidential election. Although it was conducted many decades ago in the 1940s (Franklin Roosevelt versus Wendell Wilkie), its results are still remarkably meaningful today. The emphasis was on the role of media in the political campaign, and especially on which media voters turned to for information about the candidates and their ideas. (Television was not yet a reality.) The researchers found that the media (newspapers, magazines and radio) did have effects, but they were *minor* and *selective* rather than uniform and powerful. Those findings might be somewhat different today, with both TV and the Internet added to our national media—but most

social scientists believe that the original results are still quite valid.

In the Erie County study, hundreds of citizens were interviewed in polls repeated over several months concerning their media use, how they learned about the candidates and issues, and how they made up their minds about whom to vote for .

Two kinds of effects of media were revealed: One was that the media campaign *activated the predisposed*. That is, for those whose social characteristics predisposed them to vote for a particular party's candidate, the mass-communicated messages from that source helped them reach and act upon their decision. For example, the media campaign did influence poor, Catholic, urban, blue-collar workers (the characteristics of many Democratic voters at the time) to go to the polling place and vote for Roosevelt—the Democrat's candidate. Similarly, rich, rural, Protestant farmers (typically Republican voters) were also activated by exposure to the media campaign to vote for Wilkie. Thus, *activation* was a major effect of the media.

A second, and different, influence was also detected. Many citizens in Erie County had already decided tentatively for whom they would vote, even before the campaign started. For these people, mass communications provided for **reinforcement** of a tentative decision they had already made. Thus, the campaign messages had the effect of keeping the party faithful from changing to the other side. Very few were converted by the media campaign from the Democratic to the Republican side, or vice versa (which would have been a powerful effect). Thus *reinforcement* was a clear effect of the media campaign.

Still another important finding from this historic study was that people's attention and interest in the media campaign was *highly selective*. Few indeed attended equally to both party's campaign messages. They selected the stories, speeches, and radio programs that were consistent with their own predispositions. Those predispositions, in turn, were influenced by their *social relationships*. Their ties to other people, in other words, influenced how much and how often they attended to the campaign's media messages. Specifically, family ties, friendships, and relationships at work or school often led people to listen to or read political media messages that they would otherwise have ignored. Thus, the web of social relationships in which a person is involved causes selective exposure.

These three effects—*activation, reinforcement and selectivity*—as well as the significance of predispositions and social relationships, have since that time been confirmed by studies as important effects of a mass-mediated political campaign. They will remain as important influences in many elections to come that rely on the mass media to convey candidates' messages to voters.

An unexpected outcome of *The People's Choice* research was that the media are not the only channel by which political messages reach voters. What the Erie County study showed clearly was that many voters got their information about the campaign *indirectly from other people* during discussions of candidates and issues. Many paid little attention to the news stories, speeches, and political ads presented by the media. They got their ideas and interpretations from other people by word-of-mouth.

Those exposed directly to ideas from the media were passing on information and interpretations to many others who did not attend to the campaign. This process came to be called *the two-step flow of communication*. The first stage in that flow was from the media to those who attend to the media more avidly. The second stage was the interpersonal transmission of ideas and influences from those people to others. Political messages, then, moved along word-of-mouth chains of tellers and retellers, influencing people as they went on. This discovery led to numerous studies of the diffusion of information by word-of-mouth, and the theory of the **two-step flow of communication** became well established. It will clearly be a part of elections in the decades to come.[30]

From these political studies, and many later ones that investigated other forms of mass communication content, came a new general theory of media effects, called *a theory of selective and minimal influences*. It completely replaced the older and outmoded *magic bullet theory*. The new theory explained that there were three major factors determining (1) *exposure* to particular presentations by mass media and (2) the *effects* such exposure would have on individual members of an audience. These three factors are:

1. *Individual differences*. People's psychological makeup—their personal configuration of interests, attitudes, intelligence, opinions, and prior beliefs—causes them to attend selectively and to interpret and respond to media messages in different ways. (This set of factors came to be called "consumer psychographics" in advertising and market research.)

2. *Social category memberships*. People's distinctive positions in the social structure—their age, race, education, political affiliations. income, gender, religion, and so on—lead them to share orientations with others like them. These produce selective patterns of attention and response to messages presented by the mass media. (Such category memberships are now called "audience demographics" by market researchers who assess radio and TV use and print media circulations.)

3. *Social relationships*. The web of ties to other people, such as family and friends, brings people to attend selectively to particular media content. Those ties also expose them to a two-step flow of ideas and interpretations of mass communication content in ways related to patterns prevailing among friends and family.

Above all, it became clear that when people were exposed to a particular movie, newspaper story, advertisement, television show, or other mass-communicated message, it was very unlikely indeed that they would suddenly be changed in any significant way.

Research support for selective and minimal influences. Thousands of studies of the effects of mass communication have supported the above interpretations, including intensive research on the influences of television on children.[31] Many studies explored the same issues—violence, sexual depictions, and antisocial behavior—that were the focus of the early research on films.[32]

In 1960 there was a massive study based on systematic observations of more than 6,000 children, plus 1,500 parents and teachers in both the United States and Canada.[33] People were startled to learn from this research that, even by 1960, children were, on average, devoting about one-sixth of their waking hours to television—more time than they spent in school! Still, *no direct and powerful influences on these children were identified!*

Perhaps no other research has had as much impact on the thinking about television and children as the 1971 government-sponsored *Report to the Surgeon General*.[34] This was a five-volume report on a related set of 23 independent projects (including some 60 specific studies), plus reviews of hundreds of prior investigations. It was funded with $1 million by the federal government (a massive outlay at the time). The goal was to determine whether portrayals of violence on television created a "public health problem" by causing children who were exposed to become more aggressive.

Violence shown on television did seem to influence some children, but not others, and only under some circumstances. Furthermore, the influences were often subtle and hard to identify. Overall, the Scientific Advisory Committee (composed of distinguished social scientists) concluded that television could lead *some* kinds of children to *some* kinds of aggressive conduct under *some* conditions. Thus, the theory of minimal and selective influences was generally supported. This less-than-clear conclusion was a disappointment to many critics of television, who "just knew" that it was harming the nation's youth.

At the end of the 1980s, there was a new *Report to the Surgeon General* on the issue of television and children.[35] The government-funded report did not sponsor new research but thoroughly reviewed the findings of more than 2,500 studies on the issue that had been published between 1979 and 1981. A major conclusion was that television did have some influence in raising rates of aggressive behavior among children whose viewing tended to be high. On the other hand, it appeared that viewing prosocial behavior tended to increase the probability of altruistic behavior. A considerable variety of other influences and effects were studied, but the bottom line was that although some influences could be detected, they were not powerful and uniform but limited and selective.

Conclusions. The 60 years of research between the late 1920s and the 1990s support the overall conclusion that *the magic bullet idea has no merit,* even though many people outside the scientific community still believe it. Far more strongly supported by research is the *selective and limited influences theory*—that people's individual psychological differences, social category identities, and web of social relationships lead them to attend to some media content some of the time. When they do so, they interpret the meanings of media messages within frameworks related to their psychological, social, and cultural backgrounds. Overall, however, the influence of any particular exposure to a specific mass-communicated message is likely to be minimal.

During more recent years, attention has focused on the Internet as a new medium. It is still too early to decide whether some new type of theory will be needed to interpret the influences of content that children or adults encounter on this medium. At present, the **theory of selective and limited influences** still seems a valid way to interpret the consequences of attending to messages from this source.

The Power of the Media: Alternative Interpretations

Although an impressive accumulation of research offers compelling evidence that our media are limited in their influences, everyday observation seems to suggest a different conclusion—that they are actually quite powerful! In fact, there does seem to be evidence that this is the case. But how could two such totally contradictory conclusions both be true? The experiments and surveys done in past decades seem both valid and impressive. However, a number of significant changes in both society and culture over the past years suggest that mass communications probably have had some significant influences.

The answer to this paradox lies in recognizing the difference between *short-term* and *long-term* effects. This section considers explanations of *long-term* and *indirect* influences of the media. It will look at both audiences in the United States and at people in other countries who have access to mass communication entertainment products depicting Americans and their ways of life. The purpose is not to refute the findings from the 60 years of research but to show that the situation is different when examined within a long-term perspective.

Long-Term Influences on Society and Culture

One way to understand long-term media influences is by considering how *minimal effects add up.* That is, over a long period of time, the media can have a great deal of influence in shaping people's shared ideas and interpretations, even though any particular message received by audiences on a specific day will probably have only minimal immediate effects. Two processes are involved in this adding-up effect. They are the **accumulation process** and the **adoption process.** Both have been explained by specific theories.

Mass communications have played a vital role in bringing about social and cultural changes over extended periods of time.[36] One need only look back at what has happened since World War II to see a number of long-term modifications in the way people interpret certain conditions in society. These could not have occurred without the mass media. Note

carefully that this does not mean that the media directly *caused* these changes, but they served as a "necessary condition" in the processes that brought them about.

A clear example of the accumulation process is provided by the great changes during the 1960s in extending civil rights to African Americans and other minority citizens. A strong case can be made that the media played a critical role at that time (a necessary condition), as the majority of the country began to redefine their democracy to provide for more equality for all citizens, regardless of race, culture, gender, and age.

As noted earlier, during the 1950s, television developed as a household medium. It thus became ready to play a key role in fostering public support among the white majority for the civil rights movement of the 1960s (which focused mainly on black Americans). The movement, led by Dr. Martin Luther King, Jr., and others, truly changed our society.

It is not difficult to understand why television was especially important: Night after night, the TV network news showed scenes of people being denied basic rights. Their reports showed racist and segregationist treatment of African Americans—how they had to go to the back of buses, how they were refused service in restaurants, how they were not allowed in "whites-only" public schools, and how they were kept from voting by unfair laws.

As change was resisted by some segments of society, vivid and horrifying scenes were shown via TV in the nation's living rooms—scenes of men, women, and children being menaced by dogs, blasted with fire hoses, and mistreated in other ways. Television also showed both black and white people gathering in dramatic but nonviolent demonstrations to protest the existing situation of unequal status based on skin color. TV carried live the memorable "I Have a Dream" speech of Dr. King, which touched emotional chords in millions of viewers of all colors.

These portrayals did not immediately change everyone. But slowly, *public support began to accumulate* for changes in laws that would protect the rights of African Americans to vote, to work, to go to integrated schools, and to exercise freedom of choice in housing. It was an old cause, but the new medium played a critical role in increasing the pace of change. In time, then, change came. The principles at stake—freedom and equality for all, regardless of gender, age, and other personal characteristics—were defined in law.

Another classic example of accumulated effects leading to change is the historic Watergate scandal of 1972, in which an inept team of burglars tried to bug the Democratic National Committee Headquarters in the Watergate building in Washington, DC.[37] *The Washington Post*—and later the news media in general—presented *consistent* and *persistent* reports about political wrongdoing and cover-ups, said to be engineered by the White House. Eventually, these media reports resulted in the resignation of Richard Nixon—the first time a president of the United States had been forced out of office.

The news media did not do this alone; they did not create the actual events that finally led to the resignation of Richard Nixon. What happened was that for almost two years the press engaged in relentless investigation of Watergate and repeatedly disclosed their findings in newspapers, on television, in magazines, and in books. This went on day after day and month after month, as the story unfolded. Thus, multiple exposure by various media created a *corroborative* effect, making the charges seem more valid.

At first, the public was not aroused, but President Nixon slowly lost support as the reports in the press raised more questions about his honesty. Finally, Nixon's political adversaries were about to start an impeachment process. President Nixon resigned on August 9, 1974, rather than face impeachment. By any measure, bringing down a president of the United States—the most powerful country in the world—is a remarkable effect.

Other examples could be added. A number of scholars have suggested that consistent, persistent, and corroborative presentations by the media played a part in changing the American population's beliefs, attitudes, and actions regarding the war in Vietnam. At first the war was portrayed and interpreted as a gallant effort to keep evil Communists from overwhelming a small ally. As the conflict escalated and dragged on year after year, television presented bloody war scenes and grim body counts, on a nightly basis, along with scenes of antiwar demonstrations, draft card burning, and campus protests. These reports—plus corroborating accounts in newspapers, magazines, radio, and film—helped bring about widespread negative interpretations of the morality of the war. As these interpretations accumulated, public support for the war gradually eroded. Finally, the nation's political leaders had little choice but to terminate it. By any measure that was a significant effect.

The accumulation process is common in our society. For example, during the past 25 years, large proportions of the population gave up smoking, developed a concern for the environment, began to worry about fat and cholesterol in their diet, began to wear seatbelts in the car, and changed their views about drunk drivers. Obviously, the media did not single-handedly invent and bring about these changes, but their messages clearly played *a necessary part* in altering our collective thinking and behavior patterns in each case. Without the media's attention to each of these issues, many more people in our society would probably be smoking, trashing the environment, eating fatty foods, ignoring seatbelts, and driving while under the influence. These were standard behaviors three decades ago. Insofar as the media helped bring about these changes, they had a powerful influence.

Influences on Other Societies: Negative Images of Americans

The accumulation process can also be identified in more recent events. It is widely understood that at present many citizens in other countries have negative feelings about the people of the United States and about their government, its leaders and its policies. The events of September 11, 2001, were dreadful testimony to how strong those negative feelings can be. The nation's present concern with terrorism and security are one result.

Why is it that so many people in so many countries envy, criticize or even hate Americans and their government? One answer is that the United States is the most militarily powerful, technologically advanced, and economically wealthiest society in the world. Envy, resentment, and even hate can be generated on that basis alone. It is easy for people in a less developed society to assume that the enviable position of the United States has come about at their expense—and that Americans are forcing their ideas and ways of life on the rest of the world, for their own gain. Few in such countries have visited the United States or have had direct contact with ordinary Americans.

What does happen is that most people in such countries have very limited sources of information about Americans as people. They receive reports in the news about official policies and actions, but they know almost nothing *in any direct or first-hand sense* about ordinary Americans and their daily ways of life. For the most part, the only source they have from which to build their conceptions of what we are like as a people are the *media entertainment products* that they view—films made in or about people in the United States; television programs, such as soap operas or serial dramas, that are imported and shown on their systems; MTV; and other popular culture products. These products are all readily available, and are especially popular among youth. Young people in other countries see the same movies we see, view the same television programs, and get the same news reports that Americans see at home.

How do they get these popular culture products? There are about a dozen major multinational corporations that produce and distribute globally the movies of the type that are typically produced in Hollywood and the television programming, much of which is prepared in New York City. Since many of the receiving

countries lack production facilities, they import such media content for their populations. Those media products are designed to appeal to the young, in particular, as they represent the most numerous audience. The goal is to maximize profit by attracting the largest audiences.

Research on the influences of mass communication content on various kinds of people, both in the United States and abroad, continues today. Studies reveal that what people see on television, in the movies, or in other media provides *incidental lessons* about various aspects of the society in which they live, or about the nature of people with whom they have no other links or contacts. The term **incidental learning** indicates that media content contains lessons about something—lessons that are neither sought by the audience nor intended by those who create the media content.

Incidental lessons can sometimes shape the beliefs and attitudes of audiences in ways that are unrealistic and flawed. For example, teenagers in many countries enjoy popular media entertainment products that depict Americans—and present versions of you and your family. Young people around the globe see much the same television programs and movies that are seen by audiences in the United States, because these are distributed worldwide. Thus, a teenager in Saudi Arabia or Taiwan (who has no other contacts with Americans) can learn about the nature of family life in the United States by viewing *The Sopranos,* or about the life of young women who live in New York by viewing *Sex and the City.* Not surprisingly, as a result, they develop seriously flawed **social constructions of reality**—beliefs and attitudes derived from mass communication that are totally unrealistic and in many ways harmful to the interests of the people of the United States.

Some of the long-term consequences of this flow of mass-communicated popular entertainment around the world were seen in a recent large-scale research project investigating the beliefs and attitudes toward ordinary American people held by teenagers in 12 countries. As reported in their study entitled *Learning to Hate*

	Very Negative		Generally Negative			Neutral			Generally Positive		Very Positive	FIGURE 14.7
	−5	−4	−3	−2	−1	0	+1	+2	+3	+4	+5	Overall Attitudes toward Americans
				Negative				Positive				
1. Saudi Arabia			−2.13									
2. Bahrain			−1.86									
3. South Korea			−1.76									
4. Mexico			−1.50									
5. China				−1.06								
6. Spain				−0.89								
7. Taiwan				−0.79								
8. Dominican Republic					−0.50							
9. Pakistan					−0.46							
10. Nigeria					−0.05							
11. Italy							+0.08					
12. Argentina							+0.69					
OVERALL:				−1.23								

Americans, DeFleur and DeFleur identified a number of subtle, long-term, but powerful effects of mass communications that had not been suspected.[38] These were the attitudes and beliefs of teenagers about American *lifestyles and personal characteristics* of the people who live in the United States (not the U.S. government, its actions or policies).

The study was conducted on a total of 1,313 high school students in 12 countries in various parts of the world. These young subjects responded to a set of 12 evaluative statements about ordinary Americans. Their median age was 17 years; approximately half were males and half females. The students were asked to indicate the degree to which they believed that Americans were violent, generous, materialistic, peaceful, criminal, respectful of others, and sexually immoral; the degree to which they have strong religious or family values; and other characteristics. Overall, the students held very negative beliefs about Americans. Figure 14.7 shows the overall configuration of attitudinal beliefs obtained in the countries studied. An attitude score (indicating positive or negative views) was obtained for each subject, based on whether the person "agreed strongly," "agreed," was "neu-

tral," "disagreed" or "disagreed strongly," with each statement. The resulting individual scores were averaged over the (approximately 100) teenage subjects assessed in each country.

The results present a troubling picture. It is obvious that the members of the "next generation" who were studied do not view Americans in a positive way (with the exception of those in Argentina). Their views are shaped, not by realistic contacts with Americans or the actual way of life as it exists in the United States, but by incidental lessons they received while being entertained with depictions they encountered in movies, television soap operas, MTV, and other popular entertainment products.

It would be easy to criticize these youths for entertaining negative views, but one must remember that they lack other sources of information from which they can develop more accurate understandings. The media content that they see is designed by producers whose goal is to *maximize profits.* The content has to be exciting and lively to appeal to the tastes and interests of the young. The young are far more numerous than conservative older people. Thus, they represent the best bet to enhance profits.

The multinational corporations that produce and distribute such media content face a highly competitive media environment in which they must make a profit to survive (an approved goal in an capitalistic economic system). There is no easy way to prevent or prohibit them from producing and distributing entertainment products that depict Americans in ways that will be seen as despicable and immoral in other countries. The First Amendment of the Constitution of the United States prevents any official agency of the government from exercising censorship or control. Because of this, producers and distributors of popular culture are free to continue to promote very negative images of Americans and their ways of life.

The bottom line here is that over a long period of time, young people in these societies see repeated depictions of Americans in media entertainment behaving violently, flagrantly engaging in sexual acts, shooting at each other in the streets, using dirty words, having materialistic values, lacking stable families, and having little interest in religion It comes as no surprise, then, that teenagers in many nations who receive these incidental lessons do not see us in a positive way. An unfortunate and unanticipated consequence is a *culture of hate* in at least some nations—which can play a part in the recruitment and training of the young to engage in terrorist acts by religious extremists. This will not change over time. Our current concerns with such dangers, then, may continue into the years ahead.

The Adoption Process as Long-Term Influence on Change

A second form of media-related behavior that illustrates the role of mass communications in long-term change is the *adoption process*. Theories of how it works originated in sociological studies of how new technology comes into use in a society. The central concept is *innovation*—anything new, borrowed from other people, or invented within the society. It might be technology, an idea, a word, or even a new way of dancing. The patterns of adoption of the mass media themselves are illustrated by Figures 14.2 through 14.6.

Obviously, people do not immediately adopt every innovation as soon as it becomes available, even if it is rational to do so. Innovations come into use individual by individual as people make up their minds to change. The pattern is easily recognized in such innovations as VCRs, instant breakfasts, microwave ovens, cable TV, cellular phones, and home computers. Other innovations are social rather than material; that is, innovations need not be things. New meanings, slang terms, and shared ways of thinking also qualify.

How does the adoption process actually take place, and what is the part played by mass communications? By the 1950s, research on this process was an established tradition, and the process was well understood.[39] Adoption theory states that innovations spread in an accumulating pattern of use as a result of specific decisions made by growing numbers of individuals—a pattern similar to that of accumulation theory.

This process takes place under certain conditions. First, potential adopters become *aware* of the innovation's existence. Second, this arouses their *interest,* bringing them to *seek further information.* Third, the innovation is then *evaluated* in terms of possible *uses and costs versus benefits.* Fourth, if feasible, it may then be *tried briefly.* Fifth, *adoption takes place,* and the innovation is routinely used.[40]

These five stages do not apply exactly to every individual and every innovation. Some new things—opinions, for example—cannot be tried out on a small scale but require an all-or-none decision. Others may be adopted temporarily but then abandoned.

What is the role of the media in this process? The stages discussed above suggest that the presentation of information via the media and the adoption and diffusion of innovations are closely related. Although information about a new thing, idea, or form of behavior can be provided without people adopting it, the first stage in adoption is learning about its existence (and potential utility). This is precisely what mass media provide in modern society. If they present new ideas and interpretations of realities under the conditions outlined in the accumulation process, they can play a significant role in bringing about social change.

Socialization Theories

At least two additional influences of the media can be identified that would be difficult to document in experiments or surveys. Both are examples of media contributions to mass communication's long-term influences. Two aspects of *socialization*—the learning process by which the rules of behavior and all the demands of general and specialized cultures are acquired by an individual—are particularly influenced by portrayals in media content. In one, people are exposed to depictions of behavior that are seen as attractive and worth copying. In the other, people learn patterns of social expectations.

Modeling. This perspective derives from a general psychological theory of *observational* or *social learning* that explains how new patterns of behavior are acquired by seeing them acted out by others (whether in media presentations or elsewhere).[41] In connection with mass communications, **modeling** explains how actions that are observed in media portrayals can be adopted by people to become part of their personal habit patterns.

The basic idea is that various actions are "modeled" (that is displayed) by attractive people in media content. If these are imitated by an individual and prove to be rewarding by solving a problem for them, they can become a permanent part of that individual's habitual activities.

Thus, over time, an individual can adopt a number of habit patterns from observations of behavior portrayed in media presentations—ranging from how to dress for various occasions to what to order in fancy restaurants.

Social expectations. Another way of looking at the long-term accumulation of influences on audiences is to point out that people learn the *rules* and *requirements* of various groups by seeing them portrayed in the media. That is, by seeing such groups as families, courts, the army, police departments, or law offices, receivers can see in action their norms, roles, ranking patterns, and systems of social control. They can even learn how to behave as a member of a criminal gang.

By seeing such portrayals in media content, then, even though they have never been members of a criminal gang or any of the other groups, they have a pretty good understanding of what behaviors are accepted or punished within such settings. This kind of long-term influence on people is the **social expectations theory of media influences.**[42] These effects would not be easily detected in a short-term experiment or survey, but they are very real nevertheless.

Generally, then, contemporary mass media may have only limited and selective influences on people in a short-term and immediate sense. However, if audiences attend to media content over a long period of time, they can be profoundly influenced as they construct interpretations of reality, adopt new forms of behavior, imitate models, and learn how to behave in group settings.

Chapter Review

- Each of the major print media grew out of the technological, social, and cultural changes that produced modern capitalism and the Industrial Revolution. Books, newspapers, and magazines have a common origin of print development. The electronic technologies in radio, television, and computer networks are more recent.

- Early research on mass communications was based on the magic bullet theory of media effects. Some early research seemed to indicate that the media had immediate, universal, and powerful effects.

- A huge accumulation of research over several decades indicated that on a short-term basis the media actually have minimal and highly selective effects.

- A number of long-term influences can be identified: the accumulation of minimal effects, adoption processes, the social construction of reality, the modeling of behavior, and the learning of social expectations.

Key Terms

dependency	penny press	theory of selective and limited influences
pictographs	mass communication	accumulation process
parchment	legacy of fear	adoption process
vellum	magic bullet theory	incidental learning
papyrus	selective influences	social constructions of reality
manu-scripti	reinforcement	modeling
colonial press	two-step flow of communication	social expectations theory of media influences
freedom of the press		

Notes

1. For a discussion of the broad implications of the influences of media on individuals and society, see: Perse, E. M. (2001). *Media effects and society.* Mahwah, NJ: Erlbaum. For an analysis of the issue of media dependency, see: Smyth, D. W. (1981). *Dependency road: Communication, capitalism, consciousness and Canada.* Norwood, NJ: Ablex.

2. A recent example is: Brown, J. D. (2001). *Sexual teens, sexual media.* Mahwah, NJ: Erlbaum. See also: Gunter, B. (2002). *Media sex.* Mahwah, NJ: Erlbaum. For a comparison of televised violence and its implications in Britain and the U.S., see: Gunter, B., Harrison, J., & Wykes, M. (2003). *Violence on television.* Mahwah, NJ: Erlbaum.

3. Guinea, M. A. G. (1979). *Altamira: And other Cantabrian caves.* Madrid: Silex.

4. See: Gauer, A. (1984). *A history of writing.* London: Scribner's.

5. Jackson, D. (1981). *The story of writing.* New York: Taplinger.

6. The Sumerians who lived in what is now Iraq took this important step around 1700 B.C., making use of a system of *cuneiform* writing. They made impressions in soft clay tablets that could be baked. They used a stick with a wedge-like end to form stylized symbols that stood for what we would call syllables. This required hundreds of separate symbols. The Greco-Roman alphabet we use today is much simpler, with each of our 26 letters standing for a brief sound element. See: Naveh, J. (1982). *The early history of the alphabet.* Jerusalem: Magnes.

7. See: Innes, H. A. (1950). *Empire and communications.* New York: Oxford University Press.

8. McMurtrie, D. (1943). *The book: A history of printing and bookmaking.* New York: Oxford University Press.

9. Madan, F. F. (1920). *Books in manuscript: A short introduction to their study and use* (2nd ed.). Oxford: Oxford University Press.

10. Clapper, R. H. (1934). *Paper: An historical account of its making by hand from the earliest times down to the present day.* Oxford: Oxford University Press.

11. Moran, J. (1974). *Printing presses: History and development from the fifteenth century

Professional Communication

D amn it!" Jennifer exclaimed as she fiddled with the car radio. "All I get is commercials." She turned to Gary, who was driving, and said, "I'm sick of it. I just want to listen to some nice music on the way to work, but I get 'in-your-face' ads for everything from mattresses to vacation specials in Bermuda. We don't need a mattress and we sure don't intend to go to Bermuda. On our income we couldn't even get to the U.S. border."

"I know," Gary replied. "Ads drive me nuts too. Just driving along here, the whole highway is littered with billboards. Even though I work in advertising, it can sometimes be a pain. The whole world seems to be filled with ads."

"Yeah, Jennifer said, "While you were surfing the Internet last night, I tried to watch a rerun of *Friends* on TV, and most of what I saw seemed to be one kind of pitch or another. If it's not cosmetics it's soft drinks or cars, or some cleaning product I don't use."

"You think you've got a problem?" Gary asked. "Try catching a football or baseball game on TV. My finger gets sore just clicking the remote on and off as the commercials come pouring out. Sometimes I wonder if I should change to another field, maybe like truck driving."

Gary and Jennifer arrived at the building where they both worked. Jennifer had her office on the same floor as Gary's. Jennifer saw that they were just in time to encounter a public relations (PR) team whose project she had designed. The team was in the lobby handing out free samples of a new kind of potato chip. Jennifer asked how it was going as they each took the little bag that the team gave them. Actually, the snacks were rather tasty, but neither thought they should actually buy any because they contained a lot of fat.

Gary was a bit nervous because he had to make a presentation to a group of executives from some of his firm's clients. He and his colleagues had prepared a great ad campaign that Gary felt would sell their product. He had polished his presentation carefully, but still felt a bit of apprehension. At the same time, he knew that his brief video conference with his counterparts in their West Coast branch, later in the afternoon, would be impressive.

Jennifer was also nervous. She was not having problems with any of her clients, but she knew that she had to do something about Elaine, whose office was down the hall from hers. The two of them were in a kind of competition for promotion, and Elaine had been quite hostile during their last staff meeting. It was time, Jennifer thought, to try to cope with the conflict that she saw developing. She would take the initiative and do her best to calm Elaine down by compromising on the differences between their respective plans for handling the new account that the boss had brought in.

Later, during their lunch hour, both Jennifer and Gary went into a huge room just off the lobby, where there was a public relations trade show put on by various manufacturers. Jennifer had helped design some of the displays. Gary was interested in one because it was of new computer products. There were a lot of booths, each of which had representatives of different

computer manufacturers. Gary collected a lot of pamphlets that described the different desktops, laptops, scanners, and printers that were on display. At each of the booths he was invited to try out the product, and the people there explained what a great company made the things.

When they arrived home, they found their mailbox full of advertising pamphlets, a couple of which Gary had designed. Gary sat down for a few minutes to read the paper that he had not had time to glance through earlier. He scarcely noticed that about 80 percent of it consisted of ads. Much of the other content consisted of stories that had been initially prepared for press releases by public relations agencies, but that was not particularly obvious. Jennifer looked through a fashion magazine that she liked. The majority of its pages were also devoted to advertising. That evening, just as they were sitting down to eat their dinner, the phone rang. It was a pleasant young woman who tried to interest Jennifer in a new credit card. After they finished eating, two other calls came, each anxious to interest them in buying a product or service.

In the work that Jennifer and Gary do in public relations and advertising, all the communication concepts and generalizations that have been discussed in the various chapters of this book play an important part in their daily activities as professional communicators. Verbal and nonverbal communication skills as well as an understanding of the processes and effects of mass communication are obviously essential.[1] **Practitioners** in both fields must also be aware of problems that can arise in intercultural communication. Obviously, advertising messages are prepared for different categories of consumers. The same is true of public relations promotions and activities that attempt to influence many kinds of people about many kinds of **clients.** Other communication skills are also important: In each field, conflicts always arise within the workplace and skills must be used to cope with them. In all their interpersonal communication with bosses, subordinates, colleagues, and clients, they have to listen with care. In speaking before large groups, or even small ones, they have to overcome shyness and apprehension. A constant part of daily routines requires using interpersonal media, such as written memos, letters, the telephone, e-mail, and fax. Preparing persuasive messages is a central part of their work, and understanding the mass media is very important. The messages are disseminated in print, broadcast, and other media. Thus, the professional fields of advertising and public relations illustrate the significance in the workplace of much that has been presented in this book. In addition, these two fields may be of particular interest to students of communication who are thinking about where they will seek employment.

There are two reasons for this chapter's focus on advertising and public relations: First, these two professional fields are among the most *media-intensive* and *communication-intensive* in the entire labor force. Neither produces any "product" other than *persuasive symbols* and *messages* that are designed to *influence people.* For this reason, communication skills are critical for success in both. Second, both advertising and public relations are *foundation fields* for those who work in other communication-intensive employment. There are, of course, many of these—fields in which well-developed

Advertising is an essential feature of the American economy. Organizations that produce goods or offer services have to make their products known to consumers. Without advertising, the products would never be sold, the industries that produce them and the businesses that sell them would fail, and many people would be out of work.

communication skills are the keys to success. Among them are health communication, political communication, retailing and other types of sales, and human resources management. Each of these is dependent on a thorough understanding of advertising and public relations. The communication strategies used in both provide ways to inform and to persuade clients, customers, employees, investors, politicians—and even the public at large—to think, believe and act in ways desired by the communicator.

An example of such a related field is *health communication.* In earlier times it was a simple process. The neighborhood doctor, carrying a black bag, called on the patient in his or her home. The doctor diagnosed the problem, selected a therapy, and discussed the steps the patient needed to take. Today, the process is more complicated. The patient checks in at a medical facility according to the provisions of his or her insurance policy—or those covered by Medicare or Medicaid. The patient may not have previously met the doctor, or any of the other medical providers, who will attend to his or her needs. The medical personnel employed by the facility must diagnose and prescribe a therapy as efficiently as possible—while keeping costs down. In a for-profit system, time is money. Providers may have less time for extended discussions or an amiable chat with patients. Because of such constraints, *effective communication* becomes even more important.

People in health communication fields work in many settings. They may be employed by a for-profit health maintenance organization (HMO), an insurance company, a hospital, a government bureau, a foundation, an international agency, a nonprofit charitable group, or a pharmaceutical company. In all such settings, employees' basic work is to design and disseminate messages to relevant audiences and various kinds of **stakeholders** about health issues of concern. The messages may be intended to persuade people to adopt healthier lifestyles, such as exercise and diet, or to adopt safe sex practices. They may be designed to enroll more

members in an HMO, or to try to get existing members to understand and view the organization more favorably. Or they may attempt to facilitate better communication between physicians and patients.

Whatever the goals and purposes of people who work in a field like health communication, they will have to make use of at least some of the basic skills and persuasion strategies employed in the fields of advertising and public relations. For this reason, the focus of the present chapter is on this type of professional communication.

Advertising and public relations communications not only are related to other mass media and communication-intensive fields, but also are *a significant part of modern life.* Their messages are so ever-present that many people never even think about them. Most people scarcely notice that they have been exposed to hundreds, even thousands, of advertisements throughout their day. They may be unaware that journalists get much of what they report in the news from public relations representatives of the thousands of industries, agencies, and other groups that make up the economic, recreational, and political systems of the United States. Certainly, most citizens do not think much about how truly dependent both the advertising and the public relations industries are on people like themselves.

For the reasons indicated, the intent of this chapter is to take a brief look at what advertising and public relations activities are all about.[2] Both employ bright, energetic, and hard-working people who have acquired high competence in communication. The services that these professionals provide are essential to the smooth functioning and success of contemporary urban-industrial society. A major factor is what David Potter calls "abundance."[3] In a competitive situation with an **abundance** of choices available, organizations that produce goods or offer services for the marketplace have to make their products known to consumers. Otherwise they would never be sold, and the industries that produce them, or businesses that sell them, would fail—and many people would be out of jobs. For this reason, advertising is an essential feature of the American economy.

The same is true of public relations. People who consume goods and services must have confidence in the industrial and service establishments that provide them. If they saw them as exploitative and dishonest, they would have no part of them or their products. The goal of public relations specialists, then, is to create, maintain and, if necessary, restore favorable public views of those organizations (if things go wrong). If there was no public relations industry to create and maintain such favorable views, those organizations could not accomplish their goals. They would be likely to founder and more jobs would be lost.

Perhaps looking at advertising and public relations in this positive way seems altogether too kind or idealistic. Many people have negative feelings about both of these fields. Critics complain that advertisers constantly convince people to buy things that they really don't want, don't need, and probably cannot afford. Those who criticize public relations use pejorative terms like *spin doctors* and *hype* to suggest that such communication specialists are making exaggerated or even false claims about the merits, intentions, and actions of their clients.

In some cases, such critics may be right. There are among advertisers and public relations specialists a certain number of rascals. However, the same can be said about lawyers, doctors, bankers, professors, stock brokers, and any number of other professionals. For the most part, however, those who work in these two communication specialties are no more deceitful or dishonest than people who serve clients in other ways.

The first task in looking at these fields, as we will in overview, is to note that they are really *quite different* from each other. At first glance, they may seem very similar in that both use mass communications extensively, both make use of techniques and strategies of persuasion, and both serve paying clients—usually through some type of agency. All this is true. But there the similarity ends. As you will see, the goals pursued by these two occupational groups and the communication strategies they use to accomplish them are definitely not the same.

Advertising as Professional Communication

Given the way that the economic and political institutions of the United States have developed over the last four centuries, it not possible to imagine American business enterprises or the mass media without advertising. This robust industry persuades consumers to buy virtually every kind of product and service that the society produces. Certainly, many people find ads on TV, in newspapers, and elsewhere annoying. Nevertheless, advertising keeps the economy going. It also provides a **financial foundation** on which our system of mass communication rests. Advertisers pay communications media well to present their messages.

In some societies advertising does not play this role. For example, the former Soviet Union and a number of other nations with Marxist governments had no advertising as we know it. In such "command economies" the media were both funded and controlled by the state and used for their own purposes. There simply was no need for media advertising of products or services. With the collapse of communism in many such countries, advertising appeared almost overnight. In only a few places today, such as North Korea, is commercial advertising unknown. The lesson here is that *advertising is essential to any modern market economy*. There is no known combination of a free market *and* an advertising-free society.

A Brief History of the Industry

Some forms of advertising have been a part of human activity since ancient times. Even in the Roman era, simple signs above doors indicated that products or services were available. Similar signs were common during the Middle Ages. Roaming criers or simple signs above shops communicated about wares and services to the public. Trademarks were also used by early crafts workers and merchants to distinguish their wares from those of others.

In colonial times Americans saw many advertisements for such products as coffee, chocolate, and tea. These were hawked in messages on printed pamphlets or announced in almanacs, early newspapers, and other printed periodicals. Even so, advertising in colonial times was primitive by modern standards.

Mass media advertising begins. It was when the Industrial Revolution began that advertising began to change from primitive messages on simple handbills, signs above doors, and crude outdoor messages painted on barns. It quickly became a vital part of the new kinds of newspapers and magazines made possible by the steam-driven printing press.

A truly major factor was that world trade expanded with the **Industrial Revolution.** A huge increase in the production of factory-made goods made advertising essential to the growing economy. All during the 1800s, the need for advertising grew as manufacturers, importers, and retailers sought to market their expanding variety of goods. During the 19th century, advertising in newspapers brought in an increasing percentage of their earnings. During the 1800s, newspapers became the ideal medium for all kinds of announcements about locally marketed goods and services.

In the late 19th century, the desire of business for national markets stimulated the growth of *national magazines*. At first the magazines were little interested in advertising but gradually they began to follow the lead of newspapers and became financially dependent on advertising revenues. By the 1890s, magazines were inexpensive and contained large amounts of advertisements. This allowed subscription and mailing costs to be reduced and circulations to increase greatly. The result was that some had huge circulations, especially

among women, and became a truly effective way of presenting products to consumers—especially those marketed nationally, rather than just locally.[4]

Still another consequence of the Industrial Revolution and the expansion of world trade in the late 1800s was the **department store.** These were remarkable new establishments at the time. Unlike small shops specializing in one type of merchandise, they displayed a dazzling variety of consumer goods conveniently available to be examined in one place. Shoppers could just walk through the floors and aisles, gazing at things that they might decide to purchase. This was a new and exciting adventure, particularly for women, who became their major customers. However, to get consumers into the store and to encourage them to buy, it was necessary to advertise what they would encounter when they arrived. Newspapers were, logically enough, the advertising medium of choice. Department stores were local, as were the newspapers themselves. Thus, before the age of the automobile, which currently accounts for a huge part of the revenues of newspaper advertisers, the department stores were steady and profitable purchasers of advertising space.

Establishing the advertising agency. As the advertising industry grew, newspapers and magazines developed their own internal advertising departments catering to commercial interests that wanted to buy their advertising space. Publications began to compete aggressively for the advertiser's business, especially in towns where there were competing media. Retail organizations that placed large amounts of advertising also began to establish their own advertising departments to plan and place their ads.

What was to come was an independent *agency* that worked neither for the media directly nor under the control of businesses that needed to advertise their wares. What was to emerge was an organization that would coordinate the activities of both—and derive a profit from each. The idea was slow in catching on.[5] The very first advertising agent using this strategy to open shop in the United States was Volley Parker. In Philadelphia in 1848 he began soliciting orders for advertising for newspapers. His customers produced their own copy that touted their wares. What Volley did was to buy large blocks of newspaper space cheaply and then sell it at a profit to those who wanted to advertise their products. Within a few years, others launched similar firms in Boston and New York.[6]

During the later decades of the 1800s, various kinds of intermediaries were facilitating the relationship between commercial enterprises and media organizations. As was the case with Volley, at first these intermediaries were merely space brokers who arranged for the placement of ads. Later they expanded their operations to provide other kinds of services and became the world's first *advertising agencies*—organizations that specifically provided advertising copy, creative assistance, and management of advertising strategies to large numbers of clients.

By 1910, a number of such agencies had been established in New York, Boston, and other large cities. They had begun to provide their customers with full services in creating advertising messages and campaigns, as well as in buying media space in newspapers and magazines that were likely to be read by audiences likely to be interested in their products.

Advertising and the Media: A Relationship of Dependency

In the 20th century, as new mass media were developed, the importance of advertising in promoting products accelerated greatly. Radio and television were ideal media to carry both national and local advertising, and they were especially effective. As we have seen in earlier chapters, the broadcast media soon became almost totally dependent on advertising revenues. One reason they were effective was that their audiences paid nothing. A newspaper or magazine required the receiver to purchase a subscription, or at least a copy on the street. Broadcast messages were not only free, but also were difficult to avoid. Thus, broadcasting for both local and national advertising was added to print as a major transmitter of persuasive messages.

Generally, then, as the industrial society developed and matured during the 19th and 20th centuries, a **symbiotic relationship** developed to provide the financial foundation of the American system of mass communication. Many would agree with David Potter, who in 1969 said that: "Marconi may have invented the wireless and Henry Luce may have invented the news magazine, but it is advertising that has made both wireless and news magazines what they are in America today."[7]

Thus, the main features of the modern advertising industry were already in place by World War II. The industry's development depended on and stimulated the growth of both the old and the new mass media. It could not have flowered without businesses eager to make profits, without media eager to earn revenue by carrying their advertising messages and without consumers with money to spend. But they had income earned from jobs in the great industrial growth that was taking place in the United States. Thus, advertising became a deeply established social institution linking our nation's productivity, our mass media and our consuming public.

The Advertising Industry Today

Viewed in a simple way, the contemporary advertising industry exists for one basic purpose: It puts businesses who want to market and distribute goods and services in touch with consumers who want to buy and use them. In other words, it is a kind of *facilitator* between the advertiser and the public. However, it is not a simple industry. Its parts or components include: (1) *agencies* of various kinds, (2) *media service* organizations, (3) suppliers of *supporting services* (ranging from research to commercial art), and (4) advertising *media*. Media that carry advertising messages include print, broadcast, digital, outdoor surfaces, direct-mail and a number of others. Each of these components comes in several versions and sizes. For example, some national advertising agencies are huge, with offices in numerous cities in the United States and abroad. There are also many small, local agencies with only a few employees and a few accounts.[8]

The advertising industry is made up of many kinds of independent business interests, and is by no means a tightly controlled national entity. Like other commercial and business segments of the economy, it is held together by various voluntary organizations and associations. These include the important American Association of Advertising Agencies (the 4As) and the Association of National Advertisers (the clients of agencies), as well as regional and state groups. A number of media associations are concerned with advertising—the Newspaper Advertising Bureau, the Outdoor Advertising Institute, the Television Bureau of Advertising, and the Cable Television Advertising Bureau, to name only a few. These groups produce regular publications carrying news of the advertising industry. Each category of advertising (direct mail, outdoor signs, packaging, and so on) has its own publications.

Overall, it is a huge industry that has a considerable economic influence on the society. Annually, American businesses spend some $126 billion per year on advertising, and this sum is likely to grow. Industry analysts predict that this number will approach $200 billion within a few years. Generally, of the total amount of advertising spent, media get about 60 percent. The rest goes to such activities as sales promotion, direct marketing, package design, and other activities. The top 100 advertising agencies are the big winners. These principal "middlemen" get about 36 percent of this amount. Well over a quarter of a million people work in advertising. Half are in agencies in the United States. The U.S. Bureau of the Census currently estimates that there are nearly 15,000 establishments engaged in the advertising business, including nearly 10,000 large and small advertising agencies.

Types and Functions of Advertising Organizations

There has been a clear trend toward concentration of ownership in the industry, paralleling that in the communication media as a whole. The top advertising agencies, which make up only a fraction of the total number, handle about one third of all of the nation's advertising business! For example, Young & Rubicam, the largest agency in the United States, now has worldwide billings over $8 billion annually, with 40 U.S. offices as well as over 200 offices in foreign countries.

These various elements of the advertising industry are interrelated parts of a dynamic and very competitive system. In the movies and on TV, the advertising account executive is often depicted as a person of intense energy engaged in fervent competition. That image has some validity as agencies and firms battle for accounts.

The advertising agency. In many ways, the **advertising agency** is at the center of the industry, and the most advertising agencies were once located in New York City—typically on or near Madison Avenue. There were strong regional centers—Chicago, Boston, Los Angeles, and a few others—but serious national advertisers looked to New York for big-time agencies. During recent decades, with the advance of Internet technologies, many local and regional agencies have located in smaller cities, such as Atlanta, Minneapolis, Seattle, Portland, and Kansas City. The industry is still largely in New York, which is the capital of most mass communications industries. In the future, however, this may change.

Advertising agencies are no longer what they were in the 19th century—essentially space brokers. Today, there are a number of different types. For example, the *full-service agency* performs virtually every aspect of the advertising process for its clients. The much smaller *creative boutique* provides creative ideas for ads and executions of those ideas. The *specialist agency* focuses on particular products or services—such as foods, women's products, or financial services. Finally, the *in-house agency or department* serves a single industry, or perhaps a chain of stores, large manufacturer or other business.

The full-service agency employs writers, artists, media experts, researchers, television producers, account executives, and others as part of the organization. Advertising scholars have identified three main functions for the full-service advertising agency:

1. *Planning.* The agency must know the firm, its product, the competition and the market well enough to recommend plans for advertising.
2. *Creation and execution.* The agency creates the advertisements and contacts the media that will present them to the intended audience.
3. *Coordination.* The agency works with sales people, distributors, researchers, and retailers to ensure that the advertising works.

The administrative operations of the agency, including public relations, are concentrated in one department. An administrative *director* actually runs the agency. Of course, large agencies have a board of directors and the usual trappings of any big business. However, within the full-service agency there are several major functions and groups that work as a team to accomplish their overall goals. These can be summarized in the following terms: The *account executive* and his or her staff provide services to a firm or for a product. An *account management director* is responsible for relations between the agency and the client. The *creative director* supervises writers, directors, artists, and producers, who write and design the ads. A *media director* heads a department in which the specific media to be used for particular ads are chosen. The *research department* pretests messages and gathers data to help the creative staff fashion a specific design and message. The research director supervises in-house research

and hires outside research firms for more extensive national and regional studies.

What an advertising agency offers is *service,* and it is clients' confidence in that service that causes them to pay 15 percent of their total billings (costs of their advertising efforts) to the ad agency. Just what happens from the time of the initial contact between an agency and a client to the finished advertising campaign varies considerably, depending on the size of the agency and the nature of the account; but, essentially, this is how it works:

To establish a relationship with a client, either the *account management director* calls on a business—say, a local company that manufactures solar heating devices—or someone from the business contacts the advertising agency. Indeed, the company may contact several agencies and ask all of them for proposals—with the understanding that only one will receive the account. The account management director then selects an *account executive* from within the agency, who arranges a meeting between *company executives* from the solar heating firm, his or her boss (the account management director), and other appropriate people from the agency. They discuss potential advertising objectives, the budget, and the timetable. In many ways, this strategy can be compared to the process of planning a military operation or campaign. The first step is *intelligence gathering.* Every conceivable set of facts about the product and its consumers, as well as the expectations of the client, is reviewed before any attempt is undertaken to design ads or a campaign. Questions such as the following are asked: Exactly what does this device do? What kinds of people use it and for what purpose? How is it better than its competitors? Who are likely future customers for the device? What advertising has been done in the past, with what media, what appeals, and what results? How can the likely consumers best be reached, via what medium? What persuasive strategies and appeals are likely to be effective in a new campaign?

Once the full set of background information and facts about the product are understood, the account executive goes to work inside the agency. The *research department* conducts studies or assembles information to answer some of the questions about potential consumers. The agency's *creative department* holds brainstorming sessions, discussing ideas for a potential campaign. *Artists and writers,* who have been informed of all background facts and research results, draw up sample ads. These may be rough sketches of newspaper or magazine advertisements, broadcast storyboards for television (which are a series of drawings on a panel indicating each step of a commercial), or other preliminary versions of ads being prepared for other media. Depending on how complex and detailed the campaign will be, a variety of other specialists may be involved, such as sound engineers, graphic artists, lighting experts, and actors.

The results of all this creative activity are the *preliminary versions of ads* from which the final versions will be chosen. These candidates are then *pretested* on potential consumers. The agency's research department conducts or supervises this pretesting and suggests which of several approaches would probably work best for the client. In recent years copy-testing research has grown in importance, wherein all elements of a print ad or broadcast commercial are tested carefully for consumer reactions. This process removes some of the financial risks of advertising and generally pleases the client. Research also guides the agency and the client in deciding what media to use. There are various options, including print, broadcast, Internet, outdoor advertising, matchbook covers, and subways.

The account executive then consolidates this information and, along with his or her colleagues, makes a *presentation* to the representatives of the client company. The costs of what is proposed are set forth clearly so that the company can evaluate the proposal. This type of presentation is often very detailed, with visual presentations and sample ads. Creative and research personnel are brought in to discuss various features of the ads, and other specialists discuss the advantages and disadvantages of using particular media for the campaign. Final decisions are now up to the client company. Their executives either accept or reject the agency's proposal. If they do accept it, the acceptance may be conditional on various modifications that they prefer.

Once acceptance is given, the account executive coordinates the activities within the agency to produce the actual ads. This means working with the *media department* to contact the appropriate media by which the advertising campaign will reach the public. Then, research plans are prepared for studies that will *evaluate* the campaign. The agency will need to present evidence about whom the campaign has actually reached and with what results. If all goes well, these will ensure that the account will be renewed in the future.

Finally, the advertisement comes to the attention of the *consumer,* as he or she reads a newspaper or magazine, views TV, listens to the radio, surfs the Internet, or uses some other medium. This, as they say, is the "bottom line," where "the rubber meets the road." The real test of the effectiveness of any advertisement or campaign is not whether the client likes it, but whether there is an actual and measurable increase in the sales of the product. The whole purpose is, after all, to motivate the largest possible number of consumers to buy the product. Some ads succeed in this. Others fail.

Creative boutiques. A **boutique agency** differs from its full-service counterpart. It has more limited goals and offers fewer services. It is basically a *creative department* and it may hire independent groups or other agencies to provide various kinds of advertising services for particular clients and products. A boutique sometimes works closely with an in-house agency—that is, a small ad group or department formed by a business to handle its own products. Most boutiques are like small agencies. Often, they have been established by people who once worked for full-service agencies.

Media service organizations. Media placement is important. Obviously, to reach just the right target audience, advertisements must be placed in exactly the right place in the right medium. In those media, space or time has to be arranged so that the ad can appear in just the right position. **Media service organizations** provide this specialized service for advertisers. These groups buy space in print media or time in broadcast media at reasonable rates. Then they negotiate with advertising agencies who want to place their ads in those media.

One category of this type of organization is the *national advertising representative*. This specialist is knowledgeable about network television rates and knows the ideal times to display particular kinds of products. They buy blocks of television time in advance and then sell the time to various advertising agencies for particular accounts. Usually, they do not get involved with an account until a lot of planning has already been done. There are several kinds of media service organizations. These include television production companies and independent design firms. These groups seldom work directly with the advertiser, but do so with the advertising agency.

In-house advertising departments. Many entire industries, and even large department stores or other businesses, have their own in-house agencies or advertising departments. Unlike full-service agencies, which are independent organizations that serve a number of accounts or businesses, the internal advertising department of a business works only with that firm's products. Essentially, it is part of its staff. Those who work in this department have an intimate knowledge of the business or industry. They make proposals for advertising plans and strategies. Their main concern is the final outcome—increasing sales or increasing public awareness of a particular product or service. Often, such internal advertising departments work closely with independent advertising agencies, which compete for their business, and present alternative proposals for an advertising campaign. Some of these departments are organized and function just like a small advertising

agency and they place their advertising directly with local media. If a plan calls for more complicated transactions that involve research and other specialties, however, they are likely to look to independent agencies for assistance.

Transmitting Advertising Messages via the Media

All the standard mass media are, of course, used to transmit advertising messages. Newspapers, magazines, television stations, radio stations, cable companies, the Internet, and other media are all involved. Some outlets have advertising departments. At both the national and the local level, the media compete vigorously for advertising dollars. Each of the major media has some kind of national advertising association that gathers data and tries to show that its medium is the "best buy" for reaching particular audiences. At the local level, advertising salespeople who work for media organizations—such as newspapers, radio stations, or TV stations—sell space or time, either directly to a business or to a business through an advertising agency or a media service organization.

In selecting a medium, the business or advertising agency considers what target audience is to be reached, the cost of advertising, and the effectiveness of a medium for reaching the desired consumers. While various sources report slightly different data, it is clear that newspapers get the largest share of the advertising dollar among the traditional mass media—currently about 25 percent. This is followed by television, with about 20 percent. Other media are direct mail (just under 20 percent), the yellow pages (less than 10 percent), radio (only about 6 percent), magazines (around 5 percent), and all other types (about 15 percent). Since the late 19th century, media that carried advertising dominated the communications industry and produced the lion's share of advertising-derived media revenues. During the 1990s, however, this began to change. Such segments of the media industry as the World Wide Web, videocassette stores, pay-per-view TV cable channels, television shopping networks, and business information services became increasingly important factors in the media mix.

Increasingly, audiences are being asked to pay more of the costs of their media fare. For example, newspapers and magazines have steadily raised their prices in recent years, and pay-per-view events such as prizefights and wrestling matches may charge as much as $50 for a single evening's event. Internet newspapers and various specialized digital newsletters are used instead of the traditional forms. Advertising is not central to such media. In such a climate, it is probable that advertising will play a slightly less significant role than in the past, and certainly the idea that people pay little or nothing for their media because of advertising will no longer be true. Other types of advertising media include *retail signs* and displays in stores; *specialty advertising,* as on pencils, calendars, and similar items; *outdoor advertising* on billboards and other large surfaces; *transit advertising* in the form of cards on buses and other vehicles; and *business site advertising* in such settings as trade shows. There are even rather exotic forms, such as an *electronic headline advertising* service in taxicabs, and even commercial messages posted over urinals in men's rooms. But this list gives only a hint of the diverse media available for advertising. There are even firms that specialize in skywriting and towing of banners by aircraft, or messages on blimps.

Also important as major advertising media are *direct mail and telemarketing* (via the telephone). Both are growing very rapidly. Direct mail began with low rates offered by the post office for deliveries of catalogs, brochures, broadsides, and other materials. Advanced technologies are now being used to call potential customers on the telephone (automated dialing, etc.). As further advances are made in communications technologies, it is virtually certain that they will be added to the list of advertising media.

Advertising Strategies

The idea of *persuasion* has ancient roots. Centuries before mass communication became available, when the human voice was the only medium that could be used, *rhetoric* was used as a strategy for influencing the beliefs and actions of people. It was a time when the words used in a speech, the ways in which arguments were presented, and the elegance of composition of messages were the only means available to sway the judgments and conduct of listeners. In this sense, rhetoric is as important today in the world of advertising, political campaigns, and fund-raising drives as it was in Shakespeare's *Julius Caesar* when Marc Anthony delivered his classic speech honoring the death of Caesar. In any promotional message devised today, the message must be constructed with exquisite care if it is to achieve its goal. Words have to be carefully selected; arguments explaining why people should take the recommended actions must be skillfully organized; and the overall composition of the message must fit easily into the cultural habits of the target audience.

In more modern times, social scientists have studied various strategies that have been used to persuade populations to believe or behave in a host of different ways.[9] The process of persuasion lies at the heart of such widely studied activities as *propaganda*—using media to sway peoples' commitments to such matters as loyalty to a particular leader, acceptance of a specific political system, and willingness to make personal sacrifices in times of war. Persuasion also is the basic process of the *political campaign* in countries within which ordinary citizens can play a role in selecting their leaders as they compete in elections. It is also fundamental to shaping or changing *public opinion* as legislators need to seek popular support for particular social programs or economic policies.

In such contexts, a very large body of research and theory has accumulated revealing the *persuasive strategies* that communicators have used in seeking to accomplish their goals. Such strategies are based on underlying psychological and sociological assumptions about how human beings can be motivated to adopt particular beliefs or to take actions that are desired by the communicator.

Not all advertising focuses on a specific product, like diapers, oatmeal, or soap. Such ads are the mainstay of the industry and the goal is to motivate purchases. Another form, called *institutional advertising,* is much less direct. For example, a firm that makes paper and other forest products presents a television commercial or full-page magazine picture in color about the virtues of a beautiful, well-managed forest showing cute animals but says nothing about its specific product, providing only the corporation's name. The goal is, of course, to get the public to associate the corporation with the "selfless" ad and lovely images—fostering beliefs that here is a company that "really cares."

One of the basic issues in designing any form of persuasive message regardless of the strategy employed is to define exactly what it is expected to accomplish. There are at least two ways to define success in terms of persuasion. One would be that some *personal orientation* has been changed—as in the institutional example above—where some opinion, belief, feeling, or attitude of members of a target audience has been altered in ways desired by the communicator. A more demanding definition would be that a particular form of *overt behavior* on the part of audience members has been triggered. This means that a person actually buys the product, votes for the candidate, gives a donation, or engages in some other form of action that the message is intended to motivate. Both of these outcomes can be important, often for different types of clients, but the underlying strategies on which they are based may have much in common.

Persuasive Strategies Used in Advertising Messages

What basic strategies are available for the persuasive communicator who wants either to alter personal orientations or to motivate a specific overt action? While there are many strategies that can be used, the first problem is to get the target person or audience to attend.

Capturing attention. Advertisements that are not seen and understood by consumers are wasted and costly efforts.[10] Therefore, the first—and most essential—objective of an advertiser is to *gain and retain attention.* For this reason, ad creators strive try to use words, colors, images, and sounds that they believe will capture and focus the potential consumer's attention on the message. Strategies for accomplishing this vary according to whether the ad is designed for the TV viewer, the magazine or newspaper reader, the Internet surfer, or the radio listener. A very real problem is "clutter"—the sheer volume of media content carrying ads that exists today. There is only a limited amount of time that people can spend attending to the media. Therefore, it is essential that advertisers have a detailed understanding of the exact nature of their target audience, the kinds of media to which they attend, and the pattern of interests and tastes that will lead such people to attend to a particular advertisement positioned among dozens, even hundreds, of competitors. The success of any ad, therefore, begins with its ability to break through the clutter to gain and hold the attention of potential consumers. This factor alone can spell success or failure for any particular ad.

Once attention has been obtained, the next problem is to convince the person attending to act—buy, donate, visit, or whatever. This is the most difficult part to accomplish. It is also the most important. An advertisement is successful if it brings those who see or hear it to act in ways desired by the communicator. There are two classic ways in which those who design such messages try to accomplish this goal. One is to use a psychological strategy. The other is based on a sociocultural approach.

The "learn-feel-do," or cognitive-emotional strategy. Modern advertising messages often use either emotional appeals or those based on reason (a cognitive strategy) to try and persuade members of a target audience to purchase a particular product. An example of the use of reason would be an ad for an automobile that stresses economy of purchase and operation—claiming that "the [brand of car] is the choice of those who want the lowest initial price, the best gas mileage available, the highest trade-in value, the best record of repair costs," and so on.[11] Not all products lend themselves to this approach. Far more common is the use of what are called *appeals*—which are presumed to arouse and offer satisfaction for emotional needs, wants, and desires. Rather than reason or rationality, these ads are based on such inducements as sexual themes—indicating that "using this product will make you more attractive to members of the opposite sex and that purchasing it will bring you more opportunities for engaging in the behavior that you desire." Other commonly used appeals are based on greed, humor, fear, pride, envy, or other psychological states that presumably can be aroused by the message to motivate the desired action.

A simple interpretation of how such advertisements work is this: First, the persuasive message is *learned* by the recipient. This learning then arouses some sort of *feeling* or emotional state within the individual's psychological functioning, and this, in turn, increases the receiver's motivation to *behave* in the manner desired by the advertiser. It is an old idea, but it does illustrate the *cognitive-emotional strategy*. As advertising scholar John Jones explains this rather elementary theory:

> To understand how advertising works, we need to know the order of events. . . . The earliest theory was based on a simple chain of causality described by Charles Raymond as "**learn, feel, do.**" In this theory, people receive factual knowledge about a brand. As a result, their [feelings] toward the brand change and they develop a preference for it. Then they buy it.[12]

A second strategy is not based on the psychological functioning of the target person, but

on the assumption that he or she will be responsive to what other people expect him or her to do. This is more complex, but it is based on the social requirements that people understand exist in their groups.

The "conform-or-be-punished," or cultural expectations strategy. It is obvious that the socioculture context within which an individual makes decisions about action has shared rules for behavior—norms that are profoundly important in shaping his or her actions. Simply put, cultural norms, roles, and other expectations shape actions, even though to someone looking on from outside some actions may seem bizarre or even insane. In traditional India, for example, the culturally approved practice of *suttee* dictated that it was the duty of a faithful wife to kill herself when her husband died by throwing herself on his funeral pyre. During World War II, Japanese aviators deliberately dove their bomb-filled aircraft onto U.S. naval vessels. Other Japanese military personnel killed or sacrificed themselves in a parallel manner. Many Americans could not understand these actions, but they were dictated by the normative requirements of the Bushido code—a set of cultural rules defining the proper acts of a warrior.

In the United States, culture also dictates action. In any group—family, work, education, the military, and so on—strong cultural norms, role definitions, requirements of social ranking, and many forms of social controls (rewards and punishments) are deeply understood by the majority of members. Compliance is routine. Advertisements that call attention to cultural requirements and urge the purchase of particular products to conform to them are based on a cultural expectations strategy.

An example would be an ad that urges the use of a particular mouthwash or a brand of deodorant. In such cases, the risk of offending accepted norms about bad breath or body smells provides a motivation for purchasing the product. Other ads may be based on role definitions, such as a mother's duty to provide appropriate medications to her child who is suffering from a cold or flu. Ranking is used in ads that show some high-ranking celebrity endorsing a product. This assumes that the consumer wants to be thought of as like that prestigious person. In the case of social controls, advertisements for greeting cards are based on the culturally accepted concept that sending such missives is a requirement on birthdays, anniversaries, Valentine's day, and so on. Violate these norms and you risk criticism or even rejection (social control). Thus, the basic approach is straightforward: A persuasive message defines a cultural requirement. It indicates the negative consequences of failing to conform. It shows that use of the product will allow the consumer to avoid those consequences. In contrast to the simple *learn-feel-do* formula of the psychodynamic strategy, it is based on a **learn-conform-or-be-punished** approach.

There are obviously many other ways in which persuasive messages can be designed. Advertisers are some of the most creative professionals in the American labor force today. They constantly invent new ways to advertise and promote the wares of their clients. Some ads work enormously well and become a part of the popular culture. Others are less effective, and some are simply duds. Whatever strategy they use, advertisers are following in the steps of ancient orators like Cicero, Socrates, and Aristotle, who couched their arguments in persuasive rhetoric to persuade people to adopt their ideas.

One of the most creative challenges that exists in the contemporary communications world, then, is the ability to prepare ads that will both capture attention and present the persuasive appeals to motivations that will sell the product or service. People who can do this are well paid indeed. If an agency cannot provide this type of service, it will soon go out of business.

Advertising styles, content, and strategies have changed in many ways over the years. During the late 1880s, advertising styles tended to be ornate and highly decorative. Those promoting soap and cosmetics were especially so. In the 1920s these were replaced by a new style—clean lines incorporating art deco designs. In time, these gave way to the more psychedelic posterlike ads of the 1960s and the early 1970s. During the 1980s and early 90s, the clean and orderly Swiss Gothic look was more common. This, in turn, yielded to the more traditional and formal design we see today. There is no real explanation for why such changes take place. Design experts claim that it comes about as a consequence of coordinating art and typography with content. In many ways, then, advertising styles that become common provide an index of popular culture. That conclusion is not new. As far back as 1917, writer Norman Douglas claimed, "You can tell the ideals of a nation by its advertisements."[13] In this sense, then, changes in advertising styles over the years have been closely tied to changes in American society as a whole.

Public Relations as Professional Communication

Much of what has been said about the kinds of people who work in advertising is also true of those who work in public relations. Both verbal and nonverbal communication skills are valued and required. Both fields constantly confront problems that can arise from problems of intercultural communication as different types of messages are prepared for different kinds of audiences. In both fields, communicators attempt to persuade many kinds of people on behalf of many kinds of clients. As is the case in any professional field, conflicts always arise and skills with coping with them are an asset. Also in both fields, effective interpersonal communication is a must with bosses, subordinates, colleagues, and clients. Listening, therefore, is also an essential skill, and practitioners have to listen with care. In both fields, many occasions arise requiring speaking before groups, both large and small. In such work it is essential to overcome shyness and apprehension. In both advertising and public relations contexts there is a constant flow of messages via interpersonal media, via written memos, letters, the telephone, e-mail, and fax. These media must be used with care and responsibility. In each field, preparing persuasive messages is an important part of the job, so understanding the mass media is crucial. In short, all the topics covered in the present book have value for people who work in these professional fields.

Public relations is scarcely a new field. For centuries those in power have sought to influence the beliefs, attitudes, and actions of their followers by using a variety of communication strategies. Almost universally, their goal has been to inspire awe and respect on the part of their supporters and fear among their enemies. To accomplish those purposes, they have had their scribes record—on stone, papyrus, parchment, and other media—glowing accounts of their accomplishments. They have built palaces, pyramids, and monuments; staged elaborate parades and ceremonies; and monitored carefully what both their friends and their enemies said about them.

Some have claimed divine status. For example, almost 4,000 years ago the Babylonian king Hammurabi had his scholars develop a set of 283 laws to govern his empire. He had the laws inscribed on huge square blocks of stone that were placed in the center of each city in his domain. On the tops of each side, he had carved a representation of himself receiving those laws from the Sun God. This communication was designed to convince his people of his special status and the lofty origin of his laws. This strategy was as modern and successful as any public relations communicator could devise today to enhance a leader's image.

It is clear, then, that even though it was not called by that name, the practice of public relations through communication has been around a very long time. Even today, the purpose behind many public pronouncements and displays of power is *publicity*—expanding the number of people who are aware of, and have positive beliefs about, some person, policy, or program.

Public relations is often associated with *propaganda*—persuasive communications designed to gain people's approval—or as we might say today, to "capture their hearts and minds"—concerning some action taken or planned, or some person, policy, or cause. While the word **propaganda** today arouses interpretations of misleading or even false claims, it did not always have that connotation. Originally, the term referred to the Roman Catholic Church's efforts to "propagate the faith" through the communication efforts of missionaries (which in many respects was a kind of public relations campaign).

Publicity and propaganda, then, are traditional strategies for trying to shape or modify peoples' beliefs (with the hope that it will modify their actions). Certainly both strategies played major roles in the American colonies before the Revolution, when Committees of Correspondence (patriots advocating separation from England) published pamphlets designed to win the support of the public. Also, many American presidents have had a need to sway public opinion in a direction favorable for their policies. Abraham Lincoln, for example, had a definite "public relations problem" with his Emancipation Proclamation of 1862. It freed all slaves in states and territories at war with the Union—but not in those fighting on the Northern side. Several states that were not in the Confederacy were reluctant to give up the idea of slavery, and Lincoln had a "hard sell." If he had been able to use public opinion polls at the time (they did not exist) he might not have issued his Proclamation until he had prepared the population for it with effective public relations efforts.

Similarly, in 1939, President Franklin D. Roosevelt began (unsuccessfully at first) to persuade the American people that it was in the country's best interests to come to the aid of the British in their fight against Hitler. By 1941, he had begun to turn the situation around somewhat with his speeches and policies. However, the need was eliminated after the Japanese bombed the Pacific fleet at Pearl Harbor. During the 20th century, other national leaders, such as Ghandi and Martin Luther King, Jr., became masters of communications designed to promote approval of their social and political goals. Thus, throughout both ancient and recent times, efforts to change public beliefs, attitudes, and behaviors through the use of effective messages and communication strategies have been a part of human society.

A Brief History of the Industry

Public relations (at least with that name) has only a brief history. As a professional field, it came into being because of protests concerning the "public-be-damned" attitude that was common in American big business as the 1900s began. At that time, those who led the nation's large corporations really did not care much about public opinion or attitudes. They did as they pleased regardless of what people thought of them. In time, however, the public became upset with their excesses. Early in the 1900s, many of their practices were exposed by the "muckraker" journalists of the time. These disclosures led those in charge of corporations to see a need to try to head off this negative trend. Public anger was being translated into legislation (antitrust laws) that corporations feared. It was at that point that many of the big businesses began to use public relations in one form or another to try to modify public attitudes.

The beginnings. An example of an early group providing public relations services was the Publicity Bureau of Boston. It was the brainchild of three former newspapermen who founded it in 1900. The Publicity Bureau established a new and important pattern for providing public relations services for clients, and one that would be followed in the future. Their idea was that (for a fee) they would get favorable stories placed in newspapers that would promote a company's causes and business interests. In addition, they would use other forms of *managed communication* to achieve the same goal. Among the group's early clients were AT&T, Harvard University, the Fore River Shipyard, and Boston Elevated trolley lines.

Emergence of the public relations agency. The Publicity Bureau went out of business by 1911, but other similar agencies were quickly formed. One pioneer in the field was Ivy Lee, a former journalist. He had served as a publicist for political candidates and for the Pennsylvania Railroad. Lee understood the importance of a positive public image for a business and he also understood how such an image could be systematically created through favorable publicity. Just before World War I, then, he established a **public relations agency** to provide services that we would now call public relations activities. Its goal was to help businesses communicate with the public. It was a great success. One of his clients was John D. Rockefeller, Jr.—perhaps the most famous of all "captains of industry." Lee's agency managed publicity for his (then) infamous Standard Oil Company. Another pioneer publicist was Pendleton Dudley. At Lee's urging, he opened an office on Wall Street. The muckraking journalists appear to have played a part in establishing a need among corporations to improve their public image. If people do not trust them, and see them as a negative force in society, their future can by no means be assured.[14]

When the early agencies were being established, public relations specialists were not called by that name. They were referred to as "publicity men," or sometimes "press agents." By the end of World War I, their numbers were skyrocketing. For example, in 1919, one of the New York City newspapers, *The New Republic,* undertook a census to determine the number of people in the city who worked regularly in that capacity. The paper reported that there were about 1,200 publicity men and press agents actively employed.[15] By that time, the functions were becoming increasingly well understood. For example, in 1922, journalism scholar Walter Lippmann described their task as using the media (which were mainly newspapers at the time) to provide the public with "interpretations" of events related to their clients:

> The development of the publicity man is a clear sign that the facts of modern life do not

spontaneously take a shape in which they can be known. They must be given a shape by somebody, and since in the daily routine reporters cannot give a shape to facts, and since there is little disinterested organization of intelligence, the need for some formulation is being met by [press agents and publicity men].[16]

There was, then, a thriving public relations industry by the beginnings of the 1920s. Even though their title was different, they were professional communicators performing the same services as their contemporary public relations counterparts. All they had in terms of media, however, were newspapers and magazines with which to attempt to create favorable public images and interpretations concerning those whom they represented.

Public Relations as Distinct from Advertising

Public relations and advertising may seem somewhat alike. Both design controlled communication processes that are carefully planned and organized to influence peoples' beliefs and behavior. In addition, both depend in large part on the mass media to convey their messages. But there the similarity ends. Advertising makes use of *purchased slots of media space and time.* Public relations, on the other hand, does not make much use of "paid-for" time and space in the mass media. Thus, advertisers buy and use media space or time in ways under their control—after all, they are paying the bill. Public relations practitioners, on the other hand, offer their messages persuasively, hoping that they will get through the "gatekeeping" process. Editors, news directors, and others then determine whether or not the information is worth including in their agenda. In other words, public relations specialists often use more indirect, persuasive means to build a favorable climate of opinion or to achieve other goals.

Because of this, public relations efforts are not always easy for the public to identify. Advertisements are obvious. We know them im-

mediately when we see them on television or in a magazine. However, we do not always know the source of a news article—who is actually staging a fishing tournament, an art exhibit, or some other public event reported in the news. Often, these turn out to be part of a carefully planned public relations effort. In other words, public relations people do not always announce exactly what they are doing or for what purposes. Thus, while public relations personnel may sometimes use paid advertising as part of their overall activities, they are much more involved than are advertisers in the total process of communication, from initiating the message to getting feedback from the public.

The number of people employed in public relations is growing. In 1950 there were 19,000 people engaged in public relations and publicity work according to the U.S. Department of Labor. In only 20 years, by 1970, this had grown more than 300 per cent to 76,000. Today there are more than 180,000 people working in jobs where they do this type of work. Indeed, this may be a very low estimate because the figures include only the rather narrow category who use the label "public relations and publicity writers." In contrast, another agency, the U.S. Bureau of the Census, reports that nearly *half a million persons* are currently engaged in this type of work.

In summary, both advertising and public relations are complex professional fields in which paid communicators design and distribute messages for a great variety of purposes. While critics often complain about both, they are clearly essential for the adequate functioning of the society. Both advertising and public relations are deeply dependent on the use of the mass media to get their messages to audiences. Advertisers, whether or not one likes their messages, play a critical role in alerting the public to the availability of goods and services and in persuading people to pay for them. Without advertising, the capitalistic economy could not function. In the final analysis, public relations can be thought of as a set of strategies for *deliberately manipulating meanings* in ways that are not always apparent to the target audience. The most common goal is to influence peoples' interpretations of a person, group, or policy represented by the communicator. This does not necessarily mean, however, that such manipulation is necessarily deceptive or unethical. Indeed, like advertising, public relations plays a key role in keeping the economy going. If a large part of the public became completely disillusioned with government agencies, educational institutions, manufacturers, health care providers, and so on through the extensive list of those whom they serve, the economy could not function.

Practicing Public Relations

Today, the field of public relations has grown into a sophisticated and complex occupational field, with a large part of the work carried on either by relatively large agencies or by public relations departments located in many kinds of corporations, government agencies or nonprofit groups. However, some old-fashioned "publicity agents" (still using that name) continue to work, especially in New York City, serving the needs of people and groups in such high-visibility fields as the entertainment and fashion industries.

Although it is a complex field, it is not difficult to define the basic nature of public relations in terms of what its practitioners actually do. Public relations is an organized communication process, conducted by people who make a living as professional communicators. It can be defined somewhat formally in terms of conducting the following activities: *Paid professional practitioners design and transmit messages, on behalf of a client, via a variety of media to relevant and targeted audiences in an attempt to influence their beliefs, attitudes, or actions regarding some person, organization, policy, situation, or event.*

While this is a complex definition, it sets forth the basics of what practitioners actually do. However, it does not provide enough details so that nonspecialists can actually understand the field in greater depth. Taking each of the ideas in the definition and explaining them more fully will help.

Public relations practitioners. Those who become professional public relations practitioners tend to be people whose education has been in a field in which writing and producing other forms of messages using other media has been a major focus. Many enter the field after prior employment in other media professions. Others have completed undergraduate or graduate degree programs in public relations. Many types of clients are served by such practitioners. Some work in agencies that contract for services, in the manner discussed earlier. Others may be salaried employees of a particular corporation, a government agency, or a even a nonprofit group—such as a charity, museum or university. Titles vary. Depending on where they work, some may be called an "information specialist," a "public affairs officer," or a "press secretary." Whatever their title, their activities are similar in the various settings in which they work and regardless of the clients that they serve.

The clients that they serve. Many kinds of clients are served by public relations practitioners.[17] These differ considerably among the individuals and groups in the United States that produce materials and services for the public. Among them are corporations and industries that manufacture goods. Also included are local, state, and federal government agencies; the military; institutions that provide health care services; investment firms and banks; schools, colleges and universities; organized charities; religious groups; and so on. Individuals can also be clients. Among these are public personalities, such as prominent actors, sports figures, singers, politicians, preachers, and musicians—all of whom need a constant flow of publicity in order to stay in the eye of the public and have people retain beliefs about their importance.

Media used in public relations. All the media used for communication today play some role in the activities of public relations specialists. Various kinds of messages are transmitted via newspapers, magazines, radio, and television. Increasingly, the Internet is being used to transmit information about clients or employers. Other messages are prepared for distribution via videotape or CD-ROM. Another important strategy used by practitioners is what they refer to as "special events." These include trade show displays, contests, and many other formats and contexts in which favorable images of clients or their products can be presented.

Public relations messages. Many kinds of message formats are used by public relations communicators. They write speeches and prepare news releases, newspaper articles, and magazine stories for their employers. Some serve as spokespersons for their clients, giving speeches and holding press conferences. Others prepare their clients or employers to give formal speeches. They provide guidance for public appearances and meetings. They prepare clients for press conferences by conducting practice interviews. Some help their clients or employers sponsor sports events—ranging from golf competitions to bass fishing contests. All are designed for public relations purposes.

Most of what is prepared by practitioners is fairly routine. Common are printed materials like *brochures* that provide information about a corporation, government agency, or nonprofit group. Other print material examples are *newsletters* that are distributed to various "stakeholders," such as alumni, employees, and stockholders. *Annual reports* are often prepared by public relations specialists. These report on the status, activities, and accomplishments of the organization. Central to their work, however, is the more traditional task of preparing *news stories* and other information to be released to the press, and trying to get these on the media agenda so that they appear in the paper or news broadcast in such a way that readers, listeners, or viewers will come to have favorable views of those whom the specialists serve.

An important task and objective for public relations practitioners can be *crisis communication* or *damage control* through the use of well-designed communications. Public relations specialists are needed when an airplane crashes, a train derails, oil is spilled, or a CEO is arrested for cooking the books. On such unhappy occasions, public relations practitioners disseminate messages intended to limit the negative consequences. It would be wrong to assume that they are trying to either avoid responsibility or misrepresent the situation. The goal is to design information releases that explain what happened and to show that management is focusing on steps that the public sees as meeting the client's responsibilities. PR specialists are not trained to "cover up" or distort the truth. Cover-ups and distortions do not pay. People in public relations know full well that serious mistakes can be made by those who try to deny or lie when a bad situation arises.

Targeting specific audiences. Public relations specialists prepare and transmit different types of messages to different categories of people. Some are intended to be read or viewed by the public at large and are broadly defined. Typical would be a news release prepared for the readers of a local newspaper, or an interview designed as a local TV news story. Other messages are designed for more narrowly defined groups, such as voters or the constituents of an office holder. Still others are aimed at the employees of a large company or the personnel of a major military organization. Investors are another special audience. Specialized messages are designed for investors who hold stock in a large corporation. Indeed, sometimes the intended audience is very specific. Information may be prepared specifically for the surviving family members of a disaster, such as a hurricane, a flood, an air crash, or a military accident. In any of these cases, the public relations practitioner must fully understand the nature of the audience and the impression that is likely to result from receiving the specific information.

Types of influences sought. Obviously, public relations practitioners want to have the messages accomplish the purposes for which they were designed. There are many different situations, and the purposes depend on the complexities of what is at stake. In some cases, a *long-range goal* is sought. If so, a public relations campaign may be designed to alter the behavior of the public over time regarding some specific topic or issue. A good illustration is the campaign to prevent forest fires conducted by the U.S. Forest Service. Starting back in 1949, Smokey Bear, a cartoon characterization of a forest agent, wearing the wide-brimmed hat, told the public for more than a half-century, "Only *YOU* can stop forest fires!" Smokey's message became known by virtually everyone in the United States. In fact, the campaign was so effective that in recent times the public reacted very negatively when the Forest Service proposed setting fires deliberately in order to burn accumulated dry materials on forest floors. The goal was to reduce the danger of more serious fires caused by lightning, but it got a negative response from the public.

Most public relations messages do not have such dramatic goals. The majority are intended to influence the public regarding some person, issue, or event—often about something that has taken a negative turn. For example, a film star, a sports figure, or a prominent person's son or daughter may became the object of a well-publicized scandal concerning drugs or an improper sexual encounter. An effort must be made to redeem the person's reputation. At this point, the help of public relations specialists may be enlisted to plan a carefully orchestrated strategy to restore the person's public image.

For the most part, public relations messages are much less dramatic than these examples. In fact, many have the goal of *informing* rather than persuading. The majority are news stories about some new leader, director, or CEO who has just taken charge of an organization. Others may document the release of a new model of a product, or may provide a briefing about a campaign by a military spokesperson.

The Press and Public Relations: A Symbiotic Relationship

Public relations practitioners and the press live in a state of *symbiosis,* or *mutual dependency.* A careful examination of any daily newspaper or a television news broadcast will reveal that a very large proportion of what appears in the news has its origin in someone's news conference, news release, or some other form of material originally prepared by a public relations or public affairs specialist and released to the press. This does not mean that the press blindly makes public whatever practitioners provide. Reporters follow up, interview people with other points of view, and so on. Nevertheless, much of the agenda in the daily press has its start in information prepared and released by public relations specialists. To illustrate, if a plane crashes, public money is misappropriated, or a corporation is caught harassing women or mistreating minorities, some spokesperson for the relevant organization (airline, government agency, corporation) will hold a news conference. Their purpose in appearing before reporters is not just to provide information. It is to put the best possible interpretation on what happened, how it happened that they did not foresee it, what they are doing about it, and so on. Such press conferences are not casual appearances. Most such presentations are *carefully rehearsed* ahead of time with the aid of public relations specialists who warn of damaging questions that are likely to be asked and who develop ways of deflecting questions that are likely to create harm to the agency or authorities.

The reporters, on the other hand, *must have news to report.* On most days there may be little going on that is truly newsworthy. While minor events (a fire in a home, a mugging, a pie-eating contest, or an automobile wreck) can sometimes be made interesting by clever writing, such relatively routine happenings seldom provide enough exciting copy to fill out the day's news agenda. Thus journalists turn to what public relations people have supplied to them. The point is that *something* has to appear in the paper so that subscribers can read about it, or be reported in the newscast for viewers to see. Reporters must meet deadlines. They often have very little flexibility or time to dig up alternatives to what the public relations practitioners provide for them.

In spite of their basic distrust of each other, public relations practitioners and journalists continue to live in a state of uneasy symbiosis. One need only to make a casual examination of the agenda produced by most daily papers or newscasts to discover that many stories—often the majority—are products of public relations practitioners who report routine happenings in business, government, entertainment industries, education, politics, and so on. In this way, reporters have to rely on spokespersons for politicians, personalities, corporations, and other special interests in the society. Whatever the merits of such stories, it is out of these complex and symbiotic exchanges that much of the daily news is shaped and reported.

Chapter Review

- Both advertising and public relations can be defined as a profession in which paid practitioners work to design and transmit messages and to achieve outcomes on behalf of clients. Both use a variety of media to transmit messages to relevant and targeted audiences in an attempt to influence their beliefs, attitudes, or actions regarding some product, service, person, organization, policy, situation, or event.

- Many of the communication strategies used today in these fields have ancient origins. Advertising messages have been found on Roman ruins. Even earlier, the sun-god strategy was used by Hammurabi to characterize both himself and his laws.

- Both fields make extensive use of mass communications. Advertisers purchase time and space to display their messages. Public relations practitioners try to draw attention to their clients by information transmitted in news reports, on talk shows, or in other forms of print or broadcast where they can get their messages accepted.

- Both advertising and public relations are essential in modern capitalistic economies. People must be made aware of goods and services, and must be persuaded to purchase them. The public must have confidence in the businesses and agencies that provide these goods and services.

- An uneasy symbiotic relationship exists between public relations and journalism. However, each needs the other. Much of what appears in the news has origins in events or information released by public relations practitioners. At the same time, such practitioners are deeply dependent on the media as means of transmitting their messages to their desired audiences.

Key Terms

practitioners	Industrial Revolution	media service organization
clients	department store	learn-feel-do
stakeholders	symbiotic relationship	learn-conform-or-be-punished
abundance	advertising agency	propaganda
financial foundation	boutique agency	public relations agency

Notes

1. The number of colleges and universities offering formal programs in advertising and public relations has grown sharply in recent years. See: Johnson, K. F., & Ross, B. I. (2000). Advertising and public relations education: A five year review. *Journalism and Mass Communication Educator, 56,* 66–72.

2. This chapter is based in part on a more extended discussion of the nature of these two industries in DeFleur, M. L., & Dennis, E. E. (2002). *Understanding mass communication* (7th ed.). Boston: Houghton Mifflin. See chap. 11. (pp. 290–323), Advertising: Using media in the market place; and chap. 13 (pp. 324–353), Public relations: Influencing beliefs, attitudes and actions.

3. Potter, D. M. (1968). *People of plenty* (2nd ed., p. 172). Chicago: University of Chicago Press.

4. Harvey, E. G. (1996). *The adman in the parlor: Magazines and the gingering of consumer culture, 1880s to 1910* (p. 8). New York: Oxford University Press.

5. See: Fox, S. (1984). *A history of American advertising and its creators.* New York: Vintage Books, Random House.

6. Ibid., pp. 13–39.

7. Potter, *People of plenty,* p. 168.

8. For a description of various types of advertising organizations, see: Arens, W. F. (1996). *Advertising* (6th ed., pp. 76–80). Chicago: Irwin.

9. Miller, G. R. (1987). Persuasion. In C. R. Berger & S. H. Chaffee (Eds.), *Handbook of communication science* (pp. 446–483). Newbury Park, CA: Sage.

10. Colley, R. H. (1961). *Defining advertising goals for measuring advertising success* (p. 35). New York: Association of National Manufacturers.

11. This strategy has been used for prosocial purposes as well as to sell goods. See, for example: Austen, E. W., et al. (2002). The effects of increased cognitive involvement on college student's interpretations of magazine advertisements for alcohol. *Communication Research, 29,* 155–179.

12. Jones, J. P. (1986). *What's in a name: Advertising and the concept of brands* (p. 141). Lexington, MA: D. Heath.

13. Douglas, N. (1917). South wind. In *Bartlett's familiar quotations* (13th ed., p. 840). Boston: Little, Brown.

14. Cutlip, S. M., Center, A. H., & Broom, G. M. (1985). *Effective public relations* (6th ed., pp. 138–230). Englewood Cliffs, NJ: Prentice-Hall.

15. Cobb, F. (December 31,1919). *The New Republic,* p. 44.

16. Lippmann, W. (1922). *Public opinion* (p. 34). New York: Harcourt Brace.

17. Clients can be persons, groups or even communities. See: Vale, L. J., & Warner, S. B. Jr., (2001). *Place marketing: Using media to promote cities* (pp. 33–85). New Brunswick, NJ: Center for Urban Policy Research.

16

Understanding Communication Research

"How can you make such a silly claim?" Martin protested. "What you are saying is impossible! There is no way that you are going to convince me that you can study human communication scientifically. It just won't work. Communication is far too complex. Besides, people have free will and that means they do not follow regular patterns, like trained seals, in any of their behavior, including communication."

"Well," Hanna replied, "first of all, it depends on what you mean by science. If you think of science only in terms of white coats, laboratories, microscopes, or electronic instruments that go bleep, bleep, bleep, then you're absolutely right. However, if that were the only type of setting in which science could be pursued, you would have to leave out about 75 percent of the fields that are now conducting scientific research. Only a few of today's sciences use that kind of stuff.

"Take astronomy or meteorology," Hanna continued. "You can't get solar systems and galaxies, or warm fronts and hurricanes, into a laboratory—and microscopes would make little sense for studying them. Indeed, in the majority of scientific fields, it is not the place where investigations are pursued, not the instruments that are used for various purposes, and certainly not the clothing worn by the researchers that defines it as a science."

"You will have to admit, though," Martin countered, "that people really are unpredictable. They can choose whether, when, and how they will communicate, and with whom. Because all that behavior is so random, there is just no way that you can develop any kind of formulas or laws that govern communication. After all, that is precisely what they do in the real sciences—like biology, chemistry, and physics. Look at Newton's laws and the atomic table. What do you say to that?"

"I say that they are wonderful examples of how the scientific method paid off long ago in physics and chemistry, and why it is so important to use it now in other fields," Hanna replied. "However, because those traditional sciences have already developed such laws does not mean that parallel discoveries cannot be made in newer areas, such as the study of communication. They will come in time. After all, the use of a scientific approach in studies of communication began only a generation or so ago. The physical and biological sciences got their start centuries earlier."

"Maybe," said Martin, still resisting, "but I still say that communication research just can't be scientific because it studies how people talk and act, and everybody knows that it is impossible to predict human behavior."

"Martin," Hanna sighed, "if you are willing to make the effort, I can show you how the scientific method has already revealed patterns in human communication, as well as explanations that help predict how people are likely to communicate in a great variety of contexts and circumstances."

Like Martin, many people are reluctant to accept the idea that human communication can be studied using the logic and methods of science. That is understandable, because communication behavior is indeed very complex, difficult to observe, and not always predictable. But difficult is not the same as impossible, and few would argue that the search for better ways to communicate is unimportant. The development of a body of trustworthy knowledge concerning ways to communicate more accurately and effectively is essential, which is why it is important to conduct research on the process and effects of human communication.

The present chapter has the goal of *providing an understanding* of how the rules, logic, strategies, and methods of science are applied to the systematic study of human communication and its consequences. It is not designed to train you, the reader, as a research specialist. However, the use of **research** to try and find answers to important problems is increasingly common in almost all fields.

Science had its beginnings in the study of the physical world—where it obviously has had remarkable success. It then came into use in medical fields—with additional great success. Later, during the later 1800s, the logic and procedures of science came into use in such fields as psychology, anthropology, sociology, and the study of political behavior. In these fields valuable insights into and understandings of human behavior were developed using scientific strategies. At present, communication scholars make use of scientific methods and procedures to study a great variety of problems in human communication.

At the same time, the scientific perspective provides one way to examine human communication; the humanistic or rhetorical perspective offers another. Humanists focus on how internal, psychological processes affect how we communicate. To observe, report, and explain objectively how we communicate is insufficient to humanists; instead, they want to know how we subjectively interpret the world we live in.

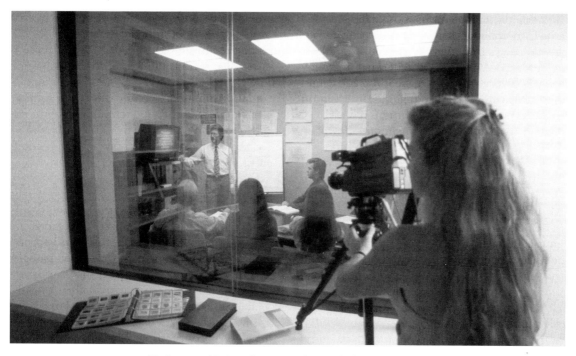

To the unsophisticated eye, most human behavior seems like a jumble of random activity. Social scientists, however, assume that there is an order and that cause/effect relationships can be discovered by careful studies in what may appear to be merely chance behavior.

Humanists argue that we cannot exactly observe how people feel, how they love or hate one another, and why a film should be interpreted in a particular way.

Both perspectives offer important methods for understanding how and why we communicate. Although humanistic methods continue to be used to inform the study of communication, increasing numbers of scholars in the field examine human communication using scientific strategies of measurement, theory building, and testing from the scientific perspective. This chapter will focus exclusively on the scientific perspective.

As noted, the use of a scientific approach to understanding human communication began only a few decades ago. Great strides have been made in developing methods of research that can be used effectively in this important task. Many of these methods were originally devel-

oped for use in the physical sciences (for example, the experiment). Later they were adapted for the basic social sciences, such as psychology and sociology. Other methods originated in the social sciences themselves (the survey) and were found to be very practical for communication research. Still others have been invented by communication researchers themselves.

Whatever the origins of these methods, researchers who study human communication within the scientific perspective now use procedures that can be called *the scientific methodology of communication research*. Collectively, those procedures can be thought of as a kind of "tool kit." The kit has many useful methods for gaining knowledge. These consist of logical strategies of observation, techniques of measurement, criteria for assessing the quality and importance of what is observed, and rules for making conclusions known to others. Through the use of that methodological tool kit, trustworthy knowledge can be accumulated about how people communicate and what consequences such behavior has for them. This chapter describes some of the main features of communication research methods and provides examples of how studies are conducted when these tools are used. It adds an important dimension to knowledge about the human communication process that is so important in daily life.

The Postulates of the Scientific Research Perspective

We begin by asking a very basic question: What is meant by *research*? As the opening vignette suggests, for some people the term conjures up images of nerds with thick glasses wearing white coats and working in laboratories with electronic gadgets and glass tubes that make gurgling sounds. This image misses the point completely. Research has little to do with where it is conducted, what gadgets are used, or how people are dressed.

In its broadest sense, research is simply a strategy for studying some aspect or feature of the real world in such a way that trustworthy knowledge can be gained and errors can be minimized. What is studied may be physical or biological, or it may be a form of human behavior—such as communication. Thus, it is not the object of study that defines research but the *way one goes about it.*

Simply stated, then, *research* (in any field) can be defined as *a set of systematic procedures for gathering credible information about some object or process.* In our discipline, the object or process consists of the verbal, nonverbal, and contextual features of human communication that have been discussed in previous chapters. Moreover, research requires that we study communication under carefully controlled conditions of observation in such a way that objective conclusions can be reached with a minimum of error.

Communication researchers conducting a scientific investigation are committed to three essential *assumptions* about the nature of what they are investigating and how they go about it. Broad assumptions of this kind are sometimes called *postulates,* and they apply to all fields in which scientific research is conducted.[1] The term **postulate** means a shared belief of a very fundamental nature—so basic that it is not subject to proof or disproof. The following assumptions are the postulates of the scientific research perspective. (Box 16.1 gives an overview of these assumptions.)

The Assumption of an Orderly Universe

Communication researchers using the scientific method must first assume that what they are studying *follows regular and discoverable patterns.* Indeed all researchers must assume there is order in what they study. Human communication behavior is no exception. It follows orderly patterns, just as physical and biological phenomena do.

The importance of making the assumption of an orderly universe is that it provides the basic reason for the very existence of science. Without this assumption, scientific research on any subject would be completely unnecessary. For example, in a chaotic world of communication behavior, no patterns could be discovered—it would be merely a jumble of random events. This is clearly not the case. Each of the chapters in this book has shown that a great deal of order in communication behavior has been identified.

Research aimed at revealing and describing order—stages, tendencies, configurations, or processes of human communication—is called **descriptive research.** Descriptive research studies reach conclusions that demonstrate some significant pattern or other orderly way in which people relate to one another using verbal, nonverbal, contextual, or mediated communication. The models of the communication process presented in Chapter 1 are examples of the end product of such research.

BOX 16.1 🔍 *A Closer Look*

Research Postulates about Communication

Communication researchers using the scientific method agree on the following postulates or assumptions about the nature of human communication and the methods they use to investigate it:

1. *The assumption of an orderly universe.* Communication behavior is not a jumble of random events. How and what people say, with whom, and when they say it follows some orderly, discoverable rules or patterns.
2. *The assumption of cause-effect relationships.* Communication behavior does not just happen. There are identifiable, discoverable causes for why people communicate the way they do, when they do it, and with whom. Theories help explain the probable causes and consequences of a particular communication event.
3. *The assumption of scientific integrity.* Science is self-policing. To trust research findings and conclusions about human communication, studies must be made public with all the procedures, findings, and interpretations spelled out. Such studies are then screened by experts before they are accepted for publication. Unpublished studies that do not disclose their methods or findings are ignored.

The Assumption of Cause-Effect Relationships

A second assumption (postulate) subscribed to by communication researchers is that it is possible to discover, through scientific investigation, *why* events occur. That is, their causes can be uncovered. This postulate is common to all fields of science—whether they are researching dreaded diseases, financial recessions, nuclear reactions, or failures in communication between people who are not alike. At any particular time in the ongoing development of science, their causes may be poorly understood or even unknown, but scientists reject the idea that things just happen randomly and that there are no causal sequences in events.

The need to develop explanations of causes and effects points directly to the role of **theory** in the research perspective. Theories are the form in which cause-effect relationships are stated, once they are discovered. In other words, if they have been verified, theories provide *explanations* of how one set of events brings about or influences another. Even before they have been verified, candidate theories provide invaluable *guides* to what needs to be studied in order to gain understanding. Much research is focused on testing and evaluating theories to see whether they really work. Thus, one major goal in communication research is to formulate (put together) theories that explain the consequences and influences of various kinds of communication. A related goal is to test and evaluate those theories to see if they are adequate. Throughout this text, theories have been used to explain particular effects in communication.

The Assumption of Scientific Integrity

The third assumption (postulate) of the research perspective is based on what researchers call the rule of *experto credite*, which means literally "have confidence in the expert." The assumption of scientific integrity refers to the confidence that scholars have in one another's published research findings. Scientists are perhaps the world's greatest skeptics, and they demand the highest standards of proof to ensure the information is credible. They abhor the idea that anyone would falsify data or findings.

The assumption of *experto credite* rests on three requirements concerning the nature of research reports, plus the skeptical and self-policing nature of science. These requirements are that science must be *public,* research reports must be rigorously *screened* before publication, and secrecy in research is *unacceptable.*

Science must be public. Scientific skepticism is nowhere more evident than in the requirement that research findings be published—spelling out exactly what was being studied, the methods used, the findings observed, and their implications. To meet this requirement, research reports are usually submitted as articles for publication in technical journals. Such journals are specialized magazines devoted to reporting research findings and related matters in various fields.[2] An acceptable article must describe in detail how the research was done and exactly why the conclusions were reached. One benefit of this requirement is that it enables other researchers to check the author's conclusions by **replication** of the study using the same methods and conditions. Findings that cannot be duplicated in this manner are regarded as controversial and are under suspicion.

Research reports must be screened. Editors of scientific journals receive many reports for publication from researchers all over the world. Each report is then *assessed* (screened) by a panel of peers, selected by the editors. These are experts in whatever has been studied. This means that the report is closely scrutinized by highly qualified researchers to detect errors in procedure or in how conclusions were reached. Only if the research report gets by this demanding review can it be accepted for publication. To protect the integrity of the assessment, this is almost always done "blind": That is, neither the author of the report nor any of the judges know the names of the others. Because many journals reject 90 percent or more of the reports they receive, this is a rigorous system.

If reports on scientific findings and conclusions survive this screening process, they become *public* knowledge. Those that are published are usually referred to as being in the "literature"—the body of research reports on any particular topic that appear in reputable journals, dissertations, or other publications. In this manner, *a body of trustworthy knowledge accumulates.* This accumulative feature keeps the cutting edge of science moving forward.[3]

Secrecy is unacceptable. The requirement that research reports be made public eliminates from the literature secret findings of projects conducted by industry, government, advertising agencies, or any other organization that does not publish its reports. Although this type of **proprietary research** (research owned by those who pay to have the research conducted) can provide a competitive edge to the particular industry that generates it, such studies may not be conducted with meticulous attention to scientific procedures and methods. Because they escape scrutiny, proprietary studies may sometimes be the work of sloppy researchers or even outright quacks or frauds. Whatever their quality, they contribute nothing to science as a "shared" body of knowledge.

One of the advantages of these self-policing features of science is the belief that published research reports have *scientific integrity.* Although misconduct such as deception or fraud does occur, it is quite rare.

This system for achieving scientific integrity does not mean that there are no inconsistencies or controversies in published research reports on various topics. They are abundant. Honest researchers, diligently using sound methods, often reach different conclusions on the same issues. However, the system described above, which is based on accepting conclusions only after they are consistently supported by a body of research, is the best one yet devised to develop shared, accumulated, and trustworthy knowledge.

Steps in the Research Process

Communication research is conducted step by step. The six basic stages listed here are followed by researchers in all fields, from planning

BOX 16.2 〇 *A Closer Look*

Steps in the Research Process

Research is a systematic process. Six basic steps are followed when conducting a formal research study.

1. *Specify the goals of the research.* The researcher begins by asking, "What problem do I want to solve? What exactly do I want to look at? What are the variables that I want to observe? What do I want to find out?"
2. *Review prior research reports.* The researcher searches the relevant literature to see what is already known about the research problem. This way, the researcher avoids duplicating research or reinventing the wheel. The literature can also give the researcher clues about procedures or special problems to consider in designing the study.
3. *Make the necessary observations.* The researcher is now ready to observe the relevant phenomena and record observations in some symbolic (often numerical) way. The researcher does this directly—by observing what people are doing or saying now—or indirectly—by noting what people say they did after the fact.

4. *Analyze the data.* To make sense of the obtained observations, the researcher must input the numerical data into the computer and perform statistical calculations. In this way, the researcher can reduce large amounts of information into a manageable index, average, or quantitative summary.
5. *Reach conclusions.* After statistically analyzing the data, the researcher must interpret the results by asking, "What does this mean? Do I accept or reject my hypothesis? Was the theory correct? Given these results, what alternative theoretical explanation can I make?"
6. *Report the results.* Finally, the researcher is obligated to make the study public by presenting and reporting each of the five previous steps. In this way, others can judge the merits of the study, learn more about the topic investigated, and teach or use the obtained information. Over time, this study and others like it contribute to the accumulated body of knowledge.

what they are going to study to publishing their results. Box 16.2 provides a brief overview of each of these steps.

Specifying the Goals of the Research

One of the most critical steps in the research process is specifying the objectives of the investigation—the reasons for which it is being undertaken. This includes stating exactly what is to be studied and why. First, the problem has to be identified in a general way. Then, each phase has to be stated clearly in a carefully defined *plan* so that the research can be conducted realistically with the greatest level of precision that resources will allow.

Identifying the relevant variables. The first consideration in planning a research project is to understand what *variables* are to be observed. A variable is a concept, factor, or condition that can take different numerical values. Recall from the meaning triangle in Chapter 2 that each concept has a label (name) and some set of meanings that people experience in response to that label. A simple example would be age. By convention, this term labels the number of birthdays an individual has had since birth. Other variables may be level of education, household income, or amount of time spent viewing television.

Looked at this way, age, income, education, and TV viewing time are concepts, and they can vary quantitatively from one individual to another. Thus, each is a variable concept. Researchers shorten this phrase and say that age, income, and so on are variables.

When relationships between variables are studied, some are *independent* and others are *dependent*. These terms can have two different implications. In some cases, variations or changes in the **dependent variable** are thought to be due to the presence and influence of a particular **independent variable**. That is, the two variables are in a relationship that implies cause and effect. For example, in a medical study the number of fatty hamburgers a person eats in a week can be related in a causal way to the probability that the individual will get fat. However, the reverse would not be considered causal. In other cases, two factors might merely vary together in some coordinated manner with each other (a correlation), without implications of causation. In communication terms, a variable like communication apprehension might influence an individual's level of social efficacy. On the other hand, such apprehension might be correlated with an individual's lack of education, which it could not possibly have caused. It is very important for the researcher to understand which of these two cases is implied by the findings—potential cause or only a correlation.

In a research project, variables are *observed*—following the scientific requirement that knowledge is founded on observation, as opposed to traditional wisdom, speculation, or religious interpretation. Observation in research usually consists of *measurement in some form*—deciding whether a variable is present or absent or present to some degree. The measurement process is discussed in greater detail in a section that will follow.

Identifying the general objectives. Research begins with a decision as to the project's overall goals. If it is simply a descriptive study, the problem is to specify what must be observed and described. If the research is designed to develop, or to test, one or more theories, the problem becomes more complex: The researcher has to identify the exact observations that will be needed, how each variable will be measured, what patterns are expected in the results, and how to decide whether the findings support the theory being considered.

Often, a research problem can be formulated in terms of a **hypothesis**—a statement that poses tentative and expected relationships between variables. Ideally, a hypothesis is derived from a theory that predicts what variables are related to others. Assembling careful observations on those variables makes it possible to *accept* or *reject* the hypothesis, as long as standard procedures for making such judgments are followed. If the hypothesis can be accepted, then it provides *support* for the theory. If it must be rejected, then the theory is called into question.

In many research projects, it is difficult to derive hypotheses in this way because there are no well-articulated theories from which to obtain them. In such cases, researchers turn to the body of evidence that has been accumulated by other researchers about what they want to study. If the evidence is not sufficiently clear, researchers can formulate a "working" hypothesis that indicates what they expect to find, given the evidence to date.

Reviewing Prior Research Reports

Researchers review the all available sources to locate reports of others who have already studied the problem. Reviewing the previous research prevents duplication and can help researchers avoid the problems of the earlier studies. Such reports can be found in many sources. In addition to the technical journals in the field, research may be reported in books, monographs, convention papers, and government documents. All of these sources must be scrutinized before finalizing research plans. This is no easy task. One aid to review the literature is the *Communication Abstracts,* which abstracts (summarizes) all the articles in communication journals each month. This source is available by subscription, or it can be found in most college libraries and online. Other electronic databases, such as *PsycINFO, Social Sciences Full-Text,* and *Sociological Abstracts,* also are helpful for finding previous studies on a topic.

With computers, a review of prior publications that formerly would have taken days or weeks to accomplish can be done in a few minutes. Commercial database providers offer electronic duplicates of printed abstracts and publications. Such databases can be quickly and efficiently searched with a desktop computer. Summaries of virtually all journal articles, books, reports, and monographs are posted promptly into these databases soon after publication. In these sources, all earlier research findings can be quickly located and reviewed.

Making the Necessary Observations

Yogi Berra, the famous baseball player, perhaps said it best when he reportedly remarked, "You can observe a lot by just watching!" His analysis actually has a great deal of merit. In scientific research, watching is called **empirical observation.** More specifically, researchers observe whether certain behaviors under investigation are present (in some amount) or absent. This means that researchers watch and make judgments as to how to classify what has been observed by deciding where the behavior fits in some set of qualitative categories, or along some numerical continuum. To illustrate, imagine a researcher who is watching a person talking to another individual in a small group experiment. One goal of the researcher's observations is to decide whether that person has played an *active* or a *passive* role as a communicator. On the basis of those categories, the judgment is recorded. A series of such recorded observations are *data.*

The nature of "data." The term **data** means *information known as fact.* To make something known as fact requires that it be communicated. Therefore, observations that are to become sci-

entific data must be *recorded* in symbols in some way, so that other scientists can see and understand what was observed. This can be done with detailed verbal descriptions for subtle qualitative observations, or it can be done with numbers for quantitative observations.

Transforming observations into recorded data can introduce distortion and change, so the procedure has to be designed with care. For example, when researchers depend on interviewing subjects, *questionnaires* are normally used for recording purposes. Traditionally, these pose each question in a standardized way so that all subjects are asked the same questions in the same way. This, in turn, helps the interviewer to observe each case uniformly.

However, such standardization can obscure subtle and important information. For example, suppose the interviewer asks, "Are you single, married, divorced, or widowed?" Suppose that a male participant is still legally married but has long since separated from his wife. Suppose further that he is now living with another woman and they intend to marry. All of these subtleties are lost when he answers, "Well, technically I'm married." The interviewer then records the observation "married" on the form—missing all the rest. Later, when the data are analyzed for interpretation, that particular subject will be included in the "married" category, presumably living in a stable marital relationship with his legal spouse. If a number of such cases were encountered, the conclusions drawn from the category "married" might be incorrect, based on such responses.

Qualitative versus quantitative observation. There is no perfect way to make empirical observations. Many techniques and strategies can be used to observe communication behavior, and each has its advantages and limitations. Some scales and questionnaires produce remarkably precise numerical data that can be analyzed with statistics, but such procedures may miss subtle aspects of communication and may fail to explain very much about why people communicate as they do. On the other hand, purely qualitative techniques may provide sensitive insights into complex human feelings and values, but they do not produce numerical data that can be easily summarized and subjected to statistical tests. This means that it may not be possible to evaluate the truth of a conclusion reached from purely qualitative observation. Despite the limitations of these approaches, both play an important part in the accumulation of knowledge about human communication.

Direct versus indirect observation. Behavior can be observed *directly* or *indirectly.* In direct observation, researchers watch communication behavior as it is openly acted out by the subjects. Here, the subjects know that they are being observed, and this condition can alter their behavior in some circumstances. In indirect observation, the participants do not know that they are being watched, so their behavior is not affected by the research. However, indirect observation without subject awareness is difficult, if not impossible. Few people would want to be observed communicating in natural settings—as they eat, cook, watch TV, feed the cat, have sex, work, play sports, and generally carry on their daily routines.

A less direct form of observation is *unobtrusive* measurement. Here, communication activities are "inferred" from information obtained after the fact. For example, people's preferences in radio stations were studied by having auto repair shops record the stations to which their customers' car radios were tuned when the vehicles were dropped off.

Although there is no ideal observation method, **participant observation** has many advantages.[4] In its classic form, the investigator actually joins the group that is under study and participates fully in its activities—so as to observe its communication patterns directly. The group may or may not know that the person is a researcher. This form of unobtrusive data gathering is called *participant observation.*

Participant observation is both difficult and time consuming, because the researcher must learn the special language, norms, roles, and lifestyle of those being observed. It's also difficult for the researcher to make an accurate and secret record of the behavior under study. Consider the researcher studying communication behaviors among prison inmates (which has been done). Participant observation in such circumstances would be dangerous as well as difficult.

Analyzing the Data

Once recorded, data must be processed in various ways before they can be analyzed to determine their implications. In quantitative research, **data entry** generally refers to transforming recorded observations (such as from questionnaires) into numbers that can be entered into statistical software in a computer. The next step, **data analysis,** takes the numbers and subjects them to a variety of statistical tests, with a computer doing the drudgery of extensive calculation.

Not all communication researchers use a quantitative approach with computers and statistics to determine what they have found in a research project. If participant observation or some other qualitative data gathering has been used, the findings do not consist of a mass of numbers to be manipulated. Many sensitive and significant studies have been completed by communication researchers using qualitative observational strategies for complex problems.

Where computers and statistics are used, extensive planning is always completed *before* the research is undertaken. This is always at the beginning, rather than at the end, after the data have been obtained. This means that a complete plan for data entry and analysis must be developed before observations begin. The reason for this is that computers are incredibly stupid. They blindly follow orders, like the mechanical robots they are. They cannot create, imagine, advise, suspect, hypothesize, or conclude anything. Although they are unbelievably good at storing information, manipulating it, and printing it out in neat reports, they cannot interpret what any of it means.

Whatever the topic of the research, when the analysis is complete, the researcher has reduced large numbers of observations to numerical indexes, coefficients, averages, or other convenient quantitative summaries. Findings of a qualitative nature usually are set forth in more lengthy descriptive reports with verbal summaries provided at the end.

Reaching Conclusions

The bottom line in research is the set of *conclusions and interpretations* that the data imply. However, moving from data analysis to interpretation is done with great care. Various criteria may be used to ensure that unwarranted conclusions are not reached.

Descriptive generalization. In descriptive research, where theory testing and hypothesis acceptance or rejection are not at stake, conclusions are likely to be stated in the form of a **generalizations.** *Generalizations* are accurate statements that communicate in precise language what was found with respect to any regularities or patterns observed. Generalizations do not address any specific case or subject under analysis. They focus on what was "generally" the case in the observations—what tendencies, trends, relationships, or differences between categories of subjects seemed to thread through the findings.

Many generalizations apply only to the particular people or situations that were involved in the study. However, based on the assumption of the research perspective that there is "order in the universe," investigators may think that what was found in their particular study is an accurate description of what exists among similar people and situations. In such a case, the generalization may extend beyond the data. There is always the danger of **overgeneralizing**—extending the implications of the results too far by claiming that the study's conclusions also apply to categories of people who were not examined and who are not sufficiently similar to those studied.

Accepting or rejecting hypotheses. In testing hypotheses to determine whether they can be accepted, statistical procedures are invaluable. Statistics provide information based on *probability* for making a clear-cut decision about whether the results of a data analysis are likely to have occurred "by chance alone," rather than as a result of a cause-effect relationship between variables. If chance seems to be as good an explanation as any other, the rule is to conclude that chance has indeed been at work. That means rejecting the hypothesis that the findings are due to causal influences. It is a good system, primarily because the standards for accepting a hypothesis are very conservative. Thus, the use of statistical reasoning and difficult standards of proof is another example of the skeptical nature of science.

Assessing the theoretical implications. There are several stages when the goal of the study is to test a theory: First, researchers must decide what conclusions are indicated by the findings. Were the research hypotheses accepted or rejected? Then, researchers need to determine the implications of those results for the theory. Are the findings *consistent* with the theory? What *alternative* explanations might account for the same results? Finally, researchers must consider any limitations or *flaws* in the study that may have contributed to the obtained results.

The role of replication. Repeating the study—that is, *replication*—helps researchers achieve reasonable conclusions. If the same kind of communication behavior is repeatedly studied and the same general conclusions emerge time and time again, the trustworthiness of the findings is enhanced greatly. This is particularly true when independent investigators arrive at the same results.

Sometimes in research a single study has dramatic findings, and the conclusions are taken as trustworthy, in violation of the principle of necessary replication. A classic example of this is a well-known study of fear appeals in persuasion. Social psychologists Irving Janis and Seymour

Feshbach exposed high school youngsters to slide-illustrated lectures about dental hygiene.[5] In one condition the lectures contained a strong fear appeal, with gruesome slides showing terrible mouth conditions caused by poor dental hygiene. A second condition presented similar subjects with a moderate fear appeal. Here, the slides showed troublesome but less severe mouth problems. Finally, a third group of subjects received a minimal fear appeal, with slides showing only very minor mouth difficulties and cavities caused by poor dental practices. The goal was to see which level of fear produced the greatest personal concern and actual change in dental practices. The results were dramatic: Those subjects who were exposed to the strongest fear messages changed the least. Those who received minimal fear messages changed the most.

This topsy-turvy conclusion took on a life of its own and was quoted as gospel in textbook after textbook, even after replication studies found opposite results.[6] In the end, the strange finding was not well supported and is no longer widely accepted as valid.[7]

Reporting the Results

When a research project has been completed, it must be made public and reported to other interested scientists. Their assessment of the importance of the findings is in a real sense the ultimate test of its merits. A lone genius working in isolation may solve the communication problems of humankind, but if he or she never makes the results public, they do not become part of the accumulated knowledge of science.

Research reports published in journals have a standard organization. Although there are variations, most good articles contain the following: (1) a statement of the problem under investigation, (2) a summary of what previous researchers have found, (3) a description of the research methods used, (4) a presentation of the findings, and (5) a section on conclusions, implications, and interpretations.

The accumulated "literature" is of critical value to researchers, but many others use it too. College and university professors may use such information for their lectures and presentations, and people in business and government may also rely on research journals. Although some reports generated by communication researchers are written in technical language, many can be understood by those outside the field.

Research Designs as Strategies for Controlled Observation

A research design is a *detailed plan* that indicates very specifically how each of the preceding steps in the research process will be carried out. Among the designs frequently used by communication researchers are *experiments, surveys, field observational studies,* and *content analyses.*

Experiments

Experiments originated in the physical sciences many centuries ago. They remain the major research strategy of modern physics, chemistry, and biology. However, experiments were not considered a suitable strategy for observing human behavior until well into the 1900s. They were pioneered by social psychologists who brought small groups of subjects into laboratory-like settings to simulate real-life experiences so that they could be studied under highly controlled conditions. After World War II, small group experiments were adopted for research in many other fields, and they have become a standard observational strategy suitable for communication research.

The logic of experiments is straightforward: Empirical observations are made on a number of human subjects, some of whom are designated as a *control group* and others as an *experimental group.* There may be more than one experimental group. An experimental group receives some sort of "treatment" deliberately introduced by the experimenter. The control group does not receive this treatment but usually undergoes some experience of a neutral nature. The treatment applied to an experimental group is some *manipulation of an independent variable that is suspected of having an influence on a dependent variable.* Measures of the dependent variable are made both before and after the treatment. The goal is to see whether the experimental group exhibits a change in the dependent factor. If a change occurs, it will be attributed to the independent variable involved in the treatment. Because the control group did not receive the treatment, it (logically) should not show any change.

There are dozens of variations, including several independent variables, a number of different treatments, and elaborate controls. Nevertheless, the underlying logic is the same: With extraneous variables eliminated or controlled, researchers can see if the treatment caused some observable effect or consequence. The experiment is an enormously powerful research design for assessing cause-and-effect relationships. Communication researchers rely on small group experiments conducted in laboratory-like settings. They also conduct large-scale experiments "in the field" (natural settings), and **quasi-experiments,** in which the so-called treatment occurs naturally.[8]

Small group simulations. Studies of small groups in laboratory settings can be used for a variety of research purposes. The laboratories are rooms where small numbers of subjects can be carefully observed as they engage in particular forms of communication behavior. These labs are often equipped with elaborate technical apparatus that present various independent variables to subjects and measures dependent variables. Often, the labs are equipped with one-way viewing screens so that direct observation is possible without the subjects' awareness.

In such experiments, the investigator typically tries to create a miniature version of some important communication process and study it within a tight system of controls. For example, beginning in the 1960s, a substantial number of experiments has been conducted on the process of decision making in juries.[9] Because it is

neither ethical nor legal to observe juries actually deliberating real cases, the laboratory experiment provides a way to study this important practical problem.

Jury deliberations are recreated *in simulation* in the laboratory by first selecting participants and instructing them that they are to act "as though" they were a jury. The mock jury is usually shown a summary of a legal case via videotape, film, or some other medium and asked to render a verdict after suitable discussion. By selecting subjects with specific characteristics, or by presenting different versions of a trial, a considerable amount of control can be exercised over the situation. A host of independent and dependent variables that can influence jury deliberations has been studied with this experimental strategy.[10]

One limitation of such experimental simulations is that, even though they do provide for a great amount of control over the variables under study, they are by no means *natural* settings for studying communication behavior. Many impose **demand characteristics**—activities the subjects are required to perform, or other conditions they experience, that are not the same as they would be in normal circumstances. Such characteristics can potentially produce influences other than those brought about by the independent variables. This is a troublesome issue because researchers may not suspect their influence. Moreover, subjects may suspect that they are serving as guinea pigs and misbehave deliberately. In many cases, they are convinced that some form of behavior is *expected* of them. This can lead them to either comply with what they think the researcher wants or to deliberately resist. Even if subjects are prevented from guessing the true nature of the research goals, biases may be introduced. There can be no assurance that the communication behavior being observed is identical to what would be found by an invisible observer in a completely natural setting. Thus, simulation experiments have many limitations.

Large-scale experiments in natural settings. Another type of experimental design—and one that has fewer problems concerning simulation versus real life—is the large-scale **field experiment**. In this research design, the subjects to be treated and observed are people living in a community, working in a factory, going to school, or carrying on their normal activities in some natural setting. The control group is a similar community, factory, school, or the like that does not get the treatment. Although this tends to avoid the issue of simulation, problems of measurement and control can be difficult.

An interesting example of a large-scale field experiment was conducted by mass communication researchers Sandra Ball-Rokeach, Milton Rokeach, and Joel Grube.[11] In overview, two communities in Washington State (Tri-Cities and Yakima) were designated as Experimental City and Control City, respectively. The investigators used a survey approach to measure sample residents' attitudes from each community before the experimental treatment. Then, the treatment was presented to the Experimental City, but not to the Control City. The treatment consisted of a special 30-minute television show that included persuasive messages aimed at changing viewers' attitudes and persuading them to donate money. Afterward, the same residents from both cities completed the survey again. The differences between the two groups regarding attitude change, and the amount of money donated, showed the influence of the treatment.

Quasi-experiments. This research design is difficult to use because it depends on applying the logic of the experiment without actual intervention by the researcher. To illustrate, suppose that you want to do research on how people communicate after a large-scale natural disaster strikes. Your goal is to find out what communication networks survivors rely on to get medical attention, find loved ones, seek shelter, obtain food, and understand what happened.

Obviously, there is no way you can (or would want to) intervene and cause a flood, an earthquake, or a volcanic eruption. But such natural events do occur. If you are in an area where such a disaster does strike, you could organize a research effort to interview survivors and record their accounts of how they communicated, with whom, and so on. Fairly elaborate data could be gathered in this way, using questionnaires, possibly supplemented with in-depth interviews for more qualitative assessments of what happened.

At this point, however, you would merely have interesting *descriptions* of what people did after the disaster. You would not have any way of comparing your findings with what they did before, to really assess the differences. To turn your descriptive study into a quasi-experiment, you would have to take additional steps. First, you would have to identify a community or an area that is *very like the one in which the disaster occurred,* but one in which no such event took place. This can serve as a control group. You can interview people in that area who are like the survivors (in a sampling sense) whom you questioned. It is reasonable to assume that they will behave the way those in the disaster community behaved *before* the tragedy struck. By looking at your project in this way, you have "before" and "after" data to compare. Thus, the logic of the experiment can sometimes be applied after the event through the use of a quasi-experimental design.[12]

Surveys

This research strategy developed out of the idea of a *census*—a procedure for counting and assessing attributes of an entire **population**—and out of *statistical theory,* especially the concept of **sampling**.[13] Essentially, surveys provide ways of selecting a *limited and manageable number* of people from populations in such a way that they have the same distribution of personal and social characteristics as the entire population itself. Then, researchers can contact and question that limited number.

Sample surveys are used frequently in communication research, including public opinion polling, election trends, response to persuasive techniques, personality and attitude assessments, and a variety of other topics. For example, a recent study investigated whether adults in a Midwestern community believed that certain kinds of television programming, such as news magazines, situation comedies, science fiction, or law enforcement shows, had influenced their views about the federal government. The researchers cited the fact that, in earlier decades, most people felt that the "government" could do just about anything, from putting an American on the moon to solving major social problems such as poverty. In contrast, many people today feel that there is little that the government can do, or can do well. In recent years, media depictions of the federal government have become increasingly negative, and the researchers wondered whether such depictions were at least partly responsible for negative perceptions of, and a lack of confidence in, the federal government. The results of their survey indicated modest support for their hypothesis.[14]

Thus, surveys are one of the central strategies used by researchers for investigating communication behavior when the purpose includes uncovering relationships between independent and dependent variables in relatively large populations that cannot be observed otherwise.

As in any kind of investigation, the initial steps in conducting surveys are to ensure that the purposes of the surveys are entirely clear, that the independent and dependent variables have been fully identified, and that decisions have been made concerning procedures for analyzing the results and reaching conclusions. Once these have been achieved, additional steps must be taken, including (1) using a procedure for picking the specific people to be studied, (2) contacting those selected and getting their cooperation, and (3) extracting the relevant information from them and recording it as data.

Selecting representative samples. *Sampling* is a procedure for picking from a population (usually a very large number of people with clearly defined characteristics) an adequate and manageable smaller number who, on average, are like those in the larger population. This

smaller number can then be contacted and observed. A *population* (for research purposes) is *all the people about whom generalizations are to be made from the results of the survey.* Obviously, it is not possible to study every member of a large population, given the resources of most researchers. For example, the residents of a small city of 25,000 people would pose a formidable task if each one had to be contacted personally. Even contacting a few thousand people who work for a large corporation could take considerable time. Fortunately, researchers discovered that careful study of a small part of such a population can yield results nearly identical to those obtained from observing all members. For example, public opinion pollsters and market researchers (all of whom use the survey design) know that a meticulous study of 1,200 to 1,500 people selected with great care from the entire U.S. population can reveal the basic patterns of behavior and belief that characterize the entire nation. Doubling or tripling the number of people studied might make the results slightly more stable, but it is not always worth the expense or trouble because it certainly would not double or triple their accuracy.

The key to obtaining accurate results from the study of a relatively small number of subjects, rather than the entire population, is to select them so that they "represent" the population as a whole. A **representative sample** is one that has been chosen in such a way that the people included are like those in the entire population in all important aspects relevant to the research. Usually this means that on average they are generally of similar age, gender, income level, years of education, religious affiliation, political preference, and so on.

Choosing a representative sample is not easy because researchers usually do not know the exact nature of the personal and social characteristics of the population. Even if these characteristics are known, it would be difficult to screen people one-by-one to pick a small number who accurately represent the population as a whole. Fortunately, a representative sample can be obtained in a much more efficient way—

by using a *random sampling procedure* to select people to study, even if the characteristics of the population are not fully known. To do this, researchers apply the same laws of probability that make games of chance—like poker, roulette, and dice—so much fun.

There are many different **random** procedures for selecting samples that are likely to be representative. All are supposed to ensure that *only chance factors* dictate the specific individuals who are selected. A completely random sample is one in which every person in the population has *an identical chance of being selected*. This can be accomplished in several ways. The simplest is the classic (but not practical) idea of using slips of paper and a big rotating drum. Suppose, for example, that small slips of paper could be placed in the drum—one for each member of the population, with that person's name written on it. When all the slips and all the names have been placed inside, the drum is closed and turned over and over until all the slips are thoroughly mixed. Finally, the sample is drawn out (one slip at a time) until the number wanted for the sample has been obtained. Although the slip and drum procedure illustrates the idea, it is not practical because the mechanics are very cumbersome. Although it was used historically, today, computer-based procedures can accomplish the task with great efficiency.[15]

A purely random and totally representative sample is more of an *ideal* than a reality. It is a sort of "model" that one works toward—such as the concept of a perfect score on the SAT, a flawless performance by an athlete, or a straight-A record through four years of college. Such events are rare in real life. The same can be said about the samples used in actual research, which approximate, but probably never attain, perfection. A number of practical alternatives have been developed, because of this problem, to approximate the results obtained from purely random sampling.

Face-to-face interviewing. Once the people who make up the sample have been identified, obviously they must be *contacted*. Although this sounds simple, the question is *how*? One way is to go to the address of each person and conduct an in-depth, face-to-face interview. This ensures that those selected are actually those studied.

The face-to-face interview as an observational strategy has its problems. For one thing, it is expensive: Interviewers have to be recruited and trained; they have to travel to where the subjects live. They have to be paid; and they might just cut a few corners if not closely supervised. There is also the problem of those subjects who are not at home. It becomes prohibitively expensive to return many times trying to catch a missing survey subject. And, when subjects know that they are being studied, they may change what they claim. In addition, interviews often probe recollections of past behavior, which may or may not be recalled accurately. The interaction between interviewer and subject may also have an influence on the answers that are obtained. For example, a subject who is asked a question about his or her annual income by an attractive member of the opposite sex may exaggerate to impress the interviewer. These problems are well understood by researchers.

On the other hand, most people *like* to be interviewed and have their opinions known. As a result, they are usually willing to cooperate and provide interviewers with lots of information. When interviewed face to face, they tend not to exaggerate or conceal information excessively. Thus, this procedure is the observational strategy of choice for surveys—if resources permit.

Telephone interviewing. If it is impractical or too expensive to interview subjects face to face, telephones may be used. Many surveys are conducted in this manner, but the quality of the results is often in question. For one thing, a sample drawn from a telephone book cannot truly represent the entire population in an area, since many numbers are unlisted. Furthermore, it is not always clear who is being interviewed. If the subjects are supposed to be female heads of households, it may actually be a grown daughter or the next-door neighbor who answers the phone. Also, in this age of dual-income families, it is increasingly difficult to reach people by phone. Finally, what about answering machines? Many people screen their calls!

To get around the problem of unlisted numbers, survey researchers can use computer programs that select and dial telephone numbers randomly—reaching potential respondents even if their numbers are not listed. Some researchers even use program computers to ask the questions! All this gets a mixed reception. Some subjects find it amusing; others are offended. Some people love to talk on the phone, even to a computer; others resent the interruption.

Although telephone surveys are widely used for many legitimate research purposes, they have gotten a bad reputation in recent years. Many salespeople pitching their wares by telephone begin by claiming that they are "conducting a survey." This deception has resulted in suspicion, a loss of credibility, and frequent unwillingness by respondents to cooperate in legitimate research.

Mailed questionnaires. A survey technique that can potentially limit costs and avoid many other problems is to send subjects questionnaires by mail. This technique is a lot cheaper per subject than face-to-face interviews, and subjects can complete the questionnaires at their own convenience. On the other hand, the people in the sample may or may not cooperate. The number of people who voluntarily return a mailed questionnaire can be hopelessly low. What if only half the people in the sample send their questionnaires back, even after repeated appeals? They may be quite different from the others who did not respond, and there is no way to know this. Any loss to the sample, and especially an exceptionally low return, reduces the researcher's confidence in the final results.

On the other hand, for some purposes the mailed questionnaire works reasonably well. A study conducted recently illustrates the point. The research problem was to discover whether bachelor's degrees earned online from a "virtual" university (one that has no campus or classrooms, and that provides instruction only via the Internet) were an acceptable criterion to gain admission to a graduate program in a traditional university. A questionnaire requesting views on this issue was mailed to a population of graduate deans, associate deans, and other administrators of graduate programs. Well over two-thirds returned the questionnaires carefully filled out. This was a return rate high enough to give confidence to the results. (The majority would not recommend that applicants with such degrees be admitted to their programs.)[16]

Using structured questionnaires. Most surveys—whether conducted face to face, over the phone, or by mail—use formal and highly "structured" questionnaires. These familiar printed lists of questions with response options vary in flexibility; some are open-ended, allowing the person to give more elaborate answers. Most, however, require the subject to check boxes, answer "yes" or "no," or similarly fit themselves into the structured way in which the questions are posed.

Structured questionnaires have advantages and disadvantages. Critics maintain that highly structured questionnaires lead participants *lockstep* through a series of rigidly posed questions, reducing their answers to categories and boxes to be checked. As a result, the participants' subtle meanings, feelings, and perceptions are either lost or distorted. Defenders of such questionnaires maintain that they efficiently transform observations into data, and they make it easy to perform numerical computer analyses. Clearly, each side has a point.

Field Observational Studies

Sometimes referred to as **field research,** this design type for *qualitative* investigation is much less formal than the experiment or the survey. Field observational studies were pioneered by cultural anthropologists who went to live among peoples in remote parts of the world, often learning their languages and spending long periods of time learning to understand the subtleties of their cultures. Communication researchers are more likely to employ this approach to study various kinds of contemporary specialized cultures or sensitive social situations in urban societies.

The central observational strategy of the field study is *participant observation*. As indicated previously, this means that the investigator enters and becomes a member of—or at least is accepted by—some group. The first problem is to gain *rapport* with the other group members, which means gaining their trust so that they open up and talk. After this, the researcher seeks intimate familiarity with the communication patterns under study. The researcher comes to understand the communication strategies, tactics, assumptions, and meanings used by the members. If successful, the researcher can prepare detailed descriptions about how the members communicate and even think about the situations that occur.

An interesting example of the use of the field observational study design focused on instruction in the college classroom. Communication researcher Ann Darling studied ways that college students signal to professors that they fail to understand something in class. She sat in on and observed three different undergraduate classes for an entire academic quarter. She was introduced to the students as a researcher studying classroom interaction. At first, students were very aware of her presence, and this inhibited their behavior. However, within two weeks they were ignoring her. Darling then began to observe, code, and record all failures to understand—every time a student signaled "noncomprehension." By the end of the quarter, she had compiled an extensive body of data. Thus, by observing participants in a natural environment, and not imposing anything on the students, this researcher was able to describe accurately how students signal problems when they don't or can't understand the instructor.[17]

In another study, researcher Alexandra Murphy used the method of participant observation combined with interviews to study ways to improve communication between flight attendants and pilots. Her interest in this topic resulted from an airline tragedy in which 24 people were killed, including the pilot, the co-pilot, and a flight attendant. The official cause of the accident was attributed to "ice on the wings," but a National Transportation Safety Board (NTSB) investigation found that a lack of crew communication contributed to the accident. Apparently, a flight attendant did not convey information to the pilot about a build-up of snow on the wings that a passenger had brought to her attention. Thirty seconds after takeoff, the airplane crashed.

The researcher, who had been an employee of another airline, observed and interacted with flight attendants and pilots on 50 flights to a variety of destinations. She then conducted in-depth interviews with flight attendants in their homes. She wanted to understand the barriers to effective communication during in-flight emergencies, and made recommendations for facilitating communication.[18]

Content Analysis

Content analysis as a strategy for research began in World War II with Allied intelligence units routinely monitoring radio broadcasts from occupied Europe. They discovered that when the stations stopped playing music that was popular among the local population and began broadcasting songs that were popular among German soldiers, troops had moved into the area.

During the 1950s, communication researchers developed content analysis designs for systematically studying virtually any kind of message. These analyses begin with definitions of "units" relevant to the research goal. Such units might be a particular *word*, a *theme*, a *depiction of a social role*, an *act of violence*, or some other identifiable entity or episode. Once a set of categories defining such units has been developed, an analyst can count the frequency of each. These frequencies can then be subjected to various calculations and analyses. Content analysis is a useful way to obtain an objective summary of exactly what a complex message contains.

An interesting application of the content analysis design is in the study of suicide notes. It is a grim topic, but researchers have analyzed the themes and other content of hundreds of such messages left behind by people who have taken their own lives. Typically, research has found that such notes contain advice, instructions, and requests, as well as expressions of hostility, sorrow, and guilt. The expressions in such notes provide important insights into the thoughts of suicides.[19]

In recent years, the content of video games has received considerable attention. Researchers have used the method of content analysis to investigate the nature of the violent acts in such games, the lessons that may be learned concerning appropriate behavior, and other related topics.

Interest in the content of video games has increased, especially since the introduction of more realistic games. For example, in October 2001, RockStar Games released an entertainment product called Grand Theft Auto III, to be used with Playstation 2. This game takes the player into a (virtual) American city. It is remarkably realistic, and the graphics are described as superb. The player is depicted on the screen as a young male who is casually dressed in a leather jacket and jeans. He holds a baseball bat. The player, guiding the virtual surrogate, can walk around the city and engage in a variety of violent and illegal activities. The player can pick up prostitutes, beat them senseless and take their money. The user can commandeer a police car, and can be a bank robber, a hit man, or a car hijacker. One person, after playing the game for the first time, reported the following:

> The world you roam is stunningly realistic, shadowy and gritty. When you drive beneath a streetlight, a pool of light reflects on your car. When you pass people on the sidewalk, you hear snippets of their conversation: "Damned foreigners." "Got any doughnuts?" If you jostle them, they glare at you. . . .

> I walk around the streets with my bat until I spot an old lady and decide to see what happens if I hit her. She falls down. A pool of blood forms around her. A police officer arrives. In a panic, I hit him repeatedly until he appears to be dead.[20]

The portrayal of women in such games has also been a focus of content analysis. For example, researchers Berrin Beasley and Tracy Collins Standley examined depictions of women in games from the Nintendo 64 and Sony Play Station console gaming systems. Their analysis found a significant difference in the number of male versus female characters, and in the ways in which they were dressed. Less than 14 percent of the characters were women, and the majority of the female characters wore clothing that exposed more skin than the male characters. Nearly half of the female characters had big busts and were dressed in ways that called attention to their bodies, especially their breasts. Women who were described as "voluptuous" appeared in games rated E, which means these games are suitable for even young children.[21]

Observing by Measuring Variables

Measuring variables is the process of *observing numerically*. It results in data that can be analyzed quantitatively. Empirical research cannot be conducted without measurement. Even participant observation results in determining whether there are certain qualities, repetitions, or patterns present in particular messages or behaviors. At the simplest level, then, **measurement** may be little more than deciding whether some quality is *present* or *absent* in what is being observed. This is the most basic form of measurement (symbolized as a 1 or a 0) in a particular instance under observation. At the most complex level, it may involve the use of sophisticated scales or tests designed to assess numerical differences among people in their personal or social characteristics. In these senses, measurement in some form is at the heart of almost any investigation of human communication, re-

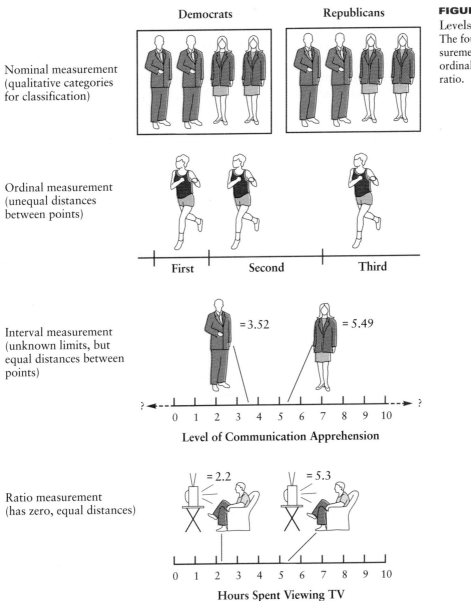

Nominal measurement (qualitative categories for classification)

Democrats   Republicans

Ordinal measurement (unequal distances between points)

First   Second   Third

Interval measurement (unknown limits, but equal distances between points)

= 3.52   = 5.49

? 0 1 2 3 4 5 6 7 8 9 10 ?

Level of Communication Apprehension

Ratio measurement (has zero, equal distances)

= 2.2   = 5.3

0 1 2 3 4 5 6 7 8 9 10

Hours Spent Viewing TV

FIGURE 16.1

Levels of Measurement
The four levels of measurement are nominal, ordinal, interval, and ratio.

gardless of the research goals, designs, or the specific features under study.

Levels of Measurement

There are four distinct levels of measurement commonly used in research: *nominal, ordinal, interval,* and *ratio.* Figure 16.1 shows the basic differences among these four. Each has advantages and limitations.

Nominal measures. The first and simplest form of measurement widely used in communication research *classifies people into meaningful categories.* Examples are religious preference, gender, political affiliation, rural versus urban residence, employed versus unemployed, and so on. The number in each category can be counted, and simple percentages or other indexes can be calculated. In this way, **nominal measurement** provides a useful way for researchers to look at similarities and differences between categories of people.

Ordinal measures. In **ordinal measurement**, each person often has *more* or *less* of some quality or attribute than others in the same category. This permits them to be "ranked"—from first to last or most to least—with respect to the same attribute (for example, "class standing," a ranking system based on grade point average). This was not the case with the nominal measurement example above. There, the people being studied were assigned to a particular category because they had an observable attribute (Republicans or Democrats, senders or receivers, males or females). Ordinal data can provide valuable information on the relative position—high, low, or somewhere in between—of subjects with respect to any variable being assessed.

Interval measures. At a more sophisticated level, **interval measurement** is based on a regular scale or *continuum* that is divided into equal intervals along that continuum. Subjects can be observed to see how much of a variable they have and then be assigned a particular point on the scale corresponding to that number. A familiar example would be assessing how attractive a person is on an interval scale between 1 and 10. Suppose you assign the individual an 8; another assessor gives the same person a 6. The average score, 7. is the numerical point where that individual is placed on the attractiveness scale. In communication research, many questionnaires are used to provide interval measurement.

The only limitation on the numbers yielded by interval scales is that they *lack a true zero point*. Thus, even if you assigned a zero rating to a target, it would not mean that the person had absolutely no attractive qualities. This

poses a problem only when sophisticated mathematical manipulations of the data are required.

Ratio measures. Although this is the most sophisticated level of measurement, it seems the simplest because it so familiar. Examples of variables assessed by **ratio measurement** are age, income, years married, and number of hours of TV viewing daily. Ratio measures are widely used in communication research.

Judging the Quality of Measurement

Whatever the level of measurement used in a research project, problems creep in. Measurement in communication research—or in any other field for that matter—is never perfect. There are always two basic questions to be asked concerning the *quality* of recorded observations: (1) Are they *valid*? and (2) Are they *reliable*? These may sound like two versions of the same question, but they are not. Each is an important quality of measurement as a means of observation in research.

Validity. A major concern about any procedure for measurement is whether it actually measures the variable for which it has been designed. For example, let's assume that you're studying meetings called by the administrators of a town, to allow citizens to comment on some proposal for the community. Your hypothesis is that high-prestige individuals are usually allowed to interrupt such a meeting or conference more than low-prestige individuals. But how can prestige or status be measured? One way would be to go ask everyone in the community under study to identify the level of prestige or status of all the individuals who might attend the meeting. If you had this information, you could calculate the average assessment or prestige ranking for each person present. Unfortunately, that approach would involve a massive undertaking, conducting hundreds of interviews.

Now suppose that you know the *assessed value of the home* of every family in the town (readily obtained from town records). You could decide to use home value (which is highly correlated with income) as a *measure of each individual's status*. So far, so good! You could justify this procedure by claiming that home value (and related income) is an important aspect of people's level of status prestige in the American society.

But wait a minute! Here is a question. Is home value based on income always a valid measure of prestige? The answer is probably not. Some people might have high incomes and expensive homes derived from socially disapproved sources—drug sales, gambling, or occupations to which people assign limited prestige (junk dealer or used-car salesman). Others might have low-cost homes—for example, esteemed ministers, priests, and rabbis—but high social status. Thus, a person's home value and income would not be a true reflection of that person's prestige or status in the community. In other words, this particular measure could have *low validity*. Researchers may or may not know the **validity** of their measures. If they do not know it, this is a shortcoming that reduces the quality of the results.

Reliability.   Measurement quality is also determined by **reliability.** Does the procedure used for measurement yield the same results *if used repeatedly* on the same subjects? Repeated measurements would be unusual, but if a procedure were repeated and if it gave one result today but a different result tomorrow—on the same people and using the same variables—it would not be a very useful way of recording observations. *Reliability,* then, is *the degree to which a measurement procedure yields consistent results with the same individuals.*

Importantly, a measure must be highly consistent (reliable) if it is to be valid. These two features of measurement quality—validity and reliability—are interrelated in this particular way. For instance, a bathroom scale that measures your weight consistently is reliable; but can it be reliably wrong—that is, invalid? Sure! The scale could consistently read 5 pounds low. Thus, reliability would be high but validity low.

Besides issues of measurement, the terms *reliability* and *validity* are also used to judge overall qualities of a research project and its findings. Researchers and critics alike are compelled to ask whether the project actually addresses the questions it is supposed to address. Can the results from the sample used in the study generalize to the greater population? For example, are laboratory simulations of jury deliberations in small group experiments really valid representations of actual jury deliberations? If so, the experiment is valid. If it is consistently found that male jurors almost always find the attractive, young female defendant innocent and the old, unattractive male guilty, does this generalization characterize real juries? If so, the conclusion is valid.

Ethical Issues in Communication Research

Suppose that an enthusiastic researcher wants to understand how real juries work in reaching their decisions. One way to proceed would be to place hidden video cameras in jury rooms and secretly tape the deliberations. Doing this without telling the jurors or the judges might be considered devious, but our society needs to know whether there is anything wrong with the legal system. Would not this need justify the deception?

To take another example, assume that in a highly controlled, sophisticated experiment, the research findings did not support the investigators' theory. This would be a major disappointment—after all, a lot of time, effort, and money went into the project. Inconclusive results provide little glory. It would be easy to throw out some of the cases that do not fit the theory. Perhaps some data could even be invented so that the research findings look impressive. No one would ever know, and where's the harm? In a society where advertisers, politicians, and businesses all make exaggerated and deceptive claims, would such minor misrepresentation be so bad?

Both of these procedures would violate critical ethical norms governing scientific research and would not be permissible under any circumstances. Communication research is done within the same set of ethical norms that apply to all the social sciences.[22]

These norms are particularly important because human beings are the subjects of investigation. One category of scientific concern is for the *truth in research findings*. The second focuses on the *protection of human subjects from harm*—including deception, loss of privacy, and violation of confidentiality.

Truth in Findings

As this chapter has indicated, conducting research is a lot of work, and it takes a great deal of time. It can be very expensive, and often it yields results that are inconsistent with the researcher's personal theories. Because researchers' reputations are built in large part on publishing reports on significant research problems, some may feel a temptation to falsify findings to reap the rewards of scientific fame. However, there is an ironclad rule that research findings must be reported honestly, even though faked results might not be detected in the rigid screening described earlier.

Although hoaxes are extremely rare in any area of research, if they do occur they are cruel for several reasons. For one thing, they mislead other investigators who study the same issues. Naturally, they usually come up with different findings, which confuses everyone and wastes a lot of time and money. In addition, legitimate evidence consistent with the falsified findings will always be clouded by suspicion. Even more important, the central claim of science—that its data, conclusions, and explanations are *the most trustworthy* that can be obtained from any source—brings respect and financial support from the public. It is little wonder that scientists are outraged by the rare violations of ethical rules that do occur. They destroy the integrity of the research process and violate the rule of *experto credite*.

Protection of Subjects

Communication research is usually benign in a physical sense: It does not involve dangerous drugs, surgery, or confinement, as may be the case when human beings or animals are used in medical experiments. Nevertheless, there are several ways in which the research process may harm human subjects. Research projects may be based on deceptions that result in unusual stress and anxiety. Investigators may intrude on privacy to an unacceptable extent. Confidentiality may be violated concerning behavior that is socially disapproved, with a resulting loss of reputation. Communication researchers are concerned with all of these issues.

Risks versus benefits. A very real problem that has no clear solution is the issue of potential risk to people versus probable benefits to society from a particular research project. Where should the line be drawn? Clearly, research that results in death, injury, or illness is not tolerable under any circumstances, even if important information can be gained from it. The Nazis and the Japanese in World War II conducted medical experiments on human beings, and these experiments were widely condemned. This end of the scale is clear; but what about research that may merely annoy people or cause them embarrassment? If useful findings can be obtained, are such harms acceptable? Again, there are no clear answers to such questions. Every specific project must be carefully evaluated before it is conducted by responsible and independent judges who determine whether the cost–benefit ratio is acceptable. In fact, most colleges and universities and major private or government agencies that fund research conduct formal analyses for the protection of human subjects before allowing research to be conducted.

INFORMED CONSENT AND DECEPTION IN RESEARCH

Is it ever ethical to deceive research subjects? One ethical position is that *informed consent* should always be obtained before any human being becomes a research subject: Obtain the subject's permission to agree to participate. In some cases, however, if the subjects know the purpose of the research before they participate, it may be pointless to conduct the study. Perhaps the most dramatic case addressing this issue was psychologist Stanley Milgram's famous study of obedience to authority (mentioned also in Chapter 10).

In Milgram's experiment, subjects were ordered to administer electric shocks to individuals in another room. The design involved deception: No shocks were actually received by anyone. However, the subjects who complied thought that they were really administering powerful jolts to people. After administering a number of "shocks," subjects heard their "confederates" in the next room scream and cry out for relief. Even though many of the subjects were deeply disturbed at what they were told to do, they obeyed nevertheless, and continued to administer more shocks. Some bit their lips, dug their fingernails into their flesh, stuttered, trembled, or groaned. In some cases, anxiety continued long after the experiment.

Is it ethical to cause such distress? As a result of the debate over this study, scientists now conclude that such deception was unethical. Recognizing that the reality factor would have been lost if the subjects had been fully informed about the nature of this particular experiment, it's better to abandon the experiment rather than cause people undue harm and anxiety.

Source: Milgram, S. (1974). *Obedience to authority: An experimental view.* New York: Harper & Row.

Privacy, confidentiality, and deception. There are occasions when the disclosure of information gained in a research project may have serious consequences for the people involved. A classic case was sociologist Laud Humphreys's study of male homosexual activity.[23]

The initial observations were made in a public restroom located in a park. The researcher observed some 100 men participating in homosexual activities, even serving as a lookout on occasion. As the subjects left, the researcher noted the license numbers of their cars. Later, after obtaining their addresses, he appeared at their homes (with a different appearance) posing as an interviewer for a survey. He obtained additional information about their family lives, work, and so forth.

Information about the research was later reported in a local newspaper. Many of the subjects were understandably concerned. At that time, unwanted exposure of their homosexual activities could have had a devastating effect on their families and jobs. Humphreys had burned the records of their names and addresses, so no disclosure occurred. Yet, a raging controversy arose over the violation of privacy of these subjects, plus the fear and anxiety that the research caused. This case helped clarify the ethical rules, making a similar situation unlikely today.

Generally, then, any research using human beings as subjects can raise complex ethical questions. In many cases, there are no clear answers to questions about what should or should not be done. The rules concerning faking evidence and causing substantial harm to people are clear enough. However, it is not always easy to calculate an acceptable cost–benefit ratio, and the development of adequate ethical rules remains an unfinished task. (See Box 16.3.)

Chapter Review

- The purpose of this chapter is not to train students to be competent researchers. Its goal is to provide in summary a framework that will enable them to understand how research is conducted and to provide ways in which they can assess the methods and conclusions of particular research reports that they read.

- Research can be defined as a set of systematic procedures for gathering reliable information under controlled conditions of observation. The process is designed and conducted in such a way that objective conclusions can be reached with a minimum of error.

- The perspective used in communication research rests on a set of broad postulates or assumptions. It is assumed that human communication exists in an orderly universe and that there are cause-effect relationships between independent and dependent conditions. It is assumed that the system for scrutinizing research reports supports the belief in *experto credite.*

- There are six general steps in the research process: (1) specify the goals of the research and the variables to be studied; (2) review prior relevant research on the topic; (3) make the necessary observations; (4) analyze the data; (5) reach appropriate conclusions; and (6) publish the results.

- A number of formal research designs are available to communication researchers, including laboratory experiments, large-scale field experiments and quasi-experiments, surveys, field observations, and content analyses. Whatever the design used, observations must be measured and recorded in one of four ways: nominal, ordinal, interval, or ratio levels of measurement.

- The quality of any given measure is judged by its validity and reliability. A measure is valid when it accurately assesses the variable under study. It is reliable when the same results are obtained repeatedly with the same subject.

- Ethical considerations are critical in communication research. Scientific integrity demands that findings be reported truthfully. Other ethical considerations concern the protection of human subjects.

Key Terms

research	empirical observation	quasi-experiment	content analysis
postulate	data	demand characteristics	measurement
descriptive research	participant observation	population	nominal measurement
theory	data entry	field experiment	ordinal measurement
replication	data analysis	sampling	interval measurement
proprietary research	generalization	representative sample	ratio measurement
dependent variable	overgeneralizing	random sampling procedure	validity
independent variable	experiment	field research	reliability
hypothesis			

Notes

1. These postulates are set forth in this section to explain clearly the logical foundation of science. Those who use humanistic, rhetorical, or other approaches to the analysis of human communication have the obligation to set forth their postulates, whether they are based on ideological convictions, shared frameworks of moral values, or personal opinions.

2. Most of the several hundred journals in which communication research reports appear are published regularly by professional organizations, universities, government agencies, foundations, or other private groups. Most are published in the United States and are in English. Articles tend to run from two or three pages long up to perhaps 25 pages. They are intended for professionals who are familiar with the technical terms and research methods of the field. Many of the technical journals in which the results of communication research are published have been cited in previous chapters of this book.

3. The accumulation and moving forward feature of any science is critical. The opposite is stagnation and obsolescence. Few people would be satisfied to stop research in their field and be content with a body of knowledge that would grow increasingly obsolete. This is as true in communication research as it is in physics or medicine.

4. Whyte, W. F. (1979). On making the most of participant observation. *The American Sociologist, 14, 1,* 56–66. A classic work is: McCall, G., & Simmons, J. (1969). *Issues in participant observation.* Reading, MA: Addison-Wesley.

5. Janis, I., & Feshbach, S. (1953). Effects of fear-arousing communication. *Journal of Abnormal and Social Psychology, 58,* 78–92.

6. Unfortunately, most current communication texts still claim that minimal or low-fear appeals will result in the greater behavior change, even though the opposite is likely to be true. For example, a recent analysis of over 40 current texts on persuasion and public speaking revealed that of the 25 texts mentioning fear appeals, only six made accurate claims; that is, high, not low, fear appeals are the most persuasive. An additional four texts were unclear,

whereas 15 continued to report the claims of the original Janis and Feshbach study—the claims of which are now believed to be invalid. See: Allen, M., & Preiss, R. W. (1990). Using meta-analysis to evaluate curriculum: An examination of selected college textbooks. *Communication Education, 39,* 103–116.

7. See, for example: Higbee, K. L. (1969). Fifteen years of fear arousal: Research on threat appeals: 1953–1968. *Psychological Bulletin, 72,* 426–444. See also: Leventhal, H. (1970). Findings and theory in the study of fear communications. In Berkowitz, L. (Ed.), *Advances in experimental social psychology* (vol. 5, pp. 119–186). New York: Academic.

8. See: Saslow, C. (1982). Designing the experiment. In Saslow, C. A. (Ed.), *Basic research methods* (pp. 71–93). Reading, MA: Addison-Wesley.

9. Typical of such simulated jury studies is: Villemur, N. K., & Hyde, J. S. (1983). Effects of sex of defense attorney, sex of juror, and age and attractiveness of victim on mock juror decision-making in a rape case. *Sex Roles, 9,* 879–889.

10. For a review of an entire program of simulated jury studies, see: Miller, G. R., & Fontes, N. E. (1979). *Videotape on trial: A view from the jury box.* Beverly Hills, CA: Sage.

11. Ball-Rokeach, S., Rokeach, M., & Grube, J. (1984). *The great American values test.* New York: Free Press.

12. Actually, the responses of a community to such an event were studied after Mount Saint Helens erupted in 1980. See: Pennebaker, J., & Newton, D. (1983). Observation of a unique event: The psychological impact of the Mt. St. Helens volcano. In H. Reis (Ed.), *Directions for methodology of social and behavioral science* (no. 15). San Francisco: Jossey-Bass.

13. See: Tankard, J. (1984). *The statistical pioneers.* Cambridge, MA: Schenkman.

14. Pfau, M., Moy, P., & Szabo, E. A. (2001). Influence of prime-time television programming on perceptions of the federal government. *Mass Communication & Society, 4,* 437–453.

15. Classic and technical works on sampling are: Kish, L. (1965). *Survey sampling.* New

York: Wiley; Cochran, W. G. (1963). *Sampling techniques* (2nd ed.). New York: Wiley.

16. DeFleur, M. H., & Adams, J. (2004). Acceptability of Online degrees as criteria for admission to graduate programs. Journal of Computing in Higher Education, 16, 150–163.

17. Darling, A. (1989). Signaling non-comprehension in the classroom: Toward a descriptive typology. *Communication Education, 3,* 34–40.

18. Murphy, A. G. (2001). The flight attendant dilemma: An analysis of communication and sensemaking during in-flight emergencies. *Journal of Applied Communication Research, 29,* 30–53.

19. Cohen, S. L., & Fiedler, J. E. (1974). Content analysis of multiple messages in suicide notes. *Suicide and Life-Threatening Behavior, 4,* 75–95. See also: Henken, V. J. (1976). Banality reinvestigated: A computer-based content analysis of suicidal and forced-death documents. *Suicide and Life-Threatening Behavior, 6,* 36–43.

20. Weiss, J. (January 13, 2002). Connecting with your inner thug: Grand Theft Auto III gives you an on-screen crime spree—and too much fun. *The Boston Globe,* p. E1.

21. Beasley, B. & Collins Standley, T. (2002). Shirts vs. skins: Clothing as an indicator of gender role stereotyping in video games. *Mass Communication & Society, 5,* 279–293.

22. For a discussion and overview of such issues, see: Beauchamp, T. (1982). *Ethical issues in social science research.* Baltimore: Johns Hopkins University Press.

23. Humphreys, L. (1975). *Tearoom trade: Impersonal sex in public places.* Chicago: Aldine.

Glossary

accommodating style   A strategy for handling conflict in which people give in to their opponents. Accommodators are the opposite of competitors. They tend to be passive, and often allow their opponents to reach their objectives.

accumulation process   A pattern in which mass communications have selective and minimal influences on a population, but over time they add up, and large numbers of people are changed when the messages are consistent and persistent.

accuracy   In communication, the degree to which all elements of meaning incorporated into the message formulated by the sender are reconstructed in the interpretation of the meaning of the message constructed by the receiver.

adaptation   Various ways in which message senders and receivers independently modify how they think and behave toward each other during the transmitting and receiving processes.

adoption process   A pattern by which innovations spread through a population of potential adopters. They first become aware of the innovation's existence, which arouses their interest, causing them to seek further information. This leads to evaluation of possible uses and costs versus benefits. If feasible, it may then be tried briefly. Finally, adoption takes place, and the innovation is routinely used.

advertising agency   A professional group that provides advertising services to individuals or businesses.

affinity-seeking   The use of various communication strategies to get people to like you.

anomie (personal)   A feeling of anxiety or distress arising from confusion concerning the social expectations of others.

arbitrary selection   The random means by which sounds and letters used to form words within a given language are selected. Once selected and established in use, however, the relationship between words and their referents becomes fixed.

artifacts   Physical objects—such as jewelry, handbags, pens, and briefcases, or even homes, cars, and offices—that provide meanings to others about our personal and social attributes.

assertiveness-training group   A specialized discussion group in which participants learn how to stand up for their rights and be more demanding in ensuring they are treated with dignity and respect.

assignment-based cohesion   A type of cohesion based on the fact that members of a group have been asked or ordered to serve by their boss, are voted into membership by a valued constituency, or must serve for some other valid obligation.

assimilation   A feature of the embedding process by which a message is reshaped into new interpretations (distortions) by the psychological characteristics and culturally learned habits of the receiver.

attitude   A relatively enduring organization of affective beliefs about some broad object (such as a policy, social category of people, or situation) that increases the probability that an individual will respond consistently to that object.

attribution process   The assignment to another individual of various personal qualities, conditions, dispositions, or external social pressures that we believe are the causes of or influences on that person's behavior. (see *implicit personality theory*)

audioconferencing   Connecting people by long-distance telephone lines (sometimes with the parties in special rooms where they can make use of high-quality speakers) so that they can conduct a meeting.

authority   The basis of legitimacy for the exercise of power.

avoidance style   A strategy for handling conflicts in which an individual chooses not to be part of the confrontation or chooses to stay away from situations in which disagreements are likely to occur.

behavior-alteration techniques Persuasive strategies designed to arouse feelings of reward and punishment. These techniques are based on principles of behavior modification in learning.

belief A kind of statement of truth that an individual accepts about some object (thing, situation, or event). Some are factual (not involving positive or negative judgments or implying emotional orientation); others are affective (involving a positive or negative judgment).

body language The idea that body actions, gestures, and other nonverbal behavior reveal more of our true thoughts and feelings than does our verbal behavior.

boutique agency A small advertising agency that offers specialized services to clients.

bureaucracy A deliberately designed plan of the goals, norms, roles, ranks, and controls in an organization.

charismatic authority An individual's unique personal attractiveness that makes people willing to accept the individual's leadership.

chauvinism A boastful, exaggerated form of ethnocentrism leading some groups to maintain that they are superior.

chronemics The study of the way in which people use time to transmit nonverbal messages.

Clever Hans effect The mistaken belief that an animal can use language as humans do because of the animal's responses or behavior. The animal may be responding to subtle cues, or its behaviors may be simply random occurrences.

client A person who employs another to provide specific services.

coercion Compelling or restraining behavior that includes threatening people with unacceptable consequences.

cognitive reorganization A modification of an individual's feelings, beliefs, attitudes, or motivations (as a result of persuasion in the present context).

cognitive restructuring A form of treatment for fears (which can be used to reduce communication apprehension) involving changing a subject's personal interpretations of an anxiety-producing situation.

cohesion (group) The set of factors in every kind of group—large or small, intimate or formal—that motivates the participants to maintain their membership and to perform the activities required of them.

collaborative style A strategy for handling conflict in which people work willingly in cooperation with an opponent. The collaborative style is characteristic of those who have a sincere concern for their opponents as well as for their own goals.

collectivism A cultural orientation in which the group and its interests are valued over individual interests.

colonial press Generally, those newspapers that were published during the colonial period. They were small, usually subject to "prior restraint" laws, relatively expensive, and circulated to a small audience of elite subscribers.

communication (human) A process during which source(s) initiate messages using verbal and nonverbal symbols and contextual cues to express meaning by transmitting information so that similar understandings are constructed by the intended receiver(s).

communication apprehension Fear experienced in anticipation of or during communication encounters.

communicator A person who either sends or receives a message during the communication process.

comparative perspective A strategy for studying behavior that assesses and contrasts modes of conduct (including communication) among various animals and human beings.

comparative psychologist A person who studies animals (including humans) as a strategy for recognizing laws of behavior common to many species.

competitive style A strategy for handling conflict in which people narrowly view all conflicts as win-lose events. Winning is their only goal and being concerned for their opponent is unnecessary.

compliance Yielding publicly or observably to an influence attempt without actually accepting the change privately.

compounding pattern A pattern of distortion whereby an original message passed word of mouth through a grapevine grows larger and more complex, gaining additional details and interpretations that were never part of the original message.

compromising style A strategy for handling conflict in which participants reach agreement by making mutual concessions.

computer conferencing The use of a computer network to enable people at diverse sites to hold a meeting. The participants type messages for one another that can be read on their screens, or they hear and see one another on the screen.

computer network A number of computers linked by wires or a radio system so that their users can transmit data files or messages from one to another. Some are local and serve a given organization; others are large scale and reach many sites in a country.

conflict A dispute concerning rewards or resources that are in limited supply, when the participants' objective is to either neutralize or eliminate the opponents' prospects of winning what is at stake.

conflict style The manner that an individual is likely to exhibit when anticipating or engaging in a confrontation.

connotative meanings   Personal or unshared meanings that an individual uniquely associates with a referent because of past experience.

consciousness-raising group   A group in which people discuss their mutual problems to help them define and deal with those problems.

constructive resistance   A resistance to persuasion that contributes positively to a situation, especially when the behavior being solicited is against ethical norms.

content analysis design   A research plan in which recorded messages are the subject of the investigation. Various units of analysis are defined, whose occurrences can be identified and counted in the message.

context   A physical setting or a sociocultural situation in which communication takes place. Examples are a church or an office (physical setting) and a wedding or a sales meeting (sociocultural situation). As a cultural factor, the relative amount of information implied by the setting or conditions of a communication exchange. In high-context communication, the message is inherent in the setting and is understood by the participants; in low-context communication, the information is communicated explicitly through the spoken word.

controls (communication)   Messages that provide sanctions—rewards for compliance and punishments for deviation from the communication rules of the group.

convention   A rule adopted within a particular cultural group (or language community) that specifies what patterns of meaning are to be labeled with what particular word or nonverbal sign.

corroborative effect   An influence of mass communications in which presentation of the same facts and interpretations of news stories by different media adds credibility to what is being presented.

cost–benefit ratio   The ratio of the efforts that have to be made in establishing or maintaining a relationship to the rewards that the relationship brings. (see *utilitarianism*)

credibility   With regard to a source, the degree to which a receiver regards a source as trustworthy and a message as truthful; a perceived characteristic of a source based on a combination of beliefs about that source's competence, trustworthiness, extroversion, composure, and sociability. Also, the degree to which a message is judged to be valuable or worthless, critical or trivial, true or false, depending on the perceived sincerity and honesty of the source as evaluated by the audience.

criteria (in listening)   The standards by which people decide whether a source is credible and whether a message is believable and important.

cultural exclusion   An attitude or behavior based on people's belief that their way of thinking and acting

is the only right way and those who think or act differently are wrong.

cultural inclusion   The commitment to acknowledge, respect, and, when possible, adapt to others who may think, feel, and behave differently.

cultural pluralism   A condition in a society in which members of diverse groups maintain their cocultural affiliations and identities within the larger framework of a common, shared culture.

cultural relativity   A perspective for judging other people's cultures—recognizing and accepting the idea that people do things differently and that what works for them is all right; no absolute standard for how people should think or act.

culture   An umbrella term that includes both the general or mainstream culture and specialized, unique co-cultures. A culture is not a group of people; it is their way of life, their language, the things they use, their traditional beliefs, and their distinctive norms and customs of behavior.

cushioning function   The benefit derived from having friends or family members who provide emotional support when events make life difficult.

data   Information known as fact. In science, this requires that the information be communicated. Therefore, observations that are to become scientific data must be recorded as symbols for other scientists to see.

data analysis   The process of subjecting numerical data to a variety of statistical tests. Other, more qualitative analyses are sometimes performed.

data entry   The process of assigning numbers to observations and feeding those numbers into a computer for subsequent data analysis.

decision-making group   A group in which the goal is to arrive at orderly judgments, usually through a formal process of evaluation and discussion.

decoding   The assignment of meaning to symbols perceived by a receiver in the communication process.

demand characteristics   The activities of an experiment that subjects must perform, or conditions they experience, that may produce influences other than those brought about by the independent variables. These can be problematic if the researcher is unaware of their influence.

denotative meanings   The meanings that by established convention are to be aroused and experienced by a particular symbol.

dependency   With regard to mass communication, a condition in contemporary society in which people rely on mass media content—such as news, advertisements, and entertainment—for decisions they make in daily life.

dependency-based cohesion   A type of cohesion characteristic of organizations with a complex division of labor. Members are bound to the organization and to one another because all members perform specialized tasks that are linked to and dependent on the tasks performed by others.

dependent variable   A variable that is influenced by the presence of particular independent variables. In a cause-and-effect relationship, the dependent variable is the effect.

descriptive research   Research aimed at revealing and describing some order—the stages, configurations, or processes of human communication.

destructive resistance   Negative, subversive, or rebellious behavior in response to legitimate attempts at persuasion.

disassociation   A strategy of transmitting messages to another that aims at reducing the use of the pronoun *we* and reverting to the individualistic *you* and *I*.

disengagement   The communication strategies people use when they are attempting to withdraw from a close association with another.

distancing   A strategy of transmitting verbal and nonverbal messages to another with the goal of increasing both physical and psychological distance between the two.

distortion   An outcome of communication in which the source's intended meanings become compounded with, or displaced by, unintended interpretations as the receiver reconstructs the meanings of the message.

dyad   Two persons in a relatively enduring social relationship.

e-mail   A system for sending and receiving typed messages on a computer network. It consists of software that permits word processing and hardware that allows a message that is displayed on the sender's screen to be sent to the receiver's computer, where it can be displayed on screen and stored in both computers' memories.

embedding pattern   A particular set of distortions—leveling, sharpening, and assimilation—that may occur in a message when it is transmitted orally from one person to the next serially.

emblems   A category of nonverbal gestures that have established conventions of meaning, providing direct verbal translations.

empirical observation   For the purpose of data gathering in scientific research, empirical observation is based on recording with the senses the presence or absence of certain attributes of a particular variable under study.

encoding   The assignment of symbols to meanings that a source intends to transmit to a receiver.

encounter group   A group in which participants meet to identify and seek ways of coping with their difficulties, such as discrimination and harassment.

enculturation   The process of acquiring understandings of a person's general culture, including not only language skills but also shared beliefs, emotional orientations, attitudes, and values that make a person an accepted member of society.

engagement   The communication process by which people move their relationship from an impersonal to a personal basis.

ethnocentrism   A belief that one's own group and way of life are superior to all others.

exchange theory   A formulation originally developed by George Homans to explain all forms of human social interaction. Applied to communication, it argues that people implicitly keep track of the history of benefits received from interacting with the other person, weigh that against the history of costs, and make an estimate of the worth of the relationship. If benefits outweigh costs for both individuals, the relationship is likely to continue; if not, the relationship is likely to terminate.

experiment   A research design that involves systematic observations on a number of human subjects, some of whom are designated as a control group and others as an experimental group. The experimental group receives treatment deliberately introduced by the experimenter. The control group does not receive this but usually undergoes a neutral experience. Measures of the dependent variable are made before and after the treatment to see whether only the experimental group has changed. There are many variations to this design.

fax (facsimile)   An electronic device for reading, transmitting, and reproducing documents, graphics, or photographs over long-distance telephone lines.

feedback   The messages provided in an ongoing manner by a receiver in response to a message being transmitted by a source.

femininity   A cultural orientation that emphasizes a traditional female gender orientation in which nurturance, cooperation, empathy, and collaboration are valued and sex roles are flexible.

field experiment   A large-scale research design in which subjects to be treated and observed are people living in a community, factory, school, or other natural setting. The control group is a similar group that does not get the treatment.

field research (field observational study)   A type of qualitative research in which the investigator lives, works, or regularly interacts with those being observed.

financial foundation   The economic basis by which a group or organization makes profits.

formal communication   A controlled communication among parties who are allowed or required by the group's coded rules to transmit particular messages to specific receivers using officially designated rules and restrictions.

forum   A type of discussion group usually based on brief presentations by members of a small group, who are introduced by a chairperson. The presentations are followed by considerable participation by audience members, again coordinated by the chair.

frame   The use of nonverbal gestures or other actions while talking so as to emphasize, complement, and reinforce what is said.

freedom of the press   A person's right to speak out in print or otherwise as specified in the First Amendment of the Constitution. This is an individual right, not a collective one giving newspapers special protections.

general culture   The overall culture developed by a people within a society who speak a common language and share the same basic social institutions.

generalization   An accurate statement that communicates in precise language what was found with respect to the tendencies, relationships, or patterns among variables being studied.

grapevine   The complex social pathways within an organization through which informal messages are transmitted by word of mouth.

group   Two or more people who repeatedly interact, regulating their conduct within some set of rules for communication and social activity that they mutually recognize and follow.

haptics   The study of touch as a means of nonverbal communication.

human relations perspective   A theory for managing organizations in which the personal and social characteristics of workers as individuals are critical factors in the work process. Managers try to motivate, encourage, and foster worker performance by taking advantage of human factors that make work more tolerable, under the assumption that this will increase output.

human resources perspective   A theory for managing organizations based on assumptions that bonds of loyalty can be created between worker and employer and that workers have insights into production processes that offer valuable clues as to how both quality and efficiency can be improved.

human use perspective   A theory of management in which workers are thought of not in humanitarian terms but simply as things that can be used, like machinery, and exploited, like raw materials.

hypothesis   A statement that poses possible relationships between variables. Ideally, hypotheses are derived from theories that predict the relationship between variables if the theory is correct.

identification   A yielding to influence that occurs because of a person's desire to emulate a particular individual or group.

implicit personality theory   An explanation of how assumptions are quickly formulated about a person one has just met. These assumptions are beliefs about qualities and motives that are projected onto an individual on the basis of limited information obtained in an initial encounter.

impression management   A transmittal of verbal and nonverbal messages that are deliberately designed to create a particular set of impressions.

incidental learning   Acquiring ideas and understandings about people, things or situations (without realizing it) by viewing either other peoples' behavior or viewing depictions in mass communication content.

independent variable   A variable that exerts influences on the dependent variable. In a cause-and-effect relationship, the independent variable is the cause.

individualism   A cultural orientation in which the individual is emphasized, and autonomy, independence, and individual success are valued.

Industrial Revolution   A major change in a society or societies in which the production of goods in factories replaces agriculture as the major economic activity.

informal communication   Communication that takes place in the absence of deliberately designed barriers or constraints—communication that is spontaneous and unrestrained. In communicating informally, people feel relatively free to say what they feel and do not constantly worry that their meanings will be misunderstood or that they will arouse hostile responses.

information   Physical events that span distance—such as sound or light waves, electronic impulses, or electromagnetic radiations—into which symbols or other signs are encoded when a source speaks, writes, or uses electronic media to transmit messages to receivers.

informed consent   A requirement that research subjects know the nature of the treatments they will receive in a study and that they agree in writing to participate under those conditions.

intercultural communication   An exchange of messages between people of different co-cultures under conditions in which their co-cultural backgrounds influence the process.

internalization   A yielding to influence because it is personally rewarding or useful.

interpersonal communication   A communication that takes place between two people who come to know each other better as their relationship moves from impersonal to personal.

interval measurement   A rating that determines how much of a variable exists along a continuum and then assigns it a numerical point on a scale. Variables are placed in relationship to one another, and intervals on the scale are equal.

intimate group   People who make up either a human family or a peer group of close friends. The communication in intimate groups is extensive, self-disclosing, and uninhibited.

kinesics   The study of body movements—including gestures, posture, and facial expression—that are used to communicate nonverbally.

labeling theory   An explanation of the way people interpret an individual's characteristics and social worth after that person has been given a negative label by an official agency. For example, the term *mental patient* causes people to assign numerous negative characteristics to those so labeled, whether or not they have those attributes.

language   The shared words, nonverbal signs, and rules for their use and interpretation within a particular group or society.

language community   Members of a human group that speak a common language.

learn-conform-or-be-punished   A strategy for designing ads that show the possible customer why he or she must use the product or face social rejection.

learn-feel-do   A strategy for designing ads that instruct the possible customer, influence his or her emotional feelings about the product and indicate how to obtain it.

learned helplessness   A feeling of inadequacy and stress arising from an inability to communicate in a predictable way with people who are inconsistent in their responses to messages.

legacy of fear   A widespread conviction in U.S. culture that the mass media have the power to harm their audiences.

legal-rational authority   The basis of legitimate authority in organizations whereby leaders are selected for technical managerial skills that qualify them to exercise power within the limited sphere defined by official definitions.

leveling   A general shortening of a message—such as a rumor, story, or other verbal account—as it travels by word of mouth through a grapevine.

linear   Moving like a straight line, from a beginning to an end through specific stages.

linguistic relativity   The principle that people of different cultures, using different languages, may define and label features of reality in different ways.

listening   An active form of behavior in which individuals maximize their attention to, and comprehension of, what is being communicated through the use of words and actions.

Machiavellianism strategy   A strategy for ending a relationship in which a manipulative individual desiring that goal is able to convince an unwilling partner, who is unaware of the strategy, that termination was the partner's idea and is in his or her best interest.

magazine   A publication with many of the characteristics of a newspaper, usually with smaller dimensions and bound at the left. It can have either general or specialized content. A magazine is a "storehouse" of ideas, opinions, and other content.

magic bullet theory   An explanation of the effects of exposure to mass communications based on assumptions that media messages reach virtually every member of an audience and penetrate every mind equally, influencing everyone's ideas and conduct in powerful ways.

mainstream culture   A culture that consists of the most common language, the basic social institutions, the material artifacts and technologies in use, and the basic values to which most participants subscribe.

manu-scripti   Books made by copying pages by hand in a careful script, letter by letter and line by line.

masculinity   A cultural orientation that emphasizes a traditional male gender orientation, in which achievement, success, ambition, assertiveness, and competitiveness are valued and sex roles are clearly differentiated.

mass communication   A process by which professional communicators use media to disseminate messages widely and rapidly, arousing meanings in large and diverse audiences to influence them in various ways.

mass media   The media that disseminate messages from professional communicators to large and diverse audiences. The major point-to-multipoint media are books, newspapers, magazines, radio, and television in its various forms. The Internet is a mixed case, incorporating some aspects of a mass medium.

meaning   The subjective responses that individuals learn to make to the things they directly experience in reality or to the particular symbols used to label that reality.

meaning (deep)   The basic ideas implied by a message that can be understood well enough for practical purposes.

meaning (surface)   The entire set of meanings encoded in a message, whether or not essential to understanding its basic ideas.

meaning triangle   A diagram showing that meaning, symbol, and referent constitute a system, with each element linked by a convention.

measurement   A process of observing that assigns numerical values to observations so that they can be quantified.

media service organization   A commercial organization or agency that purchases large amounts of media space or time and resells them to advertisers.

medium   Any device that extends the distance or time over which people can communicate. Media carry or store information into which symbols are encoded by senders and decoded by receivers.

melting pot policy An early U.S. policy geared toward eradicating cultural differences among people and promoting rapid assimilation of immigrants into mainstream U.S. culture.

memorandum From the Latin *memoro,* meaning "to call to mind." A stylized written document, widely used in organizational communication for the purposes of transmitting significant messages to one or more receivers.

message ordering The question of whether or not it is more persuasive to put arguments favoring a position early in a message. Often called the primacy–recency question: Does more change result when arguments are inserted at the end of the message?

message sidedness A feature of a persuasive message concerning the degree to which the arguments it presents explain one side only or refute opposing arguments as well.

modeling The acting out, description, or portrayal of behavior in mass communications in such a way that those activities serve as models for receivers.

natural sign An event or situation occurring in nature to which an animal learns to respond or adjust.

negotiation A process of conflict resolution that communicates back and forth between opponents.

nominal measurement The method of measurement that names what is observed and places it into some qualitatively defined category, such as female or male.

nonsocial constraints The nonsocial factors that reduce the consistency between attitude and action. For example, the act may be inconvenient, involve financial loss, pose risks, or be difficult to perform. Also, the person may lack opportunity or competence.

nonverbal communication The deliberate or unintentional use of objects, actions, sounds, time, and space to arouse meanings in others.

nonverbal immediacy A physical and psychological closeness with others; a condition that can be established through the deliberate use of nonverbal signals and actions.

normative confusion A basis of group disorganization that occurs when communication norms have not been effectively clarified or when consensus breaks down about which messages, topics, or issues are approved or disapproved.

norms (communication) The general rules that each participant in a group is expected to follow concerning the issues, topics, and modes of transmission that are acceptable to the other members.

oculesics The study of eye contact and pupil dilation in nonverbal communication.

ordinal measurement A rank ordering for what is being observed that assigns a number, such as first, second, and so on.

organization A human group that has been deliberately designed to achieve a desired objective. Usually, an organization has a large number of participants whose activities are coordinated by complex rules for communication.

organization chart A graphic representation of the chain of authority and command in an organization, which also provides a guide for the flow of formal messages. It is especially helpful in understanding the vertical flow of communication—up and down the organization.

organizational cohesion The cohesion that binds members of an organization to one another and to the group as a whole. It is based on sentiment-based cohesion in small groups of work associates, reward-based cohesion in more temporary groups, assignment-based cohesion in decision-making groups within the organization, and dependency-based cohesion that is a product of task interdependencies in the overall structure.

organizational communication The transmission of messages through formal and informal channels of a large, deliberately designed group, resulting in the construction of meanings that influence both individual members and the group as a whole.

overgeneralizing The act of claiming that what prevailed among the subjects observed in an investigation also applies to people who were not actually studied.

panel A more formal type of discussion group in which participants are often experts or representatives. The panel is usually coordinated by a moderator, and the discussion usually takes place before a live audience.

papyrus A smooth writing surface first made in ancient Egypt from thin slices of a reed. When the slices were laid criss-cross and mashed together by pounding, and then rolling, pressing, and drying, a paperlike surface was produced. The word *paper* comes from this source.

parchment A thin and smooth writing surface prepared from the skin of a sheep.

participant observation A strategy of observation in which an investigator joins a group under study and participates fully in its activities in order to observe the group's communication patterns. The group may or may not know that the person is a researcher.

peer group A small group of close and intimate friends, often of the same general socioeconomic characteristics, age, and gender.

penny press The newspapers that followed the model of Benjamin Day's *New York Sun*—selling cheaply, making their profits on advertising, and aiming at large circulations by suiting the tastes of the common people.

perception The psychological process of seeing, hearing, or feeling with the senses and then attaching meaning to what has been apprehended based on what is learned from the culture.

person perception The processes by which an individual comes to know and to think about other people—their characteristics, qualities, and inner states.

persona (personal idea) A set of beliefs, meanings, and understandings that an individual develops about another as a result of communicating with her or him. (see *implicit personality theory*)

personal space The immediate zone people carry around during their daily interactions with others.

personality The individual's enduring organization of meanings, motivations, emotional patterns, orientations, skills, and other attributes that make that person different in psychological makeup from all others.

personality trait A person's individual characteristic, such as being smart, stingy, friendly, and so on. Specific attributes that make up his or her overall nature.

persuasion The efforts to change people in some way by using strategies of communication. A transactional process in which a source encodes and transmits messages designed to influence a receiver's constructions of meanings in ways that will lead to changes desired by the source in the receiver's beliefs, attitudes, or behavior.

phylogenetic continuum The idea from evolutionary theory that animals can be arranged along a scale in terms of the complexity of their bodily structures and organization.

pictographs Crude drawings that are intended to represent objects or situations in reality. These were typical of the earliest attempts at writing.

population A statistical term meaning the entire aggregate of what is being studied. In communication research, mainly all the people about whom generalizations are to be made in a study.

postulate A shared belief of a very fundamental nature—a given that is so basic that it is not subject to proof or disproof.

power distance As a cultural factor, the relative importance a group places on power, rank, and status. High power-distance cultures value social status, birth order, and occupational or political rank. Low power-distance cultures value equality and minimize the importance of power and status differences among members.

practitioner A person who practices (works as a member of) a specific profession, such as advertising, law, education, etc.

predispositions The tendencies to approve of some things and disapprove of others that are shaped by attitudes, values, opinions, preferences, and so on.

These factors modify perceptions and interpretations because they lead people to like some stimuli and dislike others.

prejudice A configuration of emotionally held beliefs that results in a person making judgments about another individual before he or she even begins to communicate or interact.

presentation of self A way of formulating and transmitting verbal and nonverbal messages to other people about the kind of person you are.

primary groups The intimate groups that are earliest in the experience of the human individual and that play a critical part in the person's psychological and social development. Essentially, these are the family and early peer groups. Peer groups in adult life can also be considered primary groups.

principle of delayed gratification A belief that accepting costs or guarding resources in the present will pay off in significant long-term rewards.

propaganda Messages, usually transmitted by media, that have the goal of shaping a receiver's interpretation or behavior toward a topic, issue or action.

proprietary research Research conducted by industry, government, advertising agencies, or any other organization in which the findings are kept secret.

proxemics The study of the meanings communicated by the use of space and distance.

psychodynamic strategy A traditional approach to persuasion resting on the assumption that the route to achieving behavioral change lies in achieving cognitive reorganization. If feelings and beliefs can be changed by persuasive messages (cognitive reorganization), overt behavior will be changed correspondingly.

psychological reactance The strong feelings of determined resistance that cause a person to react against an attempt at persuasion.

public relations agency A professional group whose task it is to improve public perceptions of the nature or activities of their clients by placing (usually non-paid) news releases or other messages in media.

quality control circles The small discussion groups composed of individuals from a particular unit in an organization (usually devoted to manufacturing) whose members all face the same production task. They meet with their supervisor to find ways in which their particular assembly work can be done more efficiently and at a higher level of quality.

quasi-experiment A research design that incorporates the logic of the experiment without actual intervention by the researcher. The treatment is a naturally occurring condition.

random sampling procedure A set of steps for selecting a sample from a population in such a way that each subject has an equal probability of being included.

rank (communication) The rules that define communication patterns based on authority, power, and privilege within a group. For example, rank determines who issues orders and whose messages are regarded as important.

rank ineffectiveness A situation in which members of a group come to believe that the messages transmitted by those in positions of power and authority lack legitimacy.

ratio measurement A measurement system that rates the value of what is being observed and then assigns it a number along a scale. The scale begins with a zero point, and the distances between any two numbers are the same.

receiver A person who attends to, perceives, and interprets (decodes) the message information transmitted by a source.

receiver eccentricities The personal attributes and individual differences that help or hinder a person's capacity to receive and interpret messages accurately.

referent The object, situation, or event to which a symbol refers.

regulating The use of nonverbal signs and signals as informal rules of order to regulate the flow of talk among people.

reinforcement A term from psychological theories of learning, which implies that when a response to a stimulus is positive or rewarding, people will continue with the behavior, and it will become part of their repertoire, to be repeated in similar circumstances. Should the consequence be punishing, however, the behavior is likely to be dropped and replaced with some alternative response.

reliability A quality of measurement in research referring to whether a procedure will yield the same results if used repeatedly on the same subjects.

replication The repetition of a study under the same general circumstances and with the same types of subjects to see whether the findings of the first investigation will prevail in the second.

representative sample A sample that has been chosen so that the personal and social characteristics of those included are like those in the entire population in all important respects relevant to the research.

research A set of procedures for gathering trustworthy information about some object or process that is studied under controlled conditions of observation in such a way that objective conclusions can be reached with a minimum of error.

resiliency factor The propensity of human beings to be flexible in their learning histories and not to be rigidly shaped by a few negative consequences of their actions.

reward-based cohesion A type of cohesion based on the personal satisfactions or rewards that flow to

individuals because they participate in a group. This leads them to maintain membership and work toward the goals of the group.

roles (communication) A cluster of rules in a group that define who has the right to transmit particular kinds of messages and who must pay attention to them.

role-taking An activity whereby a source assesses the likelihood that a receiver will be able to interpret the intentions and meanings of a particular form of a message.

round table A common format for informal discussion groups in which there is usually no audience and the participants are arranged in some sort of circular pattern.

salient characteristic A feature or aspect of an individual that stands out in an initial encounter with another person and that serves as a dominant attribute around which that person constructs a pattern of initial impressions.

sampling A procedure for picking from some population an adequate and manageable smaller number of people who can be contacted and studied, given the researcher's resources.

schema A pattern or configuration of traces of meaning that have been organized and recorded in a person's memory.

scientific management A theory for managing organizations in which managers themselves look systematically at the design of their group and its processes to try to communicate to workers ways in which incentives, work flow, and exercise of authority can operate most effectively and profitably. Early versions were concerned with time and motion studies.

scripted or stereotypic conversations Conversations that are like highly standardized and predictable lines rehearsed in a play. These may follow clear, even rigid, rules in certain welldefined communication situations.

selective influences An explanation of why only certain types of people attend to particular forms of media messages, based on assumptions about their individual differences, social category memberships, and social affiliations.

perception An individual's assignment of a personally unique pattern of denotative and connotative meanings to some person, activity, situation, or thing. These personal stamps of meaning arise from people's different memories of meanings linked to signs, signals, and symbols, and to human characteristics, stored through experience.

self (self-image or self-concept) The pattern of beliefs, meanings, and understandings each individual develops concerning her or his personal characteristics, capacities, limitations, and worth as a human being. A personal conception of who and where the individual is in the social order.

self-disclosure The individual's communication to another that reveals the nature of the individual's past, private thoughts, personal views, or deep feelings. Also, the individual's telling another about beliefs, attitudes, values, accomplishments, status, and other personal and social characteristics.

seminar A small discussion group now commonly used in advanced courses in universities. Usually, each student takes a turn at addressing a central question that is the focus of the discussion, and the mentor draws the important lessons out of various comments.

sender-receiver reciprocity The successful adaptation to each other in a communication encounter by engaging in both role-taking and feedback simultaneously.

sender-receiver similarity A condition in which the message's sender and receiver have similar learning experiences in their language community so as to have acquired parallel meanings for verbal and nonverbal signs and symbols.

sentiment-based cohesion A type of cohesion based on bonds of affection that exist among members of a group.

sharpening The counterpart of leveling in the embedding process. A verbal message shrinks as it is passed on by word of mouth. With each retelling, it becomes increasingly organized around its more salient details, becoming more and more concise until it is only a summary of the original message.

sign An event that animals and human beings learn to associate with and use to anticipate subsequent events. Examples: clouds are followed by rain, the dog dish is followed by the dog getting fed, a red light indicates that one must stop.

signal The noises or patterned movements that animals make to which others of their species respond. Examples: cries or postures that imply danger, the presence of food, or readiness to mate. Human beings also use many signals: whistles, bells, and waving flags.

signs Stimuli to which people have learned to make a patterned response.

skills training The form of treatment for communication apprehension based on the assumption that limitations in people's skills in communicating influence their apprehension levels. To reduce the apprehension, people receive training in public speaking skills or other communication behaviors.

small group A group in which the number of members varies from two to perhaps a dozen or more; optimal size with all members participating fully in communication is five members.

small group conference A small discussion group in which several participants are brought together, usually under private conditions, to share technical information or to discuss a problem in their area of expertise.

small talk Discussions that focus on topics of general interest and have little emotional or personal significance, such as the weather, sports, or other matters not requiring self-disclosure.

social categories A number of people who have a characteristic in common by which they can be classified. Examples are gender, age, education, occupation, and race. People in such categories are often said to be characterized by certain regularities in their behavior.

social construction of reality A cognitive process by which a person acquires understandings of and meanings for some aspect of reality by communicating about it with other people (or from observing depictions of it in mass communications).

social efficacy The condition of being competent as a social person—that is, being able to form, manage, and maintain all kinds of social relationships in an effective manner.

social expectations The shared rules for conducting social activities within a group—norms, roles, ranking, and controls. These can be learned vicariously from media sources as well as by actual participation in a group.

social institution A broad configuration of closely related cultural elements and organized social activities that are essential to fulfillment of a perceived need of the social order.

social learning theory (observational learning theory) An extension of earlier, more general reinforcement theories that was originally developed to explain how individuals learn—not by performing actions themselves but by observing the behavior and reactions of those who are important as models in their lives.

social pressures The needs and desires to comply with social rules for behavior that are expected by others whose approval is sought in a situation of action. (see *social expectations*)

socialization The long-term processes of communication within which deliberate or indirect lessons are internalized, enabling the person to become a unique human being, a functioning member of a society, and a participant in its general and unique culture.

source or sender A person who formulates, encodes, and transmits a message to one or more receivers. In some cases, groups or agencies can serve as sources.

specialized culture A specialized or unique culture that characterizes a particular group within a society; such groups are distinguished from one another by such factors as race, ethnicity, gender, age, or profession.

specialized organizational culture The total pattern of beliefs, sentiments, attitudes, values, rules, and special languages shared by the members of an organization. These cultural elements set the organization off from other organizations and from the society as a whole.

stage fright   A special category of the more general condition of communication apprehension that specifically focuses on anxiety about a public performance or speech before a group or audience.

stakeholders   Persons who have some interest in the services provided by an agency or business.

stereotypes   Rigid and usually negative assumptions about personal and social qualities of people who are members of a particular social category.

stereotypic   (see *scripted or stereotypic conversations*)

susceptibility   The degree to which a person is influenced by others because of his or her personal characteristics.

symbiotic relationship   A relationship between two entities based on mutual dependency.

symbols   The labels used by participants in a language community to arouse standardized meanings for aspects of reality. The initial selection of a label for a referent is often made arbitrarily, but, once established, the connection between the label and its referent is permanent.

symposium   A very formal discussion group whose participants are usually a small group of experts. They are individually introduced by a moderator, and each makes a speech about the theme. During or between presentations, the participants seldom talk; they simply take their turns in delivering their views.

syntax   The rules for ordering words in a sentence so that their meaning is clear.

systematic desensitization (SD)   A form of treatment that has been used to reduce many kinds of fears, including communication apprehension. It seeks to reduce apprehensions through muscle relaxation techniques.

task-oriented group   A group in which people participate in order to get something done.

teleconferencing   The use of media to link spatially dispersed people for the purpose of communicating in ways that approximate the conditions of a face-to-face meeting.

territoriality   A common tendency or characteristic of both animals and humans in which they define or claim some space as their own.

theory   The form in which cause-effect relationships are stated in scientific analysis. A theory provides an explanation of how one set of events brings about or influences another.

therapy group   A specialized discussion group in which participants who share a common difficulty meet with a coordinator who has some insight into the problem. The underlying assumption is that if these people get together and disclose their feelings to one another, it will help them feel better.

trace   The imprinted records of experience registered in the brain by electrochemical or other activities of its nerve cells.

trait (personality)   A relatively stable and predictable pattern of behavior that characterizes a person; a feature of an individual's personality that makes her or him different from others, such as stingy, honest, smart, and happy-go-lucky.

transaction   Any kind of exchange. An activity that occurs between, and mutually influences, all individuals acting together in some way.

two-step flow of communication   A process by which some individuals (opinion leaders) directly receive messages from the mass media and then pass them on to others by word of mouth, often influencing their interpretations.

unclear role definition   The confusion that results from inadequate, ineffective, or unclear definitions about the roles played in a group. Whatever the type of group—from a family to a vast corporation—such role confusion can be a major factor leading to a loss of cohesion.

validity   A quality of a measurement referring to whether it actually measures the variable for which it has been designed.

vellum   A writing surface similar to parchment, except prepared from the skin of a calf.

vertical transmission   The flow of formal messages either up or down in an organization, with clearly graded levels of power and authority.

videoconferencing   The use of videocameras, long-distance cables, or satellite relays and television screens to enable people to see and talk to one another in a close approximation to having them face to face in the same room.

vocalics   The study of the way in which vocal cues signal meanings to others, such as showing people's happiness, nervousness, and so on.

voice mail   A telephone-based system in which a network of users share a sophisticated answering machine so that they can leave and store messages for others and themselves.

wage incentive system   A formula for paying workers in production settings in which wages are tied to personal output. Earnings for a worker in a production shop are determined by the number of units the individual produces in a given time period.

withdrawal and avoidance   A strategy of indirect distancing and dissociation in which parties telephone less frequently, are too busy to get together, and avoid making future plans. The parties see less and less of each other without the strain of confrontation, and their relationship simply fades away.

Credits

Name Index

Subject Index

Beliefs, 214, 456
  shaping, 310–311
  shared, 214, 215
Believability, of sender, 108, 322
Bell Telephone Laboratories, 24
Bill of Rights, United States, 381
Blame, assigning, 138–139
Body language, 66–67, 71–72, 77–78, 456.
  See also Nonverbal communication
  personal characteristics and, 71
Books, development of, 380–381
Boston Elevated trolley lines, 421
Boston Globe, 371
Boutique agency, 414, 456
Brain structure, and speech, 38
Brainstorming sessions, 163
Breakdown, of group, 171–172
British Parliament, 169
Broca's area, 38
Bureaucracy, 456
  theory of, 183–186
    emergence of rational society, 184–185
    Weber's principles, 184, 186
Burka, 219
Bushido code, 418
Buzz groups, 163

Cable Televison Advertising Bureau, 412
Cable TV, and advertising, 415–417
California, immigrants in, 216
Caucasians, 229
Cause-effect relationships, assumption of, 432
Cell phones
  etiquette for users, 362, 363
  number, in use, 360
Cha-be-u, 235–236
Character, guidelines for assessing, 322
Characteristics of, 121–122
Charismatic authority, 185, 456
Chauvinism, cultural, 218, 456
Child development, 85, 158. *See also* Learning, theories
Children
  discipline of, 235–236
  immigrants, 216–217
  personal space and, 81
  sarcasm and, 70
Chile, 226
Chinese Americans, 220
Chronemics, 86, 456
CIA (Central Intelligence Agency), 190
Civil rights movement, 396–397
Clever Hans, 35–36
Clever Hans effect, 36, 39, 456
  attempts to rule out, 40
Clients, 407, 456
  public relations, 423
Closeness, psychological, 88–89, 131
Clothing, as instrument of communication, 74–76
Co-cultures. *See* Specialized cultures
Coercion, 305–306, 456

Cognitive-emotional strategy, in advertising, 417–418
Cognitive functioning, 308
Cognitive processing, 308
  language and, 50–51, 55–56
Cognitive reorganization, 307–308, 310, 456
Cognitive restructuring, 292–295, 456
Cohesion, group, 170–171, 456
  basis of, 184–185
  organizational culture and, 204–205
Collaborative style, 341, 456
Collectivism, 222–223, 456
Colliers (magazine), 383
Colonial America, 410
Colonial press, 456
Comfortable self, 264
Communication
  animal (*see* Animal communication)
  defining, 6–7
  importance, in social life, 3–6
Communication Abstracts, 435–436
Communication apprehension, 275–299, 407, 456
  causes of, 279–282
    contextual, 279–282
  definition, 277
  public speaking and, 289–291
  reducing, 291–296
    cognitive restructuring, 292–295
    skills training, 276–277, 295–296
    systematic desensitization, 291–292
  social consequences of, 287–289, 295
Communication, human, 3–5, 456
Communication process
  defining, 7–8
  linear model of, 10–20
    deciding on the message, 11–12
    decoding and interepreting, 19–20
    encoding meanings, 12–19
    perceiving information, 19
    simultaneous transaction model of, 20–24
Communications, study of, 1–3
Communicator, 5, 456
Comparative perspective, 7–8
Comparative psychologist, 456
Competitive conflict style, 340–341, 456
Compliance, 318, 456
Composure, and believability, 322
Compounding pattern, of distortion, 201, 202–203, 203
Comprehension, 105
Compromising conflict style, 341, 456
Computer conferencing, 371–372, 456
Computer network, 456
Computers. *See* Internet; World Wide Web
Concensus, 271
Concentration, controlling, 114–115
Confidentiality, in research, 451
Conflict, 329–348, 456
  causes of, 336–339
    contextual, 337–338
    social expectations, 338–339

characteristics of, 331–332
competition and, 332–333
consequences of, 334–336
coping with, 339–342
  negotiation, 342–347
definition, 332
organizational cultures and, 204
productive vs. unproductive, 334–335
between specialized cultures, 331–332
Conflict resolution, 103
Conflict style, 456. *See also* Conflict, coping with
Conform-or-be-punished strategy, in advertising, 418–419, 460
Confrontation, and disengagement, 142
Connotative meanings, 46, 309, 457
  barrier to listening, 112
  vs. denotative, 14–15
Consciousness-raising groups, 164, 457
Consensus, reaching, 162
Consent, informed, of research subjects, 451
Constitution, United States, 381
Constructive resistance, 317
Content analysis, 445–446, 457
Context, 3, 6, 9–10, 87, 457
  communication apprehension and, 279–282, 289–290
  conflict and, 337–338
  distortion of meaning and, 25, 26
  first impressions and, 254–255
  high and low, 223–224
  importance of, 99–100, 107, 107–108
  media as, 99
Control, in affinity-seeking strategies, 264
Controls, social, 152, 153, 457
  expectations and, 306, 307
  persuasion and, 323
Convention, 12, 457
Conventions, principle of, 47, 48–49
Conversation, rules of, 67–68
Conversational rule-keeping, 264
Coping, with problems, 127–128
Core information, disclosing, 135–136
Cost-benefit ratio, of interpesonal relationships, 125–128, 133–135, 457
  assessing, 133–135
  benefits, 126–128
  costs, 126–127, 128
Covarying attribution, principle of, 269–270
Credibility, of sender, 108, 457
  influencing others and, 321–322
Criteria (in listening), 457
Cro-Magnon people, 41
Cross-cultural communication, 14–15
Crusades, 15
Cues, nonverbal. *See* Nonverbal communication
Cults, religious, 165
Cultural differences
  barrier to listening, 111
  distortion of meaning and, 200
  meaning of eye contact, 131
Cultural diversity, 212, 216